The Fourth President

A LIFE OF

James Madison

The Fourth President

A LIFE OF

James Madison

BY IRVING BRANT

The Bobbs-Merrill Company
Indianapolis   New York

The Bobbs-Merrill Company, Inc.
A Subsidiary of Howard W. Sams & Co., Inc.
Publishers / Indianapolis — Kansas City — New York

PREFACE

In 1938 I undertook to write the biography of James Madison, expecting to center it on his leadership in framing the 1787 (and present) Constitution of the United States. The work was to be completed in two years and in one volume. So vast was the discovery of previously unused material, and so greatly did it exalt Madison's rightful place in American history, that the undertaking stretched out to twenty-three years and six volumes, published seriatim from 1941 to 1961. The first volume deals with Madison's boyhood and early public service in Revolutionary Virginia; the second with his service in the Continental Congress during the Revolution and later in the Virginia legislature; the third with the framing of the Constitution and subsequent service in the Congress of the United States; the fourth with his eight years as Secretary of State. The fifth volume covers his first term as President. The sixth embraces the War of 1812 and nineteen post-presidential years, actively devoted to farming, running a university, combating the Southern doctrine of nullification and secession, and trying to put an end to slavery, to which he was unwillingly chained for a livelihood.

The conversion of my six-volume biography of James Madison into a single volume may be described as a process of selective condensation and minor omissions. In writing the original work I was compelled to correct misappraisals inherited by post-Civil-War historians from earlier Federalist writers and from Federalist politicians who systematically misrepresented both Presidents Madison and Jefferson during their administrations. Research developed the need of a further corrective, called for by the universal acceptance, by worshipers of Thomas Jefferson, of the Federalist myth that Madison was Jefferson's office boy.

So deeply were these fallacies planted in historical writings (most deeply in Henry Adams), that every challenge had to be supported and nailed down by incontrovertible evidence. That is one reason the work required six volumes. Another reason lies in a further historical fallacy—

the myth, fostered by State Rights zealots from about 1820 (the year of the Missouri Compromise on the spread of slavery) that the United States was not regarded as a nation during the War of the American Revolution, and that the Constitution of 1787 represented a victory for the defenders of state sovereignty. The corrective process required extensive treatment of Confederation history, in which Madison played an important interpretive and constructive role, and of pre-independence Virginia events in which also he was prominent.

The need is no longer acute to refute disparagement of Madison's place in history. The disappearance of that need is implied in a remark President John F. Kennedy made to me in 1962, when I was invited to autograph the six Madison volumes in the White House library: "Madison is the most underrated President in American history." Acceptance of that fact, by historians and informed statesmen, permits me to present the life of James Madison in a different manner—straight narrative and appraisal, embodying the same once-challenged presentation of character and activities, but with no overpowering need to prove them a second time.

In the preparation of this work I have avoided skeletonizing, with its rigid adherence to prior form. There is a great difference in the degree of condensation of the six volumes. They contain a total of 3,049 pages of text and notes, 458 in the first volume, *James Madison: The Virginia Revolutionist*. In the present work the proportion devoted to that period —slightly less than one-sixth of the whole—is reduced to a little more than one-fourteenth. In contrast, the final volume of the full work, *James Madison: Commander in Chief*, contains 580 pages of text and notes—something less than one-fifth of the whole. The same period comprises between one-fourth and one-fifth of the one-volume work. The difference arises chiefly from condensation of background and collateral events in the first volume, contrasted with imperative concentration on Madison's personal activities in the period of the sixth volume.

The result of this method of condensation is that, despite a drastic shortening, virtually nothing of pertinence and importance is ignored. The whole, I hope, comes into sharper focus and produces a clearer illumination of the character and work of the Fourth President.

March 20, 1969   Irving Brant

TABLE OF CONTENTS

Part I

1 / FROM CRADLE TO COLLEGE

The spring of 1751 was well into the redbud season when a carriage turned off the Rapidan River road near the mouth of Blue Run in Orange County, Virginia. The horses slowed to a walk as they pulled up the heavily wooded slope of the Southwest or Little Mountain. They stopped before a solidly built, twenty-year-old wooden house on an open hillock from which, toward the west, the endless forest reached to the heights of the Blue Ridge. Black slaves hastened out for the unloading, and a swarm of their children came running from the line of cabins north of the house.

This was the homecoming of James Madison, Jr., born a few weeks earlier in the house of his maternal grandmother, across the Rappahannock River from the little settlement of Port Royal. The farm to which he came remained his home for eighty-five years.

To this spot, eighteen months earlier, James Madison, son of Ambrose, had brought his seventeen-year-old bride, Nelly Conway. Their marriage united two families who typified diverging trends in a tobacco-growing colony—those who clung to tidewater plantations through successive generations, and those who cut farms out of the Piedmont forest.

In 1652, forty-five years after the first landing at Jamestown, ship carpenter John Maddison stepped off a vessel from England. By paying the passage money of twelve emigrants, including himself, he obtained "head rights" that entitled him to six hundred acres of unallotted lands. He chose a site on the Mattapony River, at a place called Mantapike. Clearing and cultivating the land and building small vessels, he used his earnings to obtain more head rights, expanding his estate to nineteen hundred acres during the remaining thirty years of his life.

John Maddison's son John married Isabella Todd and rose to the position of sheriff, but as his three sons (John, Ambrose, and Henry) neared maturity his thoughts turned to the uplands. In 1714 he and a neighbor patented two thousand acres along the upper Mattapony. Well to the northwest was Germanna, Governor Alexander Spotswood's colony of Teutonic ironworkers. Beyond lay the unbroken wilderness; but that wilderness was penetrated in 1716 by Spotswood and his twelve Knights of the Golden Horseshoe, accompanied by their servants, rangers, Indian guides, and seventy-four horses. Naming the rivers as they rode, they ascended the Rapidan, the Rivanna, the Swift Run, and crossed the Blue Ridge where no white man had been. On the banks of the Shenandoah they took possession of its broad valley and whatever else lay between the Blue Ridge and the Western Ocean in the name of King George the First of England.

The political force of Spotswood's proclamation was debatable, but the effect on Virginians was not. The returned Knights led the rush to survey and patent new lands. One of them, James Taylor, began the building of a 13,500-acre estate straddling the northern extremity of the Southwest Mountains. He had a daughter, Frances, whom Ambrose Madison married in 1721. Their first child, destined to be known in history as James Madison, Sr., was born on March 27, 1723.

In that same year James Taylor deeded 4,475 acres (his southernmost holdings) jointly to his sons-in-law, Thomas Chew and Ambrose Madison. Patented lands had to be occupied and developed. James Taylor, Jr., moved onto the paternal acres in 1722, Chew went next, and Ambrose followed in 1729.

In the division and development of their 4,475 acres, Thomas Chew built his house at the northern edge of the southern half and Ambrose Madison, at the southern edge of the northern half. Thus, they were close neighbors, on high lands divided by a gentle valley, when Ambrose, Frances, and their three children moved into their new home in 1730. A few miles to the north were the Taylors. In the sparsely settled Piedmont this could be called a compact family grouping.

Ambrose Madison died in 1731, while his first cleared land was still raw with stumps and slash. Frances Madison, a thirty-two-year-old widow, was left with a son and two daughters, aged nine, seven, and six. The slaves numbered twenty-nine—ten men, five women, and fourteen children. The situation was not one to daunt a woman of intelligence and fortitude. Within a few years Frances was marketing her tobacco in England and putting in orders for religious tracts. Eight volumes of *The Spectator* were shipped to her in 1749.

One can only conjecture the age at which the first James Madison took over the farm management. An early responsibility was to carry tobacco to Francis Conway's warehouse on the Rappahannock. James

Madison, bringing each year's crop to the warehouse, could not help noticing that little Nelly Conway, nine years his junior, was growing up. When she reached seventeen he married her. Their oldest son, born March 16, 1751, was given his father's name, James.

For later generations, James Madison's birthdate fell into a bit of confusion because it came in the very year that England, after a century of parliamentary resistance, emulated the continent by switching from the Julian to the Gregorian calendar. According to the Julian calendar James Madison, Sr. and Nelly Conway were married on September 23, 1749, and James was born on March 5, 1750. That has caused sundry readers of family history to count on their fingers. However, calendar reform turned March 5, 1750 into March 16, 1751. The infant Madison, therefore, had eighteen months of parental matrimony to justify his existence.

Highly embarrassing to nineteenth-century Virginia historians was the plebeian quality of Nelly Madison's given name. She is "Nelly" in Conway Bibles, in real-estate transfers, in her mother's will, and in her own will. James Madison wrote about himself for Meade's *Old Churches*: "The name of his mother was Nelly Madison." In the dying days of slavery, however, "Oh my poor Nelly Gray" made that name taboo. So Nelly Conway was posthumously rechristened "Eleanor," with the addition of a "Rose" apparently plucked from a descendant, Nelly Madison Rose.

James Madison's attitude was not that of the Virginia social apparatus. He himself did not fare too well at the hands of those who decided who was who. There is no Madison family listed in Hayden's *Virginia Genealogies*. The Madisons were merely an appendage of the Conways who, although they came from a different English county, were given a guessed-at connection with Sir Edward Conway, knighted by Queen Elizabeth I after his soldiers looted the city of Cadiz.

Twelve children, spaced two years apart, were born to James and Nelly Madison. Five died in infancy. In the order of birth, those who reached maturity were James, Francis, Ambrose, Nelly, William, Sarah, and Frances.

The play circle in early years included Chew and Taylor second cousins and a host of Negro children too young to work. Blacks and whites of all ages made up what Madison always called "our family." Boys in that day rode horses before they could lift a saddle, and "Jemmy" acquired a dexterity that attracted comment only because he retained it in old age. Family excursions by chaise for afternoon dinner covered a radius of fifteen miles (when roads were hard), bringing the Madison youngsters into contact with other cousins, the Willises and Beales.

Madison probably was taught to read and write by his grandmother, Mrs. Ambrose Madison. She died on November 25, 1761, when James was ten years old. A simple burial in the family cemetery was followed five weeks later by the usual formal funeral services to which written invitations were sent out. A new Brick Church rector, James Marye, performed his first official act when he preached from Revelations 14:13 that those "which die in the Lord . . . may rest from their labours; and their works do follow them."

It was about this time that the Madison family moved into the brick mansion, half a mile north of the old house, that bears the name of Montpelier. (Originally Montpellier, for the city in France.) It could not have been built much earlier, for Madison told a grandnephew that he carried light furniture from one house to the other, and his own movements prohibited a later date. The chosen site, where the western slope of Little Mountain leveled off, overlooked a broad expanse of meadows and forests above which, in the distance, rose the great Blue Ridge.

For half a century Montpelier remained a majestic two-story rectangle eighty feet across the front. During Madison's presidency it was enlarged by the addition of symmetrical one-story wings. A century later the wings were brought up to the central height—the gain in utility offset by a sacrifice of architectural perfection. A central hallway bisected the interior, with two large rooms on each side of it in the original design. Such was the setting of Madison's home life for three quarters of a century.

The death of Madison's grandmother may have hastened a decision on schooling, incited by his eagerness for learning. His reading until then had been such as the parental library afforded. Small nourishment could have been drawn from the *Gospel Mystery of Sanctification* and Floxer on *Cold Bathing;* but *The Spectator* should have been available, and he soon had other access to that magazine. In 1829 he wrote to an eleven-year-old grandnephew about the great influence of this work upon him "at an age which will soon be yours." He thought it the best ever written for stirring in young minds "a desire for improvement, a taste for learning and a lively sense of the duties, the virtues and the proprieties of life."

In June of 1762—three months after his eleventh birthday—Madison was enrolled in the boarding school of Donald Robertson, on the eastern shore of the Mattapony, four miles above Dunkirk. His cousins, James and Francis Taylor, already were attending. Robertson, richly equipped

with the learning of Aberdeen and Edinburgh universities, had opened
his school in 1758. Madison studied for five years under Robertson,
whom he afterwards called "a man of great learning." There seems no
reason to question the remark attributed to him by Virginia historian
John H. Gwathmey: "All that I have been in life I owe largely to that
man."

After one year in the English course, "Jamie" (as Robertson called
him) was enrolled in Latin. From Ruddiman's *Rudiments* and Cornelius
Nepos he progressed rapidly through Virgil, Horace, Justinian, Ovid,
Phaedrus, Terence, and Sallust. The final year brought Greek, from
Plutarch to Plato. At the nonclassical level he acquired a reading knowledge of French and Spanish, pronouncing French with a broad Scotch
burr of which he was unconscious until it mystified a Frenchman some
years later. Studies mentioned by himself covered the common branches
of mathematics, Salmon's *Geography* (which included history), and "miscellaneous literature." Robertson's library gave him access to the works
of Montesquieu, Montaigne, Locke, Fontenelle, *The Spectator,* and
other philosophical and political writings.

Among the papers left by Madison is a copybook of 122 pages, stitched
into a cardboard cover. Its main text, entitled "A Brief System of Logick," was drawn from such sources as Isaac Watts' widely used 1725
treatise on logic, Locke's *Essay Concerning Human Understanding,*
Aristotle, and Plato. The contents clearly represented school work,
with no indication of original thinking by Madison. Heavily inked
on the cover are the name and address of James Garlick of King Williams County, whose two sons, Samuel and Camm, became Madison's
schoolmates in 1767. On a blank front page Madison doodled
"1766yy666666666," which can hardly be dissociated from the year
1766. Nevertheless, because of the mental maturity required for organizing the thoughts of others on such a subject, scholars have tended to conclude that although Madison acquired the notebook in boarding school,
he filled it out in college. Also, it has been pointed out, Robertson's catalogue of his library does not include Watts' *Logick*, commonly used in
college courses.

These objections all fail in the light of further facts. The notebook
could not have been filled after it was bound because the written lines
run into the fold. Moreover, during the writing process Madison's handwriting changed, imperceptibly page by page, but conspicuously when
the first dozen pages are compared with the last dozen. It progresses
from large and careful juvenile lettering into smaller, casual, easy writing. No similar change took place in his college correspondence. What

then about the absence of Watts? That proves the very thing it is supposed to disprove.

In his Robertson genealogy William Kyle Anderson wrote: "Owing to the scarcity of textbooks, our ancestor was obliged to prepare those used by his pupils." Obviously, Madison copied the "Brief System of Logick" that Robertson had prepared where books were available. This simple origin eliminates the requirement of mental precocity. Needed for its production were comprehension, interest, and pertinacity, all of which Madison possessed.

The same explanation may account for a dozen astronomical drawings and charts that fill the final pages of the notebook. They were in all probability reproductions of what Anderson called Robertson's "beautiful chirography." In one drawing Madison doodled a human face in the blazing center of the Copernican solar system. He drew this after reading Fontenelle's *Plurality of Worlds,* which had all Europe and America stirred up over the probability of human or humanoid inhabitants of all the planets. Since the charts Madison copied were strictly Copernican, it does not follow that he believed in Fontenelle's neo-Cartesian prelude to "flying saucers."

Madison's connection with the Robertson school ended on September 9, 1767. Little remained for him in its curriculum except more Greek, and there were other reasons for coming home. Three younger Madisons needed schooling, and the Brick Church was receiving a rector competent and willing to provide it for all ages. Thomas Martin was an Anglican minister three years out of the College of New Jersey (now Princeton), a "New Side" Presbyterian school. He lived at Montpelier for the next two years, teaching the younger children and guiding James's studies and reading. These ranged as widely as the books the rector brought with him.

Combined with *The Spectator,* Martin's library need have contained only three particular works to account for the full contents of Madison's "Commonplace Book," compiled at some period of leisurely reading in his early youth. The notebook opens with short excerpts (124 of them) from the *Memoirs of the Cardinal de Retz,* who rose and fell in the France of Louis XIV. Retz had a gift for aphorisms, and Madison picked out many that carried a warning for public men:

> "It is more unbecoming a Minister to speak foolishly than to act foolishly."
> "In some cases it is harder to please those of our own Party than to act against our Adversaries."

"A man shows himself greater by being capable of owning
a fault than by being incapable of committing it."
"Patience works greater effects than activity."

The last two of these aphorisms, applied to Madison's own career,
give him a mixed rating. Unwillingness to confess a fault was his most
conspicuous political frailty. Patient persistence underlay his most notable achievements.

Extracts from the *Essays of Montaigne* demonstrate a growing ability
to analyze and synthesize literary material. Bringing together from different parts of an essay the common thought of Socrates and Plato that
men should treat slander with silence and overthrow it by their conduct,
Madison injected the thought: "A reputation grounded on true virtue is
like the sun that may be clouded, but not extinguished." Throughout his
life he ignored slanders.

A keen interest in literature was displayed in excerpts from the Abbe
Dubos's *Critical Reflections on Poetry and Painting*, preceded and followed by poems from *The Spectator*. In condensing both Montaigne
and Dubos he occasionally sharpened their utterances. A long and pon-
derous sentence by Dubos was cut to read, "the most delicious banquet
without an appetite is insipid."

By the time he was ready to go to college, Madison was better edu-
cated than many a present-day holder of a baccalaureate degree.

2 / COLLEGE AND CLOISTER

In the colonial period young Virginians were expected to obtain their higher education at William and Mary College in Williamsburg, the provincial capital. James Madison went to Princeton. Tidewater malarial climate had something to do with that, but more important was the good account given of the College of New Jersey by tutor Thomas Martin and his visiting brother Alexander, who stopped at Montpelier on journeys from and to the latter's North Carolina home. Both of these recent graduates of the twenty-three-year-old school were alive to the forward push of scholarship under President John Witherspoon, lately arrived from Scotland. No less significantly, the Martins had the same repugnance to attempted British control of the Anglican church in America that swayed vestryman James Madison, Sr.

President James Horrocks of William and Mary reputedly hoped to become the first American bishop. In contrast, Presbyterian Witherspoon had been fighting against church authoritarianism in Scotland even before he was ordained as a minister. He had been at Princeton but a year when an observer wrote that "our Jersey College is now talking as if she was to be a bulwark against Episcopacy."

In June 1769 James Madison set forth on horseback, accompanied by Alexander and Thomas Martin and a trustworthy slave, Sawney. Their 300-mile journey led them through Fredericksburg, Georgetown, and Philadelphia. From Princeton, on August 10, Madison wrote his first preserved letter. It was fortunate, he told Thomas Martin, that he had enrolled at once, even with the September commencement so near, because it enabled him to reread half of Horace and acquaint himself with the principles of versification—subjects he would have to neglect in the next two years. He was perfectly pleased with "the prospect before me of three years confinement," in view of the advantages expected from it. The slave Sawney, on his way home, would pay some Martin bills and carry seven grammars, to be used by the Brick Church rector in expansion of his Montpelier tutoring into a glebe-house school.

Also to be carried was a letter to the senior Madison, accompanied by a pamphlet on the founding and functioning of the college. For the Martins, Madison sent two copies of a 1769 London publication, *Britannia's Intercession for John Wilkes*. Between 1764 and 1769 this champion of civil rights had been three times expelled from the House of Commons, outlawed, and imprisoned for seditious libel of the king and private publication of an obscene *Essay on Woman*. This pamphlet, Madison remarked, "perhaps may divert you."

His next letter to his father (whom he addressed throughout his life as "Honored Sir") promised to heed the parental caution to keep expenses down because of crop losses caused by a great drouth. (A September hurricane completed the destruction.) Every trifle he bought cost far more than was to be expected.

The curriculum at Princeton put the usual heavy stress on Latin and Greek and emphasized mathematics and natural philosophy in the middle years. Madison's advanced position in the classics gave him more time for a new and attractive subject, the Law of Nature and of Nations, for which Witherspoon's qualifications were outstanding. With Harrington, Locke, and Montesquieu as guides to the study of government, and Grotius, Pufendorf, and Vattel as authorities on international relations, Madison laid the groundwork for a lifelong devotion to public law. He profited from the president's insistence that clarity in thinking and speaking was fundamental to education. To support this, Witherspoon expanded the system of public disputations in English and Latin. Many a student heard the Scotch pedagogue lay down two imperative rules for conduct in public life: "Lads, ne'er do ye speak unless ye ha' something to say, and when ye are done, be sure and leave off."

Princeton histories record that upon the retirement of freshman tutor Ebenezer Pemberton, James Madison, as spokesman for his classmates, delivered a eulogy of him in Latin. Asked about this sixty years later by Dr. Benjamin Waterhouse, Madison replied that he well remembered Pemberton's qualities, but had no distinct recollection of taking part in the memorial. This leaves the story in doubt. Yet he was so far beyond the average freshman in his Latinity that he would have been a likely choice for the assignment.

Closely connected with public speaking in college courses were the activities of two literary societies of lasting renown. Madison joined the American Whig Society, organized two months before he reached Princeton, and became one of its principal satirists in the "paper war" with the still younger Cliosophic Society. (Both were reincarnations of earlier societies, destroyed by their conflicts.) The name "Whig" led to the imputation that the Clios were Tories, and the Whigs hammered heavily on that unwarranted insinuation, made in a day when "Tory" was nearly akin to "traitor."

Madison proved himself fluent in verses that fell one foot short of iambic pentameter and several miles short of Homeric heights. Rhymed verses jumped in pairs over purling streams and skipped through flowery Miltonian fields while chamberpots bounced off the heads of base and villainous Cliosophs. President Witherspoon has been quoted as saying that he had never known Madison "to do or say an indiscreet thing" in his college years. If that was true, prevailing standards did not make it indiscreet for Madison to consign Clio's founder, "Great Allen," to Pluto's realm, wherein

> The lecherous rascal there will find
> A place just suited to his mind
> May whore and pimp and drink and swear
> Nor more the garb of christians wear
> And free Nassau from such a pest
> A dunce a fool an ass at best.

Either this was good clean fun or Madison afterwards revised his opinion of his fellow student, for when the Reverend Moses Allen spent two or three days at Montpelier in 1775, he was urged to remain through the entire winter. The warfare of the literary societies was so intense that at times it almost disrupted school work. The public reading of rhymed satires was the top event of the week. Partners of Madison in this activity were two of his close friends with decidedly greater poetic talents than his own—Philip Freneau, master of scurrilous invective, and Hugh Henry Brackenridge, whose strictly proper pen lifted the average in that respect.

The time given to lambasting Clio "Tories" did not prevent Madison from setting a record for swift progress in his studies. He took examinations in his first term that earned him a year's credits. The four-year course was completed in two years. So severe was the strain, he wrote late in life, that his sleep "was reduced for some weeks to less than five hours in the twenty four." Overstudy and lack of exercise took such a toll of his health that five years passed before he made a full recovery.

During Madison's college days Princeton was drawn into the full current of American politics. It was a period of recurring crises between England and her North American colonies. The obnoxious Stamp Act, passed in 1765, was repealed one year later, but not before the American Stamp Act Congress denied the power of the British Parliament to tax the colonies without their consent. England challenged that declaration by passing the Townshend Acts of 1767, imposing specific duties on American imports of half a dozen standard articles, including tea.

The answer to the tax was a general agreement among Boston merchants not to import British goods. Merchants in other cities followed suit. In July 1770, however, Madison was writing to his father about "the base conduct of the merchants in New York in breaking through their spirited resolutions not to import." Their letter to Philadelphia merchants requesting similar action, he said, "was lately burnt by the students of this place in the college yard, all of them appearing in their black gowns and the bell tolling." Twenty-two seniors were to receive diplomas in September, and all of them had agreed to wear American cloth. It was no slight thing for young men to sacrifice English broadcloth for rude homespun on such an occasion, and the New York *Gazette* was led to hope "that many at this critical juncture will follow their laudable example, in encouraging our own manufactures."

The "critical juncture" was the Boston Massacre, in which trigger-jittery British soldiers shot to death five taunting throwers of bricks and snowballs. To this event and to the defection of New York merchants, the students, the press, and Madison all reacted as continentalists. The whole country felt that it had been attacked.

One year later, on the last Wednesday in September 1771, Madison and eleven other seniors received their bachelor degrees from the College of New Jersey. The tone of the commencement exercises was set by the patriotic spirit of the times and received its highest expression in a metrical dialogue written by Brackenridge and Freneau. Their poem on "The Rising Glory of America" struck one of the earliest notes of nationalism and won continental fame. Newspapers listed the contributions of eleven seniors to the program. The only mention of Madison was his inclusion among the twelve who received diplomas. A hundred years afterwards, reproducing the press account in his history of Princeton University, President Maclean wrote into it: "Mr. James Madison was excused from taking any part in the exercises."

No doubt he was, but no newspaper said so. The presumption of illness is heightened by what Madison wrote in his brief "autobiography" at the age of eighty. He remained in Princeton for studies through the winter, "his health being at the time too infirm for a journey home." The determination to remain until spring was disclosed to his father in a lost letter and re-affirmed on October 9 with no mention of the reason. He expressed joy at his mother's "happy deliverance" of another son (Reuben, who lived four years), and hoped for his father's relief from rheumatism. He told of local visiting plans. It seems probable that even though his state of health did not permit an arduous 300-mile journey on horseback, incapacitating illness was not the cause of his nonparticipation in the exercises. That could be accounted for by his weakness of voice and resulting diffidence, which prevented him from addressing public gatherings of any sort until his thirtieth year.

In his 1831 "autobiography," Madison said his half year at Princeton after graduation was employed "in miscellaneous studies; but not without a reference to the profession of law." He also took this opportunity "of acquiring a slight knowledge of Hebrew, which was not among the college studies." It was at this time, possibly, that he studied the law reports of William Salkeld, published in 1717-18, covering the Court of the King's Bench from 1689 (the year after James II was dethroned) to 1714. Or, more likely, he combined Coke and Salkeld in 1784.

Madison's notes on Salkeld have been lost, but twenty years after his death they were in the possession of Inman Horner, a lawyer of Warrenton, Virginia. He wrote to William C. Cabell that Madison's digest of several intricate cases furnished evidence of an acute, strong, and discriminating intellect, which if applied to the law as a profession would have given him a rank at the bar "coequal with his eminence as a statesman." Considering the variety of talents required for pre-eminence at the bar, that judgment may be taken with reserve, but it points unmistakably to his subsequent mastery of *public* law.

Madison's brief study of Hebrew denoted an interest in theology that was further manifested in copious extracts made by him from William Burkett's *Expository Notes* on the New Testament, a book acquired by his father in 1770. The predominant character of the excerpts was proof to biographer William C. Rives that Madison explored Christianity "through clouds of witnesses" and surpassed all but a few theologians in laborious inquiries that "show both his orthodoxy and his penetration." If Madison proved his orthodoxy by jotting down "Christ's Divinity appears by St. John," what did he prove by writing "Sadducees, deny the Resurrection and the existence of Angel or Spirit"? His notes record what he read with no self-revelation except of keen interest and application. The picture of saintly piety transmitted by Rives is slightly scarred by Madison's comment when he heard that his "old friend Dod," lately ordained as a clergyman, had become a father before he became a husband. "I agree with you," he wrote to Bradford, "that the world needs to be peopled but I should be sorry it should be peopled with bastards . . . Who could have thought the old monk had been so lecherous." Editor Hunt expurgated this from Madison's *Writings*.

Madison's affirmative attitude toward theology was expressed in November 1772, after Bradford asked for advice on a puzzling choice between Law and Divinity. He preferred the latter but felt better qualified for the law. Divinity, Madison replied, was the most sublime of all sciences, and Bradford ought in any case to keep it obliquely in view. Religion received its strongest testimony from men rising in reputation and wealth who became "fervent advocates in the cause of Christ." He commended Bradford for his determination to adhere to truth and probity in the practice of law, but doubted whether that would be practicable. Doubt, ignorance, and misrepresentation by clients too often left truth to be extracted in the course of debate. That remark reflected his own reading in the law.

Madison's home studies were mixed with a teaching chore. Thomas Martin had died in 1770, leaving the younger Madisons without a tutor. James undertook the work himself. Nelly, William, and Sarah, aged twelve, ten, and eight, were his only pupils, unless seventeen-year-old extrovert Ambrose could be dragged in by the heels.

Tutoring and studying left too little time for exercise but not too little for brooding. The shock of the rector's death was more than doubled by a letter from Bradford after the 1772 Princeton commencement: "I had some expectation of seeing you and Ross there. But alas!— You have doubtless heard of poor Joe's death." Joseph Ross had been Madison's partner in doing four years' work in two, and the penalty Joe paid menaced James. "As to myself [he replied] I am too dull and infirm now to look out for any extraordinary things in this world for I think my sensations for many months past have intimated to me not to expect a long or healthy life. . . . But you have health youth fire and genius to bear you along through the high tract of public life. . . ."

Five months later, in April 1773, Madison wrote that his health was "a little better owing I believe to more activity and less study recommended by the physicians." He never defined that illness, nor could physicians of that day have named it accurately; but in the draft of a posthumous sketch his brother-in-law John C. Payne wrote and scratched out the statement that Madison was deterred from military service by "a constitutional liability to sudden attacks, of the nature of epilepsy." His mature age at the onset of the seizures, and the complete disappearance of them, identify the illness as epileptiform hysteria. This could not have developed at Princeton without Bradford knowing of it, and there was no sign of that in the surprise and alarm with which he reacted to Madison's letter, nor in his statement that he thought Madison had injured his constitution while in college. Persons of the weakest constitution, he cheeringly added, often outlive those of the strongest, and Madison seemed "designed by Providence for extensive usefulness."

A few months after advising Bradford about law and divinity Madison wrote that he himself intended "to read law occasionally" and had procured books for the purpose. "The principles and modes of government," he observed, "are too important to be disregarded by an inquisitive mind." Bradford could help by sending a sketch of the origin and principles of the Pennsylvania constitution, "particularly the extent of your religious toleration." Here Madison revealed the channeling of his legal studies into the realm of public law; also his immediate purpose, to combat the persecution of dissenters from Virginia's established Anglican church.

This was made more evident as he proceeded. He wanted Bradford to answer two questions: "Is an Ecclesiastical Establishment absolutely necessary to support civil society in a supream government? and how far it is hurtful to a dependent State?" These inquiries, worded to avoid exerting influence on Bradford, did not point to uncertainty in Madison's own mind. Implicitly he was asking: "Why should an established church be necessary to support the British government when it is obviously hurtful to Virginia?" Bradford's reply, regretting that he could not spare time for the inquiry, led Madison to unburden himself:

> If the Church of England had been the established and general religion in all the Northern Colonies as it has been among us here and uninterrupted tranquility had prevailed throughout the Continent, it is clear to me that slavery and subjection might and would have been gradually insinuated among us. Union of religious sentiments begets a surprizing confidence and ecclesiastical establishments tend to great ignorance and corruption all of which facilitate the execution of mischievous projects.

In the same letter (January 24, 1774) he described the "state and liberty" of Virginia:

> Poverty and luxury prevail among all sorts: Pride, ignorance and knavery among the priesthood and vice and wicked-

ness among the laity. This is bad enough but it is not the worst I have to tell you. That diabolical Hell conceived principle of persecution rages among some and to their eternal infamy the clergy can furnish their quota of imps for such business.

In an adjacent county (Culpeper), Madison went on, five or six well-meaning men (Baptists) were in close jail for publishing their religious sentiments which in the main were very orthodox: "I have squabbled and scolded abused and ridiculed so long about it, to so little purpose that I am without common patience. So I leave you to pity me and pray for liberty of conscience to revive among us."

His next letter (April 1) reported that "the persecuted Baptists" were circulating petitions for greater liberty and the Presbyterians planned similar appeals, but he did not anticipate success. Virginia legislators were "too much devoted to the ecclesiastical establishment to hear of the toleration of dissentients." Pennsylvania's "liberal catholic and equitable way of thinking as to the rights of conscience" was but little known among the zealous adherents to the Virginia Hierarchy. Happy it was for Bradford to live in a land where the people enjoyed religious as well as civil liberty. Under that inspiration foreigners had been encouraged to settle; commerce and the arts had flourished. In contrast: "Religious bondage shackles and debilitates the mind and unfits it for every noble enterprize, every expanded prospect."

Although Madison asked Bradford about "toleration"—permissive liberty granted by law to deviate from an established religion—he stated his own attitude and described Pennsylvania's spirit in terms of "the rights of conscience." Concepts of liberty that were to govern him throughout his life and be implanted in constitutional law took shape in the years of quiet study and reflection that followed his return from college.

3 / REVOLUTION

Although at times Madison wrote of his isolation from news and events, the preliminaries to the American Revolution actually crowded upon him at Montpelier. "I congratulate you," he wrote to young Bradford in January 1774, "on your heroic proceedings in Philadelphia with regard to the tea. I wish Boston may conduct matters with as much discretion as they seem to do with boldness."

In Madison's opinion, apparently, Boston merchants resisting taxation by Parliament were bold but indiscreet in raiding three British teaships and dumping their cargoes into salt water. Philadelphia merchants displayed heroism and a discreet regard for private property in merely handing the captain of the teaship *Polly* a cartoon appropriate to the accompanying text: "What think you CAPTAIN of a halter around your neck, ten gallons of liquid tar decanted on your pate with the feathers of a dozen wild geese laid over that to enhance your appearance?" Captain Ayers sailed down the Delaware on the next ebb tide.

Madison blamed the "obduracy and ministerialism" of Massachusetts' royal governor and observed that political, as well as military, contests were sometimes necessary to instruct in the art of defending liberty and property. He verily believed that the frequent assaults on America would, in the end, prove of real advantage. "But away with politicks!" he exclaimed. "Let me address you as a student and philosopher and not as a patriot now." In doing so, he gave patriotism a larger field by contrasting monarchy at its remembered worst with republicanism at its expected best:

> I am pleased that you are going to converse with the Edwards and Henry's and Charles &c &c who have swayed the British Sceptre though I believe you will find some of them dirty and unprofitable companions unless you glean instruction from their follies and fall more in love with liberty by beholding such detestable pictures of tyranny and cruelty.

The Stuarts were American as well as English kings. The condemnation of them was sweeping enough to imply a repudiation of the monarchic form of government.

A decision to put William Madison in the Princeton preparatory school took elder brother James back to his college in the early summer of 1774. Returning, he visited Bradford at Philadelphia and reached home at the end of June, "not a little disturbed," he wrote to his friend, "by the sound of war blood and plunder on the one hand and the threats of slavery and oppression on the other." The bloody war was on the frontiers, where "the savages are determined on the extirpation of the inhabitants." (He had not heard of the earlier butchery of Indians by the white marauders, Cresap and Greathouse.)

On the political front, Madison reported, native Virginians were unanimous and resolute in support of the Bostonians. Resolves were being adopted in every county, indicating a willingness to join the other colonies even in a universal prohibition of trade. By a lucky mistake, some of Dean Josiah Tucker's tracts had been included with books just imported from England, and he read with peculiar satisfaction what they said regarding "the interests of America and Britain." That remark put him in the vanguard of the independence movement. Tucker's proposal concerning America and Britain was that they should separate, completely and forever, by voluntary agreement. The step was short from there to armed revolution.

Actions in Virginia were more comprehensive than Madison indicated. Radicals in the General Assembly had "cooked up" (Thomas Jefferson's term) a proclamation of June 1 as a day of prayer and fasting in support of Boston, whose port was to be closed by royal order on that day. Governor Dunmore responded by dissolving the Assembly. The radicals thereupon gathered at the Apollo room of the Williamsburg tavern and sent out an appeal to committees of correspondence to summon a Continental Congress.

As the convening day (September 5) of Congress approached, Madison and Bradford exchanged appraisals of their delegations. Pennsylvania's, the latter lamented, included several "known to be inimical to the liberties of America." Virginia's seven delegates, Madison was able to reply, were mostly "glowing patriots and men of learning and penetration." Nevertheless, one or two of them, in the opinion of some good judges, could be changed for the better. His remark reflected the unjust suspicion widely felt toward Richard Bland who, as revolution neared, marched behind others in a procession he once had led.

The most radical of the seven were Patrick Henry, Richard Henry Lee, and George Washington. Yet the relatively conservative members—Bland, Peyton Randolph, Benjamin Harrison, and Edmund Pendleton—were able to pull forward great number of Virginians who looked askance at zealots. Deaf to arguments were "some interested merchants among the natives" who, Madison reported, were doing as much as they dared to prevent an interruption of trade. Also, "Scotch clergymen" disregarded the appointed day of prayer and fasting.

Pennsylvania's holdback attitude seemed to Madison much more serious. The inclusion of Joseph Galloway and another like him in the congressional delegation tended to "frustrate the generous designs and manly efforts of the real friends to American Freedom." The Pennsylvania committee of Safety, Madison thought, presumed too much on the generosity and justice of the British crown, when it proposed to defer all active endeavors until concessions were made. Instead:

> Would it not be advisable as soon as possible to begin our defence and to let its continuance or cessation depend on the success of a petition presented to his majesty? Delay on our part emboldens our adversaries and improves their schemes; whilst it abates the ardor of the Americans inspired with recent injuries and affords opportunity to our secret enemies to disseminate discord and disunion. But I am mounting into the sphere of the general Congress to whose wisdom and judgment all private opinions must give place.

Running through these letters is the thread of a swiftly rising continentalism. "*American* freedom" was threatened. "The ardor of the *Americans*" must be maintained. In praise as well as blame, the conduct of individual colonies was appraised in terms of common rights and general security. "Disunion" must be combated, but how could disunion arise unless union already was conceived to exist? With union about to be formalized, Madison endowed Congress with a wisdom and judgment to which all private opinions must defer. Here was the well-sprouted seed of American nationality.

Thinking of the momentous events that lay ahead, Madison envied his friend's "happy situation" as a prospective listener to illuminating debates. Before his own northerly trip he had longed to breathe "the free air" of Pennsylvania as an antidote to Virginia's religious bigotry. Now he yearned for the breath of continental freedom at Philadelphia. "I assure you," he wrote to Bradford, "I heartily repent of undertaking my journey to the North when I did. If I had it to perform now, the opportunity of attending the Congress would be an infinite addition to the pleasure of it." He besought Bradford to inform him of all "singular and important" proceedings that could not be gathered from the public press.

Both the regret and the request were wasted, for the Congress met behind closed doors and delegates divulged nothing without the consent of the majority. The body was in session from September 5 through October 26, 1774—three weeks and a day more than a month. Its powers were based on the credentials of its delegates, diversely derived from revolutionary assemblies, conventions, committees, and county electorates. Virginia's delegates were given no instructions, but the convention stated the intended purposes of the Congress in exceptional detail. It resolved unanimously that, for the security and happiness of the British Empire, a General Congress of deputies assemble quickly "to consider of the most proper and effectual manner of co-operating on the commercial connexion of the colonies with the Mother Country, as to procure redress for the much injured province of Massachusetts-Bay, to secure British America from the ravage and ruin of arbitrary taxes, and speedily as possible to procure the return of that harmony and Union, so beneficial to the whole Empire, and so ardently desired by all British America."

Measured by precise wording, the Virginia delegates had no power except to "consider" such measures. Among the twelve delegations (Georgia sent none) the powers specifically put on paper graded from zero for New York and New Jersey up to New Hampshire's plenipotentiary authority to attend and, with others, "to devise, consult and adopt such measures" as might be most likely to extricate the colonies from their difficulties, secure and perpetuate rights and liberties, and restore harmony. Historians have wrangled over the precise effect of these disparities, to which the delegates themselves paid no attention whatever. One and all, they construed their powers as broadly as those given by New Hampshire. *The real powers of the First Continental Congress were those it exercised*—a fact recognized and judicially declared by the United States Supreme Court in 1794.

Madison heard not a word about the course of events at Philadelphia until, in the *Virginia Gazette* of October 6, he read the Massachusetts "Suffolk Resolves," published by order of the Continental Congress. In nineteen numbered resolutions, Suffolk County rejected late actions of the British Parliament "to enslave America." It pledged nonintercourse with the British Isles and West Indies, and nonconsumption of British merchandise. Confiding in the wisdom and integrity of Congress, the Suffolk convention promised "all due respect and submission to such measures as may be recommended by them to the colonies," for the establishment of American rights and restoration of harmony. Published also by order of Congress was Suffolk County's letter to British Governor-General Thomas Gage, saying that the people had "no inclination to commence a war with his majesty's troops," but they were resolved never to submit to such injuries as were being inflicted.

The handling of these Suffolk Resolves was a masterstroke of strategy. Congressional publication and approval gave them continental distribution and added weight. Local initiative was made the basis of congressional action. The country was given an example of "due respect and submission" to whatever that action might be. Finally, the hard threat of economic reprisal and intimation of armed resistance were sheathed in an appeal to all Americans to support "*their countrymen in the Massachusetts-Bay.*" Congress trusted that the effects "of the united efforts of North America in their behalf, will carry such conviction to the British nation, of the unwise, unjust, and ruinous policy of the present administration, as quickly to introduce better men and wiser measures."

One week later came another indicator of major congressional policy. A resolution was published requesting merchants and others to place no more orders for British goods "until the sense of the Congress on the means to be taken for the preservation of the liberties of America, is made public." A month passed with doors closed. Not until November 4—nine days after the dissolution of Congress—did the Williamsburg newspaper convey the momentous decisions to the people of Virginia.

In this manner the Madisons were introduced to "The Continental Association," through which Americans were to unite for the recovery of their rights and liberties. Agreed to by Congress on October 18, signed two days later by all the delegates as initial members, the Association was to be made universal through the same system of individual signature. Persons who refused to sign, or who violated the agreement after signing, were to be stigmatized and ostracized as the enemies of freedom.

The articles of Continental Association described the "ruinous system of colony administration pursued since 1763." To obtain redress of grievances that threatened to destroy the lives, liberty, and property of British Americans, the signers agreed on their sacred honor that after

December 1 they would not import any goods or merchandise that originated in the British Isles; nor certain other goods that figured in British trade. After the first of March 1775, the ban would extend to nonconsumption of British goods. Nonexportation was postponed until September, to give time for prior repeal of the obnoxious acts of Parliament.

To enforce these rules, Section 11 provided that a committee be chosen in every county, city, and town, by qualified voters, "attentively to observe the conduct of all persons touching this association." When a majority found that any person had violated the Association, it was to publish this fact in the gazette, "to the end, that all such foes to the rights of British-America may be publicly known, and universally contemned as the enemies of American liberty; and thenceforth we respectively will break off all dealings with him or her."

Section 14 forbade any trade or intercourse whatsoever "with any colony or province in North-America, which shall not accede to, or which shall hereafter violate this association." The agreement was to remain binding until specified acts of Parliament were repealed. Provincial conventions and committees were advised to establish further regulations for carrying the Association into execution.

In all American history, no congressional enactment has rivaled the Continental Association in its drastic control of the lives, property, and conduct of the people. It operated as a virtual bill of attainder, inflicting punishment by infamy without judicial trial. The line of authority ran directly from Congress to county committees elected by the people. Provincial assemblies (some of which were unreliable) had no role at the outset except to accede to the Association or, by rejecting or violating it, to subject a whole colony to the same commercial boycott that was directed against England.

Success of the Association depended on acceptance by the people, and that was not left in doubt. Madison reflected more than the Virginia response when he wrote on November 26:

> The proceedings of the Congress are universally approved of in this province and I am persuaded will be faithfully adhered to. A spirit of Liberty and Patriotism animates all degrees and denominations of men. . . . In many counties independent companies are forming and voluntarily subjecting themselves to military discipline . . . Such firm and provident steps will either intimidate our enemies or enable us to defy them.

Virginians moved swiftly to implement the Association. Orange County freeholders, meeting in December, elected Justice of the Peace James Madison chairman of an eleven-man committee that included James, Jr. Late in that month Governor Dunmore wrote that a committee had been chosen in every county, to inspect books, interrogate merchants, and stigmatize all persons transgressing "what they are now hardy enough to call the laws of the Congress." The legal government of the province "is entirely disregarded, if not overthrown. There is not a Justice of the Peace in Virginia that acts, except as a Committeeman." Military companies were being organized in every county "for the avowed purpose of protecting their committees."

Madison recorded the same facts from an opposite point of view. "We are very busy," he wrote in January 1775, raising men and materials for defense against a possible invasion. The extensive demands of Congress, coupled with British pride and ministerial wickedness, required a preparation for great events. By spring several thousand well-trained, high-spirited men would be under arms at their own expense. The Quakers were the only people in Virginia who refused to sign the Association, but he thought them "too honest and simple to have any sinister or secret views." Signing, he said, was "the method used among us to distinguish friends from foes and to oblige the common people to a more strict observance of it."

Reference to "the common people" did not imply a political distinction or rigid social caste like that in England. Suffrage, in spite of a freehold requirement, was almost universal in that Piedmont farming community. (James Madison, Jr., qualified four times over in 1774 by purchasing two hundred acres from his father for thirty pounds.) Yet education and wealth—both of them sources of power—were blended in a minority to whom the generality of citizens looked for leadership. Foremost of such in Orange County were the Madison and Taylor families, each of which produced a President of the United States.

At the borderline of revolution neither James, Jr., nor his associates recognized the right of dissent by the few who felt like exercising it. "Some of our old bigots," he observed to Bradford in March 1775, did not altogether approve the spirited pamphlet attributed (correctly) to General Charles Lee. In it the Anglican church hierarchy was excoriated for want of truth and zest for power, but Lee's pamphlet "was generally, nay with this exception, universally applauded."

Madison wished most heartily that Virginia could lay hands on James Rivington, the New York publisher supposedly subsidized by the British ministry. He would get what he deserved. "A fellow was lately tarred and feathered for treating one of our county committees with disrespect; in New York they insult the whole Colony and Continent with impunity." In another county, a Scotch parson's conscience would not allow him to preach on a fast day appointed (he said) "by unconstitutional authority." The committee closed his church and stopped his salary. Should this parson's insolence not abate he might "get ducked in a coat of tar and a surplice of feathers" and be told to go in his new canonicals and act under the lawful authority of General Gage.

At this point the War of the Revolution began. British regulars and Massachusetts minutemen exchanged their running fire on April 21 at Lexington and Concord. One day earlier, Governor Dunmore transferred Virginia's powder supply from the Williamsburg magazine to a ship in the James River. To reclaim it, Patrick Henry rode to Williamsburg with his Caroline County company. Madison, exulting to Bradford over this action, said nothing about a tributary incident that is recorded in the memoirs of Philip Mazzei.

The Albemarle Independents, Mazzei wrote, set out to join Henry and were met at the Orange County line by "two young men sent from that county's company for the purpose of bringing the two companies together." He identified them as "the two Madison brothers, the elder of whom . . . is now President of the United States."

On May 9 the Orange County Committee adopted resolutions praising Henry for his "seasonable and spirited proceedings in procuring a compensation for the powder fraudulently taken from the country magazine, by command of Lord Dunmore." The only known manuscript of the resolution is in Madison's handwriting, and the style is unmistakably his. The closing words reflected the impact of the news of Lexington and Concord: "We take this occasion also to give it as our opinion, that the blow struck in the Massachusetts government is a hostile attack on this and every other colony, and a sufficient warrant to use violence and reprisal, in all cases where it may be expedient for our security and welfare."

Patrick Henry's exploit, Madison remarked to his Philadelphia friend, had gained him "great honor in the most spirited parts of the country." It contrasted strongly with the "pusillanimity" of tidewater gentlemen, who were extremely alarmed lest their property be exposed to governmental reprisals. Weeks of anxious uncertainty and wild stories followed these events. Bradford forwarded the rumor current in Philadelphia that Benjamin Franklin, home from England, had been installed in

Congress as a spy to report its secret proceedings to the British ministry. Madison shuddered at the thought of such perfidy; yet, directed against a man of such high repute, "the bare suspicion of his guilt amounts very nearly to a proof of its reality." "But [he continued] when I consider the united virtue of that illustrious body every apprehension of danger vanishes. The signal proofs they have given of their integrity and attachment to liberty both in their private and confederate capacities must triumph over jealousy itself."

The Second Continental Congress, convening on May 10, speedily justified that trust. On May 13 it declared a total boycott of the colony of Georgia, except St. John's Parish, for refusing to adhere to the Continental Association. On May 26 it voted that "these colonies be immediately put into a state of defence."

On June 3 the Continental Army came into existence as a title. In mid-June George Washington was commissioned "General and Commander in chief of the army of the United Colonies."

Congress next voted to emit two millions of Spanish milled dollars in bills of credit to be called "Continental Currency" and pledged "the twelve confederated colonies" for their redemption in gold or silver. Michael Hillegas and George Clymer were then appointed "joint treasurers of the United Colonies," each of them under a bond of $100,000 to be held "in trust for the United Colonies."

In the face of these actions some historians have contended that no such entity as the United Colonies ever was thought of by those who used the term. "The expression 'united colonies,' " wrote Claude A. Van Tyne, ". . . simply meant 'united efforts.' " That contention, refuted by hundreds of congressional actions and thousands of documents, is totally shattered by a resolution adopted on September 9, 1776: "Resolved, That in all continental commissions, and other instruments, where, heretofore, the words 'United Colonies' have been used, the stile be altered, for the future, to the 'United States.' "

Turning to diplomacy, Congress on July 6, 1775, adopted Thomas Jefferson's declaration on the causes and necessity of taking up arms. This was followed by an address of "the twelve United Colonies" to the people of Great Britain and a "humble petition" to the King, written by and adopted to satisfy John Dickinson. The number "twelve" was about to disappear. Stung by the continental boycott, the people of Georgia elected a new convention. The Association was signed, and Congress admitted a Georgia delegation.

The course Congress followed ran closely parallel to the views James Madison had been expressing for many months. As far back as August

1774 he wanted the colonies to put united defensive measures ahead of petitions to the Crown. He recognized the authority of Congress before that body came into existence. He referred to congressional delegates in their *confederate* capacity three days before Congress pledged the *confederated* colonies to redeem the continental currency. Now, reading the July "Declaration" and "Address," he concurred with Bradford "in every encomium that can be bestowed on them." Such eloquence "vied with the most applauded oration of Tully himself."

At this time Madison was fully engaged in military activities, to which he turned on hearing of the fighting in Massachusetts. By June he had become expert enough with the rifle (though considerably below the best) not often to miss "the bigness of a man's face at the distance of 100 yards." However, the rigors of training took such a toll of his health that he was forced to turn to the organization of forces and the gathering of supplies.

The Virginia convention, he wrote after praising the congressional pronouncements, was planning to reorganize the armed forces of the province, paying all those in active service. Preparations for war were going on in a most vigorous manner, but "the scarcity of ammunition is truly alarming." In October 1775 the Virginia Committee of Safety appointed James Madison, Jr., "Colonel of the Militia of the County of Orange." His superior officer was County-Lieutenant James Madison, Sr. Under the law of the convention, this force was to be kept in constant readiness but not called into service "except in cases of the most urgent and immediate danger." No such order ever was issued, so "Colonel James Madison" took no part in the fighting. Neither, after his service ended, did he ever employ or court the title of "Colonel" by which he often was addressed.

The position, however, was no mere honorary one. The duties were great enough, in organization and supply, to make his correspondence a total blank from July 28, 1775, until late the following May. By that time he was entering into a succession of public offices that covered the next forty years.

4 / INDEPENDENCE AND
HUMAN RIGHTS

> At a convention of delegates from the counties and cor-
> porations in the colony of Virginia, held at the Capitol in
> the city of Williamsburg on Monday, the sixth day of May
> the year of our Lord 1776; present . . . For Orange: James
> Madison and William Moore esquires. [Journals.]

A succession of events, all tending toward a final break with England,
produced this meeting. In August 1775 the Virginia Convention decreed
that annual elections be held thereafter in every county, on April "court
day," to choose convention deputies. Governor Dunmore abandoned
Williamsburg, set up government on a ship of war, and tried to make
the Norfolk-Hampton area a bastion of British strength. The reaction
of residents was such that late in November he put that region under
martial law.

A messenger from the Eastern Shore raced to Philadelphia with the
news. Congress at once did what it already had done regarding Massachusetts, New Hampshire, and South Carolina. With the approval of the
Virginia delegates it declared on December 4 that Lord Dunmore was
"tearing up the foundations of civil authority and government" in that
colony. It was "*Resolved*, Therefore, that if the convention of Virginia
shall find it necessary to establish a form of government in that colony,
it be recommended to that Convention to call a full and free representation of the people, and that the said representatives, if they think it necessary, establish such form of government as in their judgment will best
produce the happiness of the people, and most effectually secure peace
and good order in the colony, during the continuance of the present dispute between Great Britain and these colonies."

The final words formed a slender cord of possible reconciliation
between the colony and mother country. Two fires burned this away.

Dunmore celebrated New Year's Day by setting a match to the city of Norfolk. Thomas Paine lighted the other fire with the blazing torch of *Common Sense*, his anonymous exhortation for a declaration of independence. George Washington connected them: "A few more of such flaming arguments as were exhibited at Falmouth [Massachusetts] and Norfolk," he wrote on January 31, "added to the sound doctrine and unanswerable reasoning contained in the pamphlet *Common Sense*, will not leave numbers at a loss to decide upon the propriety of a separation."

An America divided three ways became within weeks a two-party continent as the vast middle group, revolting but desiring reconciliation, surged forward under the banner of independence. Paine made British monarchs, even more than Parliament, the repulsive symbol of American grievances. In adopting this tactic, he struck at the only admitted legal tie between the colonies and the mother country. "A masterly, irresistible performance," General Charles Lee called it, one that would "give the coup-de-grace to Great Britain."

Common Sense did more than that. It made independence synonymous with American nationhood. "Now is the seed-time of Continental union, faith and honor," cried Paine. Nothing but "independence, *i.e.*, a Continental form of government, can keep the peace of the Continent." Let us, said he, frame "a Continental Charter, or Charter of the United Colonies . . . Always remembering, that our strength is Continental, not Provincial." A traveler passing through Virginia wrote in April: "I hear nothing praised but *Common Sense* and independence." It was in this atmosphere that the Virginia Convention assembled on May 6, backed by the permission of the Continental Congress to establish a plan of government and inspired by the vision of independence and continental union.

James Madison and older William Moore set out for Williamsburg in the last days of unseasonable cold and drouth that left many cornfields unplanted. They splashed into the capital during a three-day downpour that turned flat lowlands into "a welkin of water." Here, for the first time, Madison encountered the panoply of war and the full feeling of the Revolution. The little city was guarded by Continental troops and Virginia minutemen under British-born General Charles Lee. Uniformed army officers and convention delegates mingled in Capitol corridors and fraternized in the Raleigh Tavern. Leather-breeched "shirtmen" bearing musket or rifle sloshed along Duke of Gloucester Street, the mile-long link between William and Mary College and the Capitol. Fifteen miles away, in the York River, lay the armed ships of Governor

Dunmore, who was building up landing parties of American Tories and runaway slaves.

James Madison looked quite a bit younger than his twenty-five years. In Virginia, anybody less than six feet tall was a midget, and Madison was only five feet six. The impression was increased (one could not say heightened) by his slender frame and boyish features. He was still beset with the fragility of long illness. Natural shyness and a voice that did not carry barred him from a speaking role in the big assembly. By the laws of politics he was slated to be a silent back-seater, with little to do but listen and cast his vote.

The youth from Orange had one possible offset to these handicaps. The first action of the delegates was to elect as their president Edmund Pendleton of Caroline County, who had headed the 1775 convention. He was the intimate friend and legal counsel of the elder Madison. James Jr. had met Patrick Henry and knew a few delegates from neighboring counties, including his cousin James Taylor of Caroline. Others he must have met at Montpelier, a favorite stopping place of Virginia gentlemen who timed long journeys to reach hospitable homes before sunset.

Youth was in itself no bar to prominence in that convention. Henry Tazewell, two years younger than Madison, was made its secretary. Edmund Randolph, three years Madison's junior, was elected Attorney General late in its session, a post that was virtually hereditary in the Randolph family. Edmund's grandfather held it, as did his father until he turned Tory and took refuge with Dunmore.

Madison was appointed to the important Committee on Privileges and Elections, which settled some hot election disputes and reported on persons accused of being "inimical to the rights and liberties of America." Madison's appointment hardly sustained the adulatory conclusions of early historians and biographers. The committee embraced more than half of the convention delegates, including all of those whose counties ranged alphabetically from Louisa to York. Madison was put on because Orange was sufficiently far from Accomac.

The business for which the convention was called—framing a plan of government—was left for action after the deeper issue of independence was decided. That subject reached the floor on May 14 in committee of the whole. Madison and Randolph sat together through much of the debates—a fact that remained clear in Randolph's memory when he undertook, thirty-five years later, to write a history of Virginia. His florid literary style did not interfere with accurate observation and honest impression.

His diffidence [he said of Madison] went hand in hand with his morals, which repelled vice, however fashionable. In convention debate, his lips were never unsealed except to some member, who happened to sit near him; and he who had once partaken of the rich banquet of his remarks, did not fail to wish to sit daily within the reach of his conversation. . . . When he thrilled with the ecstacies of Henry's eloquence, and extolled his skill in commanding the audience, he detected what might be faulty in his reasoning. Madison was enviable in being among the few young men who were not inflated by early flattery and could content themselves with throwing out in social discourse jewels which the artifice of a barren mind would have treasured up for gaudy occasions.

The reference to Patrick Henry touched one of the strangest features of the convention. It was expected from the outset, wrote Randolph, that a declaration of independence would be passed, "and for obvious reasons Mr. Henry seemed allotted to crown his political conduct with this supreme stroke." Yet he talked on the subject at length "without committing himself by a pointed avowal in its favor or a pointed repudiation of it." When the attitude of the delegates was fully revealed, Henry drafted an independence resolution and became "a pillar of fire" in advocacy of it.

That course of action was in accord with Patrick Henry's invariable rule—never to ride and direct the storm until he knew that its course was unchangeably set by public opinion. So it had been in the Virginia convention of 1775, when his famous peroration, "I know not what course others may take; but as for me, give me liberty or give me death," was uttered in support of an arm-the-colony resolution already adopted and published by the Fairfax County Committee. That was not the case with Henry's reputed Stamp Act utterance of 1766, "If this be treason make the most of it." However, in the only contemporary record of that speech, written in English by a French listener, Henry answered the cry of "Treason" by saying that "the heat of passion might have lead him to have said something more than he intended, but again, if he had said anything wrong, he beged the speaker and the house's pardon." Outside of mythical heroics, any subject of King George III who wanted to keep his head on his shoulders would have said just that.

Never after 1766 did Henry undertake to lead a crowd unless it already was abreast of him. Then why did he argue for delay by a convention that was clearly ripe for American independence? The key to that mystery is found in a letter written to him by congressional delegate Richard Henry Lee on April 20, 1776. Lee urged a speedy declaration of independence and foreign alliances, lest Great Britain "seal our ruin by signing a treaty of partition with two or three ambitious powers that may aid in conquering us."

Patrick Henry knew all the ins and outs of Virginia politics, but Europe was outside his ken. Instead of impelling him to action, Lee's letter smote him with a vision of England buying French aid by dividing the American colonies with her. These fears governed his early position in the May convention, as shown by a May 8 letter from General Charles Lee (no relation to R.H.L.). This dealt with "the objection you made yesterday, if I understood you rightly, to immediate declaration" of independency. "Your idea that [France] may be diverted from a line of policy which assures them such immense and permanent [commercial] advantages by an offer of partition from Great Britain appears to me, if you will excuse the phrase, an absolute chimera."

General Lee failed to convince Henry, but finally, with the convention about to surge ahead, the great orator seized leadership by drafting and supporting a motion instructing the delegation at Philadelphia to seek "an immediate, clear and full Declaration of Independency." This was molded by Pendleton into a more comprehensive resolution, unanimously approved. Still beset by his groundless fears, Henry wrote to John Adams and Richard Henry Lee opposing early action by Congress on the Virginia resolve. "The half of our Continent offered to France," he told Adams, "may induce her to aid our destruction, which she certainly has the power to accomplish."

These letters to Adams and Lee (both of the same tenor) testified as much to the intensity of Henry's patriotism as they did to his muddled thinking. They also foreshadowed one of Madison's future tasks—to combat the unreasoning fear of France that gripped a powerful Virginia faction (not including Patrick Henry) after the alliance with her became a fact.

There was no hesitancy in the independence resolution unanimously adopted by the Virginia Convention on May 15, 1776:

> Resolved, unanimously, That the delegates appointed to represent this Colony in General Congress, be instructed to propose to that respectable body, to declare the United Colonies free and independent States, absolved from all alle-

giance to, or dependence upon, the Crown or Parliament of Great Britain; and that they give the assent of this Colony to such declaration, and to whatever measures may be thought proper and necessary by the Congress for forming foreign alliances, and a Confederation of the Colonies, at such time and in the manner as to them shall seem best. Provided, That the power of forming Government for, and the regulations of the internal concerns of each Colony, be left to the respective Colonial Legislatures.

Employing the words of this resolution, the Virginia delegates in Congress offered their independence motion on June 7. It was adopted on July 2. The formal Declaration of Independence was adopted on July 4 and signed by the congressional delegates on August 2.

Following its call to Congress on independence, the convention resolved unanimously, "that a committee be appointed to prepare a Declaration of Rights, and such a plan of government as will be most likely to maintain peace and order in this colony, and secure substantial and equal liberty to the peole." This was the all-important committee of the convention, and appointments were made at once. Madison listened to Clerk Tazewell read twenty-eight names, including all the potentates of the convention. Tazewell read his own name and that of Edmund Randolph, but not Madison's.

A day-and-a-half recess was planned, with Thursday afternoon and evening (May 16) devoted to a grand celebration at Waller's Grove. Friday would be "Congress Sunday"—a Continental day of fasting. Well along in the Thursday morning session the convention "ordered, that Mr. Madison, Mr. Rutherford and Mr. Watkins, be added to the committee" on rights and government. It is not hard to guess who was the happiest celebrant at Waller's Grove. There three toasts were offered containing instinctive recognition of national union: "The American Independent States"; "The Grand Congress of the United States and their respective legislatures"; and "General Washington, and victory to the American arms."

George Mason, tardy as usual because of temperament or gout, took his seat on May 18. Appointed to five committees, he took charge of the one that counted. Relying almost entirely on his pen, the committee on May 27 reported a Declaration of Rights that embodied the libertarian thought of centuries. Its articles tapped Magna Carta and the 1689 English Bill of Rights, drew from Locke and Montesquieu, Wycliffe and

St. Augustine. The central political thought followed that of Nicholas of Cusa, who wrote in the fifteenth century: "Since all men are by nature free, government rests on the consent of the governed."

Mason drafted all but three or four of the sixteen articles but the original wording and committee alterations were thrown into confusion for about 175 years by a quirk of vanity in the chief author. Pleased by some changes, disliking others, he put out, in 1778, a purported "original" draft that was a composite of the true original, the committee version, and the final draft. Half a century later Madison attempted to clear this up, not from recollection but from a comparative study of the three available documents. Had the asserted original been genuine it would have been a brilliant analysis, but as it was, he only compounded the confusion. He gave Mason credit for part of the committee changes and concluded that in other instances the committee had altered the text and the convention restored the original phrasing.

The truth became evident with the identification (which happened to be made by the author of this book) of the true original, given by Mason to Thomas Ludwell Lee, who sent it to Richard Henry Lee in Philadelphia on May 25, 1776. The only actual change of any importance in Mason's draft was made by Madison himself in the article on freedom of religion.

Mason, a conventional Anglican, shared the Lockean idea that an established church should permit (in Mason's words) "the *fullest toleration* in the exercise of religion, according to the dictates of conscience." Madison believed that all men had *equal and unalienable right* to that free exercise of conscience. He might, perhaps, have carried that sole point in committee, but he linked it with an attempt at total disestablishment of the state church. The committee turned down his draft (now lying among his papers), proclaiming freedom of conscience and providing that "no man or class of men ought on account of religion to be invested with peculiar emoluments or privileges." A second draft, also preserved, contained the innovating words that went into the final version. This was worked out in partnership with Edmund Pendleton, who offered it on the floor. Preserving the opening and closing provisions of Mason's draft, it was given meaningful force by Madison. His contribution is here italicized:

> That religion, or the duty which we owe to our CREATOR, and the manner of discharging it can be directed only by reason and conviction, not by force or violence, and there-

fore all men *are equally entitled to the free exercise of religion*, according to the dictates of conscience; and that it is the mutual duty of all to practice Christian forbearance, love and charity towards each other.

Madison's deep concern over religious liberty, implicit in his low opinion of Tudor and Stuart monarchs, was intensified by the cruel and senseless persecutions he had witnessed in his own neighborhood, but his thinking went far beyond this. All history verified for him the aphorism of James Harrington that "where civil liberty is entire, it includes liberty of conscience. Where liberty of conscience is entire, it includes civil liberty." Conversely, Madison reasoned, without freedom of conscience there can be no freedom of speech, press, assembly, or association; no equality before the law; but he rejected Harrington's illogical conclusion that a national religion furnishes an avenue to freedom of conscience.

Similarly, Madison recognized the dangers inherent in Locke's argument that an established church, by its toleration of other sects, proved itself to be the true church. Ahead of his times, he was unable to bring about a separation of church and state; but he was able, at the age of twenty-five, to bring others abreast of himself in recognizing freedom of conscience as an inborn human right. With this and other rights established, the convention took up its initial business, the framing of a plan of government suited to a commonwealth on the road to independence and republican self-rule.

5 / LEGISLATOR AND COUNCILLOR

By the congressional resolution of December 4, 1775, the Virginia delegates elected in April 1776 were authorized to set up a form of government to operate "during the continuance of the present dispute between Great Britain and these colonies." That limited objective was rendered inadequate by the Virginia convention's May 15 resolution asking Congress "to declare the United Colonies free and independent states." The dilemma ended the moment it began. On that same day, May 15, Congress adopted a far more drastic resolution on government. It was necessary, Congress resolved, "that the exercise of every kind of authority under the said crown [of Great Britain] should be totally suppressed" and all the powers of government be exerted under the authority of the people of the colonies. Therefore all colonies whose governments were inadequate should adopt such government as would "best conduce to the happiness and safety of their constituents in particular, and America in general."

That resolve of Congress furnished the declared basis of Virginia's subsequent action. A form of government drafted almost entirely by George Mason was placed before the convention on June 24 and unanimously adopted five days later. A lengthy preamble, sent from Philadelphia by Thomas Jefferson, was given this additional paragraph:

> We, therefore, the Delegates and Representatives of the good people of Virginia, having maturely considered the premises, and viewing with great concern the deplorable condition to which this once happy country must be reduced, unless some regular, adequate mode of civil polity is speedily adopted, *and in compliance with a recommendation of the General Congress*, do ordain and declare the future form of govermnent to be as followeth.

The new governmental system reflected acute distrust of the Executive, which was linked in the public mind with kings and royal governors. Legislative and appointive powers were concentrated in an elected House and Senate. The governor, chosen annually by the legislature, could not buckle his shoes without the approval of an eight-man Council of State. The Executive possessed no veto power. Annual elections furnished the only check on an otherwise omnipotent legislature. The right of suffrage was to "remain as exercised at present," which meant a restriction to freeholders.

By "ordaining and declaring" the Constitution, the convention put it into effect without ratification. It then converted itself into a one-house legislature, elected Patrick Henry governor, and proceeded to enact laws for the commonwealth.

Madison played no discoverable role in the formation of this plan of government and left no contemporary comment upon it. Eight years later he assailed it in the Virginia House of Delegates as improper and invalid. The convention, he said in a speech known from the notes he used, was without due power from the people. Acting from the "impulse of necessity," it passed the ordinance "on recommendation of Congress of May 15, 1776, prior to declaration of independence: as was done in N.H. and N.J."

Madison stressed these grounds of invalidity by stating them a second time in his notes: "Before independence declared by Congress. Power from people no where pretended." By putting the Constitution into effect without ratification, the convention let its validity rest solely "on acquiescence, a bad basis." Because the delegates converted themselves into a branch of the legislature, alterable laws came from the same body that produced a supposedly unalterable constitution.

This charter of government, Madison declared, flouted Montesquieu's principle that a union of powers in one department is tyranny. Executive and judiciary were both dependent on the legislature. Equality of representation was not provided for. The Senate, badly constituted, could not initiate legislation. With suffrage vaguely defined "as exercised at present," an old law might possibly disfranchise "popish recusants." If not revised to cure these defects, the Constitution should still be referred to the people for approval or rejection, to secure it against prevailing "doubts and imputations."

Passing years sustained Madison's indictment, as worsening malapportionment and a growing landless urban population made Virginia's legislative autocracy (in the words of Jefferson) a usurpation of the minority upon the majority. Nevertheless, Madison's argument was not flawless. His principal thought in 1784 was to secure a ratification that would protect religious freedom against threatened invasion by the legislature. Then when did the idea occur to him that any charter of state government was invalid if adopted before Congress declared the independence of the United Colonies on July 4, 1776? That thought, it is safe to say, was a belated by-product of his concern over the defects of the Constitution.

Madison was contending, apparently, that Congress itself had no right to recommend state government before it adopted the Declaration of Independence. This took no account of the May 15 preamble, in which Congress resolved that every kind of authority under the British crown "should be totally suppressed." That was a virtual declaration of independence. A revolutionary Congress had the right to make it, and the states to act under it, as fully as if there had been a complete formal break.

From Richard Henry Lee and George Wythe, home from Philadelphia, Madison and his associates learned that congressional action on independence was held off until July to enable certain states—Pennsylvania, Maryland, and New York—to replace reluctant delegates or give new instructions. At length came President John Hancock's official copy of the declaration of July 4. Governor Henry being absent, it was immediately proclaimed by Lieutenant Governor John Page and the governor's council. Executives of nine other states made similar proclamations. New York, whose delegation had abstained from voting because uninstructed, put the declaration into effect by legislative action, as did Rhode Island and Connecticut.

The Declaration, written chiefly by Jefferson, was a virtual composite of his preamble to the Virginia Constitution, the "freedom and equality" concept of the Virginia Declaration of Rights, and that state's May 15 resolution calling for a break by Congress. It was a declaration by the "Representatives of the United States of America, in Congress, Assembled . . . That these United Colonies are, and of right ought to be Free and Independent States," having full power to levy war, conclude peace, contract alliances, "and to do all other acts and things which independent States may of right do."

Madison would have been mightily astonished had he heard, from an American source, the denial of Professor Van Tyne that this declaration created any such entity as the United States. It merely meant, Van Tyne wrote, that "the representatives of the *states* of America, *united* to aid each other in attaining independence, . . . [proclaimed that] *they* have full power to levy war," and so on. That theory had two eminent sponsors during the Revolution. The highest of them was King George III, who on December 22, 1775, issued a proclamation against "the present rebellion within the said colonies *respectively*." When British commander Lord Howe addressed the American commander-in-chief as "George Washington, Esquire," the letter was returned to him unopened, along with a copy of the Declaration of Independence. Howe's re-addressed letter brought from Abraham Clark of New Jersey the ecstatic remark: "He gave General Washington the title of General and called us the United States."

Although his thoughts were attuned to the national struggle, Virginia was the scene of Madison's public activities for nearly four years after the proclamation of independence. In October 1776, after spending the summer at home, he returned to Williamsburg as delegate-turned-legislator. There he had his first contact with Thomas Jefferson—the beginning of a lifelong friendship and close political association.

Jefferson, shifting his operations from Congress to the State Assembly, rose to immediate leadership of it. Madison became his righthand man in furthering what were partially Madisonian policies. Native to Jefferson's genius was his successful assault on the ancient laws of entail and primogeniture, through which Virginia had long maintained a political and social aristocracy; but in attempting to disestablish the Church of England he turned to a subject on which there is no record of his attention before Madison made it an issue in the emerging state.

Arriving a few days late, Madison was appointed to the conservative committee on religion. There he read with delight the petition of Prince Edward County citizens who described his contribution to the Declaration of Rights "as the rising sun of religious liberty." They asked that, "without delay, all church establishments might be pulled down, and every tax upon conscience and private judgment abolished."

Delegates from Augusta County, the stronghold of Scotch-Irish Presbyterian Dissenters, were instructed that the free exercise of religion required "that no religious sect whatever be established in this commonwealth." They hoped that interested bigots and illiberal politicians would be too few to perpetuate the existing system, but if it proved otherwise the people of Augusta would never be governed by the slavish notion that everything enacted by the supreme legislative body of the state "must in all cases be implicitly obeyed." Here was due notice that the American Revolution was more than an uprising to throw off British rule; evidence also that Madison's declaration of religious freedom had touched one of its deepest chords. The threat of disobedience was a protest against tidewater domination through the "rotten borough" system.

Dissenters alone could not have carried the day, but many Anglicans were tired of paying taxes to maintain a dissolute clergy. They joined the Presbyterians, Baptists, and others in removing the question from the do-nothing committee on religion to the floor of the House. There Jefferson put through a resolve that all acts of the assembly for support of the clergy "ought to be repealed." Anglican leaders toned the repeal down to a suspension of tax levies for religion until the next session. Practically speaking, that ended the Anglican establishment. The tithe levy, once broken, was soon wiped out by law. To Jefferson and Madison it was a successful session, bearing the stamp of social revolution.

Up for re-election in 1777, Madison refused to set up barrels of free whisky in the courthouse square. Attributing this violation of sacred custom to "a mean parsimony or to a proud disrespect," (he wrote later), the angered voters roundly defeated him, electing a man deficient in every nonalcoholic qualification. The new legislature promptly elected Madison to the governor's council—sure evidence that his work in the 1776 session was of greater import than the record he left of it. He was high man in a first vote spread among seven nominees, then defeated Meriwether Smith 61 to 42. The selection, made without his knowledge or solicitation, was said by his later secretary, Edward Coles, to be due to the willingness and skill he had shown in the preparation of state papers.

Taking up his new work on January 14, 1778, Madison found himself in a "much better accommodation than I could have promised myself." His second cousin and name-sharer, President James Madison of William and Mary College (lately returned from England), invited him to live in his house and eat with the college faculty. To make "some little return for the culinary favours," James of Montpelier asked his father to ship quantities of dried fruit, of which his cousin was very fond.

In law, the Council of State consisted of the governor and eight councillors. In reality, wrote Madison, it was made up of eight governors and a councillor. "The grave of all useful talents," he called it. That verdict had overall validity, but there was plenty of work for all nine members in the manifold tasks created by the war. Militarily, the Revolution was moving from brilliant achievement into "the time that tries men's souls," as Thomas Paine wrote in *The Crisis*. General Washington had won the victories of Trenton and Princeton. General Burgoyne blundered down the Hudson Valley from Lake Champlain, met with no support from the incompetent General Howe, and surrendered to the American army of Generals Gates and Arnold. Victories lulled patriots to sleep. Short-term enlistments and militia calls made the army a coming-and-going concern, mostly going. General Howe, moving his troops by sea up the Delaware, drove Congress out of Philadelphia. General Washington bedded his men down at Valley Forge, eighteen miles from that city, to watch and wait out a winter of torment.

On the first day Madison attended the council, Governor Henry submitted a letter from a committee of Congress, then sitting at York, conveying Washington's warning that the Continental Army must either "starve dissolve or disperse" unless it secured supplies immediately. The committee, speaking through Virginian Francis Lightfoot Lee, suggested that the state consider whether "an immediate seizure of all cattle, hogs, pork and salt" was not indispensably necessary. Unwilling to take this action, but distrusting the continental commissariat in Virginia, the council advised Governor Henry to appoint three special agents to make the purchases and delivery. Henry wrote to Lee that the purchases would be executed with great loss to the public. The urgency of the occasion "puts the price of meat etc. in the power of wicked, avaricious and disaffected men." Yet the whole country, particularly the area near headquarters, "abounds with the provisions for which the army is said to be almost starving."

Congress authorized impressment, but the army could not reach out beyond the near neighborhood. The states had the military forces needed for such seizures, but public opinion was not ripe for it. The highest obstacle to impressment was the same thing that made it necessary. Continental currency, unsupported by states taxes, was depreciating fast. Farmers and merchants who sold supplies to the government were paid in paper that continued to lose value while they held it. A new Virginia law made it a crime for any person to demand more in bills than in coin. It was a dead letter from the day it was signed.

Likewise, on the first day he attended the council, Madison joined in approving a step by Governor Henry to promote American occupation of the West. Colonel David Rogers was ordered to recruit thirty soldiers and go by flatboat down the Ohio and Mississippi to New Orleans for a load of goods. He bore a letter to Spanish Governor Galvez requesting a loan to Virginia and asking him to consider "whether by uniting West Florida to the Confederation of the States of America, the English settlements will not be reduced to an extremity." Two weeks earlier the council had sanctioned Henry's plan to send Colonel George Rogers Clark with three hundred men to attack the British post of Kaskaskia (Illinois) and thus gain control of the upper Mississippi Valley.

The letter to Galvez has been described by some as evidence of Virginian foreign ventures and diplomatic relationships independent of Congress. In reality the stimulus to the whole undertaking came from Congress. Governor Henry opened the correspondence in response to "a letter from his Excellency the Governor of New Orleans, directed to the Congress, and by the president transmitted to me as governor of this commonwealth." Madison, who approved this initial move to acquire West Florida, brought that province under American jurisdiction as President of the United States.

Multiply Madison's first day on the council by two years and it spans a period in which the Virginia Executive worked in faithful harmony with Congress, against heavy difficulties growing out of legislative shortcomings, state and federal. The trait that brought him to the council—his willingness and skill in writing—was utilized by Governor Henry to saddle on him the writing of official letters—something the Governor detested. Henry's matter-of-fact stride pervades the most important of his papers, especially those addressed to George Rogers Clark.

More onerous was a task imposed on Madison by his command of written French. With New York and Philadelphia in British hands and Boston harbor menaced, French war supplies came in a stream to Norfolk, which also was the port of debarkation for officer volunteers from France. This followed French recognition of American independence and the signing of a treaty of alliance on February 6, 1778. News of Dr. Franklin's treaty was relayed by Madison to his friend Colonel William Bradford on March 23, along with other reports (concerning co-operative action by Prussia and Portugal) which "carry the face of great improbability."

When French correspondence became too heavy for Madison to add to his other duties, he was given relief by the appointment of Carlo Bellini as "clerk of foreign correspondence." Bellini, an Italian vineyard worker, was an expert linguist. His work for the council involved no discretion, but the "state sovereignty school" of historians seized on his title as evidence that he headed a department of foreign affairs. Wrote Professor Van Tyne: "Virginia ratified the treaty with France, and her diplomatic activity was so great that she established by law a clerkship of foreign correspondence."

The "ratification" was a belated propaganda move that occurred in the *third legislative session* after the treaty went into effect. In June 1779 a wild rumor spread in Williamsburg that Congress was breaking the French alliance. Faced with this "most dreadful calamity," wrote Governor Jefferson to congressional delegate William Fleming, the legislature ratified the treaty "to satisfy the mind of the French minister." Of such flimsies is built the historical fiction of a nonexistent nation and all-sovereign states.

The State Council's work was complicated in the spring of 1778 by an Indian war. A witless fort commander locked up, as hostages, Shawanese chiefs Cornstalk and Red Hawk, who came to warn that British officers had turned nearby tribes against the Americans. "I can die but once," said Cornstalk. Die he did, shot down, along with Red Hawk and Cornstalk's visiting son, by militiamen who disregarded their officers' protests. The "treacherous Shawanese" promptly went on the warpath. Madison approved Governor Henry's proposal to offer rewards of $200 for the arrest of the *known* persons who committed the "atrocious and barbarous murder." The guilty men were acquitted, and the Indian war continued for twenty years.

In that same spring the repentant voters of Orange County re-elected Madison to the legislature, *sans* free whisky and without his consent. The House of Delegates, with probable reluctance, held him to be ineligible to be elected to one office while holding another.

For four months in one stretch, Madison was the only member of the council who did not miss a day's attendance because of sickness. Then illness hit him intermittently, and his attendance totally ceased from July to November, Williamsburg's "sickly season." That happened again in 1779, when (as probably in 1778) he spent those months at Montpelier and either Berkeley or Warm Springs. To Bradford, forced out of the army in 1779 by ill health, he advised a resort to the springs, whose waters, he said, had proved beneficial to himself.

In the summer of 1778 Philip Mazzei sought employment by Congress to procure a continental loan of one million pounds from his native Tuscany. Richard Henry Lee suggested that "if Mr. Madison were sent to Genoa" with Mazzei as his secretary there might be a good chance to raise the million. Congress had other ideas and Mazzei proposed that he seek a Tuscan loan for Virginia.

The State Council approved and Madison took a leading part in arranging the contract with Mazzei. The latter soon found himself spending his own money before getting an expense allowance. He wrote from a seaport to express hope that Madison, "as a lover of justice," would propose what he thought was right "as soon as you have a majority capable of deciding on disinterested principles." He agreed with Madison that it was best for him to say nothing of this, himself, and he found it noble of Madison "to offer, and very disagreeable to ask" for, such aid in "the unpleasant business." The mission failed, and Madison spent many hours, after the war, helping Mazzei recover his salary from the state.

In 1779 Jefferson became governor of Virginia, a circumstance that brought Madison into daily contact with him. After Jefferson's death Madison wrote in response to a query: "With the exception of an intercourse in a session of the Virginia legislature, rendered slight by the disparity between us, I did not become acquainted with Mr. Jefferson till 1779, when being a member of the Executive Council, and he the Governor, an intimacy took place." Jefferson in his autobiography listed George Mason, George Wythe, and Madison as the principal supporters of his 1776 legislative program, calling Madison "a new member and young; which circumstance, concurring with his extreme modesty, prevented his venturing himself in debate before his removal to the Council of State in Nov. 77." In 1812 Jefferson wrote to an unfriendly critic of the then President:

> You probably do not know Mr. Madison personally, or at least intimately, as I do. I have known him from 1779, when he first came into the public councils, and, from three and thirty years trial, I can say conscientiously that I do not know in the world a man of purer integrity, more dispassionate, disinterested, and devoted to genuine Republicanism; nor could I in the whole scope of America and Europe point out an abler head.

That intimacy must have developed swiftly, for Jefferson became governor on June 1, Madison was absent from the council from July to November, and on December 14 he was one of four men elected to fill a seven-man delegation in Congress. A year earlier General Washington had begged Speaker Harrison to send "your ablest and best men to Congress," where, the public believed, "the great, and important concerns of the nation are horribly conducted." During the next twelve months several Virginia delegates resigned, others went home, and by December Cyrus Griffin was alone in Philadelphia, voteless, since Virginia law made three delegates a quorum.

National affairs slumped steadily during that year. In the months he spent at home or at the springs, Madison studied the published reports of continental finances and found them alarming. The difficulty, he wrote to William Bradford, lay in the progessive depreciation of a vast quantity of federal money, forcing the emission of even greater sums to offset the earlier decline. If this continued, said Madison, the emissions for the year would amount to $100 million, exceeding by $40 million the federal requisitions on the states.

Unknown to Madison when he wrote this was the fact that an alarmed Congress, on September 13, 1779, had voted to stop the money presses altogether. This was expected to halt the depreciation of existing bills by inspiring confidence, but it had the contrary effect. By mid-December, when Madison was elected to his new federal post, flour sold at a dollar a pound and, wrote Delegate William Ellery of Rhode Island, "Congress are at their wit's end."

Madison, accepting his appointment, assured Speaker Harrison and the assembly "that as far as fidelity and zeal can supply the place of abilities the interests of my country shall be punctually promoted." Madison's frequent reference to Virginia as "my country" has been seized on by zealots of state sovereignty as proof that he disbelieved in the existence of the United States as a nation. On the contrary, all through the Revolution and for years afterward, the term "my country" was habitually applied by him and others both to the United States and to an individual state. So utterly natural was this duality of terms that Americans wrote occasionally of "our country" (the state) and "our country" (the United States) in the same sentence. Whenever they referred to "this nation" they meant the United States.

Although public policy bade Madison hasten to Philadelphia, storms, deep snow, and probably his state of health held him at Montpelier until March of 1780. At home he devoted himself to a study of finance, with particular reference to the current crisis, yet in such general terms that it was given newspaper publication in 1791. He challenged David Hume's contention that a fivefold increase in money would make prices five times as high. That would be true, he said, only in a country isolated from world trade or if money multiplied equally everywhere. Otherwise, a flood of imported commodities would put prices in equilibrium.

The value of American paper money, he said, was not proportionate to its quantity, but was determined by the credit of the state issuing it and the time of its redemption. The disastrous decline of continental currency was due to the vague and general nature of the pledge of redemption and to the absence of any specific provision of taxes for that purpose. Distrust of the *public ability* to redeem the money induced the initial fall in value. The French alliance relieved this, but by that time the magnitude of the emissions "begat a distrust of the *public disposition* to fulfill their engagements."

With such thoughts on his mind, James Madison entered the federal arena, to join in the attempt of Congress to solve the unsolvable.

Part II

Heavy rains and deep mud kept Madison's two-wheeled chaise twelve days on its way from Montpelier to Philadelphia. He arrived on Saturday, March 18, 1780, accompanied by his black servant Billey, and took his seat in Congress on Monday. The youngest delegate, he looked considerably less than twenty-nine. Shyness and a weak voice kept him from taking the floor for six months. Shortly after that, newly arrived Thomas Rodney of Delaware wrote in his diary:

> I take notice of a Mr. Madison of Virginia, who with some little reading in the law is just from the College, and possesses all the self conceit that is common to youth and inexperience in like cases—but it is unattended with that gracefulness and ease which sometimes makes even the impertinence of youth and inexperience agreeable or at least not offensive.

Rodney, a shallow egotist, could have profited from a later observation by Louis Otto, French legation secretary. Madison "is a man one must study for a long time in order to make a fair appraisal of him." Otto's superior, the Chevalier de la Luzerne, made that study and wrote in a survey of leading members:

> James Madison junior—of a sound and just mind. A man of learning, who desires to do good works and to improve himself, but who is not overly ambitious. Of honest principles; zealous, without going to excess, for the honor of the thirteen states . . . not free from prejudices in favor of the various claims of Virginia . . . He is regarded as the man of the soundest judgment in Congress.

On the day Madison reached Philadelphia, Congress revised the currency system of the United States. The discredited continental dollar, outstanding as a $200 million national debt which Congress was pledged to redeem in gold or silver, was devalued forty for one to halt the spiraling inflation of prices. Unsupported by state or federal taxes, it plunged so low that Madison's bill at the popular lodging establishment of Mrs. Mary House totaled $21,372⅔ for his first six months. That was about two dollars a day in hard Spanish money.

Progressive depreciation of the paper currency, wrote Madison to his father, had introduced such disorder into public affairs and threatened such an intolerable burden of debt "that Congress have thought it expedient to convert the 200 million of dollars now in circulation into a real debt of $5 million by establishing the exchange at 40 for 1." Taxes for calling in the old money at that comparative level were to be levied by the states. New money was to be emitted "under the combined faith of Congress and the several States, secured on permanent and specific funds to be provided by the latter." Congress had advised the states to repeal their laws making the old money legal tender at face value for payment of debts, and to take measures for preventing injustice during the transition.

The new system called on the states to emit not more than $10 million in paper money, issuing it as fast as the old money was called in and destroyed. This new currency was to be redeemed by the states in gold or silver within six years, through special state taxes. Meanwhile it would bear six per cent interest to be paid by Congress in bills of exchange drawn on the American loan commissioners in Europe. (That is, France would be asked to pay it.) Sixty per cent of the new money was to be retained by the states, the remainder to be delivered to Congress in payment of requisitions.

Success of the new system depended completely on the willingness and ability of the states to levy adequate taxes, payable in specie, for combined national and local purposes. Surveying the general situation from the seat of government, Madison's apprehension mounted daily. At the end of one week he outlined to Governor Jefferson "the various conjunctures of alarm and distress" that were producing a never-exceeded crisis:

> Our army threatened with an immediate alternative of disbanding or living on free quarter;
> The public treasury empty;
> Public credit exhausted, nay the private credit of purchasing agents employed, I am told, as far as it will bear;
> Congress complaining of the extortion of the people [in sale of supplies]; the people of the improvidence of Congress, and the army of both;

Our affairs requiring the most mature and systematic measures, and the urgency of occasions admitting only of temporizing expedients, and these expedients generating new
difficulties;

Congress from a defect of adequate statesmen more likely
to fall into wrong measures and of less weight to enforce
right ones, recommending plans to the several states for
execution, and the states separately rejudging the expediency
of such plans . . . ;

An old system of finance discarded as incompetent to
our necessities, an untried and precarious one substituted,
and a total stagnation in prospect between the end of the
former and the operation of the latter.

"Believe me, Sir," Madison concluded, "as things now stand, if the
States do not vigorously proceed in collecting the old money and establishing funds for the credit of the new, that we are undone." Reflecting
on the causes of the current crisis Madison wrote on May 6:

It is to be observed that the situation of Congress has
undergone a total change from what it originally was. Whilst
they exercised the indefinite power of omitting money on
the credit of their constituents they had the whole wealth
and resources of the continent within their command, and
could go on with their affairs independently and as they
pleased. Since the resolution passed for shutting the press
[September 13, 1779], this power has been entirely given
up and they are now as dependent on the States as the King
of England is on the parliament. They can neither enlist pay
nor feed a single soldier, nor execute any other purpose but
as the means are first put into their hands.

That statement totally refutes the common historical notion that
Congress from the first was the impotent agent of all-powerful sovereign
states. George Washington testified to the same shift of power. "I see
one head gradually changing into thirteen," he wrote to Joseph Jones
of Virginia. "I see the powers of Congress declining too fast for the
consequence and respect which is due to them as the grand representative body of America, and am fearful of the consequences." For the
next four years Madison labored to restore the lost powers of Congress,
hold on to those still retained, and confer new authority.

As a first assignment, the new delegate from Virginia was elected to the lately established Board of Admiralty, consisting of two members of Congress and three paid commissioners (two of whom declined to serve). He joined at once in a demand "that the flag of the United States shall be protected from insult" in neutral harbors. With five ships in the Navy that was merely a wish. The Board's chief task was to complete, without money, the 74-gun ship-of-the-line *America*, long on the ways at Portsmouth, New Hampshire. When urged by the Chevalier de la Luzerne to get the big ship launched, in order to co-operate with a promised French fleet, the Board suggested that France buy and equip the vessel. From Paris came the response that it was easier to put cannon and sailors on a ship in France.

Madison escaped from the Board in June 1780 but not from the *America*. In 1781 he made a vain attempt to sell the hull to Spain, France's ally, thus getting back the $60,000 expended. Congress agreed, but Spain did not. Another year passed with the *America* weathering on the ways. Then the huge French warship *La Magnifique* was wrecked in Boston harbor. Here was an opportunity, said Madison, to show American gratitude. Congress resolved, in his words, "to present the *America*, a 74-gun ship, in the name of the United States, to the Chevalier de la Luzerne, for the service of his Most Christian Majesty." The ship, Madison wrote to Edmund Randolph, could not be launched before "she would be scarcely worth launching." New Hampshire shipwrights bit hard on French silver and the transferred guns of the beached *Magnifigue* soon thundered on sea-plowing *L'Amerique*.

The thirteen states speedily emitted the $10 million in paper money called for by the plan of March 18, 1780 but provided no taxes to support it. Down in value went the new money, plunging in Virginia, late in 1781, to $1,000 in paper for one hard Spanish dollar. Congressional delegates struggled to pay thousand-dollar laundry bills with the meager funds received from the states.

The real sufferer was the army, both from this cause and the incompetence of the supply departments. In April 1780 a committee was appointed to reside near Washington's headquarters and reform the supply system, which was extravagantly based on commissions in lieu of salaried staffs. The higher the price, the larger were the profits of the purchasing agents. The committee frightened Congress by asking that Washington be given "dictatorial powers." His powers were already too great, protested a dominant North-South combination.

In contrast, Madison and William Ellery of Rhode Island wrote a jocular letter to the headquarters committee, concerning their "dictator" proposal, and Madison praised the Pennsylvania legislature for investing the state executive "with a dictatorial authority from which nothing but the *lives* of their citizens are exempted." The army, he wrote, was on short allowances or none at all. A mutinous spirit was rampant, engendered by hunger and want of pay, and all of Washington's endeavors had proved unable to prevent an actual regimental eruption of it. As one of several "momentary expedients," Congress shifted from the requisition of state moneys to specific quantities of army supplies. There being no storage or transport facilities, these "specs" were rotting, mildewing, or being stolen wherever there had been an effort to collect them. The quartermaster and commissary staffs must be paid salaries, Madison declared, or they would disintegrate.

The issue of reorganization was placed before the young Virginian in his first important committee assignment, junior to the veterans Oliver Ellsworth and James Duane. For months, Quartermaster General Nathanael Greene had alternated between threats to resign and demands for draft horses, storage warehouses, and salaries for his agents. Congress threw the problem to the Committee at Headquarters, from which the highly competent Philip Schuyler presented so meritorious a plan that it was promptly torn to pieces by amendments.

These final developments were reported to General Greene in the form of a rumor that he was to be held personally accountable for the financial actions of his subordinates. Under such a doctrine, he told Congress, he would not consent to hold the office a moment. His duty was to demand an accounting of all public money delivered to under-agents, but if his best efforts failed to secure it, the public must bear the loss.

It was to deal with this ultimatum that the Ellsworth-Duane-Madison committee was set up. Two days later Ellsworth and Duane left for home, and Madison became chairman of a reconstituted committee. Its report, written by him, held that those entrusted with money for public uses "should be held accountable for its due application." Congress adopted the report, which held Greene responsible but promised such allowances as justice might require. Greene promptly resigned and barely escaped ouster from the army for referring to Congress as "administration," a word rendered anathema by chronic application to the British government. Washington rebuked Congress by making Greene temporary commander of the main American army.

Madison's contention about responsibility was logical enough, given peacetime conditions. However, subagents buying supplies had to make instantaneous critical decisions, often in violation of state laws, and their personal bonds furnished a drop of security in a bucket of risk. Fraud by subordinates was properly a war cost, not a charge to be assessed against a commanding officer. After the action on his report, Madison helped to defeat a motion to reduce the quartermaster general's salary, and he was one of only five members who opposed the recall of the headquarters committee as punishment for its vehement support of Greene.

During this time Benedict Arnold's treason sent a shudder throughout the nation. Madison approved the hanging of his British accomplice in treason, Major André, whose manner of submitting to his fate "showed him to be worthy of a better one." The infamous Arnold, wrote Madison, "although he may for the present escape an ignominious death, must lead an ignominious life which if any of his feelings remain will be a sorer punishment."

Thrilling news offset Arnold's defection. A French fleet had sailed into Newport harbor, Rhode Island, bearing General Rochambeau's army of five thousand regulars and a commission for General Washington as marshal of France. This put him in supreme command of French forces. Madison, assigned to the task, wrote a glowing testimonial to the zeal of the French troops, the vigilance of their chief, and the benevolence of their illustrious sovereign, all helping to promote the mutual "glory of triumphing over a ruthless and powerful enemy to the rights of mankind." This eulogy, calculated to thrill the Gallic breast, was cut by Congress to colorless praise of French prudence and military discipline.

By this time the military front had shifted to the South. A sea-borne army under Lord Cornwallis captured Charleston, South Carolina, and spread over the hinterland. Congress met the crisis by giving the Southern command to General Horatio Gates, the idolized hero of the battle of Saratoga. (He had reached the scene just in time to receive the surrender of General Burgoyne after General Arnold won the fight—a gnawing fact that may have widened the way to the latter's treason.) Gates tested horse and spurs in the battle of Camden. They carried him two hundred miles in four days to Hillsboro, North Carolina, leaving behind him a cut-up, demoralized, and scattered army.

At this point Madison's committee report, which stimulated the resignation of the quartermaster general, produced an unanticipated dividend. General Washington, directed by a humbled Congress to name a new Southern commander, appointed General Nathanael Greene. Madison strongly approved the nomination and was placed on a committee headed by John Mathews (the man who angered Congress into dissolving the headquarters committee) to correspond with the new commander. Studying closely the general's skillful operations—sudden advances and elusive fade-aways before a more numerous foe—they successfully moved a resolution informing Greene that his military measures "afford such proofs of his judgment, vigilance and firmness, as recommend him to the entire approbation of Congress." A week later General Gates, a Virginian, was lamenting to Governor Jefferson that a motion to cancel his court-martial "to my astonishment was prevented from being carried by a Mr. Madison of this state, a gentleman I do not know, and who I am satisfied does not know me." Any true Virginian would have come bravely to his rescue.

The American victory at Iron Mountain was cheering (900 North Carolinians killed or captured 1,100 British) but 2,500 troops under the renegade Arnold had sailed southward from Sandy Hook. Madison predicted to Edmund Pendleton that this army would reinforce the troops in South Carolina rather than land in Virginia. At any time, he said, the British could regain or strengthen their position in Chesapeake Bay, "but every retrogade step they take towards Charlestown proves fatal to their general plan." Madison's reasoning was sound, but his conclusion was incorrect. Instead of giving Cornwallis power to sweep the Carolinas, General Arnold's army was sent up the James River by General Clinton (Howe's successor) and achieved nothing except the burning of Richmond. It was a blunder in strategy comparable to Howe's failure to link up with Burgoyne.

General Washington realized this fully and wrote to Governor Jefferson that no danger from Arnold should divert Virginia from reinforcing the Southern army. Mathews and Madison undertook to give Washington unneeded advice along the same line. First Mathews moved that Congress request Washington to take personal command of the Southern army. On the defeat of this, Madison moved that Washington be informed of the desire of Congress that he "immediately make such a distribution of the forces under his command, including those of our allies under the Count de Rochambeau as will most effectually counteract the views of the enemy and support the southern states." In other words, he should do at once what he intended to do as soon as his army was fit for action. Madison almost said this himself in telling Pendleton that it was "not so much the want of men as the want of subsistance arms and clothing . . . that gives the greatest alarm." Congress converted the resolution into a simple inquiry about the feasibility of ordering the French forces to take post in Virginia. Nine months later Washington took them there.

7 / WESTERN LANDS AND
IMPLIED POWERS

The British invasion of Virginia proved a multiple stimulus to patriotic action. It induced that state to recruit soldiers for the duration of the war —an action heartily endorsed by Madison, although he objected to a proviso that every soldier be given a bounty of one Negro slave in addition to money and lands. "Would it not be as well," he advised, "to liberate and make soldiers at once of the blacks themselves, as to make them instruments for enlisting white soldiers? It would certainly be more consonant to the principles of liberty, which ought never to be lost sight of in a contest for liberty." The legislature in its terror followed both courses —granted the slave bounty and authorized the creation of a Negro regiment.

Madison held to his principles when his own servant, Billey, ran away and was recaptured. He could not be sent back to Virginia, he wrote to his father, because "his mind is too thoroughly tainted to be a fit companion for fellow slaves." The usual course would be to ship him to the West Indies (and a dismal mortuary prospect), but "I . . . cannot think of punishing him by transportation merely for coveting that liberty for which we have paid the price of so much blood, and have proclaimed so often to be the right and worthy the pursuit of every human being." Madison sold Billey for a small sum under Pennsylvania law, as an indentured servant who would be free in seven years. He at once hired him back as his own paid valet.

Arnold's invasion produced its most drastic effect in a nonmilitary field. For three years a feud between Maryland and Virginia, over the ownership of western lands claimed from England, had frustrated the effective ratification of the Articles of Confederation. Virginia, by charter definitions, had a southerly boundary running straight west, and a northerly boundary running northwest to the western ocean. Under it (stopping modestly at the Mississippi) she claimed title to what are now the states of West Virginia, Kentucky, a slice of Pennsylvania, Ohio, Indiana, Michi-

56

gan, Illinois, Wisconsin, and part of Minnesota. These charter limits over-
lapped western claims by Massachusetts, Connecticut, and New York.
The Carolinas and Georgia also claimed lands as far as the Mississippi,
and New Hampshire feuded with New York over title to Vermont. Four-
sided and "landless" were Maryland, New Jersey, Delaware, Rhode
Island, and Pennsylvania.

As early as 1776, Maryland threw out the challenge "that the back
lands claimed by the British crown, if secured by the blood and treasure
of all, ought in reason, justice and policy, to be considered as a common
stock, to be parceled out by Congress into free, convenient and independent governments, as the wisdom of that body shall hereafter direct."
Maryland, New Jersey, and Delaware would not ratify the Confederation without a cut in the great western treasure.

Virginia observed that in these landless states and in Pennsylvania
great speculative land companies were being formed, with titles to millions of acres sold to them by rum-inspired Indian tribes. Never, exclaimed the Virginians, would they yield to such chicanery. Never,
replied Maryland, would Virginia be allowed to drain off her neighbor's population through low priced lands and taxes reduced by the
sale of them. The public positions of both sides were morally unassail-
able, but the political strength in back of them came from a few big
speculators in small states and a horde of little speculators in one big
state.

As far as congressional power was concerned, it mattered little
whether the Articles of Confederation were ratified or not. That document conferred less authority than Congress had exercised without it;
however, furnishers of European credit—the French government and
Amsterdam bankers—looked with apprehension upon a group of states
that were unable to agree upon the terms of their own unified existence.
The need of a formal charter was dinned into American ears by French
Minister Gerard and his successor, the Chevalier de la Luzerne.

Unable to do anything effective about that, Congress attempted to
counteract the adverse impression in Europe. For every purpose essential to the objects of the war, it declared on September 13, 1779,
"these states now are as fully, legally, and absolutely confederated as
it is possible for them to be." New Jersey and Delaware, trusting to
future adjustment of the land problem, finally ratified the Articles,
but that "froward hussy," Maryland, still held out. There was a note
of concession, however, in Virginia's denunciation of her neighbor's
recalcitrance. Triumph of the land companies, she declared, would rob

the states of a treasure expected to pay the national debt and provide bounties for Revolutionary veterans. Such words recognized a national interest in the vacant West.

When Madison entered Congress in March 1780, he had available a stentorian resolve of the legislature. Written by George Mason, it denied the right of Congress to consider the petitions of the Indiana and Vandalia companies, which asked that their Indian titles to the West Virginia country be recognized. Men of great influence, Mason averred, were seeking to convert the public lands to private purposes "under color of creating a common fund." Virginia would listen to any just and reasonable propositions, but she must protest against any right of Congress to adjudicate the matter.

Underneath its wordy violence, this was an invitation to Congress to negotiate a land cession by Virginia to the nation. This memorial was held back until the arrival of Joseph Jones, in April, gave the Virginia delegation a quorum and voting power. Jones arrived just after James Duane presented a document in which the state of New York ceded to the United States the same lands north of the Ohio River that were claimed by Virginia. New York's action was inspired by fear that Congress in sweeping up the West would interfere with state acquisition of upper New York Indian lands. However, Jones, Madison, and Duane teamed up to make it the instrument of an adjustment with Virginia. The Virginia delegation placed their state's December protest before Congress. On a motion by Duane, it and the New York cession were referred to a committee dominated by Duane and Jones. Their report urged the landed states to make a liberal surrender of territorial claims whose maintenance endangered the Confederacy.

The moment the Duane-Jones report was approved (September 6, 1780) Jones and Madison offered a motion covering the terms of cession. In case the request of Congress should be satisfactorily complied with, the territory so ceded should be laid out in separate and distinct states at such time as Congress should direct. Congress should guarantee the remaining territory of the ceding states and reimburse them for expenses incurred in subduing British posts in the ceded lands. All purchases and deeds from Indians within the ceded territory, for the use of private persons, should be absolutely void. All of the ceded lands not disposed of as bounties to the American army, "shall be considered as a common fund" for the use of the United States and no other purpose whatsoever.

Jones then returned to Virginia to work for a land cession (the state was too large for successful administration), and Madison undertook to steer the project through Congress. It was instantly assailed by the Maryland, New Jersey, and other delegations tied up with the land companies. The speculators tried to stir up Vermont-type insurrections in Vandalia (*i.e.* West Virginia) and Kentucky. To cope with that, Madison injected himself into the Vermont controversy itself. New York and New Hampshire having a common boundary, he argued, Vermont must lie in one state or the other. He moved that Congress determine their claims. His real interest, however, was in a preliminary resolve "that every attempt by force to set up a separate and independent jurisdiction within the limits of any one of the United States, is a direct violation of the rights of such state, and subversive of the union of the whole, under the superintending authority of Congress." The context involved Vermont, but Kentucky and Vandalia were in his mind.

Madison's current companions at the Virginia table were John Walker, a well-intentioned man of little force, and Theodorick Bland, called by Minister Luzerne a vain, imprudent braggart, "having pretensions to eloquence." Bland also was honest and obstinate, and possessed a beautiful, party-loving wife who described Madison as "a gloomy, stiff creature, they say he is clever in Congress, but out of it he has nothing engaging or even bearable in his manners—the most unsociable creature in existence."

Martha Bland's description fitted one facet of a later observation by Margaret Bayard Smith, that Madison was lively and charming in a congenial company, "mute, cold and repulsive" if a single "indifferent person" was present. Theodorick Bland, making up for Madison's unquestionable lack of pomposity, attacked his Vermont resolution as an unlawful assumption of power. This brought Madison to his feet with his first recorded speech in Congress. He denied unfairness in the attempt to fix Vermont's place within a state and declared that Congress, by the original union of the states, must have a superior power of decision in such a matter. That was a far reach in the direction of implied power. With Virginia's position weakened by Bland's defection, the motion produced a preliminary tie and was dropped.

Madison had better luck in the committee report on the land-cession motion, but when the crucial section nullifying Indian deeds came up the land companies centered their fire upon it and sought action on petitions to validate the titles. Madison denied the right of Congress to pass upon memorials concerning lands that still belonged to Virginia—a strange argument, coming from a man who contended that

Congress had power to set up new states and admit them to the Union. Surely that included the power to inquire into their eligibility for statehood.

To Madison's amazement, Bland took the floor against the Indian clause and carried Walker with him, putting Virginia in the negative. The clause lost by a tie vote, after which Congress struck out the clauses guaranteeing nonceded state lands and absorbing military costs. That done, Congress easily passed the Jones-Madison motion.

In his chagrin, wrote Madison to Jones, his first thought was to have the delegation place the whole matter before the Virginia Assembly. On cooler reflection he concluded that this would merely stir up Virginia's opposition to the land cession. Furthermore, not all the votes against the Indian clause were designed to aid the land companies. Some delegates (and this presumably included Bland and Walker) merely argued that if Congress had power to nullify purchases from Indians it could do anything else with the land.

Madison did not realize what a victory he had won. Three more years of arduous work were needed to implement it, but the motion as passed contained the whole substance of national land policy as maintained in coming centuries. Under it, state after state was added to a Union that ultimately stretched from ocean to ocean. The public domain was set up and opened to settlement; national forests and national parks were established—the basic title vested and remaining in the entire American people instead of in the states so added.

At the moment, however, the consent of Virginia was yet to be won. Maryland remained adamant. Then, on the first day of January 1781, Benedict Arnold's British army sailed past the capes and brought the threat of war's desolation to both of the feuding states. That made completion of the Confederation the foremost order of the day. The Virginia legislature, before fleeing to the foothills, voted to cede the Northwest Territory to the United States under the terms Madison had put through Congress. That action, combined with the push by Arnold and a final pull by the French minister, induced still-kicking Maryland to ratify the Articles of Confederation. Thus, on March 1, 1781, after three years of obstructive delay, the new system of government went into effect.

In the opinion of the *Pennsylvania Packet*, that day would be "memorable in the annals of America to the last posterity." The United States, two other newspapers declared, was growing up "into greatness and consequence among the nations." James Madison would have subscribed to that last sentiment, but he could have said in advance what he did after six years' trial, that the Articles failed because Congress was unable to enforce their provisions either by direct sanctions upon the people or by coercion of the states. Thus, the Confederation lacked "the great vital principles of a Political Constitution. Under the form of such a constitution, it [was] in fact nothing more than a treaty of amity, of commerce and of alliance, between independent and Sovereign States."

So fatal an omission, wrote Madison in 1787, resulted from a mistaken confidence in "the justice, the good faith, the honor, the sound policy, of the several legislative assemblies"—a confidence "which does honor to the enthusiastic virtue of the compilers, as much as the inexperience of the crisis apologizes for their errors." The first draft of the Articles was relatively strong. Congress worked on the text for nearly a year and a half, gradually weakening it. The principal change was wrought by Thomas Burke of North Carolina, who in April 1777 succeeded in rewriting the second article to make it read: "Each state retains its sovereignty, freedom, and independence, and every Power, Jurisdiction and right, which is not by this confederation expressly delegated to the United States, in Congress assembled."

Many historical writers have construed those words as a declaration that the states were and remained separately independent. Such a construction denies the Articles *the form* (which Madison said they possessed) of a political constitution, and it is totally at variance with the construction Burke himself placed upon the amendment, then and later.

At first, wrote Burke to Governor Caswell of North Carolina, this article expressed only a reservation to the states "of the power of regulating the internal police, and consequently resigned every other power" to Congress. He proposed, therefore, an amendment "which held up the principle, that all sovereign power was in the states separately, and that particular acts of it, which should be expressly enumerated, would be exercised in conjunction, and not otherwise." This finally won the support of all the states except Virginia and New Hampshire, and Burke was "much pleased to find the opinion of accumulating powers to Congress so little supported."

In other words, Article II was designed to limit Congress to the acts of sovereign power expressly delegated to it, and these acts were perpetually forbidden to the states. Under such terms they constituted national sovereignty. The undelegated residue of powers constituted state sovereignty.

So too Burke's letters dissipate the idea that the "independence" of the states in his amendment meant individual national independence. The difficulty in maintaining their "separate independence," he wrote to Caswell, was due to their inequality. The problem was to give the large and small states their proper weight in Congress, and yet maintain the independence of all of them. His own plan for that purpose was to create a two-house legislature, one branch allotted in proportion to population, the states having equality in the other. Thus, "independence" meant the power of self-protection against oppression.

With Burke's own attitude thus clarified, it is easy to understand why Madison, in his continuing assaults on the "imbecility" of the Confederation, paid no attention to the "sovereignty" and "independence" features of the second article. They did not mean to him, or to Burke, what has been read into them by stateminded historians and politicians.

Madison in 1781 well knew Burke's attitude, which had been made perfectly clear by him in 1779, as chairman of a committee dealing with Pennsylvania's defiance of the admiralty power of Congress. This was the famous "Olmstead Case," thirty years in the courts. A 1775 resolution of Congress authorized the colonies to set up admiralty courts whose decisions could be appealed to Congress. Pennsylvania refused to obey a decree of the Committee on Appeals reversing the court's award of the sloop *Active* to the State of Pennsylvania instead of to the privateersman who captured it. Thomas Burke wrote the report of the committee that investigated the defiance.

"Congress," Burke declared, "is by these United States invested with the supreme sovereign power of war and peace," which covers the legality of all captures on the high seas. This control being essential to the supreme power of war and peace, *the Congress could not divest themselves of it.*" The words here italicized were too strong for Congress, which cut them down to the still-decisive statement that "no act of any one State can or ought to destroy the right of appeals" to Congress from state courts of admiralty. The United States Supreme Court in 1794 quoted and upheld that report. It was completely in harmony with Article II of the Confederation, as explained by Burke at the time he wrote it; completely at variance with the modern "state rights" interpretation of the article.

No sooner were the Articles of Confederation brought into effect than Madison undertook to remedy their most obvious defects by interpretation. The substantive powers of Congress were broad. It was to have exclusive power to make war and peace, to enter into treaties and alliances, to send and receive ambassadors, to regulate captures on land and water, and to establish courts of appeal in prize cases and courts to try piracies and felonies committed at sea. Sole power was likewise given to regulate the alloy and value of coin, to fix the standard of weights and measures, to establish and regulate postoffices, and to appoint all federal army officers above the rank of colonel and all officers of the naval forces. Congress also was to decide on appeal all disputes or differences between the states arising from any cause whatever.

However, one glaring omission and two procedural rules threatened to reduce federal power almost to a nullity. Congress was given no power to levy duties or taxes but had to rely on the system, already broken down, of requisitions on the states for needed money. No final action could be taken on any important subject (these were itemized) without the assent of nine states, and no other action could be taken, except for adjourning from day to day, "unless by the votes of a majority of the united states in congress assembled." Finally, no state could cast a vote unless at least two of its delegates were present.

The practical effect was that every absent state, and every state with only one delegate present, automatically voted "no" on every proposition. With nine states present, one could outvote eight. Nothing could be done about that, but what was the meaning of the rule on preliminary voting? Did it require a majority of all the states or a majority of a quorum—seven states, or five as in the past?

Madison, Duane, John Witherspoon of New Jersey, and two or three others contended for a majority of a quorum, the rule in practically all parliamentary bodies. They prophesied that Congress would be half-paralyzed by a seven-state requirement on every incidental motion. Burke replied (correctly) that the original wording specified seven and this number was struck out because of the expectation that Canada would enter the Union. A majority appeared to side with Madison and his allies, verifying the maxim, wrote hostile Thomas Rodney, that "all men would be tyrants if they could git the power." Nevertheless, the seven-state rule was temporarily adopted because only five states had delegations of voting strength present and it was thought unwise that less than seven should decide that seven were not necessary. That action fixed the rule permanently and made it a "chaos clause," obstructing legislation, reducing the morale and prestige of Congress, and accelerating the shift of power to the states.

It was in this debate that newcomer Rodney saw in Madison the self-conceit "common to youth and inexperience." Congress, however, put him on a three-man committee "to prepare a plan to invest the United States in Congress assembled with full and explicit powers for effectually carrying *into execution in the several states* all acts or resolutions passed agreeably to the Articles of Confederation."

Madison wrote the committee's report and struck at the heart of the problem—financial dependence on states that for years had resisted lawful requisitions. Searching the Articles of Confederation, he found an apparent instrument of coercion. Article XIII stipulated that "every State shall abide by the determinations of the united states in congress assembled, on all questions which by this confederation are submitted to them." It further declared that the articles "shall be inviolably observed by every state." By these provisions, Madison's report asserted, "a general and implied power is vested in the United States in Congress assembled to enforce and carry into effect all the Articles of the said Confederation against any of the States which shall refuse or neglect to abide by such their determinations." Since that was not particularly set forth, the want of such a provision might be made a pretext to question the legality of exercising that implied power; and since it was "most consonant to the spirit of a free constitution" that the exercise of power be explicitly and precisely warranted, the committee proposed an amendment "to cement and invigorate the federal Union."

The amendment provided that in case one or more states should refuse or neglect to abide by the determinations of Congress or to observe all the Articles of Confederation, Congress "are fully authorized to employ the force of the United States as well by sea as by land to compel such State or States to fulfill their federal engagements."

This was not a proposal to *give* Congress this drastic power. It was a declaratory amendment affirming that the power already existed by implication. The necessity of arming Congress with it, Madison wrote to Governor Jefferson, "arises from the shameful deficiency of some of the States" in yielding their apportioned military supplies. Without such powers in the general government, "the whole confederacy may be insulted and the most salutary measures frustrated by the most inconsiderable State in the Union." (He cited Delaware's defeat of an embargo designed to halt trade with the enemy.) The expediency of submitting the amendment to the states, however, would depend on the probability of their complying with it:

If they should refuse, Congress will be in a worse situation than at present: for as the Confederation now stands, and according to the nature even of alliances much less intimate, there is an implied right of coercion against the delinquent party, and the exercise of it by Congress whenever a palpable necessity occurs will probably be acquiesced in.

By what means could Congress exercise such a power? As long as there was a regular army on foot, Madison remarked to Jefferson, a small detachment from it would suffice, but there was "a still more easy and efficacious mode. The situation of most of the States is such, that two or three vessels of force employed against their trade will make it their interest to yield prompt obedience to all just requisitions on them."

Since every state of the Union was guilty and the amendment required unanimous ratification, there was not a chance of its adoption. The report was sent to its death by reference to a "grand committee" of one from each state. The significance of this drastic proposal lies in Madison's sponsorship of it. He introduced the term "implied power" into the American political vocabulary nearly forty years before Chief Justice John Marshall placed it in the Constitution by judicial intepretation.

8 / *LETTER TO JAY*

Madison's rise to leadership in Congress was especially rapid in foreign affairs, where congressional committees performed the work of a Secretary of State. His first assignment was to deal with a report from John Adams, who had been sent to France as peace commissioner, concerning a reputed British suggestion of a truce. Adams was advised to consent to a long truce if it included the removal of all British land and naval forces from the country. He was relied on "to hold up the United States to the world in a style and title not derogatory to the character of an independent and sovereign people."

A few weeks later Duane, Witherspoon, and Madison drafted instructions to Francis Dana, minister to Russia. He was given power to sign a treaty "consistent with the dignity and sovereignty of the United States as a free and independent nation." The Empress Catherine headed a group of nonbelligerents known as the "armed neutrality," from which came rumbles of support for a peace based on *uti possidetis*—each side keeps what it holds. To combat this dangerous doctrine, Dana was to emphasize that the states were "reciprocally bound to sustain the sovereignty, rights and jurisdiction of each of the thirteen states inviolably." Thus, three months before the Articles of Confederation went into effect, national and state sovereignty were proclaimed in a common bond, with the nation upholding the sovereignty of the states in their individual spheres.

These nationalistic utterances came from committees of three, none of which Madison headed. Their language and thought, however, were precisely those to which he gave individual utterance when word reached the United States that former President of Congress Henry Laurens, captured at sea while en route to a diplomatic post in Holland, was being held in "rigorous imprisonment" in the Tower of London on suspicion of treason. Madison declared in a resolution offered on December 3, 1781, that "the dignity of the United States, as a sovereign and inde-

66

pendent nation," required that relief be procured for Laurens and others similarly held, wherefore he moved the immediate imprisonment of paroled British officers "most eminent for birth and rank." Such reactions make it easy to understand why Congress so quickly looked to him for defense of national rights and maintenance of American territorial claims in the peace settlement.

In the treaties that ended the Seven Years War, France ceded Western Louisiana to Spain and Eastern Louisiana to England. The latter embraced the territory between the Appalachian Mountains and the Mississippi River, north of Florida. Spain acknowledged England's right to free navigation of the Mississippi.

Thus, at the outbreak of the American Revolution, Spain held both banks of the Mississippi for two hundred miles above its mouth, and the western bank from there to the river's unknown source. In 1779, after France drew Spain into the new war against England, Spain served notice on the United States that use of the lower Mississippi was a Spanish monopoly. Furthermore, Spain challenged the American claim to lands between the mountains and the Mississippi on the ground that a royal British order of 1763 against the sale of such lands marked them as possessions of the crown of Great Britain and proper objects of conquest by Spain. Spanish capture of three British posts in the Natchez area gave point to the claimed right. The French government came to Spain's support, urging the United States to cement the new wartime alignment by going lightly on territorial claims.

John Jay had been sent to Spain as minister with firm orders to uphold American navigation and territorial claims. The entry of Spain into the war induced him to ask for fresh instructions. A movement in Congress to cede southwestern lands to Spain, in order to win a military alliance, produced strong Southern protests, but these weakened when the American defeat at Camden made Spanish aid seem more important.

Madison and his allies now attempted to postpone action indefinitely, since Jay already was bound by strong instructions. This plan was upset by the return to Congress of Daniel of St. Thomas Jenifer, Maryland spokesman for the Illinois-Wabash Company. He promptly made a motion that Spain be given satisfaction both on territory and river navigation but, wrote Chargé d'Affaires Marbois to his government, "the eloquence of Mr. Jenifer could not effect its passage." Instead, the baldness of his action jolted Congress into a renewal of Jay's instructions. Jenifer, wrote Marbois, was not disheartened: he had some new measures in prospect.

The chargé described these measures in his next dispatch. The Spanish agent Francisco Rendon, Marbois said, had given him a strong defense of Spanish territorial claims. This paper he disclosed to Jenifer, and the observations "were redrafted in concert with this delegate." Jenifer then circulated the paper in Congress as *a set of instructions from the king of France to the French minister*. They opened with an urgent plea for a triple alliance to retrieve the defeats at Charleston and then strongly assailed state charters as a claim to the West. The cession of this territory by France, it was emphasized, was to the British king, not to the colonies.

It was not the arguments, but the pretended royal French sponsorship of them that gave weight to the paper. A motion to reconsider the vote on Jay's instructions was carried by a two-state majority, throwing the whole proposition back into Congress. Marbois reported the new alignment. New England and New York delegates, fearful of being deserted as to their own boundaries, upheld the westward claims of the Southern states. The Middle states caved in. "Virginia, whose vote is directed by Mr. Madison, of English stock, well-informed and moderate, but bound by the orders of his constituents, maintained an unvarying adherence to the old instructions."

Madison and company carried the day. The old instructions were fully upheld except that Jay was authorized to accept control of contraband by Spain, with a free port of entry for American goods, if he could not obtain completely free navigation of the river. The outcome, wrote Madison, was "entirely to my satisfaction."

Concerning this knockdown battle there is not a word in the *Journals of the Continental Congress*. The story is told only in the French Archives. Jenifer, wrote Luzerne, "is considered to be self-interested." He was indeed. The stockholders he was serving included Royal Governors Dunmore and Tryon. Could England and Spain be united at the peace table, they might divide the West between them, and the speculators could hope to win from the British government what they had a diminishing prospect of obtaining from Congress.

Following this victory, Madison was commissioned to draft a letter to Jay in Madrid, to be sent also to Franklin in Paris, explaining the reasons and principles of the new instructions. He showed the initial draft to Marbois. At first, wrote that diplomat, "it displayed a little too much of the ambitious aims pursued by Virginia, which he represents. His intelligence and his moderation aided me in inspiring him with sentiments more conformable to the circumstances." If Madison did in fact tone down Virginian ambition, he strengthened the American claim in doing so. In the previous January, a committee conferring with Luzerne had staked the American claim to the West almost entirely on state charters. In the new letter, Madison made it the duty of Congress to uphold such charter claims. He affirmed (rather than admitted) that all the territory now claimed by the United States was ceded by France to the king of Great Britain; but when Americans were British subjects, they held firmly that the sovereignty, rights, and powers of the king of England extended to them because of his position "as king of the people of America themselves." It followed that all of the territory lying within the limits of the states, as fixed by the sovereign, was held for their particular benefit and devolved on them "in consequence of their resumption of the sovereignty to themselves."

All but a few small spots in this territory, Madison asserted, had been wrested from England by American forces and was subject to American civil administration. Spain's capture of British posts at Natchez carried no title to the vast hinterland, nor even to the points so occupied, these being within the charter limits of American states.

Even if the vacant land adjacent to the Mississippi should be surrendered to Spain, Madison argued, the fertility and convenience of the well-watered soil would produce intrusions by American citizens which distant Spain would be unable to restrain. This might interrupt that harmony which both nations wished to be perpetual. Already the territory contained numerous Americans who could not be transferred to a foreign jurisdiction without manifest violation of the common rights of mankind and American principles of government. More important still:

> As this territory lies within the charter limits of particular States and is considered by them as no less their property than any other territory within their limits, Congress could not relinquish it without exciting discussions between themselves and those States concerning their respective rights and powers which might greatly embarrass the public councils of the United States and give advantage to the common enemy.

Turning to the Mississippi, Madison contended that England's 1763 treaty rights of free navigation devolved on the United States. Under the usage of nations, Spain's control of both banks near the mouth of the river gave no right against those bordering its upper reaches, except the right of imposing a moderate toll for the expense and trouble of mutual use below. Here again, any exclusion from free use must be a constant and increasing source of irritation and trouble which it was the interest and duty of both parties to guard against. However, the United States was willing to accede to regulations against contraband, "provided the point of right be not relinquished and *a free port or ports below the 31st degree of N. L. and accessible to merchant ships be stipulated to them.*"

There was a remaining consideration, said Madison, which deeply concerned both France and Spain. With the Mississippi as a boundary, the singular fertility of the Ohio Valley would occasion a vast inrush of settlers. Agriculture would be their employment, but their consumption of foreign manufactures would be proportionate to the produce of their soil—provided the exchange could be made. For this there were two routes—one down the Mississippi, the other by the Great Lakes and down the St. Lawrence. By way of the Mississippi, the market would be open to the rising commerce of France and Spain. Should trade be forced into the other route, France and Spain not only would lose this trade but would give the advantage to Great Britain. Thereby Britain's loss of her exclusive trade with the United States "might prove a much less decisive blow to her maritime preeminence and tyranny than has been calculated."

Madison's arguments were unlikely to influence Spain. His theory of the devolution of crown sovereignty would not impress the exponent of divine right who occupied the Spanish throne; but the letter was not aimed primarily at Spain. Except in its denial of the right of conquest and its forecast of trouble on an obstructed river, the whole document was written for effect on France. The pictured alternatives were a huge French market in the American West, and a corresponding growth of British trade accompanied by heightened maritime power. The copy of this letter that counted was the one sent to Franklin in Paris.

Madison's letter won easy approval in Congress, but events dashed his hope that the Mississippi issue would be put aside until Jay was heard from again. Europe was talking of *uti possidetis*, and England was intriguing in Madrid to detach Spain from the war. With Georgia and South Carolina in enemy hands these reports presented a terrifying prospect. The delegates of those two states moved to revise the instructions to Jay.

Whatever the fate of this motion, Madison lamented to Joseph Jones, by the mere offering and support of it American demands would lose the weight derived from unanimity and decision. He and Bland, the only Virginians present, were bound by their instructions to vote against it, but Bland, over Madison's protests, dispatched a one-man "delegation letter" asking that the state legislature reverse its stand. Madison was barely able to obtain a postponement until the attitude of the Virginia legislature should be known. He himself then drafted a letter, signed also by Bland, asking for the "precise, full and ultimate sense" of the assembly on navigation of the Mississippi and territorial claims. The answer came, in effect, from General Benedict Arnold. On the same day that news reached Richmond of his invasion of Virginia, the panic-stricken legislature voted to rescind the state's old instructions.

Once more Congress commissioned Madison to address Jay, this time much against his will. His letter instructed the minister to recede from the instructions of October 4 on free navigation and a free port, provided Spain "unalterably insisted" on refusal, and provided the free navigation of the upper river be acknowledged and guaranteed. It was "the order of Congress at the same time" that Jay exert every possible effort to secure a free port.

This instruction was so negative in tone, Marbois reported to his government, that delegates predicted Jay would not dare to exercise the discretion thus given him. And so it turned out—with the aid of a Spanish *faux pas*. Diplomatic dispatches were invariably sent in multiplicate, and the Spanish Foreign Office (which had the American cipher) always filched one from the mails. In this instance they took the only copy that reached Spain. Months later, Jay learned of the instruction in a private letter. Utterly disillusioned by this time about Spanish purposes and fearing (he wrote to Congress) that "little half-created doubts and questions" would be raised against him in America, he stalled action.

Twice more, Madison was commissioned to draft letters to Jay. One praised the address and discernment with which the minister had reconciled "the respect due to the dignity of the United States with the urgency of their wants." The final instruction conditioned a treaty of alliance on either a large grant of money, Mississippi navigation, or American indulgences in the commerce of Spanish-American provinces—alternatives Spain was certain to reject.

By his own adroitness and persistence, Madison re-established the American claim to Mississippi River navigation before it was formally re-asserted by Congress and before Virginia renewed her instructions to defend it. His and Jay's course eliminated Spain as a factor in the territorial settlement at the peace table, leaving that issue to be decided solely between the United States and England.

9 / NATIONAL DEVELOPMENT

In February 1781, just before the Articles of Confederation were ratified, Congress took up the long-dormant power to establish government departments. Delegate Robert Morris of Pennsylvania, already "the financier of the Revolution," was an easy choice for Superintendent of Finance, including the two-ship Navy. The War Department went to General Benjamin Lincoln, who had just been freed by exchange after his excusable surrender of Charleston, South Carolina.

The great fight was over the Secretaryship for Foreign Affairs. Thomas Burke wrote in February that the choice would probably fall on Madison, "a young gentleman of industry and abilities, but I fear a little deficient in the experience necessary for rendering immediate service in that department." His refusal of it left an unresolved contest between Chancellor Robert R. Livingston of New York and Dr. Arthur Lee of Virginia, a fanatic hater of Franklin. Madison's problem was to assist in procuring the election of Livingston without voting for him against Lee.

The foreign service was torn by faction. Early in the Revolution Arthur Lee and Franklin were made joint commissioners to France, along with Silas Deane of Connecticut, who had preceded them. Lee deluged Congress with accusations that Deane and Franklin were engaged in a fraudulent conspiracy in the purchase of supplies. Deane and Lee were recalled in 1779 to answer each other's charges. Franklin, appointed minister in 1778, ignored the charges against him and performed the work all three were sent to do, yet barely escaped inclusion in the recall.

While Lee was in France his two brothers and Samuel Adams—the old Lee-Adams Axis—undertook to place Arthur in charge of peace negotiations. Minister Gerard upset that by furnishing "the Paca-Drayton Information"—the comment of Foreign Minister Vergennes that "I fear Mr. Lee and those around him." So John Adams was commissioned to make peace and negotiate a treaty of commerce with England.

73

Madison had been five months in Congress when Arthur Lee returned from France. The recalled diplomat with seeming innocence requested permission to retain a snuffbox bearing "a picture of the King of France set with diamonds," given him "as a mark of his majesty's esteem" upon his leave-taking. He asked for a full hearing to prove the falsity and malice of the charges that led to his recall. Duane forced a day's delay and Chargé d'Affaires Marbois blocked the coup by resurrecting the Paca-Drayton Information. Lee's letter was referred to a committee chaired by Madison.

Although he knew nothing of paranoia, Madison did realize the need to smother the old factionalism without creating a Lee vendetta against himself. His committee report was presented in the handwriting of Thomas Bee of South Carolina. Honeyless and stingless, it authorized Lee to retain the picture presented "as a mark of his Majesty's esteem," recognized his "zealous and faithful exertions," and assured him that "his recall was not intended to fix any kind of censure on his character or conduct abroad."

Besides displeasing Lee (because it did not condemn Franklin) this report embarrassed Minister Luzerne. He had been specially warned by Vergennes that Lee "may make a big showing of the present which he has received from the king. If this happens, you will simply remark that this present was given to Mr. Lee, not as a special mark of the king's satisfaction in his conduct, but because he [with others] signed the treaties of commerce and alliance."

Luzerne's disclosure delayed action on the Madison-Bee report. Lee's charges against Franklin spread over the country and made any praise of Lee dispraise of Franklin. Congress cut down the resolutions to mere permission to retain "the picture" (unidentified) and assurance that no censure was intended. Lee reacted with such monumental falsehoods about Franklin as a supposed thief of public money that the magnitude of the lies inspired shocked belief. Congress created an investigating committee chaired by Theodorick Bland, Lee's alter ego, and ordered young Major John Laurens to France as a special minister to secure supplies and loans. Bland's committee accused Franklin of trying to steal prize money and recommended that he be recalled.

Madison, retaining faith in Franklin, managed to put a clause in Laurens' commission and instructions requiring him to communicate with the minister "and avail yourself of his information and influence." A copy of the instructions reached Franklin a month before Laurens' wind-buffeted ship arrived in port. The old, decrepit, dissolute, thieving minister obtained all the supplies and loans Laurens was to ask for before the special envoy arrived. After that he soothed French pride, ruffled by the young army officer's brusqueness, and finally wrote to Congress praising Major Laurens' "indefatigable endeavors" and asking to be relieved of his own post.

Home from France at this juncture came Captain John Paul Jones, hero of the victory of the *Bon Homme Richard* over the *Serapis*. Blood was in his eye. He revealed that Arthur Lee had engineered a mutiny of the crew of the frigate *Alliance* and shifted the command from Jones to Captain Pierre Landais, who refused to load the vessel with offered supplies (a misdeed Lee charged against Franklin) and set sail for America with the heroic crew of the *Bon Homme Richard* chained in the hold. Bland's report and Franklin's resignation lay in forgotten pigeonholes. Landais was tried and broken.

Such was the background of Arthur Lee's bid for the post of Foreign Secretary. On the first ballot Madison and Joseph Jones decided to join Bland in a state-loyalty vote. The outcome alarmed them: Lee, five; Livingston, three. (Seven were needed.) The two met that dilemma by putting up another Virginian, Dr. James McClurg. Late in July, with twelve states present, Congress voted again: Livingston, five; Lee, four; McClurg, three. Madison concealed his motive from the French minister, who described McClurg as "a phantom put up by the friends of Mr. Lee" to defeat Livingston. Lee recognized the truth. Virginia, he complained to absent Samuel Adams, "was prevailed on to throw away its vote." Luzerne settled the matter by informing President Huntington that if the distrusted Virginian was elected, he would continue to transact affairs directly with the President or with committees. The final ballot resulted: Livingston, seven; Lee, three; McClurg, two.

Establishment of a Foreign Secretary did not affect the omnipotence of Congress in the peacemaking field. From France came news that Vergennes and John Adams were at odds. Adams wanted to display his treaty-making powers at once to the British government. The ministry would spurn him, but think how the prospect of a treaty of commerce would stir the people! Vergennes replied that to propose a treaty of commerce in the midst of war would make the United States the laughing stock of Europe.

Disputes continued on one point after another, until Adams, rebuked by Vergennes for trenching on the duties of American Minister Franklin, truculently replied that he would take up anything he pleased with the Foreign Office "without the intervention of any third person." Vergennes responded that he would neither see Adams again nor answer his letters. Luzerne was instructed to inform Congress, confidentially, that Adams had revealed "a rigidity, a pedantry, an arrogance and a self-love that render him incapable of dealing with political subjects." Informed by Franklin of the dispute, Congress on January 10, 1781, gave Adams a mild reprimand.

The full extent of the impasse was not realized until May, when Luzerne submitted memorials telling of future French aid and asking Congress to join France in accepting Russo-German mediation on the basis of complete American independence. A committee was told what Vergennes thought of Adams: a zealous patriot but possessed of "an inflexibility, an arrogance and a stubbornness that would lead him into a thousand vexatious incidents and drive his fellow negotiators to despair." If Congress put any confidence in the King's friendship they would direct Adams "to take no step without the approbation of his majesty."

This crisis came at the lowest point of American military fortunes. The army of Cornwallis was ravaging the South. Continental currency was finding new depths to drop into—from four hundred down to nine hundred for one in a single week. Unfriendly European neutrals were threatening armed intervention. Only French military, naval, and financial aid kept the Revolution from collapsing. The committee report was written in the presence of the French minister. It revoked all previous instructions except as a guide to American wishes, demanded the independence of the United States (with a blank left for boundaries), and directed Adams "in all other points to conform yourself to the advice and opinion" of the French negotiator.

Madison (not a member of the committee) rewrote one clause, making it forbid any treaty which did not "effectually secure the independence and sovereignty of the thirteen states." The figure "thirteen" furnished protection against *uti possidetis*, while the full phrase embraced all the charter claims to the West. This brought up John Witherspoon, a leader of the anti-Virginia land-company forces, with a more sweeping revision. As to "disputed boundaries and other particulars," the American negotiator should use his own judgment and prudence. He was to make "the most candid and confidential communications upon all subjects" to the ministers of France and *undertake* nothing without their knowledge and concurrence.

The clause toning down French guidance was readily adopted, but Madison fought for two days against the weakening boundary provision, which failed for lack of a seventh affirmative state. Witherspoon then shifted to a mere instruction that the best possible boundary settlement be obtained. Massachusetts helped Virginia defeat the proposal, the two states uniting in defense of boundaries and fisheries.

The situation looked bad to Madison. War conditions made the United States dependent on France in peace negotiations, and France, through Luzerne, was taking a stand against American acquisition of the West. Madison offered a series of motions to find a stopping point in surrender. Virginia alone (as on a lesser concession) voted to forbid the relinquishment of lands south of the Ohio or recognition of an exclusive British claim north of that river. In the rebound against these efforts, Witherspoon put through his original instruction leaving boundaries to the discretion of the peace negotiator.

Luzerne was dissatisfied. The instruction on guidance, he told a committee, gave France the power of preventing but not of acting. The only way to cope with "the peculiar disposition of Mr. Adams" was to place him entirely under French direction. France would make no concessions to England unless it was impossible to avoid them. Neither Great Britain nor the neutral powers would receive Adams, except perhaps as the agent of a rebelling people, unless the approach was made through the French court.

The pressure was too heavy to resist, and five southern states joined New Hampshire and New Jersey in adding a clause to the instructions. In addition to consulting with the French ministers, the American negotiator was "ultimately to govern yourself by their advice and opinion." Madison, Jones, and Meriwether Smith of Virginia reluctantly furnished the seventh state. Bland voted 'No.'

With confidence in Adams badly shaken, Congress transferred the peace negotiations to a five-man commission: Adams, Franklin, Jay, Henry Laurens (if released from his British prison), and Thomas Jefferson (whose going was frustrated by ice). Then came the belated thought: with Adams curbed, the reason for French guidance had disappeared. By that time, Madison observed in a later debate, the instructions had been communicated to the French minister and it was too late to alter them.

Actually, Luzerne reported, an attempt was made to reconsider the instructions and friendly delegates came to him in deep distress, asking him to approve a middle course. He shrewdly replied that the less responsibility France had, the better for France, since she would escape the blame for what might happen at the peace table. That pointed to the underlying factor—low American military fortunes—and the attempt to reconsider evaporated.

Madison stood by the French instruction as a matter of national good faith but undertook to reduce its scope by building up the substantive peace demands of the United States. Primarily, this involved territorial claims and New England fisheries. Originally, Adams was given an ultimatum on both points—on western lands in the peace treaty, on fisheries in the treaty of commerce. The territorial ultimatum was revoked in the panic over *uti possidetis*, but the fisheries demand was unimpaired and solely in the hands of Adams. Madison undertook to change that. He first attempted to forbid a treaty of *commerce* unless it upheld all of the objects lately dropped from the *peace ultimatum*. Protect both fisheries and western lands, or neither. His motion was beaten, six to three, by a combination of fisheries advocates and frightened Southerners.

Thereupon Madison seized leadership of the Southern group. He pointed to the danger of leaving any power whatever in the sole hands of John Adams, whose instability and fanatic zeal for the fisheries might upset the whole peace negotiation. On Madison's motion, Adams' commission to negotiate a treaty of commerce was revoked. This put western territories and fisheries on a new parity. Neither one had any protection. To get fisheries restored, New England would have to support Virginia on western land claims.

The great diplomatic need at this time (July 1781) was for a striking military victory. There was no sign of that when Madison summed up the situation for Philip Mazzei in Tuscany, yet he thought the prospects "very flattering." Cornwallis had rashly advanced into Virginia, pursuing General Lafayette and "abandoning his southern conquests to their fate." A little army under General "Mad Anthony" Wayne had moved down from Pennsylvania to reinforce Lafayette. The French volunteer major general then "faced about and advanced rapidly on Cornwallis, who retreated to Richmond, and then precipitately to Williamsburg, where he lay on the 27th ultimo."

Madison did not mention the part that he himself played in this development. For six weeks he and John Mathews had been trying to "unfreeze" Wayne's detachment from the paralyzing effect of the currency collapse. They were blocked, wrote Mathews, by men "whose souls are confined within the compass of a nutshell." At last, on Madison's motion, General Wayne was "authorized and directed, in case the supplies of provisions and forage necessary for the immediate march . . . to the southern department cannot be otherwise obtained, to impress the same." Seven states voted 'Aye'; Pennsylvania, 'No.' The loss of a single vote, in any of five states, would have defeated the motion. Its passage enabled Wayne to move, and his fateful march turned Cornwallis down the road to tidewater siege and surrender.

That was not immediately in prospect when, in the first week of September, congressmen watched the southward march of the main investing force—three thousand ragged Continentals in faded overalls, followed by the spick-and-span French army of General Rochambeau. "Nothing," wrote Madison, "can exceed the appearance of this specimen which our ally has sent us of his army, whether we regard the figure of his men, or the exactness of their discipline." As they passed the State House the French officers let fall the point of the sword and dipped their colors, and the members of Congress took off their hats.

Generals Washington and Rochambeau rode southward with the troops (the former to stall off a threatened mutiny of unpaid soldiers until French money should reach them) while subordinate French and American officers mingled with congressional delegates at an eighty-guest dinner given by the Chevalier de la Luzerne. The afternoon banquet was interrupted by a dust-laden courier from Virginia. The long-awaited Admiral de Grasse had sailed into Chesapeake Bay with twenty-eight French ships of the line. Three thousand French regulars had landed to reinforce Lafayette before the entrenchments of Lord Cornwallis at Yorktown.

Weeks of tension followed, during which Washington and Rochambeau built up the investing forces. Madison scoffed at reports that huge new British naval squadrons were approaching to lift the siege. Tricky stories spread by the enemy, he called them, "to buoy up the sinking hopes of their adherents, the most staunch of whom give up Lord Cornwallis as irretrievably lost." The day after Madison penned that prediction a British drummer boy climbed the parapet at Yorktown and beat out the signal for a parley. An officer joined him, bearing a white flag. General Cornwallis was capitulating.

Sending "fervent congratulations" to Virginia, Madison remarked that "if these severe doses of ill fortune do not cool the frenzy and relax the pride of Britain, it would seem as if Heaven had in reality abandoned her to her folly and her fate." Unless succored by other powers of which he saw no prospect, "it seems scarcely possible for them much longer to shut their ears against the voice of peace."

Congress distributed eulogies to almost everybody—but forgot Lafayette, whose investment of Cornwallis led to the capitulation. Madison repaired the oversight when the marquis, a major general in the Continental Army, asked Congress for permission to return to France. Madison's resolution, giving him both permission and a maritime conveyance, told him where he stood in the esteem of Congress. New proofs had been furnished of his "zealous attachment to the cause he has espoused, and of his judgment, vigilance, gallantry and address in its defense" against far superior numbers. A request by Madison that the Virginia legislature "pay some handsome compliments" to Lafayette led to an order that he be presented with a bust of himself, to be made in Paris of the finest marble, "as a lasting monument of his merits and their gratitude."

Peace prospects did not look bright in the spring of 1782. Lord North's ministry reacted to the Yorktown defeat by a chilling response to neutral mediators. Madison dealt with a warning by Luzerne that the British government was still bent on conquest. This communication, Madison advised, should be sent in confidence to the states, that they might be stimulated to expel the enemy and disprove the false assertions "that the people of these states are neither united nor determined in support of their national independence." The result was an appeal to the governors for soldiers, for taxation, and for resolutions of fidelity to the alliance. Only the last were furnished.

Madison (blushing, wrote Marbois, at the degradation into which Virginia had sunk), sent a special appeal to his state. "Fidelity to our allies, and vigor in military preparations—these, and these alone," he wrote, "will secure us against all political devices." This plea, Edmund Randolph told him, arrived just in time to quench anti-Gallic fires being set by Arthur and Richard Henry Lee. Madison, in response, asked for a unanimous declaration by the legislature to offset rumors of Virginian defection. Action was taken before the appeal reached Richmond. British peace proposals directed to any other body than Congress, the assembly resolved, were insidious and inadmissible, and if received, would be rejected as "inconsistent with their national faith and federal union."

These actions were related to reports (soon verified) that British peace commissioners were on their way to New York—presumably to make proposals for a separate peace. There was urgent need to reassure France. By pre-arrangement with Luzerne, Congress chose the arrival of the British commissioners as the signal for a magnificent (though delayed) celebration of a blessed event in France—the birth of the dauphin to Marie Antoinette after a vexing succession of girl babies. "It was deemed politic at this crisis," wrote Madison, "to display every proper evidence of affectionate attachment to our ally."

The British commissioner proved to be the new commander-in-chief, Sir Guy Carleton, who brought word that Lord North's ministry had been overthrown. Lord Rockingham, North's successor, had appointed Carleton and Admiral Digby joint commissioners to treat of peace. Madison saw little to hope for in this development. Carleton, he wrote to Governor Benjamin Harrison on May 14, announced the pacific disposition of Great Britain and his own similar inclination. This was offset, in Madison's view, by the avowed repugnance of Lord Shelburne, the new Secretary of State in charge of American affairs, "to a recognition of our independence and of our alliance with France." He suspected that the object of the mission was "to seduce us from the latter if not from both of these essential preliminaries to peace." However, the unanimity and firmness of Congress furnished assurance against that.

Madison's appraisal was correct as to the purpose of the Carleton-Digby mission, but he did not realize that the fall of Lord North, an immediate consequence of the surrender at Yorktown, stemmed also from mounting revulsion of the British people against the futility and cost of the war. Dispatches from Paris confirmed the divisive purpose of the peace mission, and Madison drafted congressional assurances to France on that subject. Congress pledged itself anew "to hearken to no propositions for peace which are not perfectly conformable" to the alliance. If proper proposals should be made to the United States, they would be discussed only "in concert and in confidence with his Most Christian Majesty."

During these developments Madison was making progress with his parity program for western territories and fisheries. Responsive to a legislative outcry from Massachusetts, Lovell of that state, Madison, and Daniel Carroll of Maryland were appointed late in 1781 to deal with an appeal for an ultimatum on fisheries in the peace treaty. Madison and Carroll turned down Lovell's motion to that end. Madison then wrote the committee report, presented to Congress on January 8, 1782, linking the two subjects. Without enlarging the peace ultimatum, it proposed that the king of France be informed of the extent and foundation of the American claim to the West. The limits of the colonies were established by the British Crown, and "to these limits the United States, considered as independent sovereignties, had succeeded." In this territory British posts had been seized, American government was being exercised, bounties had been promised to the army, land sales were relied on for discharge of the war debt. Britain's retention of the territory might furnish "a new nursery for her marine." (This to alarm France.)

On the Newfoundland fisheries, Madison's report set up a common right based on freedom of the seas more than three leagues from shore. Such a right had been exercised by Americans prior to the war, and was now "incident to the United States as a free and independent community." It could not be given up without renouncing an attribute of that sovereignty which they were bound by their interests and dignity to maintain in its entirety. Both of Madison's recommendations conflicted with warnings from the French minister that France was committed only to support American independence.

Congress displayed varying degrees of support for the report but sent a strong directive to the American envoys in France to contend for both claims. It then referred the report to a three-man committee charged to support it with "facts and observations" on fisheries and territories. The committee left the job to Edmund Randolph, a newly arrived delegate from Virginia, with the result that Randolph and Madison worked on it for two months. Randolph then went home, as did another committee member. Madison, a nonmember, had the report in his hands, but the committee lacked a quorum, so it could not be presented to Congress.

The stalemate lasted until August. By this time Arthur Lee was at the Virginia table, along with likeminded Bland, and the report contained material that Madison dared not let these state-oriented colleagues see. In this quandary he went to Dr. Witherspoon, who was both his personal friend and his chief antagonist in the conflict over Virginia's title to the Northwest. Witherspoon, wrote Madison to Randolph, was easily persuaded of "the innocence and expediency" of the report. Witherspoon in fact needed no persuasion. The remark suggests the need to keep Randolph persuaded of its "innocency."

Working together, Madison and Witherspoon first secured an enlargement, with Madison as chairman, of the depleted committee that produced the "facts and observations" on Madison's January 8 committee report. Next, they secured their own election to a committee to reinforce the American peace demands. As chairman of the third committee, Madison submitted a report advising that anything the second committee might have collected, on the subject of the first committee's report, be transmitted to the envoys in Paris.

Bland was on his feet in an instant. He wanted to see this material before it was transmitted. Madison suavely explained that it was to go merely for the information of the envoys. If read and approved by Congress, that would convert the paper into instructions. He withdrew his motion but re-offered it next day as chairman of the second committee, this time declaring specifically that the material was for information. By this time the whole Congress was burning with curiosity, and the fifty-page report was ordered read. The reading droned along with familiar arguments until the secretary came to this: "Thirdly, that if the vacant lands cannot be demanded upon the preceding grounds, that is, upon the titles of individual states, they are to be deemed to have been the property of his Britannic Majesty immediately before the Revolution, and to be now devolved upon the United States collectively taken."

As Madison described the affair to Randolph, the business "was going on smoothly" when the reading of this paragraph "presented to Bland a snake in the grass." His and Lee's arguments "raised up the advocates for the federal pretensions"—a development so fatal to the report that "I have no longer any hope of its success." Madison tried to smooth things out in the debate by saying that although he was satisfied that the federal argument lacked validity, it should remain in the report because otherwise, sundry states would object to the portion based on charters. This plea availing nothing, he cut off debate by raising a point of order against the interruption of a reading. When the reading was resumed, four days later, there was far more to anger Lee and Bland. Our diplomats, the report said, would not need to prove that the king was seized of the Western lands before the Revolution—his own ministers would be quick to make that claim; but—"The character in which he was so seized was that of king of the thirteen colonies collectively taken. Being stript of this character, its rights descended to the United States for the following reasons:"

> 1. The United States are to be considered in many respects as one undivided independent nation, inheriting those rights which the king of Great Britain enjoyed as not appertaining to any one particular state, while he was what they [the United States] are now, the superintending governor of the whole.
> 2. The king of Great Britain has been dethroned as king of the United States, by the joint efforts of the whole.
> 3. The very country in question hath been conquered through the means of the common labors of the United States.

In the vitriolic argument that followed, Madison kept silent while Witherspoon ripped into Lee's doubts about American national sovereignty. "The several states," he boomed, "were known to the powers of

Europe only as one nation under the style and title of the United States."
European powers cared little whether one state or another owned the
uncultivated wilderness. The question with them was whether the security
of the United States required the exclusion of other nations, especially
Britain, from these territories. Lee and Bland moved to strike out all
sections relating to the federal title. The Madison-Witherspoon forces,
not wanting a vote of any kind on its contents, referred the report to a
new committee.

A week later in a petition from Kentuckians, the issue of a federal
land title came before Congress once again. Declaring that British crown
rights had devolved on the United States collectively, they prayed that
Congress erect Kentucky "into a separate and independent state and
admit them into the federal Union." This put Madison on a redhot seat,
and he got off in a hurry. Kentucky, he agreed, ought to be made a
separate state, but Virginia would judge when that was proper. "As to
the supposition that the right of the crown devolved on the United States,
it was so extravagant that it could not enter into the thoughts of any
man." Witherspoon retorted that it had entered into his thoughts, the
thoughts of the Kentuckians, and of many others from the very beginning
of the Revolution. He was too polite to mention how recently it had been
in the thoughts of Madison himself.

The "facts and observations" were submitted to Congress in the handwriting of Edmund Randolph. In spite of that and in spite of Madison's
politically imperative implied disclaimer, there can be little doubt that he
was the author of the federal-title portion of their joint product. Randolph
was so ardent in defense of Virginia's charter claim that he spent the
next year, by request of the state legislature, building it up. Regardless
of which one wrote it, Madison had put before Congress the obnoxious
doctrine of Maryland as a reasonable argument to be presented at the
Paris peace table. Thereby he finally and irretrievably destroyed Virginia's charter claim to ownership of the lands.

This result was in full harmony with Madison's desire that the Western
lands be nationalized. "Every review I take of the western territory," he
wrote to Randolph two weeks after the flareup over Kentucky, "produces
fresh conviction that it is the true policy of Virginia as well as of the
United States to bring the dispute to a friendly compromise." Thereafter
he warned Congress that the claimant states had "both the will and the
means" to open land offices and dispose of the territory regardless of
congressional clamor. He warned the governor of Virginia that hordes
of civilians and discharged soldiers, freed of the menace of war, were

sweeping over the mountains and staking out claims in disregard of either state or national sovereignty.

This brought a further compromise by Virginia, enabling Madison (aided by Witherspoon) to work out a formula for acceptance of the cession with Indian titles tacitly rejected. The land companies fought desperately and delayed action until 1783. Then soldiers still in uniform raised a cry for disappearing bounty land, and General Washington became their spokesman. The speculators were overthrown. Eight states to two (Maryland and New Jersey still recalcitrant), Congress voted to accept the compromise Madison had worked out. His victory ended seven years of divisive strife and gave the Union the cementing bond of a national heritage of Western lands.

10 / THE TORTUOUS ROAD
TO PEACE

All through 1782 and on into 1783 Arthur Lee engaged in a running attack on Franklin and Finance Superintendent Morris. Madison persistently defended both men and was soon included in the attacks, but his personal integrity was too well established to be assailed. Pursuant to the Yorktown capitulation, certain sums of money had to be sent from Virginia to British-held New York for the benefit of captured Loyalists. Superintendent Morris suggested that to save Virginia specie, tobacco from that state be sold in New York City. A passport for that purpose was granted on Madison's motion. Arthur Lee thereupon wrote to his brother Richard Henry that Morris and the Secretary of Congress were conspiring to reap speculative profits by trading with the enemy. Richard Henry Lee put a resolution through the House of Delegates denouncing Morris and denying the power of Congress to issue passports. This, Madison commented, was the more preposterous because Virginia herself had previously sought and obtained the permission of Congress to make similar shipments for a similar purpose. Concerning the assault on Morris he wrote:

> My charity I own cannot invent an excuse for the prepense malice with which the character and services of this gentleman are murdered. . . . I have seen no proof of misfeasance. I have heard of many charges which were palpably erroneous. I have known others somewhat specious vanish on examination. Every member in Congress must be sensible of the benefit which has accrued to the public from his administration.

Fidelity to the public interest, wrote Madison, required its guardians to pursue with every vigor a dishonest servant and to "confront the imputations of malice against the good and faithful one." Arthur Lee was a member both of Congress and the Virginia legislature. When he suddenly left for Richmond during the conflict over passports, Madison and Joseph Jones reviewed "certain characters and circumstances" and concluded that his chief purpose was to eliminate Madison from Congress in December 1782 by invoking a Virginia law limiting consecutive service to three years. The Articles of Confederation contained an identical limitation, but the earliest date of exclusion would be March 1, 1784. Edmund Randolph verified Madison's prediction and revealed that the alleged ineligibility included himself on the ground that he could not be both congressional delegate and Virginia Attorney-General.

Launched in secrecy, wrote Randolph, the move had a chance of success when Richard Henry Lee publicly raised the issue of ineligibility; but "the wicked and malevolent" did not dare to attack their characters. "You were assailed under . . . such a fervor of compliment that it was unpleasant to distrust its sincerity." Randolph received similar treatment. It was a situation made to order for Patrick Henry, perennial rival of the Lees. His defense of Randolph was so effective that Arthur Lee, to protect himself, spoke against his brother's motion. The assembly then kept Madison in Congress by repealing the three-year limitation.

When Arthur Lee returned to Philadelphia after his discomfiture, Madison's first conversation with him "clearly betrayed how much it rankled in his bosom." No delegate who refused to league with him in the war against the financier could "expect to be long at ease in his post."

While Lee was raising fictitious charges against Morris of trading with the enemy, Madison was leveling his sights against merchants who actually were doing so. Privately, he had little hope of choking off shipments through New York, but as a committee chairman he denounced those who "by a sordid attachment to gain, or by a secret conspiracy with the enemies of their country, are wickedly engaged in carrying on this illicit traffic." He advised Congress to ask for state laws and use of regular army troops to suppress the trade. Timid Congress adopted the report with military enforcement stricken out.

On July 24 Arthur Lee moved to revise the peace instructions by eliminating Franklin and Jay from the American delegation and removing Adams and Laurens from French guidance. Madison took the floor against the motion. The objection, he pointed out, was to a single instruction, but the motion would unseat the ministers. Congress should consider the critical circumstances under which the instructions were adopted. No harm could come from them, but their alteration might reduce the zeal of France in the American cause.

No action was taken on Lee's motion and he chafed in silence until August 8, when he declaimed that the interest, honor, and safety of the United States demanded revocation of the instructions. Madison, replying, granted that the instructions sacrificed national dignity, but "it was a sacrifice of dignity to policy." Only if France lost confidence in the United States would she oppose the enlarging of American boundaries, and nothing would tend more strongly to produce that jealousy than a withdrawal of these instructions. Would national dignity be repaired by convincing Europe that Americans were "governed wholly by circumstances, *abject and profuse* of promises when in distress and difficulties," but so ready to veer about that no reliance could be placed on their promises?

However, said Madison, he was impressed by what Lee said about strengthening the objects of American interest. He moved that Lee's motion be postponed and that a committee be named to "report to Congress the most advisable means of securing to the United States the several objects" not included in the peace ultimatum. Witherspoon seconded the motion, which carried almost unanimously, and Madison was made committee chairman. He utilized the assignment to bring before Congress his and Randolph's "facts and observations" on Western territories and fisheries.

Shifting ground, Lee charged the "dishonest and incapable" Franklin with squandering diplomatic funds. Lee was appointed to a committee which drafted a demand that Franklin sustain every expenditure by the particular invoice of every bale and package—an impossible requirement. When one member left town, Madison obtained his own appointment to the committee, which then upset the report, substituting a simple grant of authority to bring suits when the facts warranted it.

Lee's henchman, Bland, chairman of a committee on the detention of certain goods in Holland, next produced a report described by Madison as "one of the most signal monuments which party zeal has produced. By mutilating and discoloring facts in the most shameless manner it loaded Franklin with the whole guilt and proposed finally a sweeping reprehension of him." Congress added Madison and Daniel Carroll to the committee and they squelched the recommitted report. Wrote Madison on October 8: "Doctor Lee set out the day before yesterday for Virginia. He left this place I believe in not the best of humors."

In his rage at this succession of defeats, Lee wrote so violent an anti-French letter to Mann Page that motions of censure and recall were made in the Virginia legislature. Lee summoned Theodorick Bland from Philadelphia to answer a question: are not most of the members of Congress under the influence of the French minister? Bland merely disclaimed any such influence over himself. Madison was so immune to the insinuation, the Reverend James Madison informed him, that nobody even thought of him in connection with it. Lee escaped recall by a two-vote margin. Some years later, replying to a nephew's glowing praise of Madison's conversational gifts, Arthur Lee wrote to Thomas Lee Shippen:

> It is his political conduct which I condemn, that without being a public knave himself he has always been the supporter of public knaves, and never, in any one instance has concurred to check, censure, or control them—that he has had such vanity to suppose himself superior to all other persons, conducting measures without consulting them and intolerant of all advice or contradiction—that in consequence he has been duped by the artful management of the rapacious Morris and the intriguing Marbois.

Coming from Arthur Lee, this was almost a panegyric. In no other instance did he ever acquit a chronic opponent of willful wickedness. Madison had as intense a feeling against genuine misconduct as Lee did toward the imagined variety. Coupled with it was an overriding regard for national obligations. These emotions came into sharp conflict in 1782 in relation to two men whose own fortunes were at odds, former President of Congress Henry Laurens and Lord Cornwallis, both prisoners of war, the latter on parole in London.

A year earlier Madison had proposed the imprisonment of highranking parolees to offset the holding of diplomat Laurens in the Tower of London. In September 1782 he informed Congress that he had in his hands a humble petition from Laurens to the House of Commons, published in London, praying for his release. "This petition," said Madison, "is stated not as coming from a citizen of the United States but a native of South Carolina. What is this but indirectly relinquishing the claim of independence which we have so solemnly declared and pledged ourselves to maintain at the risk of our lives and fortunes?" Commissioned to represent the sovereignty of the United States, Laurens had "prostrated the dignity of his country, wounded its honor, and as far as in him lay denied its sovereignty and independence."

Madison moved that a just-authorized notice to Laurens of his appointment to the peace commission be held up. The motion was defeated by Southerners sectionally loyal to Laurens and New Englanders who knew him as a supporter of the fisheries. They pleaded (truly) that his conduct was the result of illness and long lonely confinement. Congress stood by Laurens.

A few days passed and news came from London that Franklin, honoring an implied promise made by Laurens, had exchanged Lord Cornwallis for him, subject to the approval of Congress. South Carolinians, bitter against the devastator of their state, turned also against fellow-citizen Laurens and demanded a rejection of the exchange. Madison had long since given his opinion of Cornwallis. "No description," he had written, "can give you an adequate idea of the barbarity with which the enemy have conducted the war in the southern states. . . . Rapes, murders, and the whole catalogue of individual cruelties" had been systematically perpetrated.

Now, simply by voting with John Rutledge in committee, Madison could strike a double blow against two men whose conduct he reprobated. Instead, he joined in a two-to-one report that in spite of the earl's barbarities, the commitment to free him should be honored; and since they had voted to keep Laurens in office, it would be preposterous to "stigmatize him by a disavowal of his conduct and thereby disqualify him for a proper execution of the service." Six states voted against the exchange, but lack of a seventh made Franklin's action final. Cornwallis, gaining full freedom, continued the advice he was giving the British government—to abandon a hopeless war.

Alarming news came from England in September 1782, via enemy-held New York. The moderate Lord Rockingham was dead, succeeded as Prime Minister by Lord Shelburne, the avowed opponent of American independence. Charles James Fox, open advocate of independence, was out of the Cabinet. Shelburne and Fox had been fighting for control of the American peace negotiations. This new revolution in favor of the Shelburne party, wrote Madison, "has a sinister aspect on peace."

Prospects appeared worse next day, when a New York newspaper brought an account of a speech by Shelburne. He "speaks out his antipathy" to American independence without being able to deny its necessity, commented Madison. Luzerne reported Vergennes' conclusion that Shelburne aimed "above all to incite the Americans to acts of perfidy." Dispatches from Holland stated that the English mail "breathes war."

These upsetting developments were referred to Duane, Rutledge, Montgomery, Madison, and Carroll. "We are still left by our ministers in the most painful suspense," wrote Madison. *The last letter from them was six months old.* France must be reassured that there would be no separate peace. The committee report reaffirmed the American claim to the fisheries, a Mississippi River boundary and navigation of that river, denounced enemy agents, and repeated a Madison resolution adopted twice before: "Resolved, unanimously, that Congress will not enter into the discussion of any overtures for pacification, but in confidence and in concert with his most Christian Majesty." Even Arthur Lee and Bland joined in reknotting French ties at this moment of deep anxiety.

Unknown to Congress were certain pertinent facts. Shelburne had called American independence "a fatal necessity" whose recognition was "the first principle" of his administration. Canny Dr. Franklin, foreseeing North's fall and Shelburne's rise, had seized the opportunity, by letter, to reaffirm his "ancient respect" for the earl's "talents and virtues," and to congratulate him on the tendency toward a general peace. Shelburne promptly sent elderly Richard Oswald, Scotch merchant and former Afro-American slavetrader, to Paris for informal peace discussions. Fox sent young, ambitious George Grenville.

Franklin weighed the rival emissaries and their rival masters. He did not know that Grenville had secret orders from Fox to produce an excuse for breaking off the negotiations. To test Oswald, Franklin suggested that England cede Canada to the United States in reparation of damages inflicted by Indian allies. Oswald's warm endorsement of that idea was enough for Franklin. He wrote to Shelburne that he desired "no other channel of communication between us than that of Mr. Oswald, whom I think your Lordship has chosen with much judgment." Shelburne, when he came into power, made Oswald sole negotiator, accompanied by two advisers, one of whom replaced Grenville.

Not until *two weeks after the treaty was signed* did dispatches reach Congress *recording the start* of formal discussions. These chiefly disclosed the discord among the American envoys themselves. Although joined in the same commission, wrote Madison, they "wrote *separately* and breathed opposite sentiments as to the views of France." Franklin's letter, quietly factual, told of a two months' dispute over Oswald's commission. As first written, it authorized Oswald to treat with the thirteen American "colonies or plantations." Franklin, supported by Vergennes, argued that British acceptance of credentials describing them as representatives of "the United States of America" constituted national recognition. Delay was dangerous. Jay, who had just arrived from Madrid, replied "that we neither could nor would treat with any nation in the world on any other than an equal footing." The French purpose, Jay believed, was to postpone recognition of independence until a general peace was concluded, in order to keep negotiations under French direction and satisfy the claim of

Spain to the West. An intercepted letter from Marbois, published in London, gave weight to his fears.

Jay's attitude, Madison remarked, displayed "great jealousy of the French government." His own feeling was that France was using artifice, purposing to leave America exposed to her enemies in order to gain the credit of relieving her; but America was "more in danger of being seduced by Britain than sacrificed by France."

Far more extreme was the general reaction of congressional delegates, whose eyes were fixed on the Marbois letter. So great was the jealousy, Madison observed, that it might completely reverse the American attitude toward France. Foreign Secretary Livingston tried to calm the tumult, pointing out, in a mild reprimand of Jay, that Marbois had always made such hostile arguments about boundaries. If Vergennes designed to postpone recognition of American independence, he should have accepted Grenville's proposal that independence be dealt with in the Anglo-French negotiations. Instead, he disclaimed the power of France to speak for America.

This failed to cool the anti-Gallic heat. A motion was made to repeal the instruction that required the envoys to follow the advice of France. Madison explained the reason for its adoption—the dark military outlook, the collapse of continental money, French distrust of John Adams. When this made no impression, he asked what good would be served by revoking the instruction. If England resisted American claims, France alone could secure them. "To withdraw our confidence would lessen the chance and degree of this aid." This made sense, and Congress postponed the revocation motion without a vote. Unknown to Congress, Vergennes had rejected Marbois' advice.

Silence, long and worrisome, followed the receipt of the December diplomatic sheaf. During that interval Congress received a treaty of Commerce and friendship with Holland, negotiated by John Adams before he belatedly left for Paris. Madison headed the committee to pass on it. Though approving the substance of the treaty, Madison disliked its style intensely. "The language of the American column is obscure," he reported, "abounding in foreign idioms and new coined words, with bad grammar and misspellings." He advised that the treaty be immediately ratified, but that Adams be advised "to substitute with the consent of the other party a more correct counterpart in the American language." During the Revolution, Americans did not speak the English language.

Adams followed up the treaty with letters (wrote Madison) "not remarkable for anything unless it be a display of his vanity, his prejudice against the French court, and his venom against Doctor Franklin." Adams' next letter (February 5, 1783) drew this comment from Madison:

> He animadverts on the revocation of his commission for a treaty of commerce with Great Britain, presses the appointment of a minister to that court with such a commission, draws the picture of a fit character in which his own likeless is ridiculously and palpably studied, finally praising and recommending Mr. Jay for the appointment provided injustice must be done to an older servant.

This passage, like almost every other critical comment by Madison about fellow Americans, was expurgated from his writings when they were published in 1840. His editors thus helped present him to posterity as the passionless possessor of a disembodied brain.

American uncertainty about the peace gave way substantially in February 1783, when New York papers carried a December 5 address of George III to Parliament. The King said he had offered to declare the American colonies free and independent states. Provisional articles were agreed upon "to take effect whenever terms of peace shall be finally settled with the court of France." More weeks passed and doubts crept in: some trick might have upset the negotiations. Five months had gone by, Madison recorded, since the American envoys wrote their last-received report.

The next day—March 12, 1783—the provisional treaty was laid before Congress. It contained everything that counted—independence, the Western territories, the fisheries.

Madison with his microscopic vision detected one flyspeck. The treaty pledged Congress to recommend to the states a restitution of confiscated property. This "had the appearance of sacrificing the dignity of Congress to the pride of the British king." However, there was no likelihood that the states would comply. Also, he was perplexed to find a separate article, separately signed, defining the boundary between the United States and West Florida. This was to come into effect if that territory, seized by Spain in the war, should be restored to Great Britain. It took four days to read the accompanying dispatches, and delegates gasped when they read how the envoys had obeyed the instruction to act "in confidence and in concert" with the French court: "As we had reason to imagine that the articles respecting the boundaries, the refugees, and fisheries did not correspond with the policy of this court, we did not communicate the preliminaries to the minister [Vergennes] until after they were signed, and not even then the *separate article.*"

Franklin, Jay, and Adams also wrote separately, Franklin offering no explanations. Adams, in letters and journal, rationally defended the departure from instructions (changing scenes demanded instantaneous decisions), then accused the French of trying to dupe them on every item of the peace treaty. They puffed submissive Franklin up to the clouds and left every other man depressed in the dust. He told of a little French dinner party at which the guests gave him the "most sublime" compliment possible: "*Monsieur, vous etes le* Washington *de la negociation,*" on which he commented: "A few of these compliments would kill Franklin, if they should come to his ears." They might indeed have proved fatal, if laughter could kill, for Franklin was at that dinner, and the French host and guests were, without exception, his most intimate friends.

Franklin, Jay, and Oswald actually completed the first treaty draft, embodying nearly everything, before Adams arrived from Holland. Laurens reached Paris the day before the signing. Jay's letters praised the firmness, acuteness, and spirit of Franklin and breathed deep distrust of France.

The communications, as a whole, put Congress in a quandary. Many of the most judicious members, Madison observed, thought that all of the envoys had "been in some measure ensnared by the dexterity of the British minister." They particularly disapproved the conduct of Mr. Jay, who communicated his jealousy of the French by letter to Lord Shelburne "without even the knowledge of Dr. Franklin." The separate article on West Florida "was most offensive, being considered as obtained by Great Britain . . . as a means of disuniting the United States and France . . . and a dishonorable departure from the candor, rectitude and plain dealing professed by Congress." The separate article "made the safety of their country depend on the sincerity of Lord Shelburne," which was suspected by all the world.

These comments were in the notes of debates Madison had lately begun to make. Writing to Randolph, he said that in this business "Jay has taken the lead and proceeded to a length of which you can form little idea. Adams has followed with cordiality. Franklin has been dragged into it"—their combined actions producing a tormenting dilemma. The torment increased when Luzerne disclosed the comment of Vergennes on the secrecy. The king "did not think he had such allies to deal with." Congress cheered up when later word came from Vergennes that Franklin had offered explanations which persuaded him to "let the misunderstanding be well buried in silence and forgetfulness." Franklin sealed the reconciliation by wangling a new 6 million livres loan out of France.

Appraising the reports, Madison eulogized "the judgment, acuteness and patriotism" displayed by Franklin. His correspondence with the British minister was remarkable for strength of reasoning, of sentiment, and of expression, especially for a man of his age. Arthur Lee read the same correspondence and denounced "the treachery of old Franklin," the most "meanly envious and selfish" man that ever existed.

Madison and others gave too much weight to the disregard of the instruction on French guidance. Although born of French distrust of John Adams and desired by France in part to further her own purposes, it was not designed by Congress to give France a veto over American demands. The aim was to provide a support for them that proved not to be needed. Franklin was not "dragged into" the policy of nondisclosure. He originated it, sedulously concealing from Vergennes the proposals he made to Oswald in the early stages of negotiation. The first treaty draft had been six days in the hands of the British Cabinet when Vergennes wrote to Luzerne: "Messrs. Jay and Franklin maintain the most absolute reserve in respect to me. They have not yet even sent a copy of Mr. Oswald's [revised] commission."

Franklin's own explanation, made to Secretary Livingston a few months later, was that the instructions did not bar the commissioners from using their own judgment, and their course did not sustain French fears that excessive American demands would prolong the war. Congress paid no attention to the one really dangerous American error—Jay's insistence on revision of Oswald's commission. Negotiations were held up for two months, during which time public and parliamentary opinion in England was turning steadily against the Shelburne ministry on account of its conciliatory attitude.

With every motive to protect himself by stiffening Britain's position, Shelburne overrode his Cabinet. Compelled against his will to give up the colonies (he said later) he voluntarily sacrificed the British-American West for the sake of future amity. In doing so he assured his own political downfall, which was swiftly on its way when the signing of the American treaty, without waiting for an Anglo-French settlement, put the agreement out of danger. The outcry in England was substantially the same as Vergennes' comment on the treaty: "The British buy the peace more than they make it."

Nobody in Congress could attack such peace terms, but Arthur Lee assailed "the perfidy of France" and blamed American discord at Ver-

sailles on the instruction to follow French advice—"the greatest oppro-
brium and stain to this country," he cried, that it had ever exposed itself
to. Madison recognized this as a shot at himself and Joseph Jones, the
only original supporters of the instruction still in Congress. He was surprised, he said, at such a fixing of the blame, since the court of France
had made no use of the instruction and the Americans had construed it to
leave them at full liberty. He believed they had construed it correctly, as
relating only to concessions that might be needed to obtain peace and
independence. The instruction they actually violated, he said, was the
one that required them "to act in concert and in confidence with our
ally." This instruction, Madison pointed out (with a hot shot at his adversaries), had been repeatedly and unanimously confirmed by Congress,
supported the last time by "several of the gentlemen present" (meaning
Lee, Bland, and Rutledge).

Turning to the principal violation, Madison declared that "national
honor and national security" required that the secret and separate article
be communicated to France. Only absolute necessity or French perfidy
could justify a breach of this obligation, and the charge of perfidy had
nothing behind it but "suspicions and equivocal circumstances." Our
war would not end, he warned, until France and England signed a peace
treaty.

Strong resistance met Madison's motion to disclose the article, and
Congress adjourned for the weekend without a vote. By Monday the
issue was moot. On Sunday night, March 23, 1783, citizens ran through
the streets of Philadelphia shouting "Peace! Peace in Europe, peace in
America! The war is over." All countries had signed and the separate,
secret article was buried by the Anglo-Spanish treaty, which transferred
West Florida from Britain to Spain.

The war in America did not actually end with the news of the French
and Spanish treaties. It was to end "at the terms and epochs" fixed in
them; but those epochs were six days apart in the two treaties, April 3
and April 9. What to do and what a to-do! Secretary Livingston furnished
an ingenious solution—a proclamation by Congress that ended the conflict on "April 3 April 9." The proclamation produced an uproar in Richmond, not over the "absurdity" (as Madison called it) of the double
date, but over the affronting show of "high powers" by Congress. That
upstart body had the temerity to "further require all governors and others,
the executive powers of these United States respectively, to cause this our
proclamation to be made public." There was talk, Randolph reported,
of wresting from Congress some of its constitutional authority. Madison

soothingly sent word that "the offensive passages" escaped correction only because of the general eagerness for action.

A few months later Madison was commissioned to write a proclamation announcing a treaty with Sweden—a treaty sought by the Swedish king (Europe gossiped) for the honor of dealing with Franklin. Avoiding offensive phrases, Madison clamped down on the states with an assertion of federal authority lumping state governors with other citizens:

> Now therefore to the end that the said treaty may . . . be performed and observed on the part of these states, all the citizens and inhabitants thereof, and most especially all officers and others in the service of the United States, are hereby enjoined and required to govern themselves strictly in all things according to the stipulations above recited.

Theoretically, very theoretically indeed, a commercial treaty with Russia was up for discussion in the spring of 1793. Francis Dana, still unrecognized ("one Dana," the Empress Catherine called him, concerning whom she knew nothing), casually requested Congress for nine or ten thousand pounds with which to soften up the ministers in accordance with Russian custom. Madison, in a report, forbade Dana to enter into a treaty unless he had already engaged the faith and honor of the United States, and "permitted" him to come home as soon as propriety permitted—a recall. The report was rejected (Madison said) by a combination of shipbuilding states and South Carolina, allured by Dana's promise of import and export markets. Foreign Secretary Livingston thereupon sent Dana so stiff a reprimand that he construed it as a recall. This drew from Stephen Higginson—Massachusetts merchant and congressman—a comment to Theodorick Bland more revealing as to the two correspondents than as to Madison: "Mr. Madison's report was rejected; but the junto had determined that Mr. Dana should come home, and that no treaty should be made with Russia, perhaps by the order of the Count de Vergennes, and the views of the junto must not be defeated; if Congress could not be brought to order him home, Mr. Secretary would do it himself."

"Junto" was any disliked combination of public men, and Higginson himself was a shining light of the famous Essex Junto. Madison was forming close ties with a new member of Congress named Alexander Hamilton. In this instance, after Madison's report was rejected, Hamilton incorporated part of its provisions in a resolution designed to check Dana without recalling him. Opposed by the hemp and iron states, it lacked one vote of passage. Madison then dropped the attack on Dana and re-offered a set of safeguards over treaties of commerce. Adopted seriatim, they limited such treaties to moderate periods and required that they be submitted to Congress for approval with full liberty to accept or reject.

This put an end to the system by which Congress was pledged to accept treaties signed by authorized negotiators, if in accord with instructions. Independently of these decisions, yet growing out of the Dana controversy, Madison offered the following resolve, unanimously adopted on June 12, 1783: "The true interest of these states requires that they should be as little as possible entangled in the politics and controversies of European nations."

Here was the fullblown doctrine of "no entangling alliances," originating not in the Farewell Address of President Washington, not in President Jefferson's first inaugural, but formally declared in the words of Madison thirteen years before the earliest reputed date of origin. It was also the first step in a growing independence of France, taken by Madison in the first year of fully established independent nationhood.

11 / ADDRESS TO THE STATES

During his first three years in Congress Madison received not one cent of salary. State law allowed him $20 (Spanish) per day and expenses. By the end of 1781, $20 had the buying power of two cents. In his first year, Virginia sent him £39,000 in paper currency for expenses. Its cash value was £547.16.3, a bit over half of his living costs. Small remittances from his father kept him going during the next two years in which receipts from the state treasury amounted to less than thirty pounds in gold or silver.

To pleas that he come home for a visit, Madison replied that public duties forbade it, but anyway he could not leave without paying his debts. His plight was so bad, he informed Randolph in August 1782, that he had "for some time past been a pensioner on the favor of Haym Salomon, a Jew broker." His kindness "will preserve me from extremities, but I never resort to it without great mortification, as he obstinately rejects all recompense."

This runaway inflation was the effect of American abhorrence of taxes and the inability of Congress to levy them. To remedy this Thomas Burke, in February 1781, moved that the states be requested to vest Congress with power to lay a five per cent duty on imports. Madison, thinking it unwise to ask for powers the states were almost certain to refuse, proposed instead that the states lay duties for federal purposes and Congress collect them. Burke's plan carried, and Madison was soon chafing at Virginia's inaction on it. "What a prodigious sum we are losing," he exclaimed to Edmund Pendleton, "from the delay of the states to authorize the collection."

In a year's time the amendment needed only the approval of Massachusetts, Rhode Island, and Maryland. During that year not a penny had been paid into the federal treasury by any state except Pennsylvania. Finance Superintendent Morris drafted an excoriating circular to the states. If the army disbanded "I am guiltless; the fault is in the states;

99

they have been deaf to the calls of Congress, to the clamors of the public creditors, to the just demands of a suffering army, and even to the reproaches of the enemy, who scoffingly declare that the army is fed, paid and clothed by France." That charge, dishonorable but true, would soon give way to an army, unfed, unpaid, unclothed, which would subsist itself or disband itself.

Of course, no such blunderbuss could be fired at proud states, and Madison (who made the motion) headed a committee to confer with the financier. The upshot was the dispatch of two-man delegations to the South and East, to portray the government's desperate plight and plead for money. All they secured could have been brought back in a snuffbox. Massachusetts and Maryland ratified the impost, leaving only tiny Rhode Island blocking it, but under the Confederation, a mouse had the blocking power of an elephant.

Rhode Island fortified its stand by sending a new delegation headed by demagogic college professor David Howell. He exhorted his state to preserve the noble system under which "you are to grant your money like freemen, from time to time, bound only, as a sovereign and independent state, by your sentiments of justice, of virtue and by your sacred honor." In brief, go right on paying nothing at all.

Madison's prediction was quickly verified that such obstructive delays would soon draw "the most bitter reproaches from the public creditors." The clamors from unpaid soldiers and influential lenders soon took the form of demands that their own states pay the federal debts directly to them. Several states yielded, and Madison drafted the congressional protest. If individual states undertook to dispense moneys requisitioned for the Union, "the federal constitution must be so far infringed" and plans for a uniform revenue system subverted.

Rhode Island's final rejection of the impost, in November 1782, led to passage of a motion written jointly by Hamilton and Madison, that Congress send a delegation to "this perverse sister" (as Madison privately called her) to plead for justice to creditors and the need "to maintain our national character and credit abroad." Hamilton wrote a congressional letter to the Rhode Island legislature, logical in argument but so aggressively nationalistic that Madison's support of it seems surprising. Hamilton's basic position was that Congress, being empowered to fix the sums of money to be paid into the general treasury, "have in effect the constitutional power of general taxation." Madison, in debate, reworded the principle more emphatically. "A requisition on the states for money," he asserted, "is as much a law to them as their revenue acts when passed are laws to their respective citizens."

The junketeers to Rhode Island had jolted over frozen roads for half a day when Abner Nash of North Carolina casually mentioned something Madison told him that morning. *Virginia had repealed her assent to the impost.* The carriages jolted back to Philadelphia. "The most intelligent members," Madison wrote, were deeply affected by Virginia's action. They predicted "a failure of the impost scheme, and the most pernicious effects to the character, the duration and the interests of the Confederacy." It was in truth the tolling of the Confederation's death knell.

Ostensibly, the repeal was a reaction to Rhode Island's rejection of the impost, but what was the real motive? If the Lees had done this as a stab at Morris, Madison observed to Randolph, it would hardly have been done so quietly. There had been noise enough in Richmond, Randolph's reply made clear, and it came from the Lees. Fanciful appeals to fear were employed with the malicious purpose "of piquing Morris." In spite of his pessimism, Madison responded: "Congress cannot abandon the plan as long as there is a spark of hope. Nay, other plans on a like principle must be added. Justice, gratitude, our reputation abroad and our tranquility at home require provisions for a debt of not less than $50,000,000."

Revenue laws, he declared, must operate at the same time through all the states and be exempt from the control of each. Without this, both foreign and domestic creditors would be defrauded. The need to act was spurred by rumbles of revolt in the unpaid, bitterly resentful army. A memorial from Major General McDougall and others, Madison reported in January 1783, was proper enough in spirit, but the unrest of armed thousands behind it was quite another matter.

The Treasury was empty, Morris told a committee—Rutledge, Osgood, and Madison—and not a cent could be paid to the soldiers. More bills had to be drawn on France, without that nation's knowledge or consent, or civil government would collapse. The committee and Morris agreed, recorded Madison, that France would rather pay the unauthorized bills than force the United States to borrow from the enemy! (The peace treaty had not yet arrived.) Congress authorized Morris to draw the bills. Madison wished also to tap France for the army's back pay, and Congress approved his resolution. Morris choked it off: too much pressure might rupture the well.

The army's demand was referred to Hamilton, Madison, and Rutledge, who supported a pledge, made in the black days of Valley Forge, that officers would receive half pay for life. But to ease the strain they proposed a choice between this half pay and commutation of it to full pay for six years. New Englanders protested that any funding of the public debt would create and perpetuate a dangerous moneyed interest, poisoning republican institutions. Madison answered that the way to get rid of debts was to pay them. The half-pay commutation was approved after a month's struggle.

Madison now faced a critical decision. Virginia's repeal of the impost had, in effect, instructed the Virginia delegation in Congress to oppose any grant of taxing power to Congress. Bland of Virginia took the lead against a Hamilton-Madison-Rutledge committee motion that Congress endeavor to obtain from the states "general and substantial funds" adequate to funding the entire national debt. Wilson of Pennsylvania offered a clarifying and strengthening substitute. At this moment Arthur Lee re-entered Congress and forced a public reading of Virginia's impost repeal and instruction against federal taxing power.

Madison's decision on the instruction came in the form of a substitute for Wilson's motion. Its wording, he pointed out, was negative. In place of it he moved the following: "Resolved, That it is the opinion of Congress that the establishment of permanent and adequate funds to operate generally throughout the United States is indispensably necessary for doing complete justice to the creditors of the United States, for restoring public credit and for providing for the future exigencies of the war."

This brought Arthur Lee to his feet with a cry that federal taxing power subverted liberty by placing the purse in the same hands with the sword. Wilson corrected him when he assailed Madison's motion as if it proposed to lay federal taxes without a prior grant of authority by the states. Hamilton "imprudently" (Madison noted) argued that federal revenue collectors would enable the general government to pervade and unite the states. Bland and Lee jubilated: "Hamilton had let out the secret."

Madison undertook to repair the damage. "The idea of erecting our national independence on the ruins of public faith and national honor must be horrid to every mind which retained either honesty or pride." Could adequate funds be obtained by requisitions? Nobody would say so. Could permanent state funds be set up for federal purposes? The diversion of them by one state would lead to suspension by others. A general revenue superintended by Congress would end the jealousy; make diversion impossible; stop the appropriation by the states, to their own citizens and soldiers, of money requisitioned. The patience of the soldiery had been equal to their bravery "but that patience must have its limits; and the results of despair cannot be foreseen, nor ought to be risked."

Turning to Lee's chief argument, Madison asserted that Congress already was invested with authority over the purse as well as the sword, through the binding force of federal requisitions. He acknowledged that he was violating the instructions given by Virginia to its delegation. Members of Congress, he said, represented their states, but also "owed a fidelity to the collective interests of the whole." When clear conviction required it, they should act in accord with their judgment and be ready to "hazard the personal consequences." This issue entailed the preservation of the Confederacy, our reputation abroad and tranquility at home.

Madison's motion carried, but the strength of the opposition was ominous. A new Virginia delegate, John Francis Mercer, swung to support of his former enemy Arthur Lee. "From what motive God knows," wrote Madison, he "says that he will crawl to Richmond on his bare knees" to prevent renewal of Virginia's assent to the impost. Mercer soon revealed the source of his agitation—shock at Madison's assertion that the requisitions of Congress were laws to the states. If the federal compact had such a meaning he would "immediately withdraw from Congress and do everything in his power to destroy its existence." Gorham of Massachusetts retorted that if justice to creditors could not be obtained through the general Confederacy, some states would soon be forming new ones. To Madison, this was no empty threat. If financial conflicts were not straightened out, he remarked to Randolph, "a dissolution of the Union will be inevitable," with the weak and opulent Southern states falling prey to the "powerful and rapacious" East.

To reduce the unrest Madison supported a disliked limitation of the impost to twenty-five years, and Congress took up specific duties. A committee was appointed—Gorham, Hamilton, Madison, Fitzsimons, and Rutledge—to frame the revenue plan. The committee approved the five per cent impost and specific duties. Madison then suggested that the revenue system be united with "equitable objects" of other sorts, of interest to various states, in order to gain the concurrence of all. The committee gave him the drafting job. In two days he produced the first "logrolling" bill in American history—the whole to be submitted as an amendment to the Articles of Confederation.

The plan opened with the already approved five per cent impost and specific duties. He added a provision asked for by others: the states should furnish $1.5 million a year from revenues of their own choosing.

Then followed provisions which he described to Jefferson as "bait" for
the states:

A clause calling on the landed states to cede their Western lands: bait
for Rhode Island, Maryland, New Jersey, Delaware, New York, and
Pennsylvania.

A proposal (by Hamilton) that war costs of states ravaged by the
enemy be abated: bait for New York, Virginia, the Carolinas, and Georgia, although Virginia had blunderingly instructed her delegation to
oppose it.

A proposal originating with Madison that the United States assume
and pay all war costs incurred by the states without congressional sanction. This would be "bait" for Massachusetts, New York, Virginia, the
Carolinas, and Georgia.

Next came a proposal that land valuation as a means of apportioning
federal expenses (never put into practice) be replaced in the Articles of
Confederation by apportionment according to free population and a
portion of those "who are bound to servitude for life." (He first wrote
"who are deemed slaves," but the word, like the institution, repelled
him.) This was bait for the slave states, but he did not say so.

Finally, Madison bound the whole plan together by a concluding declaration that none of its provisions should take effect until all of them were
agreed to by all the states. The committee shifted the position of this to
the end of the revenue clauses, leaving the "bait" subject to acceptance
or rejection without affecting the raising of money. In this form the plan
was reported to Congress.

Conditions were favorable (distress worsening) when the report came
up for action in March 1783. Finance Superintendent Morris publicly
submitted a conditional resignation, to be withdrawn if public debts were
provided for by May. This, if adhered to, Madison recorded, was looked
on "as producing a vacancy which no one knew how to fill, and which no
fit man would venture to accept." Arthur Lee declared that a man who
"published to all the world such a picture of our national character" was
unfit to hold office. Hamilton and Wilson eulogized him. Madison was
put on a committee to urge him to stay, but the decision depended on the
fate of the revenue plan.

Here the prospect was alarmingly improved by the menace of an army
officers' insurrection. Circulated among them were the anonymous "Newburgh Addresses," written (it was disclosed years later) by Major John
Armstrong, Jr. He described their failure to his chieftain General Gates.
The "timid wretch" they chose to carry on the plot "betrayed it to the

Commander-in-Chief," whose overwhelming influence put it on the rocks. "Such a villain!" exclaimed Armstrong. Madison, denouncing these "anonymous and inflammatory exhortations," could hardly have suspected that he would some day appoint their author Secretary of War.

The army menace converted two delegates, minor in talents but mighty in position. Holten of Massachusetts swung his state to the impost. Mercer, the Virginia jumping bean, hopped the fence and put Lee and Bland in a minority. Congress labored for a month on the Madison report. It approved the revenue provisions and then, one by one, struck out the sweeteners. The only one that survived was *nauseous to Virginia*—the call upon the landed states to make or complete their land cessions. On the apportionment of the $1.5 million Madison produced the winning compromise formula: five slaves should count as three persons in fixing state contributions according to population.

The Madison plan carried every state delegation on April 18, 1783, but the author of it felt little expectation of unanimous ratification. "As it now stands," he observed to Jefferson, "it has I fear no bait for Virginia. . . . A respect for justice, good faith and national honor is the only consideration which can obtain her compliance." That was true generally and Madison, Hamilton, and Ellsworth were commissioned to prepare an address to the states. Written by Madison without prior consultation (so said his friend Hamilton), it was unanimously approved by Congress on April 26, 1783.

Successful termination of the war, said Madison, combined with the crisis in public affairs, called for gradual extinction of the $42,000,375 public debt and a search for "means of obviating dangers which may interrupt the harmony and tranquility of the Confederacy." Certain proposals, he said, deviated from the strict maxims of public credit but were found necessary to remove objections. These were the twenty-five-year limitation of the impost, its collection by state-appointed officers, and the reliance on the states for $1.5 million to be raised as they pleased. (That is, not raised at all.)

Madison defended the clause binding the revenue provisions into "one indivisible and irrevocable act." Without it, rejection of one clause by one state, another clause by another state, might reduce all to a nullity; and if the grants were revocable, any state could at any time involve the nation in bankruptcy.

Justice and good faith, said Madison, entitled the public creditors to immediate payment of their principal. That being impossible, solid security should be given to payment of the interest, so that holders might transfer their stock at full value until it was paid off through the natural growth of commerce, new requisitions, and the sale of Western lands. To speed that day he urged the landed states (that especially meant Virgina, North Carolina, and Georgia) to cede the West to Congress.

The heart of the address was an eloquent plea to the states to work for the happiness of the confederated republic and "render the fruits of the Revolution a full reward for the blood, the toils, the cares and the calamities which have purchased it." The national debt was great but should be borne with cheerfulness and pride. To whom were these debts to be paid? To an ally who had contributed both arms and treasure; to foreign individuals who gave a precious token "of their confidence in our justice and of their friendship for our cause;" to the army, "fellow-citizens whose blood and whose bravery have defended the liberty of their country." Finally, to those who either lent their money or manifested confidence in their country by receiving transfers from the lenders; and to those whose property had been devoted to the public service.

To discriminate among the several classes of creditors, Madison said, would be equally unnecessary and invidious. "If the voice of humanity plead more loudly in favor of some than of others, the voice of policy, no less than of justice, pleads in favor of all." A wise nation would never allow those who relieve its wants, or who rely most on its faith, firmness and resources, to suffer by the event:

> Let it be remembered finally, that it has ever been the pride and boast of America, that the rights for which she contended, were the rights of human nature. . . . In this view the citizens of the United States are responsible for the greatest trust ever confided to a political society. If justice, good faith, honor, gratitude and all the other qualities which ennoble the character of a nation, and fulfill the ends of government, be the fruits of our establishments, the cause of liberty will acquire a dignity and luster which it has never yet enjoyed; and an example will be set which cannot but have the most favorable influence on the rights of mankind.
>
> If on the other side, our governments should be unfortunately blotted with the reverse of these cardinal and essential virtues, the great cause which we have engaged to vindicate will be dishonored and betrayed; the last and fairest experiment in favor of the rights of human nature will be turned

against them, and their patrons and friends exposed to be insulted and silenced by the votaries of tyranny and usurpation.

Madison's address to the states has rightly found a place among the great documents of the American Revolution. His is the plea for national unity, calling upon the people of the "thirteen independent states" to think and act in their collective capacity for the salvation of the nation. His is the voice of liberty, pleading that the United States be kept before the world as a political society dedicated to the noblest of principles and passions. Here, both in reasoning and emotion, Madison testifies that American nationhood was born in the American Revolution, not a product to be subsequently manufactured by the Constitution of 1787. Here is the relativity of states and nation that was given legal substance decades later in the great nationalizing decisions of the Supreme Court, which harked back to Revolutionary principles.

Congress ordered the address distributed in pamphlet form. Private reprints were made in Massachusetts, Connecticut, New Jersey, and Virginia; also in England. Joseph Jones and Arthur Lee both carried the address to Richmond, where Richard Henry Lee was assailing the revenue plan as an attempt "to overleap those fences established by the Confederation to secure the liberties of the respective states." And Patrick Henry? He as usual, wrote Jefferson, was waiting to see which way the tide would run in order to fall in with it.

Henry found the tide rising and leaped into leadership of the impost supporters. Then a mass of flotsam came into view: Hamilton's letter to Rhode Island, injudiciously published by Madison as one of eight appendices to his Address, set off a panic with its unabashed call for high federal power. The tide reversed itself and so did Patrick Henry, who began whipping up new terrors against the impost. His crippling amendment, subjecting the impost to state collection, went through the legislature without a recorded vote.

George Washington partially salvaged the situation in a circular to the states. Now was the time, he cried, in accents reminiscent of Thomas Paine, to choose whether the United States was to be "respectable and prosperous or contemptible and miserable, as a nation." This was the moment to decide "whether the Revolution must ultimately be considered as a blessing or a curse." With the assembly about to adjourn, friends of the revenue plan succeeded in postponing the whole subject to the October session.

Madison saw little to hope for in the last-minute gain. Twelve states in hearty unity might have overborne Rhode Island. Now all hope of early pressure was dashed. The interval of inaction, he prophesied to Randolph, "will give full scope to malignant insinuations."

America did indeed present a strange phenomenon. In military matters, the patriotic majority in the thirteen states were as one man. In international relations, national policies found overwhelming support. Only in economics were the patriots discordant, and revulsion against taxes was nearly universal. Yet prosperous America was so alluring to foreigners that the French regulars ordered back to France had to be tricked to get them on shipboard. Captive Hessian troops, recalled by their German sovereign, broke out of barracks and were hidden by sympathetic Americans in their homes. The weaknesses of government were both the cause and the result of popular fear of governmental power. Narrow vision, self-interest, and local bias, plus political ambitions feeding on those traits, were the principal forces that had to be combated by the Madisons, Hamiltons, Jeffersons, and Washingtons.

12 / BOOKS AND ROMANCE

Madison's service in the Continental Congress convinced him that the greatest need of that body was to be better informed. To bring that about he set out in January 1783 to establish a Library of Congress. The motion to appoint a committee was made by his colleague Bland, but its report, embodying an actual list "of books proper for the use of Congress," is entirely in Madison's handwriting.

It was indispensable, he wrote, that Congress should have works at command on the law of nations, treaties, negotiations, and so on. In addition, no time ought to be lost in collecting every book and tract relating to American antiquities and affairs. These were needed both as materials for a history and to combat the territorial aspirations of Spain. The recommended book list was far broader in scope, embracing world history and culture, with a notable leaning toward the works of European freethinkers, heretics, antimonarchists, and dissident Catholics.

Madison led off with the *Encyclopédie Méthodique*, which was conditioning France for a social revolution, and followed with such devil's advocates as Bayle, Voltaire, Gentili, Barbeyrac, D'Ossat, Jeannin, Mably, Vertot, Le Clerc, Hutcheson, Priestley—works whose modern counterparts, found in possession of a university professor turned bureaucrat, would inflame Congress into a raging furnace of denunciation.

In the field of international law, Madison included such standard authorities as Grotius, Vattel, Pufendorf, and Bynkershoek. The monarchists Hobbes and Selden were offset by Hume, Cudworth, Cumberland, and others. The list covered politics, geography, law, war, languages, general history, national histories (eighteen classifications) and Americana. From consecutive positions and other details it is evident that Madison was aided by a list of 2,640 books, compiled by Jefferson for intended purchase in Europe. Also, extensive catalogues of Philadelphia booksellers were available.

Congress paid no attention to the subversive character of Madison's recommendations, but spending dollars from an empty treasury was something else. Defeated on purchase of the full list, Wilson of Pennsylvania and Madison moved to buy "the most essential part of the books." This also was negatived; but the idea persisted, and the Library of Congress came into being a quarter of a century later under President Jefferson.

Thomas Jefferson was in Philadelphia for several months in the winter of 1782-83 and lived within the "Virginia circle" in the boarding house of Mrs. Mary House. Here he witnessed and encouraged an event in Madison's life that turned from happiness to pain. Late in November, 1782, Delegate William Floyd and family returned from Mastick, Long Island, after a six months' absence. Kitty Floyd, five months short of her sixteenth birthday, was flowering into young womanhood. Thirty-one-year-old James Madison fell in love with her.

The wooing apparently was a community affair, presided over by Mrs. Elizabeth Trist, the talented daughter of Mr. and Mrs. House and a magnet of congressional interest. Jefferson watched and promoted the match. Writing to Madison during his return journey to Monticello in April, he included the following in cipher:

> Be pleased to make my compliments affectionately to the ladies and gentlemen. I desire them to Miss Kitty particularly. Do you know that the raillery sometime experienced from our family [the House-Trist dwellers] strengthened by my own observation, gave me hopes there was some foundation for it. . . . I often made it the subject of conversation, more exhortation, with her and was able to convince myself that she possessed every sentiment in your favor which you could wish.

Madison replied in a ciphered passage of a letter that came back into his possession after Jefferson's death, more than forty years later. He inked out the ciphered lines and wrote "undecipherable" alongside them, but in the course of years, a difference in fading of the two inks brought out the underlay. This is what Madison wrote:

> I did not fail to present as you desired your particular compliments to Miss K. Your inference on that subject was not groundless. Before you left us I had sufficiently ascertained her sentiments. Since your departure the affair has been pursued. Most preliminary arrangements, although definitive, will be postponed until the end of the year in Congress.

The end of the congressional year would come in November, which also marked the terminus of Madison's service. The plan, evidently, was that he should go then to Long Island for the wedding. Colonel Floyd and his family left for home on April 29, and Madison rode with them as far as Brunswick, New Jersey. There he said a fond goodby to his sixteen-year-old fiancee—and never saw her again.

There was no thought of this at the parting, after which Madison forwarded a letter "with a copy of a song," from Kitty to eleven-year-old Martha Jefferson. On July 17 he acknowledged receipt of "a letter for Miss Floyd," presumably from Martha. By August 11, all was over. On that day he wrote to Jefferson, not in cipher this time, but in cryptic terms which, nevertheless, he heavily inked-out when the letter came once more into his possession. Partially legible, it says that after an uncertainty produced "by one of those incidents to which such affairs are liable . . . the necessity of my visiting the state of New York no longer exists." A hint of the young lady's state of mind is given in the decipherable words "a profession of indifference at what has happened."

There was stoicism in a concluding reference to "a more propitious turn of fate," but the careful obliteration of the record after almost half a century indicates the deepness of the hurt. The winning suitor was a nineteen-year-old medical student. The "more propitious turn of fate" came eleven years later, and not only gave Madison a dearly loved life partner, but endowed the United States with the most popular "first lady" in American history.

After the adoption of Madison's "Address to the States" the transition from war to peace became the first order in Congress. Hamilton headed a committee, including Madison, whose main task was to deal with the shout of the soldier: "Pay—but no discharge without pay." Osgood of Massachusetts, the only "economy man" on the committee, wanted to get rid of army expense, pay or no pay. Madison urged that the army be held together until the country was entirely free of enemy troops. He and Hamilton won a compromise: enlistments for the war were binding until the definitive treaty was signed but the commander-in-chief could grant furloughs or discharges. This angered the troops and dissatisfied the economizers who, joined by Hamilton, called for immediate discharge of all troops enlisted for the duration. Madison then took the lead in obtaining a unanimous compromise—immediate furlough, through which, he said, the country might "be not wholly unprepared" for a resumption of fighting.

The economy bloc next denied that Congress had power to maintain any military force in time of peace. This argument, Madison commented, represented the "penurious spirit" of Massachusetts, "fatal to every establishment that requires expense." Hamilton's report, supported by Madison, Wilson, and Ellsworth, pointed out that if military authority belonged solely to the states in peace, the United States would have to begin to create an army at the very moment they had to employ it; but if Congress had doubts it should leave the general power in full force until the states, or a majority of them, declared otherwise. The purpose of this, as Madison explained it, was to throw the dispute into the future, lest "the present paroxysm of jealousy" might lead to disappointment if an immediate attempt were made to assert the power. Both purpose and method suggest Madison's authorship of the compromise.

Madison looked to a future "pregnant with difficulties." On the arrival of the definitive treaty, he wrote on June 17, Congress must "suffer the whole military establishment to be dissolved, every garrisoned post to be evacuated, and every stronghold to be dismantled." There was trouble right at hand. The troops in the Philadelphia barracks had "sent in a very mutinous remonstrance to Congress," signed by the noncommissioned officers, painting "the hardships which they had suffered in defense of their country and the duty of their country to reward them." They gave Congress until afternoon to make "a satisfactory answer."

Two days later, soldiers ordered home by platoons were refusing to go and (wrote the French minister) "they talk loudly in the cabarets of plundering the bank, of doing violence to Congress, and of bringing the city to a contribution." Another day came and with it an express from Lancaster bringing word that an armed column of troops was marching on the city. Madison recorded their arrival with seeming unconcern: "The soldiers from Lancaster came into the city under the guidance of sergeants. They professed to have no other object than to obtain a settlement of accounts, which they supposed they had a better chance for at Philadelphia than at Lancaster." The next day (June 21): "The mutinous soldiers presented themselves, drawn up in the street before the State House, where Congress had assembled."

How did the Philadelphia press report this grave menace to Congress? With total silence. The Chevalier de la Luzerne gave a visual account of the approach of about three hundred men, who marched up "in good order, led by their sergeants, drums beating, bayonets on their muskets." They encircled the State House "with the intent of not letting anyone leave." Madison told how it looked and felt from the inside:

The soldiers remained in their position, without offering
any violence, individuals only occasionally uttering offensive
words, and wantonly pointed their muskets to the windows
of the hall of Congress. No danger from premeditated violence was apprehended, but it was observed that spirituous
drink from the tippling houses adjoining began to be liberally
served out to the soldiers, and might lead to hasty excesses.
None were committed, however, and about three o'clock, the
usual hour, Congress adjourned; the soldiers, though in some
instances offering a mock obstruction, permitting the members to pass through their ranks.

Madison's calmness was not typical of Congress. Reassembled for an
evening session, they concluded that politics prevented the Pennsylvania
executive council from furnishing protection. Notifying that body that
they had been "grossly insulted" by disorderly troops, they voted to move
at once to Princeton, New Jersey, and did so. Madison returned to Philadelphia three days later to find that the mutineers had submitted and
accepted furloughs. They betrayed their secret leaders, Captain Carberry
and Lieutenant Sullivan, who made their escape (to Ireland), while
"some of the most active of the sergeants also ran off." Ultimately, in
line with army justice, Carberry was condemned to accept half pay for
life, Sullivan went free on a technicality, while the sergeants were sentenced to death. Congress pardoned them.

Madison's opinion of the flight of Congress was evidenced in his return to Philadelphia and is implicit also in his refutation of a charge that
Hamilton engineered the move. On the contrary, he declared, Hamilton
yielded only to "the peremptory expostulation of others." Madison spent
the rest of the summer in Philadelphia, broken by short trips to Princeton when his presence was particularly needed. He took this course, he
explained, in order to do some writing that required access to his papers.

The fruit of this was two anonymous articles published in the *Pennsylvania Journal* (the organ of his friends the Bradfords) of September 17
and October 8, 1783, under the heading "The North American No. 1
and No. 2." Their purpose was to advance the two measures he had most
in mind, the granting of taxing powers to Congress and the transfer of
Western lands from the states to Congress, but he took occasion to portray the critical condition of the country in strong and general terms.
Sending the first of the articles to Jefferson, he said he was "leaving the
author to your conjectures," a conventional method of piercing anonym-

ity when public disclosure would be embarrassing—in this instance politically calamitous.

Why, he asked, "at an era so awful and so critical," were the civil institutions of America "cursed with the impotence of old age, when they should enjoy the vigor of youth"? Why did the horrors of anarchy and domestic confusion threaten to follow the dissolution of the British bond? Ambition, and the desire to exalt communities, furnished the explanation:

> Unhappily then for America, the separate sovereignties of our respective states have left these principles to act with a force but feebly restrained by the weak barrier of a nominal *union*. An undeviating adherence to state interests, state prejudices, state aggrandizement, (or, to comprehend the evil in a term, to state politics) is the sad prognostic of that discord, confusion and never ceasing war, which has been the invariable lot of separate sovereignties and neighboring states.

The honor of Congress and the nation hung on the fate of a general revenue plan. There *was* an American army in the *late* war, but it had become unpopular to mention it or the unpaid claims of soldiers. Once let individual states, by paying their soldiers, become possessed of their claims, and "the style will be instantly changed. It will be then, 'do us justice, or we will pay ourselves' "—out of the rich commerce, perhaps, of the weak Southern states, who would seek foreign protection. "What a prospect does this idea present for America."

Safe in anonymity, Madison was able to use the language of Maryland in warning his own state against a further denial of justice to others. "Will they not with an united voice, and the voice of truth allege, that these lands were wrested from the crown of England . . . not for the benefit of any class of citizens . . . but . . . by their joint expense of blood and treasure." A similar choice was faced between commercial duties levied by Congress for the benefit of all, or by individual states to gain advantages over their neighbors.

In "North American No. 2," Madison unfolded the situation of his countrymen "in the character they have assumed, as one of the nations of the earth." In Europe, the great inland powers had divided Poland among themselves after discord and anarchy rent asunder the bonds of empire. So it would be in America "if ever civil dissension should loosen that Gordian knot, which binds these states together, and leave them resting on their individual impotence and insignificance." Lack of a general legislative power for regulating commerce would enable England—already convinced "that we could not act as a nation"—to sow the seeds of disunion, restrict trade, and cut off "a Rising Navy of America," the whole policy constituting an "insult on our national character."

He warned the country not to rely on the friendship of foreign powers, not even France. Be too wise to believe that "vindication of the rights of man can be pleasing to despots, on whose government it is a satire—or that the haughty monarchs of Europe are in haste to prostrate their dignity at the feet of untitled citizens, whom education and habit have taught them to contemn." This article closed with a peroration to a personified "Liberty!" to whom this pledge was offered: "The band of patriots who are here thy votaries . . . will instill this holy truth into the infant minds of their children, and teach them to hold it sacred, even as the divine aphorisms of religion, that the SAFETY OF AMERICA will be found in her Union."

Madison took up his residence in Princeton in September 1783, oppressed by cramped quarters. His single room, shared with Joseph Jones, was ten feet square. He had two objects in view—to complete congressional acceptance of Virginia's revised land cession and to promote the establishment of a permanent national capital on the Potomac River. The first went through easily on September 17.

Six states (one too few for success) favored Trenton for the permanent seat of government. Madison, working for Georgetown, believed that "the best chance for both Maryland and Virginia will be to unite in offering a double jurisdiction on the Potomac." The Southerners, according to President Elias Boudinot (from New Jersey), "maneuvered in such a manner as to take in the Eastern members" completely. Playing on their intense dislike of Philadelphia, they obtained New England's support of a motion to divide the national capital between two locations, six months on the Potomac, six months on the Delaware. Nobody expected this decision to hold. The purpose and effect, wrote Jefferson after a talk with Madison, was to unhinge the decision for Trenton and throw the whole matter into the future. That being achieved, Congress voted to move temporarily to Annapolis.

With deferred victory for the Potomac under his belt, Madison ended his career in the Continental Congress on October 25, 1783—three years and eight months after he took his seat. In that entire time, he had been absent from the seat of government only twice—during his brief ride with the Floyds into New Jersey and during the weeks he spent in Phila- delphia after Congress fled from that city. It was a record of attendance unmatched and unapproached. Louis Otto, French legation secretary during those years (and afterwards of high diplomatic rank) wrote in a 1784 survey of delegates:

> [Madison] Well-educated, wise, temperate, gentle, stu- dious; perhaps more profound than Mr. Hamilton, but less brilliant; the intimate friend of Mr. Jefferson and sincerely devoted to France. He entered Congress very young and seems to have concerned himself particularly with public affairs. He may one day be governor of his state, if his modesty permits him to accept that office. Not long ago he refused the office of President of Congress.

Closing, Otto made his comment that one must study Madison "for a long time in order to make a fair appraisal of him." That remained true throughout his life and no less true in historical perspective. Nowhere in his writings is there any reference to overtures to make him president of Congress or state governor. On the latter subject, Jefferson wrote to Mrs. Trist that the place was his for the taking. Eliza replied that Madison "deserves everything that can be done for him," but this was "too great a sacrifice for a man to make" under the present forms of government in America:

> He has a soul replete with gentleness, humanity and every social virtue and yet I am certain that some wretch or other will write against him. . . . Mr. Madison is too amiable in his disposition to bear up against a torrent of abuse. It will hurt his feelings and injure his health, take my word.

Madison ultimately reached an office that subjected him to a thousand times the torrent of abuse encountered by any governor, and it affected him not at all. He ignored the slanders and laughed at the lampoons. In the Continental Congress, the qualities listed by Otto and Mrs. Trist com- bined to build up his influence and hide it from the public. To these may be added a freedom from personal self-interest that put him above suspi- cion on that score. From the time he entered Congress in the spring of 1780 until he left in the fall of 1783, he was the champion of American nationhood against narrow provincialism, of republican self-government against monarchy and aristocracy, of the general welfare against local and personal interferences with it, of governmental powers measuring up to the responsibilities of government.

Possessed of a national pride and sense of national dignity that fell not far short of chauvinism, and loyal to the true interests of his native state, Madison was fundamentally not a Virginian but an American who chanced to be born in Virginia.

13 / PATRICK HENRY, LAFAYETTE, AND GRASSHOPPER

Stopping in Philadelphia during his return to Montpelier, Madison was overtaken by the trek of Congress to Annapolis and rode to that city with his congressional successor Thomas Jefferson. He resumed his journey at the outset of torrential November rains that flooded creeks and rivers and made the roads a quagmire. Nine days later a cry ran from cabin to cabin behind the Montpelier mansion: "Massa Jemmy's come!"

News of his arrival in the Rapidan Valley produced a new flood of dinner and overnight visitors—his brothers Francis, Ambrose, and William; his sister Nelly Hite, innumerable Taylor cousins, in-laws Bell, Lee, and Throckmorton, and "nextdoor neighbors" up to fifteen miles away. Some winter guests had gripes, shared and recorded by Cousin Francis Taylor. One visitor lay awake all night because the Madisons put guests between cotton sheets.

Paralyzing snowstorms frustrated Madison's plan to spend the first winter in concentrated reading. All of his trunks, shipped by water from Philadelphia, lay snowbound at Fredericksburg. They contained the fifty-six volumes of Buffon's natural history and many other wanted works. Deep snows prevented him from tapping the rich resources of Monticello, freely offered by Jefferson. For his main purpose, the study of law, he had only Coke on Middleton "and a few others from the same shelf." But good news came from Richmond, cutting off a dreaded trip to the capital. The legislature had ratified the federal impost and approved the congressional terms of the land cession to the United States.

When the Buffon set finally arrived, Madison challenged the French scientist's contention that American mammals were invariably smaller than their European counterparts. Servants brought him a wounded woodchuck, a mother opossum with seven young, dead weasels, moles, and other small animals. Thirty-three measurements of the weasel were made for comparison with Buffon's belette and hermine. As soon as he could obtain a thermometer, he added records of temperature to those already started of wind, sunshine, clouds, and precipitation.

Jefferson went to Paris in 1784 as American minister and bookbuyer for Madison. In particular he was asked to send "whatever may throw light on the general constitution and droit public of the several confederacies which have existed," also books on the Law of Nature and Nations. During the next few years, books came from Paris by the trunkful, including works in the international field by Burlamaqui, Wolfius, Bynkershoek, Wicquefort; twelve volumes of Mably, many other histories, and the thirty-seven volumes so far published of the great *Encyclopédie Méthodique.*

The rapport between Jefferson and Madison was further indicated by a 1784 proposal of the former that Madison take up his residence near Monticello, as James Monroe and William Short were doing. With Madison joining that circle, Jefferson solicited, "I could once more venture home and lay myself up for the residue of life, quitting all its contentions which grow daily more and more insupportable." Madison expressed pleasure at the "affectionate invitation," which he could not "altogether renounce," though "still less can I as yet embrace it." A few more years might prepare him "for giving such a destiny to my future life." Did that represent the desire to escape the cares of a huge estate maintained by slave labor, or was it a considerate refusal to recast his life for Jefferson's comfort and convenience? A few months later, in August, Madison accepted a gift of 560 acres from his father and began a study of a new wheat pest, identified by him as the chinch bug.

Madison's concentration on public rather than private law, in building up his library, revealed his deeper inclinations. He *thought about* the practice of law, but his most active studies of it were in the field of government. His neighbors had some thoughts concerning him on that subject. In the spring of 1784 they re-elected him to the House of Delegates, again without free whiskey, but in company with the man whose brimming barrel defeated him for that office in 1777. This development, he wrote to Edmund Randolph, was "most noxious" to his project of reading law, except as it would bring him in contact with Randolph himself—a living legal oracle.

The oracle had just asked him whether Virginia was bound to deliver up one George Hancock, who fled from South Carolina after beating up a member of the state legislature—a crime classified by the Carolina governor as a "high misdemeanor." Was it really that, or mere assault and battery? If the governor said it was a high misdemeanor, Madison replied, respect for the chief magistracy of a confederate state required an admission of the fact; but there was a tighter bond among the states than that created by the law of nations:

> By the express terms of the Union, the citizens of every state are naturalized within all the others, and being entitled to the same privileges, may with the more justice be subjected to the same penalties. This circumstance calls for a 'droit public' much more minute than that comprised in the federal articles, and which presupposes much greater mutual confidence and amity among the societies which are to obey it, than the law which has grown out of the transactions and intercourse of jealous and hostile nations.

In other words, the existence of a common United States citizenship furnished a tighter bond of union than the act of Union itself. Madison's argument, made in the period of the Confederation, pulverizes those of historians and legal writers who see proof of multiple nationhood in the extradition of criminals between state and state.

Late in April, Madison was driven to Richmond by his brother William, in a two-wheeled chaise with a riding horse behind. The German traveler Schoepf, visiting Richmond in that same year, likened it to an Arabian village, with "saddled horses at every turn . . . for a horse must be mounted if only to fetch a prise of snuff from across the way." No college-president cousin furnished homelike luxury here. Madison joined the throng at Formicola's tavern, where dozens of legislators slept, ate, drank, and told ribald stories before the fires (so said Schoepf) in two enormous rooms on each of two floors.

Attorney General Randolph briefed Madison on the legislature. Unlike the usual assembly, divided by the rivalry between Patrick Henry and Richard Henry Lee, this one contained many "children of the Revolution" who disdained the old factions but needed a better strategic leader than Speaker John Tyler. Describing the situation to Jefferson, Randolph predicted "that our friend of Orange will step earlier into the heat of battle, than his modesty would otherwise permit. For he is already resorted to, as a general of whom much has been preconceived to his advantage."

As chairman of the Committee on Commerce, Madison launched a campaign to make Norfolk the rival of Baltimore and Philadelphia. By making that city the only port of entry, the state could build up import and export facilities, check smuggling, and develop strong financial houses. Also, by keeping British ship captains out of little ports and warehouses, it would prevent a return to the old "Scotch monopoly," which started in small favors that fastened the chain of big debts. In no time at all Madison found himself facing inter-city rivalries. "In order to gain anything," he told Jefferson, it was necessary to add Alexandria, York, Tappahannock, and Bermuda Hundred.

Madison's principal purpose, at this time, was to promote "new grants of power to Congress" in order to rescue "the Union and the blessings of liberty staked on it from an impending catastrophe." The outcome depended on Patrick Henry, and for a time the prospect looked surprisingly good. The great orator helped ratify Madison's amendment to the Articles of Confederation, basing federal requisitions on state population instead of land valuation. Madison and Henry then put through a resolution to grant Congress power to retaliate in kind against Great Britain's exclusion of American vessels from the West Indies.

These federal measures cost Virginia nothing. Finally Madison moved that the state pay during the current year 1784, three-quarters of its defaulted requisition for 1781. The commonwealth was rolling in riches. Revived European markets and soaring tobacco prices, wrote Madison, had "brought more specie into the country than it ever before contained at one time." And how did Patrick Henry react? He moved that the collection of all 1784 taxes be postponed until the following year.

Passage of that resolution, of course, would be fatal to the federal requisition. Madison joined Richard Henry Lee and Speaker Tyler in fighting it, but the mightiest orator in the land was telling the people what they most wanted to hear—that they could not afford to pay taxes. The moratorium was voted. "We shall make a strange figure," commented Madison to his father, "after our declarations with regard to Congress and the Continental debt, if we wholly omit the means of fulfilling them."

Working against nearing adjournment, Madison induced the legislature to shorten the tax suspension period and allocate minor funds to Congress. "Nothing," he observed to Jefferson, "can exceed the confusion which reigns throughout our revenue department." For this and kindred evils he saw no remedy except a revision of the state constitution. His efforts in that direction won the support of Richard Henry Lee, but Lee was *flattened* by illness and Patrick Henry *flattened* the motion.

There was time for one more clash, and it came on the clause in the treaty of peace opening state courts to British pre-war creditors. Young John Marshall united with Madison in a planned move to call for compliance. Speaker Tyler and Henry forestalled this with a motion that collection of British debts must wait until Congress should act against British violation of the treaty by shipment of slaves to Canada. Madison moved to substitute his own report asserting "the duty and determination of this

Commonwealth, with a becoming reverence for the faith of treaties," to give effect to the article on debts by making them payable in four installments. Henry's resolution was adopted.

Just before the July 1 adjournment, the legislature passed Madison's resolution for a joint commission with Maryland to frame "liberal and equitable regulations" for bistate control of the Potomac River. The task, assigned to Mason, Randolph, Madison, and Alexander Henderson, was still unfinished 175 years later. Likewise, near the end of the session, a bill secretly backed by Patrick Henry was thrown into the hopper, to levy a tax (in the words of supporting petitions) "to restore and propagate the holy Christian religion." That launched an effort which, in less pious terms, was revived nationally in the last third of the twentieth century. At the moment, Madison was able to report that "the friends of the measure did not choose to try their strength in the house." A companion bill to incorporate the Episcopal church (in order, Madison believed, to prevent the laity from removing rectors) "was preserved from a dishonorable death by the talents of Mr. Henry. It lies over for another session."

Early in August, motivated by "some business [and] the need of exercise," Madison set off on horseback for Philadelphia. At Baltimore he fell in with the Marquis de Lafayette and his aide the Chevalier de Caraman, revisiting America. Lafayette pressed Madison to join him on a trip to Fort Stanwix (Rome, New York) on the Indian frontier, where the marquis planned to attend the making of a treaty with the Six Nations. Madison willingly extended "my ramble into the eastern states which I have long had a curiosity to see." As they journeyed, the marquis received "the most flattering tokens of sincere affection from all ranks," and listened to some urgent words from Madison, who wrote to Minister Jefferson from Philadelphia:

> The relation in which the Marquis stands to France and America induced me to enter into a free conversation with him on the subject of the Mississippi. I have endeavored emphatically to impress on him that the ideas of America and of Spain irreconcilably clash; that unless the mediation of France be effectually exerted, an actual rupture is near at hand.

Lafayette promised to write to the Count de Vergennes about it, and did so, showing his letter to Madison. Five months later, unsettled by Washington's fear that immediate opening of the Mississippi would block development of the Potomac and James River waterways, Lafayette sought Madison's opinion on that subject. His reply rejected the "very narrow and very delusive foundations" of such a belief. Navigation of the Mississippi, Madison declared, would determine "the value of that vast field of territory which is to be sold for the benefit of the common treasury. . . . If the United States were to become parties to the occlusion of the Mississippi they would be guilty of treason against the very laws under which they obtained and hold their national existence."

At Philadelphia Madison found the House family worrying over "poor Mrs. Trist," who embarked on an Ohio River flatboat to join her husband at New Orleans, not knowing that he was dead. Madison's letters to her—the first that she received from anybody outside her family—gave her "joy in the extreme" (so she wrote to Jefferson) at finding that her friends had not forgotten her.

From New York, Madison, Lafayette, and Caraman (with their servants and horses) sailed up the Hudson River in a barge. The tide helped, but two hurricanes held them back six days, making it a nine-day journey to Albany. There the party was overtaken by Chargé d'Affaires François de Marbois, who was traveling to the Indian treaty in a "honeymoon phaeton" after leaving his bride (Elizabeth Moore) at New York. Marbois joined them, abandoning the phaeton en route. At the Shaker village of Niskayuna they listened to a declamation against marriage by a speaker who cited the example of a Savior who "never had any carnal connection with a woman." In developing that theme (so Marbois wrote to his former fiancee in France) he used "expressions which even the least chaste writer" would avoid repeating.

In a division of labor, Madison directed the four-day march, Lafayette took care of the horses, Caraman looked after lodgings, and Marbois supervised the cooking. His specialty was a soup so marvelous (he himself admitted) that they often found themselves feeding the innkeepers. A final fifty miles of frosty wilderness travel and camping-out brought them to Fort Stanwix, to which Indians were flocking from every quarter. The American treaty commissioners had not yet arrived, so the four travelers went with guides to the Oneida Nation, eighteen miles distant, while Indians built a bark cabin for them at Stanwix. They traveled through rain, "now fording the streams, now swimming our horses," and arrived "very wet and very tired" (wrote Marbois) at the main village.

Here Madison renewed his congressional acquaintance with Chief Grasshopper and turned over to him five breasts (small kegs) of brandy. Stimulated by their contents, young warriors announced an all-night dance, which Grasshopper by custom could not shorten. Lafayette, at length, spotted a dancer who had been his servant during the war, and the young Indian ended the dance with a stirring oration. Caraman, speaking for all four men (but not for their servants) refused an offer of temporary wives.

Lafayette proved to be the hit of the Stanwix conclave. His address to the Indians, arranged for by Madison, eclipsed all others, and "even during the whole stay of the Marquis, he was the only conspicuous figure." The commissioners jealously tried to hasten the quartet's departure. The attachment of the Indians to Lafayette gave Madison hope that this would offset the pro-British influence of Chief Joseph Brant, but he expected little from the badly managed conclave. Marbois itemized the defects: skimpy presents, bad housing, ragged soldiers; to which Madison added the ill-timed efforts of New York to make new land purchases ahead of the treaty. He was surprised at the ultimate result: relinquishment of all territorial rights from Buffalo to the Mississippi in exchange for a (worthless) guarantee of their eastern lands.

The return of the four travelers was swift and delightful. On October 6, eight days after their arrival, they sent their horses to Schenectady in the charge of servants and swept down the beautiful Mohawk in an eleven-man boat with five hired oarsmen. The journey by horse was resumed to Albany, through rich autumn coloring. There Madison and Marbois took a boat to New York, while Lafayette, Caraman, and an Indian boy headed to Boston, thence by sea to Virginia. The boy was to be "given a gentleman's education," returning after that to civilize his tribesmen. Madison encountered the young Indian on his return, "a complete *petit maitre*," exquisitely clothed. He returned to his tribe, Madison recorded, and in two weeks became "to all appearances an Indian hunter that had never stirred out of his native forest."

The time Madison spent with Lafayette gave him (he wrote to Jefferson) "a thorough insight into his character. With great natural frankness of temper he unites much address and very considerable talents." He rides (he says) three hobbyhorses—the alliance between France and the United States, the union of the latter, and manumission of the slaves. "The last does him real honor, as it is a proof of his humanity." Madison took him to be "as sincere an American as a Frenchman can be; one whose past services gratitude compels us to acknowledge and whose future friendship prudence requires us to cultivate."

Arriving in Richmond two days after the fall session of the legislature found a quorum, Madison was placed on a reception committee to welcome Lafayette to the state of his military exploits. During the ensuing display of idolatry Madison reminded the assembly that it had never carried out the three-year-old resolve to present the marquis with a marble bust of himself. He obtained a unanimous doubling of it—two statues, one to be given to the city of Paris, the other to be placed in the Virginia State House. Lafayette's admirable conduct in the face of adulation caused Madison to write (again to Jefferson) that his zeal and unquestionable attachment to the United States could be usefully employed, wherever it was not opposed to the essential interests of France. That prospect was destroyed by the same French revolutionary mob that smashed the Houdon marble of Lafayette in the Paris City Hall. The duplicate still graces the Richmond State House, with the inscription Madison wrote for it.

On his trip up the Mohawk Valley Madison had been struck with the richness of the soil—fertile loam twelve feet thick in creek beds—and by the drop in land prices from ten pounds to the acre in occupied lands to a dollar and a half as one entered the wilderness. Raw lands held until the country was settled would produce a tremendous profit. This thought merged with the desire expressed to Randolph to find "a decent and independent subsistence" depending "as little as possible on the labor of slaves." Two weeks spent in Randolph's office, gaining "insight into the juridical course of practice," dispelled his thought of entering that profession.

In 1785, after arranging in Philadelphia to market the family's tobacco, Madison stopped for several days at Mount Vernon. Here, besides watching Houdon cast the plaster model of his statue of Washington, he asked the general what he thought of the Mohawk Valley as a spot for real estate speculation. That struck a chord. If Washington had the money to spare it was the very spot he had selected. James Monroe was thinking along the same lines as Madison. They searched for a joint project in the Mohawk Valley and heard of it.

Madison had no money, but Monroe (for a moment) was flush. They bought nine hundred acres at a dollar and a half an acre, stretching north from the Mohawk River nine miles east of Fort Stanwix. Monroe paid half of the cost, the balance coming due in one year. When the note became payable neither man had money. The seller extended it three years. With Monroe still broke, Madison offered to carry Monroe's share and split the profits. That being declined, Madison bought out his partner and fixed the terms—full repayment of Monroe's half interest at seven per cent plus $150. Madison held the property for six more years and sold it for $5,250—a profit of $3,311.52 after the payment to Monroe. That was hardly enough to reduce his dependence on the labor of slaves, nor was such generosity the road to wealth.

14 / FREEDOM OF RELIGION

Pressing heavily upon the Virginia legislature when it convened in October 1784 was the issue that arose late in the spring—state support of religion. Madison had undermined this in 1776, and Jefferson swept it out of existence in 1777. Now a flood of petitions called for a return to state support broadened to include all denominations. Seduced by the prospect of easy money, the Presbyterian clergy joined the Anglicans. Not a solitary opposing petition lay on the table of the Committee on Religion when Madison ran through the sheaf.

This evidence of sentiment was enough for Patrick Henry. He offered a seductively worded resolution that the people "pay a moderate tax or contribution annually for the support of the Christian religion or of some Christian church, denomination or communion of Christians or of some form of Christian worship." Backing this were the two influential Carter Harrisons, Philip Barbour, Joseph Jones, John Marshall, and Chairman William Norvell of the Committee on Religion. Madison had the support of the Nicholas brothers (Wilson Cary and George), Zachariah Johnston, Archibald Stuart, French Strother, and Spencer Roane.

Patrick Henry supported his resolve (so Madison said) with "all his eloquence." He named city after ancient city which had fallen after religion decayed and blamed repeal of the tithe law for the alarming decline of morals in Virginia. Madison, in reply, denied that the assembly had power to pass such a law. Religion lay wholly outside the purview of civil authority. Tax support of it violated the Virginia Declaration of Rights. The church was established in all of the ancient states whose downfall was described by Mr. Henry. The Christian religion, on the contrary, flourished most in conflict with prevailing laws, as in primitive Christianity, in the Protestant Reformation, and in the days when Dissenters were being persecuted in Virginia.

Moral decay, Madison averred, was the result of war and bad laws. It was complained of in New England, which had an established church.

The true remedy for declining religion and morals lay in fair laws, proper administration of them, the education of youth, and better adult example. The microscopic notes from which his speech is known conclude with a directive to himself: deliver a "panegyric on [Christianity] on our side."

The principal hazard was Henry himself. If only they could get rid of him—by some less pious method than Jefferson suggested, "devotedly to pray for his death." Madison found one: work on his love of distinction and elect him governor to succeed retiring Benjamin Harrison. Friends and foes united in placing him on that pedestal of honor and impotence. The father of the religious scheme, wrote Madison to Monroe, "will no more sit in the House of Delegates, a circumstance very inauspicious to his offspring."

By this time opposing petitions were coming in, especially from Presbyterian laymen of the Shenandoah Valley. The bill's emphasis shifted from preacher-support to aid of glebe-house schools. The measure became "a bill establishing a provision for teachers of the Christian religion." To let public opinion develop and to cool the "warmest votaries," Madison withdrew his opposition to the companion bill to incorporate the Protestant Episcopal church. He still disliked the bill, although it was modified to give lay vestries power over rectors, but the defeat of it "would have doubled the eagerness and the pretexts for a much greater evil." With that measure passed, the House voted forty-five to thirty-eight to postpone the taxation controversy until the following November.

The year 1785 was two or three days old when Madison received a letter from Richard Henry Lee, president of Congress, announcing that the post of minister to Spain was open, John Jay having been elected Secretary for Foreign Affairs. Lee informed Madison that "Mr. Madison has been nominated for Spain, and is much approved by the southern states." Madison had before him, at that moment, a letter from Monroe giving the same information and adding that Richard Henry Lee "earnestly advocated the appointment of Jefferson to the Court of Spain," in order to open the British and French posts to himself and his brother Arthur. Madison had his name withdrawn.

Looking at the situation in Virginia just before the April elections, Madison found the Episcopal clergy and laity strongly for the religious bill; all other lay groups against it. The Presbyterian clergy displayed a "shameful contrast" between their former memorials against an establishment that shut them out and their present eagerness to set up an establishment that would take them in. The elections sustained his optimism;

many supporters of the measure were defeated. Presbyterian clergymen began to change their tune. Throughout the middle and back counties, Madison wrote in June, people were saying that although the General Assembly might give this bill "the form, they will not give it the validity of a law." Considering the Declaration of Rights, "I own the bill appears to me to warrant this language of the people."

George Nicholas did not share Madison's optimism. A great majority of the people, he wrote, were against the bill. If passed, an attempt to enforce it would bring about a revolution; but it was supported in counties that were over-represented in the legislature. Hope of deterring that body must arise "from their fears, and not their justice." Identical petitions against the bill, from all parts of the state, would attain that end, and Madison was the one to write such a paper.

The result was Madison's famous "Memorial and Remonstrance Against Religious Assessments," sent to Nicholas in June. Not a word should be changed, Nicholas replied, adding that 150 freeholders signed it in a day. George Mason, an Anglican, had it printed in Alexandria for statewide distribution.

The Remonstrance contained fifteen reasoned objections to religious assessments. First was the right of every man, guaranteed in the state constitution, to exercise religion according to the dictates of his own conscience. This was a right unalienable by nature and "a duty towards the Creator," much older and deeper than the claims of civil society, and "wholly exempt from its cognizance." The preservation of free government, Madison declared, forbids any branch of it "to overleap the great barrier which defends the rights of the people. The rulers who are guilty of such an encroachment . . . are tyrants. The people who submit to it . . . are slaves."

It is proper, said Madison "to take alarm at the first experiment on our liberties." That was one of the noblest characteristics of the American Revolution. "The freemen of America did not wait till usurped power had strengthened itself by exercise, and entangled the question in precedents. They saw all the consequences in the principle, and they avoided the consequences by denying the principle." Who does not see that "the same authority which can force a citizen to contribute three pence only of his property [the tax on tea] for the support of any one establishment, may force him to conform to any other establishment in all cases whatsoever?"

Madison assailed the assessment as a source of animosities and jealousies; a corrupter of churches. Religious establishments had erected a spiritual tyranny and upheld the thrones of political tyranny. In the Virginia Declaration of Rights, the citizen's right of religious freedom was set forth with studied emphasis. Either, then, we must say that the legislature "may sweep away all our fundamental rights; or, that they are bound to leave this particular right untouched and sacred." Either we must say "that they may control the freedom of the press . . . may swallow up the executive and judiciary powers of the state; nay, that they may . . . erect themselves into an independent and hereditary assembly: or we must say, that they have no authority to enact into a law the bill under consideration. We the subscribers say, that the General Assembly of this Commonwealth have no such authority."

Circulated throughout the state, the petitions rolled back upon Richmond like a crunching avalanche, each copy bearing a dozen to a hundred signatures. In the fall, the "bill establishing a provision for teachers of the Christian religion" never was taken out of its pigeonhole.

The "Memorial and Remonstrance," however, kept on with its work. In another pigeonhole for six years had lain Jefferson's model "Bill for Religious Liberty." Madison pulled it out and pushed it to passage by an overwhelming majority. "I flatter myself," he commented to Jefferson, that its provisions, by their unaltered adoption, "have in this country extinguished forever the ambitious hope of making laws for the human mind."

Madison's "Memorial and Remonstrance" looms large in the background of the clause on religious liberty in the First Amendment to the United States Constitution. It was repeatedly republished early in the nineteenth century, during the progressive disestablishment of churches in the several states. A hundred years after that it took a central position in the series of cases through which the Supreme Court upheld the First Amendment as a "wall of separation" between state and church.

Madison attempted to expand his success with the Bill for Religious Liberty by getting action on the entire code revision, made in 1779 by Jefferson, Edmund Pendleton, and George Wythe and stalled by the "courthouse crowd" that fattened on defects in justice. Progress was made until the revisal of criminal laws came up, restricting capital punishment to murder and treason. "The rage against horse stealers," Madison reported to Jefferson, led to its defeat by a single vote. "Our old bloody code is by this event fully restored."

After two years of uneven progress, Patrick Henry's return to the legislature stopped the revisal cold. Jefferson did not share Madison's disappointment. The co-author of the revisal wrote in his autobiography that it languished until "by the unwearied exertions of Mr. Madison, in opposition to the endless quibbles, chicaneries, vexations and delays of lawyers and demi-lawyers, most of the bills were passed by the legislature with little alteration."

Co-incident with this effort, Madison undertook to fulfill George Washington's dream of making the Potomac River an effective channel of commerce between the Atlantic seaboard and the expanding West. Washington's plan, as Madison described it, was to slope Great Falls by clearing away rocks, "and by means of ropes fastened to the rocks, to pull up and ease down the [sixty-foot] boats where the current is most rapid." The same principle was to be applied to canoe navigation in mountain creeks—thus making the river navigable to its very source. A short roadway would furnish a link with the headwaters of the Ohio.

Charters from both Virginia and Maryland were needed, and Washington sent Madison a model bill. Madison reported that the Assembly "lent a ready ear to the project," but to take care of jealousy he proposed a similar development of James River navigation. Favoring government ownership, Madison framed the James River bill to turn the canals, and so on, over to the state after the subscribers received twice their original investment. An "exuberant harvest," he called this return. "Confiscation," cried the prospective investors. He shifted to a provision giving the state a first right to buy stock at the going price and both bills sailed through the legislature. Virginia bought the James River canal in 1820.

A similar concern for public rights was shown by Madison when the inventor James Rumsey applied for a patent on a "poleboat" he had invented for upstream travel on the Potomac. (A paddlewheel, turned by the current, pushed rows of setting poles against the river bottom.) Madison's bill, first laughed at and then passed, gave Rumsey a ten-year monopoly which the state could take over for ten thousand pounds. Ever after, Madison considered this bill a model for encouraging invention and checking monopoly.

Under the Potomac and James River charters, the state purchased stock in the companies. On Madison's motion, the state made a gift of stock to Washington for his Revolutionary War services. The general refused it, except for devotion to some public trust. At Madison's suggestion, the Potomac shares were legislatively dedicated by Washington to establishment of a university in the national capital, and the James River shares to endowment of an academy that became Washington and Lee University at Lexington, Virginia.

Throughout the three years when "Mr. Henry was out of the way," Madison worked for repeal of the laws that barred British debtors from the Virginia courts and thus violated the treaty of peace. Early in January 1785, he reported, one bill was "laid asleep by the refusal of the interested members" (British debtors) to help make a quorum; but both houses accepted a compromise on the day before final adjournment. Nothing remained but to order it enrolled. That night eight members crossed the James River to Manchester and sent back word next day, via canoe, that they could not return because of floating ice. (The canoe could cross!) Again there was no quorum. The assembly waited three days and then adjourned.

A year later Madison drafted a new measure honoring the treaty. The House turned the effort into "a scene of mockery" by refusing to exempt such suits from the statute of limitations. To save national honor Madison let the bill die. Virginia's conduct delayed British evacuation of the western military posts another ten years. A similar spirit came to the fore when Carter Harrison attempted in 1785 to repeal a three-year-old law that permitted owners of slaves to set them free. This attempt was made, Madison reported, in rage against a universal emancipation petition that was supported in principle "by sundry respectable members." A motion to "throw it under the table [was] treated with as much indignation on one side as the petition itself was on the other." The bill was defeated.

The failure of Madison and others who hated slavery to make a fight for its abolition was explained by the *Encyclopédie Méthodique* in an article clearly influenced by Jefferson's contacts with the editors. In the assembly "one could find men courageous and honest enough to ask for it . . . (we shall cite but one, Mr. Maddisson, who at the age of 30 astonished the new republics with his eloquence, his wisdom and his genius); but they . . . feared that a futile effort would only clamp down the chains of slavery and would not hasten the day when the Negroes would be set free."

Madison's hopes that a few years of tobacco prosperity would "put our credit on a decent footing" were dashed in 1785, when the price of Virginia's staple dropped fifty per cent. The legislature not only postponed tax collection but allowed payment in tobacco and other commodities. "The wisdom of seven sessions will be unable to repair the damage of this single act," exclaimed Madison. In June 1786 he predicted that a cry to emit paper money "will be rung in our ears by the very men whose past measures have plunged us into our difficulties." November found him combating that cry in the legislature. Paper money without taxes to back it, he asserted, was an unconstitutional confiscation of property. It fostered luxury, cut off funds for Congress, destroyed confidence, enriched sharpers, vitiated morals. If Virginia joined the paper money states—Pennsylvania, New York, Rhode Island, the Carolinas—she would be conspiring "to disgrace republican government in the eyes of mankind."

By the overwhelming majority of eighty-five to seventeen, the House of Delegates condemned paper money as unjust, impolitic, destructive of confidence and virtue—the very terms Madison had used against it. He took little comfort in the result, which he ascribed to one of Patrick Henry's intermittent absences from the legislature. Should Henry on his return (in 1787) erect the standard he would accomplish his purpose. "Shame and remorse are but too feeble restraints on interested individuals against unjust measures, and are rarely felt at all by interested multitudes."

In upholding the federal treaty power, Madison stood for national honor against the self-interest of fellow Virginians. In taking a stand against unbacked paper money, tax postponements, and debt moratoriums, he acted against the self-interest of himself and family. His father, land-rich but heavily in debt, had refused to pay off his creditors in depreciated money. As the system of avoidance spread, Madison saw in it a new menace to the Union. Paper money, he wrote in 1786, "is producing the same warfare and retaliation among the states as were produced by the state regulations of commerce." Commercial warfare also was increasing. The interplay of these incentives to disunion turned his efforts more and more to the only visible remedy—the building up of the federal government.

15 / THE ROAD TO PHILADELPHIA

The Maryland-Virginia conference on control of the Potomac River met in March 1785 with two Virginia commissioners present. Governor Henry forgot to notify the members. After waiting two days in Alexandria for Madison and Randolph, everybody accepted Washington's invitation to hold the conference at Mt. Vernon.

Maryland, by its charter, owned the Potomac from shore to shore. The new compact declared the river to be a common highway for the whole American people. Fishing rights were regulated and joint criminal jurisdiction established.

Madison secured acceptance by the legislature and saw an opening for much broader interstate gains. The compact recommended annual conferences on commercial problems. Why not, he suggested, use that as a handle to attack the defects of the Confederation? Keeping out of sight because of his nationalistic reputation, he induced John Tyler to move to vest Congress with a general power to regulate the commerce of the United States.

> If it be necessary to regulate trade at all [commented Madison to Monroe] it surely is necessary to lodge the power where trade can be regulated with effect; and experience has confirmed what reason foresaw, that it can never be so regulated by the states acting in their separate capacities. They can no more exercise this power separately than they could separately carry on war, or separately form treaties of alliance or commerce.

Aiding the project was the fact that Britain had cut off American trade with the West Indies, and tobacco sales in Europe carried "the most visible and shameful frauds in every article." Madison rejected the prevalent belief that congressional power over commerce would expose the

133

South to a Northern shipping monopoly. Had diversity of state interests been listened to, he commented to Monroe, there would have been no Confederation.

These arguments, Madison conceded, would be little relished in the Virginia Assembly. He hoped to carry the proposition because England was the offender, and old animosities were still strong. In debate he cited the system of tribute collected by the states with good harbors from importers in other states. Power over commerce, he warned, was essential to preserve the federal Constitution. Without it there would be a dissolution of the Confederacy and a settlement of every petty squabble with the sword.

The resolution introduced by Tyler but drafted by Madison called for a perpetual grant to Congress of power to establish uniform commercial regulations. Speaker Harrison and his allies made a fearful bogie of the *perpetual* grant. They beat it down to twenty-five years, then to thirteen, at which point Madison and Tyler discarded the resolution and shifted tactics. Wasting time on futile alternatives, they held back their real plan until the last day of the session. Then, with merchants all over the state clamoring for action about the West Indies, Tyler offered a Madison resolution that carried almost unanimously. Commissioners were appointed to meet with those of other states and "consider how far a uniform system in their commercial regulations may be necessary to their common interest and their permanent harmony; and to report to the several states such an act relative to this great object as when unanimously ratified by them will enable the United States in Congress effectually to provide for the same."

The blanks in the resolution were filled with the names of Edmund Randolph, James Madison, Jr., Walter Jones, St. George Tucker, and Meriwether Smith. Thus, the path was opened to the Annapolis Convention of 1786. The time was the first Monday in September. Should the meeting fail, commented Madison, all the world would know "that we are not to be respected nor apprehended as a nation in matters of commerce."

As the months passed, conditions grew worse. Connecticut, New Jersey, and Delaware, by declaring their ports free, wrecked the import duties of Massachusetts, New York, and Pennsylvania. Virginia, from which Congress received nearly the whole of its financial support in 1785, cut off every penny of it. Commercial anarchy, Madison predicted, would reduce exports and drain out more specie, thus furnishing "pretexts for the pernicious substitution of paper money, for indulgencies to debtors, for postponement of taxes." The only counter-hope was that such a crisis would produce the necessary unanimity.

In April, long-erring Rhode Island surprised everybody by approving the impost, whereupon New York killed it by a vitiating half-acceptance. Even if it had been adopted, Madison observed, the door would still be open to commercial warfare among the states and to foreign machinations. In such a commercial and political climate, and through midsummer thunderstorms and exhausting heat, Madison and a servant set off on horseback for Annapolis. They went in a great circle by way of Harper's Ferry, Philadelphia, and New York. Nothing, Madison wrote to his brother Ambrose from this last city, "can bear a worse aspect than our federal affairs as viewed from this position. No money comes into the public treasury, trade is on a wretched footing, and the states running mad after paper money."

There was much talk in and out of Congress, Madison reported, of a plenipotentiary convention to amend the Articles of Confederation. "Though my wishes are in favor of such an event," he wrote to Jefferson, "yet I despair so much of its accomplishment at the present crisis that I do not extend my views beyond a commercial reform. To speak the truth I almost despair even of this." Nevertheless, deputies had been appointed by eight states and four of the others displayed no hostility to the *object* of the Annapolis Convention. "Of the affairs of Georgia I know as little as of those of Kamskatka."

Reaching Annapolis on September 4, Madison found only two commissioners there. Lodging in George Mann's Inn cost only a shilling a night as he settled down to wait, shifting from wine, punch, and porter to tea, as fatigue wore off. By September 11, Delaware, New Jersey, and Virginia alone had quorums, plus two New Yorkers and one Pennsylvanian. The twelve who attended were all federal-minded, including Alexander Hamilton and Egbert Benson of New York, Tench Coxe of Pennsylvania, Abraham Clark of New Jersey; Madison, Randolph, and St. George Tucker of Virginia.

Absence of the Massachusetts deputies was a blow, but it eliminated the dragging influence of Stephen Higginson, who complained that the measure "originated in Virginia and with Mr. Madison" and was supported by "great aristocrats" who probably knew or cared little about commercial objects. Aristocrat Randolph headed a committee to report "measures fit to be taken" by so small a gathering. While he wrote, the others talked and decided on a drastic change of plan, cutting off Randolph in mid-sentence.

Regulation of commerce would be included in an enlarged objective: a recommendation that Congress call a second convention to make a general revision of the system of government. Partial cures had been tried and failed. The time had come for radical action. Almost all of the delegates felt that way, Madison recorded in retrospect, each one's opinion being reinforced by the attitude of the others.

The writing assignment was transferred to Hamilton, who penned so fierce a blast about the "imperative necessity for a powerful government" (the description comes from Hamilton's biographer Morse) that it produced a violent protest by Randolph. As they debated, Morse reported, "Madison said to Hamilton: 'You had better yield to this man, for otherwise all Virginia will be against you.'" Hamilton did yield, and produced a mild and disarming letter to Congress, sounding much more like Madison than Hamilton.

The project of a general constitutional revision was carefully concealed. The deputies from New Jersey, it was explained, were authorized to consider commercial regulations "and other important matters," and had moved an expansion that improved the plan. Also, to make the commerce power effective, other parts of the federal system might need adjustment. To set forth the reasons "would be a useless intrusion of facts and observations" already well known to Congress. "They are however of a nature so serious" that the commissioners "with the most respectful deference, beg leave to suggest their unanimous conviction that it may essentially tend to advance the interests of the Union" if Congress and the states concur in calling a convention to meet at Philadelphia on the second Monday in May 1787. The function of its commissioners should be "to take into consideration the situation of the United States, to devise such further provisions as shall appear to them necessary to render the constitution of the Foederal Government adequate to the exigencies of the Union," and to report an act for that purpose to Congress for confirmation by all the states.

Thanks to Randolph's protest, Madison's warning, and Hamilton's un-Hamiltonian writing, there was not a thing to attack except the basic idea. Virginia's acceptance was crucial, and Madison rode directly to Richmond to take on that job. One omen was good. Patrick Henry, retiring as governor, decided to stay on his farm for a year. But John Jay, now Foreign Secretary, had reversed his stand on navigation of the Mississippi and was promoting a treaty abandoning the claim for twenty-five years.

Jay's motive, avowedly fear of war, was chiefly economic: to trade the right of navigation for a Spanish market for fish. Such a deal, Madison told Monroe, "would be a voluntary barter in time of profound peace of the rights of one part of the empire to the interests of another part." Figure to yourself, he wrote to Jefferson, "the effect of such a stipulation on the Assembly of Virginia, already jealous of northern politics," with many members attached to the West by interest. Would not the Western people themselves, feeling sold by their Atlantic brethren, be likely to "consider themselves absolved from every federal tie" and court foreign protection?

To make the situation far worse, Jay had induced Congress to revoke the instruction to demand the right of Mississippi navigation in any treaty with Spain. Nine states were required to give that instruction. Seven repealed it—an unconstitutional action, in Madison's opinion, which added "the insult of trick to the injury." What could he say now to the Kentucky members of the Virginia legislature, after arguing to them that Congress must be strengthened to enable them to protect Western rights? There was need to say plenty. He had been in Richmond but one day when he wrote to Washington that even if Jay's projected treaty should be frustrated, "the effects already produced will be a great bar to an amendment of the confederacy, which I consider as essential to its continuance." He assured the Kentucky members that the views of Congress were likely to be changed.

At this moment another factor was projected into the public scene— Shays' Rebellion. "Great commotions are prevailing in Massachusetts," Madison reported to his father. "An appeal to the sword is exceedingly dreaded." The rebellious elements professed to aim only at reform of abuses, "but an abolition of debts public and private, and a new division of property, are strongly suspected to be in contemplation." George Washington heard the news and instantly called on Madison to secure attention to that "great and most important of all objects, the federal government." All should see that "thirteen sovereignties pulling against each other . . . will soon bring ruin on the whole, whereas a liberal and energetic Constitution, well guarded and closely watched, to prevent encroachments, might restore us to that degree of respectability and consequence to which we had a fair claim, and the brightest prospect of attaining."

Neither Washington nor Madison heard of the realities that lay behind the seizure of muskets and pitchforks by Daniel Shays and his embattled farmers—mortgages bearing interest of twenty-five to forty per cent;

taxes exceeding the average farmer's cash income ($200); twenty times as many men in jail for debt as for all other offenses combined; seizure laws that took the debtor's land, homestead, livestock, tools, furniture—all sold to the creditor at a fifth of its value and the debtor clapped into jail for the deficiency. Those were the hard facts that lay behind the forcible closing of courts by Daniel Shays, veteran of the battles of Lexington, Bunker Hill, Ticonderoga, Saratoga, and Stony Point.

National policy, however, was not determined by these hidden facts but by the terror inspired by an apparently unprovoked uprising of "desperate and unprincipled men," intent on overthrowing orderly society. The Virginia legislature forgot John Jay's treaty machinations, forgot the perils of an over-powerful federal government, forgot its own sacred sovereignty, and voted *unanimously* to send seven delegates to the Philadelphia Convention. To assist in this, Madison took the liberty of placing Washington's name at the head of the delegation without his consent.

After the appointment, Madison set himself to overcoming various objections Washington offered. Citing the critical importance of the convention's work, he said it was the opinion of every judicious friend "that your name could not be spared from the deputation." Washington agreed to go; Patrick Henry refused a place. The delegation ultimately consisted of Governor Randolph, Washington, Madison, Mason, George Wythe, John Blair, and Dr. James McClurg. There was not one "small power" man in the group.

The convention would open in five months, and much was to be done. Realizing that the Mississippi affair was crucial, Madison in November had secured his own re-appointment to Congress to succeed the now-ineligible Monroe. He then obtained unanimous instructions to the delegates in Congress to uphold the right of navigation. Surrender of the Mississippi would be regarded "as destroying that confidence in the wisdom, justice and liberality of the federal councils which is so necessary at this crisis, to a proper enlargement of their authority; and finally, as tending to undermine our repose, our prosperity and our Union itself."

That resolution virtually staked the continued existence of the Federal Union on defeat of Jay's projected treaty. Unless that project could be reversed, Madison told Washington, "the hopes of carrying this state into a proper federal system will be demolished." With these instructions in his pocket, he set out for New York, shifting from horseback to stage at Fredericksburg and ending the journey in a blinding northeast snowstorm, on February 9, 1787.

He found the Spanish situation better than expected, as far as Congress was concerned. His missionary work en route to Annapolis had converted the New Jersey delegation, and Pennsylvania was expected to swing over. Congress was in a stew over the Shays uprising, and was proposing (Madison wrote to Washington) measures "for *disarming* and *disfranchising* those concerned in it"—measures through which a new crisis might be brought on. The Shaysites were winning Massachusetts elections. Terrified New Englanders were indulging in "undigested ideas" of monarchy. Madison voted reluctantly to give Massachusetts requested military aid. *Intervention against a majority*, he said in a speech, was hard to reconcile with the principles of republican government, but *popular commotions had to be subdued.*

Twelve states and Congress approved the Philadelphia convention; Rhode Island alone rejected it. "Nothing can exceed the wickedness and folly which continue to reign there," exclaimed Madison. "All sense of character as well as right is obliterated. Paper money is still their idol, though it is debased to eight for one."

Nobody in Congress, Madison found, knew anything about Jay's negotiations with the Spanish agent, Don Diego de Gardoqui. He asked Jay about them and was told nothing. He then called on Gardoqui and found him voluble and assertive. The Mississippi was closed and would remain so. Without a treaty, Spain would buy no fish. Madison quizzed him about Spain's territorial claims east of the Mississippi and got vague and evasive answers. At last he learned what he wanted to know: Gardoqui and Jay had disagreed regarding territorial claims and had held no talks since October. Gardoqui would soon leave for home. "The Spanish project sleeps," wrote Madison to Jefferson.

Nothing less than death and public burial, however, would salvage the situation in Virginia, with Patrick Henry on a rampage against the convention and displaying "disgust [that] exceeds all measure" (so wrote Randolph) on the treaty matter. Madison's next step was to bypass Jay and present Gardoqui with an official disavowal, by the Virginia Executive Council, of the looting of Spanish mercantile property during a march on Natchez by George Rogers Clark. Clark's unauthorized actions were called uncontrollable. Madison's intent was not to flout "the federal sovereign," as Jay charged, but to let Gardoqui know that Spain "has no option but between concession and hostilities." In this meeting Gardoqui denied that Spain would make concessions concerning the Mississippi but no longer revealed "a real inflexibility."

Jay's reaction to Clark's looting was the opposite of Madison's. He advised Congress that the United States must make a yielding treaty to escape war with Spain. This heightened Madison's feeling that the seven-state repeal of the Spanish instruction must be revoked. The first step was to call for a report from Jay on the state of the negotiations, but this required the aid of Jay's supporters. To obtain it Madison arranged with William Pierce of Georgia to make the motion, saying "it had been hinted by Mr. Madison" that this was proper. Rufus King of Massachusetts, head of the fishery forces, jumped up with a protest against haste. To the surprise of everybody except Pierce, Madison supported King's protest. Pierce withdrew his motion, re-offered it a few days later, and Massachusetts gave silent assent.

The Foreign Secretary revealed an agreement that the United States would not use or navigate the lower Mississippi during the life of the projected treaty. This, said Jay, was to avoid war; but the treaty was stalled by a disagreement over boundaries. The report turned Rhode Island and Pennsylvania against the treaty. Madison, thereupon, moved that the 1786 repeal of the instruction, being adopted by seven states when nine were required, did not authorize "any suspension of the use of the River Mississippi." With several states absent, there was no chance of obtaining the required seven affirmative votes. The objective, Madison wrote, was to establish a formal record of "the paucity of states who abet the obnoxious project." The attempt to surrender the Mississippi, he felt, was at an end, a point "of great importance in reference to the coming convention." The objective was achieved after his departure from New York, when Congress fell but one state short of the required seven for repeal, and only three—Massachusetts, New York and Maryland—adhered to the "noxious project."

With this in prospect, Madison made a final entry in his notes of congressional debates. On May 2, 1787, "I left New York for the convention to be held in Philadelphia." That entry marked an ending and a beginning in the life of the nation.

Part III

16 / THE VIRGINIA PLAN

Madison took with him to Philadelphia two manuscripts written in preparation for constitutional revision, "Of Ancient and Modern Confederacies," and "Vices of the Political System of the United States." They embodied several years of study of Old World institutions and American experience.

The confederacies were dealt with one by one—the Lycian, the Amphictyonic, and the Achaean in the ancient world; the Helvetic, the Belgic, and the Germanic of modern times. What were their elements of strength and weakness? What vices made the old ones fail? Why were the modern feeble? Citations of authority reveal Madison's sedulous study of the books that flowed to him from Paris—more than a hundred references to Felice's thirteen-volume *Code de l'Humanité*, many to the *Encyclopédie*, Mably, Stanyan, Temple, Gillie, Montesquieu, and Treviux. Ancient sources included Polybius, Ubbo Emmius (in Latin), Plutarch, and many others.

Madison found one fatal defect common to all of the confederacies—weakness of the federal head. This allowed strong states to oppress the weak and foreign tyrants to subvert the whole. Athens and Sparta waged their wars inside the Amphictyonic Confederacy. Its weakness exposed Greece to the wiles and strength of Philip of Macedon. The Belgic Confederacy was paralyzed by the requirement of unanimity among seven republics.

From this background Madison proceeded to describe the "Vices of the Political System of the United States." It was like a catalogue taken out of antiquity and contemporary Europe, starting with failure of the states to comply with constitutional requisitions. This evil, resulting from the number and independent authority of the states, was so uniformly exemplified in every similar confederacy that it could be considered inherent in the existing American system and fatal to the object of it.

Then came (2) encroachment by the states on the federal authority, illustrated by Georgia's Indian wars and unlicensed compacts between states, and (3) violations of the laws of nations and of treaties with England, France and Holland. (4) "Trespasses of the States on the rights of each other," as in the laws of Virginia, Maryland, and New York favoring their own vessels and commerce. Classed also as aggressions on the rights of other states were emissions of paper money, installment of debts, occlusion of courts, and making property a legal tender. (5) "Want of concert in matters where common interest requires it"— notably in commercial affairs. Power also was lacking to establish uniform rules of naturalization, literary copyrights, national seminaries, canals and other objects of general utility. (6) "Want of Guaranty to the States of their Constitutions and laws against internal violence." Republican theory made right and power synonymous, both being vested in the majority. But an armed minority might seize power, especially if joined "by those whose poverty excludes them from a right of suffrage." Where slavery exists the theory that right and power are synonymous "becomes still more fallacious." (7) "Want of sanction to the laws, and of coercion in the Government of the Confederacy." Lacking these essentials, the federal system possessed only the *form* of a political constitution, and was in fact nothing more than a treaty of amity, commerce, and alliance between independent and sovereign states. This never was intended by the constitution's compilers, whose virtuous intentions and inexperience "apologizes for their errors."

Madison went on with his list of evils—want of ratification of the Articles by the people, multiplicity and mutability of state laws—and closed with the "Injustice of the laws of the States." This was the more alarming because it "brings more into question the fundamental principle of republican Government, that the majority who rule in such governments are the safest guardians both of public good and private rights." The causes of unjust laws lie both in the people and their representatives. Men seek office because of ambition, personal interest, or public good. Unhappily, the candidates who feel the first two motives are most active and successful. In office, they join in a perfidious sacrifice of their constituents to self-interest, often aided by the honest dupes of a favorite leader who professes public good. A still more fatal cause of unjust laws, Madison asserted, lies among the people themselves:

> All civilized societies are divided into different interests and
> factions, as they happen to be creditors or debtors—rich or
> poor—husbandmen, merchants or manufacturers—members
> of different religious sects—followers of different political

leaders—inhabitants of different districts—owners of different kinds of property &c &c. In republican government the majority however composed, ultimately give the law. Wherever therefore an apparent interest or common passion unites a majority what is to restrain them from unjust violations of the rights and interests of the minority, or of individuals?

Three motives only, said Madison: a prudent regard to their own good as involved in the general and permanent good; respect for character; and religion. None of these sufficed to restrain individuals from injustice, and they would have less influence on the multitude. The remedy, he concluded, lay in enlarging the sphere of government, not because the impulse of a common interest or passion was less predominant, but because it is harder to build up the requisite combinations. In a large territory, "the Society becomes broken into a greater variety of interests, of pursuits, of passions, which check each other, whilst those who may feel a common sentiment have less opportunity of communication and concert."

He concluded: "As a limited monarchy tempers the evils of an absolute one; so an extensive Republic meliorates the administration of a small Republic." This last thought was dominant in Madison's mind as he prepared for the work of the Federal Convention. It rendered safe the concentration of power necessary to remedy the great vices that he found in the American political system: lack of power in the central government; discord, jealousy, and oppressive rivalry among the several states; and injustice of the states to their own citizens.

Applying these principles to the task before the convention, Madison outlined the results to his closest Virginia collaborators, Governor Randolph and George Washington. The first need was to wean Randolph from his expressed idea that the new system should be built into the existing one. The way to deal with the malleable Randolph was first to agree with him, then diverge.

"I think with you," wrote Madison on April 8, "that it will be well to retain as much as possible of the old Confederation, though I doubt whether it may not be best to work the valuable articles into the new system, instead of engrafting the latter on the former." If presented to the states as separate amendments, all might fail through partial acceptance. "In truth, my ideas of a reform strike so deeply at the old Confederation, and lead to such a systematic change, that they scarcely admit of the expedient."

With Washington, Madison used no circumlocution. "Temporizing applications," he wrote on April 16, "will dishonor the Councils which propose them, and may foment the internal malignity of the disease . . . Radical attempts although unsuccessful will at least justify the authors of them." In almost identical words he laid his specific proposals before the two men. This to Randolph:

> I hold it for a fundamental point, that an individual inde-pendence of the States is utterly irreconcilable with the idea of an aggregate sovereignty. I think, at the same time, that a consolidation of the States into one simple republic is not less unattainable than it would be inexpedient. Let it be tried, then, whether any middle ground can be taken, which will at once support a due supremacy of the national authority, and leave in force the local authorities so far as they can be subor-dinately useful.

The first step, he thought, was to abandon the system of state equality in Congress, which gave little Delaware an equal voice with Massachu-setts or Virginia. Already unfair to the larger states, it would be unsafe to them once Congress was given real instead of nominal power. That done, "Let the national Government be armed with a positive and com-pleat authority in all cases where uniform measures are necessary, as in trade, &c, &c. Let it also retain the powers which it now possesses." Then came this drastic proposal:

> Let it have a negative, in all cases whatsoever, on the legis-lative acts of the States, as the King of Great Britain hereto-fore had. This I conceive to be essential and the least possible abridgement of the State sovereignties. Without such a de-fensive power, every positive power that can be given on pa-per will be unavailing. . . . Let this national supremacy be extended also to the Judiciary department. . . . [Otherwise] the intention of the law and the interests of the nation may be defeated by the obsequiousness of [state] tribunals to the policy or prejudices of the States.

A government "of such extensive powers ought to be well organized." He proposed a legislature of two branches, one chosen by the legisla-tures or the people at large, the other smaller, with members holding office for a longer term and going out in rotation. "A national Executive will also be necessary," but he had not yet formed an opinion concerning its makeup or powers. The states should be expressly guaranteed against internal as well as external dangers.

"I am afraid," he concluded, "you will think this project, if not extravagant, absolutely unattainable and unworthy of being attempted. Conceiving it myself to go no farther than is essential, the objections drawn from this source are to be laid aside." Unless the Union was organized efficiently on republican principles, monarchic innovations might be obtruded, or the empire divided into rival and hostile confederacies.

Madison reached Philadelphia on May 3, eleven days ahead of the convention's scheduled opening. Not another deputy was there, except the Pennsylvanians, and it was May 25 before the required quorum of seven states was reached. During that interval Madison drafted "the Virginia Plan" for submission to his state colleagues. It was a virtual expansion of his letters to Washington and Randolph into a groundwork of government, in the shape of numbered resolutions. The first three set guiding principles:

> (1) Resolved, That a Union of the States merely federal will not accomplish the objects proposed by the articles of Confederation, namely common defence, security of liberty, and general welfare.
>
> (2) Resolved, That no treaty or treaties among the whole or part of the States, as individual Sovereignties, would be sufficient.
>
> (3) Resolved, That a *national* Government ought to be established, consisting of a *supreme* Legislative, Executive and Judiciary.

It is evident from the course of events that Randolph protested against this total discard of the Articles of Confederation, which conflicted with the views he had expressed in April. Madison shifted (for the time) to a single resolve which made it possible for the Virginia governor, as spokesman for the delegation, to present the plan to the convention: "(1) Resolved that the Articles of Confederation ought to be so corrected and enlarged as to accomplish the objects proposed by their institution; namely, common defence, security of liberty and general welfare."

The fourteen resolutions that followed began illogically, "Resolved *therefore*," which fitted only the ensuing nationalistic structure. The plan provided for a two-house legislature, the first elected by the people, the second elected by the first branch with longer tenure. The powers of the legislature, in addition to those vested in Congress by the Confederation, were described in these sweeping terms:

> . . . and moreover to legislate in all cases to which the separate States are incompetent, or in which the harmony of the United States may be interrupted by the exercise of individual Legislation; to negative all laws passed by the several States, contravening in the opinion of the National Legislature the articles of Union; and to call forth the force of the Union against any member of the Union failing to fulfill its duty under the articles thereof.

Other resolutions provided for a "National Executive" to be chosen by the legislature, and that "a National Judiciary be established to consist of one or more supreme tribunals, and of inferior tribunals to be chosen by the National Legislature, to hold their offices during good behavior." Jurisdiction was to cover various specified subjects "and questions which may involve the national peace and harmony."

It was likewise resolved that provision be made for the admission of new states, and that republican government and territory of each state be guaranteed by the United States. All state officers should be bound by oath to support the Articles of Union. Finally, the amendments to be proposed by the convention should be submitted, after approval by Congress, to state conventions "to be expressly chosen by the people."

Presentation of this plan launched the business of the convention after George Washington was elected president of it. Randolph read the Virginia Plan on May 29 and supported it with vigor. Gouverneur Morris of Pennsylvania, brilliant and mercurial, pointed out at once that the first resolve conflicted with all that followed. It was impossible to set up a supreme national government merely by enlarging the Articles of Confederation. Randolph dropped that resolution and offered Madison's original three. With eight states present, the convention voted six to one (New York divided) to establish "a *national* Government . . . consisting of a *supreme* Legislative, Executive and Judiciary."

Two crucial questions lay ahead. Who would control that powerful general government? How would the delegates feel about its powers after it was known what states would be in the best position to wield them? Fifty-five men, when all were assembled, would give the answers.

17 / LINES FORM IN
THE CONVENTION

James Madison was two months past his thirty-sixth birthday when the Philadelphia Convention began its work. Thirteen delegates were younger. The average age, forty-three, was lifted considerably by Benjamin Franklin's eighty-one years. Charles Pinckney was twenty-nine; Hamilton, thirty-two (two years older than he thought he was); Rufus King, thirty-two; Randolph, thirty-three; and Gouverneur Morris, thirty-five. Young men were shaping the destiny of a youthful nation.

In the country at large French Chargé d'Affaires Otto saw four groups: (1) those who desired a strong central government over the states; (2) those who would break the country into three allied confederacies; (3) army officers who favored throwing the states into one mass under Washington; (4) those who wanted nothing done at all, headed by Governor Clinton of New York and Samuel Adams.

If there were indeed four such groups, the second and third were not represented in the convention, and the fourth only by Robert Yates and John Lansing, who were sent to outvote Hamilton and preserve New York's regional monopoly of import duties. Madison testified at the close of the convention to its fundamental unity: "It appeared to be the sincere and unanimous wish of the convention to cherish and preserve the Union of the states. No proposition was made, no suggestion was thrown out, in favor of a partition of the empire into two or more confederacies."

Madison, at thirty-six, was at a lifetime peak of physical fitness and health. The historian H. B. Grigsby described his appearance in 1788 as muscular, well-proportioned, and ruddy complexioned. The weakness and pallor of early youth had disappeared. Horseback riding and long walks (for which he imported a pedometer from Paris) kept him in trim. He needed physical stamina now to sustain double duties, for besides taking full part in the convention he determined to keep a record of its debates.

In pursuance of this task, he wrote in a preface to his notes, he chose a seat in front of the presiding member and took notes, partly in a self-invented shorthand. The notes were written out between the daily adjournment and reassembling of the convention. "It happened, also, that I was not absent a single day, nor more than a casual fraction of an hour in any day, so that I could not have lost a single speech unless a very short one."

Fragmentary notes were taken by several other delegates and a fairly full account—replete with biased opinion but accurate in substance—by Yates of New York, during the brief term of his attendance. A rule of complete secrecy imposed by the convention both during and after its sessions, and protracted by Madison's political discretion, prevented publication of his notes until four years after his death. They remain the principal source of the history of the convention.

That same secrecy, of course, kept the country completely in the dark during the three and a half months the convention was at work. This concealed the basic division, which was inside the party that wanted a strong government. This cleavage developed when the convention took up the resolve of the Virginia Plan that representation ought to "be proportioned to the quotas of contribution, or to the number of free inhabitants, as the one or the other rule may seem best in different cases."

This was an indirect way of counting slaves in fixing the South's proportional strength in Congress. To ease the way toward it, Madison moved simply that equal representation of the states "ought not to prevail in the national legislature, and that an equitable ratio of representation ought to be substituted." This would have been agreed to, he recorded, except that George Read of Delaware said his delegation was instructed against any change of the rule of suffrage. Should such a change be fixed on, "it might become their duty to retire from the convention."

Madison replied that under the new system, with legislative acts taking effect regardless of state attitudes, there was the same reason for different numbers of representatives from large and small states, as from large and small counties within a state. The question was postponed with a feeling that "the proposed change of representation would certainly be agreed to." Madison would have been less sure of this had he known that Read himself asked the Delaware legislature to bind them in this manner.

The resolve that the national legislature consist of two branches was readily agreed to, and only New Jersey and South Carolina (with Delaware divided) opposed the election of the first branch by the people. Popular election of one branch, asserted Madison, was "essential to every plan of free Government." He favored successive filtrations in other branches, but to be stable and durable "the great fabric to be raised . . . should rest on the solid foundation of the people themselves."

Wilson of Pennsylvania opposed Madison's proposal that the popular house elect senators, without regard to state lines, from persons nominated by state legislatures. Wilson suggested that they be elected by the people from interstate districts. Madison protested that the larger state, in such a district, would monopolize the office. Wilson's idea was not pressed, but the convention defeated the resolve for a selection of one body by the other. Leaving that subjected undecided it proceeded to the resolve on congressional power.

Nobody opposed a continuation of all the powers of the existing Congress. On the proposition for giving legislative power "in all cases to which the separate States are incompetent," South Carolina (alert in defense of slavery) wanted an enumeration of them and "called on Mr. Randolph for the extent of his meaning." Not having written the clause, Randolph stated his personal attitude. He "disclaimed any intention to give indefinite powers to the national Legislature," declaring that nothing could change his mind.

Madison, author of the resolve, took a different stand. He had brought with him "a strong bias in favor of an enumeration and definition of the powers necessary" to the national legislature; but he "had also brought grave doubts concerning its practicability. His wishes remained unaltered; but his doubts had become stronger." What his opinion might ultimately be he could not yet tell: "But he should shrink from nothing which should be found essential to such a form of government as would provide for the safety, liberty and happiness of the community. This being the end of all our deliberations, all the necessary means for attaining it must, however reluctantly, be submitted to."

Many years later, editing his notes, Madison struck out the word "grave"—the only weakening modification he made of his nationalistic position in the convention. His statement to the convention, however, left the meaning of the clause undetermined, and even South Carolina joined in approving it. The other clauses, giving powers necessary to preserve harmony among the states and to negative state laws contravening the articles of union, were agreed to without debate or dissent. A final clause, sanctioning the use of force against any delinquent state, was dropped on the motion of its author. It looked "more like a declaration of war, than an infliction of punishment," and Madison hoped it would be unnecessary. That is, he thought the federal veto over state laws would suffice.

At this stage, Madison favored a stronger negative than the one already approved, which covered state laws conflicting with the federal constitution. On June 8 he seconded Charles Pinckney's motion "that the National Legislature should have authority to negative all laws *which they should judge to be improper.*" Madison accused the states of a constant tendency "to encroach on the federal authority; to violate national treaties; to infringe on the rights and interests of each other; to oppress the weaker party within their respective jurisdictions." He regarded "an indefinite power to negative legislative acts of the States as absolutely necessary to a perfect system." The convention disagreed.

When the resolve that the Executive be chosen by the national legislature came up, Wilson proposed an election by the people. The reaction was negative. Any system that made the Executive independent of the legislature, declared Roger Sherman of Connecticut, was "the very essence of tyranny." A majority voted that the legislature make the appointment.

The convention then defeated the proposal in the Virginia Plan that the Executive and judiciary be a council of revision, exercising a veto power over legislation. Judges should not have a hand in the making of laws which might come before them later in a test of constitutionality. Wilson called for an absolute Executive veto; Madison, a qualified one. This brought a unanimous decision that vetoed bills could be repassed by a two-thirds majority. Madison continued to urge that judges be given a share in the veto power, but his motion was voted down, seven states to three.

On the selection of federal judges, Madison agreed with Wilson and turned against his own original plan of appointment by the national legislature. That, he said, would allow incompetent legislators to choose unqualified men for improper purposes. Should judges be appointed by the Executive or the Senate? Madison wanted that question left to maturer reflection, but the convention voted to give the power to the Senate.

An attempt to eliminate lower federal courts brought an emphatic protest from Madison. "Unless inferior tribunals were dispersed throughout the republic with *final* jurisdiction in *many* cases, appeals would be multiplied to a most oppressive degree." Federal courts must be at hand to deal with "improper verdicts in state tribunals." On Madison's motion, the legislature was *permitted* (not required) to establish lower courts.

The convention endorsed Madison's proposal that the new constitution be ratified by conventions instead of by legislatures. If it were put into effect "by the supreme authority of the people themselves," he contended, there would be less of a tendency to decide uncertainties in favor of the states, as had occurred in conflicts between acts of the states and of Congress.

Charles Pinckney and Rutledge of South Carolina then attempted to reverse the decision for popular election of one branch of the national legislature. "The people," said Pinckney, were less fit judges than state legislatures. Sherman supported the move in order to preserve harmony between national and state governments. "The objects of the Union, he thought were few": national defense; maintenance of internal security; treaties; regulation of commerce and drawing a revenue from it. All but these and a few lesser matters would be better in the hands of the states. Wilson and Mason took the opposite stand.

Madison sensed a crisis in this debate of June 6 and drew on his heaviest artillery. He considered an election of "one branch at least of the Legislature by the people immediately, as a clear principle of free government." Also, it would avoid "too great an agency of the State Governments in the General one." Sherman, he said, had not adequately covered the objects that required a national government. It was essential also to provide for the security of private rights and the steady dispensation of Justice. "Interferences with these were evils which had more perhaps than any thing else, produced this convention."

Madison picked up an admission by Sherman that "in a very small state, faction and oppression would prevail." The remedy for that was to enlarge the sphere of government. *"This was the only defence against the inconveniences of democracy consistent with the democratic form of Government."*

From this premise Madison repeated the major argument of his "Vices of the Political System of the United States," that the injustice of state laws proceeded from the rivalries of different sects, factions, and interests in a too-small political society. In Greece and Rome, the rich and poor alternately oppressed each other. Slavery exemplified the evil. In the most enlightened period of time "we have seen the mere distinction of colour made . . . a ground of the most oppressive dominion ever exercised by man over man." What was the source of the unjust laws of the states? "Has it not been the real or supposed interest of the major number? Debtors have defrauded their creditors. The landed interest has

borne hard on the mercantile interest. The holders of one species of property have thrown a disproportion of taxes on the holders of another
species."

The only remedy was to enlarge the sphere, and thereby divide the
community into so great a number of interests and parties that one would
offset another. It was incumbent on the convention to try this remedy
and "frame a republican system on such a scale and in such a form as
will controul all the evils which have been experienced." Try this remedy
they did. A convention made up of conservative defenders of property,
brought together by the twin spectres of national collapse and social
chaos, proceeded to build a democratic government, stabilized against
the historic evils of democracy by its continental sphere, its strength,
and its federal organization.

Madison's speech was the turning point of the convention on democratic government, but it did not produce unanimity on the issue before
the house. Read of Delaware said they must look beyond the continuance
of the states. "A national Government must soon of necessity swallow all
of them up." Wilson challenged that assertion. "He saw no incompatibil-
ity between the National and State Governments provided the latter were
restrained to certain local purposes." The Pinckney motion for election
of the first branch by state legislatures was defeated eight to three, South
Carolina, New Jersey, and Connecticut supporting it.

The convention turned next to the Senate and John Dickinson moved
for election by state legislatures. Its membership, he said, should be distinguished for rank in life and weight of property, as nearly like "to the
British House of Lords as possible." Wilson disagreed. A national government "ought to flow from the people at large." He returned to his
earlier suggestion and moved that senators be elected by the people in
large districts—that is, some of them interstate. Madison, who previously had opposed this, now gave it inferential support. If state legislatures chose the senators, he said, "we must either depart from the doctrine of proportional representation; or admit into the Senate a very
large number of members." The first was unjust, the second inexpedient:
"The use of the Senate is to consist in its proceeding with more coolness,
with more system, and with more wisdom, than the popular branch. Enlarge their number and you communicate to them the vices which they
are meant to correct."

Madison could see no reason to prefer election by legislatures. The
great evils complained of were that the legislatures had run into schemes
of paper money. "Their influence then, instead of checking a like pro-

pensity in the National Legislature, may be expected to promote it." Every state except Pennsylvania voted against Wilson's motion, after which the convention unanimously approved the selection of senators by state legislatures.

In this debate, Madison recorded in a footnote, neither side dealt directly with the true issue. Dickinson wanted election by state legislatures to promote state equality in the Senate. Wilson desired interstate districts to keep the Senate small and in ratio to population. The outcome was a blow to the large-state forces, which up to this time had appeared to be thoroughly in control of the convention. Their opponents, however, were receiving accretions in strength. Governor William Livingston brought prestige to New Jersey's capable but obscure delegation. Dr. James McHenry, called home by his brother's illness, was replaced by Luther Martin, a zealot for paper money and the carving up of Virginia. His vote divided Maryland.

Thus fortified, William Paterson of New Jersey moved that the convention take up the rule of suffrage in the national legislature—that is, both branches of it. He and his colleague David Brearly then launched an attack on the concept of a national government. At the formation of the Confederation, said Brearly, the question of representation "had been rightly settled by allowing each sovereign State an equal vote." When the proposition for destroying the equality came forward he was astonished and alarmed. Substitute a ratio based on population and Virginia would have sixteen votes, Georgia only one. He would not say it was fair that Georgia should have an equal vote with Virginia. What remedy then? "Only one, that a map of the United States be spread out, that all the existing boundaries be erased, and that a new partition of the whole be made into thirteen equal parts."

Paterson took up the theme. Proportional representation struck at the existence of the lesser states. A confederacy supposed sovereignty in its members and sovereignty supposed equality. "If we are to be considered as a nation, all State distinctions must be abolished, the whole must be thrown into hotchpot, and when an equal division is made, then there may be fairly an equality of representation." New Jersey would never confederate on the plan before the convention. "She would be swallowed up."

Replied Wilson: if the small states would not confederate on this plan, Pennsylvania and he presumed others would not confederate on any other. "A new partition of the States is desirable, but evidently and totally impracticable." Adjournment and a soothing speech by Benjamin

Franklin cooled rising tempers, but when the subject was resumed Connecticut laid down a *sine qua non.*

Sherman moved that each state have one vote *in the second branch.* "Every thing he said depended on this." The smaller states would never agree on any other principle. The motion was defeated six to five, and by the same division the convention voted that the ratio in the second branch be the same as in the first.

With that question insecurely settled, the convention hastened through the remaining resolves of the Virginia Plan. Madison seconded a motion that members of the first branch be elected for three years. Instability, he said, was one of the great vices of state legislatures. In the more extensive national legislature, three years would be required for members to gain knowledge of the problems of other states than their own. Gerry replied that the people of New England would never give up annual elections, their only defense against tyranny. Nobody, Madison rejoined, could say what his constituents thought now or would think in twelve months. "We ought to consider what was right and necessary in itself for the attainment of a proper government." The three-year term was upheld.

Madison supported a motion that senators be elected for seven years, saying that would not give too much stability. "His fear was that the popular branch would still be too great an overmatch for it." A stable and firm government organized in the republican form should be held out to the people. Otherwise they would be likely, in universal disgust, to "renounce the blessing which they have purchased at so dear a rate." Seven years carried, eight to one. Randolph and Madison put through a resolve that jurisdiction of federal courts extend to "questions which involve the national peace and harmony."

That completed the consideration of the Virginia Plan in committee of the whole, and its revised form was placed before the convention on June 14. Paterson secured a day's postponement to enable him to place a "purely federal" substitute before the house. Coming in the wake of his and Brearly's speeches on state equality, this was an ominous notice that the fundamental conflict of the convention was just emerging into view.

Paterson placed the New Jersey Plan before the convention on June 15. It was a cleverly conceived document, primarily designed to preserve state equality and to unite Maryland with the small states. A study of various preliminary drafts reveals that the powers of Congress were drawn up by Lansing of New York and Sherman of Connecticut; the executive and judiciary articles were slightly modified by Paterson from the Virginia Plan, and Luther Martin contributed a drastic article on national supremacy.

Paterson made an ironic stroke by leading off with Madison's temporary opening resolve of the Virginia Plan, calling for correction and enlargement of the Articles of Confederation. The national legislature was to possess all the powers of the existing Congress, plus the authority to levy import duties and stamp taxes; also to regulate trade and commerce with foreign nations and among the states.

The plan called for a plural executive. The judiciary was to consist of a supreme tribunal appointed by the executive, with appellate power in federal cases appealed from state courts. Provision was to be made for admission of new states and for uniform rules of naturalization. Capping it was this mighty provision for national supremacy, followed by a specific provision for enforcement by military power:

> Resolved that all Acts of the United States in Congress made by virtue and in pursuance of the powers hereby and by the articles of Confederation vested in them, and all Treaties made and ratified under the authority of the United States shall be the supreme law of the respective States so far forth as those Acts or Treaties shall relate to the said States or their citizens, and that the Judiciary of the several States shall be bound thereby in their decisions, any thing in the respective laws of the Individual States to the contrary notwithstanding.

The purpose of this article, as revealed by Martin's later strategy, was to give the national government judicial and military power to enforce acts of Congress dividing up the states against their will. In spite of her previous land cession, Virginia still extended to the Mississippi, as did North Carolina and Georgia. The small states and Maryland were still land-hungry, a state of mind that underlay New Jersey's "hotchpot" proposal. Three days before the New Jersey Plan was introduced, congressional delegate Grayson of Virginia "lamented that the desire of dismembering states prevails in so great a degree among the citizens of the Union."

That desire was no less evident in the stand of Delaware's convention delegates for state equality in the national legislature. "I conceive our existence as a state will depend upon our preserving such rights," Read had written to Dickinson in January, "for I consider the acts of Congress hitherto as to the ungranted lands in most of the larger states, as sacrificing the just claims of the smaller and bounded states to a proportional share therein, for the purpose of discharging the national debt incurred during the war." He would trust nothing to the candor, generosity, or public justice of the larger states. That was the state of mind behind the New Jersey-Delaware-Maryland scheme of throwing the states into "hotchpot" for redivision.

To put the two plans on a procedural parity, both were referred to the committee of the whole. There Paterson quickly got down to cases. The small states, he said, acceded to the Articles of Confederation "reluctantly and slowly. New Jersey and Maryland were the two last, the former objecting to the want of power in Congress over trade: both of them to the want of power to appropriate the vacant territory to the benefit of the whole." If state sovereignty was to be maintained, with representatives drawn immediately from the people, the only expedient "is that of throwing the States into Hotchpot," and redividing them. The people at large, Paterson declared, were not complaining of the set-up of Congress. "No, what they wish is that Congress may have more power."

Wilson compared the two plans point by point, finding far greater governmental effectiveness in the Virginia Plan. He could not persuade himself that the people were so devoted to state sovereignty as some supposed, nor that a national government was so obnoxious to them. Where did the people look for relief from present evils? From a reform of state governments? "No, Sir. It is from the national councils that relief is expected." However, it would be with extreme reluctance that he would give powers to the existing Congress. Its inequality of representation "has ever been a poison contaminating every branch of Government."

Charles Pinckney remarked that the whole small-state argument came down to one point: "Give New Jersey an equal vote, and she will dismiss her scruples, and concur in the National system." Edmund Randolph said he "was not scrupulous on the point of power. When the salvation of the Republic was at stake, it would be treason to our trust, not to propose what we found necessary"—immediate repair of the imbecility of the Confederation through substantial reform.

Alexander Hamilton, hitherto silent, now declared himself "unfriendly to both plans." No amendment that left the states in possession of their sovereignty could possibly answer the purpose. The general power "must swallow up the State powers [or] be swallowed up by them." The Virginia Plan lacked firmness. It was his private opinion, supported by "so many of the wise and good, that the British Government was the best in the world. . . . Their House of Lords is a most noble institution." Let us, he advised, go as far in this direction as republican principles will admit. "Let one branch of the Legislature hold their places for life or at least during good behavior. Let the Executive also be for life." Hamilton closed by reading, but did not offer, a plan of government along these lines.

Madison stayed out of the debate on the New Jersey Plan until the fourth day (June 19) and then delivered the final and conclusive speech against it. To refute the claim that the convention lacked power to frame a government bearing directly on the people, he pointed out that the Articles of Confederation did exactly that in relation to piracy and felonies at sea. In Connecticut and Rhode Island, delegates to Congress were elected by the people. So it was already, in part, a national government. He described the weaknesses of the New Jersey Plan. It provided no means of enforcing treaties. It failed to check encroachments on the federal authority. Lacking ratification by the people, it did not make the federal constitution supreme over state constitutions. It would not halt insurrections nor cure the multiplicity, the mutability, the injustice, the impotence of state laws.

Turning to the remedy—federal military coercion—relied on by the small-state delegates, Madison told them that it never could be exerted except against the small states themselves. The great ones would be impregnable. If the Union were dissolved, would the small states be more secure against the ambition and power of their larger neighbors than they would be under a general government pervading every part of the empire? If dissolution led to formation of two or more confederacies, could the smaller states expect equality to be granted them by their larger associates?

The only great difficulty, Madison observed, lay in the affair of representation. It was admitted that it was *unjust* to give Delaware an equal vote with Virginia, sixteen times as populous; but, it was said, it would be *unsafe* for Delaware to allow Virginia sixteen times as great a vote. New Jersey proposed that all the states "be thrown into one mass and a new partition be made into 13 equal parts." Would such a scheme be practicable? The dissimilarities in property laws, manners, habits, and prejudices of the different states forbade it. However, said Madison, admitting this redivision to be practicable and the danger in proportional representation to be real, would not a voluntary coalition of the small states with their neighbors be more convenient and equally effectual for their own safety?

That wound up the debate in committee of the whole. The delegates then rejected the Paterson plan by "postponing generally" its first proposition, New Jersey and New York alone supporting it. By the same vote, except that Maryland divided, the revised Virginia Plan was "re-reported without alteration."

This was an overwhelming inferential decision for a "supreme national government," but it was far from deciding the crucial question of who would control that government. The plan consisted now of nineteen amended resolves which had to be debated and voted on anew. Wilson, discussing the first resolve, said that "by a National Government he did not mean one that would swallow up the State Governments as seemed to be wished by some gentlemen." This brought Hamilton to his feet to say that "he had not been understood yesterday. By an abolition of the states, he meant that the national legislature ought to have indefinite authority. As *States*, he thought they ought to be abolished . . . leaving in them, subordinate jurisdictions."

Rufus King said the terms "States" "Sovereignty" "national" and "federal" were being used inaccurately and delusively. "The States were not 'Sovereigns' in the sense contended for by some. . . . they could not make war, nor peace, nor alliances, nor treaties." They were dumb and deaf, for they could neither speak nor listen to any foreign sovereign whatever. On the other hand, a Union of the states comprised the ideas of both confederation and consolidation. "A Union of the States is a Union of the men composing them, from whence a *national* character results to the whole." If the states formed a confederacy in some respects, they formed a nation in others. "He doubted much the practicability of annihilating the States; but thought that much of their power ought to be taken from them."

Luther Martin challenged this view. The separation from Great Britain, in his opinion, "placed the 13 States in a state of Nature towards each other." Confederation ended that and placed them on the footing of equality, and they were met to amend it on the same footing. Wilson disputed Martin. He "could not admit the doctrine that when the Colonies became independent of Great Britain they became independent also of each other." He read the Declaration of Independence, declaring "the United Colonies . . . to be free and independent States." From this he inferred "that they were independent, not *individually* but *Unitedly*, and that they were confederated as they were independent, States." Hamilton agreed with Wilson.

On the motion of Ellsworth, the word "national" was unanimously struck out of the opening resolve, which was then revised to read "that the *Government of the United States* ought to consist of a supreme legislative, Executive and Judiciary." That, said Ellsworth, employed "the proper title" of the nation. The motive for the change, Madison explained when jubilant State Righters discovered it in 1819, was merely to get rid of a term that might be liable to mistake or misrepresentation.

On the second proposition, small-state delegates argued vigorously against a two-house legislature. Their purpose was to open the way to Sherman's rejected compromise: two branches, and a proportional representation in one of them; each state to have an equal voice in the other. The large states spurned the offer. Jealousy, said Wilson, would continue to exist between state and national legislatures, but both represented the same people and the national legislature would leave the state governments in possession of what the people wished them to retain. On the contrary, he conceived that "the general Government would be in perpetual danger of encroachment from the State Governments."

Madison (on June 21) carried this farther. Not only was there less danger of federal encroachment on the states, but "the mischief from encroachments would be less fatal" if made by the general government than if made by the states. The history of all confederacies, he said, showed a greater tendency to anarchy in the members than tyranny in the federal head. Suppose for a moment that the states were reduced to corporations dependent on the general legislature. "Why should it follow that the general government would take from the states any branch of their power as far as its operation was beneficial, and its continuance desirable to the people?" The objection to general federal power lay not against its probable abuse, but against the imperfect use of it in so vast a country and over so great a variety of objects:

> Were it practicable for the General Government to extend its care to every requisite object without the cooperation of the state governments, the people would not be less free as members of one great Republic than as members of thirteen small ones. . . . Supposing therefore a tendency in the General Government to absorb the State Governments, no fatal consequence could result. Taking the reverse of the supposition, that a tendency should be left in the State Governments towards an independence on the General Government, and the gloomy consequences need not be pointed out.

Had such words come from Madison in the Virginia of 1830, when slavery was deified and nullification extolled, he would have done well to escape lynching. He let them stand as recorded, but made sure that they reached only the eyes of posterity.

The convention reaffirmed the two-branch legislature, the first to be elected by the people. Madison resisted a motion to have the members elected annually. Distant members would have to travel seven or eight hundred miles and go home to seek re-election. New members needed more time to gain the required knowledge. The vote was for two years.

Madison, Randolph, and others beat down an attempt by Williamson of North Carolina to perpetuate the system of state payment of congressional salaries. Williamson argued that the nation ought not to pay the expenses of men sent from the poverty-stricken western states solely to thwart the measures and interests of the older ones. Madison vigorously protested the policy "of leaving the members from the poor States beyond the mountains, to the precarious and parsimonious support of their constituents." If new western states were admitted to the Union, "they ought to be considered as equals and as brethren."

Election of senators by state legislatures was confirmed on June 25 without debate, Virginia and Pennsylvania alone voting no. In this division, Madison recorded in a footnote, these two states were influenced by a feeling that election by legislatures would interfere with proportional representation. His own position was revealed a few minutes later during the attempt (which failed) to have senators paid by the states. As recorded in part by Yates, in part by himself:

By the vote already taken, will not the temper of the state legislatures infuse itself into the Senate? Do we create a free government? . . . . The motion would make the Senate like [the existing] Congress, the mere agents and advocates of State interests and views, instead of being the impartial umpires and guardians of justice and general good.

On the subject of tenure, proposals were put forward that senators be elected for four, six, or seven years, going out in rotation. The six-year term failed in a tie vote, Madison supporting it. Read then moved for tenure during good behavior. When that was rejected he moved that the term be nine years and on this the main debate took place, Madison leading off.

The proper function of the Senate, he said, was to protect the people against their rulers and against their own transient impressions. Men chosen for a short time, as the more numerous house would be, might share the popular errors. "A necessary fence against this danger would be to select a portion of enlightened citizens, whose limited number, and firmness might seasonably interpose against impetuous councils." The same defense was needed to check sudden impulses of the majority to commit injustice on the minority.

An increase of population [said Madison] will of necessity increase the proportion of those who will labour under all the hardships of life, and secretly sigh for a more equal distribution of its blessings. These may in time outnumber those who are placed above the feelings of indigence. According to the equal laws of suffrage the power will slide into the hands of the former. No agrarian attempts have yet been made in this country, but symptoms, of a leveling spirit, as we have understood, have sufficiently appeared in a certain quarters to give notice of the future danger. How is this danger to be guarded against on republican principles?

Among other means, he answered, "by the establishment of a body in the Government sufficiently respectable for its wisdom and virtue, to aid on such emergencies, the preponderance of justice by throwing its weight into that scale." That called for considerable duration in the second branch of the legislature. "He did not conceive that the term of nine years could threaten any real danger" to republican principles if accompanied by "a perpetual disqualification to be re-elected."

Hamilton and Wilson agreed with Madison, but Sherman declared that government was instituted for those who live under it, and "the more permanency it has the worse if it be a bad Government." Gerry warned that a longer term than four or five years "would defeat itself. It never would be adopted by the people." Nine years was defeated—Pennsylvania, Delaware, and Virginia supporting it. All three of those states then joined in a seven-to-four majority fixing the term at six years, one third to go out biennially.

On June 27 the convention took up, or attempted to take up, the tentative decision to make the Senate proportionate to the population. The result was an oratorical exhibition by Luther Martin who, Madison recorded, "contended at great length [a day and a half] and with great eagerness that the General Government was meant merely to preserve the State Governments, not to govern individuals;" that to refer a new government to the people would "be throwing them back into a State of Nature," thereby dissolving the state governments.

Madison opened the debate when it got back on the track. He was convinced that state equality in the Senate was neither just, nor necessary to the safety of the small states. Brearly and Paterson had admitted its injustice. "The expedient proposed by them was a new partition of the territory of the United States." The reasoning behind it was fallacious. They confounded the making of mere treaties, specifying certain duties of the parties, "with a compact by which an authority was created paramount to all the parties, and making laws for the government of them." France, England, and Spain would not hesitate to treat on an equality with the Prince of Monaco and four or five other little sovereigns, in regulating commerce and so on; but would thirty million people submit their fortunes into the hands of a few thousand, if they were forming a council of deputies with authority to raise troops, levy taxes, and so on, for all of them?

By the plan proposed, "a compleat power of taxation, the highest prerogative of supremacy is proposed to be vested in the National Government." It would have many other powers. But he saw no need to secure the small states against the large ones. Mere size would not unite the large states. Religion and manners did not set them against the others. No common production of staples linked them: "The staple of Massachusetts was *fish*, of Pennsylvania *flower*, of Virginia *tobacco*." Large counties in a state showed no tendency to combine. Among independent nations, the large ones tore each other to pieces. Among confederacies not possessing a strong central authority, large states, rivals of each other, trampled on their weaker neighbors.

"The two extremes before us," Madison went on, "are a perfect separation and a perfect incorporation, of the thirteen States." In the first instance they would be independent nations; in the last, mere counties of one entire republic, subject to one common law. In the first case the smaller states would have everything to fear from the larger. In the last they would have nothing to fear: "The true policy of the small States therefore lies in promoting those principles and that form of Government which will most approximate the States to the condition of counties."

It was of course futile (except as irony) to present that argument to small-state delegates whose real purpose was to gain control of a government powerful enough to carve up their larger neighbors. Without making that direct accusation, Madison said that the large states would never consent to a partition as long as their importance and security depended on their own size and strength. Give the general government sufficient energy and permanence, and gradual partitions of the large states and junctions of the small states would be facilitated.

Wilson, following Madison, likened state equality in the Senate to "the representation of the boroughs in England which has been allowed on all hands to be the rotten part of the Constitution." Sherman resurrected the sophistical argument that giving a populous state more votes than a small state was like giving a rich man more votes than a poor man. Franklin, taking note of the rising acrimony, remarked that "*God governs in the affairs of men*" and moved that henceforth prayers be held each morning "imploring the assistance of Heaven." Madison recorded Hamilton's protest that the hiring of chaplains would spread reports of dissension but not his reputed remark that he saw no need of invoking "foreign aid." A vote was avoided by adjournment.

In the absence of a cooling breeze from Heaven the next day's debate was hotter than ever. Gorham advised Delaware to seek safety in a union with Pennsylvania. Read retorted that Delaware would not fear proximity to Massachusetts, weak as that state had proved herself to be (in confronting Daniel Shays). "These jealousies," Read declared, "are inseparable from the scheme of leaving the states in existence. They must be done away. The ungranted lands also which have been assumed by particular states must be given up."

The large states, Dr. Johnson of Connecticut observed, saw the states only as "districts of people composing one political Society." However, they also "exist *as* political Societies," and must therefore be armed with some power of self-defense. This brought up Madison. He agreed with Johnson "that the mixed nature of the Government ought to be kept in view; but thought too much stress was laid on the equal rank of the States as political societies." As Yates recorded Madison's remarks:

> Some contend that States are sovereign, when, in fact, they are only political societies. There is a gradation of power in all societies from the lowest corporation to the highest sovereign. The States never possessed the essential rights of sovereignty. These were always vested in congress. Their voting, as States, in congress, is no evidence of sovereignty. The State of Maryland voted by counties—did this make the counties sovereign? The States, at present, are only great corporations, having the power of making by-laws, and these are effectual only if they are not contradictory to the general confederation. The States ought to be placed under the control of the general government—at least as much so as they formerly were under the king and British parliament.

Judge Yates's notes were published in 1821, a year when the nation was torn apart over the admission of Missouri as a free or slave state. Virginia was storming against nationalistic decisions of the Supreme Court. Editors of the Washington *National Intelligencer* and Richmond *Enquirer*, expressing disbelief of the Yates record, asked Madison for comment. His own notes substantially agreed with those of Yates. Not daring to admit this, in the political storm then raging, but deeply averse to telling an outright falsehood, Madison (not for publication) inaccurately paraphrased the Yates report, then disparaged it with rhetorical questions.

"Who can believe," he wrote to Joseph Gales of the *Intelligencer*, "that so palpable a misstatement was made on the floor of the convention, as that the *several states* were political societies, *varying* from the *lowest* corporation to the *highest sovereign;* or that the states had vested *all* the essential rights of sovereignty in the old Congress?" Yates, he said, did not wilfully misrepresent, but his notes were full of egregious errors and sprang from prejudices which gave "every tincture and warp to his mind of which an honest one could be susceptible." Actually, Yates did not quote Madison as saying that *the states* varied from the lowest corporation to the highest sovereign, nor that *all* the essentials of sovereignty were vested in Congress. Having made this irrelevant disclaimer, Madison revised his own notes, not to eliminate the record of his nationalism, but to expand it for posterity by incorporating in it an additional nationalistic utterance credited to him by Yates. The addition is italicized below, in Madison's record of his words:

> Mr. Madison . . . thought too much stress was laid on the rank of the States as political societies. There was a gradation, he observed from the smallest corporation, with the most limited powers, to the largest empire with the most perfect sovereignty. He pointed out the limitations on the sovereignty of the States, *as now confederated their laws in relation to the paramount law of the Confederacy were analogous to that of bye laws to the supreme law within a State.* Under the proposed Government the powers of the States will be much farther reduced. According to the view of every member, the General Government will have powers far beyond those exercised by the British Parliament, when the States were part of the British Empire.

Brief notes kept by King sustain the Yates account. Wrote King, quoting Madison: "The States are not sovereign in the full extent of the term. There is a gradation from a simple corporation for limited and specified objects, such as an incorporation of a number of Mechanicks up to a full sovereignty as possessed by independent nations, whose powers are not limited. The last only are truly sovereign."

Following these nationalistic remarks, Madison warned against giving *unequal* portions of the people an *equal* voice in a government of such powers. To do so "would subject the system to the reproaches and evils which have resulted from the vicious representation in Great Britain." He entreated the small states to renounce a principle confessedly unjust, which if admitted "must infuse mortality into a Constitution which we wished to last forever." They should "ponder well the consequences of suffering the Confederacy to go to pieces."

Alexander Hamilton spelled out one of those consequences—multiple partial alliances with rival and hostile European powers. Then he put his finger on the real issue before the convention: "It has been said that if the smaller States renounce their *equality*, they renounce at the same time their *liberty*. The truth is *it is a contest for power, not for liberty.*"

That contest was partially resolved when the convention, six states to four, reaffirmed proportional representation in the first branch of the legislature. Ellsworth promptly moved for state equality in the second branch and "trusted that on this middle ground a compromise would take place." Deprive the small states of this and the body of America would be cut in two "somewhere about this part of it." (That is, the Delaware River would separate two confederacies.) This measure of self-defense, Ellsworth asserted, was necessary to protect the small states from large-state combinations.

Wilson replied that there were "no coinciding interests" among the large states that could produce a coalition of them against the small ones. "No answer has yet been given to the observations of [Mr. Madison] on this subject." The argument was "all a mere illusion of names. We talk of states, till we forget what they are composed of"—people.

Madison challenged the whole concept of a conflict between large and small states and foresaw a different one arising. The states were divided into different interests not by relative size, but partially by climate and other causes, "principally from the effects of their *having or not having slaves.*" The great division of interests in the United States lay not between the large and small states, but "between the Northern and Southern, and if any defensive power were necessary, it ought to be mutually given to these two interests." Such a defense, he suggested, could be furnished by counting slaves in fixing representation in one branch of the legislature and basing the other on freemen only, although, he pointed out, this would destroy the equilibrium of interests in the two houses.

Wilson then proposed that each state have at least one vote in the Senate, and the larger states one for each 100,000 souls. Madison was ready to acquiesce in this concession "on condition that a due independence should be given to the Senate." The plan with election by legislatures made the Senate absolutely dependent on the States—"only another edition of Congress," with all its faults. "Still he would preserve the State rights, as carefully as the trials by jury."

That last sentence, taken out of context, has been cited over and over as evidence that Madison's principal effort, and indeed the principal effort of the convention, was to safeguard state sovereignty. In reality it was a minor detail and was not even in his original notes. He picked it out of Yates *to replace one of his own.* Combining the marked-out sentence with the one from Yates, the full relevance of his remark becomes clear: "Make it [the Senate] properly independent and it is of little consequence from what states the members may be taken. I mean, however, to preserve the state rights with the same care as I would trials by jury; and I am willing to go as far as my honorable colleague."

That is, he would *preserve state rights* by giving each state at least one senator. The small-state response was a total and violent rejection of Wilson's compromise. "Look at the votes," shouted corpulent, bull-voiced Gunning Bedford of Delaware. "Have they not been dictated by interest, by ambition? Are not the large States evidently seeking to aggrandize themselves at the expense of the small? . . . Can it be expected that the small States will act from pure disinterestedness? Look at Great Britain." The borough system there was called the rotten part of the Constitution, but "have not the boroughs however held fast their constitutional rights? and are we to act with greater purity than the rest of mankind?" The large states, roared Bedford, "dare not dissolve the Confederation. If they do the small ones will find some foreign ally of more honor and good faith, who will take them by the hand and do them justice."

This was a confession of what Madison, Wilson, Hamilton, King, and others had come close to charging. King grieved that such thoughts, expressed "with a vehemence unprecedented in that House," had entered into the honorable member's heart. It could only be excused on the score of passion.

A tie vote followed on Ellsworth's motion for state equality in the Senate. Five for it: Connecticut, New York, New Jersey, Delaware, Maryland. Five against: Massachusetts, Pennsylvania, Virginia, North Carolina, South Carolina. Divided: Georgia.

General Charles Cotesworth Pinckney on July 2 moved the appointment of a committee of one from each state "to devise and report some compromise." Madison and Wilson considered this a waste of time, as the *mere opinion* of such a committee would not influence the house. The proposal carried, and in the selection of the committee by ballot, Madison and Wilson were left off. Two delegates strong for compromise, Mason and Franklin, represented Virginia and Pennsylvania.

Mason, a zealot for giving the popular house exclusive power to originate money bills, made that the price of acceptance of state equality in the Senate. Madison assailed the committee compromise. He "could not regard the exclusive privilege of originating money bills as any concession on the part of the small States. Experience proved that it had no effect." It did not touch the objections to state equality in the Senate. The convention must either depart from justice in order to conciliate the small states and a minority of the people, or it must do justice to the larger states and the majority of the people. He himself could not hesitate:

> The Convention with justice and the majority of the people
> on their side had nothing to fear. With injustice and the mi-
> nority on their side they had every thing to fear. It was in
> vain to purchase concord in the Convention on terms which
> would perpetuate discord among their constituents. . . . But
> if the principal States comprehending a majority of the peo-
> ple of the United States should concur in a just and judicious
> plan, he had the firmest hopes, that all the other States would
> by degrees accede to it.

The words "by degrees" carried a plain threat that the large states
would report a plan embodying proportional representation and wait for
the pressure of necessity to bring the small states into line. Gouverneur
Morris endorsed that course and presented a grim picture of the results
of small-state resistance:

> Let us suppose that the larger States agree; and that the
> smaller refuse: and let us trace the consequences. The oppo-
> nents of the system in the smaller States will no doubt make a
> party, and a noise for a time, but the ties of interest, of kin-
> dred and of common habits which connect them with the
> other States will be too strong to be easily broken. . . . This
> country must be united. If persuasion does not unite it, the
> sword will.

Turning to the effects of state equality, Morris predicted that large
states outvoted in the Senate would resist laws so enacted. "State attachments, and State importance," he declared, "have been the bane of this
country. We cannot annihilate; but we may perhaps take out the teeth of
the serpents." In the ensuing debate Wilson opposed the compromise,
Franklin, Mason, and Gerry upheld it.

On a preliminary test of strength (July 7) the compromise was upheld, six states to three, with Massachusetts and Georgia divided. Their
tie votes, plus outright loss of North Carolina, marked the disintegration
of the "large and to-be-large" combination of states on which Madison
had based his strategy from the outset. This affected at once his attitude
toward federal powers. He objected to an effort by Gerry to have those
powers defined before the composition of the Senate was decided:

> Mr. Madison observed that it would be impossible to say
> what powers could be safely and properly vested in the Gov-
> ernment before it was known, in what manner the States were

to be represented in it. He was apprehensive that if a just representation were not the basis of the Government it would happen, as it did when the Articles of Confederation were depending, that every effectual prerogative would be withdrawn or withheld, and the New Government would be rendered as impotent and as shortlived as the old.

Paterson replied that the small states had yielded too much in giving up state equality in one house. They never would be able to defend themselves without equality in the second branch. "His resolution was fixt. He would meet the large States on that ground and no other." Morris said the compromise made the national legislature "another Congress, a mere Wisp of straw. . . . Among the many provisions which had been urged, he had seen none for supporting the dignity and splendor of the American Empire."

Madison reminded Paterson that his hotchpot doctrine of representation was sound in principle, based on population. It must "for ever silence the pretensions of the small States to an equality of votes with the large ones." He suggested as a proper ground of compromise that in the first branch the states be represented according to the number of free inhabitants, "and in the second, which had for one of its primary objects the guardianship of property, according to the whole number, including slaves."

This meant three-fifths of the slaves, as in the "wealth and numbers" ratio of Confederation requisitions. The subject was referred to a grand committee, which reported an initial apportionment state by state, of sixty-five representatives, with partial account taken of slaves. Madison moved that the total number be doubled. In a membership of sixty-five, a majority of a quorum would be only twenty—too few to win the confidence of the people. Too expensive, came the objection from New England, and only Virginia and Delaware voted, 'aye.'

In the debate on a permanent rule counting three-fifths of the blacks, Gouverneur Morris objected both to their inclusion and to proportional representation of future western states. "If the Western people get the power into their hands they will ruin the Atlantic interests." Apportionment should be entrusted to the duty, honor, and oaths of the house members themselves. Madison, replying, was "not a little surprised to hear this implicit confidence urged by a member who on all occasions, had inculcated so strongly, the political depravity of men," and the necessity of placing one vice and interest against another. If the popular house could be so trusted, what need was there of a Senate? Morris, he said, wanted the South to trust the Northern majority, yet exhorted all to distrust the West. "To reconcile the gentleman with himself, it must be imagined that he determined the human character by the points of the compass."

The truth was, averred Madison, "that all men having power ought to be distrusted to a certain degree. . . . With regard to the Western States. he was clear and firm in opinion, that no unfavorable distinctions were admissible either in point of justice or policy." He saw no substantial objection to representation according to numbers, which in the United States were a sufficient measure of wealth; but when a vote was taken on counting three-fifths of the slaves, it was voted down by the Northern states aided by South Carolina, which wanted to count them all.

Morris, of all people, bridged the chasm. The South wanted to include slaves in apportioning the legislature, but not in reckoning taxes. Link them together; let them choose both or neither. Perhaps to his surprise, the Carolinians and Georgians chose both. The result was almost unanimous approval of a resolution that both representation and direct taxation should be proportionate to population, including three-fifths of the slaves.

With this decided, the convention swung back on July 14 to the thornier problem of the Senate. Madison endorsed a proposal by Charles Pinckney that states have from one to five senators. He apprehended "that if the proper foundation of Government was destroyed, by substituting an equality in place of a proportional representation, no proper superstructure would be raised." There was no weight to the argument that one branch of the legislature should have state equality because the new government was to be partly federal, partly national. "He called for a single instance in which the General Government was not to operate on the people individually." It seemed now to be pretty well understood, said Madison in conclusion, "that the real difference of interests lay, not between the large and small but between the Northern and Southern States. The institution of slavery and its consequences formed the line of discrimination."

This diversionary argument left the small states unmoved. Joined by Massachusetts, they defeated Pinckney's motion for a one-to-five allocation of Senate seats among the states. Then on July 16, with Massachusetts divided, the convention approved the whole revised report. Five to four, they voted for proportional representation in the first branch of the legislature, counting three-fifths of the slaves; and for state equality in the Senate. Virginia, Pennsylvania, South Carolina, and Georgia cast the negative ballots. New York did not vote. Her three delegates had gone home, Hamilton vexed at the futility of his position; Yates and Lansing followed in disgust at their inability to wreck the convention.

The large states were now in a quandary. Randolph moved an adjournment "that the large States might consider the steps proper to be taken in the present solemn crisis." This was agreed to and the large states caucused next morning. "The time," Madison recorded, "was wasted in vague conversation." Several delegates (including himself, to judge from his past remarks) wanted the principal states, representing a majority of the people, to stand firm and "propose a scheme of Government to the people . . . in a separate recommendation, if eventually necessary." Others, however, seemed inclined to yield, and the consultation probably "satisfied the smaller States that they had nothing to apprehend from a union of the larger, in any plan whatever against the equality of votes in the second branch." In this atmosphere of small-state triumph and large-state confusion, the convention turned to the theme of power in the new government.

19 / SMALL STATES TURN
TO HIGH POWER

Controlling the Senate, the small states as such had nothing to fear from the large ones. Controlling the popular house, the large states as such had no reason to fear the small ones. Each group had a check on the other. This dissolved the two blocs as far as federal power was concerned. That subject came before the convention at once, in the shape of Madison's resolve that the national legislature be empowered "to legislate in all cases to which the separate States are incompetent; or in which the harmony of the United States may be interrupted by the exercise of individual legislation."

Should those words go into the Constitution? At the outset Randolph said no. Madison had leaned reluctantly toward their inclusion. Now from South Carolina came a motion that the clause be committed "to the end that a specification of the powers comprised in the general term" might be reported. The motion was defeated in a tie vote, five to five, with large and small states intermixed on both sides. For enumeration: Connecticut, Maryland, Virginia, South Carolina, Georgia. Against: Massachusetts, New Jersey, Pennsylvania, Delaware, North Carolina.

Among the ardent nationalists, Madison took a stand for enumeration; Wilson, Morris, and King stood for general power. Among the recent champions of state equality, Paterson, Livingston, Brearly, Bedford, and Dickinson blossomed out as high nationalists. Madison's final stand apparently was determined by failure of the large states to control both houses.

It became evident next day that the five-to-five alignment was not basic. Sherman, who voted for enumeration, moved that the national legislature have power "to make laws binding on the people of the United States in all cases which may concern the common interests of the Union," but not to interfere with the internal police of the States in matters wherein the general welfare of the United States is not concerned.

Sherman intended this to go into the Constitution; his draft made it the final item in his enumeration of powers. His motion was defeated, eight to two, after Morris protested that in many cases, as in paper money, the internal police of the states ought to be infringed.

Next, Bedford of Delaware moved (seconded by Morris) that the resolve of the Virginia Plan be amended to read: "and moreover to legislate in all cases for the general interests of the Union, and also in those to which the States are separately incompetent, or in which the harmony of the United States may be interrupted by the exercise of individual legislation." Randolph rose in alarm. "This [said he] is a formidable idea indeed. It involves the power of violating all the laws and constitutions of the States, and of intermeddling with their police."

Randolph's protest leaves no doubt that they were discussing the Bedford clause as a part of the Constitution. Neither his nor Madison's resolve, as a mere guiding principle, would violate state constitutions or invade state police power. Bedford's motion passed, six states to four, the opposition coming from Connecticut, Virginia, South Carolina, and Georgia. The amended resolution, blending the words of Bedford and Madison, was then adopted eight to two, only South Carolina and Georgia voting no.

Thus, apart from the extreme defenders of slavery, every delegation in the convention wanted a national legislature that would in fact— either by a general power or by adequate enumeration—be competent "to legislate in all cases for the general interests of the Union." With that stand taken, the convention took up the previously approved resolve empowering the national government to negative all state laws contravening the articles of union.

Madison clung to his original position. He considered the negative "essential to the efficacy and security of the General Government." Without it, the states "can pass laws which will accomplish their injurious objects before they can be repealed by the General Legislature or be set aside by the National Tribunals." Laws of immediate necessity might be given temporary effect "by some emanation of the power into the States" —that is, by a federal censor.

Morris declared himself "more and more opposed to the negative." It would "disgust all the states," and a law that ought to be negatived would "be set aside in the Judiciary department." The clause was eliminated, seven states to three.

Luther Martin then offered the national supremacy clause which he had embedded in the New Jersey Plan. Approved unanimously, it declared all laws adopted pursuant to the Articles of Union, and all treaties, to be "the supreme law of the respective states," and the state judiciaries were bound thereby. This completed the projected pyramid of federal legislative power backed by the judiciary. Both the all-powerful Bedford resolution and the national supremacy clause emanated from delegates who supported the New Jersey Plan, men who conjured up phantoms of federal tyranny when the large states were riding high but who took the lead in the same direction when they got into the saddle.

This record knocks to smithereens the long-prevailing assumption of historians and politicians that the small-state victory was a triumph for state sovereignty and for a weak federal government. Historian George Bancroft vainly attempted to set this right. He "received it from the lips of Madison and so it appears from the record," that from the day the smaller states achieved an equal vote in the Senate, they "exceeded all others in zeal for granting powers to the general government." All that did was give Bancroft a reputation for unreliability; but Madison put the same thing on paper three months before his death, in a letter addressed but not sent to Senator B. W. Leigh of Virginia.

Taking up the election of the Executive, all states except Pennsylvania opposed the plea of Wilson and Morris for a choice by the people rather than by Congress—necessary, they said, to make him independent. The convention then reversed an earlier decision and made him eligible for re-election. This rendered him still more dependent. McClurg of Virginia drove that fact home by moving that the Executive hold office during good behavior. To protect McClurg from the expected cry of monarchism, Madison came to his support. Respect for the mover entitled the motion to a fair hearing "until a less objectionable expedient should be applied for guarding against a dangerous union of the Legislative and Executive departments." The motion was defeated, four to six, Virginia supporting it. The vote, Madison wrote in a footnote, was no index of opinion. The purpose was chiefly "to alarm those attached to a dependence of the Executive on the Legislature."

When the subject was resumed on July 19, it was moved once more to make the Executive ineligible to re-election. Morris, Randolph, Wilson, and Madison spoke for the motion. Wilson "perceived with pleasure, that the idea was gaining ground, of an election mediately or immediately by the people."

Madison concentrated on "the fundamental principle of free government," that the legislative, executive, and judiciary powers should be *independently*, as well as *separately*, exercised. The Executive could not be independent if appointable by the legislature. "The people at large was in his opinion the fittest" source of appointment. Days of debate produced first a decision for a choice by electors appointed by state legislatures, then (on July 24) selection by the legislatures themselves. Gerry moved an appointment by state governors. Madison thought this equally bad.

"There are objections," he told the convention next day, "against every mode that has been, or perhaps can be proposed." Objections were insuperable to a choice by the national legislature. Besides making the Executive dependent, it would cause violent contention. Candidates would intrigue for election. Ministers of foreign powers would mix in as they did in Germany and Poland. Choice by state governments would render the national Executive subservient to the states and promote their pernicious measures. That left an option "between an appointment by Electors chosen by the people—and an immediate appointment by the people . . . or rather by the qualified part of them, at large. With all its imperfections he liked this best."

Mason objected to election by the people. That would cause the Executive to be chosen by those who knew the least about eminent characters, instead of those who knew the most. On his motion, the convention went back to the original decision for a one-man executive, elected for seven years by the national legislature, and ineligible to re-election. The motion carried seven to three, with Virginia divided: Mason and Blair, aye; Washington and Madison, no; Randolph off the floor. (McClurg had gone home, too long away from his wife, delegates said.)

Other decisions were made in the course of this long debate. The convention took up once more Wilson's proposal, strongly supported by Madison, that the Supreme Judiciary should be associated with the Executive in vetoing legislative acts. Linking them, Madison argued, would help the judiciary defend itself against encroachments by the legislature and would inspire additional confidence and firmness in exercise of the veto. Instead of violating the doctrine of separation of powers, he contended, it would strengthen that principle by adding defensive powers to the judiciary and executive departments. Even so aided, he thought "the Legislature would still be an overmatch for them." The proposal was rejected as improper and "a dangerous innovation."

Madison moved that federal judges should be nominated by the Executive and confirmed by the Senate. The Executive, he said, would be more likely to select fit characters. He would act for the whole nation, while a choice by the Senate would enable a majority of the states representing a minority of the people to select a biased tribunal. Over the opposition of Virginia, Pennsylvania, and Massachusetts the convention voted that the Senate appoint the judges.

Madison fared better with the final resolution of the Virginia Plan— that the new instrument be ratified by state conventions chosen by the people rather than by legislatures. The Federal Constitution, he said, "would make essential inroads on the State Constitutions." A state legislature had no power to change the constitution under which it held its existence. To achieve such a change, a ratification must be obtained from the people:

> He considered the difference between a system founded on the Legislatures only, and one founded on the people, to be the true difference between a *league* or *treaty*, and a *Constitution*. . . . A law violating a treaty ratified by a pre-existing law, might be respected by the judges as a law, although an unwise or perfidious one. A law violating a constitution established by the people themselves, would be considered by the Judges as null and void.

Thus Madison, like several others in the convention, endorsed the doctrine of judicial review of state laws. Furthermore, he went on, the law of nations freed all the parties to a treaty if one party violated it. "In the case of a union of people under one Constitution, the nature of the pact has always been understood to exclude such an interpretation." By that statement Madison excluded the right of a state to secede from the Union.

A motion by Ellsworth for ratification by legislatures was beaten seven to three, newly arrived delegates from New Hampshire forming part of the majority. All states except Delaware then voted that the Constitution, after being approved by Congress, be submitted to state assemblies "expressly chosen by the people to consider and decide thereon."

On July 26 the Virginia Plan as amended was unanimously referred to a Committee of Detail "to prepare and report a Constitution conformable thereto." Referred also were Paterson's New Jersey Plan and a scheme of government introduced by Charles Pinckney but never considered by the convention. Committee members, elected by ballot, were Rutledge of South Carolina, Randolph of Virginia, Gorham of Massachusetts, Ellsworth of Connecticut, and Wilson of Pennsylvania. To give the committee time for its work, the convention adjourned until the sixth of August.

Among the five members of the Committee of Detail, James Wilson was the only recorded advocate of a general power to legislate for the interests and welfare of the Union. Rutledge and Randolph were strongly for enumerated powers, and Ellsworth and Gorham appeared to have such a preference; but in the forming of a government, the committee consisted of Wilson and four others. He was the only delegate who equaled or possibly surpassed Madison in that respect.

The committee quickly decided upon an enumeration of powers, ignoring the Bedford resolution. Randolph made a verbose draft based on the Virginia Plan. Wilson rewrote it, drawing also upon the New Jersey and (slightly) the Pinckney plans, and produced a document not sharply different from the Constitution as finally adopted. It endowed Congress (here so called for the first time) with seventeen specific powers. These began with the power "to lay and collect taxes, duties, imposts and excises," followed by power "to regulate commerce with foreign nations, and among the several States." Closing the list was the broad power to "make all laws which shall be necessary and proper for carrying into execution" all the powers vested in the federal government or its officers.

Structural provisions followed the convention's mandate. "The United States of America" was to have a government "to consist of supreme legislative, executive, and judicial powers." The legislative power was vested in a two-house Congress—a House of Representatives elected every two years by the people, and a Senate with two members from each state. These were to be chosen by state legislatures for six years, one third to be elected every two years. All money bills were to originate in the House. The Senate was to have power "to make treaties, and to appoint Ambassadors, and Judges of the Supreme Court."

The executive power was vested in a President elected for seven years by Congress and ineligible to re-election. He was to *receive* (not send) ambassadors; command the army, navy, and state militia; make all appointments not otherwise provided for; and take care that the laws of the United States were faithfully executed.

The judicial power was vested in one Supreme Court and such inferior courts as Congress might from time to time establish. All judges were to serve during good behavior. The jurisdiction of the Supreme Court was to be original in actions involving foreign diplomats or American states; appellate in all other cases, "with such exceptions and under such regulations as the Legislature shall make."

The national supremacy clause was broadened to make the Constitution, laws pursuant to it, and treaties, *"the supreme law of the land,"* instead of the supreme law of "*the respective states*," and superior to state constitutions. The committee went beyond its directive in sections forbidding the states to coin money, grant letters of marque and reprisal, enter into any foreign alliance or treaty, or grant (nor could Congress) any title of nobility. Also the states were forbidden, without the consent of Congress, to emit bills of credit, lay import duties, keep troops or ships of war in time of peace, enter into interstate or foreign compacts, or engage in war unless invaded or in such imminent danger of invasion that Congress could not be consulted.

Representatives in Congress were to be apportioned among the states in the same ratio as direct taxation—according to the total number of free inhabitants and three-fifths of all others. The states were to prescribe the times, places, and manner of electing members of the House, subject to the power of Congress to alter the provisions at any time. Qualifications of voters were to be the same as for the more numerous branch of the state legislature. Congress could not tax exports, nor tax or forbid the importation of slaves; nor pass a navigation act without the assent of two-thirds of those present in each house. The crime of treason was strictly defined and limited. The United States guaranteed to each state a republican form of government, protection against foreign invasion and (when applied to) against domestic violence (such as Shays' Rebellion).

The Constitution as reported fulfilled the desire for a supreme and strong federal government, but weakened the Executive by exalting the Senate in foreign affairs and judicial appointments, and by giving Congress power to "make war"—not merely to declare it. The South received special protection for slavery and in the two-thirds requirement for regulation of foreign commerce. The "necessary and proper" clause admitted sweeping powers by implication. The document left plenty of room for disagreement.

As soon as the draft-constitution was taken up on August 7, Morris sought to restrict voting for congressmen to freeholders. Admit the poor to suffrage and the rich would buy their votes. Franklin struck the opposing keynote. "It is of great consequence that we should not depress the virtue and public spirit of our common people." Madison helped to defeat the motion, pointing out that several states allowed landless men to vote:

> Viewing the subject in its merits alone, the freeholders of the country would be the safest depositories of republican liberty. In future times a great majority of the people will not only be without landed, but any other sort of property. These will either combine under the influence of their common situation; in which case, the rights of property and the public liberty will not be secure in their hands: or which is more probable, they will become the tools of opulence and ambition, in which case there will be equal danger on another side.

Disturbed by these words in later years, Madison appended a lengthy footnote saying that he "felt too much at the time the example of Virginia." His "more full and matured view of the subject" was that a limitation of suffrage to freeholders "violates the vital principle of free government that those who are to be bound by laws ought to have a hand in making them. And the violation would be more strikingly unjust as the lawmakers become the minority." Where property and personal rights are both at stake, he concluded, it is better that those possessing both interests should be deprived of half of their share in the government, than that those having the interest "of personal rights only, should be deprived of the whole."

Madison strongly supported a motion by Charles Pinckney to strike out the clause giving the House of Representatives sole power to originate money bills. It was of no advantage to the large states, he said, but

merely fettered the government and furnished a source of serious alter-
cation between the houses. It was eliminated, seven states to four, but
Randolph and Mason declared they would attempt to reinstate it.

Morris and Pinckney attempted to require fourteen years' citizenship,
instead of four, for election to the Senate. They saw "peculiar danger
and impropriety" in opening it to persons with foreign attachments.
Madison regarded any constitutional restriction as improper. This one
would give a mortifying notice to great numbers of respectable Euro-
peans "who love liberty and wish to partake its blessings" that they were
under suspicion. He ridiculed the idea that state legislatures would appoint "any dangerous number of strangers," while as for bribery, that
was most likely to be attempted by seducing persons least open to suspicion. Wilson, a native of Scotland, remarked that this restriction would
bar him from office. Morris replied that "we should not be polite at the
expense of prudence." Every nation, like every club, had a right to
choose its members, and he would not trust any of these philosophical
"Citizens of the World, as they call themselves." Fourteen years was
defeated, but the citizenship requirement was lifted from four to nine
years.

The South Carolinians attempted to strike out the power of Congress
to alter state regulations governing "the times, places and manner" of
electing members of Congress. Protests came from Gorham, Madison,
King, and Morris. "These were words of great latitude," said Madison.
"It was impossible to foresee all the abuses that might be made of the
discretionary power." Legislatures could mold their regulations to favor
the candidates they wished to succeed. The inequality of representation
in some state legislatures would foster a like inequality in the national
representation. The motion failed.

Pinckney and Rutledge then moved that property qualifications be
required for public office, suggesting $100,000 for the President and
lesser amounts for judges and legislators. The motion was rejected without a rollcall, but a clause remained giving Congress power to fix property qualifications for its own members. Madison opposed the whole
section as improper and dangerous. If the legislature could fix qualifications, it could by degrees subvert the Constitution. "A Republic may be
converted into an aristocracy or oligarchy as well by limiting the number
capable of being elected, as the number authorized to elect." Witness the
abuse of both powers by the British Parliament. The section was eliminated by a seven-to-four vote. On Madison's motion, the convention

required two-thirds, instead of a simple majority, for expulsion of a member of either house.

On August 13 Madison seconded a motion by Hamilton (who intermittently returned to the convention) that mere citizenship and inhabitancy, for no fixed period, be required for eligibility to Congress. Madison said he "wished to maintain the character of liberality which had been professed in all the Constitutions and publications of America. He wished to invite foreigners of merit and republican principles among us." Some with foreign predilections might attain office, but similar feelings would cause our own people to prefer natives. Wilson took a similar stand, but Butler of South Carolina (a native of Ireland) "was strenuous against admitting foreigners into our public councils." So was the convention, seven states against four.

Morris moved that the seven-year citizenship requirement for House membership should not affect the rights of persons at present citizens: they had come to this country on a pledge of equality. Such pledges, Sherman remarked, were given by individual states. The United States could make any discriminations it judged requisite.

That peculiar doctrine, Madison replied, "was a subtlety by which every national engagement might be evaded." Grant that the states alone were bound by pledges of equality. "Will not the new Constitution be their act? . . . will not the States, be the violators?" A breach of faith would bring reproaches that would soon be echoed from the other side of the Atlantic. The Morris motion lost by a margin of one state. Seven years of citizenship for the House, nine for the Senate, were then confirmed.

Randolph and Mason sought to limit the Senate's power to amend money bills, denying it the right to increase or diminish taxes or appropriations. Surely, remarked Madison, the Senate should be allowed to *diminish* expenditures. Why restrain it from checking extravagance? And who could tell the primary purpose of amendments: whether to alter the amount of money or to regulate commerce?

The convention struck out the limitation, although Virginia voted for it—Madison and Blair, no. Washington, Madison recorded, gave up his own convictions to reduce the danger that Randolph and Mason, "if disappointed, might be less cordial in other points of real weight." That danger was emphasized a few days later when Mason indicated distrust of Madison because of his contention that the states should be reduced to "mere corporations."

In an effort to force a compromise that would get rid of the two-thirds rule on navigation acts, Morris, Wilson, and King joined Mason and Martin in a drive against the slave trade. On August 24 a grand committee linked the two propositions: importation of slaves must not be prohibited before 1800, and the two-thirds rule should be stricken out. South Carolina obtained a postponement of the ban until 1808, over Madison's prophetic forecast: "Twenty years will produce all the mischief that can be apprehended from the liberty to import slaves."

Mason and Randolph then united with Pinckney and Martin in defense of the two-thirds requirement to pass navigation acts. Without it, declared Mason, the Southern minority would be bound hand and foot to the Eastern states. Madison met this with quiet analysis. Exclusion of foreign shipping by act of Congress might temporarily raise freight rates but would stimulate shipbuilding in both North and South. That would bring a southward migration of seamen and merchants. The Southern states would find security in American maritime strength. Passage of laws by a simple majority would make foreign intrigue less probable. Even if the East should benefit from navigation laws more than the South, its contribution to taxes would be that much greater, and a national benefit.

Randolph, veering farther on his tangential course, declared that present features of the Constitution were so odious that he doubted whether he could agree to it. Drop this two-thirds requirement and it "would complete the deformity of the system." The convention dropped it.

On Madison's motion, the power of Congress to "make war" was changed to "declare war," thus placing the waging of it in the hands of the President. He sought also to give the national government exclusive authority to appoint *general officers* of the militia and control its discipline. "The States neglect their militia now," he asserted, "and the more they are consolidated into one nation" the less each will rely on its own forces. Furthermore, "as the greatest danger is that of disunion of the States, it is necessary to guard against it by sufficient powers to the Common Government." (Secession must be prevented by force.) Madison won on discipline but lost on appointment of officers. Federal control of that, said Sherman, would sound the alarm to every man of discernment.

Disagreement developed over a motion by Rutledge that the United States assume state war debts—a proposal that Madison had made in Congress in 1783. Considering this, a grand committee recommended on August 21 that "The Legislature of the United States shall have power to . . . discharge as well the debts of the United States as the debts incurred by the several States during the late war, for the common defence and general welfare." The convention eliminated the reference to state debts and made payment of the federal debt mandatory: "The Legislature *shall* fulfil the engagements and discharge the debts of the United States and shall have the power to lay and collect taxes duties imposts and excises."

This brought a protest from Butler that it would compel payment to "the Blood-suckers who had speculated on the distresses of others." On a reconsideration of the clause, it was postponed in favor of a declaration that the debts of the United States would remain as valid as they were under the Confederation. Sherman then moved that the power to tax be given the following addition: "for the payment of said debts and for the defraying the expences that shall be incurred for the common defence and general welfare." Madison recorded that "the proposition, as being unnecessary, was disagreed to." These moves, insignificant in themselves, were made important four decades later by Madison's use (or misuse) of them to explain the taxing power as finally framed.

The convention on August 23 took up the clause giving the Senate power to make treaties and appoint judges of the Supreme Court. Morris and Wilson objected; the Senate was too numerous for such a purpose and was subject to cabal. Madison observed that for obvious reasons the President should have a hand in the making of treaties. Morris doubted whether the Senate ought to be in the business at all, but moved "for the present" that ratification by the whole Congress be required. Madison thought it unwise to require this of treaties of alliance and suggested that President and Senate be allowed to make them. The subject was referred to the Committee of Detail—one more step in the piling up of subjects for future consideration by that group.

At this point—August 23—Madison was stricken with bilious fever. For a week his recorded share in debate was reduced to a sentence or two at a time, and the entries of others were similarly cut down. His handwriting became shaky but, though the work "almost killed him" (he told Edward Coles, later his secretary), he did not miss a single session.

The proceedings were dominated at this time by an earlier move by Madison. On August 13, dissatisfied with the seventeen enumerated powers of Congress submitted by the Committee of Detail, he moved the addition of nine more. They comprehended power to dispose of unappropriated public lands; set up temporary governments in new states;

regulate affairs with Indians; exercise exclusive authority over the seat of national government and a district around it; procure landed property for forts, magazines, and other needed buildings; establish a university; and provide for literary copyrights. Included also were two powers of immense scope: (1) "To grant charters of incorporation in cases where the public good may require them, and the authority of a single State may be incompetent. (2) "To encourage by premiums and provisions, the advancement of useful knowledge and discoveries."

These two powers, primarily designed to provide a federal system of canals and roads and permit the granting of patents, were so broadly worded that they amounted almost to a general power of legislation for the welfare of the Union. A nearly duplicate list was proposed by Charles Pinckney (who may have seen Madison's at their common boarding house), and several other proposals came from various sources. All were referred to the Committee of Detail.

From that committee, on August 22, came a final power of sweeping scope. It blended the broad resolution for congressional power in the original Virginia Plan, the rejected Sherman substitute for it, and the all-powerful Bedford resolution adopted on July 16. The committee recommended the addition of the following to the powers of Congress:

> . . . and to provide, as may become necessary, from time to time, for the well managing and securing the common property and general interests and welfare of the United States in such manner as shall not interfere with the governments of individual states, in matters which respect only their internal police, or for which their individual authorities may be competent.

This proposed power was referred on August 31 to a new grand Committee on Unfinished Parts, along with all other reports and motions that had not been acted on. Examination of the record reveals eleven of these, including the one approved on August 23 and then reconsidered: "The Legislature shall fulfil the engagements and discharge the debts of the United States and shall have the power to lay and collect taxes duties imposts and excises." Referred also were the sections giving the Senate power to make treaties and appoint judges of the Supreme Court, providing that Congress elect the President for a *single* term of seven years; and the clause on the origin of money bills.

The committee began its work at a moment of mounting tensions and crystallizing positions. On August 30, when the subject of admitting new states came up, Carroll and Martin of Maryland moved to strike out a provision that forbade the dividing of a state without its consent. Such were the sentiments of "a considerable minority" with regard to the crown lands, said Carroll, that unless the federal claim to them was safeguarded there would be no chance of unanimity in submitting the Constitution. Unanimity, replied Wilson, could not be purchased by submission of the majority to the minority. He knew of no more alarming doctrine than that "a political society is to be torn asunder without its own consent."

The motion was beaten, eight states to three, but Martin renewed the fight. In Wilson's mind, he remarked, the small states were phantoms, but "when the Great States were to be affected, political societies were of a sacred nature." Hold to that guarantee, and some of the small states would "take their leave of the Constitution on the table." He moved the following article: "The Legislature of the United States shall have power to erect New States within as well as without the territory claimed by the several States or either of them, and admit the same into the Union . . . ."

Again New Jersey, Delaware, and Maryland cast the only 'aye' votes. Deprived of the intended fruits of the national supremacy clause he had planted in the Constitution, Martin packed his bags and left for home. He was not the only dissident. Opposing submission of the Constitution to state conventions, Elbridge Gerry declared that the document was full of errors and protested against "destroying the existing Confederation, without the unanimous consent of the parties to it." George Mason said he "would sooner chop off his right hand than put it to the Constitution as it now stands." Randolph began to talk about "another General Convention" empowered to accept or reject amendments submitted by the state conventions.

In the face of this opposition, the convention held firmly to state conventions. Madison answered the protest that some state constitutions did not permit this manner of ratification. The people, he said, were "the fountain of all power, and by resorting to them, all difficulties were got over. They could alter constitutions as they pleased."

How many ratifications should be required to bring the Constitution into force? Enough, remarked Madison, to guard against the danger that it "might be put in force over the whole body of the people, though less than a majority of them should ratify it." A majority *of the states and of the people*, he evidently believed, could act for all. The convention filled the blank with "nine," and voted that it be effective among those ratifying it.

From the Committee on Unfinished Parts, on September 4 and 5, came the final compromise of the convention. The sweeping power to provide for "the general interests and welfare of the United States" was not reported. The taxing power was revised to read: "The legislature shall have power to lay and collect taxes duties imposts and excises, to pay the debts and provide for the common defence and general welfare, of the United States."

The President was to be made elective by the people through the Electoral College, for a four-year term, and to be eligible to re-election. If nobody received a clear majority, the Senate would elect from the top five candidates.

Power to make treaties and appoint ambassadors and judges was transferred from the Senate to the President, subject to approval by the Senate.

The House of Representatives was given sole power to originate bills for raising revenue, but the Senate was permitted to amend them.

Four legislative powers proposed by Madison were added: to regulate trade with Indians; to exercise exclusive legislation over the seat of national government; to exercise similar authority over places purchased for forts, arsenals, and other needful buildings; to promote the progress of science and useful arts by copyrights and patents.

Madison, in a footnote, explained the result in this manner: Mason, Gerry, and several other large-state delegates (none of them members of the committee) "set great value on this privilege of originating money bills. Of this the members from the small States, with some from the large States who wished a high mounted Government endeavored to avail themselves, by making the privilege the price of arrangements in the constitution favorable to the small States, and to the elevation of the Government."

The *large-state members of the committee* were Madison himself, Morris, and King, all of whom strenuously supported the compromise in debate. Obviously, they were the ones who joined the small-state representatives—Sherman, Brearly, and Dickinson—in a common front for "elevating the government" by a concession to Mason and Gerry in the matter of money bills.

Among the changes reported by the committee, the only one of special advantage to the small states was the Senate's power to break deadlocks in the presidential electoral college. Contributing to "a high mounted Government" were the lifting of the President's authority and the conferral on Congress of a power to use taxation to "provide for the common defence and general welfare." Beginning with Hamilton's 1791 "Report on Manufactures" and continuing in Supreme Court decisions down to the present day, this has uniformly been construed to cover all objects pertaining to the general welfare. Madison, breaking with Hamilton, challenged this. The words, he said, were merely picked up from the Articles of Confederation, where they formed a general caption to enumerated powers. In 1830 he elaborated this claim, tracing the words to rejected motions by Sherman and others on payment of Confederation debts.

The best answer to Madison's argument lies in his selective silence. Possessing the full record in his unpublished Notes of Debates, he said not a word about the August 22 shift of the main drafting committee, capping "enumeration" with "general power." He ignored the referral of that sweeping power to *legislate* for the general welfare, to the same committee from which came the power to *spend* for that purpose. The committee's action can be construed as a meaningless pickup from the Articles of Confederation only if one disregards the alternatives that lay before it. A convention that was at a hair's breadth from a *general power of legislation* would have had no qualms about a *spending power* commensurate with the purposes for which the Constitution was being drafted.

21 / WE THE PEOPLE

The decisions on congressional and presidential power hurtled the Philadelphia Convention along toward completion of its work. Outside, in spite of or because of the deep secrecy, apprehension deepened and anticipation grew. On September 6, during the final debate on the presidency, Madison wrote to Jefferson concerning the attitude of the people:

> Nothing can exceed the universal anxiety for the event of the meeting here. . . . All the prepossessions are on the right side but . . . certain characters will wage war against any reform whatever. My own idea is that the public mind will now or in a very little time receive anything that promises stability to the public councils and security to private rights, and that no regard ought to be had to local prejudices or temporary considerations.

The *Pennsylvania Gazette* reported that commerce and manufactures were suspended. "The states neglect their roads and canals till they see whether those necessary improvements will not become the objects of a national government." Moneylenders buried their specie until they should know whether they were safe from paper money and tender laws.

Taking up the reports of the Committee on Unfinished Parts, the convention moved rapidly toward completion of the Constitution. Gouverneur Morris explained why election of the President by Congress was abandoned: to make the Executive independent of the legislature, and thus make re-election feasible without the evils of intrigue and faction. "Many were anxious even for an immediate choice by the people." The decision for electors chosen by the people avoided "the great evil of cabal" because the electors would vote at the same time throughout the United States and distant from each other.

Charles Pinckney, Wilson, Randolph, and Mason—men of disparate views—all objected to appointment by the Senate if the electors deadlocked. They said it tended toward aristocracy. The primary object,

190

Madison answered, was "to render an eventual resort to any part of the Legislature improbable." If the Senate "in which the small States predominate should have this final choice, the concerted effort of the large States would be to make the appointment in the first instance [by the electors] conclusive." Madison's own state, however, joined Pennsylvania and South Carolina in a futile attempt to strike out "Senate" and insert "Legislature." Sherman brought both sides together with a motion that the House of Representatives, "the members from each State having one vote," should decide electoral-college deadlocks.

The convention on September 7 took up the subject of succession in case of the death, resignation, or disability of the President and Vice President. Randolph moved to insert a provision that "the Legislature may declare by law" what officer should act as President, "and such officer shall act accordingly until the time of electing a President shall arrive." Madison objected to the wording of this, as it "would prevent a supply of the vacancy by an intermediate election." On his motion, the clause before adoption was changed to read "until such disability be removed, or a President shall be elected."

Time and again Congress has altered the unsatisfactory laws on presidential succession, always on the supposition that an intermediate election is not permissible. On the contrary, the wording was altered for the express purpose of sanctioning that course.

The convention approved the shift of the treatymaking power from the Senate to the President with the advice and consent of the Senate. In doing so it rejected Madison's suggestion that treaties of peace be made by the Senate alone. The President, he said, might be tempted to continue a state of war from which he "would necessarily derive so much power and importance."

Madison took the lead in defeating Mason's motion that the President be impeachable for "maladministration," as well as treason and bribery. Such a provision, he said, would "be equivalent to a tenure during the pleasure of the Senate." Mason successfully substituted "other high crimes and misdemeanors." This change caused Madison to propose that impeachment of the President be tried by a tribunal that included the Supreme Court. Trial by the Senate would make him improperly dependent on that body. Sherman replied that the change would subject him to trial by his own appointees. Virginia and Pennsylvania cast the only votes for the motion.

The convention on that day (September 8) completed the final compromise by confirming the sole power of the House of Representatives to originate money bills. A committee was chosen by ballot to revise the style and arrangement of all the adopted articles. Chaired by Dr. Johnson of Connecticut, its other members were all high nationalists—Hamilton, Morris, Madison, and King. They let Gouverneur Morris do the work, which was completed in four days.

"The finish given to the style and arrangement of the Constitution," wrote Madison forty-four years later, "fairly belongs to the pen of Mr. Morris. . . . A better choice could not have been made." Although a highflying orator, he had a gift of terse and trenchant written expression and a keen sense of organization. The twenty-three articles turned over to the committee were reshaped into seven. The committee approved his brief and eloquent preamble, setting forth the derivation, purposes, and force of the new charter of government:

> WE, THE PEOPLE OF THE UNITED STATES, IN ORDER TO
> FORM a more perfect union, to establish justice, insure domes-
> tic tranquility, provide for the common defence, promote the
> general welfare, and secure the blessings of liberty to our-
> selves and our posterity, do ordain and establish this Con-
> stitution for the United States of America.

Though not a specific grant, this was a conspectus of federal power. While awaiting the report of the Committee of Style and Arrangements, Hamilton and Madison united to revise the article requiring Congress to call a constitutional convention on the application of two-thirds of the state legislatures. Hamilton wanted to give Congress itself the power to submit amendments. Madison combined both methods in a single provision. Congress would have power to submit amendments by a two-thirds vote of both houses, and must call a convention on application of two-thirds of the state legislatures. All amendments, by either system, would be valid when ratified by three-fourths of the state legislatures or state conventions, with Congress choosing the method.

Randolph, at this point, itemized twelve objections to the Constitution. He disliked especially the power of Congress to pass all laws "necessary and proper" to carry out its powers and the absence of a two-thirds requirement for passage of navigation acts. "Was he to promote the establishment of a plan which he verily believed would end in tyranny?" His objection to a three-fourths vote to override presidential vetoes led to its reduction to two-thirds. Madison, Morris, and Hamilton opposed the change, Madison saying there was more danger in the weakness of two-thirds than the strength of three-fourths, but the motion carried.

Mason then moved that a committee be appointed to draft a Bill of Rights. "It would give great quiet to the people and with the aid of the State declarations, a bill might be prepared in a few hours." Sherman saw no need of this. The State Declarations of Rights would remain in force and were sufficient. The states voted unanimously against the motion. Reviving the subject two days later, Charles Pinckney and Gerry moved to insert a guarantee of freedom of the press. This won four states, including Virginia, but fell before Sherman's objection that the power of Congress did not extend to the press. The short shrift given these proposals, Madison said later, was due to haste and fatigue, and the presentation of them so late in the convention.

Madison and King thwarted a motion "that persons impeached be suspended from their office until they be tried and acquitted." The President, Madison declared, was made "too dependent already on the Legislature, by the power of one branch to try him in consequence of an impeachment by the other." This proposal would enable one branch alone to put him out of the way at any moment by a temporary removal.

Dr. Franklin moved (September 14) that the power of Congress "to establish post offices and post roads" be enlarged by adding a power for cutting canals. Wilson seconded the motion; Sherman said it meant national spending for local benefit. Madison moved to enlarge this into a power "to grant charters of incorporation where the interest of the United States might require and legislative provisions of individual States may be incompetent." His primary object, he said, "was to secure an easy communication between the States," to match the free commercial intercourse "now to be opened."

King thought the power unnecessary. "It is necessary," replied Wilson, "to prevent *a State* from obstructing the *general* welfare." King warned that it would stir up opponents of national banks and commercial monopolies. Wilson doubted that prejudices would be excited concerning banks, while "as to mercantile monopolies they are already included in the power to regulate trade." Mason disagreed that they were included but wanted the motion limited to canals. That was done, but only Virginia, Pennsylvania, and Georgia voted, 'aye.' The defeat took the incorporation motion with it.

Madison then moved the insertion of a power "to establish an University, in which no preferences or distinctions should be allowed on account of Religion." Wilson supported the motion; Morris called it unnecessary: "The exclusive power at the Seat of Government, will reach the object." Pennsylvania, Virginia, and the two Carolinas alone supported it.

The scope of the commerce clause came into view when Maryland delegates, on September 15, asked for a clause protecting the right of states to lay tonnage duties for clearing harbors and erecting lighthouses. Morris denied that the Constitution imposed any restraint on state tonnage taxes. Madison disagreed, saying:

> Whether the States are now restrained from laying tonnage duties depends on the extent of the power 'to regulate commerce.' These terms are vague, but seem to exclude this power of the States. They may certainly be restrained by Treaty. He observed that there were other objects for tonnage duties as the support of seamen &c. He was more and more convinced that the regulation of commerce was in its nature indivisible and ought to be wholly under one authority.

Implicit in Madison's statement were the great decisions of Chief Justice Marshall's Supreme Court upholding the exclusive power of Congress to regulate interstate and foreign commerce. His remark that the power "was in its nature indivisible" pointed toward the later extension of that power to cover activities having a bearing on interstate commerce. Finally, his comment about the use of tonnage taxes to support seamen forecast the actual levying of duties for that purpose within the next ten years—a long-jump precedent for the Social Security Act of 1936.

The last affirmative action of the convention was a fresh capitulation to the small states. Sherman moved to add a proviso to the article on amendments to the Constitution, "that no State shall without its consent be affected in its internal police, or deprived of its equal suffrage in the Senate." Madison protested: "Begin with these special provisos, and every State will insist on them, for their boundaries, exports &c." The motion was beaten, three states to eight. Sherman and Brearly moved to strike out the entire amending power. The motion was beaten, two to eight, Delaware dividing; but the minority insistence carried the threat of revolt from the entire work of the convention. Morris offered a limitation that went into the Constitution, "that no State, without its consent shall be deprived of its equal suffrage in the Senate."

"This motion," Madison recorded, "being dictated by the circulating murmurs of the small States was agreed to without debate." Thus, a minority of the convention forced a solecism into the Constitution—the absurdity that "We the People" can be perpetually enjoined from altering their Constitution by an exception from its established method of amendment. The political power of its beneficiaries, not constitutional law, is what perpetuates that confessedly unjust rotten borough system.

Following this came the apologias of the convention rebels. "Mr. Randolph, animadverting on the indefinite and dangerous power given by the Constitution to Congress," renewed an earlier motion for state amendments to be submitted to another general convention. Without it he could not sign the Constitution, though he would not then decide whether he would oppose it afterward.

George Mason dwelt on "the dangerous power and structure of the Government, concluding that it would end either in monarchy, or a tyrannical aristocracy." Elbridge Gerry listed eight flaws in structure and powers, all of which he could swallow if it were not for "the general power of the Legislature to make what laws they may please to call necessary and proper," the limitless power to raise armies and money, and the absence of trial by jury in civil cases. All three men said they would sign if a second convention were called. On that question, wrote Madison, "All the States answered—no."

On Monday, September 17, Benjamin Franklin "rose with a speech in his hand," which his colleague Wilson read for him. It was a plea that all reluctant delegates do what he was doing regarding parts of the Constitution with which he disagreed. "The older I grow," said the patriarch of the convention, "the more apt I am to doubt my own judgment, and to pay more respect to the judgment of others." He doubted that another convention would do better than this one, for it would assemble fallible men with all their prejudices, passions, and errors of opinion. "It therefore astonishes me, Sir, to find this system approaching so near to perfection as it does."

Randolph rose and "apologized for his refusing to sign the Constitution notwithstanding the vast majority and venerable names that would give sanction to its wisdom and its worth." He repeated that he had not decided to oppose it at home: he merely wished to preserve his own freedom of action in case it failed—as he thought it would fail—to be ratified by nine states.

Morris replied that the moment the plan went forth the only question would be a choice between a national government and general anarchy. Hamilton pleaded for all to sign, even though they disliked the Constitution as much as he did. The refusal by even a few might do infinite mischief by kindling latent sparks.

King then "suggested that the Journals of the Convention should be either destroyed, or deposited in the custody of the President." He feared a bad use of them by opponents of the Constitution. It was resolved unanimously that General Washington retain the Journal and other papers, "subject to the order of the Congress, if ever formed under the Constitution." The members present, minus three, "then proceeded to sign the instrument."

While the last members were signing, Madison chronicled, Dr. Franklin looked at the back of the president's chair, on which a sun was painted. To a few members sitting near him the old statesman observed that painters had "found it difficult to distinguish in their art a rising from a setting sun. I have," said he, "often and often in the course of the session, and the vicissitudes of my hopes and fears as to its issue, looked at that behind the President without being able to tell whether it was rising or setting: but now at length I have the happiness to know that it is a rising and not a setting sun."

James Madison and James Wilson stand out as constructive statesmen among the fifty-five men who participated in the framing of the Constitution. Madison had the better historical grasp of public law and displayed superior talent in applying the lessons of history to American experience. Wilson excelled in fitting the structure of government to Madison's balanced federalism. Madison led in preventing the President from being made the puppet of Congress. Wilson fashioned the link between him and the people—the Electoral College.

The ultimate structure of federal government was outlined in detail by Madison in his Virginia Plan, but it was so clearly founded on state examples that the major credit goes to him for the deviations from them —in the independence and power of the executive and judiciary. At all times Madison stood for a supreme federal government of exalted power —not so authoritative as Wilson, Morris, or Hamilton would have made it—but squarely in line with the powers discovered in the Constitution (some of them over Madison's belated protest) by Congress and the courts in later generations.

Madison's fundamental contribution was the concept of national supremacy and local autonomy in a federal republic ruled by the people, with checks and balances to guard against legislative or executive tyranny and against impetuous legislation. The excesses of state sovereignty stirred an antipathy in him that had to be curbed by his associates, but the chief limitation that he sought (federal veto) became a reality through the less drastic and more workable means of judicial review.

The title "Father of the Constitution" was first bestowed on Madison, in those precise words, in an 1827 public address by Charles J. Ingersoll. He never accepted the full implications of such expressions. "You give me a credit to which I have no claim," he wrote to a correspondent in 1831, "in calling me '*the* writer of the Constitution of the U. S.' This was not like the fabled goddess of wisdom the offspring of a single brain. It ought to be regarded as the work of many heads and many hands."

Nevertheless, Madison was given primacy by his associates in the convention. Virginia took the lead, wrote Delegate William Blount of North Carolina in July, with "Madison at their head." John Quincy Adams recorded the statement of Convention Secretary William Jackson that Madison was by far the most efficient member of the convention. Delegate William Pierce of Georgia, in thumbnail sketches of the delegates, wrote that Madison blends "the profound politician with the scholar. In the management of every great question . . . he always comes forward the best informed man of any point in debate. The affairs of the United States, he perhaps has the most correct knowledge of, of any man in the Union."

Madison himself had an exalted opinion of his associates. Whatever might be their competency, he wrote in a later year, "I feel it a duty to express my profound and solemn conviction, derived from my intimate opportunity of observing and appreciating the views of the convention, collectively and individually, that there never was an assembly of men, charged with a great and arduous trust, who were more pure in their motives, or more exclusively or anxiously devoted to the object committed to them."

That is a valid judgment, though incomplete. These fifty-five men, one and all, were men of property, and part of their "great and arduous trust" was to safeguard property against "the leveling spirit" of Shays' Rebellion and the destructive excesses of state debt moratoriums, fiat money, and impairment of contracts. This they did by specific prohibitions of such state practices, but they left the federal government unfettered. For this, Madison was responsible with his doctrine of automatic division of interests in a large federal republic. A charter of democratic self-government was built on the twin foundations of liberty and security. The real marvel is that this was done at a time when pure democracy was universally regarded as the road to immediate anarchy and ultimate tyranny.

More than a dozen convention delegates were members of Congress. Within a few days after adjournment these "fiery zealots" of nationalism, as Richard Henry Lee called them, were stringing back to New York to offset the antifederal arguments already spouting from the lips of Lee, Nathan Dane of Massachusetts, and four or five others. Soon Lee was lamenting that the patriot voice was raised in vain against a coalition of monarchists, army officers, aristocrats, and rapacious Northerners. Madison replied that Congress had directed the convention to form a firm *national government.* If, in some respects, it had gone beyond the limits of the existing Articles of Confederation, so had Congress. That body had "exercised assumed powers of a very high and delicate nature, under motives infinitely less urgent than the present state of our affairs."

The contest was fortunately terminated, Madison wrote to Washington, by unanimous adoption of a mild resolution, expressing no opinion, transmitting the report "to the several legislatures, in order to be submitted to a convention of delegates chosen in every state by the people thereof." How would Virginia react? "Much will depend on Mr. Henry," Madison observed, predicting opposition. By the end of October, Patrick Henry and George Mason were leading a formidable array of opponents, including the Lee brothers, the Nelsons and Cabells, St. George Tucker and John Taylor. Governor Randolph was uncommitted, and the Constitution had the important support of Edmund Pendleton, John Marshall, Wilson and George Nicholas, Archibald Stuart, James Innes, and other influential figures. A battle royal was assured.

Nationally, favorable reports reached Madison from the northern and middle states, except New York and Rhode Island; favorable also from the far South. Luther Martin, violating the rule of secrecy, was regaling the Maryland legislature with a blend of fact and fiction, presenting the convention's work as a diabolical conspiracy against their state and the small ones. But the small states themselves were exulting in their victory.

Concluding that Governor Randolph held the balance of power in Virginia, Madison set out to woo him, combining appeals to his reason and his vanity. Replying to Randolph's reaffirmation of his desire for a second convention, Madison praised the spirit of his letters. A second convention would be futile because the friends of a good constitution would be divided among themselves, and the opponents would be united for frustration. Had Randolph come out for the Constitution, Henry would have suppressed his enmity or been baffled in the policy it dictated. "I have for some time considered him as driving at a southern confederacy," and calling for amendments merely to promote his real designs. The great need was for leadership: "Had yourself, Colonel Mason, Colonel R. H. L., Mr. Henry and a few others seen the Constitution in the same light with those who subscribed it, I have no doubt that Virginia would have been as zealous and unanimous as she is now divided on the subject."

Informing Jefferson in Paris of the Virginia alignment, Madison wrote at vast length about the work and accomplishments of the convention. It appeared to be the sincere and unanimous wish "to cherish and preserve the Union of the States." Believing that "a confederation of Sovereign

States" could never be brought to either *voluntary* or *compulsive* observance of federal law, the convention embraced the alternative of a government operating directly on the individuals composing the states.

> This ground-work being laid, the great objects which pre-
> sented themselves were (1) to unite a proper energy in the
> Executive, and a proper stability in the Legislative depart-
> ments, with the essential characters of Republican Govern-
> ment. (2) to draw a line of demarcation which would give to
> the General Government every power requisite for general
> purposes, and leave to the States every power which might be
> most beneficially administered by them. (3) to provide for the
> different interests of different parts of the Union. (4) to adjust
> the clashing pretensions of the large and small States.

Each of these objects, wrote Madison, "was pregnant with difficulties."
The clash between the large and small states "created more embarrassment and a greater alarm for the issue of the Convention than all the rest
put together. The little States insisted on retaining their equality in both
branches, unless a compleat abolition of the State Governments should
take place; and made an equality in the Senate a sine qua non . . . . It
ended in the compromise which you will see, but very much to the dissatisfaction of several members from the large States." Madison's only
other complaint was about the absence of a complete federal negative on
state laws: "It may be said that the Judicial authority, under our new
system will keep the States within their proper limits, and supply the place
of a negative on their laws. The answer is, that it is more convenient to
prevent the passage of a law than to declare it void after it is passed."

Madison explained the refusal of Randolph and Mason to sign the
Constitution. The governor's objections turned "principally on the
latitude of the general powers," and on the connection between President
and Senate, but he was not inveterate in his opposition. Colonel Mason
left Philadelphia "with a fixed disposition to prevent the adoption of the
plan if possible. He considers the want of a Bill of Rights as a fatal
objection . . . [but objects] most of all probably to the power of regulating
trade, by a majority only of each House."

Madison's stay in New York dragged out. Virginians supplicated him
"for God's sake" to come home and run for the state convention. He
authorized his brother Ambrose to announce his candidacy, but still
stayed in New York, held there by something more impelling than watching the old government skid toward oblivion.

Late in October, Alexander Hamilton invited Madison to join him and John Jay in writing a series of newspaper articles to be signed "Publius," promoting ratification. New York, a crucial state, was the immediate target, but the thrust of the plan was nation-wide. Thus began the writing of the *Federalist Papers*, which in addition to their primary purpose became the greatest of all historical commentaries on the Constitution and republican government. Jay's serious illness, after he wrote four articles, threw the heavy burden onto Hamilton and Madison. Of the eighty-five Federalist articles published between October 27, 1787, and the late spring of 1788, Hamilton wrote fifty-one, Madison twenty-nine, while Jay was the author of Nos. 2, 3, 4, 5, and 64. From Madison's pen came Nos. 10, 14, 18, 19, 20 (utilizing some of Hamilton's materials in the last three), 37 through 58, 62, and 63. The rest were by Hamilton.

The Federalist, first published as a book in May 1788, did not reveal its authorship, nor did subsequent editions until after Hamilton's fatal duel with Aaron Burr in 1804. Preceding that event Hamilton made a listing of authorship which spread among his friends, giving those of Madison and Jay by numbers and saying "all the rest by Mr. Hamilton." In such a list, published a few years after Hamilton's death, Madison's string from "37 through 58" was cut to "37 through 48," with no reference to Nos. 62 and 63. In 1818 Jacob Gideon published a new edition, obtaining for that purpose Madison's own copy, with the initials of the author at the head of each article.

The Gideon list was used in all subsequent editions until after the Civil War, when the apotheosis of Hamilton caused publishers to revert to the "pre-duel" ascription. Later editors headed the disputed articles "Hamilton or Madison." This continued until the studies of Edward G. Bourne in the 1890's and Douglass Adair thirty years later substantiated the Gideon list, not only in the minds of scholars in general but of Hamiltonian editors.

To this the author of this Madison biography contributed an explanation that absolves Hamilton of any intention to steal credit. The earliest known Hamilton list—that in Chancellor Kent's copy of The Federalist —not only ends Madison's string at No. 48, but gives No. 53 to Madison and No. 54 to Jay, whose original draft of *No. 64* is in his papers. Add ten to all the erroneous numberings given to Madison and Jay and they agree with Madison's list. It is obvious that Hamilton merely misread or misremembered the Roman numerals that headed the articles in the 1788 edition.

The "Publius" series opened with a general outline of its scope by Hamilton. Jay followed with four articles on the value of a close and strong Union in reducing the dangers from foreign influence. Hamilton then took over with four articles on the Union as a protection against dissension among the states and hostilities between them.

Madison's opening contribution, the Tenth Federalist, published on November 23, acquired in time a fame that placed it far above and beyond its status as an argument for ratification of the Constitution. It was a treatise on the economic motivation of politics—the final and perfected form of his analysis of that topic in the "Vices of the Political System of the United States" and his June 6 speech in the Philadelphia Convention. The Tenth Federalist was written primarily to combat the widely circulated argument, based on Montesquieu, that republican government and liberty could co-exist only in a small republic, such as an individual American state. Madison contended that the contrary was true: diversity of interests promoted political freedom, and diversity of interests increased in proportion to the extent and diversity of territory and population. The resulting political principle was innate in human nature:

> The diversity in the faculties of men, from which the rights of property originate, is not less an insuperable obstacle to a uniformity of interests. The protection of these faculties is the first object of government. From the protection of different and unequal faculties of acquiring property, the possession of different degrees and kinds of property immediately results; and from the influence of these on the sentiments and views of the respective proprietors, ensues a division of the society into different interests and parties.

The latent causes of faction were "thus sown in the nature of man," and manifested themselves in differences concerning religion, government, political leaders, and many other points. "But the most common and durable source of factions has been the various and unequal distribution of property"—those with property and without property, creditors, and debtors; landowners, manufacturers, merchants, the moneyed interest—all divided into different classes, actuated by different sentiments and views. "The regulation of these various and interfering interests forms the principal task of modern legislation, and involves the spirit of party and faction in the necessary and ordinary operations of the government."

Since the *causes* of faction could not be removed, said Madison, relief must be sought by controlling its *effects*. That was to be achieved by extending the sphere of government, taking in a greater variety of parties and interests, and thus making it more difficult to give the majority a common motive to invade the rights of other citizens. This was the advantage of a republic over a pure democracy, and of the American Union over the states composing it.

Madison carried this thought farther in No. 14, while in Nos. 18, 19, and 20 he expanded the study "Of Ancient and Modern Confederacies." Hamilton wrote the next sixteen articles, concentrating on the defects of the Confederation, the necessities of national defense and a general power of taxation. Madison then took over with a string of twenty-two articles whose publication was not completed until February 22, 1788. Here he devoted himself mainly to the relationship of the Constitution to the principles of republican government, the structure of the projected federal government and its bearing on the governments of the states.

In No. 39 Madison challenged the customary application of the word "republican" to any elective representative government, no matter how oligarchic or aristocratic it might be. In its true meaning:

> We may define a republic to be, or at least may bestow that name on, a government which derives all its powers directly or indirectly from the great body of the people, and is administered by persons holding their offices during pleasure, for a limited period, or during good behavior. It is *essential* to such a government that it be derived from the great body of the society, not from an inconsiderable proportion, or a favored class of it; otherwise a handful of tyrannical nobles, exercising their oppressions by a delegation of their powers, might aspire to the rank of republicans, and claim for their government the honorable title of republic.

In No. 41, Madison refuted the widespread charge that the power to lay and collect taxes "to pay the debts, and provide for the common defence and general welfare" amounted to "an unlimited commission to exercise every power which may be alleged to be necessary for the common defence or general welfare." It would be singular indeed, he said, to use so awkward a form and place to describe an authority to legislate in all possible cases. What color could the objection have, "when a specification of the objects alluded to by these general terms" immediately followed? The phrases, he said, were taken from the language of the Articles of Confederation, where they were descriptive of the objects of the Union. What would have been thought of Congress if that body had disregarded the specifications of power and used those phrases to justify an unlimited power of providing for the common defense and general welfare?

Madison's analysis was logical as applied here, to deny an unlimited power to *legislate* for the common defense and general welfare. Not so as he employed it later, to hold down the *spending power* to the specific objects of general welfare involved in the other enumerated powers of legislation. Where, except by applying the term "general welfare" more broadly, did the Continental Congress find authority to appropriate money to educate Indian youths at Dartmouth and Princeton?

One by one, Madison justified the powers given Congress, coming in No. 44 to the sweeping "power to make all laws which shall be necessary and proper" for executing the powers vested in the federal government. Few parts of the Constitution, he remarked, had been assailed with more intemperance than this, yet "without the substance of this power, the whole Constitution would be a dead letter." He then defined it in terms that formed a preview of Chief Justice Marshall's broad construction of it in *McCulloch* v. *Maryland*. Said Madison:

> Had the Constitution been silent on this head, there can be no doubt that all the particular powers requisite as means of executing the general powers would have resulted to the government, by unavoidable implication. No axiom is more clearly established in law, or in reason, than that wherever the end is required, the means are authorized; wherever a general power to do a thing is given, every particular power necessary for doing it is included.

Had Madison held to this definition all his life he would have had a much narrower disagreement with Hamilton and virtually none at all with Marshall. He turned next to the clause making the Constitution, the laws passed pursuant to it, and treaties, "the supreme law of the land." Without this, he said, state constitutions would be paramount to the federal Constitution in many cases. National laws and treaties might be valid in some states, ineffective in others:

> In fine, the world would have seen, for the first time, a system of government founded on an inversion of the fundamental principles of all governments; it would have seen the authority of the whole society everywhere subordinate to the authority of the parts; it would have seen a monster, in which the head was under the direction of the members.

Continuing this theme in No. 45, Madison dealt with the fear that the whole mass of federal powers would be dangerous to the portion of authority left in the several states. Adversaries of the plan, instead of considering what degree of federal power was essential to the security and happiness of the American people, had been declaiming against it as a derogation from the importance of state governments.

> Was, then, the American Revolution effected, was the American Confederacy formed, was the precious blood of thousands spilt, and the hard-earned substance of millions lavished, not that the people of America should enjoy peace, liberty and safety, but that the government of the individual States . . . might enjoy a certain extent of power, and be arrayed with certain dignities and attributes of sovereignty?

Madison denied, however, that any undue sacrifice was entailed. The powers delegated to the federal government "are few and defined." Those to remain in the state governments "are numerous and indefinite." Federal power would "be exercised principally on external objects, as war, peace, negotiation and foreign commerce, with which last the power of taxation will, for the most part, be connected." In contrast, the powers reserved to the states "will extend to all the objects which, in the ordinary course of affairs; concern the lives, liberties, and properties of the people, and the internal order, improvement, and prosperity of the State."

That was true as far as it went, but it was a far cry from the distribution of powers as he described it in the Philadelphia Convention. There, the states were necessary only because "the general government could not extend its care to all the minute objects" of the local jurisdictions. There, the federal taxing power was "the highest prerogative of supremacy." Had he spoken his full thoughts in *The Federalist*, he would have said that the federal powers were few, defined, and *vast;* the state powers numerous, indefinite, and *minute.*

The remainder of Madison's share in the work, Nos. 47 through 58, 62, and 63—dealt with the structure of government and distribution of its powers among the various departments. Here, he said, the Constitution followed the principle of separation of powers, with enough of a blending to enable each branch to maintain its independence. If they were totally separate, the legislative branch, confident of popular support and sharing popular passions, would overwhelm the others. In a hereditary monarchy, the king was the source of danger, but in a representative government, "it is against the enterprising ambition of [the legislative] department that the people ought to indulge all their jealousy and exhaust all their precautions."

In the Fifty-Seventh Federalist, Madison rejected the contention that the House of Representatives would lack sympathy with the mass of the people. Who were "to be the electors of the federal representatives? Not the rich, more than the poor; not the learned, more than the ignorant; not the haughty heirs of distinguished names, more than the humble sons of obscurity and unpropitious fortune." The electors were to be "the great body of the people of the United States"—the same who elect the corresponding branches of state legislatures.

In No. 62, Madison had the difficult task of defending state equality in the Senate, contrary to his convictions. He took care of the problem by saying that this resulted from mutual deference and concession, not theory. Rejection now would leave the country with a government still more objectionable. Besides, state equality furnished a protection against consolidation into one simple republic.

This was a telling argument, but furnished a warning against full reliance on *The Federalist* as an unalloyed expression of the views of its writers. That applied still more to Hamilton, who totally suppressed his aversion to republican government. Both men, however, shared a common conviction of the necessity of adopting the Constitution, to avert national disaster; both were faithful to the duty of fair interpretation.

23 / RATIFICATION

Six states had ratified the Constitution when Madison set out for home on March 4, 1788. Delaware led off, followed by Pennsylvania, New Jersey, Georgia, Connecticut, and Massachusetts. Before leaving New York, Madison had word of formidable opposition to him for a seat in the state convention. More worrisome was an adjournment till June of the New Hampshire convention. That ended his hope of confronting Patrick Henry and George Mason with nine ratifications. To Edmund Pendleton, old, ill, undecided, but still influential, he made an appeal based on *the only issue*—"the simple one whether the Union shall or shall not be continued. . . . The opposition with some has disunion assuredly for its object; and with all for its real tendency."

Feeling no need for haste, Madison spent a week in Philadelphia and three days with Washington at Mount Vernon. At Fredericksburg he picked up a letter from his neighbor, Joseph Spencer, warning him that he faced defeat unless he hastened to offset the "vile prevarications" that were being circulated about the Constitution. On his way he should be sure to call on a Baptist leader and correct his belief that the document threatened religious liberty.

Madison reached home on March 23, the day before election. Orange County had but one polling place, so Madison addressed his entire constituency when he mounted a stand on election day in defense of the Constitution. He defeated the influential Thomas Barbour, 202 to 56. Pro-Constitution James Gordon won the other seat by a lesser margin. Edward Carrington rejoiced that Madison had turned "the sinners of Orange from their wicked ways."

Montpelier was thronged with visitors during the next few days, bearing reports of hard times in the Piedmont. Tobacco was low priced and so was corn, in spite of a short crop. These same conditions, plus usurious interest rates, prevailed in Maryland. There the sufferers turned against the Chase-Martin paper-money faction and supported the Constitution. Stability in government would bring loans from Europe and ease the money market, while federal import duties would hit only the rich. Maryland ratified on April 28 and South Carolina on May 23. Eight states, therefore, had given their assent when the Virginia Convention convened on June 2. Virginia could bring the Constitution into force among the nine.

Throughout the preceding two months Madison had been laboring to pull Governor Randolph into line and to allay the hostility manifest in Kentucky. With Randolph he employed the usual formula: Agree with him wherever possible; in answering objections, make him think the answers were his own. Also, play on his deep distrust of Patrick Henry. If anything came of *Henry's suggestion* (originally Randolph's) of a second convention, it would be "more remote from *your* ideas" than the present plan. Secret plotters of disunion would wreck a revision by demanding changes sure to be rejected in some places.

Patrick Henry had written to Randolph that he would continue his opposition if only *one half of one state* was against the plan. This veiled threat to take southern Virginia out of the Union was grist for Madison: "The declaration of H——y, mentioned in your letter, is a proof to me that desperate measures will be his game. If report does not more than usually exaggerate, Mason also is ripening fast for going every length." Every thought uttered by Madison came back to him, in Randolph's next letter, as "objections [that] have always struck me" to a second convention—his own scheme, whose rejection at Philadelphia made him refuse to sign the Constitution.

Kentucky was a harder nut to crack, for Henry had effectually transplanted the fear of surrender of the Mississippi from the old to the untried new Congress. Madison furnished arguments to be relayed to Kentucky by George Nicholas. The new Constitution would transform national impotence into national power in dealing with Spain. The "notoriously incompetent" present Congress would have successors "able to hold a language which no nation having possessions in America will think it prudent to disregard."

Nicholas urged Madison to prepare an address to the people. Madison objected, but just in advance of the Virginia convention the *Independent Chronicle* published two letters of "An American" embodying Madison's thoughts and style. The delegates were warned that rejection of the Constitution would produce the miserable alternatives of thirteen jarring sovereignties, two or three contending confederacies, or a feeble union. From abroad would come insults and injuries, while at home the dangers to liberty, prosperity, and peace would sink every American into despondency or drive him to despair.

Richmond swarmed with visitors on opening day. Edmund Pendleton was elected chairman by acclamation, his prestige discouraging the "antis." George Mason threatened more than divine vengeance if (as happened in Maryland) the convention voted on the Constitution without discussing it clause by clause. Madison eagerly concurred: debate confined to general principles would have been Patrick Henry's meat. For the same reason Madison agreed to the opposition's demand that all discussions be in committee of the whole. That doubled the chance for recovery from Henry's mesmerism and also allowed Chairman Pendleton to take part in debates.

The tone of the opposition was set in Henry's opening motion to read all resolutions of the Virginia legislature bearing on the Annapolis and Philadelphia conventions. Pendleton, rising on his crutches, choked this off with a statement that they were commissioned to decide whether the new system was a proper one, not whether the framers of it exceeded their powers.

George Nicholas opened for ratification with a speech that paraphrased Madison's *Federalist* articles Nos. 52 and 53. Patrick Henry, following, wanted to know what had stirred the citizenry from quiet repose to a sense of fearful jeopardy. Three words had done it, three little words in the preamble of the new Constitution. Who had authorized those men in Philadelphia to speak the language of "We the people" instead of "We the States"? Their purpose was to form a great consolidated government.

Governor Randolph then addressed eagerly expectant delegates. They heard a defense of his refusal to sign the Constitution. Then, to the astonishment of nearly everybody except Madison, he assailed the idea of amendments before ratification. His speech was virtually a composite of the letters Madison had written to him.

George Mason, violating his own clause-by-clause rule, tore into the federal power of direct taxation. That grant, he charged, took away the concurrent taxing power of the states and would lead to a consolidated government. Madison rose to deny both the premise and the conclusion but said that he would abide by the rules and discuss direct taxes when they reached that subject. Optimistic but not over-confident, he reported that night to Washington:

> Henry and Mason made a lame figure and appeared to take different and awkward ground. The Federalists are a good deal elated by the existing prospect. I dare not however speak with certainty as to the decision. Kentucky has been extremely

> tainted, is supposed to be generally adverse, and every piece
> of address is going on privately to work on the local interests
> and prejudices of that and other quarters.

Antifederal William Grayson was grieved but not cast down by the loss of Randolph. "Kentucky is with us," he wrote to Nathan Dane of Massachusetts. If they could gain the four other counties on the Ohio, "the day is our own."

Henry spent the next day building up the terrors of "We the people." By these words the government would be consolidated and state sovereignty relinquished. "The rights of conscience, trial by jury, liberty of the press, all your immunities and franchises, are rendered insecure, if not lost, by this change." America was to become an empire, with liberty in ropes and chains. He assailed the new taxing power, with federal sheriffs outdoing the barbarous ravages of those unfeeling bloodsuckers, the state sheriffs.

Following this, Henry rose to such oratorical heights that the official stenographer (a friend of the Constitution) sat spellbound, unable to record his words. He recovered in time to set down Henry's prediction that if Virginia valiantly refused to yield without prior amendments, the ratifying states would comply. But what did it amount to if the states were disunited? "I speak the language of thousands. But, sir, I mean not to breathe the spirit nor utter the language of secession." (Thus, he stirred the thought in disavowing it.)

Governor Randolph was not impressed. "Mr. Chairman," he said, "if we go on in this irregular manner, contrary to our resolution . . . it will take us six months to decide this question." Randolph replied to Henry by listing the evils in Virginia government that the federal constitution would prohibit. It was a virtual list of Henry's disruptive triumphs, justice strangled in the courts, debts uncollectible. As for trial by jury, the legislature, in violation of the state constitution, had passed a bill of attainder against Josiah Phillips. Was this arbitrary deprivation of life consistent with the genius of republican government? (No need to recall that Henry, as governor, had asked for this bill of attainder.)

The main reply to Henry and Mason came from Madison. Weak of voice, he spoke for the first time before hundreds of auditors. The historian Grigsby described his style as related by listeners. He always rose to speak "as if with a view of expressing some thought that had casually occurred to him, with his hat in his hand and with his notes in his hat; and the warmest excitement of debate was visible in him only by a more or less rapid and forward seesaw motion of his body."

Madison was pained, he said, "to hear gentlemen continually distorting the natural construction of language." He rebutted Henry's assertion that loss of liberty usually resulted from the tyranny of rulers. Far more often, despotism was produced by turbulence and violence, by the majority trampling on the rights of the minority. Mr. Henry had said the people of the country were at repose, everything was in perfect tranquillity and safety. If so, "why have complaints of national and individual distresses been echoed and re-echoed throughout the continent? Why has our general government been so shamefully disgraced, and our constitution violated?"

He cited Henry's statement that there was no instance in history, of power once transferred being voluntarily renounced. Eight states, he pointed out, had just made such a renunciation in their ratification of the Constitution. "The power of raising and supporting armies is exclaimed against, as dangerous and unnecessary." Far greater danger, replied Madison, would lie in the knowledge, by ambitious or avaricious foreign nations, that the United States government lacked that power. He repelled Henry's assertion that Congress could establish a national religion: the federal government, to the honor of America, had no jurisdiction over that subject.

George Nicholas, so fat that he was cartooned (to Madison's delight) "as a plum pudding with legs to it," assailed Henry with his redoubtable bluntness and wit. He ridiculed the contention that taxation by Congress against the will of its Virginia minority would be taxation without consent. As well say the same of a Virginia county taxed by the state legislature over its opposing vote. Bushrod Washington, writing that evening to his Uncle George, glowed with enthusiasm over the speeches of Randolph, Madison, and Nicholas, but found that it was the quiet reasoner between the two impassioned orators who produced results: "Mr. Madison followed with such force and reasoning and a display of such irresistible truths that opposition seemed to have quitted the field. However, I am not so sanguine as to trust appearances or even to flatter myself that he made many converts. A few I have been confidently informed he did influence who were decidedly in the opposition."

Two days later Madison assailed the Confederation. "A government," he said, "which relies on thirteen independent sovereignties, for the means of its existence, is a solecism in theory, and a mere nullity in practice." He drew lessons from ancient Greece and modern Europe and applied them to American experience. "Governments destitute of energy, will ever produce anarchy." The Confederation was so notoriously feeble that foreign nations were unwilling to form treaties with us—treaties which individual states were free to violate at pleasure. The "honorable member" (Mr. Henry) had said the federal government could rely on the punctuality of the states in meeting requisitions. For the past twelve months, said Madison, payments inadequate from the beginning had sunk to $276,641. "Suggestions and strong assertions dissipate before these facts."

Madison cut off his speech suddenly, with the statement that he would "no longer fatigue the committee at this time, but will resume the subject as early as I can." For the next four days he was in bed with bilious fever. Reports of the debate were brought to him, including some encouraging blunders by Patrick Henry. Stung by Randolph's reference to the Phillips bill of attainder, Henry defended it on the ground that the attainted man was not a Socrates. Randolph and John Marshall assailed him. Because a man was not a Socrates, was he to be attainted at pleasure? If so, who was safe?

Henry assailed the clause forbidding the states to issue paper money as needless and out of place. "I acknowledge," he said, "that paper money would be the bane of this country. I detest it." (That from the man who had attempted to ride back into power on paper money, only one year earlier!) Henry disavowed the idea of disunion but put it in the minds of others by saying that Virginia and North Carolina "could exist separated from the rest of America." He challenged Madison's contention that republican government, properly organized, could safely exist over an extensive territory. Whoever says "that a continent can be governed by that system contradicts all the experience of the world." The new system would fail because President and Congress were to be chosen by the people. There was none of that self-love which made the British House of Lords the protector of the people and the King—a feature that made him "pronounce the British government superior in this respect to any government that ever was in any country."

Still devoting himself to Madison, Henry directed all his satirical gifts against the absent delegate's description of the new government as partly national, partly federal. Some might be deceived, said he, by this anatomical curiosity in which the brain is national, the stamina federal, one limb national, another federal. The real significance was that a great consolidated government would be pressing on the necks of the people.

Light-Horse Harry Lee, answering Henry, invited him to turn away from his favorite system of "king, lords and commons," and meet the issue with solid arguments instead of ingenious oratorical bolts. "Most feelingly does he dwell on the imaginary dangers of this pretended consolidation. I did suppose that an honorable gentleman whom I do not now see [Mr. Madison] had placed this in such a clear light that every man would have been satisfied with it."

By the time Madison re-entered the debate on June 11, it was evident that Henry's "Socrates" remark had undermined the bill-of-rights issue as an argument for amendments *before ratification*. The fate of the Constitution, Madison concluded, would turn on direct taxation and the impact of the Mississippi River arguments on Kentucky members. He took up direct taxes. Without them in wartime, regular troops could not be raised; militia must be relied on, risking national annihilation. France and Great Britain would soon be at war again. America, possessing sufficient strength, could carry on trade with both of the contending powers. Without such defensive strength, she would be insulted and attacked, her ships seized. To prevent this and to enjoy the great advantage of carrying the commerce of the nations at war, it must be known to the belligerents "that our government can command the whole resources of the Union."

Madison denied that federal power to levy taxes would destroy the states. The devotion of the people to their state governments would prevent that, nor would it be attempted. Early in the Revolution, he said, Congress "had the power to trample on the states. When they had that fund of paper money in their hands [from 1775 to 1779] . . . was there any disposition to debase the state governments?" None whatever.

The powers of the general government were few and related to external objects. There was really no great increase in federal powers. The nature of them was changed. "Now they tax states, and by this plan they will tax individuals." In theory, Madison said, there was no difference between the two systems, but in practice the difference was infinite; one ineffectual, the other adequate, and necessary for the public safety.

Henry now put on record what his side had been saying in the cloak-rooms. The illustrious Jefferson "advises you to reject this government till it be amended." Could we not, retorted Madison, "adduce a character equally great on our side?" (Every listener visualized Washington.) However, he denied that Jefferson was opposed. Personal delicacy forbade him to quote the letters he had received, but he would say that this illustrious citizen strongly approved the taxing power and state equality in the Senate, which Henry called the rotten part of the Constitution.

Turning to navigation of the Mississippi, Madison denied that a majority in the present Congress were disposed to surrender it. Pennsylvania, New Jersey, and five Southern states were solid in defense of navigation. Replying that he did not want to reflect on any private character, Henry said he wished that "past and present members" of Congress (Monroe and Grayson) would describe its (secret) proceedings on the projected treaty. Madison shot back "that if the honorable gentleman thought that *he* had given an incorrect account of the transactions," he would on investigation find himself mistaken.

Monroe then told of Jay's proposal to give up Mississippi navigation for twenty-five years. Grayson assailed the treaty project as a New England bid for a Spanish market for fish. This gave Madison the choice of violating the secrecy rule or staking the issue solely on his word. He chose the latter.

The treaty, he said, was dead. Seven states had once favored a temporary alienation of the right, but the New Jersey delegates were now instructed on the other side. The real question was whether the new Congress would make it more or less secure. Under the Articles of Confederation, nine states in Congress could give up the Mississippi. Under the new Constitution, with all senators present, it would take nine states and the President. What the people wanted was not the mere right to navigate, but the actual possession and enjoyment of that right. That would never come about unless an energetic government was established.

Patrick Henry was at his scornful best in replying. The new Congress furnished no security. The Spanish ambassador could bribe senators with impunity because they could not be recalled. The President, as distinguished from the Senate, was nothing. The contrary argument was one "I would not give a single pin for." Finally, Henry argued, the United States could safely rely on the strong arms of France, who was bound to defend our claim by the territorial guarantee of the 1778 treaty of alliance.

George Nicholas shot that argument to pieces by asking why, if there was such a guarantee, France had not already acted on it. But Henry's eloquence, as his legislative career attested, often linked affirmative results with absurd arguments, so Madison displayed no undue confidence when he wrote to Washington on June 13. Kentucky opposition, if solid, might be fatal, and the whole business was "in the most ticklish state that can be imagined." Each side, Theodorick Bland reported, was claiming a majority of from three to eight.

For two weeks, opponents of the Constitution had been violating their own rule that the document be considered clause by clause. On motion of Francis Corbin, the convention voted to follow the rule, and did so, with an immense speed-up of progress and no reduction of discord. Henry asked questions about each clause, answered them himself, and then challenged Madison to answer the answers. Other opponents did likewise.

Why, after authorizing the states to fix the times, places, and manner of electing senators and representatives, did the Constitution give Congress power to alter regulations. The purpose, said Madison, was to prevent the states from dissolving Congress, and to ensure uniformity in elections and equality of representation throughout the continent. Also: "Should the people of any state, by any means be deprived of the right of suffrage, it was judged proper that it should be remedied by the general government."

George Mason, who had argued in the Philadelphia Convention for greater federal control over the militia, now reversed himself and said it was being made too great. With this he coupled a denunciation of the power given Congress to maintain a standing army in peace time—one of the greatest of all evils. That very evil, Madison answered, was guarded against by the federal power to call forth the militia, which reduced the necessity of a standing army. Henry assailed the taxing power and militia control from a new angle: it violated the ancient maxim against putting sword and purse in the same hands. That maxim, Madison responded, was being totally misapplied. Its only rational meaning was that the sword and purse were not to be given to the same department of government. So it was in Great Britain, the sword in the king's hand, the purse in Parliament's.

Mason, Grayson, and Henry dwelt on the fearful crimes and judicial tyranny that would result from federal control over the seat of government. Replied Madison: "Was there ever a legislature in existence that held their sessions at a place where they had not jurisdiction?" Ought it to be under the control of some particular state "that might at a critical moment seize it?"

Henry shifted to similar dangers in the power to pass laws "necessary and proper" to execute the specific powers. This, he said, exposed Virginia "naked to the armed and powerful," without any federal Bill of Rights to furnish a safeguard. That clause, rejoined Madison, merely enabled Congress to execute the delegated powers, whose particular applications were beyond human capacity to enumerate.

Henry's reference to the absence of a Bill of Rights gave Nicholas and Madison an opening they had been waiting for. Nicholas conceded the necessity of such a bill, but should they dissolve the Union because of its omission? All of the states wanted it. Where then was the difficulty of obtaining it *through subsequent amendments?* (Specific pledges by Madison were to come later.)

The contest went on in the same fashion. Clause after clause was presented as a source of horrendous terrors; explained as a necessary and proper cure of existing evils. Mason inveighed against the clause forbidding interference with the diabolical slave trade before 1808 and at the same time protested that the Constitution gave Congress power to tax slavery out of existence. The southernmost states, Madison replied, would have dissolved the Union if this concession had not been made. As for manumission through taxation, that was impossible because direct taxes had to be proportionate to population throughout the country.

Henry presented the chilling thought that once the proportion was fixed, Congress could lay Virginia's share entirely on slaves. There was a moment of tension, which the great orator broke up with a climactic shout: "They'll free your niggers." The convention broke into a roar of laughter, and the slavery issue vanished.

When the executive department was reached new scares developed. The President, said Mason on June 17, would be re-elected as long as he lived—kept in office by the great powers of Europe. Not once in fifty times, he predicted, would the ninety-one electors produce a majority for one man. Each voting for two men, it would take a majority of their 182 votes to elect. Madison explained that only a majority of the ninety-one electors was required, so the high man would win if he received forty-six votes.

The office of Vice President, Madison said, was an important one. If the President died, his successor, like himself, would be the choice of the people. Should both the President and Vice President die, "*the election of another President will immediately take place,*" or Congress could make an appointment to continue until the expiration of the term. (Here again is evidence of the power to hold an interim election.)

The opposition leaders—Henry, Mason, and Grayson—turned to the treaty power. The President could get a nefarious treaty ratified in special session by failing to summon senators from injured states. If he did anything so atrocious, Madison replied, he would be impeached. Henry inveighed against the clause making treaties a part of the supreme law of the land. Nowhere else in Christendom was this the case. "They are so in every country," Madison answered, citing Blackstone as to England. In England, Henry responded, the impeachment power was backed by blocks and gibbets; in this Constitution it was "a mere sham; a mere farce;" the guilty try themselves. If treaties were supreme law they were paramount to the Constitution.

Madison went into a general analysis of the treaty power. The old Congress, he said, had indefinite authority to make treaties which were recognized in many state laws to be supreme. The power, however, was not absolute and unlimited. He denied that it allowed the President and

Senate to dismember the empire or to alienate any great essential right. He endorsed Corbin's assertion that treaties were paramount only to the laws and constitutions of the states, not to the power of Congress. To allow state laws to counteract treaties, Madison declared, "would bring on the Union the just charge of national perfidy, and involve us in war." At this time, June 18, Grayson found eight delegates undecided, and five of these were needed to defeat the Constitution. He thought two could be picked up by a masterly attack on the federal judiciary. Madison wrote to Washington and Rufus King that the Federals seemed a little bit ahead. His own illness was continuing "in a degree which barely allows me to operate in the business."

George Mason launched the attack on the courts with the charge that they would protect federal officers in "the most insolent and wanton brutality to a man's wife or daughter." Then came the masterly appeal to self-interest. Every British pre-war creditor could sue for his money in federal court. A thousand debtors who had paid once (in worthless paper money placed in escrow) would have to pay again.

Able replies came from Pendleton and Marshall, but the crisis was so acute that Madison, ill though he was, made one of his longest speeches. The authority of the judiciary must be as extensive as the legislative power. It must encompass treaties to ensure their uniform application. Federal jurisdiction would protect Virginians from prejudices in the courts of other states. Ninety-nine lawsuits in a hundred would remain in state courts. He examined the appellate jurisdiction of the Supreme Court, noting that Congress was given power to determine whether it should extend to fact as well as law. A sound and uniform administration of justice, operating with celerity, would inspire public and private confidence, thereby raising the value of property and relieving debtors.

Four days elapsed before Madison took the floor again for his last major speech. He emphasized the awful nature of the alternatives— "whether the thirteen states shall unite freely, peaceably, and unanimously, for security of their common happiness and liberty, or whether every thing is to be put in confusion and disorder." George Mason had brought forward forty amendments—twenty in a bill of rights, some of the others called by Madison "improper and inadmissible." The opponents were demanding their adoption in advance of ratification. Would not every other state, Madison asked, think itself entitled to propose as many? All the amendments sought by all the states would have to be considered by all of them, including the eight states that had ratified the document. If Virginia made this demand she would be obliged to recede from it. Unobjectionable amendments could be recommended for adoption later but, said Madison, "I never can consent to his previous amendments, because they are pregnant with dreadful dangers."

Henry tried to exploit Madison's assertion that amendments could not be obtained before adoption of the Constitution. "His arguments, great as that gentleman's abilities are, tend to prove that amendments cannot be obtained *after* adoption." Madison replied that any defects could be removed by the method set forth in the Constitution. He regarded a declaration of rights as unnecessary, because the general government had no powers except what were given them. It was dangerous because an incomplete enumeration would be unsafe, but he would be the last man to oppose any amendment that would give satisfaction and was not dangerous.

Attorney General James Innes (reputed to be the largest man in Virginia) put some oratorical avoirdupois into the final debate. He had hoped to hear reasonable arguments against the Constitution and had listened to nothing but horrors and chimeras. He grieved that jealousy of the North had supplanted the spirit of 1775, when the glorious name of an American extended from end to end of the continent. The attorney general closed with a point of law. The people had commissioned them to adopt or reject the document on the table. "It transcends the power of the convention to take it with previous amendments," thereby binding the people to what they knew not.

June 26 was the day of decision. Eighty-eight to eighty, the convention rejected previous amendments. Then, eighty-nine to seventy-nine it ratified the Constitution. That done, on the motion of the Federalists themselves, the forty Mason-Henry amendments were unanimously recommended to the consideration of Congress.

Every delegate present recognized the victory of the Constitution as Madison's victory and Patrick Henry's defeat. David had slain Goliath. The greatest orator of revolutionary America had been overcome by a quiet reasoner, weak of voice and further weakened by fever and fatigue. Eight times the stenographer made entries such as "Here Mr. Madison spoke so low that he could not be heard." Delegates overcame that by leaving their seats and crowding around him.

Madison's influence reached far beyond his own speeches. Except for the arguments of Marshall and Pendleton on the judiciary, every supporting utterance bore the stamp of Madison's thought, previously expressed on the floor, in letters, or in *The Federalist*. He won by placing every disputed issue before the convention in terms so clear and logical, offered with such sincerity and fairness, that they prevailed over the oratory, the distortions, and exaggerated alarms of Henry, Mason, and Grayson.

There was a deeper reason for the victory won by Madison, Pendleton, Randolph, Marshall, Nicholas, Corbin, Henry Lee, and Innes. The great verities were on their side. The choice was between national salvation and national dissolution, but the battle was fought in a region and in a climate where unreasoning fears and emotional oratory were on the other side and were usually triumphant.

Henry and Mason, in spite of their distortions and false alarms, were basically sincere. They sensed, in the Constitution's elasticity, the coming shift of power from the states to the nation; but they saw it as the fruit of nationalist conspiracy, whereas Madison recognized it as the pressure of national necessity. The opponents were forced into a weak position—the demand for prior amendments—because it was the only possible method of reaching their true goal—rejection. They failed because their only valid objection to the Constitution—the absence of a bill of rights—was countered by the pledge of subsequent amendments. Patrick Henry's genius, applied to a weak cause, led him into a succession of improvised assaults of the passions upon the intellect. In a quick-acting convention they might have carried the day. In twenty-four days they broke down under the greatness of the national crisis and the cumulative force of Madison's relentless appeal to reason.

Unknown to the Virginia convention, New Hampshire's ratification on June 21 already had brought the Constitution into effect among nine states. In New York's convention, antifederal Governor Clinton's two-to-one majority was fading to a narrow margin. Madison rushed the news of Virginia's action to Hamilton, who had written that "Our only chance of success depends upon you." Clinton, wavering at the news, proposed that New York ratify, retaining a right to secede if the state's demanded amendments were not accepted. Would New York be received on that basis? "My opinion," Madison replied to Hamilton's query, is that a *conditional* ratification "does not make New York a member of the new Union. . . . The Constitution requires an adoption *in toto* and forever." That letter, read on the convention floor, produced a five-vote margin for unconditional ratification. All states were now in except North Carolina and Rhode Island, whose ultimate action was not regarded as in doubt.

Princeton saw reason at this time to confer the degree of Doctor of Laws on Madison for his statesmanship during and after the Revolution. The trustees and faculty, wrote President Witherspoon, "were not barely willing but proud of the opportunity of paying some attention to and giving a testimony of their approbation of one of their own sons who has done them so much honor by his public conduct." Witherspoon had the "peculiar happiness to know, perhaps more than any of them, your usefulness in an important station."

Madison carried Virginia's instrument of ratification to Congress. There, he wrote to Washington, advocates of New York as the first seat of the new government "studiously promote delay" in establishing it. He welcomed the postponement: newly elected legislatures, likely to be federal-minded, would choose the first Senate. His main object at the time was to fix the temporary site to the south of New York, as an easier transition to a hoped-for permanent seat on the Potomac.

"The only chance the Potomac has," he advised Washington, "is to get things in such a train that a coalition may take place between the southern and eastern states on the subject." Unluckily, a deadlock developed on the temporary seat. Madison swung his support to New York. The alternative, he told reluctant allies, was to see the new government strangled in its birth. All yielded except Maryland and Delaware.

Spurred by Governor Clinton, the New York convention now appealed to all state legislatures to force the calling of a new constitutional convention. The object of this "pestilent maneuver," Madison declared, was to take the amending process away from Congress and put it in the hands of men who would mutilate the whole system.

Next came news that North Carolina, spurred by a paper-money faction, had rejected the Constitution. Madison was giving a dinner for J. P. Brissot de Warville when this word came. The rejection, Madison assured the French traveler, was temporary and would have no weight in the minds of Americans. In his next book, *New Travels*, Brissot appraised Mr. Madison, "celebrated in America" and well known in Europe through the "merited eulogium" of him by his friend Jefferson:

> Though still young he has rendered the greatest services to Virginia, to the American Confederation, and to liberty and humanity in general. . . . He distinguished himself particularly in the conventions for ratification of a new federal system. Virginia balanced a long time before adhering. Mr. Madison won the members to it by his eloquence and his logic.

At the time of their meeting, Brissot went on, Madison had an air of fatigue, owing perhaps to his recent immense labors. "His look announces a censor, his conversation discovers the man of learning, and his reserve was that of a man conscious of his talents and his duties."

The French minister at this time was the Count de Moustier, who on his arrival in January had brought a fine watch, manufactured at Madison's request and Jefferson's order. Moustier also brought his sister-in-law, Madame de Brèhan, as official hostess, and her young son. "She is goodness itself," wrote Jefferson to Madison. American society saw only that the travel arrangements of the count and his hostess proclaimed her to be his mistress. Madison did not appear to share the general shock. During his absence in Virginia, President of Congress Cyrus Griffin (also unshocked) sent word to him from the "marchioness" that she had bought a slave girl, "and only wants a boy *in order that they may breed* to use her own language." Upon his return in August the request was confirmed, and Madison wrote to his father: "Tell my brother Ambrose if you please that he must draw on Mr. Shepherd for the price of the Negro boy for the French Marchioness." The purchase was to be made outside "the family"; no Madison slaves were sold in the lucrative Southern market, or anywhere else.

By the end of the year Madison was disillusioned concerning the Moustier menage. The count, he wrote to Jefferson, "is unsocial, proud and niggardly and betrays a sort of fastidiousness towards this country. He suffers also from his illicit connection with Madame de Brèhan which is universally known and offensive to American manners." Nearly all New York ladies had ostracized her. "She knows the cause, is deeply stung by it . . . and conveys impressions to her paramour over whom she exercises despotic sway." In a few months, however, he reported that "Madame de Brèhan begins to be viewed in the light which I hope she merits," and Moustier too was becoming more acceptable.

Congress set January for election of presidential electors and March 4 for the convening of the new Congress in New York. The choice for President was beyond question—every vote would be cast for Washington. A man from Massachusetts was conceded second place, but Madison did not like the choice between Governor Hancock, "weak, ambitious, a courtier of popularity, given to low intrigue," and John Adams, whose book on American constitutions, slanted toward aristocracy, made him "obnoxious to many, particularly in the southern states."

Congressional politics were seething, with Governor Clinton and Patrick Henry working for an antifederal majority that would summon a second convention. Madison welcomed the genuine demand for libertarian amendments, which came from friends of the Constitution. "My own opinion," he wrote to Randolph in October 1788, "has always been in favor of a bill of rights; provided it be so framed as not to imply powers not meant to be included in the enumeration." At the same time he had never thought the omission a material defect and was anxious to supply it only to satisfy the anxiety of others. Some who raised the issue, he suspected, had the insidious hope of subverting the plan of government altogether because of their hostility to the articles relating to treaties, to paper money, and to contracts. These "created more enemies than all the errors in the system positive and negative put together."

Patrick Henry cherished a second hope—to get revenge for his defeat in convention by keeping Madison out of the new Congress. Two senators were to be elected by the Virginia legislature, and in that body Henry put forward Richard Henry Lee and William Grayson. The latter, trailing Lee by twelve votes, received nine more than Madison, who was placed in nomination without his consent after he wrote to friends that he preferred the House of Representatives.

George Turberville implored Madison to come home before the congressional elections in February. "Your very presence," he wrote, "would shrink into nonentity almost those aspiring assassins who, triumphing in their calumnies of absent characters, have belittled themselves even in the estimation of their adherents." More specific was Henry Lee's account to Madison of the assault on him in the debate on the senatorship: "Mr. Henry on the floor exclaimed against your political character, and pronounced you unworthy of the confidence of the people in the station of senator. That your election would terminate in producing rivulets of blood throughout the land."

To keep Madison out of the House of Representatives, wrote Turberville, Henry fashioned a congressional district of eight counties (twelve on the modern map), linking Orange with the most antifederal counties that could be tied together. The district was tailored to include the home county of James Monroe, Henry's candidate. To frustrate a quickly developing move to elect Madison from a tidewater district, a law was passed confining the choice in each district to residents of it.

The main accusation against Madison was the false one that he opposed all amendments to the Constitution. To "remove the slanderous imputation" (wrote Richard Bland Lee) a pamphlet had been printed quoting from Madison's letters. Madison insisted on deletion of them: publication would look like electioneering. However, heeding Lee's appeal, he returned to Virginia.

Reaching Alexandria by stage, Madison found himself invited to spend a week with Washington at Mt. Vernon. The general in his diary recorded only the dates of arrival and departure, but their subsequent correspondence revealed that they discussed the powers and duties of the President under the new Constitution.

At home Madison learned that the campaign against him was in full swing. Monroe was writing letters at a prodigious rate. This worried him less than the news he received from his Baptist supporter, the Reverend George Eve. Patrick Henry was circulating the story through that sect that Madison not only opposed all amendments but had "ceased to be a friend to the rights of conscience." The upshot was that when Henryites Early and Banks invaded the Saturday evening Baptist church service, on January 17, primed to convert it into an anti-Madison political rally, Preacher Eve turned the tables with a written message from the candidate:

It is my sincere opinion that the Constitution ought to be
revised, and that the first Congress meeting under it ought to
prepare and recommend to the states for ratification the most
satisfactory provisions for all essential rights, particularly the
rights of conscience in the fullest latitude, the freedom of the
press, trials by jury, security against general warrants etc.

Eve's sermon eulogized Madison for the act establishing religious
liberty and for defeating the bill for a general assessment. Next day, dur-
ing the baptisms at the Rapidan River, all the talk indicated that "Mr.
Eve has given a great wound to Mr. Early's cause." Fourteen years later
Joel Early wrote to Madison about "the monstrous mistake under which
I then lay as to the tendency of your policies."

Huge Culpeper County (split today into three counties) seemed likely
to decide the battle between Madison and Monroe, and both spoke there
on "court day," January 19. The rivals were personal friends and had
an identical thought. Why not travel together for company and to fight
the bitter cold? For two weeks they went from county to county, one
supporting the Constitution, the other condemning it. Although Monroe's
supporters were vilifying Madison, the latter wrote at the journey's end
that the exclusion of personal issues "saved our friendship from the
smallest diminution." The critical meeting was at the Hebron German
Lutheran Church, whose parishioners, habitual bloc-voters, were expected to swing Culpeper County.

Madison described that meeting years later. After church services the
crowd assembled outside in the snow. Two fiddlers enlivened the gathering, which then listened patiently to the constitutional debate as if they
were spectators at "a sort of fight." After that, Madison "had to ride in
the night twelve miles to quarter," and got a frostbite that left a lifelong
scar on the left side of his nose.

The Hebron meeting paid off. Madison carried crucial Culpeper 256
to 103, and his own county 216 to 9. Monroe won his own county,
Spottsylvania, by only 74 votes, but the antifederal avalanche in big
Amherst pulled Madison's overall majority down to 336.

The victor set out at once for New York, slowed down by snow, floods,
and bad roads, and stopped once more at Mt. Vernon. There he returned a "peculiarly confidential" letter from Washington and its
equally private enclosure. Neither man left any hint of its contents, but
in a postscript to one of his letters the general said he had "not the
smallest objection to your conversing freely with colonel H—— on all

matters respecting this business." Who was Colonel H———? There have been various speculations on that, but a letter written by the general's nephew, Supreme Court Justice Bushrod Washington, identifies him as Colonel David Humphrey, former military aide and member of the Washington household. The document was the 65-page draft on an unused inaugural address. Madison's advice can easily be guessed: the proposed speech went too deeply into Washington's personal feelings and too extensively into presidential policy to be appropriate.

Madison left Mount Vernon in company with representative-elect John Page, two days before Congress was due to convene. The House did not achieve a quorum until April 1, the Senate not till the sixth, on which day the votes of the presidential electors were counted. The sixty-nine electors (Rhode Island, North Carolina, and New York had chosen none) cast sixty-nine votes for George Washington, thirty-four for John Adams, and thirty-five scattering. The two were proclaimed President and Vice President of the United States.

Madison opened the legislative business on April 8 with a call to levy import duties and regulate commerce, thus reviving "those principles of honor and honesty that have too long lain dormant." He then offered a resolve for specific duties on rum, liquors, wine, molasses, sugar, tea, cocoa, and coffee, plus an ad valorem duty on all other imports. Connected with this was a tonnage tax at three rising levels—on American vessels, on those of nations in treaty with the United States, and on the vessels of other powers.

Thomas Fitzsimons of Pennsylvania moved to expand the specific duties to "protect our infant industries." Southerners protested that the tonnage rates (by excluding British vessels) would create a New England shipping monopoly. Madison approved the protective system and defended New England shipping: its development would protect the thinly populated South. He proclaimed himself "the friend to a very free system of commerce," and wanted a free interchange between arts and agriculture, between city and country, between nation and nation. But under existing circumstances there were exceptions to free trade, some of which he would list: To prevent the driving of American ships off the ocean, discrimination in foreign ports must be met by counterdiscrimination. Duties were needed to develop domestic production of the raw materials of manufacture, to discourage luxury spending, to develop the means of national defense, for wartime embargoes, and finally, duties for revenue.

Madison added the Fitzsimons list to his own and suggested an eight-cent tax on molasses—low enough to permit American manufacture of rum, yet impose a moderate excise on the domestic product. The eloquent Fisher Ames, speaking for New England distillers, shrieked with anguish. Congress had not assembled "as at church or school, to listen to the harangues of speculative piety." Fish was sold to buy molasses. The tax would ruin both industries and reduce innocent children to starvation.

Virginia, replied Madison, imported three times as much as Massachusetts, and would pay three times as much in duties. The South imported many things for the poor. "Might not Southern children, for want of clothes, be taught to breathe this same vindictive spirit?" Were the Northern people the chosen few? No, the general government "was instituted for the protection of all," but it could accomplish this end only "by acts of justice and impartiality."

The duty on molasses was finally fixed at five cents. Ames, after this first encounter with Madison, described him to a Boston friend as "a man of sense, reading, address and integrity," very pro-French and decidedly a Virginian in his politics. Said Ames:

> He speaks low, his person is little and ordinary. He speaks decently, as to manner, and no more. His language is very pure, perspicuous and to the point. Pardon me if I add that I think him a little too much of a book politician, and too timid in his politics, for prudence and caution are opposites of timidity. . . . He is our first man.

When Jonathan Parker moved to lay the heaviest permissible tax on imported slaves—$10 a head—the cry came from the deep South that Virginia was working to build a market for surplus blacks. Madison came to his colleague's support, and both of them struck at slavery itself. Parker quoted the Declaration that all men are created equal. Madison said the tax would give expression to its intended moral purpose: "It is to be hoped that by expressing a national disapprobation of this trade we may destroy it, and save ourselves from reproaches, and our posterity the imbecility ever attendant on a country filled with slaves." The weakening effect of slavery, Madison declared, made it a matter of national concern; however, to avoid protracted delay of the revenue bill he persuaded Parker to shift from an amendment to a separate bill.

On tonnage taxes, Madison easily secured his primary levy on American vessels. It was needed, he said, for support of lighthouses, hospitals for disabled seamen (creeping socialism!), and other establishments incidental to commerce. Far more difficulty attended the motion for discriminating duties designed to counter Great Britain's exclusion of American vessels from the West Indies and limitation of them to American produce in voyages to England. He desired, he said, a system adequate "to form a school for seamen, to lay the foundation of a navy, and to be able to support itself against the interference of foreigners." What but maritime strength could defend coastal cities or repel an invading enemy?

In taking this stand Madison opposed Virginia's commercial interest and showed not a trace of the timidity Fisher Ames thought he saw in him. Confine West Indian exports to American bottoms, he said, and we should soon hear a different language from Great Britain, whose dominions were dependent on American resources. On three successive voting tests, Madison built the counterdiscrimination majority from nine to nearly forty; but in the Senate, Lee and Grayson of Virginia took the other side and the punitive tonnage tax was rejected. For Madison, this merely threw the issue into the future.

April 23 was a gala day in New York City. Thirteen pilots in white uniforms rowed a specially built barge from Elizabeth City to the Battery, with President-Elect George Washington under the flag in the stern. Behind, trailed a mile-long line of rowboats and sailing craft. Inauguration was postponed seven days, to complete the revamping of the old City Hall. The inaugural address, brief and modest, praised the talents, rectitude, and patriotism of the legislators who would devise and adopt the measures of government. The President invited constitutional amendments to fortify the rights of freedom and to promote public harmony.

The House and Senate, imitating British custom, made written replies to the "address from the throne." This required another response from the President. On May 5 Washington thanked Madison for the "good work" he had done in writing the inaugural address and asked him to complete the work he had begun. Since Madison also wrote the reply of the House, the whole sequence came from his pen—the inaugural, the reply, the response to the reply, the whole striking a note of democratic simplicity and cordial relations in the inception of government.

Not so simple, not so cordial, and decidedly less democratic were the senatorial proceedings sponsored by Vice President John Adams. At his instigation the Senate ordered its members of the joint inaugural committee to report formal titles for the President and Vice President. Madison induced that committee to return contrary advice, which the House accepted. Then, without waiting for Senate action, Madison set the style in drafting the House reply to Washington's inaugural address. He directed it simply "To the President of the United States."

The Senate, infuriated, rejected the committee report and asked for a conference. Madison soothed hotheads who wanted to refuse a meeting. He advised the House "to proceed with due respect to the Senate, and give dignity and weight to our own opinion . . . by the deliberate and decent manner in which we decide." He did not conceive titles to be "pregnant with danger." The President's powers would not be increased an iota "if you were to load him with all the titles of Europe or Asia." Elaborate titles conflicted with the nature of our government and the genius of the people, diminishing instead of increasing the true dignity of a Republic and of the chief magistrate himself.

Madison headed the House conferees; Richard Henry Lee, those of the Senate. They deadlocked and made separate reports, the senators proposing this grandiloquent monicker: "His Highness the President of the United States and Protector of their Liberties." Vice President Adams orated for forty minutes. Call George Washington merely President, he declared, and the common people of foreign lands "will despise him to all eternity." As Madison described the secret debate to Jefferson: "Adams espoused the cause of titles with great eagerness. His friend R. H. Lee, although elected as a republican enemy to an aristocratic Constitution, was a most zealous second. . . . Had the project succeeded it would have subjected the President to a severe dilemma and given a deep wound to our infant government."

With the House standing firm, the Senate rejected the Adams-Lee mouthful and voted to follow the practice adopted by the other branch. The decision followed a spreading whisper that the Vice President was picking a title for himself as Washington's successor.

On May 19 Madison moved the creation of a Department of Foreign Affairs, a Treasury Department, and a War Department. Each would be headed by a secretary appointed by the President, with the advice and consent of the Senate, and removable by the President. The debate lasted more than a month, turning on the contention of Theodorick Bland of Virginia, supported by many others, that because the consent of the Senate was constitutionally necessary to appoint, it was necessary also to remove. That plausible conclusion, Madison asserted, violated a principle of responsibility that pervaded the whole system. If the President had full power to remove executive heads, those appointees were completely responsible to him, and he was completely responsible for their behavior; but if a secretary could not be removed without the consent of the Senate, presidential responsibility was destroyed without even the shadow of a substitute.

Smith of South Carolina came back with a quotation from *The Federalist* No. 77, a work which he understood "to be the production of two gentlemen of great information." It asserted flatly that the Senate's consent "would be necessary to displace as well as to appoint." Instead of throwing responsibility for this on Hamilton, Madison intimated that it resulted from failure of the authors to consider the basic division and separation of powers. The executive power was placed in the President, and the only possible exceptions were those made in the Constitution itself. An exception was made in appointments, but none in removals. As the removal power was executive, it lay beyond the reach of Congress. Furthermore, the Constitution made it the duty of the President to see that the laws were faithfully executed. He could not do so without the power to remove faithless officers.

Replying to a suggestion that the whole issue be left to the courts, Madison acknowledged that in the ordinary course of government, "the exposition of the laws and Constitution devolves upon the judiciary," but if the constitutional boundary of the several departments was brought into question, "I do not see that any one of those independent departments has more right than another to declare their sentiments on that point." Madison's crucial words were "*declare their sentiments.*" He was not denying the superior right of the judiciary to make binding determinations of constitutionality in deciding cases. Madison, Ames, Benson, Vining, and Boudinot produced a 34-to-20 majority sustaining the President's removal power as implicit in the Constitution.

Madison's primacy in Congress, during these opening months, was attested in a long discussion of his merits and demerits carried on between Fisher Ames and George Minot of Massachusetts. During their disagreement over discrimination against British shipping, Ames called Madison cool and reflective, deducing consequences from principles with clearness and simplicity, yet at times running into declamation: "I think him a good man and an able man, but he has rather too much theory, and wants that discretion which men of business commonly have. He is also very timid and seems evident to want manly firmness and energy of character."

Minot rebuked young Ames for letting differences of opinion carry him into contemptuous expressions. Ames admitted overstatement and went on: "But did I express any contempt for Madison? Upon my word I do not recollect a word of it, and there is not in my heart a symptom of its ever having been there. . . . But I see in Madison, with his great knowledge and merit, so much error, and some of it so very unaccountable and tending to so much mischief, that my impatience may have tinctured my letter with more gall than I remember."

He still thought Madison probably deficient in that vigor of character which made Charles James Fox risk bold measures, but he was admirable for "a sound judgment, which perceives truth with great clearness and can trace it through mazes of debate without losing it." As a reasoner he was remarkably perspicuous—"a studious man, devoted to public business, and a thorough master of almost every public question that can arise. . . . Upon the whole, he is a useful, respectable, worthy man, in a degree so eminent that his character will not sink. He will continue to be a very influential man in our country."

Coming from Madison's principal antagonist in the First Congress, that left no doubt about his position in the country's new legislative body. The fact that such a discussion could be held was a testimonial to his leadership.

25 / THE BILL OF RIGHTS

On June 8, 1789, James Madison moved that the House go into Committee of the Whole to receive some constitutional amendments which he hoped would be unanimously approved. Hours of debate followed—some members calling for reference to a select committee, others urging delay; some opposing all amendments, others concealing a desire for drastic alterations in the Constitution. Shifting ground, Madison moved for a select committee. Former advocates of it switched to Committee of the Whole. Madison then stymied the opposition by simply moving the adoption of his resolutions. Both sides joined in sending them to Committee of the Whole. The situation was not really bad. Dullards on civil rights had temporarily united with intriguers for a second constitutional convention.

In framing his amendments Madison winnowed the sheaves of proposals from eight ratifying conventions. He searched state bills of rights. If five states favored a proposition approved by him, well and good. If he disliked a proposition similarly favored, it stayed out.

Virtually the full provisions of the first ten amendments, as they went into the Constitution, were embodied in his propositions. Nearly all had their counterparts in the twenty libertarian proposals drafted by George Mason for submission to Congress by the Virginia Convention of 1788. He led off with three nonessential assertions, drawn from the Virginia Declaration of Rights, concerning the popular basis of free government and the right of the people to alter it. These were ultimately dropped with no loss.

From the twenty substantive amendments, nearly all restricting federal power, that came from Patrick Henry, Madison picked two innocuous provisions relating to the apportionment and pay of Congress. Both were submitted to the states but not ratified. "Two or three contentious additions" from the Virginia list, he wrote, "would prostrate the whole project."

The heart of the Madison proposals was a ten-clause resolution covering freedom of religion, speech, press, and assembly; the right to bear arms; freedom from peacetime quartering of soldiers; immunity from double jeopardy, compulsory self-incrimination, or loss of life, liberty, or property without due process of law; security from general warrants, unreasonable search and seizure, excessive bail or fines, or cruel and unusual punishments; the right to a speedy and public trial, with assistance of counsel and other safeguards. The same resolution covered what became the Ninth Amendment preserving unenumerated rights retained by the people.

These guarantees were to protect the people against violations of their rights by Congress. Another resolution was to protect their most essential rights against violation by the states: "No State shall violate the equal rights of conscience, or the freedom of the press, or the trial by jury in criminal cases."

Subsequent sections required grand-jury action in criminal cases, guaranteed trial of crimes by an impartial jury of the vicinage, and provided for jury trials in private suits at common law with a bottom money limit on the right of appeal. Two declaratory provisions completed the sheaf. One on separation of departmental powers was dropped. The last declared that the powers not delegated by the Constitution, nor prohibited to the states, "are reserved to the States respectively."

Madison began his supporting speech with a mild affirmation of necessity. Recognizing that many "champions for republican liberty" thought a bill of rights unnecessary, some even calling it dangerous, he said that he himself "always conceived that in a certain form, and to a certain extent, such a provision was neither improper nor altogether useless." The British Bill of Rights furnished no example for America. It merely restrained the Crown, but left the power of the Legislature indefinite. "The freedom of the press and rights of conscience, these choicest privileges of the people, are unguarded in the British Constitution." In our government, where the executive was the weaker branch, the restraints must be leveled against the legislative branch, most powerful and least controlled, therefore most liable to abuse its power. Yet he conceived that in the United States the greatest danger to liberty lay "in the body of the people, operating by the majority against the minority," and against them the prescriptions of liberty ought to be leveled.

One by one, Madison answered the objections to a bill of rights. It was said that federal powers were enumerated, and Congress was given no control over civil liberties. True, but they might be invaded through the sweeping power to carry the delegated powers into effect. Congress was given no power to issue general warrants. Without a specific prohibition, might it not be contended that those were a necessary means of enforcing the collection of revenue?

Some, he said, argued that state bills of rights continued in force and were adequate to all purposes. They did indeed remain, but some states had none, others had very defective ones, "and there are others whose bills of rights are not only defective, but absolutely improper." Instead of securing some of these rights "in the full extent which republican principles would require, they limit them too much to agree with the common ideas of liberty." What Madison had in mind, presumably, was the acceptance by some states of Blackstone's narrow definition of freedom of the press as mere freedom from prior restraint, leaving people subject to prosecution for criminal libel.

It was said also that a federal bill of rights was unnecessary because those of the states were ineffectual. True, Madison agreed, there were few states in which the most valuable rights had not been violated, but it did not follow that the prohibitions had been without salutary effect. Under the new federal government there would be new force to such guarantees: "If they are incorporated into the Constitution, independent tribunals of justice will consider themselves in a peculiar manner the guardian of those rights; they [the courts] will be an impenetrable bulwark against every assumption of power in the Legislative or Executive; they will be naturally led to resist every encroachment upon rights expressly stipulated for in the Constitution by the declaration of rights."

Besides this, said Madison, "the State Legislatures will jealously and closely watch the operations of this Government, and be able to resist with more effect every assumption of power, than any other power on earth can do; and the greatest opponents to a Federal government admit the State Legislatures to be sure guardians of the people's liberties."

The thought of protecting liberty against federal invasion, through "the jealousy of the subordinate governments," had been suggested by Madison to Jefferson in 1788. Jefferson, agreeing, added that the federal courts would check unconstitutional laws. Madison combined the two propositions in a prediction that showed no signs of fulfillment within his lifetime. It was not until the middle of the twentieth century that the "independent tribunals of justice" showed signs of becoming a real bulwark against federal assumptions of oppressive power.

The Constitution, Madison observed, had wisely provided that "no State shall pass any bill of attainder, *ex post facto* law, etc." There was more danger of those powers being abused by the State Governments than by the Government of the United States. The same could be said of other powers, if not controlled "by the general principle, that laws are unconstitutional which infringe the rights of the community." He would add, therefore, "that no State shall violate the equal right of conscience, freedom of the press, or trial by jury in criminal cases." He wished for these prohibitions "because it is proper that every Government should be disarmed of powers which trench upon those particular rights."

Six weeks passed before Madison obtained halfway action: reference to a committee of one from each state. Elected by ballot, the committee was headed by Vining of Delaware, with Madison in second place, and the amendments were perfected within a week. Controversy centered on the religious article, wherein Madison had undertaken to obtain a national prohibition of religious establishments. The clause he originally laid before Congress had this wording: "The civil rights of none shall be abridged on account of religious belief or worship, nor shall any national religion be established, nor shall the full and equal rights of conscience be in any manner, or on any pretext, abridged." The committee preserved the force of this in shortening it to: "No religion shall be established by law, nor shall the equal rights of conscience be infringed."

Asked whether this did not tend to abolish religion altogether, Madison said he understood it to mean "that Congress should not establish a religion, and enforce the legal observation of it by law, nor compel men to worship God in any manner contrary to their conscience." From Connecticut, where the Congregational religion was established, came the fear that this would impede suits to collect moneys pledged to religious societies. To offset that, Madison moved to restore the word "national." That would point the amendment directly toward its object—to relieve the fear that one sect, or two in combination, might gain preeminence and establish a religion "to which they would compel others to conform."

He withdrew his motion when the protest was made that the word "national" was a bugbear to Antifederalists, who visualized consolidation of the states. Madison's choice of language, however, was significant. His apprehension that "two sects [would] combine together and establish a religion" harked back to the effort of Anglican and Presbyterian clergy to obtain, in Virginia, a general assessment in support of religion.

The House switched to a New Hampshire wording: "Congress shall make no laws touching religion, or infringing the rights of conscience." This ambiguous clause gave way to a substitute moved by Ames: "Congress shall make no law establishing religion, or prevent the free exercise thereof, or to infringe the rights of conscience." This undoubtedly came from Madison. It blended his original proposal and words he had used in support of it. Ames had just written, privately, that the religious guarantee was a "prodigious great dose" of useless medicine; but he was willing to accept a phrasing that did not curb the states. Unopposed by the now neutral Congregational establishment, Madison gained his objective—an amendment protecting the rights of conscience and barring any form of federal support of religion.

In the Senate, Anglican devotee Richard Henry Lee teamed up with New England churchmen in cutting the religious guarantee to pieces. Under the wording substituted there, Congress could "make no law establishing articles of faith or a mode of worship or prohibiting the free exercise of religion." That opened the way to financial support of churches and church schools. Madison was chairman of the House conferees. Supported by Vining and Sherman, who had been inactive in debate, he won a complete victory over the Senate and brought back the wording that went into the Constitution: "Congress shall make no law respecting an establishment of religion or prohibiting the free exercise thereof."

The history of the religious guarantee, as well as its wording, mark Madison as its author. Throughout his life he interpreted it as a total ban on any form of federal support of religion. In 1811, as President, he vetoed a grant of five acres of public land to a Baptist church on the ground that it "comprises a principle and precedent for the appropriation of funds of the United States for the use and support of religious societies, contrary to the article of the Constitution which declares that 'Congress shall make no law respecting a religious establishment.' " In his "Essay on Monopolies," written late in life, he declared that the appointment of congressional chaplains violated this principle because these were "to be paid out of the national taxes," and small and unpopular sects were excluded.

The grand committee of the House added freedom of speech to Madison's resolution, forbidding the states to violate the rights of conscience, freedom of the press, or trial by jury in criminal cases. Arguing for approval, he called this the most important amendment in the whole list. The House gave it the required two-thirds majority but it was killed in the conservative Senate—and came to life in the Fourteenth Amendment.

As the House moved toward the end of Madison's list, St. George Tucker of South Carolina attempted to insert the word "expressly" in what became the Tenth Amendment, thus stripping away the implied powers of Congress. Madison took the floor against the motion: "It was impossible to confine a government to the exercise of express powers; there must necessarily be admitted powers by implication, unless the Constitution descended to recount every minutia. He remembered the word 'expressly' had been moved in the convention of Virginia, by the opponents to the ratification, and, after full and fair discussion, was given up by them, and the system allowed to retain its present form."

The vote went two to one against Tucker, and by a narrower margin the House defeated Thomas Burke's attempt to eliminate federal control over the times, places, and manner of electing representatives. To weaken those provisions, Madison asserted, would undermine the principles and efficacy of the Constitution. At the last moment Roger Sherman insisted that the amendments be added to the Constitution instead of incorporated in its body, as Madison desired. The author of the amendments gave up on that, thereby (though he did not realize it) adding dignity and force to the collective mandates. Two trivial amendments failed of ratification. The remaining ten sailed through eight legislatures—one less than needed —but struck a snag in the Virginia Senate after passing the House of Delegates almost unanimously. Hardin Burnley, Orange County legislator, explained the hostile maneuver to Madison. Eight of the fifteen senators rejected the four most popular amendments, hoping to throw the whole issue back into Congress and revoke the power of direct taxation. The eight then issued a proclamation declaring that they defeated the amendment on religious freedom because it did not forbid Congress to "levy taxes to any amount for the support of religion or its teachers." The eight who took this stand included every recorded advocate of an established church. The seven who voted to ratify included three outstanding champions of religious liberty and no opponents of it. A Baptist leader sent word to Madison "that the amendments had entirely satisfied the disaffected of his sect." The senatorial dissenters met disaster in the next election, and the amendments were ratified in December 1791.

Of the ten amendments thus adopted, not one was reduced in force from the form in which Madison introduced them. Not a single vital proposal was rejected by Congress or failed of ratification, except for the United States Senate's defeat of curbs upon the states; and that policy triumphed after the Civil War.

Following his success with the amendments, Madison united with Ames, Smith, Benson, and Sherman—a disparate group—in defense of a comprehensive federal judiciary. Considering a court bill passed by the Senate, State-righters Aedenus Burke and Thomas Sumter of South Carolina attempted to knock out all inferior federal courts except of admiralty, imposing their duties on state judges. Follow that course, said Madison, and state judges would assume federal office through *description* instead of by presidential appointment in manifest violation of the Constitution. Many state courts could not be trusted with the execution of federal laws.

The argument brought a despairing wail from Burke. No matter which way he turned, the Constitution stared him in the face. So did a thirty-one-to-eleven defeat, but not a single state-righter objected to Section 25 of the Senate bill, spelling out the Supreme Court's power to reverse decisions of state courts—a power which most of the South ultimately denounced as unconstitutional.

Regional alignments developed swiftly when the House took up the subject of a permanent national capital. Madison, at work since 1783 for a location on the Potomac, foresaw an attempt by Pennsylvania, New York, and New England to place the permanent capital on the Susquehanna; New York being given the temporary site as bait. His forecast was soon verified by motions to those ends.

Madison countered, through Richard Bland Lee, with resolutions perfectly describing but not naming the Potomac. The seat of government should be "as nearly central as a convenient water communication with the Atlantic ocean, and an easy access to the western territory will permit." Those resolutions, cried an opponent, formed a bandage over his eyes, leading him toward an unseen object. "They appear to me," rejoined Madison, "to contain those luminous truths which ought to guide him through his embarrassment." The House defeated the Madison-Lee motion two to one. (Wonderful bass and pickerel fishing on the Susquehanna, congressmen were told.)

Madison, no fisherman, picked on Scott's admission of a deal outside the House. More than half of the United States and nearly half of its inhabitants had been disposed of without their consent or knowledge. Had such developments been foreseen at the time the Constitution was ratified, he firmly believed that "Virginia might not have been a part of the Union at this moment." Publication of this remark produced a sensation, but Madison assured alarmed correspondents that there was no new schism in Virginia. He merely meant that a controversy over the capital might have turned half a dozen crucial votes against the Constitution.

Wadsworth of New York, angered by Madison's charge of a secret deal, declared that New England members refused all overtures "till they were assured there was a bargaining set on foot to carry them to the Potomac." Madison retorted that he wished all the facts were put on paper. The Southern gentlemen acted only to block a sudden and improper decision.

This was a veiled reference to the commotion that occurred when Madison nonchalantly strolled into a house where King and Goodhue were negotiating a deal with the Pennsylvania delegation. Nobody, wrote Senator Maclay, knew whether he introduced himself or was brought in to disrupt the meeting. There, however, he was, and occupied a room downstairs, while exchanging messages with Pennsylvanians upstairs. "The result was that Messrs. Clymer, Fitzsimons, Heister, Scott and the Speaker [Muhlenberg] declared totally against any treaty with the New England men."

What happened, Madison reported to Pendleton, was that the Pennsylvanians, "full of distrust and animosity" against the more northerly states, offered to support the Potomac site in exchange for a temporary shift of government to Philadelphia. Flattering progress was made on this ground, but a day or two later the Pennsylvania-New England coalition was re-established. Key man in the upset was Senator Morris, who switched the permanent site to Germantown and won Senator King's support with a signed pledge by himself and six Pennsylvania representatives that they would work to keep Congress in New York until 1793.

The House accepted Germantown on the day before final adjournment. Affecting to surrender, Madison put through a little amendment, merely providing that Pennsylvania laws should continue in force in the ceded territory until Congress decided otherwise. The bill went back to the Senate and died there. This turn of events was not precisely coincidental. Maclay recorded the remark of Senator Izard of South Carolina that "a trifling amendment will be made in the lower House, just enough to bring it up here, and we will throw it out." They did so, and on that note Congress adjourned until January 4, 1790.

In Philadelphia Madison encountered Senator Morris, who told him that after the recess he would speak seriously to Southern members about a revival of the Potomac project. "I told him," Madison wrote to Washington, "they must be spoken to very seriously after what had passed, if Pennsylvania expected them to listen to her."

During Washington's first five months in office, while government departments were being created, the President treated Madison almost as a one-man cabinet in the matter of advice on filling it. Madison himself, a "natural" for Secretary of State, was excluded by a prohibition he himself had planted in the Constitution: excluding members of Congress, during the time for which they had been elected, from offices created in that period.

On May 27 Madison wrote to Jefferson in Paris that John Jay would be continued in foreign affairs if he desired the place, and the Treasury would go to either Hamilton or Jay. Hamilton "would be preferred by those who know him personally." The President had asked him whether any appointment at home would be agreeable to Jefferson. "Being unacquainted with your mind I have not ventured on an answer." Jefferson, about to come home on leave, had no need to reply.

Jay, it developed, wanted to be Chief Justice. Would it be safe, Washington asked Madison, to nominate Jefferson for Secretary of State without his consent? And what about Edmund Randolph for Attorney-General? Washington already had sounded Randolph indirectly, but his reply came to Madison. He would really like to *refuse* a federal office, thus showing disparagers that he could have one, but his wife was in bad health, debts were piling up, and a federal salary would helpfully supplement his law practice. "I commit myself to you," he concluded.

Six weeks later, after nominating Hamilton for the Treasury, Washington informed him "that it is my *present* intention to nominate Mr. Jefferson for Secretary of State and Mr. Randolph as Attorney General; though their acceptance is problematical." The surprising fact is that Hamilton knew nothing of this in advance.

The decision to appoint Randolph followed an evening conference with Madison, on a grist of judicial appointments and other matters. "I am very troublesome," wrote Washington next day, "but you must excuse me. Ascribe it to friendship and confidence and you will do justice to my motives." The President's reliance on Madison became so well known that the latter was deluged with appeals for aid in obtaining public office. Senator Maclay believed him guilty of paying "court to the President, whom, I am told, he already affects to govern."

Maclay had in mind the conflict over the appointive power. This was followed by a direct confrontation between President and Senate on the subject of "advice and consent" to nominations for office. The specific complaint was that President Washington had sought the advice of members of the House (i.e. Madison), concerning appointments, instead of consulting the Senate, which had the constitutional duty of giving advice. The Senate, to show its irritation, arbitrarily rejected a minor nomination. The President stingingly defended the defeated nominee, whereupon the Senate appointed a committee to confer with the President on the mode of receiving communications about appointments and treaties. Washington told the committee—Izard, King, and Charles Carroll— that he did not consult senators because they could give their advice and consent afterwards. Maclay wrote in his diary: "Mr. Izard was clearly of opinion that all the late measures flowed from the President. Mr. Madison, in his opinion, was deep in this business."

Indeed he was. The morning after this conference, the President asked Madison to call that afternoon—Sunday, August 9. On Monday, Washington furnished the Senate committee with a detailed analysis of the constitutional relations between President and Senate. Every sentence was stamped with Madison's thought and style. The Senate, in its duty to advise and consent, served as a council to the President. Consequently the time, place, and manner of consultation rested with the Executive. The Senate formally acquiesced, but when the President came before that body the next day to discuss an Indian treaty, the icy reception he received produced an equally icy decision: never again would he hold a personal consultation on that senatorial function, nor has any President ever done so since. The presidential honeymoon was over—the first and last honeymoon ever wrecked by jealousy of James Madison.

Madison and Hamilton had worked closely together in the Continental Congress, and both of them expected that relationship to continue under the new government. "When I accepted the office I now hold," wrote Hamilton to Edward Carrington in 1792, "it was under a full persuasion that from similarity of thinking, conspiring with personal good-will, I should have the firm support of Mr. Madison in the general course of my administration. Aware of the intrinsic difficulties of the situation, and of the powers of Mr. Madison, I do not believe I should have accepted under a different supposition."

That conclusion may be doubted, but the expectation of cordial relations was plainly evident in Hamilton's request to Madison, a month after his appointment, "to put on paper and send me your thoughts on . . . an addition to our revenue, and also as to any modifications of the public debt" which could be made consistent with good faith. Madison's reply voiced the general expectation that the foreign debt would be placed on a sound basis, and suggested that the domestic debt be reduced by western land sales, thus soothing those who were hostile to payment of it. The debt, he said, ought to be extinguished. He closed with affectionate regards—the last time they ever were exchanged between them.

Hamilton's 1789 Report on Public Credit disclosed a national debt of $54,124,464.56, of which $11.7 million was owed in Europe. The $42 million domestic debt, including overdue interest of $13 million, consisted chiefly of six per cent certificates to settle veterans' pay and war contractors' claims against the government. Calling on Congress to fund these debts, Hamilton said the soaring prices of public securities testified to confidence that this would be done, and funding them would win the confidence of these people, cement the union of the states, and make public securities a virtual part of the national money system, promoting prosperity.

Madison looked at the same set of figures through different glasses. The public debt was to be perpetuated, not paid off. The soaring prices represented the avidity of speculators, who had rushed to buy securities for a few shillings in the pound, and whose emissaries were still exploring "distant parts of the Union in order to take advantage of the ignorance of holders." These speculators were the people who were to cement the Union. Madison, even more than Hamilton, believed the debt ought to be funded at full value, but he wanted partial reimbursement of original holders, while still paying the speculators more than they paid for the securities they had bought up.

Hamilton in his report quoted what Madison had written in his 1783 "Address to the States," before the speculative orgy began—that there should be no discrimination between original holders and later purchasers. He also proposed, as Madison had done in 1783, that the United States assume the war debts of the several states. Here Madison saw a new situation. A number of the states, notably including Virginia, had paid off millions of dollars of these debts. Assumption in gross, without credits for such payments, would make these states pay twice.

Madison took no part in the tumultuous early debate, during which reports spread that members of Congress were deeply involved in the speculation. Wadsworth of Connecticut and Smith of South Carolina were said to have sent off money-laden ships. An arriving senator from North Carolina passed two expresses heading south with great loads of money. The speculation centered, it was rumored, in William Duer, Hamilton's Assistant Secretary of the Treasury.

The rumors told only the smallest fraction of the truth. Duer and William Constable (partner of Senator Morris) were in partnership and working separately. Duer borrowed money from everybody he could reach, pyramiding his speculative purchases. Constable, as revealed by his books in the New York Public Library, raised $5,156,479.32 from Dutch and Flemish bankers for the purchase of American securities.

As knowledge of the speculation spread, congressional radicals turned against payment of the debt. Scott of Pennsylvania and Livermore of New Hampshire moved a new devaluation. The securities, they alleged, were not an obligation of the new government. This brought Madison into the debate. The debt, he declared, had been contracted by the United States in a national capacity. The change of government had enlarged the capacity to pay, and had not diminished the obligation to do so. The amount of the debt was the amount the United States received and had promised to pay. No logic, no magic, could diminish it. The only thing to decide was, "to whom the payment is really due." Three classes deserved consideration: (1) Original creditors who still held their securities; (2) Original creditors who had alienated them; (3) Present holders of alienated securities.

The first group, said Madison, was entitled to full payment. The second and third had rival pretensions. The second group—mostly impoverished veterans of the Revolution—had a claim in which humanity reinforced justice. They had been forced to receive the securities; poverty forced them to sell. Under the plan before the House, those who had lost seven-eighths of their due were being required to contribute to those who made a sevenfold gain.

The third group—holders by assignment—Madison continued, had a valid claim upon the public faith. To reject their fair claims would be fatal to public credit; but to load the entire loss on the other group was an idea at which human nature recoiled. The only expedient was a liberal composition. Let the present holders "have the highest price which has prevailed in the market; and let the residue belong to the original sufferers," who were identifiable in the government records. Some might say that this would injure public credit. That would be prevented by the honesty of the policy, which would not save the government a farthing— also by full provision for the foreign debt and punctuality in future domestic payments.

Madison moved an amendment, in line with his policy, and the vials of wrath were poured on his head by Boudinot, Sedgwick, Ames, Smith, and Laurance. "Do not rob on the highway to exercise charity," cried the eloquent Ames. The proposed measure would destroy the property and faith of foreign investors; violate the sacred rights of property; and produce confusion, corruption, and expense in a fruitless effort to distinguish original from later owners. Ames had some hope of converting Madison. "I think so highly of his probity and patriotism," he wrote, "that if he can be made to see that these consequences will follow, or only be apprehended, he will give up his scheme."

Jackson of Georgia; Seney of Maryland; White, Page, and Lee of Virginia supported Madison's position, but he got no help from those who wished to repudiate the debt. "Esau [like the veterans] had sold his birthright for a mess of pottage," said Livermore, "and heaven and earth had confirmed the sale." If the debt had to be paid in full, he cared not who got the money.

When Madison resumed the debate on February 18, the Senate adjourned in the afternoon to listen to him. He refused to admit "that America ought to erect the monuments of her gratitude, not to those who saved her liberties, but to those who had enriched themselves in her funds." These securities, he asserted, were forced on the veterans at a time when they were not worth an eighth of their face amount. It was take this or nothing. "The same degree of constraint would vitiate a transaction between man and man before any court of equity on the face of the earth." Opponents had reminded him of his contrary position in 1783. At that period, he replied, the veterans' certificates had not been issued. Transfers of debt were few and involved little loss. Since then, the injustice had become enormous and flagrant, and made redress a great national object.

Altered circumstances, Madison averred, had destroyed the argument of 1783; but if it was to be adhered to, how could anybody justify the Treasury plan? His own proposal was to pay the debt in full. The bill before the House cut interest on part of the debt from six to four per cent and violated the pledge of redemption. If contracts were immutable, all should be enforced. If not, Congress should correct injustice. There were difficulties, but the true ownership of securities could be traced in the records.

Benson of New York asked whether an original creditor who had assigned his certificates could, in conscience, accept a further payment on it. Madison would ask in turn whether a present holder, who got his certificate from a distressed fellow citizen for one-tenth its ultimate value, might not feel some remorse in retaining so unconscionable an advantage. Benson said that involved benevolence, not right.

Senator Maclay, upon his arrival, was told that Madison had been on the floor most of the morning and "had spoken most ably indeed. He seemed rather jaded when I came in." Maclay recorded how Madison met a challenge to show a single instance in history comparable to his proposed action: "He produced an act of Parliament in point in the reign of Queen Anne. But now the gentlemen [Laurance of New York and Fisher Ames] quitted this ground and cried out for rigid right on law principles. Madison modestly put them in mind that they had challenged him on this ground and he had met them agreeably to their wishes."

Expecting Madison's motion to be defeated, Maclay thought up a recipe for turning defeat into victory and retiring the domestic debt in the process. Slash interest on the debt certificates from six to three per cent and make them and nothing else receivable in sales of public lands. His diary told how he would steer Madison into acceptance: "I think I know him. But if he is led . . . he must not see the string." Maclay broached his plan to Scott, a debt repudiator, who said it would carry if Madison supported it; but Scott refused to do the transmitting: "He was afraid of Madison's pride." So Maclay called on Madison, bluntly told him that his plan would fail, and offered his own. The result: "It hurt his *Littleness*. I do not think he believed me. I read the resolutions. I do not think he attended to one word of them, so much did he seem absorbed in his own ideas. I put them into his hand. He offered them back without reading them. . . His pride seems of that kind which repels all communication. . . The obstinacy of this man has ruined the opposition."

Maclay did not recognize the gulf between his partial repudiation of the debt and Madison's attempt at equitable distribution of full payment. Madison's plan was defeated, thirty-six to thirteen, and nine of the thirteen were Virginians. The majority was made up of congressional speculators, cementers of the rich, those who feared injury to public credit, those who thought Madison's motion impracticable, and those won over by Hamilton's scaling down of interest.

Madison wrote to his father that the division he proposed was much better relished in the country at large than in Congress. Probably he read the cry of a veteran in the *Columbian Centinel* of Boston: "Happy there is a Madison who fearless of the blood suckers will step forward and boldly vindicate the rights of the widows and orphans. the original creditors and the war worn soldier." Nor could he have missed the poetic effusion in the *Pennsylvania Gazette* "On the rejection of Mr. Madison's motion":

A soldier's pay are rags and fame,
A wooden leg—a deathless name.
To Specs, both *in* and *out* of Cong,
The four and six per cents belong.

Writing to a critic, Madison said he believed that a large part of the transactions in public securities were vitiated by fraud. Nevertheless, he had carefully refrained from attacking the title of current holders because he did not wish to stir up popular prejudice against the funding of the debt.

This reticence helped build up a misunderstanding of his position. His own and later generations have recognized the sincerity of his motives, but many historians have treated his proposal as a partial repudiation of the national debt, contrasted with a Hamiltonian plan of payment in full. In reality Madison proposed full payment, while the Hamilton plan impaired contracts by cutting interest and deferring part of the obligations until 1800. The impairment failed to damage national credit *because the funding was undertaken by a government with adequate taxing power.* The political weakness of Madison's program lay in the fact that it would hurt the rich (though leaving them with a profit), help the poor, and save nothing to the taxpayer.

The House in the same bill took up assumption of the states' Revolutionary debts. Here the full force of speculative pressure was at work. "Ship-Money Smith," whose buyers were picking up securities from the uninformed Piedmontese, called for quick action. He was fearful that delay would allow state debts to "find their way into the same channel" of speculation that had absorbed the continental debt.

Madison, who had proposed federal assumption in 1783, was repelled now by the speculative orgy and by the relative position of Virginia, Massachusetts, and South Carolina. Each of these three states had owed $5 million in 1783. Since then Virginia had paid off $2 million. The two others had paid nothing but were demanding assumption in full. Madison stayed out of the debate until he heard cloakroom threats from Hamiltonian followers that they would vote against funding the *national* debt unless the state debts were taken over. (Profits from federal speculation had been plowed back into state securities.)

Taking the floor, Madison called it preposterous and improper to demand assumption of state debts as a condition for payment of the older and deeper national obligation. However, justice between state and state required a settlement of accounts on terms fair to all. He therefore moved that states be repaid the amounts actually paid to creditors since the close of the war. Opponents protested that this would add $15 million to the cost. (Too heavy because the states, not the speculators, would get it.) The amendment was beaten, twenty-two to twenty-eight. Assumption then carried, thirty-one to twenty-six, but the arrival of North Carolina opponents produced a reversal by two votes.

Thereafter, successive defeats of assumption reduced its advocates to desperation. "The eastern members," wrote Madison to Monroe, "talk a strange language on the subject. They avow, some of them at least, a determination to oppose all provision for the public debt which does not include this, and intimate danger to the Union from a refusal to assume." The opponents would disregard "their prophetic menaces."

In an effort to link assumption with the location of government, Madison moved to make Philadelphia the temporary national capital—a preliminary to placing the permanent seat on the Potomac. The assumptionists countered successfully by substituting Baltimore for Philadelphia (a bad omen for transfer to the nearby Potomac). That threw the issue into the Senate, and Senator Morris arranged to meet Secretary Hamilton "by accident" in the Battery. He recorded the result: "Mr. Hamilton said he wanted one vote in the Senate and five in the House of Representatives [for assumption]; that he was willing and would agree to place the permanent residence of Congress at Germantown or the Falls of Delaware [Trenton] if he would procure those votes."

Morris agreed, with the stipulation that Philadelphia be made the temporary site. He secured the needed senatorial vote, but Hamilton found himself unable to complete the bargain. The New York delegation flatly refused to give up their hold on Congress, and Morris would not relinquish Philadelphia.

Hamilton realized that, to overcome the loss of Pennsylvania, he must win Virginia and Maryland to assumption. That meant he must win Madison. Thomas Jefferson had just reached New York City to take up his duties as Secretary of State. Encountering him in the street, Hamilton (as Jefferson described it in his *Anas*) "walked me backwards and forwards before the President's door for half an hour. He painted pathetically the temper into which the legislature had been wrought; the disgust of those who were called the creditor states," the danger of their secession. Some of Jefferson's friends could save assumption.

Jefferson invited Hamilton to dine with him next day. It was a threesome, completed by Madison, who listened to Hamilton's appeal and made a proposition of his own. Hamilton should abandon "assumption in gross," accept the defeated Madison amendments allowing credit for debts already paid by the states, and agree to establishment of the permanent capital on the Potomac. On his part, Madison would vote against assumption but would turn enough votes to carry it. Hamilton accepted. White and Lee of Virginia, Carroll and Gale of Maryland, reversed themselves and the bargain was carried out in full.

Madison's attitude was that of a hardboiled bargainer, so sensitive to his own reputation for consistency that he refused to include his own vote in the bargain. Apparently he had the whole compromise in mind before that famous dinner. Three days earlier he wrote to Monroe that the defeat of assumption "has benumbed the whole revenue business." He suspected that it would "yet be unavoidable to admit the evil in some qualified shape," and the Potomac might show up in the vicissitudes of the business. The "qualified shape" was formed by the amendments he forced on Hamilton's funding measure. Without mutual sacrifices on funding and the national capital, he told Monroe after the dinner, no funding bill would pass and national credit would "burst and vanish, and the states separate."

This incident has commonly been portrayed as a deal between Hamilton and Jefferson, with Madison brought in as the latter's submissive minion. It is part of the long-prevalent myth that Jefferson broke with Hamilton over funding and assumption and carried Madison along with him, thus rupturing the Madison-Hamilton friendship. Actually the break between Madison and Hamilton became complete before Jefferson reached home from six years in France. Jefferson was a last-stage observer of the crucial events by which Madison brought "Jeffersonian Democracy" into existence two years before Jefferson's political genius gave it that name.

Following the adjournment of Congress in August 1790, Madison spent several weeks regaining his strength by horseback riding in the New York countryside, then traveled to Virginia with Jefferson in the latter's phaeton. At Rock Hall, on the Eastern shore, they were overtaken by young Thomas Lee Shippen, a nephew of ten members of the Lee family, who rode with them as far as Georgetown and recounted the pleasures of the journey. "I never knew two men more agreeable than they were," wrote Shippen to his father. Waiting for a Chespeake Bay ferry, "we talked and dined and strolled and rowed ourselves in boats, and feasted upon delicious crabs."

At Annapolis a friend of Shippen guided them to the top of the State House steeple and spent three full hours "opening the roofs of the houses and telling us the history of each family who lived in them." A fine meal next day of turtle and fish at Mann's Inn preceded a thirteen-mile ride to the dirty village of Queen Anna's, with its gnats, flies, and bugs.

Bidding their "little companions" an early goodby, the trio breakfasted next morning at Bladensburgh "with an old black woman who keeps the best house in the town and calls herself Mrs. Margaret Adams." The travelers arrived a few hours after a nighttime mob, angered that President Washington and family had chosen to lodge with the Negro woman, invaded her premises and demolished her Temple of Cloacina.

At Georgetown, a cavalcade of citizens guided them through the site of the future national capital winding up with a boat trip to Little Falls. Jefferson and Madison then proceeded to Mount Vernon, where President Washington's servants were enriched by fourteen shillings in tips from Jefferson, borrowed from Madison, who financed the trip because of Jefferson's heavy transatlantic freight bill.

Reaching Montpelier, Madison loaned his friend a servant and fresh horses for the thirty-mile run to Monticello. Jefferson was so pleased with one of the animals that he bought it but feared that Madison would cheat himself on the price: "Witness the money disputes on our journey." They finally agreed on 25 pounds, but the horse died shortly after it was delivered—the commonest cause of ruptured Virginia friendships. Jefferson insisted on paying for the dead animal. Madison demurred. He had learned from his servant that the horse was taken very ill during his return from Monticello. The horse, Jefferson replied, "was fairly sold and fairly bought," his disorder was of the instant, and "I should as soon think of filching the sum from your pocket as of permitting the loss to be yours." Combining the price of the horse with two offsetting accounts, Jefferson sent a check for $95.26. Madison returned $23.26, pointing out that Jefferson had added the balances instead of subtracting them.

A candidate for re-election to Congress, Madison had no opposition and made no campaign beyond a strictly private letter to a friend in each county. He plunged into management of the two farms he owned personally—one of them overseen now by Sawney, the slave who had accompanied him to Princeton in 1769. Overseer Mordecai—a new man— was directed to choose one milch cow for himself and let the rest be milked for the Negroes. He must treat them "with all the humanity and kindness consistent with their necessary subordination and work."

Turning to agricultural matters, Madison gave instructions on the preparation of a red clover field, interplanting of corn and potatoes, forging of plows, and building of stables. He instructed Mordecai to make meadow dams to check erosion and, for the same purpose, plow along horizontal lines instead of long straight furrows. Sawney was directed to plant two hundred apple trees on top of Little Mountain and convert the tobacco field up there into Irish potatoes. Madison's three-year account, dated 1790, with Fontaine Maury's store in Fredericksburg reveals numerous purchases by "the Negro Sawney."

Jefferson rejoined Madison in November for the return to the national capital, lately shifted from New York City to Philadelphia. There they resumed their residence with Mrs. House, whose home was headquarters of the Virginia delegation. To that place came Monroe, filling out (the deceased) Grayson's term in the Senate, and William B. Giles, brilliant and erratic successor to Bland in the House. Washington's address to the new Congress was written jointly and with variant thoughts by Madison and Hamilton. The reply of the House came as before from Madison's pen, and he was advised once more by Washington "to finish the good offices" by writing the presidential response to House and Senate. Through Hamilton, Washington congratulated the country on the rise of public securities and national credit and revenues. From Madison came advice to admit Kentucky into the Union, to make the United States less dependent on foreign shipping, and to reduce the national debt through sales of public lands.

In the House, Madison's disagreement with Hamilton rose to new heights with the latter's proposal in December 1790 that Congress establish a national bank. The Senate passed the bank bill without a roll call, and the House approved it in Committee of the Whole without opposition. Madison then called for a debate on constitutionality and led off in opposition.

From what clause of the Constitution did Congress derive power to set up a bank? Not from the taxing power, for the bill did not lay a tax, and the power to devote money to the general welfare was limited to enumerated objects. Not from the power to borrow money, for it did not include the power to create the ability to borrow. Not from the "necessary and proper" clause, which only enabled Congress to carry out the specified powers. Madison pointed to the chain of reasoning employed to support the bill:

> To borrow money is made the end, and the accumulation of capitals implied as the means. The accumulation of capitals is then the end, and a Bank implied as the means. The Bank is then the end, and a charter of incorporation . . . implied as the means. If implications, thus remote and thus multiplied, can be linked together, a chain may be formed that will reach every object of legislation, every object within the whole compass of political economy.

The proposed bank, Madison asserted, was not necessary to the government; "at most it could be but convenient." Its uses to the government could be supplied by collection of taxes in advance of needs, by loans from individuals, by other banks over which the government would have at least equal control. If the power was not in the Constitution, the exercise of it was usurpation and established a precedent leveling all constitutional barriers.

Fisher Ames, in reply, declared that Madison had given his case away by admitting the utility of banks to government. European nations universally relied on them. What would happen if a war should break out? Should we send across the sea for loans? Power to establish a bank, he contended, was a necessary incident to the powers to regulate trade and provide for the public credit and national defense.

The House passed the bill, thirty-nine to twenty. The President asked his Cabinet officers to review its constitutionality. Jefferson and Randolph denied that Congress possessed this power; Hamilton affirmed it. Jefferson drew his argument from Madison's speeches and went far beyond them. The Constitution, he declared, limited Congress "to those means without which the grant of power would be nugatory." President Washington asked Madison to prepare a veto message, which he did. Two days later, Washington received Hamilton's rebuttal of the Randolph and Jefferson opinions. Not fully convinced, he decided to accept the will of Congress and signed the bill.

In effect, Hamilton used the line of thought that prevailed with Madison from 1781 through 1788. The latter had asserted the existence of implied powers even under the Confederation. Hamilton's argument, based on the "necessary and proper" clause, virtually duplicated Madison's broad interpretation of it in *The Federalist*.

Strangely enough, nobody pointed out that for two years Madison had been advocating an action that belied his own argument. Spurred by a "rude genius" named John Churchman, he sought in 1789 to send a scientific expedition to Baffin Land to determine the cause of the variations in the compass needle charted by Captain Cook in his voyage around the world. A committee advised postponement on account of the cost. Madison protested: "Well aware as I am that public bodies are liable to be assailed by visionary projectors, I nevertheless wish to ascertain the probability of the magnetic theory. If there is any considerable probability that the projected voyage would be successful or throw any valuable light on the discovery of longitude, it certainly comports with the honor and dignity of government to give it their countenance and support."

On the very eve of the bank fight Madison renewed, but in vain, his support of the Churchman project. Deeply buried in that concept of the spending power was the constitutional authority to expend billions of dollars sending three Americans to the moon. Sharing to some extent the prevalent Virginian distrust of banks, and further repelled by the growing partnership between government and predatory wealth, Madison was led into a position that conflicted with his past conception of federal power and his own vision of the country's development.

The fight over the bank bill brought Madison and Jefferson into a closer political partnership at a moment when Jefferson's entry into the Cabinet threw him into conflict with Hamilton. Early fruit of this was an invitation from Jefferson to Madison's college friend Philip Freneau to become a translator in the State Department at $250 a year, with duties so light that he could engage in other activities. Freneau was publishing the New York *Daily Advertiser,* which had supported Madison's funding policies in a running fight with the Hamiltonian organ, Fenno's *Gazette of the United States.* Fenno, sustained by government printing, moved his newspaper to Philadelphia when Congress went there, and Madison solicited Freneau to follow him.

Freneau declined Jefferson's offer of a clerkship, saying he was committed to establishment of a newspaper in his old home town in New Jersey. When Congress adjourned in April 1791, Madison sought out Freneau in New York and made him "sensible of the advantages of Philadelphia over New Jersey." In ability, Madison was convinced, Freneau was unrivaled "in the whole catalog of American printers."

Jefferson joined Madison in New York, and (as Jefferson explained later to President Washington), they looked across Mrs. Ellsworth's boarding table, *and there was Freneau.* Strangers being present, they had no conversation. Apparently, however, Freneau shook his head, for it required two months more solicitation by Madison and a promise by Jefferson of State Department printing, before Freneau finally made the decision to invade Philadelphia. Henceforth, the heavy invectives of Fenno were matched by the satiric laughter and biting jibes of Freneau, who did not wholly spare the President. This coincided with a swift rise in political leadership, revealed in the words of the *Maryland Journal* on March 22, 1791: "Keep always before your eyes the steps by which a Jefferson and Madison have gradually ascended to their present preeminence of fame. Like them you must devote your whole leisure to the most useful reading. Like them you must dive into the depths of philosophy and government . . . keeping and holding fast, as to the rock of your political salvation, their unshaken integrity and scorn of party."

The May meeting of Madison and Jefferson in New York marked the beginning of a leisurely drive into New England. Politics figured in it, but Madison described the objects as "health, education and curiosity," in search of which no itinerary could take them out of the way. They drove to Albany in three days, using Jefferson's phaeton with Madison's saddle horse as a spare. On May 29 they sailed up Lake George, "the most beautiful water I ever saw," said Jefferson. Shifting to murky Lake Champlain, they sailed northward twenty-five miles until driven back by high winds and a heavy sea. Madison became so seasick that it suggested a return of his early epileptiform ailment and caused him ever thereafter to shun overseas appointments or travel.

With Bennington, Vermont as their northerly limit in New England, the travelers came back through Connecticut, crossed the sound to Long Island, and visited William Prince's famous nursery at Flushing. Eighty maple trees bought there died in transplanting.

Followers of Hamilton had their glasses trained on Jefferson and Madison throughout this trip, in which they saw no motive except the organization of a political party. In New York, a Treasury subordinate reported, there was a passionate courtship between Livingston and Burr, Jefferson and Madison, directed, it was suspected, toward the elimination of John Adams as Vice President.

Acrimony by and against Adams was sharpened at this time by republication in Philadelphia of Part I of Thomas Paine's *Rights of Man*, assailing the denial of those rights by the British government. It bore an introductory note by Jefferson aimed at the Vice President. The note was genuine, but it was published without Jefferson's knowledge and against his wishes. Paine's work, said Jefferson, would be a useful antidote to some of the heresies that had recently sprung up. This was a clear reference to the writer "Publicola," whose Essays of Davila in a Boston newspaper, assailing Jefferson and Paine, were universally attributed to John Adams.

Madison, acknowledging Jefferson's disclaimer, remarked that Adams had no reason to complain. His 1787 book on American constitutions had attacked the system of government under a mock defense of it. Adams' attack on Paine, he predicted, would "draw the public attention to his obnoxious principles, more than anything he has published." House Clerk John Beckley, who turned up everywhere and everything, sent word from Boston that "Publicola" was in reality twenty-three-year-old John Quincy Adams, the Vice President's son. That ended Madison's puzzlement over the superior literary style of the Davila essays. This news, relayed to Jefferson, enabled him to write to Adams, explaining his accidental connection with Paine's book, and condemning, tongue in cheek, those who criminally accused Adams of being Publicola.

The Paine-Publicola imbroglio led to violent attacks on Jefferson as a supposed partisan of French Revolutionary excesses, and the northward journey of Jefferson and Madison brought the latter into the area of slander. Rumor had it that he was an invisible partner of Patrick Henry in the Yazoo land scandals, with which the Virginia orator had an early (and luckily abortive) connection. In July 1791 Madison wrote to his father: "The report in Georgia relating to me is as absolute a falsehood as ever was propagated. So far am I from being concerned in the Yazoo transaction that from the nature of it, as it has been understood by me, I have invariably considered it as one of the most disgraceful events that have appeared in our public councils."

Public sale of the national-bank stock built up Madison's dislike of the whole transaction. Shares paid for with depreciated public securities *at face value* were instantly resold at a profit of fifty per cent. "The subscriptions," he wrote, were "a mere scramble for so much public plunder which will be engrossed by those already loaded with the spoils of individuals." In August he witnessed the start of frenzied speculation in the portion of the public debt whose redemption was postponed until 1800. Add this to the preceding excesses, he wrote to Jefferson, and his imagination could set no bounds to the daring depravity of the times: "The stockholders will become the pretorian band of the government, at once its tool and its tyrant; bribed by its largesses and overawing it by clamors and combinations."

These were the words of a fighting politician, not of a political philosopher. Madison was spending months in New York City for no apparent reason, while Jefferson and Washington solicited his return. Possibly this marked the last stage of an incident recorded by Dr. Samuel Latham Mitchill. While Congress sat in New York, it was reported that Madison "was fascinated by the celebrated Mrs. Colden, of our city, she who was so noted for her masculine understanding and activity, as well as for feminine graces and accomplishments."

Madison went to Philadelphia near the end of August and left almost at once, in Jefferson's company, for a six-week stay in Virginia. The return journey in the fall was enlivened by the presence of Maria Jefferson, and by a half-broken horse, owned by Madison, that sent his carriage racing down every hill. The President and Martha Washington rode with them to Georgetown to attend the opening sales of lots in the District of Columbia. The prices caused rejoicing—so vast an increase over the purchase figure that it would cover the cost of all government buildings. Five days through a driving southeast storm completed the journey to Philadelphia.

Washington's October 25 message to Congress was thoroughly Hamiltonian, enthusing over revival of confidence and the rapid subscription of bank stock. The reply of the House, written by Madison, was mildly congratulatory but, he remarked privately, if his palate alone had been consulted, "the cooking would not have been precisely what it was." Washington's reliance on him was still in evidence. When Congress passed an apportionment bill unfairly favoring the northern states, Ham-

ilton urged that it be signed, Jefferson and Randolph advised a veto.
Washington told them he would be governed by Madison's opinion.
Madison called the bill unconstitutional, and the President, for the first
time, exercised his veto power.

At the same time, federal judges declared a pension act unconstitutional because it imposed nonjudicial duties on them. Madison hailed this
evidence that power existed to check unconstitutional acts of Congress.
It "gives inquietude," he wrote to Henry Lee, "to those who do not wish
Congress to be controlled or doubted whilst its proceedings correspond
with their views."

In the reapportionment, enlargement of the Virginia delegation forced
a drastic cut in Madison's district. French Strother and William Cabell
teamed up in the legislature to produce a district that would send Strother
to Congress. Instead, the assembly took out Cabell's stronghold, Amelia
County, vastly increasing Madison's strength.

During the winter and spring of 1791-92, Madison wrote unsigned
essays for Freneau's *National Gazette*. Six years ahead of Malthus, he
opened with a treatise entitled "Population and Emigration." Here, he
projected the outstripping of the world's food supply by man's excessive
faculty for reproduction, with emigration to underpopulated areas, while
they were available, the only alternative to infanticide, starvation, or de-
pletion by war and endemic disease. His next contribution warned against
consolidation of the states and called for united efforts to erect "one paramount Empire of reason, benevolence and brotherly affection." The
democratic drift of his political thinking was manifest in numerous
articles:

> • Republican government requires that the people be a
> sentinel over their rights and over all governments.
> • Public opinion sets bounds to every government, and is
> the real sovereign in every free one.
> • The force of public opinion has sustained the equilibrium
> of the British government through centuries of enormous
> change.
> • Charters of republican government are to be used to de-
> fend liberty against power and power against licentiousness.
> • Parties being inescapable, their evils are to be avoided
> by political equality and by the silent operation of laws which,
> without violating the rights of property, tend to equalize
> wealth.

• The hope of universal and perpetual peace is visionary, but in a republic, war should be declared only by the authority of the people, and every generation should bear the cost of its own wars.

• Division of power between the United States and the states, and separation of governments into legislative, executive and judiciary departments, may prove the best legacy ever given to the world.

• The springs of government are either permanent military force, corruption, or the reasoned will of the society. In the last class "are the republican governments which it is the glory of America to have invented, and her unrivaled happiness to possess."

• Citizens who provide their own food and raiment are the most truly independent and happy, the best basis of public liberty, and the strongest bulwark of public safety.

• A man has property in land, merchandise, money, opinions and their communication, religion, the safety and liberty of his person, the free use of his faculties. The United States should equally respect the rights of property, and the property in rights.

The spring series closed with the only article that struck directly at Hamiltonian policies. The real friends to the Union were those who were devoted to the authority of the people, to liberty, to the limited and republican system of government; those who resisted tyranny, who considered a public debt injurious, and regarded usurpation and monarchy as the dissolvers of union.

The writing was resumed in September with "A Candid State of Parties." On one side were those who believed mankind incapable of governing themselves but must be ruled by rank, the influence of money, and military terror. The others were offended at every measure that deviated from republican principles. "The Republican party, as it may be termed," would seek to banish every difference except that which divided the enemies and friends to republican government.

Here for the first time Madison applied the term "Republican party" to the entity he had created in Congress and that now was gaining national coherence under the rising leadership of Thomas Jefferson. Hamiltonians were beginning to call themselves "Federalists," but Madison had a different name for them in his final article, "Who are the best Keepers of the People's Liberties?" This was a dialogue between Republican and Anti-Republican. The former found the best keepers in the people themselves. The latter condemned the people as stupid, suspicious, and licentious: "they should think of nothing but obedience, leaving the care of their liberties to their wiser rulers." The dialogue terminated in an exchange that reflected the devastating impact of the French Revolution on American conservatives, who only three years earlier had helped Madison implant a Bill of Rights in the Constitution.

> *Anti-republican.*—. . . You have neither the light of faith nor the spirit of obedience. I denounce you to the government as an accomplice of atheism and anarchy.
> *Republican.*—And I forbear to denounce you to the people, though a blasphemer of their rights and an idolator of tyranny.—Liberty disdains to persecute.

The conflict between Madison and Hamilton reached a new peak early in 1792 after the presentation of Hamilton's "Report on Manufactures." The purpose to stimulate them was in line with his own long held ideas, but he flared up at the invocation of the General Welfare clause as the source of constitutional power. Hamilton affirmed that the power to lay taxes to promote the general welfare was as broad as the general welfare itself. Madison repeated his contention that the power was limited to objects set forth in the other enumerated powers. "If not only the *means*, but the *objects* are unlimited," he protested to Henry Lee, "the parchment had better be thrown into the fire at once."

The issue came before the House in a bill to pay bounties to cod fishermen as an offset to the duty on salt. Madison objected to the word "bounties," which tied it to "general welfare." That phrase, he averred, came from the Articles of Confederation, and never was it supposed that the old Congress could "give away the moneys of the states" in bounties or for any purpose they pleased. He voted for the measure after securing an amendment changing "bounties" to "allowances," which permitted the thought that it was a regulation of commerce.

The triviality of the change contrasted bizarrely with the import of Madison's language. Never in the old Congress would he have referred to its appropriations as "giving away *the money of the states*." In that day his emphasis was on the sovereign power of Congress to tax the states. Money was spent to put Indian boys through college. That, assuredly, was a "bounty" for the general welfare, not an "allowance" justified by the Commerce Clause.

Hamilton construed Madison's restrictive attitude as a personal assault upon himself. This was confirmed in his mind when Madison, after putting through a bill for protection of the western frontiers, objected to a motion that the Treasury report a method of raising supplies for that purpose. To maintain the independence of the House, Madison contended, it should apply to the Treasury for facts, then form its own opinions, and submit them to the Secretary. Madison well knew, wrote Hamilton, that if this course had been followed he would have resigned rather than endure drudgery without reward in public good or reputation: "My overthrow was anticipated as certain. And Mr. Madison, laying aside his wonted caution, boldly led his troops, as he imagined, to a certain victory. He was disappointed. Though late, I became apprised of the danger. Measures of counteraction were adopted; and when the question was called, Mr. Madison was confounded to find characters voting against him whom he had counted upon as certain."

It was in this letter, to their mutual friend Edward Carrington, that Hamilton said the expectation of firm support from Madison governed his decision to accept the Cabinet position; but "the opinion I once entertained of the candor and simplicity and fairness of Mr. Madison's character has, I acknowledge, given way to a decided opinion that it is one of a peculiarly artificial and complicated mind."

During a good part of the last session, Hamilton went on, Madison "lay in a great measure perdu," but prompted Giles and others to come out in open opposition to him. Madison, he said, had spread insidious insinuations that the Treasury purchased public securities at an artificial price for the benefit of speculators. This, he thought, was Madison's response to Hamilton's open declaration that he would "consider and treat him as a political enemy."

The report about "insidious insinuations" flowed out of the speculation in deferred securities, based on rumors of a general redemption before 1800. Assistant Secretary Duer, who had become a compulsive gambler, crowned his follies by plunging into this field. In an effort to save him, Hamilton bought for the Treasury $52,685 of Duer's deferred securities at the stepped-up price. But Duer kept on, disregarding Hamilton's plea: "Do not plunge deeper. Have the courage to make a full stop." Duer resigned from the Treasury, went bankrupt, and spent his last seven years in debtor's prison. Madison's comment to Pendleton on Duer's collapse clarifies the cause of his break with Hamilton:

> The gambling system which has been pushed to such an excess is beginning to exhibit its explosions. Duer of New York, the prince of the tribe of speculators, has just become

a victim to his enterprises, and involves an unknown number
to an unknown amount in his fate. It is said . . . that every
description and gradation of persons, from the church to the
stews, are among the dupes of his dexterity and the partners
of his distress.

Duer's fall produced a panic in all the money centers. "Every day,"
wrote Madison, "exhibits new victims and opens new scenes of usury,
knavery and folly." Secretary Hamilton threw $150,000 into the market
to buy securities, taking this action, he wrote to banker William Seton,
"to relieve the distressed." This produced the "insidious insinuations"
by Madison, recorded by Hamilton as calumnious, that he had employed
public funds at an artificial price (the depressed securities were bought
at par) for the benefit of speculators.

The best that can be said for Hamilton is that he himself made no
profit out of his operations, designed to cement a government partnership with men of wealth. His letter to Carrington—a 6,000-word tirade
against Madison—obviously was written to start a political fire against
the latter in Virginia. With "affected solemnity," he said, Madison
sounded the alarm against federal authority and held up the bugbear
of a faction unfriendly to liberty: "This kind of conduct has appeared to
me the more extraordinary on the part of Mr. Madison, as I know for a
certainty it was a primary article in his creed that the real danger in our
system was the subversion of the national authority by the preponderancy
of the state governments."

That was true, but Hamilton took no account of the profound effect
of his own "woo the rich" policies in precipitating the change. He won-
dered whether Madison might not subscribe to Jefferson's peculiar ideas
concerning national finance—that Congress "had no right to bind posterity" by funding the debt. Certainly the two men were united in the new
views and "Mr. Jefferson was indiscreetly open in his approbation of Mr.
Madison's principles, upon his first coming to the seat of government."

Hamilton correctly realized (as many historians have not) that the
cleavage between himself and Madison preceded Jefferson's return from
France; but his conjecture was wrong concerning acceptance, by Madison, of Jefferson's opinion that no public debt was valid beyond the life
of the generation that incurred it. When Jefferson advanced that doctrine
he received the reply from Madison that "debts may be incurred with a
direct view to the interest of the unborn as well as the living." Cancellation of debts after nineteen years—the span of a generation—would be

unjust and anarchic. All men born into society gave tacit assent to established government and laws.

The people, Madison believed, would soon awaken to the true import of Hamiltonian policies, but the explosive shock, in the year of a presidential election, might make the country's safety depend on what Washington would do about a second term. That issue was put squarely before him on May 5, when the President asked him to draft an announcement of his intention to retire. The decision had been disclosed to Madison some time earlier, so firmly stated that he merely said it would surprise and shock the public mind. Since then, the President informed him, he had revealed his intention to Hamilton, Knox, and Jefferson, all of whom protested it.

Madison now joined in the protests. Washington's retirement at this particular time "might have effects that ought not to be hazarded." He recalled their conversation four years earlier, when Washington reluctantly yielded to the plea that acceptance of the office was indispensable to establishment of the new government. "Reasons of a like kind" required him to retain it for some time longer. Washington detailed his objections: he felt unsuited to the place, his health was infirm, the spirit of party was dividing his Cabinet, popular discontent with him was rising.

Madison replied that Washington's judgment equalled and often excelled that of anybody who could have taken his place. In politics the only dangerous group—those who inclined toward a mixed monarchy—were strongly opposed by public sentiment. If Washington retired, who would succeed him? Jefferson? Adams? Jay? Jefferson seemed eliminated by his repugnance to public life and the hostility of New England and Pennsylvania. The unconcealed monarchical principles of Adams put him out of the question among republicans. Jay was regarded by the West as a dangerous enemy because of his Mississippi River negotiations.

Washington held to his determination to retire, and a month later again asked Madison to prepare an announcement. Madison advised "a simple publication in the newspapers," in plain and modest language but again pleaded for "one more sacrifice, severe as it may be, to the desires and interests of your country." He enclosed, however, the draft of an address in which Washington mildly depreciated his services, gave his blessing to his beloved country, and expressed the desire to partake, in a private station, of "that benign influence of good laws under a free Government which has been the ultimate object of all our wishes." Jefferson reinforced the appeal to Washington to remain in office, and he yielded.

Going home in the summer of 1792, Madison rode through a country in which flax and oats were destroyed by drouth, corn was dying, and no tobacco was planted. He reached Montpelier at the beginning of a week-long deluge that threatened the one surviving crop—wheat, then rapidly supplanting tobacco (to Madison's pleasure) as the cash staple of the Piedmont. At home he had good news from his brother Ambrose, who was in Kentucky on a land-buying expedition. Ambrose had bought, for both of them, seven thousand acres on tributaries of the Green River and three thousand hilly acres on Sandy River. Part of the better land lay close to ten thousand acres on Panther Creek, to which James Madison, Sr., took title from the state twelve years earlier. All was to be held for long-term profit—a form of speculation that raised no political hackles.

In July 1792, Washington, Jefferson, Madison, and Monroe all were in Virginia for lengthy stays. With these four cats away, the road was open for Hamilton to launch a long-planned newspaper war on Jefferson and Madison. The original intention, revealed by four unpublished manuscripts, was to levy assaults without using names. He railed against those (Madison) who tortured the Constitution out of personal rivalry and against "POPES in government" (Jefferson) pretending profound knowledge, yet ignorant of human nature.

Putting these aside, Hamilton entered Fenno's *Gazette* over the signature "T.L." with an attack on Philip Freneau. Was he paid a public salary for translations or for vilification of the government that fed him? Freneau replied briefly in his *National Gazette* that he "received a small stipend for services rendered as French Translator to the Department of State and, as editor of a free newspaper, admits into his publication impartial strictures on the proceedings of government."

Converting himself into "An American," Hamilton quoted Freneau's explanation but cut it off at the word "newspaper." That distorted it into a statement by Freneau that he was paid a government stipend *as editor*. From that premise Hamilton asked how Jefferson could remain in the Cabinet while sponsoring such a vilifier of men and measures adopted by Congress and sanctioned by the Chief Magistrate of the Union. It might be true, as Freneau stated on oath, that his coming to Philadelphia was neither advised, urged nor influenced by the Secretary of State, but was not this done "by a *particular friend* of that officer?"

Continuing the assault, Hamilton became Amicus, Metellus, and A Plain Honest Man, and left drafts of all the articles in his papers. His deepest thought was revealed in a paper that he decided not to publish: "Mr. Jefferson fears in Mr. Hamilton a formidable rival in the competition for the presidential chair at a future period and therefore the sooner he can ruin him in the public estimation the better for his purpose." A recent deathly malady of President Washington, Hamilton wrote and then crossed out, excited Jefferson's ambitious ardor and suggested to him that he would be a more likely successor "were the more popular Secretary of the Treasury out of the way."

Only in megalomaniac dreams could such thoughts be put on paper. Madison took horse to Montpelier on learning of Hamilton's "extraordinary maneuver of calumny." Monroe came over from his nearby residence. It was agreed that he and Madison should join in writing a series of pseudonymous articles for the Philadelphia *American Daily Advertiser*. Monroe opened with one quoting liberally from Jefferson's letters to Madison, disproving the charge that Jefferson opposed ratification of the Constitution. Jefferson delivered the article to the printer and wrote to Washington about his intense surprise at the publication of it. His own copies of the letters "were under a lock of which I had the key."

Hamilton, discomfited by publication of Jefferson's letters, converted himself into "Catullus" and asked whether they were "genuine letters or mere fabrications; how far they may have been altered or mutilated." Madison continued the series with a defense of Freneau. His paltry salary as clerk forced him to do other work. Was it dishonorable to make the rest of his living from a newspaper? Or was that complained of only because he was a Whig and a Republican? Unwilling to deny or admit the role he played in bringing Freneau to the capital, Madison handed the pen to Monroe, who merely disparaged the "slanderous imputation" that Madison would conduct a negotiation for the purpose of subverting the government which he contributed so essentially to establish.

Style and animus betrayed Hamilton's Protean name-changing and the people laughed, cheered, or jeered. Demanding a sight of the Jefferson letters and offered them if he would drop his anonymity, Hamilton proclaimed victory and fled the field.

One man who did not laugh was George Washington. Discovering at last the personal nature of the feud in his Cabinet, the President asked for mutual forbearance. Hamilton gave his promise and kept on with his anonymous attacks. Jefferson affirmed, with technical truth, that not a word of dissension had come from his pen. He promised not to write against his assailant until he retired, which would be as soon as he could do so without seeming to be driven out by slanders.

Reaching Philadelphia on November 1, 1792, Madison found himself attacked in an anonymous pamphlet, which he ascribed to Hamilton—a conjecture borne out by marked-out passages in Hamilton's drafts of his newspaper articles. The attack did not seem to distress him greatly. "I throw in for your amusement," he wrote to Judge Pendleton, "an anonymous pamphlet which makes pretty free with the characters of several of your friends. In what respects myself everything happens to be pretty notoriously false which I would not wish to be true." The pamphlet built up a picture of Jefferson, while still in France, seducing Madison into malevolent assaults on the Secretary with whom he had been so friendly.

Madison left among his papers an unpublished "Outline of Answer." The attack upon himself, he wrote, rested on two absurd suppositions— that Jefferson, in Paris, foresaw a rivalry with Hamilton, and that Madison sacrificed his principles "to the ambitious and malicious views of his friend." A resumé of Madison's congressional career rounded out the reply. Hamilton's pamphlet had one lasting effect: it helped to implant in history the fiction that Madison, who initiated the republican break with Hamilton, was led into it by the overpowering influence of Thomas Jefferson.

Washington's November 6, 1792, message to Congress, written chiefly by Hamilton, portrayed national finances cheerfully except for western resistance to an excise on distilled spirits. Madison, as usual, headed the House "response committee," but the reply was dictated by his Hamiltonian colleagues, Benson and William Vans Murray. In it, he protested, they affirmed the right to petition for redress of grievances and then prejudged the petitions. Worse still was the inflammatory insinuation, not generally true, that opponents of the excise were selfish tax-evaders. Madison recognized but did not spell out the full truth: that the excise was an exorbitant income tax levied on the western mountaineers' substitute for money—whisky.

Madison was now battling to keep the Treasury from dominating Congress. He protested in vain against a motion to ask Hamilton to report a plan for reducing the public debt. The Senate, he observed, was forbidden to originate revenue bills, but a one-sided report from the Treasury would have more weight than a Senate bill. Hamilton, who did not want the debt reduced, came back with a proposal to set up a sinking fund supported by a graduated tax on carriage horses. That, said Madison, was both a discrimination and a mockery—favoring the pedestrian East over the equestrian South, and giving the high-sounding name of sinking fund to a miserly $40,000 a year.

Madison assailed Hamilton's request for authority to borrow $2 million, which was linked with his efforts to avoid the repayment, to revolutionary France, of debts incurred during the reign of Louis XVI, lately deposed. Beaten tactically, he secured an order that the Treasury make a detailed report on the foreign balances. This disclosed repeated diversions to America of moneys borrowed to repay France. Hamilton defended himself on the ground that he had borrowed the money *under two laws combined*, and one of these permitted the buying up of the domestic debt. Partisans of the Secretary, Madison observed, saw nothing amiss in this "very blameable irregularity and secrecy," but the $2 million loan project faded from sight. Fisher Ames ascribed the whole tumult to Madison: "Virginia moves in a solid column, and the discipline of the party is as severe as the Prussian. Deserters are not spared. Madison is become a desperate party leader, and I am not sure of his stopping at any ordinary point of extremity." Wholly obsolete now, was Ames's original impression that Madison was "very timid and [wanting in] manly firmness and energy of character."

Like nearly all Americans, James Madison greeted the French Revolution with enthusiastic approval. The pleasure it gave, he wrote in 1790, must be "enhanced by the reflection that the light which is chasing darkness and despotism from the Old World is but an emanation from that which has procured and succeeded the establishment of liberty in the new." And so it appeared at the outset. The fall of the Bastille was on a par with Lexington and Concord. Madison saw a spreading of the movement. The Austrian Netherlands had "caught the flame" and renounced the imperial government. Even Spain "begins to awake at the voice of liberty." All Europe must by degrees be aroused to assertion of the rights of human nature.

A Tory minority felt as did Madison's neighbor Robert Beverly, that Americans were being infected by "this revolutionary, anarchical, democratical, tyrannical, patriotic age," drawing its spirit of reform "from the infamous sans-culottes of the terrible republic." A year and a half later, in the fall of 1791, Madison was rejoicing that the Revolution seemed to have succeeded "beyond the most sanguine hopes." The King, by freely accepting the Constitution, had baffled external machinations against it, and the peaceable election of a legislative assembly had suppressed the danger of internal confusions.

The new government was conservative, but the Revolution raced beyond it. The King and Queen fled toward Austria and were brought back. Prussian and Austrian menaces goaded France into a declaration of war. The Commune seized Paris and arrested the King. Mobs stormed the Tuileries and massacred thousands of Royalists in the streets. Danton rose to power, and the monarchy was abolished.

With these developments, in the summer of 1792, American public opinion divided virtually along the lines of domestic politics. Federalist imagination translated French mobs to the American scene. Republicans adhered to the French radicals, in spite of what Madison called their "follies and barbarities." The important fact, for him, was that the Germanic monarchs were undertaking to crush freedom, while the French nation was united against royalty and for national defense.

News that Louis XVI had been guillotined reached Madison just as he set out for Virginia in March 1793. In his neighborhood, he reported, sympathy for the King was general but based on spurious accounts of his innocence and the bloodthirstiness of his enemies. In the wake of this came a letter from the French Minister of the Interior, informing Madison that he had been made a citizen of France by the National Assembly. Among eighteen world figures thus honored, two others were Americans —Washington and Hamilton. Authorship of the *The Federalist*, revealed in a French edition, accounted in part for the selection.

Washington and Hamilton ignored the French action. Madison accepted his "honorable adoption" with peculiar satisfaction, he wrote to Minister Roland, because the United States had done so much to banish prejudice and reclaim the lost rights of mankind, and was so intimately bound to France by libertarian affinities. He ended with anxious wishes for the glory of the French nation and the final triumph of liberty by a victory over the minds of all its adversaries.

News that Great Britain had declared war on France caused Madison to hold back this letter until events were clarified. President Washington proclaimed American neutrality, calling for "a conduct friendly and impartial towards the belligerent powers." Acceptance of French citizenship would violate the spirit of the proclamation. Madison, nevertheless, asked the Secretary of State to forward the letter, saying: "I shall not trouble myself about any comments which the publication attending all such things may produce here." Roland was out of office when Madison's letter was written. It was his wife who exclaimed, just before she was beheaded: "O Liberty! What crimes are committed in thy name."

The proclamation of neutrality shocked Madison. The United States was bound by the treaty of 1778 to defend France's American territories from attack. Hamilton's attempts to "shuffle off" the treaty seemed to him "equally contemptible for the meanness and folly of it." It was a dangerous doctrine that a change of government terminated public engagements. That "would perpetuate every existing despotism, by involving in a reform of the government a destruction of the social pact, an annihilation of property, and a complete establishment of the state of nature."

The "Anglified complexion" of the neutrality proclamation preyed increasingly on Madison's mind. "It wounds the national honor," he wrote to Jefferson on June 19, 1793, "by seeming to disregard the stipulated duties to France. It wounds the popular feelings by a seeming indifference to liberty." Also, it seemed to violate the Constitution by making the Executive Magistrate the organ of the disposition, duty, and interest of the nation in relation to war and peace.

Madison ignored the fact that the Constitution put the Executive in charge of foreign affairs in matters short of war, and that Congress had overriding power to end or modify neutrality. He hoped that the American people would offset the proclamation by an enthusiastic reception of Edmond Charles Genet, the French envoy who had just landed in Charleston, South Carolina.

Genet was in fact greeted with such adulation by one party that it went to his head. He attempted to set up prize courts under French consuls and to use American seaports as bases of naval operations. Secretary Jefferson tried for three months to restrain him, then wrote in anguish to Madison: "Never, in my opinion, was so calamitous an appointment made . . . . Hotheaded, all imagination, no judgment, passionate, disrespectful and even indecent towards the President . . . talking of appeal from him to Congress, from them to the people, urging the most unreasonable and groundless propositions, and in the most dictatorial style. . . . He renders my position immensely difficult."

Madison answered in dismay: "Your account of G[enet] is dreadful. He must be brought right if possible. His folly will otherwise do mischief which no wisdom can repair. Is there no one through whom he can be *effectually* counselled?"

A few days later, from Jefferson, Madison received Hamilton's published letters of "Pacificus," upholding the neutrality proclamation and denying the binding force of the treaty with France. With them came Jefferson's appeal: "For God's sake sake, my dear sir, take up your pen, select the most striking heresies and cut him to pieces in the face of the public. There is nobody else who can and will enter the lists with him."

Madison reluctantly performed the task—the most grating in his experience, he called it—"in scraps of time, with a distaste to the subject" and with lassitude due to the July and August heat. Madison's five letters of Helvidius followed the eight of Pacificus in the same newspaper, the Philadelphia *Gazette of the United States*. Hamilton's basic contention was that it was the duty of the President to preserve peace until Congress declared war, and in fulfilling that duty he must decide what obligations the treaties of the country impose on the government. Matters of war, peace, and treaties were executive in nature. The President's power in that field was broad; the power of Congress, narrow.

Madison's five articles gave no hint of disrelish or lassitude. The pieces signed Pacificus, he said, had been read "with singular pleasure and applause by the foreigners and degenerate citizens among us, who hate our republican government and the French Revolution." The basic fallacy of Pacificus was that the powers of making war and treaties were executive in nature. They were, in fact, said Madison, high acts of sovereignty which in Europe were concentrated in the sovereign. In a republic such powers, if not purely legislative, were so nearly so that no other department could assert a rival claim.

Madison agreed that it was the President's duty to preserve peace until Congress declared war, but this did not give him the authority to decide what obligations were imposed on the country by treaties. Hamilton had admitted that the power to judge the need of war was part of the power to declare it. If that part of the declaratory power was concurrent, Madison replied, the whole must be, but it was given exclusively to Congress. He challenged Hamilton's contention that abolition of an old government threw treaties into abeyance until the new government was recognized. Such an argument challenged "the only lawful tenure by which the United States hold their existence as a nation."

At the end of August a messenger from Jefferson brought a top-secret letter. It contained the memorandum of a talk with the President about Jefferson's resignation from the Cabinet, submitted July 31 to take effect in September. Washington told him that Hamilton intended to retire late in the session of Congress, and he urged Jefferson (successfully) to postpone his departure until that time. They talked of a successor. The President "said Mr. Madison would be his first choice, but he had always expressed to him such a decision against public office that he could not expect he would undertake it." With this information, Madison could shape his plans. Washington's inference, Madison replied, was correct. Asked years later why he refused an office under Washington which he accepted under President Jefferson, he said he wished to remain in Congress to sustain his constructions of the Constitution.

Turning to relations with France, Jefferson said that Genet's conduct was inspiring universal indignation. He himself had adhered to the French envoy as long as there was a hope of setting him right, but finding him "absolutely incorrigible, I saw the necessity of quitting a wreck which could not but sink all who should cling to it." So, he said, it had been decided to insist on Genet's recall. In spite of this decision, Hamilton and Knox were eagerly pressing for an appeal to the people against Genet, Hamilton telling the President that the new Democratic Societies in the United States were agencies of sedition set up by Genet to overthrow the American government, Jefferson warning that an appeal to the people on that basis would be a declaration of war on the Republican party.

Strongly impressed by Hamilton's picture, unsettled by Jefferson's, the President repeatedly asked Jefferson what Madison thought about his proclamation. "I tell him you are so absorbed in farming that you write to me always about ploughs, rotation, etc." Such themes did, in fact, fill a good part of Madison's letters. In one of them, he asked Jefferson to hand $34.70 to William Gardner, to pay for two plows which Dr. George Logan had made for him after a special pattern. And who was William Gardner? He was Madison's runaway slave Billey, set free because Madison could not punish him for taking the Declaration of Independence seriously.

In Virginia, Madison informed Jefferson, friends of France were turning away from Genet in disgust, heightened by habitual veneration of Washington. The pro-British party was spreading poison. The only antidote was to distinguish between the nation and its agent. Let it be impressed that "the enemies of France and of liberty" were trying to drive America into the arms and ultimately the form of government of England.

Genet's conduct, Madison remarked to Monroe, "had been that of a madman." The only consolation was that his excesses were so great that people were likely to blame him rather than his government. Further tempering the effect, Great Britain was warring on American commerce by intercepting un-contraband articles bound to unblockaded ports and taking them to herself at her own price. "This must bring on a crisis with us, unless the order be revoked on our demand, of which there is not the least probability."

Yellow fever was raging at this time in Philadelphia, and Washington wrote from Mount Vernon to ask whether the President had lawful power to summon Congress to another meeting place. Madison replied (as did Jefferson) that no such power existed, but he approved Washington's alternative suggestion that he proclaim his intention to go to a safe place and *recommend* that Congress assemble there. Madison set out on horseback for Philadelphia, his journey saddened by the death of his brother Ambrose. At Fredericksburg he picked up a letter from Jefferson, in Philadelphia, saying that the epidemic had ended suddenly after torrential rains. Nobody connected its termination with the mosquito-killing frost that followed the downpour. Senator Monroe joined Madison at Fredericksburg and they bought an ancient carriage which fulfilled their hope that it would survive the trip.

Jefferson dominated the writing of Washington's message to Congress

(December 3, 1793) and it followed completely Madison's "Helvidius." The neutrality proclamation was narrowly defined to prevent acts of hostility by Americans. This enabled Madison, in the reply of the House, to approve the President's vigilance for peace and endorse the proclamation. This may have soothed the hurt of Madison's connection with "that rascal Freneau," as Washington called him. Jefferson was "sincerely sorry" about the newspaper attacks that caused the President such suffering, but he recalled that Madison had foreseen their cause: "I remember an observation of yours made when I first went to New York, that the satellites and sycophants which surrounded him [Washington] had wound up the ceremonials of the government to a pitch of stateliness which nothing but his personal character could have supported and which no character after him could ever maintain."

Swiss-born Albert Gallatin brought his fiscal talents into the new Congress as a senator from Pennsylvania. His first move was to suggest that the Secretary of the Treasury submit regular reports. The Senate—fourteen to twelve Federalist—retaliated by throwing Gallatin out of office on the flimsy ground that his citizenship (nine years required) did not begin until six years after he came to America. One good resulted. In the ensuing turmoil of public opinion, the secretive Senate opened its doors and kept them open, leading to ultimate primacy in Congress.

Jefferson left office on the last day of 1793, succeeded by vacillating Edmund Randolph. Hamilton, rid of his rival, changed his mind about resigning. William Bradford, an ardent liberal turned conservative, succeeded Randolph as Attorney-General. The Cabinet was swinging into Federalist control, Washington was guided by his Cabinet, and the strains of the French Revolution produced ever deeper cracks in American policy.

In Congress, Madison became the storm center of the conflict. For three years, his motion for tonnage tax discrimination had lain without action, awaiting a report from the Secretary of State on foreign commercial restrictions. Sent to Congress two weeks before Jefferson left office, the report built a factual case for adoption of the measures Madison had proposed—a strict system of reciprocal favors and retaliations. It arrived at a moment of angry tension. The British government had ordered seizure of American food ships, and France issued a similar decree in reverse.

On January 3, 1794, "Mr. Madison's Resolutions" were laid before the House. They called for higher tonnage taxes on vessels of nations having no commercial treaty with the United States. Port restrictions were to be met in kind. The United States had a treaty of commerce with France. The motion, if implemented, would establish counterdiscrimination, but England could escape this by means of a treaty of commerce.

The United States, Madison pointed out, exported necessities and imported luxuries. It could stand a curtailment of trade better than the countries it traded with. Four years' experience had proved the need of a moderate, firm, and decisive attitude. He would not go every length at first, but by doing no more than other nations and less than some, "our country may make her enemies feel the extent of her power."

Ames, leader of the anticounterdiscriminationists, secured a week's postponement. Smith of South Carolina then led off with an all-day speech. (The original text, in Hamilton's handwriting, lies among his papers.) The speech attacked Madison's resolutions by assailing Jefferson's report, accusing him of understating French hostility to American commerce and exaggerating that of Great Britain.

Madison spoke all the next day. He was a believer in free trade but that required freedom everywhere. British ships carried eleven-twelfths of American commerce because British law gave that country a preference and totally excluded American ships from the West Indies. Britain sold twice as much to the United States as she bought in return. Trade with France ran seven to one in the other direction. Nine-tenths of all imported manufactures came from Britain, but that country excluded both American manufactures and wheat, flour, fish, and salted provisions.

Twice, said Madison, the House had voted to correct this by retaliations. Now the extravagant objection was made that this might produce war. On what imaginable pretext could an independent nation be attacked for following the example of its adversary? If war resulted it would prove a fixed predetermination to make it.

The proposed regulations, their sponsor said, would benefit the North by stimulating manufacturing and navigation. They would temporarily injure the South by cutting exports, but he believed his own state would cheerfully concur in that sacrifice. British policy was bottomed on the belief that the United States would be ruled by conflicting local interests. Rejection of the resolutions would confirm that and "rivet the fetters on our commerce."

Ames, Boudinot, and Fitzsimons offered strong opposition, and Madison spent nearly two days in final rebuttal. His retaliatory policy, he told the House, would make it to the British interest to be just. It would increase the American marine, encourage domestic manufactures, break up the British monopoly in that field, and win the nations in treaty, notably France, into arrangements further helpful to American commerce.

Giles and newcomer John Nicholas of Virginia talked down an attempt to vote while Madison was out of the room. When he returned the first resolution carried, fifty-one to forty-six. Several New Englanders, won over to the resolutions, secured a month's postponement in order to build up backing at home. A nationwide campaign followed, with Federalist editors leveling slanderous attacks at Madison as a corrupt tool of France since 1778. He described the state of affairs to Jefferson on March 2: "The interval has produced vast exertions by the British party to mislead the people of the eastern states. No means have been spared. The most artful and wicked calumnies have been propagated with all the zeal which malice and interest could invent. The blackest of these calumnies, as you may imagine, have fallen to the lot of the mover of the resolutions."

In diplomacy the French picture was worsening in Europe, improving in America. Robespierre had overthrown the Girondists, and the Reign of Terror was on. Genet, recalled, remained in America to escape the guillotine (and later married the daughter of Governor Clinton). His successor, Joseph Fauchet, was courting Washington. Writing to his own government, he paid a dubious compliment to "Madison, *le Robespierre des Etats Unis.*" Washington received Fauchet with "affectionate solicitude for the success of the republic," but that did not prevent a decision to allow American ships to carry provisions to British armed forces in the West Indies. "This is really horrible!" exclaimed Madison. Britain was allowed to cut off American supplies to the French dominions, while we aided Britain "in taking from France the islands we have guaranteed to her . . . What can be done?"

Three days later Madison reported "a terrible slam" against the United States in the West Indies. A hundred American vessels had been seized for condemnation. This "new symptom of insolence and enmity" in Britain showed either an intent to bring on formal war, "or that she calculates on the pusillanimity of this country and the influence of her party in a degree that will lead her into aggressions which our love of peace can no longer bear."

The West Indian *putsch* reversed New England sentiment. Congressmen who had fought Madison's resolutions now clamored for more drastic action. House and Senate put through a thirty-day embargo of all shipping. Praise for Madison rang out all over the country. The Republican Society of Charleston beheld in Citizen Representative Madison, "the firm patriot and true Republican," and joined in burning a group effigy of their Congressman Smith, Ames, Benedict Arnold, and the Devil.

With the thirty-day embargo in effect but disliked by both Britain and France, Congress, in mid-April, dropped its extension and turned to more drastic measures. Bills were offered to sequester British debts, establish a lien on British imports, and suspend importations from that country until spoliations were paid for and the peace treaty of 1783 was executed. (British troops still held northwestern frontier posts.) Madison held back his resolutions until these measures should be disposed of. The House passed the nonimportation bill by a wide margin.

At this point the Hamilton wing of the Cabinet persuaded President Washington to send a special envoy to England to negotiate a treaty of commerce. Hamilton wanted to go, but congressional rumblings prevented his appointment. Secretary of State Randolph urged that Madison be sent. Madison wanted Jefferson chosen. The President selected anti-Gallic Chief Justice John Jay. All legislation, of course, had to lie in limbo until he returned.

At the height of the conflict Senators King and Ellsworth had a private talk with Senator John Taylor of Virginia, arguing for dissolution of the Union. King told him that Madison "had some deep and mischievous design." Madison dismissed the threat of dissolution, jotting on Taylor's memorandum of it, "probably in terrorem." However, to explain and justify his own position, he put out a 10,000-word pamphlet of *Political Observations*, justifying his resolutions, upholding moderate defense measures, opposing war, and defending friendship with France. The opposition, wrote Madison, was "ever ready to invoke the name of Washington" to garnish their heretical doctrines with his virtues, arousing "a fair suspicion that they who draw most largely on that fund are hastening fastest to bankruptcy of their own."

Surveying the scene as Congress approached its June 9 adjournment, Madison saw his own position dissolving. The sending of Jay had created a belief in the validity of the Federalist assertion that it was the only alternative to war with England. Confidence in the President swept aside all opposition. In the Senate, Madison affirmed to Jefferson, the Republican party "is completely wrecked, and in the House of Representatives in a much worse condition than at any earlier period of the session."

From France, at this time, came a demand for recall of Ambassador Gouverneur Morris in retaliation for the ouster of Genet. Madison headed a committee that asked the President to replace him with Aaron Burr. Instead, Washington offered the position to Madison, then to Robert

Livingston, and finally to Monroe, who took it with Madison's strong approval. Had Madison accepted, Alexander Hamilton would have whooped with joy. Had Madison coveted the office, he would have refused it. He was tied to Philadelphia at that moment by a chain stronger than steel.

When Madison wrote at Montpelier, on September 15, 1793, that "the malignant fever in Philadelphia is raging still with great violence," he had no idea that the epidemic was shaping his life. Among the victims of yellow fever was a young Quaker lawyer named John Todd, who three years earlier had married a dashingly attractive Quaker girl named Dolley Payne. She survived, and one year to the day after Madison wrote about the epidemic, Dolley Payne Todd became Mrs. James Madison.

Virginia genealogists and early Madison biographers could not allow the glamorous wife of a President of the United States to have such a name as "Dolley," so they changed it into the nickname "Dolly" and rechristened her "Dorothy." For this they discovered that she was named for her mother's aunt, Dorothea Spotswood Dandridge, second wife of Patrick Henry. Dorothea was only eight years old when Dolley Payne was born in North Carolina.

If her name *was* "Dolley," it may be asked, how comes it that in the *Letters and Memoirs* published by her own grandniece, Lucia B. Cutts, in 1886, she is called "Dolly" in forty-one places? The manuscript of those memoirs is in the handwriting of Lucia's mother, Eliza Cutts, and in forty-one places the spelling is "Dolley." The publishers changed it. The name is "Dolley" in the church birth-record in Guilford, North Carolina, "Dolley" in family Bibles, "Dolley" in all of her letters that bear her full name, "Dolley" in real estate transfers, "Dolley" in her will, and "Dolley" on her tombstone. In 1826 the sculptor John H. I. Browere wrote that his wife was determined to name their baby daughter after Mrs. Madison, but they were unsure of her name in full. He wrote after receiving the information: "Our young daughter has been named Dolley Madison Browere."

Quaker John Payne brought his family back from North Carolina one year after Dolley's birth, and some years thereafter bought "Scotchtown," a big, snub-gabled, clapboard house a hundred feet long, once owned by Patrick Henry in Hanover County. John Payne was opposed to slavery. When the Virginia legislature in 1782 legalized manumission, Payne set his slaves free, sold his plantation, and took his large family to Philadelphia. There he made and sold starch.

Dolley, at the age of sixteen, was a black-haired, blue-eyed, pink-cheeked maiden of striking figure. Although to please her parents she accepted Quaker garb and discipline, she gleefully welcomed the insurgency of two friends, writing to a former house guest: "A charming little girl of my acquaintance, and a Quaker too, ran off and was married to a Roman Catholic the other evening—thee may have seen her, Sally Bartram was her name. Betsy Wistar and Kitty Morris, two plain [garbed] girls have left to effect a union with the choice of their hearts, so thee sees Love is no respecter of persons."

John Payne's starch business failed in 1789 and, solvency being part of Quaker godliness, the Pine Street Monthly Meeting expelled him for failure to pay his debts. He stayed in his bedroom until he died, while his wife converted their home into a boarding house. Dolley was being ardently wooed, at this time, by a young lawyer named John Todd. He stood loyally by the family during its misfortunes, and on January 7, 1790, he and Dolley were married. A son was born to them thirteen months later, and another in August of 1793, just as yellow fever struck the city of Philadelphia.

John Todd took his wife and two children to the relative safety of suburban Gray's Ferry, and he went back to the city. For two months he buried the dead, helped the sick, wrote wills for the dying. In October he buried his own father and mother. Frost killed the plague on October 21, but the fever was in John Todd's veins. "I must see her once more," he cried to Mrs. Payne. And so he did, but that same afternoon he died. Dolley herself was almost fatally stricken, and her infant son died.

Widowed at twenty-five, with a child of less than two years, Dolley Todd went back to her empty house. Her sister Lucy had eloped two years before with George Washington's nineteen-year-old nephew, George Steptoe Washington, who lived at "Harewood" in the Shenandoah Valley. The Washingtons took Mrs. Payne and several of her children into their home. The two oldest boys were roaming the earth and Anna remained with her oldest sister.

John Todd left a house and other property to "the dear wife of my bosom." Dolley needed a lawyer to handle the estate, and Attorney William W. Wilkins promptly fell in love with her but had to settle for the status of brother. Aaron Burr was another legal adviser and friend. Living only one block from the seat of Congress, Dolley was a familiar figure to its members. Congressman Isaac Coles, a firm Madison supporter, was her cousin. Eliza Collins, her bridesmaid when she married John Todd, was engaged to Congressman Richard Bland Lee. One spring day in 1794 Dolley wrote excitedly to Eliza: "Thou must come to me. Aaron Burr says that the great little Madison has asked to be brought to see me this evening."

Madison was forty-three years old and at the height of his early fame. He was "the great little Madison" to the whole country, although at five feet six he was exactly as tall as John Adams, whom few called great and nobody called little. Probably Madison's slender build helped to win him the appellation. A bachelor through prior misfortune, he was no drawing-room favorite, although his stiffness in the presence of women had disappeared—witness his rapport with Madame de Brèhan and friendship with Mrs. Colden. The manner of Madison's approach to Dolley was virtually an announcement of courtship.

The wooing that followed was swift and ardent. Madison was just short of being accepted when he set out for Montpelier in mid-June. Dolley was to visit relatives in Hanover County and then go to the home of her sister Lucy Washington near Winchester. Madison planned to meet her there; but in Hanover County Dolley was stricken, probably with malaria, and Madison was held at Montpelier by the deathly sickness of a young guest from France. Weeks passed with no word from Dolley except that she was ill. Then Madison was lifted to the heights by a letter from her on her way west, to which he replied on August 18: "I received some days ago your precious favor from Fredericksburg. I cannot express, but hope you will conceive the joy it gave me. The delay in hearing of your leaving Hanover, which I regarded as the only satisfactory proof of your recovery, had filled me with extreme [illegible] inquietude, and the confirmation of that welcome event was endeared to me by the style in which it was conveyed."

Madison hoped that Dolley would never have another deliberation on the subject of marriage. "If the sentiments of my heart can guarantee those of yours, they assure me there can never be a cause for it." Dolley wrote another letter at Fredericksburg, to her lawyer and former suitor William Wilkins. Did she have his approval of her marriage with Madison and how would it affect the trust fund set up by John Todd for their son? That fund, Wilkins replied, needed only Madison's approval. About the marriage he wrote:

Mr. M——n is a man whom I admire. I knew his attachment to you and did not therefore content myself with taking
his character from the breath of popular applause—but consulted those who knew him intimately in private life. His
private character therefore I have every reason to believe is
good and amiable. He unites to great talents which have
secured him public approbation those engaging qualities that
contribute so highly to domestic felicity. To such a man therefore I do most freely consent that my beloved sister be united
and happy.

In a passage scratched out but decipherable, Wilkins admitted that
he had "not been insensible" to Dolley's charms. Few persons in his situation "would not have felt their irresistible influence; but none I will
venture to say could have mingled in their emotions more true respect
and more fraternal affection than I have." He was pleased "that an
honorable asylum is offered to my gentle friend who has been so unde-
servedly and vindictively persecuted."

The nature of that persecution was revealed when Dolley reported
to Eliza Collins that Madison had given "full approbation" to the Payne
Todd trust fund, thus relinquishing any claim of his own. You are
acquainted, she wrote, "with the unmerited censure of my enemies on
the subject." Her crime was taking property out of Quaker unity.

James Madison and Dolley Payne Todd were married at Harewood
on September 15, 1794. The date, Madison wrote to his father, reflected
the fact that "on my arrival I was able to urge so many conveniences in
hastening the event." The ceremony was performed before a quiet Payne
family gathering by the Reverend Alexander Balmain of Winchester,
whose wife was Madison's cousin. In her letter to Eliza Collins, written
before the ceremony, Dolley said: "In the course of this day I give my
hand to the man of all others I most admire. You will not be at a loss to
know who this is as I have been long ago gratified in having your approbation. In this union I have everything that is soothing and grateful in
prospect—and my little Payne will have a generous and tender protector."

She signed the missive "Dolley Payne Todd" and added: "Evening—
Dolley Madison! Alass! Alass!" It proved one of those rare marriages
that started out with adoration on his part, admiration or more on hers,
and deepened in mutual love throughout their lives.

Four days after the wedding the bridal couple drove to Strasburg to
visit Madison's sister Nelly Hite. There Dolley had a brief bout with

malaria. Upon her recovery they returned to Harewood and set off for Philadelphia with little Payne and Dolley's sister Anna. They followed a route Madison had taken eight years before, through Harper's Ferry, over rugged mountain roads that made "a perfect wreck" of Madison's "neat and costly" but infamously executed new carriage. In Philadelphia they took a house at a fifty per cent increase in rent, vacated by James Monroe when he left for Paris. Monroe was commissioned to send them second hand house furnishings and other debris of the Revolution, but two years later Madison was still looking for them "by every vessel that escapes the British depredations."

Dolley was expelled from the Friends church for marrying outside of it—the sixth member of the Payne family to be so treated in five years. Congratulations flowed in to Madison from present and past associates. Jefferson, fearing that domestic happiness would take his friend out of public life, dangled the Presidency before him. "There I should rejoice to see you; I hope I may say, I shall rejoice to see you." He adjured Mrs. Madison to keep her husband in office "for her own satisfaction and the public good."

Pennsylvania's Whisky Insurrection began and ended during Madison's marital journeys. Whisky was the only "money" known in the western mountains, and a heavy federal excise combined with distillers' charges amounted to a confiscatory tax on cash income. Farmers replied with tar and feathers, house-burnings, and guns that were not fired. President Washington, spurred by Hamilton, sent 15,000 militiamen under that newly appointed general to suppress the uprising. Hamilton, invoking the principle that "every man may of right apprehend a traitor," sent hundreds of captives back to Philadelphia. His only regret was that he could not fasten treason charges on Gallatin, Congressmen Findley and Smilie, and that "worst of all scoundrels" H. H. Brackenridge—four men who actually had persuaded the embattled farmers to go home before the army arrived. Two obscure mountaineers were tried and sentenced to death, but the President pardoned them.

Madison had no sympathy with resistance to the law, which in his sight advanced "the business of despotism" through the use made of it by Hamilton. He credited the people in general with suppressing the uprising by their wholehearted response to the President's call. By doing so they ended the talk "that a standing army was necessary for *enforcing the laws.*"

Hamilton lamented the premature ending of resistance. "The best objects of punishment will fly," he wrote to Rufus King, "and they ought to be compelled by outlawry to abandon their property, homes, and the United States." The political putrefaction of Pennsylvania was greater than he had any idea of. Without rigor everywhere "the next storm will be infinitely worse than the present one."

Madison sensed the Federalist purpose in the words Hamilton placed in the President's annual message in November. "Certain self-created societies," the message said, were behind the "designing individuals" whose "arts of delusion" misled the western counties. To Madison this meant that Washington's tremendous prestige was being used to wreck the Democratic Societies—"self-created" by ordinary people who had no business to come together politically. Organized on the model of the Jacobin Clubs of France, they were pro-French but strictly American in their objectives. The societies in western Pennsylvania supported the insurrection, those everywhere else helped to put it down. Madison outlined to Monroe the purpose of the "self-created" reference, which he called perhaps the greatest error of Washington's political life: "The game was, to connect the Democratic Societies with the odium of the insurrection—to connect the Republicans in Congress with those societies—to put the President ostensibly at the head of the other party, in opposition to both, and by these means prolong the illusions in the North and try a new experiment on the South."

Federalist editor "Porcupine" Cobbett aimed that campaign straight at Madison by resurrecting some year-old Southern toasts: "The Democratic Societies throughout the world . . . Citizen *Maddison* and the *Republican Party* in Congress." Madison headed the committee that drafted a reply to the President, denouncing the insurrection but ignoring the "self-created societies." In the House, Fitzsimons moved to insert a reprobation of them. By a two-vote margin, the word "self-created" was struck out, ruining his amendment.

To avoid affront to Washington, Madison then moved to censure "certain combinations of men" who had taken an active part in the uprising. In debate he assailed the original language. "He conceived it to be a sound principle that an action innocent in the eyes of the law could not be the object of censure to a legislative body. . . . Opinions are not the objects of legislation." Congress, Madison argued, could properly investigate persons in the public service, but the Democratic Societies were composed of private citizens. "You animadvert on the abuse of reserved rights: how far will this go? It may extend to the liberty of speech, and of the press." And consider the individuals: "It is in vain to say that this indiscriminate censure is no punishment. If it falls on classes, or individuals, it will be a severe punishment. . . . Is not this proposition, if voted, a vote of attainder? . . . If it be admitted that the law cannot animadvert on a particular case, neither can we do it."

One sentence epitomized Madison's view of the political society he helped to create: "If we advert to the nature of Republican Government, we shall find that the censorial power is in the people over the Government, and not in the Government over the people."

Federalists, in reply, warned that wild extremes of liberty would lead to anarchy and usurpation. By a two-vote margin, denunciation of "self-created societies" was put into the resolution. Then one man switched, and the tie-breaking vote of the Speaker reduced the censure to societies in four Pennsylvania counties. That destroyed its political effectiveness and it was supplanted by a meaningless substitute.

Washington came back with a call to the people to check the artful approaches to insurrection. Commented Madison: "If the people of America are so far degenerated already as not to see, or to see with indifference, that the citadel of their liberties is menaced by the precedent before their eyes, they require abler advocates than they now have to save them from the consequences." Ames was reduced to despair by his party's defeat. "Madison and Parker," he wrote to Christopher Gore, "are honorary members [of the Democratic Club]. Oh shame! Where is thy sting?"

The truth was that Congress was almost ready to follow the course of events in England. There panic inspired by the French Revolution was producing wholesale trials for seditious libel (including that of Thomas Paine), and Parliament was about to make it punishable by death to advocate abolition of the rotten borough system.

The election aftermath eased Madison's concern. New York and New Jersey, he reported to Jefferson, were swinging to Republican congressmen. Republicans were holding their own in Massachusetts, where Ames owed re-election to the smuggled-in votes of Negro and British sailors. In Pennsylvania the Republicans won nine out of thirteen seats and stunningly defeated Fitzsimons, leader of the attack on the Democratic Societies. The new Congress, however, would not meet for a year.

In the old one, an outburst of antialienism greeted a bill from Madison liberalizing naturalization. Such a law would flood America with assassins. Samuel Dexter of Massachusetts sarcastically dragged in priesthood and the Pope. This brought Madison to his feet: "He did not approve the ridicule attempted to be thrown out on the Roman Catholics. In their religion there was nothing inconsistent with the purest republicanism. . . . They had, many of them, proved good citizens during the Revolution."

Federalist opposition withered. A few weeks later Dexter sent Madison a confidential note, asking why a man of his talents and integrity should have changed his political position. He was promptly invited to Sunday dinner. Their talk may or may not have started Dexter's conversion to the Republican party. One thing was evident: Madison's marriage had given him an effective sidearm.

Hamilton resigned from the Treasury early in 1795 and in "an arrogant valedictory report" (Madison's words) submitted a plan of debt-reduction that would require thirty years to produce results. Madison, assailing it, proposed a general tax on property. Ames scoffed at this as the meaningless trick of a man out of power; but he exulted that Madison endorsed the land tax at the very time the Republican Boston *Chronicle* "asserts that the Madisonians are opposed to it." The term "Madisonians" was significant. Republican hopes of the Presidency centered in Jefferson, but the party was "Madisonian" in Congress. Jefferson and Madison were pushing each other toward the Executive chair. Jefferson once more appealed to Dolley to keep her husband in line for that promotion. Madison replied that insuperable reasons shut his mind against such an idea. It was Jefferson who should yield to "truths which no inflexibility will be able to withstand."

Jefferson came back with a direct plea to Madison to seek the Presidency, "because there is not another person in the U. S. who, being placed at the helm of our affairs, my mind would be so completely at rest for the fortunes of our political bark." As for himself, bad health, age, the delights of family life, and eagerness for farming were a total bar. "The question is forever closed with me."

Adjournment of Congress on March 3, 1796, gave the senior Madisons, aged seventy-two and sixty-three, their first sight of the new daughter-in-law, whom they knew through her friendly letters. Relieved of farm responsibilities, the senior Madisons spent a good part of the summer at Healing Springs. Meanwhile, what of Jay's mission to England? From the glumness, when questioned, of "those most likely to be in the secret," Madison anticipated ill results. "I suspect," he wrote in February, "that Jay has been betrayed by his anxiety to couple us with England, and to avoid returning with his finger in his mouth." The text of his treaty arrived after Congress adjourned. President Washington called a special session of the Senate for June 8 and kept the contents strictly secret. Madison, combining conjectures with floating wisps of information, sent Monroe an alarming outline. It was fully confirmed in June when Senator Butler, violating an order for continued secrecy, dispatched the sheets of the treaty to Montpelier as fast as they could be copied.

Madison found that it contained not a word about impressment of American seamen into the British Navy. The doctrine that free ships make free cargoes was given up. Tax preferences to American ships were wiped out. Contraband lists were enlarged. The West Indian trade was opened until two years after the war—virtual military action against France. American exports were limited. Sale of French prize goods in America was prohibited. Worst of all was the granting of favored-nation status to Great Britain with nothing in return. What nation, Madison asked Livingston, would grant the United States a trade favor, knowing that it would be passed along to Britain without being paid for? What persuaded Jay to concur in such an insidious surrender? "It seems impossible to screen him from the most illiberal suspicions, without referring his conduct to the blindest partiality to the British nation and government and the most vindictive sensations towards the French Republic."

Offsetting all this, there was little more than a repetition of unfulfilled peace treaty pledges. Such a treaty, Madison declared, would have been scorned by the United States at the time of its greatest embarrassments. It stamped the Federalists as a British party, ready to sacrifice "as well the dearest interests of our commerce, as the most sacred dictates of national honor."

Washington, disliking the treaty, was willing to sign it if the Senate approved. That body did so, by an exact two-thirds vote, on June 24, first excluding the section on West Indian trade and the ban on exports. Senator Mason of Virginia defied rules and gave the treaty to the Philadelphia press, whence, wrote Madison, "it flew with an electric velocity to every part of the Union."

The reaction, as Madison described it later, "was universally and simultaneously against it. Even the mercantile body . . . joined in the general condemnation." Addresses against it went to the President from all quarters. Madison refused to make a personal protest: his current relations with Washington made uninvited communications unwise. Secretary of State Randolph advised rejection. The President, Madison said, was shaken by the reaction and left for Mount Vernon without signing.

Accident, intrigue, and Cabinet malevolence decided the contest. British Minister Hammond handed Secretary of the Treasury Wolcott an intercepted dispatch written in 1794 by French Minister Fauchet. Timothy Pickering, the new Secretary of War, translated it. Fauchet referred to certain "precious confessions" of Secretary of State Randolph regarding the Whisky Insurrection, and mentioned some financial overtures by him that were detailed in Fauchet's Dispatch No. 6.

Wolcott, Pickering, and Bradford called Washington back from Mount Vernon. Randolph was accused of soliciting a bribe. He protested his innocence and resigned. From Fauchet, just taking ship from France, he received Dispatch No. 6 and a letter completely exonerating him. The overtures related to advance payment of three or four merchants selling flour to France. Randolph published a lengthy, inept *Vindication* in which he quoted, in English, a sentence from No. 6 concerning the flour merchants: "Could you lend them instantaneously [*momentanement*] funds sufficient to shelter them from British persecution?"

That sentence damned him. The four flour-sellers *had not then been selected*. How could they be paid *instantaneously?* The brand of infamy hung over him for the next hundred and fifty years. Yet the whole case against him rested on two mistranslations from the French: *"Precieuses confessions"* means *"useful information." "Momentanement"* means *"temporarily"*—a mere request that the unselected flour-sellers be not forced to wait half a year for their money.

Vindictive partisanship deprived Randolph of a fair hearing, but his own ineptitude completed his downfall. "His greatest enemies," wrote Madison, "will not easily persuade themselves that he was under a corrupt influence of France, and his best friend can't save him from the self-condemnation of his political career, as explained by himself." Federalists, meanwhile, were gleefully naming Republican leaders, as the "four men" of the Fauchet letter. Senator Butler wrote to Madison about "a vile underhand game playing with a view of injuring unspotted characters. In this an attempt is making to implicate you." Livingston was more specific: "The name of every man they wish to hunt down is inserted with the specific sum given to purchase him. I suppose I need not tell you that neither you nor Mr. Jefferson have escaped."

Returning to Philadelphia early in November, the family of four (Sister Anna was with them) took a three-story brick house on Spruce Street at £200 a year.

Conflict still raged over the signed treaty with England. For two months Hamilton and King had been pouring out articles under the name of Camillus, Hamilton picturing treaty opponents as a Jacobin rabble seeking to foment a war with England. Madison received an appeal from

Jefferson: "Hamilton is really a colossus to the anti-republican party. . . . For God's sake take up your pen and give a fundamental reply to Curtius and Camillus." Madison sensed that the signing of the treaty had changed public opinion. "The British party," he wrote to Minister Monroe, "were reinforced by those who bowed to the name of constituted authority," or were devoted to the President. Merchants were coerced by bankers and British creditors who threatened to call their loans. Nevertheless, he believed that the real sense of the nation was still on the other side.

Being commercial, Jay's treaty would need acts of Congress to put it into effect. Madison decided to assert the right of the House of Representatives to pass independent judgment on that legislation and thereby decide the fate of the treaty.

The Cabinet situation had worsened. Washington transferred Pickering to the State Department and made James McHenry Secretary of War. Attorney-General Bradford died and was succeeded by Charles Lee, a cipher. "Through what official interstice," asked Madison, "can a ray of republican truths now penetrate to the President?"

In the House, the Federalists ousted Republican Speaker Muhlenberg in favor of Jonathan Dayton. Madison, as usual, headed the committee to frame a reply to the President's message. His Federalist associates, Sedgwick and Sitgreaves, demanded a clause endorsing treaties "compatible with our national rights and honor." Madison accepted it when it was agreed to add "with our Constitution and great commercial interests." That established the basis of his coming attack on the treaty.

Madison delayed this attack. The President (with out-of-office Hamilton writing his message) had shrewdly omitted any request for supplemental legislation, and Madison thought it unwise to antagonize moderate treaty opponents by initiating opposition. Two months later Washington sent a favorable Spanish boundary treaty to the Senate and took that joyous moment to lay Jay's treaty before the House. Still he made no request for legislation. Newly elected Edward Livingston jumped the gun by moving that the President be asked to lay Jay's instructions and correspondence before the House. Federalists raised the cry that the House had nothing to do with treaty papers unless the purpose was impeachment.

Madison stated the basic question: Must the House pass bills to implement a treaty without consulting its own judgment? Smith of South Carolina put it differently: "Can the House repeal the treaty? No; then they must obey it."

Taken without limit, said Madison, the legislative and treaty powers clashed. The powers to regulate commerce, declare war, raise armies, and borrow money were specifically vested in Congress but came within the scope of treaties. There were two ways of looking at the relationship: (1) The treaty power could be viewed as unlimited in its objects and completely paramount—the view of the Jay treaty supporters. (2) The congressional power could be viewed as co-operative with the treaty power, on the legislative subjects submitted to Congress by the Constitution.

If the treaty power was unlimited, he argued, President and Senate could put the United States into a war. The true construction required the sanction of the whole Congress in all cases that involved powers specifically given to that body. The House, in such matters, must exercise its reason.

Ames, too ill to debate, thought Madison strangely wary. "He flinched from an explicit and bold creed of anarchy." Wariness paid off. The House, sixty-two to thirty-seven, called for the treaty papers. The President peremptorily refused to send them: inspection of the papers was irrelevant to any constitutional purpose except impeachment. House Republicans caucused and approved resolutions drawn by Madison. The House did not claim an agency in making treaties, but when a treaty dealt with subjects committed to Congress, it was the right and duty of the House to deliberate on the expediency of carrying such a treaty into effect.

Leading off in debate, Madison conceded that the President might withhold documents on grounds of national security, but the House alone could judge their relevance to legislative objects. No doubt it was true, as Washington had said, that the Convention of 1787 defeated a motion that no treaty should be binding unless ratified by a law. That had no ·bearing on a treaty which was not *made effective* by ratification. In any event, the views of the men who framed the Constitution could never be the oracular guide in expounding it: "As the instrument came from them it was nothing more than the draft of a plan, nothing but a dead letter, until life and validity were breathed into it by the voice of the people, speaking through the several state conventions."

Under this criterion Madison could not lose. In the ratifying conventions, he and others had understated the powers they had aggressively advocated in convention debate. His apotheosis of the state conventions was devised to sustain his altered attitude toward federal power.

The House, fifty-seven to thirty-five, upheld its right to refuse to implement the treaty and spent three weeks debating actual rejection. Madison riddled the treaty, much as he had done in writing to Monroe, and predicted that if the House stood firm, the Executive would seek its modification. The idea of war was visionary and incredible. He estimated on April 18 that he had a twenty-vote majority, but "the banks, the British merchants, the insurance companies were . . . sounding the tocsin of foreign war and domestic convulsions." Petitions were rolling in upon Congress, partly inspired by terror, partly by pressure. A bank director, soliciting signatures among debtor merchants, was "like a highwayman with a pistol, demanding the purse."

The fear-of-war cry echoed in Congress. Ames painted a frightening picture of war and destruction—Indians making midnight aglitter with burning homes, the desolating storm descending from Europe—and Jay's treaty a rainbow of peace at its edge. That speech has been called the decisive factor in the contest, but Madison regarded the issue as already decided by the "fever and delirium" of the preceding agitation. With defeat impending, he sought to heap coals on the other side by condemning the treaty in the act of accepting it, but half a dozen "wrongheads" among his followers would not yield an inch. "Before some were ripe for the arrangement, others were rotten." The motion lost by a single vote, and the treaty was accepted, fifty-one to forty-eight. Madison wrote to Jefferson: "The progress of this business throughout has to me been the most worrying and vexatious that I ever encountered; and the more so as the causes lay in the unsteadiness, the follies, the perverseness and the defections among our friends, more than in the strength or dexterity or malice of our opponents."

The disgusted tone of that remark suggested that Madison was fed up with life in Congress. He found little cheer in conditions outside it. The people everywhere, he continued, had been led to believe that treaty opponents aimed at war. In New England, such was the influence of Aristocracy, Anglicism, and Mercantilism, "that Republicanism is perfectly overbalanced, even in the town of Boston." Spring elections in many states showed that a crisis which ought to have strengthened the Republican cause had crippled it.

By the summer of 1796, attention centered on that year's presidential election. Hamilton leaked the information that Washington was to publish a farewell address. John Adams and Thomas Jefferson were universally looked upon as rivals for the highest position. For second place (but put forward, under the system then prevailing, as if for first) the favorites were Thomas Pinckney and Aaron Burr. Madison's strategy put Jefferson into the race without his consent. Madison had been at Montpelier three months, and the election was only six weeks off, when he wrote to

Monroe on September 29: "I have not seen Jefferson and have thought it best to present him no opportunity of protesting to his friends against being embarked in the contest. Whether he will get a majority of votes is uncertain. I am by no means sanguine. His enemies are as indefatigable as they are malignant."

Washington's Farewell Address to the people had just been published. It showed him, said Madison, to be completely ensnared by the British faction, laboring to prevent any improvement in commercial relations with France. All channels lately opened to his mind conveyed "a rancor against that country and suspicion of all who are thought to sympathize with its revolution."

The address was a composite production to which Madison made a large contribution not hinted at in his criticism of it. Washington wrote, and sent to Hamilton for perfection, a draft that opened by quoting the full text of an address (the one written by Madison) "composed and intended to have been published in the year 1792."

At a personal meeting, Hamilton advised against using the Madison draft in the form of a quotation. Washington concurred but wrote that it should be included. Use of it would show that he had no intention of aggrandizing the executive department. Hamilton embodied almost the whole of Madison's 1,200 words in the address, added his own extensive contribution, and closed with Washington's additional text.

Madison's portion forged the link between Washington and the people and gave the address its inspirational tone. Hamilton added force, amplitude, and partisan politics to the advice about public affairs. The concluding personal passages are almost as Washington originally wrote them. The shafts against the Republican party, which disturbed Madison so much, were the toned-down residue of an unacceptable onslaught by Hamilton. The warning against foreign entanglements stemmed from Madison's 1783 resolutions in the Continental Congress.

Madison went home to Montpelier in the summer of 1796 with his mind made up. He would not seek or accept re-election to Congress. Mingled in the decision were repugnance to the toils and frustrations of minority leadership, love of the farm, and the desire for quiet companionship with Dolley. The last two considerations made him refuse an offer of unanimous election to the Virginia governorship.

At home, Madison took over the management of all the farms, while his father, disabled for months by sciatica, went with his wife to Healing Springs. Madison carried out improvements he had urged his father to make—enriching the soil with clover and plenty of manure, rotating crops. Having no clover seed, he planted timothy and even used the sweepings of the hayloft to convert exhausted land into pasture. On the banks of the Rapidan he supervised the long-planned building of a new flour mill.

Returning to Philadelphia in November they were five in number—James, Dolley, Anna Payne, little Payne Todd, and Madison's sister Frances (Fannie) joining them for the winter. Unable to find an available house, the five crowded into cramped quarters and struggled to stow away the furniture, swollen by a watersoaked shipment sent from Paris by Monroe. Early December found the election still in doubt, four states unreported. Adams was carrying the North, also Delaware and Maryland. Jefferson had Pennsylvania and was winning the South; but under the preposterous system by which each elector voted for two candidates *for President,* second man to be Vice President, Hamilton was intriguing to make Pinckney President. New England responded by throwing away twenty-one Pinckney votes, making Jefferson an easy winner for second place. Final results: Adams, seventy-one; Jefferson, sixty-nine; Pinckney, fifty-nine; Burr, thirty.

Anticipating this result, Madison wrote to Jefferson insisting that he *must* reconcile himself to whichever place he won. Adams, he said, was disgusted with Hamilton and talking in friendly fashion about Jefferson, who might conceivably gain a valuable influence on Adams' policies.

Jefferson responded by sending Madison the draft of a letter to Adams —to be sent or not according to his judgment—expressing unfeigned pleasure at the latter's victory *over himself.* Madison delicately suggested that the letter betrayed difficulty in writing it, and certain phrases might be misconstrued. And what would be the reaction of Republicans who had risked the enmity of Adams by their zeal for Jefferson, if told that their candidate was glad to be defeated? The letter was torn up.

In the "lame duck" session of Congress, Madison renewed his effort to establish a national university in the new capital. Washington was offering his Potomac Canal stock as an endowment. In a momentary revival of their old relationship, the President gave Madison a supporting memorial of the capital commissioners. To outwit the economy bloc, Madison refrained from seeking a public contribution and merely moved to "enroll proper persons" to receive donations. John Nicholas of Virginia replied negatively, with the thought Madison relied on positively, that if a national university were begun with private funds, national dignity would require its completion with public funds. The motion was beaten by one vote.

A new French minister, Adet, emulating the tactics of Genet, stirred antipathy to France by a belligerent published note which Madison called "pregnant with evil." Secretary Pickering responded with a diatribe that supported the British minister's view of him as "one of the most violent anti-Gallicans I have ever met with." Madison described the effect of Pickering's reaction: "The British party, since this overt patronage of their cause, no longer wear the mask. A war with France, and an alliance with Great Britain, enter both into print and conversation; and no doubt can be entertained that a push will be made to screw up the President to that point before he quits office."

A brief message from the President on France (January 19, 1797) showed no sign of that, but it was accompanied by a 30,000-word "corrosive" dispatch from Pickering to the American minister in France (Monroe had been recalled; C. C. Pinckney succeeded him) that filled Madison with alarm. Here was the fester of an incurable gangrene. Congressional action, he concluded, was necessary yet impossible. Silence might look like approbation, but defeat of a motion to disapprove would be worse. There was still time (January 29) for remedial action by President Washington, but more might depend on President-elect Adams, of whose mind Madison knew nothing and expected little. A report was circulating which he sent to Jefferson: "It has got into the newspapers that an envoy extraordinary was to go to France, and that I was to be the person. I have no reason to suppose a shadow of truth in the former part of the story, and the latter is pure fiction."

In reality, the story was *prospectively true*, but it involved action by Adams, not Washington. Two days before the change of administration, Fisher Ames delivered to John Adams the suggestion of Alexander Hamilton that Madison, C. C. Pinckney, and George Cabot be made an extraordinary mission to France. The mission, wrote Hamilton, would need "a man as influential with the French as Mr. Madison, yet I would not trust him alone, lest his Gallicism should work amiss."

Adams asked Jefferson to find out whether Madison would go. The answer (a refusal) had not come when President Adams broached the subject at his first Cabinet meeting. Telling of it in retrospect, he said he had long wished to make use "of the fine talents and amiable qualities and manners of Mr. Madison." At the Cabinet meeting this colloquy took place:

Wolcott: Is it determined to send Mr. Madison?
Adams: No; but it deserves consideration.
Wolcott: Sending Mr. Madison will make dire work among the passions of our parties in Congress, and out of doors, through the states.

> Adams: Are we forever going to be overawed and directed by party passions?
>
> Wolcott: Mr. President, we are willing to resign.

Adams would have averted a quasi-war with France and escaped a mountain of trouble for himself, if he had let them go. During the selection of the commission (C. C. Pinckney, Marshall, and Gerry) Attorney-General Lee asked a Virginia congressman if Marshall would be acceptable in his state. Madison would be preferable, came the reply. "Nobody of Mr. Madison's way of thinking will be appointed," snapped Lee. Hamilton appealed to Wolcott, who replied that Minister Adet also wanted Madison: "If the government suffers France to dictate what description of men shall be appointed to foreign courts, our country is undone. . . . Mr. Madison would insist upon a submission to France, or would obstruct a settlement and throw the disgrace of failure on the friends of government."

A third appeal came from Hamilton, but it was fruitless. No higher tribute could have been paid to Madison, at the close of eight years in Congress, than to have this foreign mission proposed by his arch-enemies, Hamilton and Ames, and favorably received by an Executive with whom in past years he had ever been at odds. They themselves rose above partisanship.

Relieved of public responsibilities, Madison waited a month for March winds to dry quagmire roads. By water he shipped five bushels of precious clover seed, eighteen chairs, sixteen boxes and trunks, and twenty bundles of rods for the manufacture of nails. Overseer Collins brought extra horses to Philadelphia to carry more personal baggage. In leisurely fashion the party of five took a roundabout route to Harper's Ferry to visit Dolley's mother and Madison's relatives in the Shenandoah Valley. Ahead of them Madison sent a refusal to re-enter the Virginia legislature. He and his wife were going to settle into the quiet occupations of rural Virginia.

Farm management kept Madison busy until the 1797 crops were in.
He was in Richmond in December when first word came from the American envoys in France—war seemed near. If it came, it would be war with
a country moving from revolution into the imperialism of General Napoleon Bonaparte; but to President Adams and his Cabinet, this only
added the menace of military genius to the bloody excesses of the overthrown Robespierre. In February, word arrived that Talleyrand, recalled
from exile by the Directorate, had said there would be no declaration of
war on America.

Madison still saw two great obstacles to peace—lack of a cordial spirit
on either side and Jay's treaty with England. It was admitted, he wrote to
Vice President Jefferson, that American policy should put France and
England on an equality. How could this be done? Only by dissolving the
British treaty, an unwise act, or by stipulating with France as we have
with England, "that she may plunder us." By such a compact France
would give up the principle that free ships make free goods. She would be
better off, Madison thought, to equalize conditions by retaliation.

To meet that situation, he went on, the United States could declare
war, go to war indirectly by arming merchant ships, or attempt defense
through commerce regulation. The people would not tolerate the first
course, the third would injure Britain and America more than France;
so, he thought, the second expedient would be persisted in.

Blaming Adams and those around him for putting the United States
into such a hole, Madison scathingly contrasted the first and second
Presidents—"the one, cool, considerate and cautious; the other, headlong, and kindled into flame by every spark that lights on his passions."
In April came word of the solicitation by Talleyrand's agents (dramati-
cally unidentified as X, Y, and Z) of a $250,000 bribe from the American
envoys. Madison found this more incredible for its stupidity, in a man

who had spent his exile in America, than for its heinous depravity; but he was appalled by publication of the dispatch by order of President and Senate. "After this stroke in the politics of those two branches of our government [he wrote to Jefferson], no one who has not surrendered his reason can believe them sincere in wishing to avoid extremities with the French Republic; to say nothing of the internal views to which they mean to turn this extraordinary maneuver."

Those "internal views" were speedily disclosed. The next letter from Jefferson told of a bill in the Senate for deportation of aliens, and the disclosure by a war advocate, "in a fit of unguarded passion," that it would be followed by a sedition bill to shut down Republican newspapers, especially Bache's Philadelphia *Aurora,* a violent critic of Adams. Freedom of the press, Madison replied, was the only remaining check upon desperate projects. The sanguinary faction had better not "adopt the spirit of Robespierre without recollecting the shortness of his triumphs and the perpetuity of his infamy."

The Senate's alien bill arrived—"a monster," Madison called it, "that must forever disgrace its parents." He read Adams' address to the young men of Philadelphia—the most degrading language that ever fell from the lips of a Revolutionary patriot. He surveyed the President's measures. His law for capture of French privateers meant that the war was on. Food shipments to France were cut off, while Britain would be fed at the expense of American farmers through the downward plunge of flour prices. And the answers of Adams to an address of protest formed the grotesque climax of a tragicomedy. The President, wrote Madison, "is verifying completely the last feature in the character drawn of him by Dr. F[ranklin] . . . 'Always an honest man, often a wise one, but sometimes wholly out of his senses.' "

Disregarding protests that the sedition bill violated the First Amendment, Congress passed it, and the President affixed his signature on July 14, 1798. One month earlier he had signed the Alien Act, which gave him unchecked power to deport aliens whom he considered dangerous to American security. The Sedition Act made it a penal offense to publish any false, scandalous, and malicious writing against the government, President, or Congress, with intent to bring them into disrepute or stir hatred against them. The act was to terminate on the last day of Adams' term of office—*prima facie* evidence that the purpose was to terrorize press and public during the 1798 and 1800 elections. The first victim was Congressman Matthew Lyon of Vermont, who went to prison for publishing, in his newspaper, a letter charging President Adams with a grasp for power, thirst for adulation, and selfish avarice.

While this scene developed, Madison was employed in remodeling the family home, using the $5,250 received from the sale of his Mohawk Valley acreage. He bought 100,000 nails from Jefferson's home-operated factory and had 190 French-window panes shipped from Philadelphia.

In the Lyon trial, Supreme Court Justice Paterson (presiding in district court) instructed the jury that they must find the editor-congressman guilty if they concluded that his letter was designed to make the President and government odious or contemptible. In other trials, other justices progressed to vituperation. Shattered was Madison's belief that if guarantees of freedom were embedded in the Constitution, "independent tribunals of justice" would be an "impenetrable bulwark" in their defense. If this failed, Madison had said in 1789, there was a stronger resource—the power of state legislatures to resist federal actions. To this the two men turned on Jefferson's initiative, planning in concert but acting independently.

From this came Jefferson's "Kentucky Resolutions," sent to that state in October 1798, and Madison's "Virginia Resolutions," carried to Richmond in November by Wilson C. Nicholas, who arranged with John Taylor of Caroline for their introduction. The two sets of resolutions were directed to the same end—denunciation of the Alien and Sedition Acts as unconstitutional, but they differed markedly in tone and implications. Jefferson made an emotional assault on the two laws and declared that *each state* had a right to judge for itself of infractions of the federal compact and the mode of redress. The state legislature then declared the laws to be "altogether void and of no force." Madison's Virginia Resolutions opened with a pledge to defend the Constitution, proclaimed federal power to be limited by that compact, and then declared: "In case of a deliberate, palpable and dangerous exercise of other powers, not granted by the said compact, the States who are parties thereto, have the right, and are in duty bound, to interpose for arresting the progress of the evil, and for maintaining within their respective limits, the authorities, rights and liberties appertaining to them."

The resolutions protested against alarming infractions of the Constitution in the Alien and Sedition Acts and called on other states to "concur with this Commonwealth in declaring, as it does hereby declare, that the acts aforesaid, are unconstitutional; and that the necessary and proper measures will be taken by each, for cooperating with this State, in maintaining unimpaired the authorities, rights and liberties reserved to the States respectively, or to the people."

Visiting Richmond in December (during a trip to Hanover County with Dolley), Madison discovered that the resolutions as introduced declared the Alien and Sedition Acts to be "unconstitutional, null, void and of no effect." Nicholas, it developed, had shown the draft to Jefferson who persuaded him to insert the declaration of nullity. Taylor secured its elimination before the resolutions were adopted.

To supplement his resolutions, Madison drafted an "Address of the General Assembly to the People," adopted in January 1799. In it he described the Sedition Act as an artful and vicious device to stir up the people about calumny in order to conceal usurpation. "So insatiable is a love of power," he wrote, "that it has resorted to a distinction between the freedom and licentiousness of the press for the purpose of converting the First Amendment of the Constitution, which was dictated by the most lively anxiety to preserve that freedom, into an instrument for abridging it." He took note of the argument that Congress had power to create and punish the crime of seditious libel provided they allowed the accused to exhibit the truth as evidence in his defense:

> This doctrine, united with the assertion, that sedition is a common law offence, and therefore within the correcting power of Congress, opens at once the hideous volumes of penal law, and turns loose upon us the utmost invention of insatiable malice and ambition, which, in all ages, have debauched morals, depressed liberty, shackled religion, supported despotism, and deluged the scaffold with blood.

John Marshall replied with an "Address of the Minority." He refrained from asserting the existence of a federal common law. Instead he found warrant for the Sedition Act in the combined effect of the power of Congress to pass "necessary and proper" laws to carry out its enumerated powers, and in the English common law *as the law of the individual states.*

Nationally, things went badly for the Republicans from 1798 to 1800. The XYZ delirium brought heavy Federalist gains in the 1798 congressional elections. Held back until after that event were dispatches from Gerry, the only commissioner France was willing to receive. No man of candor, Madison remarked, could fail to recognize that the letters disclosed French anxiety for a friendly understanding, whereas Pickering displayed "a narrow understanding and a most malignant heart." However, he observed an anomaly. The President's message to Congress gave France an option for peace, while the Secretary of State sought through insults to exasperate France into a refusal of it.

Unknown to Madison, the Adams administration was torn to shreds by internal dissension. Hamilton ruled the Cabinet, obtained second place in the military command (under Washington), and became hot for war with France. President Adams, convinced that Talleyrand wanted peace, defied his Cabinet and sent a new mission to Paris, while the naval war continued; but the Adams "completely out of his senses" kept up the domestic war unleashed by the Sedition Act. Six congressmen appealed to Madison in 1799 to re-enter the state legislature and defend Virginia against calumnious attacks engendered by the Resolutions of 1798. Five New England states, New York, and Delaware had responded to the appeal for cooperation, none favorably and typically with defense of the Sedition Act.

Madison yielded, and in the fall went to Monticello for a strategy meeting. Jefferson in his invitation proposed a legislative address to the seven protesting states, reaffirming Virginia's position, expressing warm attachment to the Union, but declaring a determination "to sever ourselves from that union we so much value rather thán give up the rights of self-government." Describing the meeting to Nicholas, who was unable to attend, Jefferson said Madison did not concur. So from this, he added, "I recede readily, not only in deference to his judgment but because we should never think of separation but for repeated and enormous violations." Obviously, this was the argument Madison employed to scotch the secession idea; otherwise it would have deterred Jefferson from making the suggestion.

Entering the legislature, Madison, as committee chairman, wrote a 20,000-word *Report on the Resolutions of 1798*, replying to the protests of seven states. It was adopted on January 7, 1800. The *Report*, a clause-by-clause defense of the 1798 resolutions, fell naturally into four parts. Opening, it centered on the principle that since the states were the creators of the federal compact, they must be the rightful judges in the last resort of whether it had been violated. The term "States" was used in different ways, but in its ultimate sense "it means the people composing those political societies, in their highest sovereign capacity."

The judicial branch, Madison said, had power to make final decisions in relation to other departments of government, but not in relation to the rights of the people as parties to the constitutional compact. Declarations on that subject should be left to the candid judgment of the American public, but their interposition could "be called for by occasions only, deeply and essentially affecting the vital principles of their political system."

Next, Madison re-affirmed his strict construction of the General Welfare clause of the Constitution. From this he turned to the Alien and Sedition Acts, attacking the former both for its innate injustice and for its disregard of the constitutional guarantee of due process of law. Any alien, friendly or hostile, could be expelled by executive fiat on mere suspicion.

The main body of the *Report* assailed the constitutionality of the Sedition Act. He scored the contention that Congress had power to punish seditious libel on the theory that the English common law, being the law of the several states, became *ipso facto* the law of the United States. Such a construction, he said, "would sap the foundation of the Constitution as a system of limited and specified powers." This struck at John Marshall.

Besides having no constitutional basis, Madison averred, this act of Congress was positively forbidden by the command of the First Amendment: "Congress shall make no law . . . abridging the freedom of speech or of the press." He assailed Blackstone's definition of freedom of the press as merely exemption from previous restraint on publication. This idea of freedom, "can never be admitted to be the American idea of it . . . It would seem a mockery to say, that no law should be passed, preventing publications from being made, but that laws might be passed for punishing them in case they should be made." Some degree of licentiousness was inescapable but was accepted under this amendment as less harmful than restraint: "And can the wisdom of this policy be doubted by any who reflect, that to the press alone, chequered as it is with abuses, the world is indebted for all the triumphs which have been gained by reason and humanity, over error and oppression."

Coming at last to the criticisms of Virginia by other states, Madison asked where lay the impropriety of the Resolutions of 1798. The legislature in declaring the acts to be unconstitutional, did not assume the office of the judge: "The declarations in such cases are expressions of opinion, unaccompanied with any other effect, than what they may produce on opinion, by exciting reflection. The expositions of the judiciary, on the other hand, are carried into immediate effect by force."

Madison listed numerous methods by which the states might make their influence felt, either to bring about a repeal of the laws or, in the last resort, to eliminate them through a constitutional convention called at the demand of two-thirds of the legislatures. The *Report*, circulated throughout the United States, was called by John Dickinson "an inestimable contribution to the cause of liberty." Federalists complained that

Virginia had changed her attitude. The change lay entirely in elucidation. The *Report* of 1800 first re-displayed and then pulled the teeth of the 1798 resolutions. Had the explanation been offered in the original resolutions, the document would have created not a murmur of alarm.

In studied disregard of the 1800 clarification, the "interposition doctrine" was trickily revived by the South Carolina nullifiers in 1828 and again in the 1950's by resistors of the Supreme Court's decisions on racial desegregation. In valid effect, Madison's defense of freedom of the press transcends all other features of his *Report*. It became, in the mid-twentieth century, a powerful weapon in resisting congressional and judicial reversions to the oppressive spirit of 1798. In 1800 it built up the public reaction against the President who inspired the Sedition Act and the judges who executed it with unrelenting ferocity.

Enforcement of that law reached its self-destructive climax during the presidential campaign with the conviction of half a dozen editors for stinging but trivial political comments. These vicious prosecutions, Madison thought, could not fail to work a change among the people. "In this view our public malady may work its own cure." It did indeed have that effect, reinforced by Madison's *Report*, but many other factors worked against Adams and Pinckney. Farmers looked on the Federalist party as the agent of exploiting bankers and merchants. Mountaineers were embittered over the whisky excise. Adams' stand for peace with France reversed the shift to Federalism produced by the XYZ scandal and shattered the morale of his own party.

By summer the cry was in full throat that Jefferson was a vile atheist who robbed widows and orphans. Madison was dragged in. Unable to refute his *Report*, wrote Thomas Mason in June, the aristocrats were basely assailing his private reputation. "It galls me beyond description to see men whose understanding I revere, whose private virtues I love, and in whose intimacy and friendship I feel happy, thus weighed down."

Adams' worst trouble was in his own party. "Oh mad! Mad! Mad!" exclaimed Hamilton when the President fired half of his Cabinet. Hamilton, R. G. Harper, and other war zealots concocted a plan for defeating him. Lie low until electors were chosen, advised Harper, then "let those who think Mr. Adams unfit to be President drop him silently." Hamilton's scheme was to induce all South Carolina electors to vote for Pinckney and Jefferson under the two-vote system, thus cutting Adams and putting Pinckney on top of the heap.

Hamilton's intrigue for Pinckney was matched on the Republican side by that of Aaron Burr for himself. Working through David Gelston of New York and Joseph Alston of South Carolina (engaged to marry Burr's daughter, Theodosia), Burr sent assurances to Madison that the Republicans would carry Rhode Island. The four electors of that state would vote for Jefferson and Adams, thus averting a tie between Jefferson and Burr. He wanted a pledge that Virginia would be faithful to himself as well as to Jefferson.

Madison, one of the Virginia electors, gave that pledge. Burr actually was promising to throw away the votes of four men who had not the slightest chance of being elected. And so it turned out. Jefferson and Burr received seventy-one votes apiece, the Federalists trailing six votes behind. Twenty-three years later Madison recorded how he had been gulled: "It is a fact within my own knowledge that the equality of votes which threatened such mischief in 1801 was the result of false assurances dispatched at the critical moment to the electors of one state, that the votes of another would be different from what they proved to be."

Burr was plotting not for a tie but for victory. When the New York electors met to cast their votes, Anthony Lespinard refused to give a pledge to vote for Jefferson. He was held in line by adoption of a resolution requiring all twelve electors to show their ballots to each other.

The tie threw the election into the House of Representatives. Word reached Madison from John Dawson (his successor in Congress) that the Federalists were planning to support Burr but not to elect him, thus prolonging the deadlock. Dawson circulated the reply, called "a strong and angry letter," in which Madison declared that if the present House did not elect a President the next one could choose between the two highest on the list. "Revolutionary," Senator Gunn called this; but the Federalists themselves were talking about a "stretch of the Constitution" by a law putting the president *pro tempore* of the Senate into the Presidency. Commented Madison: "Desperate as some of the adverse party there may be, I can scarcely allow myself to believe that enough will not be found to frustrate the attempt to strangle the election of the people and smuggle into the chief magistracy the creature of a faction."

Congressman Harrison G. Otis saw a chance, by electing Burr, to sow "the seeds of a mortal division" among the Republicans and win Burr over to his new friends. Put no trust in Burr, replied Hamilton—"a profligate, a bankrupt, a man who laughing at democracy has played the whole game of Jacobinism." Hamilton made a pro-Jefferson appeal to Bayard, Delaware's lone congressman, but was repelled. Burr's friends had "distinctly stated that he is willing to consider the Federalists as his friends."

What of Burr himself? Hearing a false report that South Carolina had elected Jefferson, he wrote for publication that he would be dishonored

and insulted by a suspicion that he would think of competing with
Jefferson in the highly improbable event of a tie. After the tie developed,
he wrote to the same man, General Samuel Smith of Maryland, that he
was insulted at the suggestion that he withdraw his name. Publicly, he
adhered to the advice of Federalist Harper: "Keep the game perfectly in
your own hands, but do not answer this letter, or any other that may be
written to you by a Federalist man, nor write to any of that party."

The reason for that was clear. The Federalist votes were in Burr's
pocket but the slightest sign of a link with that party would make it impossible to win the Republican votes he must have to be elected. Congressman Matthew Lyon testified to the words in which his vote was
solicited for Burr: "What is it you want, Colonel Lyon? Is it office, is it
money? Only say what you want, and you shall have it!"

Voting began on February 11. Thirty-two ballots in three days produced identical results: eight states for Jefferson, six for Burr, and two
divided. Then Bayard notified the Federalists that he intended to shift
to Jefferson. For three days he was subjected to "clamor and vehement
invective." On the thirty-fourth ballot, Vermont joined Delaware, and
ten states made Thomas Jefferson President of the United States.

Hamilton has commonly been given the credit for Bayard's decisive
action. His course did him credit, but Bayard knew what Burr was while
voting for him thirty-three times. More potent than Hamilton's appeal
may have been the assurance conveyed to Bayard by General Smith that
Jefferson, as President, would leave well-behaved public officials in office.
Bayard wrote at once to Revenue Collector Allan McLane of Delaware
that his job was safe.

Madison sensed another influence—the inability of the Federalist
phalanx in Congress to hold out against the revulsion of their own partisans outside Congress at the attempt to subvert the election, and the
absence of any military force to abet usurpation. "What a lesson to
America and the world," he exclaimed, "is given by the efficacy of the
public will when there is no army to be turned against it."

Part IV

32 / SECRETARY OF STATE

Shortly after he entered the Presidency and again after he left it, Thomas Jefferson said that he never would have accepted the duties and responsibilities of that office if he had not been assured of the help of James Madison in performing them. On November 24, 1800, Jefferson stopped at Montpelier on his way to Washington, the new national capital, and asked Madison to become Secretary of State, subject to election results. Madison accepted. Other Cabinet appointments were discussed and decisions made.

On December 19 Jefferson urged Madison to come to Washington before the change of administration. Such a forecast of his entry into the Cabinet would assuage the Federalist minority in Congress and inspire the Republicans with "confidence and joy unbounded." Madison replied that his own illness (chiefly rheumatism) and the worsening condition of his father made this impossible. Also, he thought it would be awkward to appear on the political scene before he was regularly called to it, and even before election results made such a call possible.

Their prior conversation on other appointments was pointed to in Jefferson's letter: "I wrote to R.R.L. by a confidential hand three days ago. The person proposed for the T has not come yet." No need to tell Madison that Albert Gallatin was slated to head the Treasury or that Robert R. Livingston was invited to become Secretary of the Navy. This offer delicately informed the former Foreign Secretary that he would not be Secretary of State. Refusing the naval office, he accepted the post of minister to France. That too must have been planned at Montpelier, for there was no written consultation with Madison about it.

Following his election over Burr, Jefferson made an urgent plea to Madison to come immediately after March 4. He prepared to leave, as his father's health was improving, but late in February it relapsed. On the last day of the month Madison wrote that "yesterday morning rather suddenly, though very gently, the flame of life went out."

James Madison, Sr., lacked one month of being seventy-eight when he died. Fatherless from the age of nine, he had built up his Orange County estate by land purchase and the over-fecundity of slaves whose families he refused to break up or condemn to death in fever-ridden Carolina rice plantations. Foremost "squire" of the county, he had been justice of the peace, vestryman, sheriff, county lieutenant and Revolutionary committeeman, army recruiter and wagon builder for the army. The fame of his eldest son never overshadowed his own primacy in local affairs.

When his father's will was opened, Madison found himself executor with a myriad difficult tasks ahead of him, including division of the land among numerous heirs through "amicable negotiations, concessions and adjustments." Hardest to decide was whether a residuary bequest of slaves included the heirs of his deceased brothers, Ambrose and Francis. By general agreement a friendly court suit was decided upon, and the children were excluded. James, to whom the family home was left, traded with other heirs to consolidate their and his holdings. He wound up with three farms of about 5,000 acres, extending from the Rapidan River to the top of the Southwest Mountains. To attend to long-persisting details, brother William was appointed co-executor.

As a prelude to his public service, Madison expressed approval of President Adams' peace convention with France, against which Federalist senators were raging. The agreement included mutual release of captured warships and privateers, of which the United States held eighty-nine, France none. "As the stipulation is mutual," Madison observed, "it certainly spares our pride." Self-interest warned against provoking an unjust and unnecessary war by rejecting the agreement.

Madison's nomination for Secretary of State, submitted on March 5, won speedy approval by a Federalist-controlled Senate called in special session. In the heat of the presidential campaign the Boston *Columbian Centinel* had named Madison and Gallatin as two "sons of darkness" who, in State and Treasury, would help the atheistic, ambitious Jefferson destroy the Constitution. But minister William Vans Murray, predicting his own recall from Holland, wrote that: "if Madison be Secretary of State there will be more justice and liberality of opinions on party men. He is the best of them all."

To avoid the certain rejection of Gallatin, Jefferson withheld his name in order to let him settle into the Treasury through a recess appointment. Robert Smith of Maryland accepted the Navy post after it was refused by three others, including his brother Samuel. Pending Madison's arrival, Attorney-General Levi Lincoln acted as Secretary of State.

Madison was pleased with the President's inaugural address, which paraphrased his own 1783 warning against entangling Old World alliances and called for freedom of speech and press. Jefferson's conciliatory words, "We are all Republicans: we are all Federalists," foreshadowed a policy which Madison approved. All appointees would be Republicans until the Federalist monopoly was thoroughly broken, especially in the courts, but nobody would be discharged for partisan reasons.

The judicial situation was canvassed on April 3 when Jefferson stopped at Montpelier, where he found Madison in "very indifferent" health. President Adams, before leaving office, had loaded the federal judiciary with twenty-three "midnight judges" authorized by the "lame duck" Congress. The President told Madison that, finding a number of undelivered commissions in the office of the Secretary of State, he had forbidden delivery of them. That action brought on the famous lawsuit of *Marbury* v. *Madison* (of no concern to Madison himself) wherein Chief Justice Marshall's *obiter dicta* established the Supreme Court's power to declare acts of Congress null and void.

Delayed by intensified illness, Madison was unable to accompany the President to Washington, when he stopped on April 26, but followed him on a muddy chuckholed road and reached the capital on the first of May, his health improving. The oath of office was administered next day by one of the midnight judges, William Cranch, brother-in-law of Abigail Adams.

The State Department staff consisted of Chief Clerk Jacob Wagner and six other clerks, all hangovers from the Federalist regime. Wagner asked whether his resignation was desired. Honor and delicacy, came the reply, would take the place of political conformity. Publisher Duane confidentially described the staff as a collection of picaroons (Pickering men), nobodies, and a nincompoop. Madison let out one picaroon for economy reasons but the nincompoop, Daniel Brent, held office long enough to tell President Van Buren, in 1837, that his message to Congress reminded him of Mr. Madison, who he thought "understood the use and value of words better than any other man."

The city of Washington had changed decidedly since Madison passed through it four years earlier. One wing of the new Capitol was completed, and the President's white sandstone "palace" was flanked by the brick Treasury building and the still-unoccupied combined offices of State and War. Pennsylvania Avenue was a mile-and-a-half streak of mud, bordered by a stone footway, newly cut through woods and alder swamps to connect the legislative and executive branches of government. Shacks and fine houses were scattered through the forest, and a built-up section followed the roadway from the President's house to Georgetown.

The Madisons spent most of May in the presidential mansion (Federalists accusing the President of charging rent). The State Department was still in the Six Buildings, on the road to Georgetown. There, wrote British legation secretary Augustus Foster, Madison "received foreign ministers in a very indifferent little room into which they were ushered by his clerk."

Foster, later British minister, appraised Jefferson and Madison in the light of long contact. Jefferson was more of a statesman and man of the world, Madison "too much the disputacious pleader;" but Madison "was better informed, and, moreover, was a social, jovial and good humored companion full of anecdote, and sometimes matter of a loose description relating to old times, but oftener of a political and historical interest." A pornographic poem of unknown handwriting, left in Madison's papers, suggests a penchant for off-color narratives. George Tucker, whose acquaintance with him began in 1800, described his appearance at that time: "He was then nearly fifty years of age, dressed in silk stockings and black breeches, and wore powder according to the practice that still prevailed in full dress. The first [impression] he made on me was that of sternness rather than the mildness and suavity which I found afterwards to characterize [him]."

Restating that later impression, he said that Madison "had an unfailing good humor and a lively relish for the ludicrous which imprinted everything comic on his memory and thus enabled him to vary and enliven his conversation with an exhaustless fund of anecdote." In the light of such remarks, one can only marvel at the ability of Historian Max Farrand to write on what American history would be like "If James Madison had had a Sense of Humor."

One of the first foreign ministers received by Madison was Edward Thornton, British chargé d'affaires, who was notified that his country's warships could no longer use American seaports as a base from which to pounce on enemy merchantmen. An order implementing the treaty of 1794 limited belligerent warships to twenty-four hours in port. In the summer, Thornton cited that order in protesting that French prisoners on board the English snow *Windsor* captured the vessel and carried it into Boston harbor. Madison, at Montpelier, referred the case to Jefferson at Monticello, suggesting a reply "that the case is not considered as within the purview of the treaty" because the French recaptors came from a privateer, not a national vessel. The prize could be sent away under another rule which had been invoked against Spain.

The President disagreed. He thought the ship must be considered as a prize "to which no shelter or refuge is to be given in our ports according to our treaty;" but he referred his opinion back to Madison for any revision that he thought proper. Madison put his own view into force. "It was readily decided," he wrote to Gallatin, "that the treaty of '94 is inapplicable to the case." The President "has thought, as I do," that the ship should be sent away under the Spanish precedent.

Throughout his eight years as Secretary of State, Madison habitually wrote (with legal truth): "The President had decided." So completely and habitually did Madison attribute his own lines of thought to the President that it built up a belief, among historians, that Madison was a mere messenger boy. So far was this carried that Bemis' *Diplomatic History of the United States* contains only one mention of Madison as Secretary of State—the fact that he held the post.

Thornton in one of his notes to Madison used the phrase, "With your passion for chess." That precisely described his method of operation. He studied every possible motive for the moves of his opponents and looked to the future consequences of his own. Had he been a poker player he would have "held his cards close to his chest."

Work had piled up pending Madison's arrival, as Jefferson was unwilling to make important decisions in his absence. First to be faced was the question of continuing the annual tribute which Washington and Adams, emulating Europe, had been paying to the Barbary pirate nations. The Cabinet on May 15 voted unanimously to protect commerce with warships instead of dollars; but payments to the Dey of Algiers were three years in arrears and these promises must be fulfilled. The Secretary made up a list of presents including four redbirds and two squirrels. It was to be hoped, Madison wrote to United States Consul Eaton, that Algiers and Tunis would not follow the perfidious example of Tripoli, but if they should do so "their corsairs will be equally repelled and punished." The armada was still in port when the Bey of Tripoli declared war on the United States by cutting down the consular flagpole.

In a larger field, the attempt to shape foreign policy began with dispatches to Rufus King, American minister to England. Expressing a sincere desire to establish "entire confidence and harmony and good will between the two countries," Madison said this could be achieved "on no other foundations than those of reciprocal justice and respect." Of these he saw no sign in the continued British depredations on American commerce, the insulting seizures of American vessels and the number and manner of impressments committed on American seamen. These wrongs, he said, had made a deep impression on the American mind, and unless a change of conduct soon became apparent, American policy could "scarcely fail to take some shape more remedial then that hitherto given to it." The Adams policy of tolerating aggressions had come to an end.

At the same time rumors were afloat that Spain had ceded the vast province of Louisiana to France. "The fact is not authenticated, but is extremely probable," wrote Madison to Wilson C. Nicholas. The subject was being studied, with all its complexities. These involved the changing state of affairs in Europe. Bonaparte, after smashing the great continental coalition, ruled France with dictatorial power as First Consul. Spain was his vassal. The French colony of Saint Domingue (Haiti) was in revolt under the banner of black Toussaint Louverture, who was not brought to heel by a commission as French captain general. England, deprived of continental allies, carried on the war with France at sea. The communistic French Revolution, reduced to a hortatory memory in France, continued to evoke terror in Great Britain and among American Federalists.

To deal with the situation in St. Domingo (as all Americans called the French colony), Tobias Lear was sent there, contrary to French law, as commercial agent. In March, President Jefferson told French chargé d'affaires Louis Pichon that the United States could not act contrary to French rights on the island without helping to throw the region into the hands of the British. That aligned the United States against the rebels, but Madison's instructions to Lear informed him that he would "conform to the intention of the President by an amicable and conciliatory line of conduct, regulated by the principle of neutrality, towards all powers, internally or externally connected with the island."

These instructions, unknown to Pichon, contradicted the assurances given him by the President. He plied Madison with questions but found him "very reserved on this matter." The chargé persisted, seeking to discover the government's intentions either by Madison's "absolute silence or by nonequivocal clarifications." The Secretary "readily named" Lear and other new agents, but when Pichon suggested that it would be a mark of confidence in the First Consul to communicate their instructions, he replied that "*the United States took things in this colony as they found*

them, without presuming to judge, and desired only to continue their
commerce." The administration wished France to recover her colony
but could not risk getting embroiled with Toussaint who, as Pichon ought
to know, was ready to issue a declaration of independence.

"This," wrote the dismayed diplomat (July 22, 1801), "was all I could
get out of Mr. Madison." He hastened to see Jefferson, telling him that
from Madison's "equivocal and reserved language" he feared that the
United States favored Toussaint's project. By no means, the President
assured him, but since France could not act against the rebels, the United
States could do nothing. Then if France *should act* against them, Pichon
asked, would the United States act jointly with France? The diplomat
joyfully reported the answer: "Without difficulty. But for this joint action to be complete and effective it would be necessary that you make
peace with England. Then nothing would be easier than to supply everything for your army and navy, and to starve out Toussaint."

Jefferson elaborated his position. Toussaint's slave insurrection endangered two-thirds of the American states. England, he felt sure, had
no more desire than the United States to see "St. Domingo become an
Algiers [devoted to piracy] in American waters."

In their clash of opinion, Jefferson reacted instinctively to his apprehension of a slave rebellion, Madison was considering the underlying
implications of French policy. Chief of these involved a matter on which
he and Jefferson thought alike—the persisting report that Louisiana,
forcibly transferred to Spain at the close of the Seven Years War, had
been secretly retroceded to France. Jefferson called such a retrocession
unwise and very ominous. Madison told Livingston that he should seek
to make France see and shun the danger of collisions growing out of
contiguity of territory.

To hold and develop the trans-Mississippi country, in the face of
British naval power, France must have an impregnable naval bastion in
the Caribbean. St. Domingo, firmly held, would furnish such a bastion,
and there was no mistaking the effect of the promise Jefferson made to
Pichon. At the next interlude of peace, Napoleon ordered General Leclerc to St. Domingo with an army of forty thousand men and quoted
Jefferson's words in his instructions.

Pichon's fateful dispatch recounted the rest of his talk with Madison.
The Secretary, with an expression at once "circumspect and studied,"
said it was to be hoped that France would abandon the idea of reclaim-
ing Louisiana. With France holding the west bank of the Mississippi,

navigation of that river would cause daily collisions. The United States felt no concern for its own safety. The Western growth of population made it needless to worry about any forces France could send there.

Pichon asked if the United States wished to expand beyond the Mississippi. "A chimera," Madison called the idea. Surely, said Pichon, the United States would not make it a crime for France to recover lost territory. Madison repeated with studied emphasis that if the transfer took place, it would almost certainly bring on a collision between the two countries.

The young chargé had a repute in the Foreign Office beyond his years and rank. When stationed at Amsterdam, he led Talleyrand to reverse his stance by persuading him that President Adams wanted peace and that Envoy William Vans Murray could be trusted. Now he apologized to the Foreign Minister for venturing into discussion without instructions, but the conversation with Madison "was too categorical, the circumstances too urgent," for him to remain passive.

The transfer of Louisiana, Pichon warned his government, would carry the germ of a future conflict unless, from the outset, France knew how to act on all points that concerned American security and commerce. Adopting Madison's argument about military power, he pointed out that Kentucky had increased in fifteen years from 60,000 to 250,000 souls and was shipping millions of dollars worth of produce through New Orleans. On August 11 he wrote that in spite of the President's words to him concerning St. Domingo, the policy he suspected Madison of following seemed to remain in effect. Agent Tobias Lear at Cap Français was echoing Madison's purpose of maintaining good relations between the United States and Toussaint's government.

Having set these diplomatic lines in motion, Madison left for Virginia late in July, warned by a severe bilious fever to seek the curative quality of mountain air. Before departing, he gave architect William Thornton the task of finding a suitable residence for him. Thornton contracted for a house having a common wall with his own, under construction at what is now 1333 F Street, Northwest. He borrowed $600 to pay a year's rent for Madison and supervised the division of the third floor into four dormered bedrooms. Coachhouse and stables for four horses were yet to be built.

Madison was at Monticello in September when a false report arrived that French action on the Franco-American peace treaty (actually ratified on July 31) had been postponed. It was decided that Livingston should leave at once for Paris, and Madison prepared his instructions on his return to Montpelier. The minister must try to dissuade France from carrying out the transfer of Louisiana and Florida. In doing so he should emphasize the American desire for harmony with France, the danger of collision resulting from territorial contact, and the unwillingness of the United States to see this territory pass from Spain to Great Britain. He could remark that if the French presence in Louisiana led to embroilment with the Western states, this might turn American thoughts toward a closer connection with Great Britain. This could produce a crisis in which French possessions "would be exposed to the joint operation of a naval and territorial power." Should the cession be irrevocable, it would open a new objective. France might "be induced to make over to the United States the Floridas, if included in the cession to her from Spain, or at least West Florida, "through which flowed the important river Mobile."

These instructions held out a gloved hand with a sword behind. France could leave Louisiana and Florida with Spain, relying on the United States to keep England out, or she could risk the loss of the country *through a union of American land power and British sea power*. This penalty could be escaped by transferring all or part of Florida to the United States. The main objective was to obtain New Orleans, the great West Florida port of entry on the Mississippi.

Pichon sensed new hazards in the violent public reaction to Spanish seizures of American ships. "I am afraid they may strike at Louisiana before we take it over," he wrote. In November, a few weeks after Madison returned to Washington, news came that France and England were at peace. The Treaty of Amiens spread French hegemony over most of the continent west of Russia, while Britain got Trinidad and remained supreme at sea.

Peace left Napoleon free to move (jointly he expected) against Toussaint Louverture; but President Jefferson now talked stiffly to Pichon. If France took possession of Louisiana, he warned, the next war in Europe would produce an American alliance with England. France would hold the province "no longer than it pleases the United States." Blacks on the island of Guadeloupe revolted and sent a mission to seek American recognition. Madison assured Pichon that it would not be granted, but when shown a French order limiting trade to government-held ports, the Secretary told him that no direct measures could be taken to stop commerce. But, said Pichon, the *droit public* forbids trade with rebels. Public law, responded Madison, had nothing to do with it. Trade was forbidden by a valid French regulation which the United States could not help to enforce. Wrote Pichon: "Mr. Madison and I understood each other very well. In these arguments as in my replies, it was really Saint Domingue that was at issue."

Continuing the exchange, Madison said that the United States did not intend to antagonize the black population of these colonies and implant germs of enmity that could finally be brought to birth in the slaveholding states. At this reversal of Jefferson's position, Pichon "recalled to Mr. Madison" that the President, last summer, had said "positively that the United States would join in starving Toussaint." Receiving no reply the chargé hurried over to see Jefferson: "I found him very reserved and cold, while he talked to me, though less explicitly, in the same sense as Mr. Madison."

General Charles V. E. Leclerc landed on St. Domingo with 20,000 men (as a starter), the prestige of being Napoleon's brother-in-law, and orders to supply his armies from the United States. "Jefferson," wrote the First Consul, "has promised that the instant the French army arrives, all measures will be taken to starve Toussaint and to aid the army." Finding himself without money in a destroyed city and all available supplies overpriced in American ships and warehouses, Leclerc sent an agent to New York to sell drafts for a million francs. The banks, loaded with dishonored French bills, would not touch them at a thirty per cent discount. Leclerc seized American cargoes in the port he controlled. American exporters canceled sailings. Denunciations filled the American press. French officers vituperated the United States. Pichon pleaded with Leclerc and with the Foreign Office, telling both that to win the war against the rebels they must cultivate American friendship. Napoleon ordered that Pichon himself feed the army.

The chargé boldly replied that the order appeared to be a confession of incompetence in France, but he would do what he could to achieve the impossible. He began with a letter to Madison, intended for publication, warning of the danger to America from black chiefs who were refusing to submit to the white race, and saying that France expected the United States to forbid trade with the rebels.

Pichon handed this letter personally to Madison who advised him to suppress it. The American national spirit, the Secretary said, longed for expansion of trade. The Dominican revolt opened and assured an insular trade that would be ended with defeat of the rebels. The trading Northern states cared nothing about Southern fears of a slave insurrection. Pichon would do well to issue a simple announcement of the trade-restriction order and say nothing that could "stir up party men and enthusiasts." The advice was accepted.

The chargé then turned to the supply problem and was met with a barrage of questions. Why was so large an army sent to St. Domingo? Why was it kept secret from the United States? Was it true (and Madison knew it was) that part of the accompanying naval squadron was to land an occupying force in Louisiana? Pichon got past that by whipping out a friendly letter from Admiral Villaret to the President. Madison promised payment of $140,000 due to France under the recent treaty, but he balked at an appeal for a loan. Imagine the outcry in the country, he said, if Congress made such a loan while France was refusing to indemnify American merchants for spoliations at sea. Once more Pichon appealed to Jefferson, who (he wrote to Talleyrand) "spoke to me with the language of sincerity and marked interest" and said he would consult with members of Congress on what could be done. "Mr. Madison on the contrary spoke a language entirely discouraging." Two weeks later Pichon sadly recorded that all the support he received in Congress was from enemies of France endeavoring to maneuver the administration into a pro-French position.

Confirmation of the cession of Louisiana reached Washington in the spring of 1802, through reference to it in a later Spanish treaty. The effect was evidenced in the dramatic words used by the President to Livingston. From the moment France enters New Orleans, wrote Jefferson, "we must marry ourselves to the British fleet and nation." This paraphrase of Madison's 1801 instructions to the minister has been put forward again and again, by historians, as the beginning and climax of American policy toward France.

Madison saw dark prospects. "No hope remains," he wrote to Livingston on May 1, "but from the accumulating difficulties" of putting the transfer into effect and its destructive influence on Franco-American relations. The minister should exert every effort to induce France to abandon the project. If New Orleans and the Floridas were included in the cession, he should ask France to put a definite price on them.

The "accumulating difficulties" were those of Leclerc. "The prospect of a protracted and expensive war in St. Domingo," Madison told Livingston, "must form a very powerful obstacle to the execution of the project." This prospect was reported to him by Lear, whom Leclerc expelled for protesting the arbitrary imprisonment of two American ship captains. These men, wrote Madison in asking Pichon to seek their release, had been "treated as the vilest of malefactors." Pichon hastened to Madison's house, where the Secretary read aloud a letter from Leclerc to Lear reciting the crimes of the two Americans. John Rodgers (who had risked his life to rescue the French population of burning Cap Français) had calumniated the French army *while in the United States*. The other captain had a ship named the *St. Domingo Packet*, which made Leclerc think it was owned by Toussaint.

Pichon wrote to Leclerc with cold legal logic tinged with biting irony. "In law, General, a citizen of a foreign country does not have to answer before the authorities of another country for acts" committed outside the complainant's jurisdiction. "As for Mr. Davidson, allow me, General, to observe that the name of a ship and suspicions do not constitute a misdemeanor."

On receipt of this letter the husband of Pauline Bonaparte blew up completely. This man, he wrote to brother-in-law Napoleon, is *un fripon, un miserable*, a rascal who took money on the side in buying supplies. "*Je demande son changement.*" Pichon received a reprimand much milder than was called for by the First Consul. Tell him, stormed Napoleon, that he should not engage in political conversations which degrade his government; his excessive zeal has subjected him to remarks such as no French agent ought to listen to. Tell him that the proceedings of the army were blamable, but he is not to judge the motives of General Leclerc in making the arrests, as he had undisputed police power. Tell him it might be true that the French had used hard words against Americans, but American newspapers were filled with the most indecent calumnies of France and her armies.

Napoleon's outburst seemed actually to be directed more against Madison, for accurately dissecting the First Consul's policies, and against the American public, than against Chargé Pichon, who kept his post. (The corruption charge was formally withdrawn.) Livingston, to whom a protest was made against the army slanders, was instructed to reply "that our presses are not under the regulation of the government, which is itself constantly experiencing more or less of their abuse."

The French ruler notified his Minister of Marine that he intended to take possession of Louisiana with the least possible delay. To further the process he tricked Toussaint into a peace conference and sent him to die in a French dungeon. Ship me the rest of the black generals by September, he adjured Leclerc. "Defeat these gilded Africans and there will remain nothing more to desire."

The gilded Africans were not shipped to France. Guerrilla warfare spread, and yellow fever came to the aid of the rebels. Half of the French officers were dead by June. The black generals Christophe and Dessalines, who had helped to betray Toussaint, were made French commanders in regions beyond the reach of Leclerc. Their territory expanded as

Leclerc's shrank. France restored slavery in Guadeloupe, and the news of it sent revolution flaming over every hill and valley of St. Domingo.

Napoleon was now confronted with two choices affecting his coveted empire beyond the Mississippi. To hold it, he must rebuild French power in the West Indies, at a vast expenditure of men and money, and make ready for an ultimate collision with the United States. The alternative was to renew the European war, toward which Old World ambitions were pushing him, and rely on the United States to keep Louisiana out of British hands. He chose the impossible—he would follow both courses.

33 / THE LOUISIANA PURCHASE

Federalists were surprised that the first session of Congress under President Jefferson did not result in the country's downfall. At its opening, Griswold of Connecticut looked around at the ignorant Jacobin scoundrels and expressed belief that his own party members, "in consequence of their superior skill," would have a decided influence on legislation. Alas, his colleagues were soon crying that never in history was a set of men more blindly devoted to their leaders than these Republicans to the President. Congress knocked out the new circuit courts and most of the "midnight judges," abolished internal taxes, began to cut the public debt, and repassed Madison's liberal naturalization law. Jefferson freed the victims of the Sedition Act.

Black despair seized the Federalists. "We are all going the downhill road to democracy," wrote Senator Uriah Tracy, "naturally and with our whole might." Fisher Ames conceded that Jefferson probably believed in his extreme democratic principles. "Madison certainly knows better and yet there ever was a strange vein of absurdity in his head." Jefferson and Madison were the Roland and Condorcet of America's French Revolution and only accident or Federalist energy could keep a Robespierre from following.

Pichon saw another contrast between Jefferson and Madison. The President, possessing no dignity, went about on foot, on horse, without servants, and received visitors "in an unseemly negligé, very often in slippers." However, "the whole administration is not on this footing. Mr. Madison lacks nothing of dignity, but Mr. Gallatin prides himself on an absolute lack of it." Hamilton (Robert Troup recorded) regarded Madison as "in a deep decline" among surrounding demagogues and predicted his early resignation. Federalists were unable to believe that a man of obvious honesty, intelligence, and mental balance could genuinely approve what was going on.

Why did Jefferson leave Federalist minister Rufus King in London? Theodore Sedgwick had an answer. Republican leaders, "a certain little great man excepted," viewed nothing with more horror than a rupture with England. This conclusion was based on the campaign canard that Jefferson was a coward and also reflected ignorance of Madison's current view of England, as a potential ally in the Louisiana situation.

Peace in Europe cancelled the wartime advantage given to American shipping and gave full effect to Britain's heavier countervailing duties. To lay new burdens on foreign ships, Madison wrote to King, would violate the spirit of the 1794 treaty. He proposed that each country repeal its discriminatory laws, to be effective when the other country did so. The British government, hoping to build up exports, accepted the proposal and senseless panic swept New England. Jefferson left the decision to the Federalist congressmen whose constituents had everything to gain from mutual repeal. They so perverted the issue, wrote Madison, that action was postponed for a year.

In Paris, Robert Livingston was getting nowhere fast. The reason for that was made plain in June 1802 by an inspired article in the semiofficial *Gazette de France*. Accusing the United States of furnishing arms to the St. Domingo rebels, it said the rapid increase of American population, industry, trade, and wealth destined that country to rule over the new world and put all the West-Indian colonies under its yoke. Europe should put off that evil day by making Louisiana "a counter poise to the domination of the United States." The article echoed Talleyrand's 1797 forecast that France in possession of Louisiana and Florida would form a "wall of brass forever impenetrable to the combined efforts of England and America."

Pichon described the effect of the article. Federalists cried out that Paris and Madrid were deceiving and playing with a feeble administration. Madison in a "very serious discussion" said it appeared that France aimed at splitting the United States apart. It was an error to think that loss of the West would greatly weaken the Atlantic states, and a still greater error to think that the Western states wished to withdraw. With all America united, "France cannot long preserve Louisiana against the United States, and nothing would do more to unite the whole continent than having France in the neighborhood."

Instead of being a counterpoise protecting other French and Spanish colonies, Madison went on, French presence in Louisiana would weaken the hold on them. An American alliance with England in the next war would throw all of South America into British hands. The United States wanted no possessions there, but even without a war the United States and England, acting together, could within ten years divide all the export and import trade of these colonies. It was thus, said Pichon, that Madison talked, "with much coolness, much method, and as if he had been prepared." The President talked to him in the same vein.

Although he knew of Leclerc's request for his recall, Pichon calmly tore Talleyrand's basic policy to shreds. France foresaw and accepted future American power and ambition when the decision was made to help the United States win independence. Any attempt to repress American growth by force would throw the two countries together. It was necessary, in dealing with the United States, "to be resigned to their future power, to conciliate them, and acquire the merit, useful in other respects, of acceding to that which the force of events will give them in spite of us."

A few days after this interview, Pichon received a lengthy outline, to be presented to Madison, of the French complaints concerning St. Domingo. Its contents plainly stamped Talleyrand as the source of the *Gazette's* accusatory article. Pichon sent back, point by point, the Secretary's oral reply. The arming of Toussaint by President Adams, said Madison, was a byproduct of the naval war for which the Jefferson administration was no more responsible than the First Consul was for the acts of his predecessors. If the United States had cut off all supplies to St. Domingo, Great Britain would have taken the island. How could the United States break with Toussaint, a French general, when France herself had not condemned his conduct? Would not that have brought on commotions? "These conclusions, citizen minister, are irresistible."

Madison, Pichon continued, granted the general right of European powers to monopolize their colonial trade; but when those colonies were opened to foreigners, the United States claimed a right "to place national dignity and the state of commerce out of reach of all arbitrary action and injury." That required the admission of American consuls to French colonies. Secondly, the United States would no longer submit to the despotism and caprice to which their carrying trade was subjected by the European states. France would face reprisals if she did not remove discriminatory duties. Britain still required that American goods be carried to British colonies in British ships, but "we have the means to compel a more just treatment of our rights."

In the fall of 1802 and on into the spring, Madison received a string of extraordinary communications from Livingston. Late in the summer, the minister had sent two memoirs to Talleyrand. The first declared that

France could become invulnerable at sea only by dividing the empire of it with the United States. Given a proper commercial treaty, he predicted, Americans would unite with France in hostile operations against England. That was presented to men who knew that the United States had entered a naval war against France while formally allied with her.

The second memoir made a strong presentation of Madison's thesis that a Mississippi River boundary between two nations, at a vast distance from their government, would produce local collisions and lead to war. Continuing, he said that through a union of sentiments and commercial interests, France and the United States could transfer part of British commerce to more moderate nations "and deliver the world from the tyranny founded by Great Britain." The best commentary on that diplomatic masterpiece is the fact that it was expurgated from the memoir published in the *American State Papers* in 1832, edited by Robert's brother Edward Livingston.

Next came letters from Livingston suggesting that Pensacola and St. Augustine be left to the French, who desired them to prevent American control of the Gulf of Mexico, while New Orleans and the rest of West Florida would be "a cheap purchase at twenty millions of dollars." A year elapsed before Madison learned, from Legation Secretary Thomas Sumter, that the $20 million valuation was obtained from the Boston speculator Daniel Parker who added, in reply to Sumter's protest, "a man might make his own fortune too."

Dismaying information reached Washington in November 1802. Spanish Intendant Morales, using European peace as a pretext, had closed the port of New Orleans to all except Spanish vessels and prohibited the deposit of American goods. Madison sent protests to New Orleans and Madrid. To our Western citizens, he wrote to Minister Pinckney, the Mississippi is everything. "It is the Hudson, the Delaware, the Potomac and all the navigable rivers of the Atlantic states formed into one stream." If the intendant added obstinacy to his ignorance or wickedness, nothing but energetic action of the American government could temper the indignation of the Western people.

To Livingston, Madison wrote that no matter who held the mouth of the Mississippi, "justice, ample justice, to the Western citizens of the United States is the only tenure of peace with this country." There were or soon would be 200,000 militia on the waters of the Mississippi, every man of them ready to march at a moment's warning in defense of their right to free use of that river. This consideration alone ought to be sufficient "to cure the frenzy which covets Louisiana."

In March 1803 Madison received from Livingston a note which he described to Jefferson as an enigma, suggesting "some hazardous finesse or some unwarrantable project." The minister said he had "in a private memoir under the [First] Consul's eye, touched a string that has alarmed them." Cryptic advice followed: "The minister [Talleyrand] knows nothing of this. Set on foot a negotiation fixing our bound with Britain, but by no means conclude until you hear from me that all hope here is lost."

What possessed Livingston, exclaimed Madison to Jefferson, to put such a confidential letter, "not even in cipher, into the hands of a British minister" to forward from London! Weeks later came the "string" that was to bring Napoleon to heel. Livingston, after receiving a suggestion from Joseph Bonaparte that the United States seek Louisiana instead of Florida, sent a proposal directly to Napoleon through his brother. France should keep East Florida, giving her command of the Gulf of Mexico. She should sell to the United States West Florida, New Orleans, and Louisiana north of the Arkansas River. The alternative: "France, by grasping at a desert and an inconsiderable town, thereby throwing the weight of the United States into the scale of Britain, will render her mistress of the new world."

This argument undermined Madison's strategy. Instructed to persuade France that American self-interest forbade a transfer of Louisiana to England, Livingston made the United States a mere instrument of British territorial ambition. Next to come from him was a follow-up letter to Joseph Bonaparte. The plan he was proposing, Livingston said, would furnish an easy way of meeting the spoliation claims of American citizens, but secrecy was needed to "prevent the debts from being the object of speculation *other than such as the First Consul shall authorize.*" Edward Livingston omitted the words here italicized when he published this letter in 1832, thus converting Robert's bribery offer to Joseph into a moral preachment.

The American minister suggested a mode of operation. "To enter into the financial arrangements of people in power here," he wrote, "would lead me into a very delicate discussion." The better way of collecting American claims was to make "some advantageous offer" such as he had sketched in former letters. In other words, pay $20 million for Florida and let French officials split the swag above the amount of American spoliation claims.

Up to this point, Napoleon's attitude was adamant. He was set on holding and developing St. Domingo and Louisiana. Late in December he received stunning news—Leclerc's army was virtually wiped out. The

First Consul ordered a fleet and army to sail instantly for St. Domingo, but the ships froze up in Dutch harbors. He appointed General Bernadotte minister to the United States. The general, second most powerful man in France, was to hold the Americans to friendliness with France during a renewed European war and reconcile them to French ownership of Louisiana. Livingston was told that he "must consider the purchase of [New Orleans] as out of the question."

In the United States, the closure of New Orleans set the entire West to clamoring for war with Spain. Federalists denounced the administration for weakness. To take forcible possession of New Orleans, Chargé Thornton wrote on January 3, 1803, would be the most popular action the President could take. On that day Pichon called on Madison at home and was told "how uneasy and estranged they were" in regard to France. "I furnish you, Citizen Minister, word for word and without comment the conversation of Mr. Madison":

> Is it not singular, Mr. Pichon, that Mr. Livingston has not
> been able to obtain, at the date of his last letter from Paris, a
> word of response to the inquiries he has made on the subject
> of our interests and our rights upon the Mississippi? Certainly
> if people behaved thus toward you, you would regard this
> silence as a sort of declaration of war. It is absolutely neces-
> sary that our position with respect to you be clarified, or it
> will soon become more serious. We wish to live in peace with
> all the world, but I fear that in France they may not be willing
> to let us follow our inclinations in this regard.

Jefferson and Madison had now lost confidence in Livingston. In Spain, Minister Charles Pinckney was doing no better in a similar assignment—persuading Spain to sell the Floridas if she still owned them. From Madrid at this time came a confidential note from Legation Secretary John Graham, a young man Madison knew and trusted: "In my opinion nothing will be done here advantageous to the United States unless another minister is sent out pointedly charged to speak boldly . . . a man of talents and address."

To meet this double crisis Jefferson and Madison reached a decision: to appoint James Monroe as a special envoy, having joint powers with Livingston in Paris and with Pinckney in Madrid. Congress was asked for a secret appropriation of $2 million for unspecified diplomatic purposes. Madison, writing the House committee report, met the clamor for military action by asking whether we should lay the foundation for future peace or the hazards and horrors of war, "the great scourge of the human race." The Floridas and New Orleans, his report declared, "command the only outlets to the sea" for the American West, and "must become a part of the United States, either by purchase or conquest." Congress voted the money.

Madison's joint instructions to Livingston and Monroe charged them to seek, by just and satisfactory arrangements, a cession of New Orleans and East and West Florida, or as much thereof as they could. They had full power to sign a treaty "concerning the enlargement and more effective security of the United States in the River Mississippi and in the territories eastward thereof." No price limit was fixed, but the President was willing to go up to fifty million livres ($9,375,000).

The French, Madison said, could hardly fail to see that hostile measures against the United States would "connect their councils and their colossal growth" with France's formidable rival. The collisions at New Orleans should warn her against assuming the hazards of proximity. Western and Altantic people alike believe "that they have a natural and indefeasible right to trade freely through the Mississippi. They are conscious of their power to enforce this right against any nation whatever."

Without acquisition of Louisiana being made an object, its relationship to Western security put it well within the range of negotiation. Jefferson revealed the thought of it, or of seizure, a few days later when he decided upon the Lewis and Clark exploring trip to the Pacific Northwest. "We might through those agents," he remarked to Senator Plumer, "purchase land of the Indians or think of conquest."

The President put quite a different complexion on the joint mission when Pichon dined with him on January 12, 1803. Monroe was chosen, said Jefferson, because he was so well known as a friend of the Western people that his mission would operate to "tranquillize them and prevent unfortunate incidents." The administration hoped, wrote Pichon, that conditions in St. Domingo and Europe would delay the occupation of Louisiana and give time for negotiations. If these failed to halt the transfer, the United States could make alliances and act with greater vigor after ten years' growth. The costs of war would make the administration unpopular, so Monroe was sent to appease and control the ferments of the West.

Even with this long range threat, the "tranquillizing" avowal tended to undermine Madison's warning of Franco-American collisions on the Mississippi. It reached Paris in a sequence of developments which Livingston described to Madison. He learned of Monroe's appointment on March 3, just after he had made arrangements for satisfying Talleyrand's

"540.1675.1460.1541. . . . which I must now relinquish." Madison did not interline the ciphered words, which were "personal interest." That is, Livingston realized that he could not count on Monroe joining him in bribing the Foreign Minister. His colleague was, in fact, enjoined by Madison to use "honest means."

Knowledge that Monroe was coming stimulated Livingston to action. He sent Talleyrand the stiffest note yet on Louisiana and the New Orleans closure, basing it on Madison's repeated admonitions of the danger of war. Talleyrand, the minister reported, promised a reply that would take care of American rights on the Mississippi. "Unfortunately," wrote Livingston, "dispatches arrived at that moment from Mr. Pichon, informing them that the appointment of Mr. Monroe had tranquillized everything." Talleyrand decided to let the storm blow over and sent a note "which contains nothing."

Livingston was correct as to facts but not as to causes. On the day Pichon's note was received (March 22) or the next, British Ambassador Whitworth offered a $500,000 bribe to Talleyrand to be split with Joseph and Lucien Bonaparte, on condition that they persuade Napoleon to preserve the Peace of Amiens and leave Malta in British hands in exchange for a free hand on the continent. With Napoleon intent on using Malta as a stepping stone to Egypt, the only chance to collect the bribe was by persuading the First Consul to concentrate on St. Domingo, Florida, and the empire of Louisiana. Joseph and Lucien carried the argument to Napoleon even in his bathtub and won the plaudits of historians (ignorant of the bribe) for patriotic devotion to France.

It was not Talleyrand, but Napoleon, who would measure the weight of Jefferson's remark about sending Monroe to tranquillize the West. This was not the last word from Pichon. Six days later (March 28), a follow-up dispatch arrived, repeating, amplifying, and giving new direction to the earlier account. Two days after his talk with the President, Pichon said, Madison invited him to his office and gave him a very different account of the Monroe mission.

Events at New Orleans, the Secretary said, proved that navigation of the Mississippi never would be surely guaranteed until that river formed a national boundary all the way to the sea. All difficulty could be prevented by ceding the territory east of the river to the United States, and Monroe would be authorized to offer perhaps two or three million dollars, which the situation in St. Domingo might render especially useful.

Madison then warned France, in well-veiled terms, not to provoke a forcible expansion of the United States beyond the Mississippi. He dreaded to have circumstances arise (a war) that would carry its population to the western bank: "In spite of the affinities of custom and language, a colony beyond the river could not exist under the same government. It would give birth infallibly to a separate state, having in its bosom the germs of collision with the East, all the more ready to develop because there would be more connections between the two empires."

The conduct of France, Madison went on, might "determine the political combinations" (an alliance with England) that would lead to these eventualities. These would be unpleasant for the United States, but the alliances would be still more so for France.

Madison's argument was designed to deter France from attempting to hold Louisiana. The evil consequences he pictured for the United States, from a flow of American population beyond the Mississippi, were based on holding that region *as a colony*. Settled and admitted to the Union state by state, it would (and later did) fit his doctrine that stability and freedom in a federal republic increased with its size.

Pichon understood perfectly that the picture of civil war drawn by Madison for an expanded United States was actually a notification that peace was impossible between the United States and a French colony. "The implicit language of Mr. Madison," he wrote to Talleyrand, ". . . brings to light ideas too general to be neglected"—ideas whose germ he had long ago displayed to his government. French policy must be founded on these incontestable conclusions: (1) French colonies, as experience [in St. Domingo] proved, could not exist at any time without the friendship of the United States. (2) In Louisiana, "we are dependent on them in time of peace; at their mercy in the first war with England."

"The crisis [Pichon declared] grows greater every day, and we cannot push it into the distant future. . . . I should fail in my duty if I did not tell you that these feelings of concern which Mr. Madison expressed to me are generally felt and that public opinion in the latest circumstances expresses itself at least as strongly and energetically as the government."

Napoleon read Pichon's dispatch on March 28 or 29. He had just cast the die in Europe by saying publicly to Ambassador Whitworth: "I must either have Malta or war." The First Consul reacted to Madison's warning by ordering that General Bernadotte proceed at once to his ministerial post: "The necessity of his presence in America does not admit another hour's delay." His presence was essential only if Napoleon was determined to hold Louisiana.

On April 8 Livingston sent Talleyrand a clipping from the New York *Chronicle*, recording a motion of Senator Ross to appropriate $5 million and raise 50,000 troops for the seizure of New Orleans; but Livingston weakened the effect by saying it was reported that Monroe's sailing might be postponed (a damaging untruth) and telling how grateful it would be to his own feelings to announce that the friendship of the First Consul was solely responsible for restoration of American rights at New Orleans. Not a word about a land cession—that was thrown out of the window in order to get ahead of Monroe, who landed on that day at Le Havre.

The balance tipped next day when the diplomatic pouch from London brought a copy of the *Times*. The United States Senate, it chronicled, had voted to build fifteen gunboats to cruise in the Mississippi. The President was about to call out 80,000 militia. It was immaterial, the accompanying story read, whether Spain or France possessed Louisiana, "the government and people seem to be aware that a decisive blow must be struck before the arrival of the expedition now waiting in the ports of Holland." The country appeared to be on the eve of war with France.

Ignoring Talleyrand, of whose motives he had become distrustful, Napoleon summoned Finance Minister Marbois and Admiral Decrés to the St. Cloud palace. Marbois chronicled the developments in his *Historie de la Louisiane*. They remained there all that Easter Sunday (April 10) and the following night. Saying that he knew the value of Louisiana, the First Consul told them that he had not a moment to lose to put it beyond the reach of England: "I am thinking of ceding it to the United States. . . . They ask me only for one city of Louisiana, but I regard the entire colony as already lost . . . Tell me, each of you, what you think."

Marbois recorded his reply: "We should not hesitate to sacrifice what is going to slip away from us. . . . [The Americans] need but enter the country to be its masters." Decrés warned that without such colonies France could have no navy. Napoleon slept on the question overnight and then summoned Marbois: "I renounce Louisiana. It is not only New Orleans that I mean to cede; it is the whole colony, reserving none of it."

Take charge of the negotiations, Napoleon ordered. Tell nobody but Talleyrand. See Livingston today; do not wait for Monroe's arrival. What price? asked Marbois. Ask for a hundred million francs, plus American assumption of mercantile claims; but half of that would be acceptable.

Across the ocean, in these momentous April days, the Jefferson administration was moving closer to an accord with England. On the eighth, the President asked his Cabinet to vote on terms of an alliance, should one prove necessary. Madison, Gallatin, and Smith, outvoting Dearborn and Lincoln, approved a mutual pledge of no separate peace. All voted not to let England take Louisiana.

Madison sent new instructions to Livingston and Monroe. If France denied free navigation of the Mississippi, they were to assume that war with her was inevitable. The next day word came that Spain had restored the right to deposit American exports in New Orleans—a heavy blow, wrote Madison to the envoys, to those clamorous for war. He did not guess the reason for it: Godoy's spiteful resolve that France should not benefit from Spain's prior violation of American rights.

Both to the envoys and through Pichon, Madison continued to threaten an alliance with England and war with France. He regarded the Ross resolution, authorizing him to seize New Orleans, as a drive at war "through a delegation of unconstitutional power to the Executive;" but he made all possible use of the war spirit that lay behind it. Speaking loudly in a social circle, Pichon reported, Madison told the chargé that it was true that "the nation was in a ferment . . . that it felt its strength . . . that it held the balance in the new world and could decide it at any moment." There was "one power [England] which realized this perfectly, and it was to be hoped that all would realize it." Having said this, Madison added a perfect preview of the Monroe Doctrine, including the extension President Cleveland gave it in 1895:

> That the United States had no inclination to make a trial of their strength, but if they were obliged to do so, it was easy to see what the outcome would be: that in truth their interest was that the new world remain at peace; that the wars of Europe should not prolong their ravages there, and that it would depend in great part on them [the United States], one day, to guarantee it this tranquillity.

In a private letter to Monroe, which remained undeciphered until 1952, Madison called for shrewd management of the war threat to stimulate "the yielding dispositions of France." It must not be overdone, and the United States must not arm too heavily, lest France be led into an unexpected accord with England: "In case of an adjustment between them, without one between us and France, we might be on the worst of terms." France and England had been ten days at war when this was written.

Another ten days passed, and Madison received the amazing news that Louisiana had been offered and nothing remained but to agree on a price and specify the boundaries. The same pouch brought Livingston's account of happenings on April 11, the day after Napoleon announced his decision, and a joint dispatch of the two envoys confirming the proceedings.

Talleyrand, sent by Marbois, asked Livingston "whether we wished to have the whole of Louisiana. I told him no, that our wishes extended only to New Orleans and the Floridas," but that it was sound French policy to give the country above the Arkansas. Pretending that he lacked authority, Talleyrand replied that without New Orleans the upper country would be of little value. What would the United States give for the whole? Twenty million francs, Livingston ventured to say. Too little, replied the foreign minister.

Livingston told how Napoleon came to change his mind. It resulted from his—Livingston's—conversion of Talleyrand and his sending of Senator Ross's resolution to Talleyrand with "an informal note expressive of my fears that it would be carried into effect, and requesting that General Bernadotte might not go till something effectual was done."

There was not an atom of truth in this concerning himself except for the bare conveyance of the Ross resolutions. About them he wrote: "What the effect of these resolutions were was not known." He did not convert Talleyrand. That minister, when informed of Napoleon's decision to sell, wrote "*Nulle*" on the draft of a reply to Livingston's ignored memorials, telling him that Louisiana was still ruled by an independent foreign power (Spain).

Livingston's note of April 8 contained not a word about delaying Bernadotte, but four days later he begged Talleyrand to speed the general on his way "before Mr. Monroe arrives," bearing an answer to "my last note with something positive . . . couched in generous terms. You could [say that] you are charged to ask me to present some particular proposition . . . and that the First Consul is disposed to listen to such a proposition with the generosity and moderation that mark his high character."

At the finish, Livingston sufficiently recovered his sanity to write, "Please, Sir, regard this as unofficial," thus enabling him to conceal it from his own government. Livingston's contemporary dispatches correctly reported the dates of events preceding Monroe's arrival. A month later he wrote to Madison that the decision to sell was made "as I informed you, on the 8th of April." In his own Letterbook he altered the date of a note to Talleyrand, and in writing to Congressman Mitchill and General Gates he gave three false dates. Working through the Boston expatriate speculator James Swan, he flooded the American press with the story that his last memorial to Talleyrand produced the cession.

What moved Livingston to these incredible actions? *Cherchez le candidat.* When he heard that Monroe was coming he submitted his resignation, later withdrew it and wrote to his brother Edward: "To my friends who are upon the spot I wish to leave the direction of my future career in politics." His ambition: to become the Republican nominee for Vice President in 1804.

Livingston as minister was no more effective in promoting the sale of Louisiana than Talleyrand was in blocking it. Basically, the decisive force was the westward pressure of American population. Five men, however, share the personal credit: Napoleon, whose ambition to rule the Old World made him more cognizant of obstacles to ruling the New; Jefferson, whose affirmative attitude was basic to the acquisition; Madison, who corrected Jefferson's tactical errors and put steadily mounting pressure on Napoleon without stirring his antagonism; Pichon, whose courage and wisdom strengthened Madison's strategy; Toussaint Louverture, who undermined the capacity of France to hold a continental American colony. These five men set the United States on the road to empire.

34 / SEEKING WEST FLORIDA

From President Jefferson down to the last buckskinned woodchopper in the new state of Ohio, Republicans hailed the purchase of Louisiana as a magnificent and stunning victory. To Federalist leaders (except Hamilton) it signalized the crack of doom. A Pandora's box pregnant with evils, Oliver Wolcott called it, and Rufus King agreed. Gone was the supremacy of the Atlantic states, as Gouverneur Morris had foretold in 1787. Kentuckians in Congress were bad enough, moaned Josiah Quincy, but now "other like thick-skinned beasts will crowd Congress Hall—buffaloes from the head of the Missouri and alligators from the Red River."

Madison, in his usual quiet manner, wrote to the envoys of the pleasure and high expectations aroused by the dawn of their negotiations. "The purchase of the country beyond the Mississippi was not contemplated in your powers because it was not deemed at this time within the frame of probability." Though not expressly authorized, it undoubtedly would be confirmed.

Completion of this purchase, Madison remarked, would exhaust the fund appropriated for the acquisition of Florida, but that could be dealt with later. "The Floridas can easily be acquired, especially in case of a [European] war, and perhaps by arrangements involving little or no money." That is, Florida might be ceded to satisfy American claims for maritime damages inflicted by Spain as France's ally.

Later dispatches from Livingston and Monroe told of swift and easy financial negotiations with Marbois. Starting with Napoleon's figure of a hundred million francs and offered half as much, the Finance Minister came down to eighty million and warned that if the Americans held out for less, the temperamental First Consul might change his mind. They accepted, on condition that twenty million be used to satisfy the claims of American merchants and shipowners.

Under the treaty, the United States was to pay sixty million francs ($11,250,000) in stock, irredeemable for fifteen years, and twenty million ($3,750,000) in American treasury notes. France already had sold the stock to Baring Brothers of London and Hope of Amsterdam at a discount of $1.5 million, under the easy-going system by which English bankers financed countries at war with their own.

The treaty reached Washington on July 14. A hallelujah chorus resounded throughout the nation, drowning the shrill cries of Federalist congressmen who, exclaiming at the enormous price, declared that the administration was bankrupting the Treasury to buy a desert.

Accompanying the treaty and official dispatches was a private letter from Monroe praising Livingston's work in the negotiations but blaming him for his repeated and futile efforts "to conclude something before I got here." Livingston's own letters, Madison replied, "fully betrayed the feelings excited by your mission," and revealed his disregard of the measures of the government.

A few days before the treaty arrived, Madison said, American newspapers published Livingston's memoir to Talleyrand, and along with it "a letter from Paris understood to be from Swan . . . representing it as the primary cause of the cession," and treating Monroe's arrival as something that "snatched the ostensible merit" from Livingston. Swan (regarded by Monroe as "the greatest scoundrel in Europe") duplicated Livingston's misdating of the Louisiana offer.

Madison found it hard to believe that Livingston himself was responsible for publicizing his memorial, with its suggestion of a Franco-American alliance. He would not be surprised if England took notice of it. Instead of accusing Livingston, Madison asked him to "trace the indiscretion of its author." Livingston's next letter disclosed that he had authorized the French government to publish his memorial unofficially, requested to do so, he claimed, by a French minister who said it would reconcile the people of France to the cession. (The people were not thinking about their new war with England!) Madison ordered him to withdraw his authorization. French publication would give the appearance of American collusion with France against England. Livingston replied that "reflecting more fully" on the matter, he had withdrawn the request before he was ordered to do so.

Another source of trouble lay ahead. Madison was unaware that Swan, one of the major claimants to the 20 million francs allotted to Americans under the treaty, was in effect European publicity manager of Livingston's campaign for Vice President. The allocation of damages was placed in the hands of Livingston, supervised by a three-man American board.

One clause of the Louisiana treaty caused concern. Ratifications had to be exchanged by October 30, but Congress was in recess. The Cabinet voted for a special session beginning October 17. Two weeks would be enough for a quick-acting body like the United States Senate. There was also a minor stumbling block. President Jefferson concluded that the purchase was unconstitutional. In the previous January he had agreed with Gallatin that "there is no constitutional difficulty as to the acquisition of territory," but he thought it "*safer* to proceed by amendment of the Constitution." When the time for action came, he wrote to Senator Breckinridge that in thus advancing the good of their country, the Executive "have done an act beyond the Constitution."

Deciding to ratify first and get power later, Jefferson submitted an amendment to Cabinet members decreeing that Louisiana "is incorporated with the United States." Madison objected that this implied the absence of power to acquire Florida. He suggested an additional clause extending congressional power to territories "which may be acquired by the United States," thus implying the power to acquire them.

The matter stood thus when Jefferson, at Monticello, received from Livingston a hastily written letter whose nonciphered passages (the key was in Washington) seemed to indicate a threat by France to void the treaty if the whole agreement was not complied with in the time specified. Thoroughly alarmed, Jefferson sent the letter to Madison at Montpelier, saying that he still wanted an amendment but thought they had better get it *sub-silentio* without the knowledge of France.

Madison, reading the dispatch, saw no wish by France to get out of the bargain. Rather, she wanted to hasten its execution to prevent a British intrusion of Louisiana and was trying to find out whether the United States had an understanding with England on that subject. (That is, for England to seize the province and turn it over to the United States without its being paid for.) That was precisely what the envoys said in their next joint dispatch; but individually, Livingston continued to pile up warnings that France was "sick of the bargain" through which the United States gained such an immense advantage. This was self-exalting illogic: Napoleon could have upset the treaty simply by directing Spain to refuse to deliver Louisiana to France.

Such a possibility was posed to Madison when he received notice from Spanish Minister Carlos d'Yrujo that Spain regarded the sale of Louisiana as a "manifest violation" of a pledge by Napoleon that France "will never alienate it." This caveat against the purchase, Madison observed to the President, would be very serious if French or even British collusion could be suspected. That being highly improbable, he put it down as a device to obtain a price for Spain's consent to the transfer and to give Spain a talking point in fixing the boundary between Louisiana and Florida.

Disagreement on that subject loomed between Washington and Madrid. In their negotiations with Marbois, Livingston and Monroe told the French minister that their researches into ancient maps and records showed the Perdido River (twenty-five miles east of the Mobile) to be the boundary between Florida and the ancient French province of Louisiana. The Peace of 1763 gave England everything along the Gulf from the Mississippi River to the Atlantic Ocean. England split this country at the Appalachicola River into East and West Florida. Thus, West Florida from New Orleans to the Perdido was part of Louisiana. The American envoys proposed that the treaty make this clear. Marbois warned against it. "The mere name of Florida" he told them, "would produce difficulties with Spain." Livingston and Monroe then proposed that the province be transferred *in the very words* by which Spain ceded it to France in the Treaty of San Ildefonso, October 1, 1800. That idea was followed with enlargements.

The signed treaty declared that Spain had retroceded to France, and France now ceded to the United States, "the province of Louisiana, with the same extent that it now has in the hands of Spain, and that it had when France possessed it, and such as it should be after the treaties subsequently entered into between Spain and other states." The last clause confirmed the east-west boundary fixed in 1795 between the United States and the Floridas. That left two criteria, derived from the Treaty of San Ildefonso, by which to fix the boundary running northward from the Gulf of Mexico: Louisiana as it was up to 1762, in the hands of France; Louisiana as it was between 1762 and 1800, in the hands of Spain. On the day the treaty was signed, wrote Livingston, the envoys had told the French that they construed it to make the Perdido the boundary, "so that there will be no deception should we claim it in treating with Spain."

Madison met Yrujo's argument by quoting the written refusal of Secretary Cevallos to discuss a sale with Minister Pinckney. France had recovered Louisiana, and "the United States can address themselves to the French government to negotiate the acquisition of territory which may suit their interest." That, replied Yrujo, merely gave France the duty of rejecting the demand. Madison's arguments, Yrujo wrote to Madrid, "are as full of subterfuges, evasions and subtleties, as they are destitute of logic, solid reasoning, and devoid of that good faith which he always puts on display when speaking and writing, and which squares so little with his political conduct."

This personal unpleasantness did not prevent the Marchioness d'Yrujo (the former Sally McKean of Philadelphia) from riding around Washington with Dolley in the Madisons' new chariot of "neat plain elegance," glassed all around, with Venetian blinds, built for them that summer at a cost of $594. Many a congressman, trudging along Pennsylvania Avenue's stone walk felt friendlier toward the Secretary of State after receiving a lift from Dolley to the Capitol or Executive offices.

The subterfuges, and so on, to which Yrujo objected reached their summit in his argument that Spain's cession to France was invalid because Napoleon had not fulfilled the promise on which the treaty was based—to secure world-power recognition of the Spanish King's son-in-law as King of Etruria (a new name for Tuscany). England and Russia refused to recognize the king, therefore the treaty was invalid. Madison remarked to Yrujo that by ascending the Etrurian throne, the king had notified the world that the conditions on which this action depended had been fulfilled or waived. Finally, the orders signed by the King of Spain for putting France in possession of Louisiana "are an answer which admits of no reply."

French officials advised Monroe not to go to Madrid in quest of a Florida cession while Spain was balking at the delivery of Louisiana. He went, therefore, to London to work against impressment of seamen (Rufus King having resigned), leaving Livingston to press for a French definition of the boundary. Madison defined for Livingston the American position on the "rightful limits" of Louisiana: "It seems undeniable, from the present state of the evidence, that it extends eastwardly as far, at least, as the River Perdido; and there is little doubt that we shall make good both a western and northern extent highly satisfactory to us."

This reflected the tone of a Cabinet meeting in which all present— Madison, Gallatin, and Dearborn, answered yes to the President's question whether New Orleans should be taken by force if Spain refused to give it up. Jefferson sent the Louisiana treaty to the Senate on October 17. The debate there lasted two whole days. Federalists echoed Yrujo's claim that France had no power to make the cession. The overwhelming Republican majority ratified the treaty, twenty-two to seven.

Concealed from the Senate was a short-fused time bomb from Napoleon. Fearful of Anglo-American collusion, he had demanded a clause *in the exchange of ratifications* declaring the treaty void if funds were not transferred within the time prescribed. Pichon and Madison did some shadowboxing. The chargé argued in support of the insulting demand. Madison put forward a counter-clause: the United States could declare the treaty void if Louisiana was not delivered as stipulated. Take both or neither, he said. Pichon, as expected, disobeyed Napoleon's order—an action almost unique in French annals. Madison's counter reservation, Pichon explained to Talleyrand, was to open the way to seizure of the colony if Spain blocked a peaceable relinquishment.

Spanish obstruction was not a wholly imaginary menace. With the treaty ratified, documents exchanged, and financial affairs in train, President Jefferson sent regular army and militia detachments down the Mississippi, with five hundred mounted Tennesseeans as a reserve at Natchez. Territorial Governor Claiborne and General Wilkinson, Madison informed Livingston, were authorized to decide on the need of a *coup de main*. None was needed. On January 15, 1804, an express from New Orleans brought word that Louisiana had been peaceably delivered, first to France and on the same day to the United States, on December 20.

This action cleared the way for renewed pressure on Spain for payment of spoliation claims growing out of French use of Spanish seaports in the war that ended in 1801. Spain denied liability on the ground that a Spanish royal order forbade such actions. That, Madison replied, was a confession of liability, since the order had never been enforced. When French consuls condemned American ships in Spanish ports, they either did so under the authority of Spain or without lawful authority. In the latter case their actions were nonconsular and private: "As well might Spain say that a theft or robbery, committed in the streets of Madrid by a Frenchman or an American, is to be redressed by France, and not by her, as pretend that redress is to be so sought for spoliations committed by cruisers from, or condemnations within, Spanish ports."

There could be no escape from this responsibility, Madison told Pinckney, unless Spain not only pleaded duress, prostrating her national honor, but proved the reality of the duress. Meanwhile, similar depredations were being repeated in Spanish ports in the West Indies, forming a ground for additional reparations. All these claims, probably exceeding what the United States would offer for all the territory east of Louisiana, were to be brought into the negotiations for purchase of that colony.

Pinckney and Monroe had a tough assignment, to induce Spain to give up a colony she was determined to keep, in exchange for cancellation of a debt she did not intend to pay. For the time, however, American efforts centered on the part of West Florida regarded as part of Louisiana. The

French commissioner who made the transfer told Governor Claiborne, privately, that no part of Florida was included in the delivery. In regard to the western boundary, Madison reported to Livingston, he "held a language more satisfactory"—the cession extended to the Rio Bravo (Rio Grande). Livingston should gather evidence to support the American claim to the Mobile region and, in upper Louisiana, to the 49th parallel as the boundary with Canada. He must work to keep the French government "in our scale, against that of Spain." France ought to welcome a transfer of the Floridas to the United States to keep them out of the hands of Great Britain in case the war spread to Spain.

As a first step toward assertion of a boundary on the Perdido, Congress passed the Mobile Act of 1804. Sought by the President, probably drafted by Madison and Gallatin, it was steered through the House of Representatives by John Randolph of Virginia, who became chairman of the Ways and Means Committee and administration leader in his second term. Tall, thin, and ghostly pale, this shrill-voiced man was the Republicans' most effective orator. Rendered impotent by an attack of mumps in early youth, he substituted a flourish of pistols and (more deadly) invective for the conventional virtues of manhood.

The Mobile Act extended the revenue laws to all territory ceded by France and contained two sections that bore on territory still held by Spain. Section 4 added to the Mississippi customs district all the navigable rivers, bays, and inlets "lying within the United States, which empty into the Gulf of Mexico east of the River Mississippi." Section 11 gave the President discretionary power to create a separate customs district embracing "the shores, waters, and inlets of the bay and river of Mobile" and other waterways east of the Pascagoula.

Section 4 put West Florida within an existing American customs district, to the extent that it lay within the purchase from France. Section 11 authorized the President to create a district embracing the same area, with no declared limitation to lands "lying within the United States."

The wording of these two sections permitted customs jurisdiction over Mobile Bay without a prior settlement with Spain, and various historians have called this the government's intention. The record disproves it. Before the bill was signed, the Cabinet voted to extablish a customs house on the Mobile River but located it at Fort Stoddert, *north of the 1795 boundary*. Three days after the signing, Secretary Gallatin instructed Hore Browse Trist, collector of the new District of Mississippi, that it was the President's intention to negotiate for this part of West Florida, not to occupy it by force, "and you are therefore to exercise no act of

territorial jurisdiction within the said limits, though part of your district."
A fortnight later Madison told Pichon that the sole purpose of Section 11
was to provide for immediate customs control in case Spain recognized
the Perdido boundary during a recess of Congress.

To give Yrujo a chance to object, Madison had sent him two printed
copies of the bill during the weeks that it lay before Congress. The Spanish minister uttered not a word of protest, but when the signed act was
published he stormed into Madison's office and angrily denounced Section 11 as an invasion of Spanish sovereignty. Madison assured him that
the act was much less drastic than he supposed, although West Florida
was "clearly ours."

Those words drove the Spaniard to fury. He wrote to Madison, pretending that the published act of Congress was a newspaper fabrication.
It constituted, said he, an "atrocious libel" on the American government,
an insulting usurpation of the rights of his sovereign, a direct contradiction to presidential assurances. Reporting this to Pinckney in Madrid,
Madison called it "a rudeness which no government can tolerate." Remembering the minister's previous laudable conduct, the President was
not asking for his recall, but would leave it to the Spanish government to
provide a means of restoring cordial communication. In other words,
Spain should recall or censure him without being asked to do so.

In spite of his indignation, Madison made a temperate reply to Yrujo.
Section 11, he said, was subordinate to Section 4, and shared by implication the limitation to places "lying within the United States." Although
the President was given power to extend the customs district to places
beyond the acknowledged limits, if within the *claimed* limits, that would
not be done in advance of friendly adjustments with Spain. Yrujo was not
mollified. The insult of the claimed jurisdiction, he replied, was not
altered by the President's promise not to exercise it. Only repeal by Congress could remove the insult.

Yrujo was wrong on one count, right on another. He mistook the implications of the act for its purposes. But there was patent impropriety in
the failure to specify in the act that its provisions were subordinate to
negotiations with Spain. Why was that omitted? Presumably because it
would weaken the last resort—the use of force if negotiations failed.
Madison's construction, that Section 11 was ruled by Section 4, was given
the force of law by President Jefferson when he set up the Fort Stoddert
customs district on May 30, 1804. Acting under Section 11 he used the
words of Section 4, limiting the district to areas, "lying *within the boundaries of the United States.*"

Believing that Spanish policy might still be determined in Paris, Madison sent Livingston a detailed analysis of the Treaty of San Ildefonso. First amplifying the argument that Louisiana "when France possessed it" extended to the Perdido, he took up the alternative wording—the extent "that it now has" (or had in 1800) in the hands of Spain. The two definitions, he contended, covered the same extent. It was "not denied that the Perdido was once the eastern limit of Louisiana," nor was it denied "that the territory now possessed by Spain extends to the river Perdido." That river, then, "is the limit to the eastern extent of Louisiana ceded to the United States."

The word "now" in the treaty, Madison said, covered the fact that Louisiana was ceded to Spain in two installments. The portion west of the Mississippi went to her in 1762, the rest of it, and Florida, going to England at that time and to Spain in 1783. France knew it only as a unit, and that unit was restored in the retrocession. The term "retrocede," in the treaty, he said, fittingly described the return of the entire province to France.

Madison's analysis was uncannily correct, although the proof lay buried in French and Spanish archives. In the San Ildefonso negotiations, Napoleon insisted on the double definition of the extent of Louisiana, in order to set up a title to the Mobile district. Why then did he not support the American contention that it was included? The reason can be found in his remark, recorded by Marbois, that if the treaty with the United States contained no obscurity as to boundaries "it would perhaps be good policy to put it there." Spanish anger would be diverted from France to the United States.

Livingston was pleased with the partial shift of negotiations from Madrid to Paris but, he wrote, if the United States relied on a direct application to France, "a great private interest would defeat your object." He believed he could have made a better bargain for Louisiana if the appointment of Monroe had not prevented him from satisfying Talleyrand. "As it was, the the sale of Louisiana brought no profit to a shop that has not usually seen a customer pass by." East Florida by itself was "of too little moment to afford a *bon pot de vin*," but the two Floridas together would merit a good price with something "for the privy purse." The American arguments, he believed, would be "sufficiently cogent if backed by a million livres" for those who were to smooth the channel in Paris and Madrid.

This amazing letter has lain in the Madison papers open to the public for more than a hundred years. Historians who readily quoted advice in it to seize West Florida apparently thought the bribery proposal too trivial to mention. By the time Madison received the letter Livingston had left office, a new minister was on his way to Paris, and Talleyrand had come to Spain's support. Madison advised John Armstrong, Livingston's successor, that if Tallyrand's deviation from sound policy was an effort "to convert the negotiations with Spain into a pecuniary job for France and her agents," it would no doubt be pushed with temerity but might "finally be abandoned under a despair of success" and give way to something better. In other words, millions for purchase but not one cent for bribery.

Ever since he took up the task of implementing the Louisiana treaty, Livingston had been engaged in a running battle with the United States Commission of Claims appointed by himself and Monroe as part of the machinery for paying American claims out of the twenty million francs earmarked for that purpose. Under the complicated system, an American claims agent (Consul General Fulwar Skipwith) was to act jointly with French officials in approving claims. In cases where they disagreed, the Claims Commission was to *ascertain* whether the claims were eligible or not. They were to report their findings to the American Minister, who would then send his own observations to the French government, whose decision would be final.

Livingston contended that this gave him general control over the commission in spite of the word "ascertain" in the definition of its duties. The fight opened with an attempt by Livingston to have claims paid in full as fast as they were approved, pursuant to a "conjectural list" of priorities, supposedly chronological, submitted by him. The board, learning from Skipwith that the list was in a chronological jumble, voted to dig into the original records to obtain correct dates. Since the claims already in and yet to come seemed likely to exceed twenty million francs, it decided to hold back payments and prorate the ultimate deficiency, if any.

Livingston furiously protested this course. His motives were not made clear in the official records, but the course he demanded would have given priority to three of the biggest claimants, James Swan, John R. Livingston, and Peter Livingston, whose combined claims totaled 4,084,188 livres. The Livingston claims were legitimate but Swan's, amounting to about 2.5 million livres, were largely based on losses actually incurred by him, the board found, as a purchasing agent for the French government.

Swan marshaled a dozen American claimants into an attack on the board and a eulogy of Livingston, who "by his unabated zeal and unceasing solicitude effected the cession of Louisiana to the United States" together with the means of a speedy discharge of American claims. Then

Livingston received a stunning blow. Madison (enlightened by Skipwith) informed the minister that it seemed doubtful whether the twenty million francs would cover all claims. He was directed to seek *at once* an agreement with France to suspend all payments until it was ascertained whether the fund was adequate. Instead of obeying, Livingston replied with a letter so fantastic that it was placed in the files without being deciphered. It recounted a patently imaginary conversation between him and Marbois about Talleyrand's account to him of the fury of Napoleon over nondelivery of Louisiana stock (already delivered). From this Madison would see "how delicate a business it will be to ask any modification of that treaty till they get their money."

Livingston and Marbois teamed up in support of Swan's claims, the French financier rendering an opinion that the Commission of Claims was wholly subordinate to Livingston. (Madison disagreed when he heard about it.) The fractious board, nevertheless, rejected Swan's fifteen claims, eight of which, if valid, should have been paid out of the French treasury. Livingston punished Skipwith by cutting $1,000 off his salary and transferring that sum to one of his own clerks—an unwarranted action, Madison commented to the President, in which he probably consulted "his feelings rather than his instructions."

A brilliant thought now struck Livingston. Since it was too late to be nominated for Vice President, he would engineer an exchange of offices with the Secretary of State. Marking his letter private and confidential to be deciphered only by Madison, he wrote on February 8, 1804: "If it were possible to spare you from where you are, you can render your country essential services here." There were many objects of moment to be sought, and should the office be upgraded from minister to ambassador, "your rank and political standing would render them proper."

Jefferson and Madison just one day earlier had a still more brilliant thought. Relying on a long-unanswered request to be relieved, Madison invited Mr. Livingston to come home.

Meanwhile, Yrujo emphasized his break with Madison in the spring of 1804 by closing his house and leaving for Philadelphia without calling on the Secretary. "He and the marchioness called together at the houses of my colleagues," Madison reported to Jefferson at Monticello, but the lady went alone to say goodby to Dolley. For her and her husband, commented Sally, "I feel a tenderness . . . regardless of circumstances."

By midsummer Pinckney in Madrid and Yrujo in Philadelphia were in an unwitting conspiracy to make bad conditions worse. Spain, angered by the Mobile Act, refused to ratify a partial claims settlement negotiated in 1802. Pinckney, notified of this, wrote to Cevallos that if this action was final, his instructions required him to warn all Americans to leave Spain and to ask for his own passports—a virtual ultimatium of war. Guessing correctly that no such instructions existed (since none had been intercepted), Cevallos repeated his refusal (thus putting Pinckney in a fix) and sent the correspondence to Yrujo.

The Spanish minister, during this time, was flooding the press with anonymous articles, ostensibly written by Americans, furiously denouncing the administration's policy toward Spain. Ordered by Madrid to protest Pinckney's ultimatum, he drove with his wife to Monticello (passing Madison's residence without stopping, wrote Pichon to Tallyrand). Ahead of him, but unknown, went an affidavit to Jefferson from Federalist editor William Jackson swearing that Yrujo had offered him money to print a series of anti-American articles signed "Graviora Manent" which were published elsewhere. Behind Yrujo, equally unknown to him, Jackson published that same affidavit.

Jefferson, about to leave for Washington, waited two days to see Yrujo. The President disavowed Pinckney's action and told the minister to take it up with Madison. Saying nothing about the Jackson affidavit, the President invited the Yrujos to remain as the guest of his daughter Martha, and departed. October came before Yrujo, returning to Philadelphia, was hit in the face by Jackson's disclosure.

Compelled by the President to direct his explanation to Madison, Yrujo defended his conduct on the ground of freedom of the press. As for bribery, paying an editor for space was no more indelicate than feeing a physician. However, he would not waste money on an insignificant local sheet, least of all for printing such harmless ideas as those expressed by "Graviora Manent."

The implied disclaimer of authorship did not impress Madison, who had discovered that one of the articles consisted chiefly of a translation into English of one of Yrujo's letters to him. The decision was made to ask for his recall, with Monroe carrying the demand from London to Madrid.

Yrujo's own explanation, wrote Madison, "convicts him of an attempt to debauch a citizen of the United States into a direct violation of an act of Congress" (the Logan Act, forbidding communication with a foreign government to frustrate United States policy.) He had used expressions grossly disrespectful to the President and capped his "egregious misconduct" by an appeal to the people in which his pretensions were matched only by his sophistry. Relations with Yrujo were not completely severed, but communications from and to the Secretary of State were hard and uncompromising, matching the attitudes of the two governments toward the issues that divided them.

Resumption of war between France and England in May 1803 brought an immediate renewal of British impressment of seamen from American vessels. When Rufus King returned to the United States in July, he reported that the First Lord of the Admiralty agreed verbally to a mutual agreement forbidding impressment; but in writing he exempted the "narrow seas" between Great Britain and the continent, calling them territorial waters. As this was the area where most impressments occurred, King dropped the negotiations.

In August Madison sent Chargé Thornton the deposition of a native American seaman who swam ashore from a British frigate which impressed him and three others off the port of Norfolk. After the seizure, said the Secretary, the frigate sailed right back into the port "whose kindness and commerce it had insulted." The United States, he declared, "can never acknowledge a right in any other nation to take from their vessels on the high sea any persons whatever," other than military personnel of the enemy. To this he added a sharp protest against conversion of American ports into supply bases and centers of operations against American commerce.

Thornton observed in Madison "a bitterness of tone and of insinuation" like that in the newspapers. He felt sure that the President, if consulted, "would not have acquiesced in either the language or the doctrine of Mr. Madison's letter." That is, he thought Jefferson, like President Adams, would merely have protested the seizure of Americans, whereas Madison denied the right to remove seamen of any nation from American ships.

Thornton's rejoinder asserted the right to control the actions of all British subjects and accused the United States of favoritism to French cruisers in American ports. Sending the correspondence to Jefferson at Monticello, Madison said he thought it best to give no answer to these "very exceptionable remarks." The President suggested that he make a well-disposed reply and request that Great Britain act on the King-

Hawksbury agreement as if it had been signed. Madison reminded him of the exemption of the narrow sea and repeated his unwillingness to answer Thornton; but as he was coming to Monticello within a few days, he would do nothing until he had "the pleasure of being able to take your directions in person."

Taking instructions in person meant winning the President to his own policy, which he proceeded to do. A further reason for ignoring Thornton's provocative note was the impending arrival of British Minister Anthony Merry. His Foreign Office nickname, "Toujours Gai," was both a pun and a satiric commentary on his plodding, humorless devotion to routine diplomacy. With him came Mrs. Merry, large and bejeweled—a fine woman "accustomed to adulation" (so wrote Legation Secretary Augustus Foster to his mother) who suffered horribly from association with the degenerate sons and daughters of British ancestors.

"The women here [wrote Foster] are in general a spying, inquisitive, vulgar and most ignorant race. They are many of them, daughters of tavernkeepers, boarding housekeepers and clerks' wives and yet as ceremonious as ambassadresses. Even you with all your resources and powers of self amusement would absolutely be puzzled here."

Lady Elizabeth Foster was indeed a woman with great powers of self amusement. It was said of her that if she crooked her finger in the Court of King's Bench, the Lord High Justice would descend from his woolsack and follow her. The fat historian Gibbon, getting down on his knees to beg her to marry him, fell over on his side and had to be helped by her to his feet. She lived in a contented triangle with the Dutchess and Duke of Devonshire, to whom she bore two sons. When her legitimate son Augustus was promoted to be minister to Sweden, Foreign Minister Canning wrote that he received the appointment because Swedish Commander-in-Chief "Baron d'Armfeldt conceives himself to be father of Augustus Foster." The belief at least implied the opportunity. Augustus in his letters addressed the Baron as "Dear Uncle."

Merry promptly complained to Madison that President Jefferson received him in old clothes and slippers. The Danish minister, Madison replied, was received in the same manner. The Dane, said Merry, was a diplomat of the third rank; he was of the second. That was a fair portent of things to come. Merry was shocked to learn from Madison that he was expected to make the first call on other Cabinet members. That was the custom in England, Madison reminded him. His unspoken rejoinder can almost be heard: "But these are *American* cabinet members."

The real shocker came when the President entertained the Merrys at dinner on December 2. As Jefferson was a widower, Dolley Madison usually served as hostess at such functions. When the group went in to dinner, the President gave his arm to Mrs. Madison. The Marchioness d'Yrujo took the seat at Jefferson's left. Madison placed Mrs. Merry next to the Spanish minister. Merry started to sit down next to Madame d'Yrujo but was shoved aside by a congressman. The minister (like Madison) sat somewhere down the line.

Jefferson's contempt of protocol was well known and reluctantly accepted. The Madisons, at home, were meticulous in observing it. After this dinner the outcries of the Merrys forced the Secretary of State to support either the President or the enraged minister. Pichon told how the problem was handled. At a dinner for the Cabinet and Foreign diplomats, Madison gave his hand to Mrs. Gallatin, causing "a sort of derangement in the salon." Partners were chosen by the men and the Merrys, left alone, had to go in together.

This departure from Madison's custom made it evident, Pichon reported, that the Secretary wished "to make Mr. Merry feel more strongly the embarrassment of the scandal he had created. But this incident increased it." To tone things down, Madison invited the Merrys to a social dinner. The minister came alone, bringing an excuse from his wife. Merry's report to London rated Madison's offense as worse than the President's, because of his subordinate situation and the preference given to Cabinet wives, "a set of beings as little without the manners as without the appearance of gentlewomen. . . . Everything else in the federal city is equally as perfectly savage." Fully as savage, perhaps, as the minister's English.

Affairs would have died down, Pichon thought, except that Yrujo, "who is vanity personified," drew Merry into an agreement that their wives would boycott presidential dinners and be given precedence over Dolley Madison and other Cabinet wives at legation dinners. They tried to bring Pichon into the arrangement, but he continued his "respect and deference" for the President, and gave precedence in his own house to Mr. and Mrs. Madison. To cope with the possible international consequences of this "diplomatic superstition" as Madison called it, the Secretary of State asked Rufus King about precedence at British royal parties. Foreign ministers were never invited to such parties, and in the Queen's drawing room there was nothing but confusion. At dinner parties the women usually trooped ahead into the dining room, "the highest title taking the lead."

This tacit support of Jefferson's position led the Cabinet to lay down a rule of complete *pele mele* and opened the way to Madison's first talk with Merry about the imbroglio. Usage, he observed, was so different in different countries as to leave all free. In Russia, military rank predominated; at Rome, ecclesiastical; in England, hereditary. But without precedence, Merry objected, he was subject to the degrading possibility of sitting below Thornton. Distinctions among diplomats, Madison replied, were a labyrinth he declined to enter. Continuing to wave the olive branch, the Secretary finally brought Minister and Mrs. Merry back to his house for an evening visit. To Mrs. Merry's horror, she found her own haberdasher and his wife among the invited guests. Wrote Augustus Foster: "It is indeed a country not fit for a dog."

In spite of this "frivolous farce", Madison got along quite well with Merry on Anglo-American affairs. The British minister wanted to know why the United States had not ratified an 1803 convention settling the northern boundary of the United States. Because, Madison replied, it was based on the mistaken belief that a line running directly west from the Lake of the Woods would intersect the Mississippi River. The object of the clause, Merry protested, was to give Great Britain access to the Mississippi. The treaties recognizing that right, parried Madison, were based on the supposition that the Mississippi had its source in Canada. The Secretary's elusive and negative attitude, Merry reported, cloaked a design of "encroachment on His Majesty's just rights."

Merry had a happy thought when the Senate, in February 1804, ratified the convention with this article excluded. By using this as an excuse for rejecting the convention, he advised his government, Great Britain could deprive New England of important benefits contained in other articles. Congressmen from those states had told him they were secretly planning secession (because of the purchase of Louisiana). Reject the treaty, and they would go forward rapidly toward a separation from the South. Great Britain followed his advice.

Madison's early talks with Merry dealt chiefly with impressment, but other objectives were to end "paper blockades" of actually unblockaded ports, limit the definition of contraband, regulate visits and searches at sea, and abandon "the doctrine that a colonial trade not allowed in time of peace is unlawful in time of war." In return, the United States would agree to a mutual return of deserters and a ban on exportation of contraband.

To support this policy Madison emphasized the rising feeling in and out of Congress, especially over impressments. The United States would never desist from its claim "that the American flag should give complete protection to whatever persons might be under it," military enemies of Great Britain alone excepted.

Merry seemed to yield a little—enough to alarm Thornton, who was willing to see impressments *tacitly* abandoned. He warned Undersecretary Hammond in a secret note that "if we yield an iota without a real and perfect equivalent (not such imaginary equivalents as Mr. Madison mentions to Mr. Merry) we are lost." Every concession would be "ascribed to our fears; and this country is rising fast, if it be not checked very speedily and effectually, to an importance which will most sensibly annoy us."

Merry swung toward Thornton's position when he observed the progress of war-spawned bills in Congress and "found Mr. Madison prepared to defend the bills on every point," although disclaiming administration sponsorship of them. The actual function of the bills, ultimately postponed, was to give weight to Monroe's efforts in London. To furnish a basis for those efforts Madison drafted a convention in thirteen articles, supported by ten thousand words of argument. "Absolutely indispensable," he said, were suppression of impressments and definition of blockades. "Highly important" were reduction of the list of contraband and recognition of America's right, as a neutral, to trade with the colonies of belligerent nations. No person was to be taken out of a ship at sea, unless in the military service of an enemy. No port was to be considered blockaded unless investing warships created "an evident danger of entering."

Madison's argument against impressment, in this instruction of January 5, 1804, fixed the position of the United States in the eight-year diplomatic struggle that followed. Except for military personnel, he wrote, "we consider a neutral flag on the high seas as a safeguard to those sailing under it. Great Britain on the contrary asserts a right to search for and seize her own subjects." Under that cover, American citizens and other neutrals were carried off. Great Britain did not deny that the seas were free, subject to the law of nations, but "in what usage except her own" was there a sanction for taking any but military enemies from a neutral ship?

Ships and cargoes seized in war, Madison noted, had to be carried before a regular tribunal, strictly regulated by the law of nations. But seamen were taken without a trial, deprived of their dearest rights, their destiny determined by a naval officer, "sometimes cruel, often ignorant," and intent on filling up his crew. Great Britain, he could safely affirm, would be among the last nations in the world to suffer such an outrage and indignity. Yet this was being done to Americans, often in defiance of the most positive proof of their citizenship.

To meet the charge that great numbers of British seamen were serving in the American trade, Madison cited the results in 2,059 impressment cases complained of by the United States between 1797 and 1801. Of these seamen, 1,142 were released as non-British, 805 cases awaited further proof, and only two seamen were finally found to be British subjects. Sending Monroe one of the bills then pending in Congress, Madison said it probably would not be pressed if there was hope of an amicable settlement: "But such is the feeling through this country, produced by the reiterated and atrocious cases of impressment and other insults on our flag, that a remedy of some kind will ere long be called for in a tone not to be disregarded."

Turning to England's claim of jurisdiction over the "narrow seas," Madison said it was so indefensible that he could scarcely believe it was advanced. The doctrine was the residue of a claimed sovereignty once exercised over all the seas from Norway to Spain, but that was when power decided questions of right and general ignorance of the law abetted usurpation.

As to colonial trade, said Madison, all nations including England changed their regulations in wartime. (France therefore had a right to abandon her peacetime monopoly of trade with French colonies.) Minister Merry, he revealed, predicted adament rejection of the neutral right to carry French colonial goods to France. "Should that aversion be unconquerable, Monroe should seek protection of the carrying trade between hostile and neutral colonies. British aversion did indeed prove unconquerable, on everything. When the impressment negotiations finally broke down, Monroe left for Madrid.

The United States at this time was in hot water with France over the burgeoning trade with the black rebels of St. Domingo. There Dessalines and Christophe were taking seaport after seaport from the beleaguered remnants of the French army. Suppose, Pichon wrote to Madison, that Southern slaves were in revolt and France tolerated a similar trade with them. "Imagine what feelings would be excited!" Madison, instead, imagined the excitement in New England if the trade were cut off. He reaffirmed his 1802 contention that contraband trade with a revolting colony did not differ from trade with an independent warring nation.

Madison then made the countercharge that French officials, driven out of St. Domingo, had issued privateering commissions in Cuba and opened French prize courts in that neutral Spanish colony. American ships were captured, their cargoes sold, the ships scuttled, and the profits divided between the privateersmen and the prize-court judges. The American government, Pichon rejoined, was allowing its nationals to carry on a private and piratical war, conveying munitions to rebels under its very eyes, but to Talleyrand he wrote that "Mr. Madison's complaints on this subject are well founded. You will hardly conceive the conduct pursued by the many cruisers flying the French flag with which the seas are covered." A brother of the St. Domingo paymaster had set up court in Cuba, condemning prizes when he was himself interested in the armaments, and giving orders "to privateer against a nation with which we are at peace."

Pichon was on stronger ground when he protested to Madison against the arming of American merchant vessels, some carrying twenty guns. The Secretary said it could not be stopped without an act of Congress and that body was in recess. Furthermore, it was common practice to arm private ships in time of peace, to protect property. True enough, the chargé retorted, but that argument could not be applied without putting France on a level with the Barbary pirates. That would have been *touché* if Pichon himself, writing to Talleyrand, had not put the French corsairs on precisely that piratical level.

Madison directed his protests also to Yrujo, notifying him that Spain would be held responsible for the misconduct in Cuba. The marquis replied that the United States was handing poignards to assassins and torches to incendiaries in a French colony. Spain demanded "the most decisive measures" to end this trade. If the demand was ignored the United States would find some of the foremost nations of Europe sustaining King Carlos. Backed by the President, Madison asked whether France had requested this Spanish intervention. Forced to say no, Yrujo was told that the foodstuffs being sold in St. Domingo were neither poignards nor torches. By her conduct in Cuba, Madison observed, Spain did not seem to consider herself a neutral. She could not at the same time be both neutral and belligerent, nor could she, as a neutral, make demands on the United States which she could not make even as a belligerent.

The distinction Madison made between weapons and foodstuffs was repeated to Pichon. Weapons could be seized on the high seas, foodstuffs only within the limits of municipal law. Rebelling Negroes, Pichon replied, could not be accorded the same rights as other people. This difference, he explained to Talleyrand, he "did not pretend to justify," but it was a fact on which the United States established a part of its social edifice. The argument made no impression on Madison, who assured alarmed Philadelphia merchants that he was seeking a relaxation of restrictions on the "profitable trade with St. Domingo." Those who violated the regulations would have to assume the legal risks. All others would be supported against the "gross irregularities" of insular officials.

In France, Talleyrand was duplicating the stiffer part of Pichon's protests. When brigands were deluging a country with blood, he asked the American minister, did any peaceable and honorable nation have an interest in helping such people to live? This principle ought to end all thought of claiming damages, but if colonial governors had been provoked to misconduct, their regulations would not receive "the imperial sanction."

The imperial sanction! Those words represented one of the major events of history. Napoleon Bonaparte, on May 18, 1804, had made himself emperor of the French. The scattered bones of the French Revolution, two years unburied, had been scraped into a grave amid the ruins of the Bastille. Madison received the official news from Pichon with cold reserve. "I have thought it best," he wrote in asking for the President's approval, "to decline any expressions which might enter in the smallest degree into the character of the revolution in the French government or even be personal to the emperor." Accordingly, his reply to Pichon merely acknowledged the right of every nation to change its government and expressed pleasure that his Imperial Majesty temporarily recognized old letters of credence. If any higher civility was thought appropriate, he observed to Jefferson, it could be furnished through the legation in France.

The sentiment was a normal one for Madison, who had greeted Napoleon's original seizure of power as a death blow to liberty, leaving the United States as the only theater of true freedom. But when Napoleon put the crown on his head, he infused the imperial spirit into all transactions. Henceforth there was to be a whiff of grapeshot in French diplomacy.

Thomas Jefferson was unbeatable in the 1804 presidential election. What could the Federalists hope for in the face of the Louisiana Purchase, lowered taxes, reduced public debt, economy in government, and severe chastisement of the Barbary pirates?

Two years earlier Jefferson's avowed dislike of his office caused a report to spread that he would decline at the next election, and Madison would be offered as a candidate. "Is this true?" asked Thomas Law of William Eustis. The rumor merely measured Madison's position in the party. There was a foretaste of the more distant future, however, in the nomination of Governor George Clinton of New York for Vice President. In the congressional caucus, wrote Federalist William Plumer, the Virginians were zealous for the New York governor, wishing "to elect an old man who is too feeble to aspire to the Presidency."

Ratification of the Twelfth Amendment deprived the Federalists of a potent instrument of political intrigue. Henceforth, presidential electors would vote separately for President and Vice President. Despair turned party chiefs more and more toward thoughts of secession. The wicked state of Virginia, lamented Wolcott, "has been the principal cause of all our divisions. The dominion of a community composed of beggarly Palatines and insolent slaves is intolerably odious."

Among the political canards was one slightly on the comic side, directed against the chastity of Dolley Madison and her sister Anna, then the wife of Congressman Richard Cutts of Massachusetts. As the story reached Chief Justice Jeremiah Smith of New Hampshire, Postmaster General Gideon Granger leaped to the defense of the ladies against some slanderous remarks by Congressman Samuel Hunt of New Hampshire. Hunt challenged Granger to a duel. Granger declined. Madison thereupon "waited on Mr. H. with the compliments of the two ladies and an invitation to dine *en famille*."

Senator Plumer, asked about it, assured the Chief Justice that "Mr. Hunt is a great favorite with Mrs. Madison and sisters, and is well received by the Secretary of State." Certain it is that the ladies developed a loathing of Granger, whose clumsy intervention spread the story. More vexatious were the neurotic personal attacks of John Randolph on Madison, kept up for ten years. Gnawing jealousy can be seen in an 1804 letter to Monroe condemning those who "affect to talk of the prodigious weight of particular individuals merely to excite the personal feelings of individuals whom they believe indisposed to be considered as secondary characters." Jefferson, who treated Randolph with friendship but not flattery, was immune to attack. Gallatin, who cultivated an intimacy with him, was spared. Madison, having no public or social motive for such cultivation, treated him with cool detachment and reaped a harvest of hatred.

Randolph said of himself: "There *was* a volcano under my ice, but it is burnt out." George Ticknor told of the shrill and effeminate voice and extraordinary appearance of this tall, gaunt man who combined sexual impotence with the fury of other passions: "His head is small . . . To his short and meager body are attached long legs which instead of diminishing grow larger as they approach the floor until they end in a pair of feet, broad and large, giving his whole person the appearance of a sort of pyramid."

The open break with Madison came in connection with Georgia lands. Following the scandalous Yazoo purchase of a western empire from a bribed Georgia legislature, and revocation of the sale by its successor, President Jefferson commissioned Madison, Gallatin, and Attorney-General Lincoln to negotiate a transfer of the lands to the United States. Their most difficult task was to settle the claims of thousands of purchasers, mostly New Englanders, who lost lands and money by the revocation of the sale.

The joint federal-state commission reached an agreement in 1802, by which Georgia ceded most of the present states of Alabama and Mississippi to the Union for $1,250,000, with a provision that the United States could appropriate up to 5 million out of 57 million acres to satisfy dispossessed claimants. The great majority of these were innocent purchasers. The biggest were "innocent" in law only. The commissioners verified the charge that every member of the Georgia legislature except Robert Watkins had been bribed. Without affirming that Georgia was competent to repeal the sale, they held that the title of the claimants could not be supported in law. Most claims, however, were valid in equity, and the interests of the United States made it advisable to satisfy them. Sale of five million acres would not indemnify every purchaser but would nearly cover aggregate losses. The land companies themselves demanded much more.

Georgia and Congress ratified the agreement, but Randolph steadily blocked an appropriation to satisfy claims, aiming his entire attack at Madison. Why, asked the Richmond *Enquirer*, was not some of the fury directed against "Mr. Gallatin, who certainly drew up the report?"

Jefferson's re-election gave the signal to Randolph to intensify his attacks on the bill authorizing a settlement. His speeches, one listener observed, added up to "the most abusive strain of invective ever witnessed" in a legislative hall except under Robespierre. The deadlock continued until 1810, when the Supreme Court in *Fletcher* v. *Peck* denied the power of Georgia to rescind the sale, and thus forced Congress to make a vastly more expensive settlement. Madison and Randolph both abhorred the Yazoo transaction. Madison sought a settlement founded on reason and costing little. Randolph's assault on him as a "Yazoo man" was a calculated prostitution of the truth to political demagogy and neurotic jealousy.

The most sensational event of 1804—the killing of Hamilton by Burr in a duel—produced a brief and noncommittal remark by Madison to Monroe: "You will easily understand the different uses to which the event is turned." Much as Madison hated dueling, he declined to make a political exception from the accustomed public toleration of it. His reaction allowed Plumer to write in his diary a few months later: "The Secretary of State, Mr. Madison, formerly the intimate friend of General Hamilton, has taken his murderer into his carriage," on a visit to the French minister.

Personal acrimony took a reverse turn when Jefferson pressured the House of Representatives into an impeachment of Supreme Court Justice Samuel Chase for his vindictive enforcement of the Sedition Act. Did these constitute "high crimes or misdemeanors," the minimum constitutional ground of impeachment? Trial manager John Randolph said yes in his most impassioned tones. Chase's Federalist lawyers said no with cold logic. The Republican Senate fell one vote short of the two-thirds majority required for conviction. Senator John Quincy Adams wrote that he "had conversation on the subject with Mr. Madison, who appeared much diverted at the petulance of the managers on their disappointment."

Jefferson, chagrined at the failure, hit back at the Federalists three days later in his second inaugural address. This contained the famous parable in which, under the guise of pleading that the American Indians be uplifted from barbarism, he made a satiric attack on the "obstacles of habit" that kept the Federalists from rising to a civilized level. The first draft contained severe direct attacks on the Federalist press and preachers, which were toned down by advice of Madison and Gallatin. Madison furnished the final revised wording by which the "Indians" were characterized: those "who feeling themselves something in the present order of things and fearing to become nothing in any other, inculcate a blind attachment to the customs of their fathers in opposition to every light and example which would conduct them into a more improved state of existence." Following the inaugural, Jefferson returned to the presidential palace and held a levee open to all, even including, wrote Augustus Foster, "blacks and dirty boys, who drank his wine and lolled upon his couches before us all."

Relations with Great Britain, at this time, were going from bad to intolerable. That very word, indeed, had been used by Madison to describe the conduct of the warships *Cambrian* and *Driver*, whose officers, in the summer of 1804, insulted revenue officers and took fourteen seamen by force from a British merchant ship in Boston harbor. If such violence and defiance of law continued, wrote Madison to Merry, "you will see sir that the United States must be driven by the most imperious circumstances into precautions as disagreeable to themselves as they may be inconvenient to those who fail to render such measures unnecessary."

Merry supported Captain Bradley's argument that a British warship in an American port enjoyed British sovereignty for the sweep of its anchor chain. Madison's "high language," he wrote to the new and aggressive Pitt government, seemed to threaten the exclusion of all British ships of war from American ports. That was precisely what Madison suggested to the President, following similar offenses in New York harbor. Jefferon replied that, were the Navy's new gunboats completed, he certainly would make a proposition to the Cabinet to clear out that harbor. That was a wish rather than a threat, but it indicated a belief that the Executive had inherent power to use naval force in territorial waters. Also, it confirmed Jefferson's practice of resting all important decisions on a vote of the Cabinet.

Tension eased considerably when word came that the British government, in advance of any complaint, had removed Bradley from command and ordered him home. (He was given a bigger ship.) Congress, nevertheless, gave the President asked-for authority to forbid and repel the entrance of foreign armed vessels. What was meant, Merry asked, by exclusion of a warship because of "vexation of trading vessels?" That, said Madison, was to prevent the impressment of British subjects on American vessels—a position taken also by the Washington and Adams administrations. The long talk centered on impressment, the British minister promising lenity, Madison "maintaining to the last" (reported Merry) that the right could not be admitted.

Ill-feeling mounted when the British sloop of war *Busy* stripped an American ship of more than half its crew just outside New York. American seamen, Madison told Merry, did not need to carry evidence of citizenship, or to prove they were not British subjects. This doctrine, if accepted, would make irrelevant the contention that British subjects were employed on American ships—a charge, Madison contended, that was grossly exaggerated. The Secretary was jubilant when he discovered that Parliament, in 1739, adopted a resolve that the rights of British vessels were violated when they were visited "at open sea, under the pretext that they are freighted with contraband or prohibited merchandises"— searches sanctioned by the law of nations. However, turnabout was not fair play in the eyes of Foreign Secretary Lord Harrowby. He wrote to Merry that "the pretension advanced by Mr. Madison that the American flag should protect every individual sailing under it on board of a merchant ship is too extravagant to require any serious refutation."

Should Congress pass offensive bills for the protection of seamen, Harrowby threatened, England would withdraw her offer to extend the treaty of 1794 and adopt a policy of retaliation. Imagine how that would scare Madison, who had waged his hardest fight in Congress against that treaty and advocated retaliation as a substitute! Very different was the British attitude when Madison informed *Toujours Gai* that the Royal Navy had seized a ship containing a consignment of French wines and four jars of preserves destined for the President and Secretary of State. "The effects belonging to the President and Mr. Madison have been liberated," wrote Merry in June 1805. A broken jar of preserves was the only casualty.

With impressment negotiations hopelessly bogged down in London, Monroe returned to Paris, from which place he was to proceed to Madrid if—and only if—he met with "active co-operation or favorable dispositions" in the French government to influence that of Spain. With the approval of new minister John Armstrong and against the advice of Livingston, Monroe sent Talleyrand a strong defense of the Perdido boundary and asked for French support of a cession of all the Floridas to satisfy American spoliation claims. Weeks passed without an answer. Treating silence as a "favorable disposition," Monroe set out by mule train for Madrid, where he found Pinckney hanging from the limb of his self-imposed isolation. Monroe managed to cut him down and they worked together in harmony, getting nowhere.

Talleyrand's discourtesy to Monroe, Armstrong informed Madison, resulted from the indication Monroe gave that Spain would get no money for the Floridas. (No money, consequently, for Spain's annual tribute to France.) Armstrong himself had received repeated intimations "that if certain persons could be gratified," the negotiations could be transferred to Paris and brought to a satisfactory close. His reply had uniformly been that the measures of a nation like France could never be influenced "by considerations that would equally dishonor them to offer and the United States to hear."

For Madison, this letter wiped quite a blot off Armstrong's scutcheon as author of the mutiny-stirring "Newburgh Addresses." He was pleased to report to Jefferson that the new minister "understands the language in which the honorable and honest policy of this country ought to be expressed." He told Armstrong "that the President entirely approves the just and dignified answer given to the venal suggestions emanating from the French functionaries." The United States owed it to the world to furnish a protest, even though a solitary one, against the corruption that prevailed. That was the closest Madison came to official comment on Livingston's earlier appeals for bribery funds.

Talleyrand's belated reply to Monroe, supporting Spain on the Florida boundary, was followed by similar rebuffs of Armstrong. Madison wrote to Monroe that "a failure of your efforts ought to be anticipated." The choices left were war, or a course guarding against war *for the present*, "leaving in vigor our claims to be hereafter effectuated."

With France and Spain united in construction of the treaty, Madison concluded, war to gain Florida would antagonize world opinion. Also, it was a decision for Congress, not the Executive, to make. That consideration, he told Monroe, forbade the Executive to take any step "which would commit the nation, and so far take from the legislature the free exercise of its power." Moreover, facilities were daily increasing "for a successful assertion of our rights by force" at some future time.

Two factors, Madison said, were essential to maintenance of rights without an immediate resort to arms. Neither Spain nor the United States should build up settlements or strengthen their military establishments within the disputed limits. Spain must leave the Mobile and other rivers freely open to American commerce. Otherwise, the swift settlement and trade growth north of the boundary would threaten collisions leading to war.

These instructions to Monroe produced no effect in Spain, but they served well to illuminate the policies of the Jefferson administration and the bent of Madison's thinking. Force was to be avoided until circumstances made it necessary and the country's growth made it effectual. Madison laid down a constitutional rule, sound in principle but disregarded by virtually all wartime Presidents, including himself—that the exclusive power given Congress to declare forbade the President to take any steps that would make war inevitable.

Relations with France took a downward turn in Washington in November 1804 with the arrival of a French minister. The keen-minded and friendly Pichon did not suit the temper of a crowned Napoleon. To succeed him and put America in proper subordination, came General Louis Marie Turreau, the red-whiskered, 47-year-old "butcher of Vendée." Armstrong described him to Madison: very profligate, bad tempered, an ex-Jacobin notorious for cruelty in war. Senator Plumer looked at him and wrote: "I have never yet beheld a face so cruel and sanguinary."

Turreau's first effort was to heal the breach between Madison and Yrujo. He brought them together and reported his failure to Talleyrand. The two "detest each other cordially." He blamed Yrujo for starting the quarrel, Madison for the continuation of it. The Secretary of State, he wrote, "is curt, spiteful, passionate, and his private resentment, rather than difference of policy will hold him away from Mr. d'Yrujo for a long time."

Turreau's words were "*sec, haineux, passioné.*" Historian Henry Adams gave "*sec*" its ordinary meaning of "dry" instead of "curt", thus picturing Madison as a sapless (though passionate!) individual for whom Turreau, with his keen insight, had "no high respect." The general made one more effort to reconcile Madison and Yrujo, at a dinner for the former. There, the Spaniard "would have consented but the Secretary of State does not know how to forgive." Turreau included all Americans in his disfavor: "These people have been well spoiled. It is time to put them back in their place."

Dolley Madison "heard sad things of Turreau—that he whips his wife, and abuses her dreadfully; I pity her sincerely; she is an amiable, sensible woman." Madame Turreau did not take all this meekly. When five months pregnant, she hit the general with a flatiron after he danced with six naked prostitutes in front of unshaded windows, with his three-piece legation orchestra furnishing the music. Turreau responded with such a beating that it required the quick thinking of an attaché, said Senator Plumer, to drown out her screams by blowing loudly on the

French horn. (Somebody else named another instrument; it could have been an ensemble.)

Into this pandemonium, it appears, stepped Madison. Wrote Anthony Merry, after telling of Turreau's immoral conduct and ferocity: "His treatment of [his wife and children] was carried latterly to so barbarous an excess as to oblige them to fly from his house and only the mediation of, as I believe, the Secretary of State, aided by the necessity of the case, was sufficient to bring them again all together under the same roof."

Federalist politicians and editors, judging Turreau and Madison by their relative ferocity and hirsute features, pictured Madison as a shivering weakling in a tiger's grasp. The two men actually got along quite well for a time. On one occasion, recorded the New York *Herald*, Madison and Turreau were in hot debate when Madison's barber, Dixon, thrust his head through the doorway and announced that he had come to shave the Secretary. They forgot their anger in peals of laughter.

The first sharp clash between them came with Turreau's protest against the "brigandage" (i.e. the trade) of an American mercantile armada in the West Indies, too strong to be attacked. Madison offset this with the repressive orders of Captain General Ferrand. Madison's ire was stirred when the French minister, obeying instructions, wrote to him that General Moreau, banished from France as a plotter against the emperor, "ought not to be" the object of honors, or greeted with any demonstration during his stay "that goes beyond the bounds of hospitality."

This "reprehensible intrusion" into American affairs, Madison suggested to the President, ought to receive "an answer breathing independence as well as friendship . . . and I enclose one to which that character was meant to be given." Jefferson suggested a denial that the federal government had power to restrain state or local authorities. Madison replied that he thought it inexpedient "and might not even be correct, to deny it." No foreign government would be satisfied with such an explanation. Turreau received the answer breathing independence. Moreau received a tumultuous welcome, and Turreau, reporting it, breathed not a word about his discomfiting exchange with Madison.

The American mercantile armada against which Turreau had protested returned from St. Domingo with such huge profits that it led to a victory dinner in New York on board the 22-gun *Indostan*. Napoleon launched verbal thunderbolts when he read the ninth toast: "The government of Hayti, founded on the only legitimate basis of authority—the people's choice." "This system of impunity and tolerance," Armstrong

was notified, "could not continue longer." The United States should interdict all trade with the rebel ports. A similar blast came from Turreau.
Madison ignored the letter for two months, then cited the French reply
to England prior to 1778, when England protested against French trade
with the American rebels. France, as a neutral, was not bound to prevent her subjects from engaging in contraband trade with rebelling
colonies.

However, that pro-Negro Haitian toast and the vision behind it gave
Turreau powerful allies in Congress. Southern members, fearful of a
slave insurrection, rallied to the bill to cut off trade with the rebels. Jefferson's son-in-law Eppes told the House that independence of the ex-
slave colony "would bring immediate and horrible destruction on the
fairest portion of America."

Notifying Armstrong of the bill's enactment into law, Madison said it
resulted from expediency, not from any rightful demand of France "and
still less from a manner of pressing it, which might have justly had a
contrary tendency." However, its passage opened the way to a possible
trade agreement. Armstrong should renew a proposal that food be
shipped to St. Domingo in exchange for its products—a trade "obviously favorable to the true interests of France." That was very close to
saying that the true interest of France was to leave Emperor Dessalines
on his throne.

Turreau, versed in war, had no illusions about America's ability to
withstand attack. The country, he reported, lacked the means to wage
offensive war, and there was an aversion to it that did not depend on the
personal character of Mr. Jefferson. It was shared "even by those who
have the best-founded claims and hopes of succeeding [him] such as
Mr. Madison." Far different, the general went on, would be the country's
situation in a defensive war. A continental attack would instantly unite
all parties. In a vast and difficult country suitable to guerrilla warfare, the
most formidable military power in the world could have no hope of
success.

The Americans, Turreau believed, had the idea of driving the Euro-
peans from the new world. Perhaps they could do so, but Turreau disagreed with the belief held by some that England would some day relinquish Canada voluntarily. Discussing national policy with Madison,
he asked why all American efforts were directed toward the south, when
Canada, Nova Scotia, etc., could be taken.

" 'No doubt,' the Secretary of State replied to me, 'but the time has not
yet come; when the pear is ripe, it will fall of itself.' " Turreau saw only

one chance of putting a stop to American territorial expansion—by a Spanish cession of the Floridas and Cuba to France, thus placing a strong naval power in control of the Gulf of Mexico. "France alone can halt the enterprises of the Americans and frustrate their plan." In this generally sound analysis, Turreau took no account of the greatest future element in American strength—spread of an expanding population into an empire already given up by Spain and France.

James and Dolley Madison spent the late summer and autumn of 1805 in Philadelphia, where Dr. Philip Physick treated an ulcerated tumor on Dolley's leg near the knee. Since late May she had barely been able to walk, but during the drive to Pennsylvania all her concern was for her husband, who on the way was laid low with an attack of bilious fever. She thought "all was over" with her because she could not aid him, but "heaven in its mercy restored him next morning" and now "my beloved husband . . . is my unremitting nurse." Dr. Physick promised cure in a month's time, without surgery, but the healing process stretched out three times that long.

Madison carried on the business of state at Dolley's bedside, which shifted to suburban Grays Ferry when yellow fever hit the city. He learned that the Madrid negotiations had been broken off without even presentation of the minor demand (free navigation of Mobile Bay and river) with which he hoped to soften the impact of the expected rejection of the Perdido boundary. To escape a choice between national loss of face and an immediate show of force, Madison joined with Gallatin (a sudden convert) in recommending enlargement of the seagoing Navy. He had "long been of opinion" that this was wise, "and the present crisis gives a great urgency to such a policy."

From the President at Monticello came the question "whether we ought not immediately to propose to England an eventual treaty of alliance," to come into force whenever the United States should be at war with Spain or France. Such an alliance, Madison responded, would be the best of all possible measures, but he saw not the least chance of laying England "under obligations to be called into force at our will without corresponding obligations on our part." If England was to be *bound*, "we must be so *too*."

Jefferson thought Madison had misunderstood him. He meant that the treaty should come into force if the United States became engaged in war with France or Spain *during the war in Europe*. England should stipulate "not to make peace without our obtaining the objects [boundaries and spoliation indemnities] for which we go to war." He was setting a Cabinet meeting for October and hoped Madison could be there. Unable to leave Dolley, Madison furnished a statement. He was convinced that a coalition with Great Britain was unattainable without a positive commitment to enter the war.

The Cabinet found the question of a British alliance too difficult and important to be settled without "your aid and council." That council was furnished when Madison heard of Pitt's formation of the third Continental Coalition, uniting England, Austria, Russia, and Sweden against France. This development, he wrote, increased Napoleon's need for money and reopened the chance of securing the Floridas by negotiation. The risk of an alliance with England was reduced, but so was the need of it. The project was dropped.

This whole discussion, put on paper because the principals were widely separated for several months, shows clearly why Jefferson leaned so heavily on Madison, as he himself said later, in performing the duties of his office. The Secretary of State was a constant and tactful correcter of the President's unthought-out ideas.

While favoring an ultimate alliance with England, Madison had very different thoughts about current relations. In the spring he had learned that the American brig *Aurora* had been captured by the British, sent to Newfoundland, and condemned on two grounds. The court held that the carrying of Spanish produce from Havana to Barcelona violated the British "Rule of 1756," which held that trade from a colony to the mother country, closed to other countries in time of peace, could not be opened to them in time of war. (Spain was now a belligerent.) Second, the court held that the landing of this cargo in the United States and payment of duties on it, with later reshipment followed by remission of duties (as in other cases of re-export) did not break the continuity of the voyage from Cuba to Spain.

Directing Monroe to protest this action in London, Madison said that the Rule of 1756 was maintained by no country except England. It conflicted with the law of nations, was imposed solely by naval force, and was invoked or abandoned in war to suit the policies of Great Britain. As for the claim of a continuous voyage, it was contradicted by the opinion of Sir William Scott, the outstanding admiralty judge of England, in the 1800 case of the *Polly*. If the landing of goods and payment of duties did not prove a bona fide importation, Scott said "I should be at a loss to know what should be the test." Lord Mansfield had held that even a transfer of cargo from ship to ship off a neutral port broke the continuity of a voyage.

In spite of these clear precedents, Madison predicted, the *Aurora* decision would be upheld on appeal. Because, he said, the purpose of the condemnation was not to cut off trade with Spain. An act of Parliament specifically authorized British vessels to trade with the enemy, under license. The purpose of the Rule of 1756 and the continuous-voyage doctrine, as now applied, was to restrain the rising trade of the United States. England ought not to forget that the United States would counteract her unjust and unfriendly policy.

A similar protest was made to Minister Merry, and Madison resumed the subject in a chance encounter in Philadelphia. Here Merry was surprised to have him discuss the interference with colonial trade in a much more moderate manner than was expected "from his natural irritability" and the sensation which the seizures had produced. His harsh words were for "the perfidious and insolent proceedings" of Spanish officers who were kidnaping American citizens along the West Florida frontier. It did not occur to Merry that these contrasting attitudes offered a prospect that a change in Britain's naval policy might give her an ally in the war.

Madison did far more than nurse Dolley during these months. He took with him to Philadelphia a trunkful of works on the law of nations and other books including forty years of the *Annual Register* covering British politics, war and trade. After several weeks of preliminary study he launched into the writing of a 70,000-word book challenging the Rule of 1756 and the decisions of Sir William Scott, which he found to be "often at variance with each other and the arguments sometimes shamefully sophistical, at others grossly absurd." The worst of these transpired during the writing of the book—a decision in the case of the *Essex* verifying Madison's expectation.

Scott's court reversed the ruling it had made in the case of the *Polly*. To save face, Scott called in two other judges and let one of them put out the opinion. They held that the landing of colonial goods was designed to escape the prohibition against direct shipment. So it was, but that had been true when Scott held it legal under the law of nations. There could be little doubt that the great judge reversed himself under coercion from the British Cabinet.

Madison's pamphlet aimed at total destruction of the Rule of 1756. If he could establish that a belligerent had the right to alter its commercial regulations in time of war (as England had done again and again), it would make no difference whether wartime trade between colony and mother country was direct or broken. The Rule of 1756, he declared, was unknown to early writers and contrary to the law of nations. It conflicted with numerous treaties, even British treaties, and more often than not with British practice. Great Britain denied the right of her enemies to relax their laws in favor of neutral commerce, yet relaxed her own. She denied the right of neutrals to trade with the colonies of her enemies, yet "she trades herself with her enemies, and invites them to trade with her colonies." Under three 1805 Orders in Council, British subjects were importing enemy colonial goods and re-exporting them to enemy countries—the very trade she was denying to Americans.

To support his position Madison ransacked the writings of Grotius, Pufendorf, Bynkershoek, Vattel, Martens, and others. He traced European treaties through 150 years, pursued British Cabinets and courts through the eighteenth century, and capped the mass of contradictions with his own analysis. The Rule of 1756 had "*as its true foundation a mere superiority of force.*"

The bulky pamphlet, published in January 1806, was anonymous but known to be from Madison. It bore the title "*An Examination of the British Doctrine, which subjects to capture a Neutral Trade Not Open in Time of Peace.*" That fittingly reflected the book's length, microscopic exactness, penetrating logic, clear reasoning, and (today) its massive unreadability. It was lively enough in an era of thwarted American commercial ambition. John Quincy Adams and Rufus King praised it, John Randolph and Uriah Tracy damned it. Dr. Benjamin Rush wrote that "My son is now devouring it." That was, possibly, young Richard's first step toward three Cabinet positions under three Presidents.

Madison's pamphlet was still on the press when striking evidence arrived that British policy was indeed designed to throttle American trade. A London pamphlet entitled *War in Disguise*, anonymous, but written by James Stephen, read throughout as if it were written in reply to Madison's *Examination*, and so in effect it was. The core of Madison's argument, sent to Monroe, was paraphrased by him to Lord Mulgrave, who turned the letter over to Stephen.

Stephen *advocated* everything that Madison *charged* England with doing, and more. The government should cut off neutral trade from enemy colonies, thus giving British planters, merchants, and shipowners a monopoly in major articles. If the United States should retaliate by placing an embargo on British commerce, a well-regulated British trade with enemy countries, combined with smuggling of British manufactures into the ill-guarded Atlantic states, "would soon show them their folly."

With the Madison pamphlet as ammunition, President Jefferson induced Congress to pass a nonimportation act directed against Great Britain. To make it an instrument for negotiation, the effective date was postponed until November 15, 1806.

Madison left Dolley behind when he returned from Philadelphia at the end of October. She was not quite strong enough to travel when the disappearance of yellow fever made him willing to leave her. Their letters during the ensuing fortnight, written after eleven years of marriage, had some of the characteristics of puppy love. Dolley: "Adieu, my beloved, our hearts understand each other." Madison: My happiness "cannot be complete till I have you again with me." Payne Todd was nearly fourteen, and Madison wrote that he was entering him in St. John's College, in Baltimore. This school, conducted by Father Dubourg of the Sulpician order, would give him proficiency in spoken French, which Madison lacked.

Press and public at this time were clamoring for war with Spain and France. Federalists denounced the administration for not seizing West Florida and Texas. Madison, taking account of this, observed to Dolley that "the power of deciding questions of war and providing measures that will make or meet it is with Congress and that is always our answer to newspapers." To George W. Erving, sent to Madrid as chargé d'affaires, he sent word not to re-open negotiations. He might, however, teach Spain a salutary lesson by disclosing the effect of her "proud and perverse" course on American public opinion. France had been given a lesson by creation of the new coalition against her imperial career. Nor did the spectacle of folly end there: "England seems as ready to play the fool with respect to this country as her enemies. She is renewing her depredations on our commerce in the most ruinous shapes, and has kindled a more general indignation among our merchants than was ever before expressed."

The United States, he said, would "continue to pursue a steady and dignified conduct, doing justice under all circumstances to others," and seeking it for themselves. President Jefferson's annual message gave form to this aim. The present crisis in Europe, he said, disposed France to effect a settlement of the Florida issue. Means would be needed which Congress alone could furnish or deny.

On November 12 the President summoned the Cabinet to itemize a previous decision. He proposed and the Cabinet voted to offer Spain

$5 million for the Floridas and Texas, of which about $4 million would be repaid ultimately to settle spoliation claims. A few days later Madison learned from Armstrong that Talleyrand had offered informally to deliver Florida for $10 million and to fix the western boundary of Louisiana at the Colorado River in mid-Texas. The Cabinet, recognizing that this included a chunk of money for Talleyrand, held to its figure of $5 million. This was followed by a decision to ask Congress for an installment of $2 million, with the probability that it would be passed along by Spain to Napoleon's war chest.

A New England congressman, Barnabas Bidwell, moved that an appropriation bill be drafted. This notified Randolph that his implied abdication as administration leader was accepted. Protesting that no money had been asked for, Randolph went to see Jefferson and Madison. Both asked him to recommend an initial $2 million. Madison told him that hope of success lay in France's need of money and Spain's subjection to France.

To support his request, Jefferson sent a sheaf of diplomatic correspondence to Congress. In this, Randolph discovered a letter from Monroe advocating seizure of Florida and Texas by force. Earlier, Randolph had written that Jefferson's annual message "breathed war," and he would exert all his efforts against such a course. Now, with Jefferson taking the pacific course and Monroe breathing war, Randolph did a lightning reversal. He persuaded the special committee to reject Bidwell's motion and to recommend, instead, that troops be raised to protect the southern frontier and punish Spanish intruders—that is, seize all the disputed territory. The House rejected the report and voted the $2 million. The Senate agreed.

At this point Randolph's devoted follower, Congressman Christopher Clark of Virginia, tried to avert a Randolph-Jefferson rupture by having Randolph appointed minister to England. Madison told Clark that Randolph was not fitted for the post. Randolph, learning this, quickly found an opening to vent his rage.

On the day the House voted the $2 million, Madison's book defending neutral trade was placed on every congressman's desk. The Secretary, by request, gave the Senate a statement of adverse changes in British policy. Gregg of Pennsylvania moved to prohibit the importation of British goods until these evils were corrected. Randolph denounced this as a move toward war, then turned to Madison.

Some days ago, he said, "a book was laid on our tables, which, like some other bantlings, did not bear the name of its father. . . . Has any gentleman got the work?" he asked. Handed a copy, he read from it, "then cast it indignantly on the floor," extolled *War in Disguise*, and launched into a 2½-hour tirade "replete with invective" against Jefferson and more especially Madison (The description is by Senator Smith of Maryland.) Replied Smilie of Pennsylvania next day: "Notwithstanding the contempt with which a certain book was yesterday treated by the gentleman from Virginia, I will venture to predict that, when the mortal part of that gentleman and myself shall be in ashes, the author of that work will be considered a great man."

Considering Smilie's advanced age and his own frailty, retorted Randolph, that would not be very long; but, he asked, "am I the apologist of Britain because your cause has been weakly defended, or treacherously betrayed? No sir, this 'Examiner' is her apologist!" The work was "a miserable card-house of an argument which the first puff of wind must demolish." In reality, what was demolished was Randolph's position in the House. He was blown down by his own biting blasts of wind, and his rage increased as his status declined.

Randolph's purpose was clear to everybody. It was, wrote John Quincy Adams, "to prevent Mr. Jefferson from consenting to serve again, and Mr. Madison from being his successor." Pickering expressed the thought with Federalist malevolence. "The feeble timid Madison or the dull Monroe" was to extend the rule of "fools and knaves" until the government was subverted. Minister Merry joined in the universal verdict. The assault was designed to lower Madison's "political character and estimation in order that Mr. Monroe . . . might . . . succeed to the Presidency."

Madison, formally, and Jefferson, informally, gave Monroe permission to come home (to push his candidacy). The President also sought to advise him, in a letter that miscarried, to be on guard against new friends who were attacking his old ones "in a way to render you great injury." The President himself would observe "a sacred neutrality." Randolph made an open bid to Monroe: "Everything is made a business of bargain and traffic, the ultimate object of which is to raise Mr. Madison to the Presidency. To this the old Republican party will never consent . . . Need I tell you that they (the old Republicans) are united in your support?"

Randolph's reference to "the old Republicans" implied that Jefferson and Madison had turned Federalist. The Jeffersonians gave the Randolph faction a new christening, "the Quids." Meaning, "the what are theys?"

On April 5 Randolph intensified his assault on Madison. Recalling his endeavors to "protect the Southern frontier from Spanish inroad and insult," he said he found the executive department strangely unwilling to take a decided stand. "I found what was worse." The Secretary of State told him "that France would not permit Spain to come to any accommodation with us. . . . and that we must give her money." He considered that proposal a base prostration of the national character, "and from that moment, and to the last moment of my life, my confidence in the principles of the man entertaining these sentiments, died, never to live again."

To emphasize the words, Randolph threw his hat across the room. The falsity of Randolph's presentation was evident in the belated resort to it. If Madison said what Randolph said he did, why did the indignant congressman not kill the appropriation by making the charge in his impassioned speeches against the bill?

Among many vituperative innuendoes, the one substantial charge against Madison was that he attempted to send the $2 million to Europe before it was appropriated. Gallatin, in whose province that lay, formally denied the accusation. Findley of Pennsylvania said Randolph's defamation of citizens was "an outrage on decency." If he had a charge to make, he should have asked for an inquiry, "but this would not have answered the gentleman's purposes of slander" since it would have given the Secretary the opportunity of defending his own character.

Madison prepared a statement "for the public if found expedient," denying that he had ever suggested the use of money without congressional authorization, nor otherwise than "in a bona fide purchase for a valuable consideration in territory," with payment to the nation owning and conveying it. He merely left the statement in his papers. Randolph himself, reiterating the charges, bogged down in muddy contradictions. In the same breath he declared that the United States must deal with Spain alone and that "there exists no such nation." Yrujo's instructions "are signed 'Charles Maurice Talleyrand.'" If that metaphor was valid— and it was—Spain could not sell except by the will of France. Seizure of Florida by force (as Randolph and Monroe advocated) would mean war with France.

That, in fact, was precisely what Madison told Randolph, as shown by Randolph's own newspaper revision of the talk under the name of *Decius*. He quoted Madison as saying "that France wanted money, and that we must give it to her or have a Spanish and French war." This revision abandoned the charge of bribing France and substituted a yielding to Napoleonic extortion. Distorted as it was, it nevertheless revealed what Madison actually told him: *If the United States was to obtain Florida*, it must be purchased from Spain through France, or obtained by war with both countries.

In Virginia, Madison needed no defense. "Your life has been so pure," W. C. Nicholas wrote to him, that such assaults made no impression. One charge, he said, did receive credit, that Madison had shown partiality to Federalists by retaining Chief Clerk Wagner and Clerk Daniel Brent, proteges of former Secretary Pickering. A few weeks earlier, having Pickering at dinner, Madison eulogized Wagner as "fit for Secretary of State." Previously, when Wagner was incapacitated by a long illness, Madison refused to accept his resignation and held the place open for him for six months, taking on added duties himself. Some months after Nicholas made his comment, Wagner applied for a collectorship in the Treasury— a political sinecure. Not getting it, he resigned, established a Federalist newspaper, and made Madison the target of scurrilous falsehoods throughout the remainder of his political career. The friendliest hand is the one that serpents strike.

Late in the year 1805 the inhabitants of Washington heard a cannon-ading on the Potomac River at Alexandria. It was not Admiral Nelson, following up his great victory at Trafalgar, but a salute to an ambassador from Tunisia, coming to the United States (according to Barbary custom) at American expense.

Thus arrived Sidi Suliman Mellimelli, with eleven attachés and ser-vants, an Italian band, and four Arabian studhorses as a gift for the President. Secretary of State Madison put the visitors up at Stelle's old hotel and quickly received a call from Mellimelli and the carrier of his four-foot pipe. The ambassador had a demand and a request to make. The President, having sanctioned tribute to Algiers (pledged by his predecessor) must reverse his refusal to pay tribute to Tunis. And the Secretary of State should provide him with some concubines. Madison accommodated him with "Georgia, a Greek" who was put on the Trea-sury payroll as a servant. "Appropriations for foreign intercourse," Mad-ison wrote soon afterward, "are terms of great latitude and may be drawn on by very urgent and unforeseen occurrences."

Jefferson proved obdurate as to tribute but welcomed the studhorses, one of which was of Arabian royal pedigree. If Congress was willing, said the Chief Executive, this stallion might pay all the expenses of the Tunisian mission. Congress was willing and eager, but the President told Joseph Bryan of Georgia that he would have to pay the official stud fee. However, wrote Bryan to Madison, the President's groom refused "to put a couple of mares to the Barbary horse" without an order which "I pre-sume must come from you." Thus Madison became, ex officio, the first Secretary of Agriculture.

At this time, Washington was invaded by Indians from the Southwest and the Missouri River country—half a dozen blue-coated Creeks and twenty-one half-naked western warriors brought in by Lewis and Clark. Indians and Tunisians, diplomats and congressmen hobnobbed in Dolley

370

Madison's drawing room. The Indians in turn threw a party at which an Osage chief danced himself to death.

Refused tribute, Mellimelli begged for some concession that would save him from having his throat cut. The President and Madison sent him on his way loaded with presents. What, Madison asked the President, should be done with three Tunisians who deserted—the ambassador's secretary, cook, and barber? Pay their fare to England, said Jefferson. That was done, and the British government billed the United States for six months board and lodging at the home of a London Jew who had the misfortune to speak Turkish. The bill was not paid.

The next unwelcome visitor was the Marquis d'Yrujo, who came back from Philadelphia in spite of a hint that he was not welcome. Madison received him coldly, and after consulting the President, notified him that his departure was expected at the end of the wintry season. He defiantly replied that he would remain as long as it suited the Spanish king's interests or his own convenience. He then sent a protest to all foreign diplomats and published it along with a savage attack on the President. Federalists lionized him, but Madison cut him off from all further communication. He could deal with the State Department through French Minister Turreau.

The need for that was at hand. Into the United States in November 1805 had come the South American revolutionary, General Francisco Miranda, seeking American assistance (in addition to British, already pledged) in the liberation of Venezuela from Spain. Miranda found private support for an expedition but was turned down by Jefferson and Madison. As Miranda described the meeting to his supporter Rufus King, he told Madison that the refusal of sanction might deter people from aiding him. The Secretary allegedly replied "that the United States was a free country, where every one may do what the laws do not forbid." From this, Miranda said, he understood "that although the government would not sanction, it would wink at the expedition."

Far different was Madison's account of the interview, sent to Minister Armstrong. If hostilities toward Spain became necessary, he told the Venezuelan, they would not take place in an underhand and illicit way. He was reminded that "it would be incumbent on the United States to punish any transactions within their jurisdiction" that might involve hostility against Spain.

Miranda used his deceptive story with artful efficiency. He sold drafts on the British government and secured their payment by assuring Undersecretary Vansittart that the Jefferson administration "gave me a perfect, tacit consent." Similar assurances to Americans enabled him to raise large sums, with promises of profit, and to recruit several hundred adventurers of good social standing though "of crooked fortunes." So, on January 23, 1806, he sailed from New York with two heavily armed ships, using false papers of foreign registry. His principal partner, who cloaked the expedition, was Col. William S. Smith, son-in-law of President Adams and hangover Federalist surveyor of the port of New York.

At Staten Island Miranda took on board his expeditionary force and mailed an exceedingly artful letter to Madison. The "important matters" he had communicated should remain "in the most profound secrecy until the final result of this delicate affair." He had conformed "in everything to the intentions of the government." To Madison, as shown by a note jotted later on the missive, the "important matters" were Miranda's dealings with England, and the statement about conformity was marked "not true." To anybody familiar with Miranda's actions, however, the letter seemed to prove that the government backed his expedition.

This came to Madison with stunning force on February 6, when he received both an account of Miranda's operations and the violent protests of Yrujo to Turreau. After a quick conference with the President, Madison ordered prosecution of any persons within reach who had rendered themselves liable to criminal action.

Turreau came to see Madison next day, suspecting government complicity, and sent a report to Yrujo that became famous—made so by the appalling mistranslations of Historian Henry Adams. The first two sentences were accurately rendered: "I was with Madison this morning. I imparted to him my suspicions and yours." The remainder is given below, first in the words of Henry Adams, then in a translation made for this book by the French Embassy in Washington:

> (Adams) "I sought his eyes, and what is rather rare, I met them."
> (The embassy) "I looked into his eyes, and what is rather unusual, I caught the meaning in them."
> (Adams) "He was in a state of extraordinary prostration."
> (The embassy) "He was very dejected."

No doubt the errors of Henry Adams were innocent. He was a scholar who translated "*demander*" to mean "demand." Nevertheless, his presentation of Madison as a shifty-eyed weakling, shivering with fear, probably did more to blast Madison's posthumous reputation than all the deliberate misrepresentations of his Federalist adversaries.

Actually, Turreau did not even catch the meaning in Madison's eyes. It was not governmental complicity but the sense of being duped that produced his dejection. Madison told Turreau that he had no suspicion that an expedition was being organized. He supposed Miranda might attempt to export contraband of war, but no law forbade that. All possible punitive steps, he told the French minister, had already been taken. He regretted the failure of federal officers to detect the outfitting but said this was true also "of the foreign agents on the spot, whose vigilance must have been particularly excited."

Madison was wrong. Yrujo himself had been informed of the expedition in December by Jonathan Dayton, but his vigilance was not excited. On December 31 Yrujo wrote to Madrid that Madison refused Miranda's request for six frigates and three thousand marines, but told him that if private persons wished to take a discreet part in the expedition the government "would close its eyes to their conduct." To excuse his inaction, Yrujo sent Madrid a cock-and-bull story which he credited to Dayton. Madison, he alleged, told Miranda that he would refuse to treat with Yrujo, thus leaving "no way for me to thwart the departure of the ships." This nonsense was made more preposterous by the fact that between December 31, when Yrujo notified his government of Miranda's plan, and January 24, when Madison cut off relations with him, Yrujo had one talk with the Secretary and wrote two letters to him. On no occasion did he mention Miranda. One effective step the minister did take. He notified the Venezuelan authorities, who captured the whole expedition except for Miranda himself, who was in Haiti.

Colonel Smith and shipowner Samuel G. Ogden were prosecuted for promoting the expedition. The trial gave the Federalists a field day. Smith and Ogden memorialized Congress with accusations of government connivance. They were unanimously rejected as an interference with the courts; yet even some Republican members believed Miranda's tale. A Burr henchman picked the biased jury panel—thirty-three Federalists, three Burrites, and six Republicans.

The defense lawyers subpoenaed the entire Cabinet, whose testimony being irrelevant, wrote Madison, could not be received, but who were "rather themselves to be examined, as so many culprits." This view prevailing, the subpoenaed members informed the judges that the President said he could not dispense with their official duties. Justice Paterson sustained this refusal but the jury did not. Disregarding the law, the evidence, and the judge's instructions, it found the men not guilty. Pierrepont Edwards, special government counsel, wrote to Madison: "To disgrace the President and you and the present administration was the point aimed at from the start—and it is a source of infinite mortification to the friends of the administration here that conduct, springing from such motives, should be crowned with so much success and have such cause of triumph."

Of all the Americans involved in the Miranda affair, the one most at fault was Rufus King, former minister to England. He first sent Miranda to Madison, bearing a letter from British Undersecretary Vansittart to King, conditionally pledging British assistance. A memorandum by King reveals that he disbelieved Miranda's version of his talk with Madison. Yet he spread the word that "I fully credit it," and silently allowed his friends to sink thousands of dollars in the venture.

Jonathan Dayton had no thought of aiding Spain when he tipped off Yrujo to Miranda's expedition. He did so as the agent of Aaron Burr, who for a year had been soliciting Minister Merry for British funds to finance a plot to take the Southwest out of the United States by armed revolt. Miranda was his competitor for subversion funds.

After Miranda's arrival Burr intensified his pleas. All through the West, "persons of the greatest property and influence" were behind him. Let him be given 110,000 pounds by March or April, and he would detach Louisiana and the Western states, whereupon the North and South would fall apart. Delay it beyond that time and France would regain that country. All this Merry reported to his government on November 25, 1805, adding his own opinion that this result "I readily conceive may happen."

An inkling of this reached Jefferson in December, in an anonymous warning that Burr was "conspiring against the state" as a British pensioner and agent. Joseph Daveiss of Kentucky wrote to Jefferson in February 1806 that "we have traitors among us. A separation of the Union in favor of Spain is the object." But Daveiss, a partisan Federalist, destroyed his credibility by listing among the conspirators Henry Clay, Senator Adair, and Governor William Henry Harrison.

In the fall of 1806 repeated accounts of Burr's activities came to Madison—about his distribution of cash, his boat building at Blennerhasset's Island on the Ohio, his raising of a force of adventurers. Then General William Eaton, late consul to Tunis, informed Jefferson of Burr's efforts to draw him into the plot and gave full details of it. Burr, he said, named as his partner General James Wilkinson, commander-in-chief of the American Army and governor of Upper Louisiana.

This produced a Cabinet deliberation, but only led to a decision to send John Graham (home from Spain) on a trip of investigation. Then came a startling message from Wilkinson. Eight or ten thousand men were to gather in New Orleans by December, ostensibly to invade Mexico through Vera Cruz. He had no idea who was organizing them, but he believed the real purpose was to stage a revolt in Orleans territory. He intended to throw his little band into New Orleans to defend it with his "last breath" against usurpation and violence.

Wilkinson was the most unprincipled liar and scoundrel in the military annals of America and equally skillful. He had been in correspondence with Burr for months, with an arrangement to unite forces with him at Natchez. For years Wilkinson had been drawing an annual pension from Spain. He applied at this time to the Mexican viceroy for an extra $121,000 to save that country from Burr. Two roads were open to him, to outdo Burr or do him out and win undying glory. Like a praying mantis dealing with a wasp, Wilkinson drew Burr into his grasp and devoured him.

Receiving Wilkinson's warning, the Cabinet on November 25 took instant action, approving a denunciatory presidential proclamation, ordering the seizure of Burr's boats, and directing Wilkinson to block the expedition and arrest its promoters. Madison felt no alarm but was puzzled. There could be no doubt, he wrote to Monroe, that a military enterprise was being undertaken against Spain. Severance of the West also was afoot, but there was no ground to suppose that the general sentiment would countenance either.

Wilkinson then sent a treasonable ciphered letter from Burr, with a garbled decipherment that eliminated every crimination of Wilkinson himself. The President sent this to Congress, and other documents, praising Wilkinson, who had acted "with the honor of a soldier and fidelity of a good citizen."

Jefferson's vigorous proclamation stirred alarm in the East. It shattered Burr's expedition traveling down the Mississippi and sent its leaders fleeing westward as pretended land-settlers. The Senate hysterically voted to suspend the writ of habeas corpus in New Orleans, but the House defeated the resolution 113 to 19. "For what purpose everybody knew," wrote Burwell of Virginia, certain members (no need to name John Randolph) "insinuated Mr. Madison was the promoter of it." Every Cabinet member had opposed the suspension except Navy Secretary Smith.

Two of Burr's lieutenants, Dr. Erich Bollman and Samuel Swartwout, were sent to Washington by Wilkinson in defiance of a habeas corpus ruling. Madison recorded an interview Bollman had with the President. It appeared, he concluded from it, that Bollman sought the meeting only to minimize his own connection with Burr and diminish the latter's criminality. Learning that Kentuckians who had been shouting for Burr now called him traitor, Madison wrote that his enterprise "has probably received its death blow. Every additional development of it increases the wonder at his infatuation." Bollman and Swartwout, he expected, would remain in prison until tried, but Chief Justice Marshall released them on habeas corpus: the record disclosed no overt acts of treason.

A month later, in March, word came that Burr, arrested in Mississippi Territory, was on his way to Richmond under a guard of soldiers. This created both rejoicing and alarm in the administration. Marshall was holding court in Richmond and could release Burr on habeas corpus unless charges supported by evidence reached there ahead of the prisoner. Attorney-General Caesar Rodney, carrying depositions, reached Fredericksburg exhausted by bad roads. Burr had passed through. Rodney searched the town for a reliable and swift carrier. He found Colonel Tatham of Bowling Green, about to go south, but Tatham was a "little flighty." Fortunately, wrote the Attorney-General to Jefferson, the colonel had "a very faithful servant." So the slave Joseph galloped off with the precious depositions that could not be entrusted to his master. He beat Burr to Richmond.

Jefferson asked Madison to supervise the assembling of western witnesses against Burr. That task Madison assigned to his newly appointed chief clerk, John Graham. Conducting the trial in Richmond, Chief Justice Marshall proved his impartiality by remarking that "the hand of malignity" guided the prosecution. He avoided politics by issuing a subpoena, replete with belittling remarks, ordering President Jefferson to appear in court and bring certain letters of Wilkinson. Jefferson sent the letters and rejected the subpoena, saying that he had paramount duties to perform.

Nine-tenths of the witnesses were still to be heard when Marshall put an end to the testimony. The government, he ruled, must either prove Burr's physical presence on Blennerhasset's Island during the actual formation of an assembly in force for the purposes of war, or it must prove by the direct and positive testimony of two witnesses that he *procured* such an assembly. That was impossible except by self-accusation by Burr and Dayton. The angered jury found that Burr was not proved guilty "by any evidence submitted to us."

Burr and his lawyers leaped to their feet in protest, but calmed down when the Chief Justice matter-of-factly ordered that "not guilty" be entered on the record. In spite of the political bias Marshall displayed against President Jefferson, his ruling was in full harmony with the purpose and words of the framers when they defined the crime and punishment of treason. He completely knocked out "constructive treason," the ancient instrument of monarchic tyranny.

"Chief Justice Marshall has it seems acquitted Burr," wrote Rodney to Madison. Jefferson was furious, and Madison agreed with him that Burr should be tried again in Richmond for a misdemeanor, which would permit use of the excluded testimony. After Burr's second acquittal, Jefferson suggested still another prosecution in Ohio, for acts committed there, but the Cabinet persuaded him, instead, merely to submit the whole record to Congress. Publication of it would place Burr before the country in his true colors. And so it did, with nothing lacking except the overwhelming proof of treasonable intent that was hidden in the British archives.

Relations with England became critical in the spring of 1806. Three warships, persistent defiers of New York port officers, met by chance off Sandy Hook and proceeded to raid American commerce in territorial waters. A cannon shot killed a seaman and stirred national passions. Madison directed Monroe (now back in London) to protest these "violent and lawless proceedings" and demand "exemplary punishment" of the cannonading officer, Captain Whitby. The Secretary notified Merry that the President was ordering the *Cambrian*, the *Driver*, and the *Leander* to leave and stay out of American ports.

The crisis was given a public turn when Merry was overheard saying to Madison, at a social gathering, that "before we went to war, we ought to be very sure that no other measure of a conciliatory nature remained." Such a measure actually was in the wind. Jefferson appointed William Pinkney, a leading Baltimore lawyer and champion of shipowners, as a special envoy to work with Monroe in seeking a new treaty of commerce.

The choice of Pinkney astonished both parties. Republicans regarded him as a Federalist. Federalists looked upon him as a demi-democrat. Nobody was more surprised than Senator Samuel Smith of Maryland, who hoped to get the assignment himself. His brother Robert, the Secretary of the Navy, told him that not a member of the Cabinet was consulted. That meant only that Robert was not consulted, lest he stir up a row by telling Samuel.

Turreau did not believe the Smiths' story. "On the contrary," he wrote to Paris, "I am persuaded that this strange promotion is the work of Mr. Madison, the habitual wire-puller [*le faiseur ordinaire*]." It is beyond doubt, he added, "that the Secretary of State entirely directs the cabinet at Washington, and that he seizes all occasions to please the Federalists individually. His influence on the head of government is all the more powerful because the latter courts it."

The French minister quoted a remark made by President Jefferson. "He never would have accepted such a place, if he had not found in the best of his friends all the talents necessary to help him fill it." This infatuation for *un homme mediocre*, Turreau observed, was no surprise to those who knew Jefferson—a man who understood his country's interest but lacked energy and audacity and was readily thrown off balance. Congressman Nicholson credited presidential politics with the selection. The purpose, he wrote to Monroe, was "to take from you the credit of settling our differences with England."

Turreau's statement that Madison directed the Cabinet was completely at variance with the general opinion of the public, which regarded Jefferson as all in all, but it coincided with a spreading belief in Congress. John Adair of Kentucky had attended the Senate only five months and must therefore have combined report with observation, when he said to Senator Plumer in April 1806: "The President wants nerve—he has not even confidence in himself. For more than a year he has been in the habit of trusting almost implicitly in Mr. Madison. Madison has acquired a complete ascendancy over him."

Federalist Plumer replied that Madison, an honest man, was "too cautious, too fearful and too timid to direct the affairs of this nation." Disturbed, Plumer queried his Federalist colleague, Senator Gilman of New Hampshire, who told him that he believed the President was honest but lacked firmness. "Mr. Madison was much more timid, and yet he governed the President," who seldom consulted the other heads of department.

In appraising Madison, Federalists mistook caution and quiet methods for timidity; but their belief that he governed the President was a conclusion forced on them in spite of their unflattering opinion of the Secretary, and it reduced that opinion to absurdity. A timid Chief Executive would not be governed by a Cabinet member "much more timid" than himself.

In London, Monroe and Pinkney pressed their case before a new ministry formed upon the death of Pitt—the "Ministry of All the Talents." Merry tried to soothe Madison with a letter from Foreign Secretary Charles James Fox promising to seek an end to all disputes by treaty. Written after Fox learned of the nonimportation resolution, Madison commented to the President, it plainly resulted from loss of the German market, due to Napoleon's victories and fear that the United States might shut another trade door. The soothing syrup turned to acid when Merry gave notice of a "paper blockade" of all German rivers. Madison retorted that every American ship had a right to enter and depart unless a blockading fleet invested the port.

During this time a monkey wrench thrown by John Randolph landed in London. His assault on Madison's *Examination of the British Doctrine* enabled James Stephen to put out another pamphlet, "proving" the validity of his arguments by the repetition of them in Congress. British newspapers followed with Randolph's false allegation that Madison had offered Napoleon a $2 million bribe. Our affairs in London, Jefferson commented, "are in danger of being all in the wind."

Pinkney reached London on June 19 and did nothing for weeks while Foreign Minister Fox was slowly sinking in a fatal illness. Before Fox died Minister Merry was recalled, and his place given to David Erskine, thirty-year-old son of "the celebrated Erskine," champion of civil liberties. David had an American wife.

Monroe and Pinkney were given two imperative orders. They must not promise repeal of the nonimportation act unless they obtained a treaty forbidding impressment on the high seas. Also it must protect American trade between an enemy colony and the parent country when the goods were transshipped from the United States. They were to seek an end to "paper blockades," commercial discriminations, and naval insults and injuries in American waters.

Reports from them began to come in November 1806. Lords Auckland and Holland declared that forbidding impressments would make the American merchant marine a haven for British deserters. They proposed that American seamen be required by law to carry "authentic documents of citizenship." Monroe and Pinkney rejected this as a derogation of national sovereignty.

Madison was cheered (he wrote to the envoys) by Britain's request, which Congress granted, for postponement of the nonimportation act; but to newly arrived Minister Erskine, his manner "indicated disappointment and vexation" over impressment. "He did not believe that justice was intended to be done to the United States."

That portent was fulfilled, but Madison was totally unprepared for the news received on February 1, 1807, that Monroe and Pinkney had agreed *to leave impressment out of the treaty*. Erskine was notified at once that the United States never would abandon its opposition to the practice. The injury it inflicted far outweighed the brief loss to England of a few seamen who could be recovered when American ships visited English ports. Furthermore, its abolition had been taken up as a point of honor. On this the United States would never yield; but, with impressment ended, they would give every facility for restoring British deserters.

The President, though preferring no treaty to one that permitted impressment, suggested that they "take the advice of the Senate" on the issue. The Cabinet's vote was "unanimously not," both on consulting the Senate and accepting such a treaty. Putting some of his disgust into words, Madison instructed the envoys that no treaty should be signed unless it contained a formal stipulation against impressment, but the President would agree to an informal mutual understanding to the same effect.

A few days later grave news arrived from Paris. Napoleon had issued the Decree of Berlin, imposing a total blockade against the British Isles. It was to remain in force until Britain stopped seizing private property and restrained the right of blockade to seaports actually invested. Then came a joyous note from Monroe and Pinkney, hastily announcing that they had signed a treaty satisfactory on all points. This meant, seemingly, that Great Britain had yielded on impressment in order to win American support against Napoleon's Berlin Decree. Madison joyfully gave the news to Erskine.

Three weeks later, on March 3, 1807, the day Congress was to adjourn sine die, the British minister handed Madison a copy of the new treaty and suggested that the Senate be held in session to ratify it. What does it say about impressment, was Madison's first and only question. "Nothing," was the answer.

Erskine reported Madison's "astonishment and disappointment . . . he did not think it would be possible to ratify the treaty." To make matters worse, Britain in a supplemental note reserved the right to take the same measures against neutral commerce that Napoleon did. Great Britain would not be bound by the treaty unless, prior to exchange of ratifications, France abandoned her violations of maritime law or the United States gave security that it would not submit to them. This note alone, Madison told Erskine, would prevent ratification even if the treaty were satisfactory.

Jefferson, cured of a migraine headache by the startling news, told a senatorial delegation that evening that he would not submit the treaty to the Senate. He did, however, make a further suspension of the nonimportation act, and Madison instructed the envoys to work for an informal agreement against impressment. By this time, Erskine gave notice of a British Order in Council retaliating against the Berlin Decree. It forbade all trade from port to port of enemy countries and set up a "paper blockade" of virtually the entire continental coast from St. Petersburg to Trieste. This vast trade had been taken over almost entirely by American ships.

Madison dissected the British action. In the absence of a blockade—impossible to enforce along a continental coast—the forbidden trade was lawful both in peace and war. Britain acted before it was known whether France intended to violate treaties with the United States, or whether, in that case, the United States would fail to restore equality. He pointed out that Britain was cutting off her own avenue to the continent, since the (presumed) American immunity to the French decree would cover British goods carried under the American flag. It was expected, Madison told the envoys, that these truths would be reflected in remedial measures.

To aid new negotiations, President Jefferson disclosed only the general features of the rejected treaty. Federalist editors, who had been predicting secret ratification of a bad treaty, now exclaimed that a good treaty was being abandoned under French pressure or to help Madison's presidential prospects. Said the *United States Gazette:* "Whether Mons. Turreau has set his famous whiskers against a treaty with England, or whether Mr. Jefferson fears that the successful negotiation of a treaty would render Mr. Monroe more popular than consists with the views of the executive previous to the next presidential election, we are not informed."

Besides omitting impressment, the treaty gave up the weapon of non-importation and imposed various trade regulations. Studying the colonial clauses more closely, Madison found them full of tricky provisions to cut off the American carrying trade between the Orient, South America, and the Levant, even between China and Asiatic colonies. He sent this analysis to Senator Smith of Maryland who replied that war would be better than such a treaty. Monroe, defending the treaty a year later, inadvertently revealed what lay behind this. The treaty, Lord Auckland told him, had to protect the trade monopoly of the East India Company.

Madison worked out a new treaty draft, protecting trade and offering a new formula on impressment and deserters. This he held back, pending a report by Gallatin on the number of British seamen in the mercantile marine. The Treasury head reported—9,000 Britons out of 67,000 seafarers. However, these 9,000 made up almost half of the able seamen in foreign trade, enough to cripple shipping if withdrawn. Better let the negotiation take a friendly nap, Madison advised. For this course he gave Robert Livingston an additional reason: "But whatever amicable arrangements may be put on paper, harmony and good will between the parties cannot be lasting, if the most efficacious remedy be not applied to the atrocious behavior of the British ships of war on our coasts, and even in our harbors."

Three weeks later in June 1807, these words became an understatement. The 50-gun British *Leopard*, following the 36-gun frigate *Chesapeake* out of Hampton Roads, demanded three deserters reputed to be on board. Delivery being refused, the *Leopard* poured broadside after broadside into the helpless frigate, whose gun were not cleared for action. With his ship dismasted and twenty-two holes in its hull, Captain Barron struck his colors. Three Americans were killed, eighteen wounded. Four seamen were taken from the frigate.

Jefferson drafted a proclamation excluding all British warships from American waters unless in distress or on diplomatic business. Madison loaded the draft with hard words: "insults as gross as language could offer," "this enormity," "avowed and insulting purpose," "her lawless and bloody purpose." In conclusion, however, Madison linked conciliation with a demand for indemnity. Mutual desire to avoid a rupture should "strengthen the motives to an honorable reparation for the wrong," and thus maintain the existing relations of the two countries.

Jefferson accepted most of Madison's revisions but toned them down in the final draft, published while war fever swept the country. To Erskine the key words were "honorable reparation," denoting the wish to avoid war. The Cabinet voted to bring all warships home from the Mediterranean and to have 120,000 militia placed in readiness. Reparation demands were sent to Monroe, and a special session of Congress was called for October, allowing four months for a reply.

Two things, Madison wrote, were indispensable: formal disavowal of the attack and restoration of the four impressed seamen. Beyond this, the United States had a right to expect every "ingredient of retribution and respect" that was proper to repair an "insult to the rights and sovereignty of a nation." There was no alternative but voluntary satisfaction by Great Britain "or a resort to means depending on the United States alone."

Added to the final draft was an imperative requirement that total abolition of impressment be included. If reparations were refused, all American ships in British ports must be hurried home, and the ambassador of Russia (England's ally on land and victim at sea) should be notified of the probable resort "to measures constituting or leading to war."

Writing to Paris and Madrid, Madison withdrew the offer to buy the Floridas. If the United States entered the war against England or broke with her commercially, the benefit to France should greatly reduce the price asked for those colonies. Or, hostilities between the United States and England might lead to British occupation of the Floridas. He did not add Jefferson's remark that in such a case the United States would get there first.

The fact was that while demanding reparations for the *Chesapeake* attack, the government sought to gain objectives that made reparations more difficult to obtain. The conduct of British naval officers kept up the war spirit. Following the President's proclamation, wrote Madison to Monroe, some ships left. Others defied it. Their blockade of Norfolk amounted to "an invasion and a siege."

Erskine protested the President's proclamation but sent his government Madison's warning that unless reparation was granted for the attack on the *Chesapeake*, "war must be the consequence," and that preparations for it of the most extensive kind would be entered upon by the Congress. The Secretary of State summed up national feeling for Monroe: "Reparation or war is proclaimed at every meeting . . . and the reparation must . . . satisfy the just feelings of a nation which values its honor, and knows its importance."

Although Madison denied that the nationality of the four men taken from the *Chesapeake* affected Britain's liability, he gathered many affidavits showing that two were natives of Maryland. One of these, an ex-slave, bore the name of his white father, Ware. A third seamen, also a Negro, had been brought from South America at the age of six. Admiral Berkeley claimed, through Erskine, that all three Americans enlisted voluntarily on the *Melampus* after deserting their own ship. That was a confession, Madison replied, to the knowing enlistment of American deserters without consulting American law. Their later flight from the *Melampus* restored them by their own act to the country to which they owed allegiance. The Secretary called the fourth seaman an American, but the British officers were so sure he was their countryman that they hanged him.

Madison's relations with Erskine remained cordial, and he built up a friendship with legation secretary Augustus Foster, who spent some time at Montpelier at the height of the *Chesapeake* crisis. Foster described the house and its Blue Ridge setting. At the front was a portico "of the plainest and most massive order of architecture, but which Palladio gives as a specimen of the Tuscan." It was executed by Madison "without the assistance of an architect," built of ordinary materials by common workmen to whom Madison prescribed the proportions. The result was a specimen "of good and massive Doric" pillars. A twelve-inch rain carried away Madison's milldam on Blue Run, cut off Foster's expected money supply, and forced the diplomat to borrow $70 for his return journey.

Letters from Monroe, forwarded from Washington, enabled Madison to inform the President (at Monticello) that England disclaimed any right to search ships of war for deserters, but Foreign Secretary Canning's qualifying words and irritable tone suggested that he might "quibble away the proposed atonement." The British minister warned Canning that a few illegal captures along the American coast and insulting behavior in the harbors had excited more ill-will than the most rigid enforcement of British maritime rights in other parts of the world.

Grim reports followed Madison's return to Washington in October. Britain's special ambassador to Denmark, Francis James Jackson, de-livered an ultimatum backed by an investing fleet, to abandon neutrality. The Danish Prince Regent stood firm and "Copenhagen Jackson," as he was known for the rest of his life, gave the order to fire. The capital was reduced to rubble, and hundreds died.

On the continent, military defeats drove Prussia and Russia out of the coalition against Napoleon. England countered their defection with brutal use of naval power against a distant neutral. The President's annual mes-sage contained no reference to conciliatory language used by Canning to Monroe. Why was this? asked Erskine. Because, Madison told him, that language carried no indication of redress. Combined with the linking of Chesapeake reparations and impressment, this persuaded Erskine (he told Canning) that the purpose was "to prevent the effect of any apology or redress . . . from allaying the indignation of the people."

That was the precise objective Madison had outlined to Monroe months before—to obtain satisfaction at one stroke on all points in controversy. That hope faded fast. The London *Star* told of the government's intention to retaliate the Berlin Decree and "settle at once the clamors of the Amer-icans respecting their right to trade with the French colonies." From Paris came word that Napoleon had ordered the capture of every vessel bound to or from the British Isles—no exceptions from the Berlin Decree. England and France were in a grand partnership for the destruction of American commerce.

Facing this mesalliance of enemies, President Jefferson and his Cabinet turned to the thought of a general embargo to save American ships and cut off supplies from both belligerents. Madison wanted to retain the existing nonimportation act (not yet in force), extend it to France and superadd the embargo. Jefferson thought this would lead to war with

England "and give her the choice of the moment of declaring it." Bad news piled up. King George III proclaimed rigorous impressment. English newspapers confirmed the signing of an order in council countering Napoleon's decree.

Accepting this as final, Jefferson laid an embargo message before his Cabinet. Citing the actions by which "the whole world is thus laid under interdict by these two nations," Jefferson wished to submit this question "to the wisdom of Congress": "If therefore on leaving our harbors we are certain to lose them, is it not better as to vessels, cargoes and seamen to keep them at home?"

The Cabinet thought this format put the decision too much in doubt. Madison rewrote the message, citing "the great and increasing danger" in which merchandise, vessels, and seamen were being placed. To keep these essential resources in safety, "I deem it my duty to recommend the subject to the consideration of Congress, who will doubtless perceive all the advantage which may be expected from an immediate inhibition of the departure of our vessels from the ports of the United States." Congress also was invited to prepare "for whatever events may grow out of the present crisis."

The embargo bill passed both houses in four days. Randolph spoke for all dissidents with his shrill cry that America, crouching "to the insolent mandate of Bonaparte," was being dragooned into a French alliance. But Madison told Turreau that the law put France on a par with England, and the United States would provide for its proper security.

The orders of November 11, 1807, subjected all French-controlled seaports to the same restrictions *as if they were blockaded*, with certain exceptions. Neutral vessels could trade *directly* between their home ports and French colonies. Exempted also were vessels which *had last cleared from British ports* under British licenses. This was commercial warfare against neutrals, not military action against Napoleon. It forbade the "broken-voyage" American trade between French colonies and Europe. It enabled England to supply France and the whole Napoleonic empire with British goods carried by American ships holding British licenses. Madison's interpretation of the purpose finds complete support in the papers of Chancellor Perceval: "Our orders . . . say to the enemy, 'if you will not have our trade, as far as we can help it you shall have *none*.' "

Although Madison agreed with Jefferson that an embargo was needed, the two men differed in their general approach. From 1789 onward, Madison had sought to use trade restrictions and discrimination as weapons of force to compel England to cease her commercial aggressions.

Jefferson justified his 1807 embargo on the simple ground that without it, all vessels, cargoes and seamen would have been lost and war would have resulted. Better, he argued, "discontinue all intercourse with those nations till they shall return again to some sense of moral right."

Following the signing of the Embargo Act, Madison was identified both at home and in London as the author of three articles defending it in the *National Intelligencer*. Repeating almost verbatim, language he had used in 1794, Madison said that the embargo, besides guarding maritime resources, would make it "the interest of all nations to change the system which has driven our commerce from the ocean." Great Britain would feel it in her manufactures and naval stores, and in supplies essential to her colonies. France would lose colonial luxuries; Spain, imported food. Being an impartial measure of peace and precaution, there was "not a shadow of pretext to make it a cause of war." He closed the series with an appeal to the people, through national unity, to deliver a death blow to the insulting opinion in Europe that Americans would submit to wrongs of every sort rather than suspend commerce: "Let us teach the world that . . . we will flinch from no sacrifices which the honor and good of the nation demand from virtuous and faithful citizens."

At this juncture Dr. George Rose, special envoy in the *Chesapeake* affair, came up from Norfolk. "Young George" disclosed at once two points in his instructions. He could not discuss impressments, and he was positively forbidden to begin negotiations until the President recalled his proclamation of July 2, 1807, excluding British warships from American harbors. That proclamation, Madison told him, was not an act of redress but a general precaution to ensure internal quiet. Outrages later than the *Leopard*'s attack required its continuance. He would not conceal the fact that, had the United States possessed sufficient force, "it would have been employed in compelling their submission." Reporting these remarks Rose commented:

> It is but justice due to this minister to observe, that these considerations were urged in a temper and tone calculated to promote a dispassionate discussion. . . . Nor did I find in him, in this first conversation, either that acrimony of temper, or that fluency of expression, which I have invariably understood to be two of his chief characteristics in similar discussions.

To help get around the proclamation obstacle, Madison asked for an informal disclosure of the reparations offer. Navy Secretary Smith, who had an early social contact with Rose, was sent by the President to further that request. This led to a gross exaggeration, three years later, of Smith's participation. To rebut a charge that Gallatin had mixed too much in diplomacy, Jefferson asked why that was not said also of Secretary Smith, who conducted "the whole nearly, of [the Rose] negotiation, as far as it was transacted verbally." That was nonsense. Except for closing statements the entire negotiation was verbal. In the 199 pages Rose wrote to Canning, he named Madison 102 times; Smith, 3 times, and two of these in relation to social events. Jefferson had a conveniently fluid memory.

The impasse over exclusion of warships was broken, not by Madison and Rose, but by news that Russia had declared war on England. Apprehensive of similar American action, Rose backed away somewhat from his demand for prior withdrawal of the proclamation. Madison proposed that all formal papers be signed on the same day, leaving priority "a matter of uncertainty." Rose demurred, but accepted Madison's offer to show him, in advance, the *draft* of a recall proclamation, to be issued simultaneously with the reparations agreement.

That settled, Rose gradually built up British counter-demands. Madison rejected them one after the other, then was hit by a fever that caused several days' delay. The negotiations ended when Rose said the United States would be required to disavow Captain Barron's denial that he had British deserters on board. The British envoy recorded the words with which Madison broke off the talks: The United States could not be expected to make "an expiatory sacrifice to obtain redress, or beg for reparation." The Secretary, Rose wrote to Canning, positively rejected "the proposal that mutual reparations should be made . . . insisting that the attack on the *Chesapeake* should be redressed first and separately, and that other grievances on both sides should be disavowed and repaired by bilateral instruments."

To polish off the affair, Madison wrote a 5,000-word reply to Rose's introductory letter. It was a review of all British naval predations, with hardly a reference to the *Chesapeake*. Rose found it hard to believe that an American minister could put his hand to such an instrument. The motive, he concluded, was political. Madison, as a candidate for President, desired "to touch the popular feelings" and was trying also to reconcile the people to the embargo, "under which their impatience naturally increases every hour." In this conclusion "Young George" Rose displayed an acumen of which there was no hint in the negotiations ruined in advance by George Canning's incredible instructions.

Eighteen hundred eight was the first election year in which the Republican choice for President was flecked by doubt. Three candidacies had been taking shape for four years. Sixty-eight-year-old George Clinton, inoculated with the virus by the Vice-Presidency, deviated in at least one respect from the description of him by Senator Plumer: "He has no mind —no intellect—no memory." One memory was clear as the sky: Vice President Adams succeeded President Washington, and Vice President Jefferson succeeded President Adams.

The presidential ambition of James Monroe needed no outside stimulus except as to timing. Two Americans in London, comparing notes, found that Monroe made the same remark at different times: he would "sooner be a constable" than oppose Madison for President. Against that reluctance John Randolph carried on a continuous campaign, motivated less by devotion to Monroe than by hatred of Madison. Against his appeals Monroe cited the higher pretensions of men older than himself. His candidacy would tear up ancient friendships and rend the Republican party.

Such reasons, Randolph replied in September 1806, had no validity when the high merit of a Monroe was opposed to "the cold and insidious moderation" of a Madison. This last gentleman was responsible for "that strange amalgamation of men and principles" that had of late proved so injurious to the Jefferson administration. It was because of Madison's influence that the government "stands aloof from its tried friends, whilst it hugs to our bosom men of the most equivocal character," such as William Pinkney.

This was a telling shot, for Monroe deeply resented the sending of that treaty-writing associate. Things had occurred, Monroe replied, that hurt his feelings and might change his relations with the men in power. Nevertheless, he wished his friends to keep in mind the general soundness of the administration's conduct. Little as he liked the coming of Pinkney, he found in him a co-operative spirit, and he was glad that he himself elected to remain and complete the treaty rather than act on the renewed authorization to come home (and run for President).

All this changed like a flash with rejection of the treaty that was to be his path to glory. Every Randolphian insinuation turned into self-evident fact, and Randolph piled up new allegations. The request for revision of the treaty was a device to hold him in London while Madison won the Presidency. Madison's friends had "left nothing undone to impair the very high and just confidence of the nation in yourself."

Strange, that if Madison and Jefferson were scheming to keep Monroe in London, they should send him a letter of farewell to the King and give Pinkney a commission as his successor. Littleton Tazewell gave Monroe both constructive advice and a tacit warning against Randolph. He should make no announcement concerning the Presidency until he reached home and surveyed the situation: "Among those who are apparently your most zealous advocates there are some made so by disappointment actuated by sinister views . . . not because they prefer you but because they hate you less than others."

Monroe was nearing Norfolk in December 1807 when ex-Speaker Nathaniel Macon analyzed his political situation. To win either first or second place Monroe must have Governor Clinton as his running-mate. Would Clinton stoop to second place? Would Virginia throw away a Madison Presidency in order to make Monroe Vice President? Monroe had only one campaign issue—the rejection of his treaty, but, remarked Macon, "the extract of the treaty which has been published has injured Monroe more than the return of it by the President."

Clinton, too, was a one-issue candidate—too many Virginians in the Presidency. His newspaper supporters assailed Madison for keeping viperous Federalists in his office. The New York *American Citizen* accused Madison of excluding the Vice President from Cabinet meetings: "The influence of Mr. Madison over the President is known and harmony in the cabinet probably required that his wishes should be complied with."

In the Cabinet, the close rapport between Madison and Gallatin made the latter a firm Madisonian supporter after Jefferson refused to extend his service. To break their alliance became the chief object of William Duane, publisher of the democratic Philadelphia *Aurora*, who had failed to get the State and Treasury printing he asked for. His heaviest assaults were leveled against Gallatin, who nevertheless recognized that Madison was the real target. "You are not less aware than myself," wrote Gallatin to Jefferson in 1806, "that the next presidential election lurks at the bottom of these writings and of the congressional dissensions." Duane's object was to link Pennsylvania with New York in blocking Madison and creating a choice between Clinton and Monroe.

From Norfolk Monroe hastened to Washington to consult with friendly congressmen. Randolph kept away from him for several days, explaining that open association with "a proscribed individual" might mar Monroe's prospects. They met in secret before Monroe left for Richmond in January, and Randolph no doubt told him what he had been telling others, that the Virginia legislature would favor him over Madison by a big majority. Nationally that was certainly true of the Federalists, whose own party was too shattered to put up a ticket. Monroe, wrote Timothy Pickering, was "inferior in learning and discernment to Mr. Madison," but he was more practical and more upright and was cured of his attachment to France. Madison was as visionary as Jefferson, who, if Madison should be elected, "would direct all the movements of the little man at the Palace." The myth of Madison's subordination had few doubters among those who hated Jefferson.

A congressional caucus of Republicans would nominate the presidential ticket, but endorsement of either Virginian by his legislature could have a heavy impact in Washington. Virginia congressmen friendly to Madison sent assurance to Richmond that other state delegations would support Madison. Congressman John Clopton told Monroe the same from an opposite angle. Madison would get Pennsylvania, New Jersey, probably New England, also New York if Clinton was dropped. A quick Virginia endorsement of Monroe was needed.

Madison's congressional managers, Senators Giles and Nicholas, urged that the Virginia test be held back until after the congressional caucus. They regarded Clinton as the main threat and wished to avoid "carping and captious" criticism of Madison as a Virginia candidate. Impending adjournment of the Richmond body made delay impossible, so Nicholas and Giles persuaded Caucus Chairman Bradley of Vermont to speed up the congressional vote. The result was that the legislature acted on January 21, the congressmen on January 23—neither knowing of the other's action. Madison won both contests by overwhelming votes.

In Virginia the Madison and Monroe supporters caucused separately, Madison carried his group 123 to 0. Monroe took the other, 57 to 10. Counting three names signed next day, Madison won the legislative endorsement 136 to 57.

On the eve of the congressional caucus, New York congressmen offered to withdraw George Clinton's candidacy and give Madison clear sailing, provided the Madisonians would nominate DeWitt Clinton, the governor's nephew, for Vice President. They did not hide their motive—to put the younger Clinton in line for the Presidency in 1816. Such an arrangement, wrote the governor's son-in-law, "Citizen" Genet, "was treated with contempt by Mr. Madison's friends." Most of Clinton's supporters refused to vote, and the caucus produced these results: For President—Madison, 83; George Clinton, 3; Monroe, 3; not voting, 5.

For Vice President—Clinton, 79; John Langdon, 5; Dearborn, 3; John Quincy Adams, 1.

John Randolph's faction and nearly all Clintonians stayed away from the caucus—certain notice of trouble ahead. The *National Intelligencer* pleaded that the party division, if it came, should be "candid, honorable, magnanimous," with no traducing of character. It hailed Madison as the man "best fitted to guide us through the impending storm"—a man of irreproachable morals and solid talents, whose discharge of public duty had been distinguished by intelligence, fidelity, and zeal.

Monroe, spurred by Randolph, remained in the field, ignoring the warning of his other congressional supporters that this would ruin his future prospects. Jefferson (writing to Monroe) saw "with infinite grief" a contest arising between two men "who have been very dear to each other, and equally so to me." His sincere friendship for both prescribed a sacred neutrality. He had no doubt that their conduct toward each other would be chaste. "But your friends will not be so delicate," he told Monroe, and the principals would be drawn into the passions aroused by their friends. Monroe circulated this veiled plea for withdrawal as evidence "that Mr. Jefferson was not hostile."

DeWitt Clinton now planted a brilliant thought in his uncle's mind. He should run *on Madison's ticket for Vice President, and against both Madison and Monroe for President.* The plan was publicized by DeWitt as from an unnamed person to whom George Clinton replied that he could not comment on something "over which I can have no control." That left him in the competition for both offices.

Federalists took up Clinton as their best instrument for defeating Madison. John Randolph and sixteen other caucus absentees published an address denying the power to hold such a meeting (Jefferson had been nominated twice in that manner) and violently assailing Madison. The nation needed a leader combining firmness and wisdom: "Is James Madison such a man? We ask for energy, and we are told of his moderation. We ask for talents, and the reply is his unassuming merit. . . . We ask for that high and honorable sense of duty which would at all times turn with

loathing and abhorrence from any compromise with fraud and speculation. We ask in vain."

The election, it appeared, might depend on Pennsylvania and Virginia.
The Clinton machine controlled virtually the entire New York press and,
as one New Yorker described its conduct, DeWitt's "hired libellers are
again set upon the scent to defame." Madison was assailed as a weakling,
unable to fulfill the common duties of his office, and as a man who by
subtlety and guile had reduced the President to an easy submission. Clinton was a military genius (who lost two forts to the British) and his strong
leadership was essential to the nation's survival.

The Clintonians concentrated also on Pennsylvania, with a pledge to
sweep the Tories out of office. Thomas Leiper, presidential elector (and
marketer of Jefferson's and Madison's tobacco), wrote to the President:
"You cannot conceive what injury it has done Mr. Madison here, his
keeping Wagner, Brent and Forrest in his office." Duane's *Aurora* supported Madison. (Its rule was, "Never back a loser.") Duane told of the
"daily resignation" of members of Monroe's campaign committee and
published a forecast giving Madison eleven states with 107 electors; uncertain or divided, six states with 67 votes. The prediction was that Pennsylvania's electors, already appointed by the legislature, would cast their
ballots solidly for Madison.

The campaign gained new acerbity as the United States felt the full
impact of French and British decrees victimizing American commerce.
Monroe, his adherents cried, was the man who could end the trouble
with England. Federalists and Clintonians raised the cry of "French influence" against Madison. Thundered Pickering: "Why, in this dangerous
crisis, are Mr. Armstrong's letters to the Secretary of State absolutely
withheld . . . Has the French emperor declared that he will have no
neutrals?" It was now politically imperative to publish both British and
French correspondence, and Jefferson sent Congress a file amounting to
a hundred thousand words.

All day for six days the clerks in both houses read those letters aloud.
Vice President Clinton fumed. Why waste time on papers "of no significance"? To many, however, it was evident that the contest between Madison and Monroe was being decided. For two months those letters filled
newspapers throughout the continent. Before the end of that time it was
apparent that Monroe's candidacy was dead and Clinton's was dying.

Madison had given strong instructions on impressment; Monroe had
been unable to carry them out. Madison had outlined a good treaty; the
envoys had produced a bad one. Finally, contrary to a thousand rumors,

Madison had conducted the negotiations with Rose in a manner that thrilled the hearts of patriotic Americans. He has dared to meet the most celebrated British diplomats, exclaimed a Trenton editor, "and has completely vanquished, disarmed and disgraced them." William A. Burwell summarized the reaction in Virginia: "Upon the subject of the next President there is literally no division."

The dispatches from France were skimpy, due to Armstrong's chronic laziness; but the savage cynicism with which he charged and proved Napoleon's violation of the 1800 treaty was enough to undermine the Federalist allegation of subservience. Not that they dropped the charges. Former Chief Clerk Jacob Wagner, now filling the Baltimore *North American* with slanders of his benefactor, cried out that Madison's long concealment of "those wretched shreds of dispatches" (actually disclosed with unseemly haste) gave evidence of partiality to France and hatred to Britain.

The Federalists had new grist in Napoleon's Decree of Milan. This declared every ship of every nation to be denationalized and subject to confiscation, if searched by an English ship or forced into an English port. In response to Armstrong's protest, Foreign Minister Champagny (Talleyrand's successor) delivered Napoleon's ukase: he expected a declaration of war against England by the United States. Jefferson sent this blackmailing threat to Congress, with the comment that both nations were seeking to draw the United States "into the vortex of their contests" —designs that confirmed the wisdom of the embargo.

Sent in confidence, these letters produced a political fire against Madison that forced their publication. This intensified the charges of subserviency, which could have been countered by disclosure of Madison's instructions to Armstrong. "No independent and honorable nation", he had written, could yield to such pressure. Armstrong should "make that government sensible of the offensive tone employed," but leave the way open for friendly explanations. Rather than prejudice the negotiations, the Secretary elected to take the punishment.

Clintonians, Federalists, and Quids found a more solid issue in the growing antipathy to the embargo. Madison's friends in Congress consulted him and came back with a resolution. The President was to be given discretionary power to suspend the embargo against any belligerent that stopped molesting American commerce. This was supported by alternative "committee opinions" written by Madison. (1) In case the belligerent powers adhered to their destructive proceedings, an entire suspension of foreign commerce might be substituted for the embargo.

(2) The time might come when war would be preferable to the evils of further forbearance.

Coming from the Republican nominee for President, this was a semi-forecast of the War of 1812. It pointed to the ultimate scrapping of Jefferson's policy of peace through self-sacrifice; but Jefferson himself, following a Cabinet discussion, had already called it a "universal opinion that war will become preferable to a continuance of the embargo after a certain time." In the meantime, stricter enforcement measures were put through Congress along with the authority to suspend the law. They spread the discontent. Small republican evaders were hit, along with the big Federalist merchants and shipowners.

This hurt Madison so much that the Federalists put up their own presidential ticket headed by Charles Cotesworth Pinckney. That move unified the Republican party. Monroe dropped almost out of sight. Local Republican conventions all over the country came out for Madison.

Minister Turreau sensed another development in American politics. Divorcing himself from Napoleon's demand for American entry into the war, he asked Madison for friendly assurances *unrelated to an alliance*. In Spain, a mob resenting national humiliation had forced King Charles to abdicate and put his moronic son on the throne as Ferdinand VII. England, Turreau suggested, would turn to North and South America as her armies were driven out of Europe. The United States could aid or obstruct her plans. Which would they do?

Controlling Spain, Madison answered, France could make her cede the Floridas to the United States; but if England had designs on Spanish colonies, that would make the United States more important to her, and would make American neutrality more essential to France and Spain. At this hint of an Anglo-American alliance, Turreau launched an effort to draw the United States into a common stand with France. All he obtained was a pledge of "exact impartiality," and a lifting of the embargo in favor of the first power that rescinded its orders.

For three hours Turreau pursued his fruitless effort, then went to see the President. Jefferson promptly assured him that even if revocation of the British orders forced a lifting of the embargo in her favor, the United States would "never—no never" make an arrangement with them unless impressment was renounced. Elated, Turreau sought out Madison once more and renewed his urgings that the United States openly adhere to Napoleon's "continental system." When we are at war with England, Madison answered, what will be our guarantee? "The co-operation of all the states of Europe," replied Turreau. But, responded Madison, "might *you* not reach an agreement yourselves with England?" The official *Moniteur* had given such a hint. True, conceded Turreau, the *Moniteur* was official, but its views could not be balanced against the joint agreement of the sovereigns of Europe. (In other words, almighty Napoleon would be bound by his vassals.)

This was Turreau's own report in July 1808, of his discomfiture by the man he once characterized as "*un homme mediocre*." And the Secretary had taken this stand in disregard of the expressed views of the President. The minister sent his government a re-appraisal: "The secret but well assured and very constant influence of Madison develops and becomes more powerful as the time of his election draws near. . . . It seems to me that it is necessary to act from now on as if he were President."

A few weeks later an offer arrived from Napoleon via Armstrong to cede the Floridas if the United States would enter the war. Madison's refusal to depart from "fair and sincere neutrality" was coupled with satisfaction that the emperor would approve "a precautionary occupation of the Floridas against the hostile designs of Great Britain." That left the way open to acquisition by force.

On the heels of this came Napoleon's Bayonne Decree, a cynical order to seize American ships wherever found, in order to *assist in enforcement of the Embargo Act*. "If France does not wish to throw the United States into the war against her," wrote Madison to Armstrong, she ought not to hesitate a moment in revoking so much of this and other decrees as violate the rights of the sea.

For two summer months the candidate for President looked after his farms and read the newspaper assaults on him as a minion of France. "Citizen" Genet informed the country that, as French ambassador, he delivered the certificates of French citizenship to Jefferson and Madison and transmitted Madison's acceptance to "the bloody Robespierre." Clinton's son-in-law got the facts a trifle askew. Citizenship was bestowed on Washington, Hamilton, and Madison; and Madison accepted a year before Robespierre rose to power. Madison said nothing, and the charge was put down, even by the Clintonian Albany *Register*, "as the offspring of prejudice or a distempered zeal."

In the final weeks, international issues merged with a blazing opposition to the embargo that bordered on insurrection. Supporters of Pinckney, Clinton, and Monroe accused Madison of everything—subserviency to Napoleon and a hostility to England that led to the hated embargo. Gallatin wrote to Madison that New York and New England were lost and New Jersey in doubt. An answer had to be made and fast.

Jefferson's November message to Congress, rewritten by Madison, was the chosen vehicle. Bluntly stating that the "candid and liberal experiment" had failed, the message declared that the United States had demonstrated the moderation and fairness of their councils and had confirmed in all citizens the motives that "ought to incite them in support of the laws and the rights of their country." To support their fortitude and patriotism, the President was submitting to Congress the 1808 diplomatic correspondence of the Secretary of State.

Once more the newspapers were deluged with official letters disproving the charge of truckling to France and weakness or warmongering toward England. For the first time, the people learned that England had been told that repeal of her orders would end the embargo, and failure of France to do likewise would lead to war. The overwhelming national reaction was expressed by Duane's comment in the *Aurora* on one dispatch: "The man who can read this able and spirited paper, without feeling his pride increased and his indignation excited, ought to suspect his head of imbecility, and his heart of insensibility to virtue or patriotism."

There was no set day of general election. Results were tabulated state by state, week by week, on the wins and losses of electoral slates, some elected by the people, some by legislatures. By November 27 Madison's victory was assured. Pinckney narrowly carried New England and Delaware and won two electors (chosen by districts) in Maryland and three in North Carolina. Clinton duped New York Madisonian legislators by a pretended withdrawal and put two-thirds of his electoral ticket (including six last-ditchers) into office. Madison swept all the rest of the country. On December 7 the electoral college cast its vote: Madison, 122; Pinckney, 47; Clinton, 6.

Madison's victory was an approving verdict on his work and Jefferson's in guarding America's welfare and safety in a world convulsed by warring giants. It was an endorsement of Republican aims and achievements in contrast with the policies of the demoralized Federalists. It was a proof of the people's ability to penetrate sham, reject reiterated falsehoods, and measure a man by his personal qualities and his record. It was an expression of confidence in Madison as an honest man who loved and honored his country and could be trusted to defend it. Known integrity broke the shaft of slander.

Following the electoral decision, President Jefferson called himself "but a spectator" of events. The President-elect plunged into a turbulent struggle to find a substitute for the embargo. Former Speaker Macon moved to exclude the goods and warships of any belligerent power that had decrees in force violating the lawful commerce of the United States.

The committee report on it, furnished by Gallatin, was patterned on Madison's letters.

There was no alternative, the committee asserted, "but war with both nations, or a continuance of the present system." A general repeal of the embargo, without arming, would be submission to both belligerents; partial repeal would be submission to one and war with the other. The aggressions of England and France were "to all intents and purposes, a maritime war waged by both nations against the United States." Permanent suspension of commerce would not be resistance. "It cannot be denied that the ultimate and only effectual mode of resisting that warfare, if persisted in, is war." The committee left that question to the decision of Congress.

Madison, without disclosing his agency in the report, told the British minister that it "seemed distinctly to announce that the *ultimate* and only effectual mode of resisting the aggressions of the belligerents would be by a *war*." Erskine a week later reported Madison's determination "not to remove the embargo, except by substituting war measures against both belligerents, unless either or both should relax their restrictions upon neutral commerce." Should either one relax, "the United States would side with that power against the other which might continue the aggressions." The alternatives therefore, Madison went on, "were Embargo or War," and the American people would perhaps soon prefer war "as less injurious to the interests and more congenial with the spirit of a free people."

Congress had a different idea. It passed an embargo enforcement law so rigorous that it revived the secession movement in New England. Embargoites reeled before the impact. Congressman Nicholas offered a resolution (identified by Gallatin as "Mr. Madison's") for embargo repeal and future issuance of letters of marque. It declared that the United States should not delay (beyond a date left blank) "to resume, maintain and defend the navigation of the high seas, against any nation or nations having in force edicts, orders or decrees violating the lawful commerce and neutral rights of the United States."

The House voted for repeal of the embargo, effective March 4, but rejected armed reprisals, thus making repeal a submission. The Senate passed a strong measure and the House struck out the reprisal clause. The law finally enacted provided for repeal of the embargo on March 15, no letters of marque and, in place of the embargo, nonimportation from England and France with presidential power to exempt whichever country ceased to violate American neutral commerce. This, said Congressman Montgomery, was the best thing obtainable "from the imbecility and timidity" of a Republican faction that held the balance of power. From Madison's standpoint, the discretionary power given him was the one redeeming feature of a law that advertised his dilemma to the world. Congress would not back a policy of force, and the people would not sustain peaceful coercion if it hurt their pocketbooks.

As executive power shifted from Jefferson to Madison, the Republican party still held overwhelming majorities in Congress; but the cohesion that had made President Jefferson master of legislation during his first seven years had totally disappeared. The sturdily loyal A. J. Dallas stated the trend to Gallatin in the summer of 1807: "I verily believe one year more of writing, speaking and appointing would render Mr. Jefferson a more odious President, even to the Democrats, than John Adams."

Another certainty was that President Madison's foreign policy would differ widely from that of his predecessor. Partly, that was due to his more aggressive approach to international relations. Partly it was his reaction to the failure of the peaceful policies he had helped to formulate. His conduct as President could be foreseen in the appraisal of him by Gallatin who, with himself, had turned the Jeffersonian Presidency into an executive triumvirate. Wrote Gallatin after the electoral college cast its ballots: "Mr. Madison is, as I always knew him, slow in taking his ground, but firm when the storm arises."

Part V

41 / INAUGURATION

Inauguration Day, March 4, 1809, opened with a sunrise salute from the cannon at the Navy Yard and Fort Warburton. The militia produced a military flourish more symbolic of the nation's danger than of its readiness to cope with it. Domestically, too, the auguries for Madison's Presidency were far from cheerful. He faced a rebellious Congress, nominally Republican (Democratic) but riddled with factionalism. Not a trace was left of the cohesive unity which for seven years made the President's word law in the legislative branch of government.

Nothing of this was evident as ten thousand people gathered around the Capitol at noon, while thousands of others lined Pennsylvania Avenue, cheering the new President and his escort of Washington and Georgetown cavalry. Greeted by a bipartisan committee of senators, he was placed beside President Jefferson, with the full Senate and diplomatic corps on the platform. Supreme Court justices were directly in front, and House members occupied the floor.

Madison arose at once to deliver his inaugural address. He was "extremely pale and trembled excessively" at the outset, one observer recorded, "but soon gained confidence and spoke audibly." Chief Justice Marshall administered the oath, minute guns rang out, and Madison retired to his carriage through nine companies of uniformed militia.

Open house followed at the Madison home on F Street. Dolley "looked extremely beautiful . . . all dignity, grace and affability," in her long trained cambric dress and white-plumed bonnet of purple velvet and white satin. So wrote Margaret Bayard Smith. Madison was "dressed in a full suit" of wool from imported Algerian Merinos.

Festivities climaxed in "a grand inauguration ball" at Long's Hotel. Dolley "looked a queen," wrote Margaret Smith. Madison was visibly tired, though he spoke to her with "some of his old kind of mischievous allusions." Jefferson's affectionate feeling for Madison was visible to all. "I do believe," commented Margaret, "father never loved son more than he loves Mr. Madison." Jefferson escaped the crush by leaving early, and Madison remarked to Mrs. Smith that he "would much rather be in bed."

Turreau escorted Dolley to supper, and Erskine led Sister Anna. Dolley's physical amplitude kept the warring diplomats apart. The President sat facing the trio. There was no Jeffersonian *pele mele*.

Madison's inaugural address balanced France and England with no pulling of punches. "The present situation of the world is indeed without a parallel," said the new President, "and that of our own country full of difficulties." Peace and republican institutions had produced an unrivaled growth in American agriculture, commerce, manufactures, and public revenue. Trespassing on the rights of no other nation, it had been "the true glory of the United States to cultivate peace by observing justice" and to fulfill neutral obligations with scrupulous impartiality. The belligerent powers had replied with injustice and violence: "In their rage against each other, or impelled by more direct motives, principles of retaliation have been introduced equally contrary to universal reason and acknowledged law."

Nobody could foretell how long these arbitrary edicts would be continued, but Madison was confident that the nation would safeguard its honor and interests. He was going to his post "with no other discouragement than what springs from my own inadequacy to its high duties." He then outlined the principles and purposes of his administration:

> To cherish peace and friendly intercourse with all nations having correspondent dispositions;
> To maintain sincere neutrality towards belligerent nations;
> To prefer, in all cases, amicable discussion and reasonable accommodation of differences, to a decision of them by an appeal to arms;
> To exclude foreign intrigues and foreign partialities;
> To foster a spirit of independence, too just to invade the rights of others, too proud to surrender our own . . . ;
> To hold the union of the states as the basis of their peace and happiness;
> To support the Constitution, which is the cement of the Union, as well in its limitations as in its authorities.

The listing went on, to include respect for the rights of the states to avoid interference with the rights of conscience; to preserve private and personal rights and freedom of the press; to observe economy in public expenditures; to limit the standing military force; to promote agriculture, manufactures, and commerce "by authorized means;" to favor in like manner science and education; to lift the American aborigines from degradation and wretchedness into a civilized state. He closed with a tribute to Jefferson.

The wording of Madison's first principle was significant. He would cherish peace not with all nations, but with all *having a similar disposition*. He approved a limited standing army at a time when militant Andrew Jackson wanted none at all. Dominant, as always, were his devotion to the Union and emphasis on civil rights and liberties, especially freedom of religion and the press.

Republicans praised the address; Federalists damned it. But what of the democratic dissidents? That problem already had arisen in the selection of a Cabinet. For Secretary of State Madison wanted well-qualified Albert Gallatin. Gossip, probably started by the subject of it, named flighty and flamboyant Senator Giles. In mid-February Secretary of War Dearborn resigned to accept a collectorship, and Giles gave Madison a silly story that Jefferson intended to nominate his successor. At that moment, wrote Giles, the relations between Jefferson and the Senate were such "that a nomination from him is rather a signal of distrust than of confidence in the person nominated." This brought Giles to his real object. Jefferson, he wrote, was reported to be behind the choice of Gallatin for Secretary of State. Giles presented nine senatorial objections to him, omitting only the principal one—that he was born in Switzerland and spoke with a French accent. "Nothing could be more unfortunate for you during your whole administration," Giles declared, than the transfer of Jefferson's reputation for eccentricities and favoritism in appointments. The nomination of Gallatin would have that exact tendency.

The Senate on that very day fortified this appraisal by unanimously rejecting the long pending nomination of Jefferson's protégé William Short to be minister to Russia. No such unanimity was possible against Gallatin, but three Republican senators could defeat him by uniting with the Federalists. Madison knew that Giles spoke for himself, Smith of Maryland, and Leib of Pennsylvania, errand boy of Gallatin's enemy Duane. Gallatin probably would resign from the Treasury if nominated and rejected for Secretary of State. He could stay where he was without reappointment. Madison decided to keep him there.

To solve his dilemma and win the support of powerful Senator Smith, Madison decided to shift his brother Robert from the Navy to the State Department. Considering Robert Smith's qualifications, this meant that the new President would have to be his own Secretary of State, but the two men had been friendly in the Jefferson Cabinet.

Sectional politics influenced other choices. Dr. William Eustis of Massachusetts, physician and Republican leader, was chosen for Secretary of War. Wanting a South Carolinian to head the Navy, Madison drew the name of Paul Hamilton out of a hat. Caesar Rodney was retained as Attorney-General, and Gideon Granger remained as Postmaster General, a non-Cabinet office. Retiring Congressman Campbell of Tennessee doubted the qualifications of Smith and Eustis but said of the man who chose them: "There is the utmost confidence in the chief who conducts the great affairs of the nation."

All Cabinet nominations were confirmed on the day they were submitted. With them Madison sent up the name of former Senator John Quincy Adams as minister to Russia. His ex-colleagues rejected him but softened the blow with a resolve that they opposed the mission, not the man. Madison promptly notified Emperor Alexander that he intended to renew the nomination in a special session of Congress in May and expected the Senate to approve it. He did and it did.

What of late rival Monroe? Jefferson, as peacemaker, invited him to dinner. "He is sincerely cordial," the ex-President reported to Madison, "and I learn from several that he has quite separated himself from the junto . . . He and John Randolph now avoid seeing one another, mutually dissatisfied." Had this word come a few weeks earlier, Monroe might possibly have been the new Secretary of State.

All through the campaign, the Federalists had charged that Madison was too timid for the Presidency. A chance to verify that belief developed at the moment he took office. Governor Snyder notified the Pennsylvania legislature that he intended to use the militia to resist a decree of the United States Supreme Court transferring Revolutionary War prize money from the State of Pennsylvania to Gideon Olmstead—a case twenty years in litigation. The challenge came to a climax on March 25, when a United States marshal with a writ of attachment was confronted by General Bright and fixed bayonets, one of them touching the marshal's breast. The Philadelphia *True American* described the confrontation: "In the name and by the authority of the United States, said the marshal, addressing the soldiers, I command you to lay down your arms, and permit me to proceed. In the name and by the authority of the commonwealth of Pennsylvania, I command you to resist him, replied General Bright, in which he was obeyed."

The Pennsylvania legislature adopted ringing resolutions of defiance, tempered by a direction to the governor to seek a settlement. Sent by Madison, Attorney-General Rodney recommended prosecution of "the principal offenders" and secured warrants for the arrest of General Bright and his squad. The governor wrote a letter full of compliments and employed Madison's Resolutions of 1798 to justify resistance to Supreme Court usurpation.

Madison replied that he was "expressly enjoined, by statute, to carry into effect any such decree where opposition may be made to it." He was pleased, therefore, that a clause in the (protesting) act of the Pennsylvania legislature authorized the governor to remove the difficulty (by paying the claim), and he had no doubt that the governor would exercise the authority given him "in a spirit corresponding with the patriotic character of the State over which you preside."

Madison's reference was to a clause so ambiguously worded that it could mean resistance or acquiescence. By picking the latter meaning, he gave the governor an easy way to get off the hook. Snyder capitulated, but partisanship flared after Justice Bushrod Washington sentenced General Bright to three months in prison and eight militiamen to lesser terms. Appealed to by Pennsylvania Republicans, Madison pardoned them before they served a day. The governor's faction gave a jubilee dinner with toasts for everybody from the President down. Snyder became an ardent Madisonian, thanks to the depth of velvet over an iron glove on a small hand.

Dolley Madison was employed during these spring months with refurbishing the presidential domicile. Architect Henry Latrobe was authorized by Congress to spend the enormous sum of $26,000 for this purpose. He squandered $2,150 on three mirrors but Dolley disagreed with his location of the big one. Her wish was law, said he—"*tutto si fa— tout se fait.*" He also bought the $458 pianoforte she craved.

The President and his wife had living quarters in the southwestern corner of the house, Congressman and Anna Cutts in the southeastern. The maitre d'hotel was "French John" Sioussa, inherited from British Minister Merry. He was a capable chef, who on at least one occasion was too drunk to attend to his duties.

The "President's Palace" was just coming to be called the "White House." General Dearborn used the phrase on May 19, 1809, as a symbolical term for the Presidency and Cabinet positions: "The materials of which the white house and other large houses are composed are pretty well known and many of our best friends are more uneasy than I think they have any good grounds for."

On May 31, Dolley Madison held the first of her Wednesday evening levees, which swiftly became affairs of political importance. The President and his lady, wrote a British guest at this first affair, formed a striking contrast—Mrs. Madison plump, tall, and affable; the President "a very small thin pale-visaged man of rather a sour, reserved and forbidding countenance." He seemed "incapable of smiling, but talks a great deal and without any stiffness." Mr. Madison (as usual) wore black, "his hair dressed in a very old fashioned style—a large club highly powdered, his locks long without any curl or fizzing and his hair combed down on his forehead." This was the team that was to furnish an ever-available social center for the informalities of official life.

At the outset of the White House re-furnishing, Latrobe put in a claim for extra salary. Madison asked Jefferson what the arrangement was. Telling of it, the former President said that in dealing with this architect "the reins must be held with a firmness that never relaxes." In eight years of voluminous and cordial correspondence, this was the nearest Jefferson came to guiding his successor. President Madison never asked for any advice and never disclosed a controversial decision before it was made.

Relations between the United States and England were at a dangerous low when Madison became President. The embargo had failed and had been repealed. Impressment of seamen continued, and there had been no atonement for the attack on the *Chesapeake*. New England merchants, hungry for profits in British trade, saw nothing but "French influence" and hostility to themselves in the government's efforts to uphold American rights at sea.

In his final months as Secretary of State, Madison had virtually told Erskine that England could choose between war with the United States and an Anglo-American alliance against France in case Napoleon clung to his decrees. Asked by the British minister, in January, what lay behind the move to raise fifty thousand volunteers, he said it was to guard against a sudden attack by either Great Britain or France. Indeed, he added, their conduct had been such that the United States "would be justified in proceeding to immediate hostilities." Erskine saw no leaning toward France. On February 10 he wrote to Canning: "I continue to be firmly persuaded that Mr. Madison . . . would most willingly seize the first opportunity of recommending to the next Congress to assert the neutral rights of the United States against France, should His Majesty . . . cause his Orders in Council to be withdrawn."

On that same day Madison instructed Minister Pinkney to watch for some change in Canning's unfriendly attitude. If he found it, he should inform Canning that only Congress could formally avow a determination to resort to arms; but he was free to declare the Executive opinion to be, that in case the British orders should be revoked, and the decrees of France continue in force, "hostilities on the part of the United States will ensue against the latter."

Writing privately to Pinkney, Madison told him that if the British orders were enforced after the embargo was repealed, "war [with England] is inevitable, and will perhaps be clamored for in the same quarter which now vents its disappointed love of gain against the embargo."

This forecast reduces to utter nonsense the widely held belief of historians that a pacifistic Madison was dragged into the War of 1812 by rambunctious congressional War Hawks.

When Armstrong's correspondence was sent to the Senate in the fall of 1808, Madison placed a secrecy injunction on some of the letters because their intemperate wording might cause the minister to be expelled from France. He had been President but one day when the Boston *Centinel* arrived, loaded with these "suppressed documents." (Senator Pickering denied the "impudent and horrible" accusation that he was guilty of divulging them.) In substance, they contained nothing not found in the letters made public, but Federalist editors shrieked that Madison had suppressed them to provoke war with England. Publication of them virtually gave England an option between an alliance with America and continued war on her commerce.

The same option (likewise one for France) was implicit in the Non-Intercourse Act of March 1. That law prohibited importation of the goods of either nation, but the President was given power to revoke the ban against either one that should stop molesting American commerce. Dim hopes as to both countries sank lower with the arrival of couriers on March 11. A new British order suspended *nonexistent* transit duties but continued to compel American ships, trading to the continent, to put into British ports. That subjected them to seizure under Napoleon's Milan Decree.

Two weeks after President Madison took office, identical instructions were sent to Ministers Pinkney and Armstrong. Signed by Secretary of State Robert Smith, they were replete with Madison's language, and he said later that he wrote practically all of Smith's important dispatches. This was a conditional offer to enter the war on either side:

> I am instructed to state to you that if the edicts of either of the belligerents shall have been entirely revoked or even so modified as not to produce any actual infraction of our neutral rights, it is the opinion of the Executive, that Congress will, at the ensuing special session, authorize acts of hostility on the part of the United States against the other, unless he also should evince an equal respect to the just expectations of the United States by a similar revocation or modification.

In the follow-up Madison did not put the two countries on a parity. Great Britain, he observed to Elbridge Gerry, was both the prior and the greater aggressor. But he saw a better chance of eliminating the greater aggression. Once more he informed Erskine, this time through

Smith, of his readiness to ask Congress "to enter upon immediate measures of hostility against France." No counter-assurances were given to Turreau, who merely received a cheering forecast "by people who know the intentions of the Executive." Turreau's enlightenment came several months later, when Secretary Smith read to him the following sentence from a note delivered by Armstrong to Champagny, on the effect of an exclusion of American ships from the French decrees: "I am authorized to add that if France shall give such interpretation and Great Britain shall refuse an equivalent explanation of her Orders in Council, in that case the President of the United States will advise to an immediate war with the latter."

Thus, in his first fortnight in office, the new President moved from defensive embargo to threat and promise (within constitutional limits) of a resort to military action. The "weak and timid" Madison, who always (some historians say) was governed by the will of Congress, made a secret offer to draw the United States into either camp of the Napoleonic wars that would give a sufficient *quid pro quo*. Moral protest there might be, against this course, but it bore all the marks of strength and determined purpose. There was, of course, a hoped-for pacific outcome. If *both sides* repealed their decrees, peace would last and commerce would flourish.

The prospect of an accord with England bloomed quickly. On April 7, Erskine announced that he was authorized to settle all outstanding differences, starting with reparations for the attack on the *Chesapeake*. Pledged were restoration of the (three still living) impressed seamen and financial provision for the victims of the cannonading. Madison wanted more drastic punishment of Admiral Berkeley than mere recall. Erskine refused. Madison, withdrawing the demand, wrote a stinging sentence into Smith's note to the minister. While the President "forbears to insist on a further punishment of the offending officer, he is not the less persuaded that it would best comport with what is due from His Britannic Majesty to his own honor."

With the *Chesapeake* issue disposed of, the main question was taken up: repeal of the Orders in Council in exchange for revocation of the trade ban against England. Erskine made a partial revelation of his instructions. In advance of a treaty, England would immediately withdraw the Orders in Council in exchange for exclusion from all nonintercourse laws. The agreement, Erskine said, could go into effect next week.

Madison and Gallatin puzzled over this note. How could the orders be withdrawn in a week if withdrawal was dependent on a future act of Congress? At the next meeting with Smith, Erskine suggested three modifications—that the United States continue its sanctions against France, renounce all *direct* trade between the enemies of England and their colonies, and permit the British Navy to capture American vessels trading with the Napoleonic countries. Madison rejected the third condition and said the second required a treaty. Erskine dropped those two and said he was ready to sign an agreement for mutual and simultaneous revocation of the offending regulations at a date to be agreed on.

Since Erskine was not empowered to make a treaty, he was not obliged to present written instructions. The alternatives for the United States were to base immediate action on Canning's offer as presented, or let spoliations and uncertainty continue for half a year during an exchange of ratifications. Madison and his Cabinet decided on an immediate signing and proclamation of the agreement. Erskine agreed to an effective date of June 10.

So, on April 19 the President proclaimed that, whereas David Montagu Erskine, in the name of his Sovereign, had declared that the British Orders in Council "will have been withdrawn" on the tenth of June next, "therefore I, James Madison, President of the United States, do hereby proclaim" that they will have been so withdrawn, "after which day the trade of the United States with Great Britain . . . may be renewed."

The proclamation electrified the nation. Federalists and Republicans vied in heaping praise on Madison. "Never statesman did an act more popular," exclaimed the politically hostile Philadelphia *Gazette.* Madison turned his thoughts to France. The Federalists, he observed to Jefferson, probably would work to produce war with that country; but "if France be not bereft of common sense, or be not predetermined on war with us, she will certainly not play into the hand of her enemy." In other words, France would avoid war by following Britain's example.

Federalists in Congress and the press gleefully pointed to the contrast between the policies of Madison and Jefferson. Mr. Madison, observed Mathew Carey (friendly to both), was being "raised among the celestials —Mr. Jefferson sunk among the infernals." Jefferson, writing to Madison, trusted that no Republicans would countenance the Federalist suggestion that there had ever been any sensible difference in their views. Randolph, checkmated in a move to drive a wedge between the two men, confessed his purpose by crying that he would not help "to attach the sound, healthy body of the present Administration . . . to the dead corpse of the last."

This was at the opening of the special session in May. Madison's message asked both for implementation of the Erskine agreement and protection of manufactures. He said he had ordered all gunboats decommissioned except at New Orleans and had discharged 100,000 militiamen; but four additional frigates then under construction were being fitted for service.

Gallatin now moved into a headlong clash with Robert and Samuel Smith. He discovered that Robert, when Secretary of the Navy, had cashed large bills of exchange drawn by Samuel Smith's business affiliate in Leghorn, Italy, to pay expenses of the naval expedition in the Mediterranean. The money never was applied to the expenses. Knowing that accusations against the Smiths would be charged to personal bad feeling, Gallatin gave the information to his friend Judge Nicholson, with an intimation that he might resign. Nicholson begged him not to, but passed the Leghorn information along to Macon and Randolph. An investigation cleared the Smiths: a Leghorn paymaster had absconded with the money and bankrupted his firm. Gallatin realized that deeper trouble with the hostile brothers lay ahead, but Madison and Jefferson dissuaded him from resigning. He was induced to remain, he wrote to Jefferson, by the gratitude and duty he owed to the country that had received and so highly honored him, by "the confidence placed by Mr. Madison in me, my personal and sincere attachment for him," and the desire to be of further service.

Turreau gave notice of his displeasure at the Erskine agreement by moving to Baltimore without a word to the President or Secretary of State. This promoted another aim. He had divorced his wife and was courting the famous Baltimore beauty and wearer of shockingly lowcut gowns, Elizabeth Patterson Bonaparte, whose elopement marriage with Napoleon's brother Jerome had been rudely cancelled by the Emperor. Elizabeth refused, *seriatim*, to be either Turreau's wife or mistress.

From Baltimore, the minister protested roughly to Secretary of State Smith against an alleged plot by Madison to seize Mexico, Cuba, and the Floridas. Madison recognized the source of this—an injudicious remark by Jefferson to Turreau, just as the former President was leaving Washington, that the United States "must have the Floridas and Cuba." This was bolstered by a toast given by General Wilkinson during a stop in Havana en route to New Orleans: "The New World, governed by itself and independent of the Old."

To disabuse Turreau, Madison bypassed the Secretary of State and sent Gallatin to Baltimore. Directly ascribing the reports to the words of Jefferson and Wilkinson, Gallatin assured the minister that these could not be attributed to the Executive. Wilkinson's actions were due "solely

to the vanity, the indiscretions and the usual rashness of that general."
Madison had "set his heart" on the Floridas only as a means of preventing misunderstandings with Spain and securing an outlet for Southern
produce. Possession of Cuba was "a new idea of Mr. Jefferson," the
present administration would not accept the island as a gift. This left a
clear bid for Florida.

Madison took Turreau's concern for Cuba as evidence that Napoleon
coveted the island. In reality, his unauthorized intervention in Spanish
affairs brought him a sharp order from Champagny "not to display such
distrust of the Americans, founded only on suspicion . . . [especially] at
the beginning of a new Presidency." Gallatin's report, however, led
Madison to send new instructions to Armstrong. As no pretext remained
for continuing the French decrees, "let it be understood that their immediate revocation is confidently expected," to be followed at once by
the exemption of France from the nonintercourse law.

At the end of May Secretary Smith spent a week in Baltimore and
entered into an unsupervised discussion of Spanish colonies with Turreau. He repeated Gallatin's denial of American designs on Cuba and
enlarged the criticism of Jefferson into a violent attack on him for feeble-
ness, uncertainty, and lack of policy. This gave Turreau an inspiration.
"I already knew," he wrote to Champagny, "that Mr. Madison willingly
allowed [the Jefferson administration] to be attacked in the newspapers."
Convinced by this and Smith's remarks that the new President had
broken completely with his predecessor, he decided to promote that
break and at the same time demonstrate *his power to attack Madison
without doing so.* He sent Champagny an advance copy of the result:
a twenty-three-page letter to Secretary Smith ferociously assailing
Jefferson.

Had Turreau possessed the slightest understanding of American politics, he would have known that no President had any control of the press
and that the assaults on Jefferson came from Federalist newspapers seeking to produce a break between the two men. Madison read the screed
and gave Turreau a choice: withdraw the letter or go back to France.
Having sent the letter to Paris, Turreau was in a bad spot. To escape expulsion, he withdrew it—and wrote to Champagny that it produced the
desired effect.

By this time Spain had a new king. Napoleon ousted Ferdinand and
put his brother Joseph on the throne. Rival claimants for recognition
appeared in Washington, and Madison refused to decide between them.
Turreau the Terrible was ordered to present a letter from King Joseph
to President Madison. He did not do so. "I was afraid," he explained,

"that Mr. Madison would cause me to suffer a refusal, which I ought to avoid." The Butcher of Vendée had lost his cleaver.

June 10 arrived, and restoration of trade with England was celebrated in gala fashion. In mid-afternoon London newspapers reached Washington with news of a new British Order in Council. The old ones were repealed as to Russian and German ports. Neutral vessels no longer were required to enter English ports; but "paper blockades" of Napoleonic Europe were continued, and trade with French and Dutch colonies prohibited. It was an improvement, but partially contravened the Erskine agreement. Whatever "the crooked proceeding" might mean, Madison commented, "it served to check the extravagance of credit given to Great Britain for her late arrangement with us."

The President left Washington on July 20, to spend the summer on the remodeling of Montpelier, which was to be given two one-story wings. A messenger followed him. The British government had repudiated the Erskine agreement. Erskine was recalled. "Copenhagen" Jackson, the hatchet man of the Foreign Office, was to succeed him. "The attack on the *Chesapeake*," said a departmental note, "did not produce half so violent a sensation." No less was the sensation among Madison and the twenty-three guests lodged in his torn-up house.

Foreign Minister Canning had told the House of Commons that Erskine disobeyed his instructions. Madison could not guess how. The British government, he commented, seemed to have reverted to monopoly and piracy, yet he was surprised at it "in spite of all their examples of folly." Perhaps they had yielded to the clamors of London smugglers in sugar and coffee.

George Joy, Boston merchant and Madison's private ear in London, caught the departing ship with another explanation. He heard a whisper that the ministers were on the point of approving the agreement when the King read it and said that "he would not ratify anything in which he was so personally insulted." Eight years later Madison accepted this as true. The agreement was wrecked by the cutting sentence he injected into a Smith note to Erskine, relative to the King's honor. He would have eliminated the sentence, Madison said, had Erskine objected to it.

Actually, Erskine furnished ample grounds for rejection of the agreement. The three "suggested modifications" which he presented and abandoned were in reality mandatory conditions imposed by Canning. The pique given King George III was probably more of a convenient excuse than a basic reason for the decision.

At the Cabinet's urging Madison left for Washington on August 4, taking but two and a half days for the journey. Later dispatches, he found, absolved Canning of bad faith. He had disclosed the instructions in Parliament; but the very nature of them required restoration of the barriers to English trade. Did the President have power *to reinstate a law?*

There had been a legal doubt about Madison's first proclamation, since he spoke both for himself and the King of England. Validity depended on acquiescence, and this, it was decided, could be withdrawn without congressional action. So, on August 9, the President proclaimed that the British orders had not been withdrawn on June 10, wherefore the trade renewable in the event of such withdrawal was once more subject to the restrictive laws. To protect innocent commerce, it was announced, no penalties would be imposed on British cargoes or American ships whose journeys originated under the sanction of the first proclamation. "No plea but manifest necessity," Madison commented, justified that assumption of executive authority.

In the country at large, Republicans stood by the President; moderate Federalists remained moderate. The die-hards poured vials, pitchers, buckets, and barrels of wrath on Madison's head. He knew of Erskine's instructions. He conspired with that minister to betray the British government, deceive the American people and serve France by signing an agreement sure to be rejected. This second Federalist reversal, commented Madison to ex-Federalist Samuel Dexter, promised little of that internal stability, concord, and national spirit which were essential to win respect "for our character and our rights."

As Federalist assaults on the President grew heavier, Republican feeling against England mounted. Erskine remained a martyred hero; Canning gave his country a deeper stain of villainy. "My blood boils," exclaimed Dolley's congressional brother-in-law, John G. Jackson; but his colleagues, he told Madison, would act only if the people goaded them to it. "Blows, blows, blows alone will make them substitute war for words, unless it be a war of words."

43 / THE DESTROYER
OF COPENHAGEN

"Expectation and surmise is now all agog," wrote Thomas Digges to Thomas Jefferson on September 11, 1809, as to how Madison "will receive the mighty Copenhagen Jackson." No British minister ever had such a build-up. With his Prussian wife and three children, the destroyer of Copenhagen entered Hampton Roads on August 29 aboard the British frigate *L'Africaine*, which slowly beat up Chesapeake Bay against head winds, while the people waited. They were indeed all agog for Magog.

Attorney-General Rodney had a ready formula for the reception of Francis James Jackson. Notify his government, he advised the President, that his record rendered him personally obnoxious. Madison had returned to Montpelier, partly to avoid the appearance of waiting to receive the minister. Erskine presented Jackson to Secretary Smith, who informed the minister that if very anxious to present his credentials, he might go to the President's summer home. The minister preferred (he told Canning) to show equal unconcern by waiting.

Jackson and his wife spent the next three weeks in the saddle, enjoying the riverside hills and forests and studying the astonishing social habits of the white aborigines. Servants referred to the innkeeper and his wife as "the gentleman" and "the lady." The latter actually paid a social call on Frau Jackson, shook her hand, and invited both of them to return the visit. "Being in Rome," they did so, and were astounded to learn that Mrs. Erskine had been a frequent caller. She was an American, too.

The minister went through Erskine's files—"a mass of folly and stupidity" that made it charity to call him a fool. From Madison as Secretary of State, Erskine had passively endured insults in which "every third word was a declaration of war."

Erskine told him "of the most violent things said to him by the President and his minister." To these he had turned the other cheek, but Jackson would meet their insolence in a different manner. "Perhaps if I can make them believe, as they safely may, that I shall give blow for blow, they will leave me in peace."

Jackson presented his letter of credence to the President on October 2. Reading the King's wish for a satisfactory adjustment of differences, the President said that any overtures for that purpose would be received with a corresponding disposition. The call for "overtures" supported Erskine's prediction that if Jackson repeated the rejected conditions, Madison would "send [him] to the right about." So he evaded the subject, and the President, perceiving this, turned the conversation to "general and uninteresting topics."

Getting down to business with Smith on October 4, Jackson said his government would renew the *Chesapeake* negotiations in spite of the objectionable reference to the King, and would not renew the three conditions concerning the Orders in Council which the United States had rejected. If the American government wished to broach the subject, he "could receive, discuss, and *eventually* conclude upon" any substitute for them that might be offered. Smith (Jackson wrote) exhibited the utmost surprise and disappointment. No British proposal? He burst out at last, in confusion: "How shall we be able to get rid of the Non-Intercourse Act?"

Smith's own report caused the President to take the negotiation out of his hands. Henceforth there would only be written exchanges, Smith sending notes signed by himself but written by Madison. The first note told of the President's surprise and regret that Jackson could not explain the disavowal of the Erskine agreement; that he could make no proposition, but only receive one, concerning recall of the Orders in Council; that the orders would not be recalled unless the United States formally accepted Canning's three conditions. (This last was interpretation.)

Jackson was shocked by the shift to writing and the contents of the letter. He sensed a build-up for an anti-British newspaper campaign. Well, his reply (he told Canning) would put an end to the idea that "every species of indirect obloquy" would be patiently submitted to.

Writing to Smith, Jackson challenged the statement that Erskine had not revealed his instructions. The fact that the American negotiator suggested substitutes proved that the originals were "explicitly communicated to you, and by you, of course, laid before the President." Under such circumstances, His Majesty's government had every right to disavow the agreement.

Jackson flatly denied that he had said the Orders in Council would not be revoked unless the United States accepted Canning's three conditions. Being empowered only to *receive* a proposal, and none having been received, he *could not* have stated what answer he might *eventually* return. Therefore he "could not have made, *with that view*," the statement ascribed to him. In other words, he made it to indicate what the United States would have to propose.

In writing so strongly, Jackson explained to Canning, his intention was to check the spirit by which America sought to "make her will and her view of things" the criterion of approval or condemnation. The Madison administration had no spirit of mutual concession: "All is to bend to their will; nothing will satisfy them but the entire and unqualified surrender of our whole policy and an adherence to one . . . more conformable to theirs."

A week passed with no answer. "I . . . brought them in some degree to their senses," exulted Jackson to his brother George in Spain. The Jacksons were entertained at a White House dinner, where (wrote the minister) Madison settled that "foolish question of precedent" by taking Mrs. Jackson in to dinner. Jackson escorted Dolley, whom Mrs. Jackson described as "*une bonne grosse femme de la classe bourgeoise.*" Commented the minister: "I do not know that I had ever more civility and attention shown me."

Two days later Jackson's world collapsed. Reading a 4,000-word letter written by Madison, signed by Smith, he exploded with anger and frustration. "Madison is now as obstinate as a mule," he exclaimed to his brother. Nothing "will suit him but the absolute surrender of our Orders in Council. Until he gets that, he will not even accept any satisfaction for the affair of the 'Chesapeake'. If, after this, we give them any satisfaction at all, we had better send it wrapped up in a British ensign, and desire them to make what use of it they please."

The President, said his Smith-signed letter, persisted in his expectation of a formal and satisfactory explanation of the refusal to ratify the Erskine agreement. Mere violation of instructions on immaterial points, he said, quoting Vattel, was not enough. The reasons must "manifestly outweigh, not only the general obligation to abide by what has been so done, but also the disappointment and injury accruing to the other party." That was the greater in this instance, because the United States already had carried the arrangement into full effect.

Were the reasons for rejection "strong and solid," as required? The condition regarding colonial trade was utterly irrelevant. The demand that British cruisers be authorized to capture American vessels violating the Non-Intercourse Act touched a vital principle of sovereignty. Whatever the object of clinging to the old orders might be, after their avowed object had disappeared, he would only "remark that, in relation to the United States, it must be an illegitimate object." (That is, to preserve the European market for British smugglers and licensed traders with the enemy.)

Instead of reacting violently against Jackson's charge that the American government knew of Canning's conditions *as mandatory requirements*, Madison refuted it quietly. (This forbearance, he explained to Pinkney, was in the hope of restraining him from repeating the offense.) What was more common, he asked Jackson, than for public negotiations "to begin with a higher demand, and that failing, to descend to a lower"?

Madison did not know that Smith had orally denied any knowledge whatsoever of those conditions—when he saw them in print he took them to be forgeries. Jackson did not know that Madison wrote Smith's letter. So, to Jackson, Smith appeared to be confessing on paper that he had lied in person. He decided to repeat the insinuation of bad faith. Furnishing the previously refused explanation of the Erskine rejection, he added this thrust: "These instructions, I now understand by your letter, as well as from the obvious deduction which I took the liberty of making in mine of the 11th instant, were, at the time, in substance, made known to you."

Madison's reply abstained from comment "on several irrelevant and improper allusions" in Jackson's letter; but he could not ignore his repetition of a language implying knowledge that the instructions of his predecessor did not authorize the arrangement formed by him:

> After the explicit and peremptory asseveration that this Government had no such knowledge, and that with such a knowledge no such arrangement would have been entered into, the view, which you have again presented of the subject, makes it my duty to apprise you that such insinuations are inadmissible in the intercourse of a foreign minister with a Government that understands what it owes to itself.

This sharp rebuke still left Jackson an out, by mere silence. Instead, he moved from insinuation to the "blow for blow" tactic of which he had boasted. "You will find, sir," he replied, that he had drawn no unwarranted conclusions, "and least of all should I think of uttering an insinuation, where I was unable to substantiate a fact." He must "continue, whenever the good faith of His Majesty's Government is called in question, to vindicate its honor and dignity, in the manner that appears to me best calculated for that purpose."

Jackson was hardly prepared for the shattering response that came from Madison's pen on November 8: "Finding that, in your reply of the 4th instant, you have used a language which cannot be understood but as reiterating and even exaggerating the same gross insinuation, it only remains, in order to preclude opportunities which are thus abused, to inform you that no further communications will be received from you, and that the necessity of this determination will, without delay, be made known to your Government."

The astounded minister sent word, through Legation Secretary Oakeley, that he was moving the entire legation staff to New York. A note signed by Oakeley said "Mr. Jackson has seen with much regret" that his unavoidable performance of duty had led to such a result. He "could not imagine that offense would be taken" at his statement, as none was intended. Madison gave Jackson another chance. He replied through Smith, orally, that an explicit and candid statement in writing, of the real meaning of Jackson's language would efface the impression of having delivered a gross insult. It would be sufficient to change the word "conditions" to "propositions" in Jackson's last description of what Erskine had submitted.

Now Jackson was plagued by his own previous blunder in basing England's *right to disavow* the agreement on Madison's supposed knowledge of Canning's three *conditions*. To change that word to *"propositions,"* he wrote to Canning, would "do away the ground" on which he had upheld his government's course. He could not do that. So he sent Oakeley with an unsigned note saying that the minister would not resume communication until invited in writing to do so, and would not remain in Washington unless the government publicly repudiated a criticism of him in the *National Intelligencer*. Smith cut Oakeley off as he began to outline this message, and the legation secretary asked for Jackson's passports.

Reporting the final rupture to Canning, Jackson declared his belief "that Mr. Smith read every word of your original dispatch," even though Oakeley had told him the contrary. The President's course, he thought, was governed by a belief "that the sun of Britain is setting," and hope for a more friendly British ministry. Observing this, "I adopted a language which I hoped would at least make them pause. But they had from the beginning resolved to get rid of me," hoping for a more tractable successor. All they wanted was to gain concessions that would "gratify their pride and their interests." They would not go to war, but "nothing will satisfy the present administration" short of abandonment of impressment and full admission to the colonial trade.

Nothing could have been more absurd than the belief that Madison was swayed by hopes of a friendlier ministry. News had come that Canning and Castlereigh resigned after fighting a duel. Perceval, the great enemy of American colonial trade, was forming a ministry in which the moderate Grey and Grenville refused to serve. "The change in the ministry," wrote Madison, "seems likely to make bad worse . . . under the quackeries and corruptions of an administration headed by such a being as Perceval."

Federalists piled Jackson's desk with letters of support and condolence. He received (via another) Ben Stoddert's confident assertion that Smith "wrote no part of the correspondence with Mr. Jackson I am sure, yet it is most likely he concealed from Madison, who is the scribe in this correspondence, the knowledge he possessed of Erskine's instructions." Here Jackson had testimony that the entire expression of American policy was *in the President's letters*. Gone were the significance of Smith's puerile falsehoods and the inferences of bad faith on which Jackson staked his position.

By making and acting on such as appraisal, Jackson could have salvaged his position and still thrown deserved blame on Madison for not inquiring searchingly into Erskine's powers. Instead he moved slowly northward, from one anti-Madison dinner table to the next. By the time he reached Boston he had "little doubt" of the truth. A demand for his expulsion "was made by Bonaparte as soon as my appointment was known," and Madison would have willingly complied had he not thought the step "too decisive and ostensible a proof of his devotion to French interests."

To defend his position before Congress, Madison wrote a 4,500-word letter to Pinkney describing the entire affair. Correctly assuming that Jackson was bound by instructions similar to Erskine's, Madison attacked the instructions themselves. One of them violated the Constitution—a demand that he pledge continuation of the Non-Intercourse Act against France. More broadly, he sought to show that the reasons England gave for disavowing the Erskine agreement were of trivial economic or military value compared with what she would gain.

As far as the public was concerned, there was no need of a defense. A mere summary of the diplomatic exchanges brought surprising support from Federalist editors and stirred Republicans to ecstacy. "In truth I think," wrote Congressman Bacon of Massachusetts, "that James Madison's administration is now as strongly entrenched in the public confidence as Thomas Jefferson's ever was at its fullest tide," and was not likely to ebb as much as that one did.

The President's first annual message, on November 29, briefly justified his position in the Erskine rejection and Jackson expulsion, but struck a peaceful note in the wish for "a favorable revision" of Britain's policy through other channels. France, he reported, was continuing those trespasses which had "long been the subject of our just remonstrances." Owing to loss of revenue in commerce, current expenses exceeded receipts but no loan had so far been necessary. Separate departmental reports would be made but in the meantime he asked that the militia be organized for "eventual situations." Domestically, he said, there was prosperity and happiness, aided by the spread of manufactures stimulated by the "impolitic and arbitrary edicts" of the European belligerents.

This reflected a nationwide agitation for the support of home industry. Not only along the coast but on the whole western perimeter of settlement, mills and factories were multiplying in metals, textiles, glass, and paper. Exclaimed the author of a magazine's "cursory view" of this vast expansion: "Let the agriculturist and manufacturer, therefore, join hands, and bid the jarring world defiance." The President put himself at the head of this movement both in words and policies.

Chief remaining bludgeon in Federalist hands now was the aggravating conduct of Napoleon. Transmitting Armstrong's correspondence, Madison remarked in his annual message that the "posture of our relations" with France did not "correspond with the measures, taken on the part of the United States, to effect a favorable change." The mildness and brevity of his language, on top of the break with Jackson, looked to many like a portent of war with England. Ex-Senator George Logan, the Quaker pacifist, begged the President not to dissolve the Union by uniting with Bonaparte in a war on England. "Arouse, my friend," he cried. ". . . Banish from our councils that irritability of temper and false honor which has tended to widen the breach."

The nation, Congress, and the Executive, Madison replied, all had the same desire to keep out of the vortex of war. "But the question may be decided for us, by actual hostilities against us or by proceedings leaving no choice but between absolute disgrace and resistance by force." The sending of Jackson was the worst possible plaster for the Erskine wound. He outlined the easy terms by which England could match the American desire for an honorable settlement. Make reparation for the *Chesapeake* attack, drop the revised Orders in Council designed to protect Britain's trade with her own enemies—do this, and the way would be open to a larger negotiation (on impressment and colonial trade) with prospects of happy consequences.

This letter was still in Madison's hands when Logan wrote that he was about to leave for England and would be glad to carry any papers the President desired to send. Madison guessed Logan's purpose. He intended to intervene once more in diplomacy, in violation of the "Logan Act" passed in anger against his previous effort (decidedly useful) to end the naval war with France. Instead of invoking that dubious statute, Madison entrusted Logan with a note to Pinkney, to whom he sent also a copy of the letter to Logan which, said the President, the doctor was sure to take with him. This, he felt sure, Logan would show to British leaders. Thus, Madison was turning his critic into an unconscious emissary.

Both in diplomacy and politics Madison needed a clear-cut indication that France had the wisdom to offer what England took away. The best he could give Congress was an August letter from Champagny to Armstrong reiterating that American merchant vessels were subject to seizure if they allowed themselves to be searched by British warships. France gave notice that as long as the Non-Intercourse Act excluded American ships from France, they would not be allowed to enter the vassal ports of Holland, Germany, Spain, and Italy. So far so bad. But a final paragraph had a better sound:

> Let England revoke her declarations of blockade against France; France will revoke her [Berlin] decree of blockade against England. Let England revoke her Orders in Council of the 11th November, 1807; the decree of Milan will fall of itself. American commerce will then have regained all its liberty, and it will be sure of finding favor and protection in the ports of France. But it is for the United States, by their firmness, to bring on these happy results.

There were hazards unknown to Madison. The letter to Armstrong, drafted by Napoleon, had been far stiffer in language before Champagny was permitted to tone it down. The emperor then drafted a decree, as yet unsigned, confiscating all American ships entering French, Spanish, or Italian ports, in retaliation for application of the Non-Intercourse Act to France.

Unaware of this, Madison pressed for British action. There seemed, he wrote to Pinkney over Smith's signature, to be "an intentional obscurity" about the terms of withdrawal of the Berlin Decree. Was Britain required to withdraw all paper blockades, or only those proclaimed before the Berlin Decree was issued? Pinkney was to feel the British pulse on a general withdrawal. Armstrong, on the contrary, was directed to find out what the French meant but assume that nothing more was required than withdrawal of illegal blockades antedating the Berlin Decree. If that proved true, there might be progress, step by step, until all decrees and orders had been revoked.

It was a neat arrangement; the difficulty was to induce either nation to make the first jump. Federalist newspapers made this no easier by serializing John Lowell's anonymous pamphlet, "The Diplomatic Policy of Mr. Madison Unveiled," which made him the mastermind of thirty years of French villainy toward the United States. Jefferson's administration presented "one continued tissue of devotion to France," and it would eventually appear that Mr. Madison "was not the dupe or the obedient slave of Mr. Jefferson, but the principal instigator of those measures which without the slightest occasion have brought us to our present deplorable situation."

Encouraged by Lowell's onslaught, Federalists in the House resisted a bombastic resolution by Giles denouncing Jackson. They saw no insult in his truthful and valid rejoinders to American sophistry and deception. Three weeks were frittered away, said Burwell of Virginia, in this "indecision and shameful waste of time." On January 3, 1810, the administration held the House in session for nineteen hours and passed the resolution, 72 to 41.

The divisive debate and ultimate passage of the resolution, Madison predicted in a private note to Pinkney, would probably produce an unfavorable reaction in British policy. Resentment would be expressed, not by open war, but "in more extended depredations on our commerce; in declining to replace Mr. Jackson," and perhaps in the course observed toward Pinkney himself. On the slim chance that the new ministry would follow a friendlier course, Pinkney was given the same treaty power conferred on him and Monroe in 1806, with reparation for the *Chesapeake* a prerequisite and revocation of the Orders in Council the second objective. It was well, Madison observed, that precautionary steps had been taken in national defense.

The last remark reflected a disagreement between Madison and Gallatin—the only serious one in their experience. In August, Gallatin wrote to Jefferson that his continuance in the Cabinet depended partly on control of military expenditures. In December, with a Treasury deficit impending, Gallatin submitted a budget for 1810 cutting military and naval funds by $3 million (fifty per cent). To avoid an immediate resignation, Madison submitted the report to Congress. Then, after waiting three weeks, he sent a special message asking Congress to increase defense expenditures instead of cutting them. Without actually asking that this be financed by borrowing (anathema to Gallatin), he called it fortunate that the solid state of public credit made loans a convenient and adequate resort for handling the inescapable "precautionary measures involving expense."

Madison's circumspection confused Congress. "In point of obscurity," said Senator Crawford of Georgia, the message approached the work of a Delphic oracle. "Is he for war? The message breathes nothing but destruction and bloodshed. Is he for peace? The message is mere milk-and-water, and wholly pacific."

The President had a dual purpose in this obscurity. Besides being worded to keep Gallatin in the Cabinet, the message was designed to leave the way wide open for a bill just introduced by Congressman Macon. This was described by Madison, its secret sponsor, as "better than nothing, which seemed to be the alternative." Known later as "Mr. Macon's Bill No. 1," it provided for repeal of the Non-Intercourse Act (about to expire anyway), excluded British and French vessels (except in distress or on public business) from American harbors, and limited importations of British and French goods to those shipped *in American vessels* directly from the country of production. (No more smuggling via Halifax or Florida.) Like earlier measures, this one authorized the President to lift the restrictions on either belligerent in case it ceased to violate the neutral commerce of the United States.

Madison's principal concern was for the probable British reaction. If that country retaliated, he wrote to Pinkney, all trade with it would be cut off. If limited trade was kept up, British navigation would still feel the effect of exclusion from the American carrying trade. The measure would probably pass the House and might possibly go through the Senate. He did not condemn Congress for the diverse opinions and prolix debate: "Few are desirous of war; and few are reconciled to submission; yet the frustration of intermediate courses seems to have left scarce an escape from that dilemma."

Expelled Minister Jackson, still in the country, wrote to a Federalist that the congressional warriors "are cowards in their hearts. . . . We look

only to the Executive [who sees] cause of offense but not . . . for war."
He missed Madison's main thought—that the lack of other alternatives
was driving the country toward war or submission. Jackson brought that
choice nearer by assuring Foreign Secretary Bathurst that only a few
hot Democrats advocated war, wherefore: "There seems never to have
been a period at which England could with less risk than at the present
undertake to demonstrate to the world that she can better do without
American commerce than America can do without that part of her commerce which is dependent upon a good understanding with England."

For three weeks a divided House of Representatives lambasted the
Macon Bill as too weak, too strong, easy to enforce, sure to be evaded,
submissive, aggressive, pro-French, pro-British, and even, a few thought,
pro-American. The House passed it 73 to 52. In the Senate, Smith, Leib,
and Giles teamed up with the Federalists to cut it to a shadow. On the
final roll call Giles stood with the administration, but Smith marshalled a
17-to-15 majority against it. After the vote Samuel Smith said to a fellow
senator: "I have pleased you and my constituents but I have killed
R[obert] S[mith]."

44 / MUCH ADO BUT NOTHING DONE

Madison's request for additional defense funds faced multiple hurdles —Gallatin's contrary advice, the historic Republican hostility to permanent army and naval forces, fears engendered by the speeches of congressional War Hawks (a new term), and the return of John Randolph to his seat after a year's absence that began in illness and continued in leisurely sulking. During that period Randolph had been only mildly critical of Madison but vented his long pent-up fury against Jefferson—a runaway (he wrote to Madison) who threw the odium of his disgraceful and disastrous measures "from *his* shoulders upon *your own.*"

For a time it appeared that the defense measures would win easy approval. The House voted $450,000 for repair of the six frigates, and the bill seemed sure to pass the Senate since only six members had opposed the authorization. Navy Secretary Hamilton began the work and had spent $150,000 when the Senate, in a maneuver managed by Leib, killed the appropriation.

The army was worse off. General Wilkinson, ordered by Secretary Eustis (a physician) to camp on high ground, chose instead a river-delta swamp where malaria, dysentery, and bilious fever wrought fearful ravages. "Why throw more money away on sick and dead soldiers?," rose the cry in Congress.

Hostility to spending increased when the *National Intelligencer*, to influence the spring elections, summarized a private letter from Pinkney to Secretary Smith. Marquis Wellesley, the new foreign minister, admitted in conversation that Copenhagen Jackson was in the wrong and said "a successor would be sent out to the United States." Humbug! Phantom! Forgery! shouted Federalists and Quids in Congress. Produce the letter!

The excitement brought John Randolph to Washington, where he instantly moved "that the Military and Naval Establishments ought to be reduced." Ostensibly to support this, Federalists engineered a request that the President transmit any recent letters from Pinkney not requiring secrecy. Madison replied that the only uncommunicated letter was one of

428

January 4, which being private and involving delicate personal considerations, was regarded as outside the purview of the call.

To the Federalists, this meant that the letter was nonexistent. Madison did not reveal the note of gratitude from Pinkney thanking him for
preventing a publication which "would have produced serious embarrassment." London newspapers arrived with accounts of parliamentary proceedings that in effect disavowed Jackson's conduct. A ministry-inspired
motion in the House of Lords proclaimed that "the disagreement had
been that of individuals."

This was a political triumph for Madison, but it doomed his defense
program. Why spend money when England was speaking in these pacific
accents? The House adopted the Randolph reduction motion two to one.
Randolph and his committee overdid their work, advising that the Navy
be cut to three frigates and three smaller vessels and the Army to three
regiments. The House, shocked, struck out the Navy reduction and the
army bill was not even taken up.

There was, however, no increase of defenses, and the new tax bills met
with a resounding defeat. The need for borrowing should have helped
a pending bill, strongly endorsed by Gallatin and privately approved by
Madison, to renew the twenty-year charter of the Bank of the United
States. Oldtime enemies of the bank cried out against the payment of
two-thirds of the bank's dividends to foreign stockholders. Madison's
1791 speech denying the constitutionality of the bank was republished
in full.

Madison now said nothing publicly, but (wrote Gallatin later) "made
his opinion known" that he considered the question of constitutionality
"as settled by precedent." Actually it was more firmly settled by twenty
years' proof that the bank was constitutionally "necessary and proper"
as an adjunct to government finance; but the renewal bill did not even
reach a vote.

During the retreats from military strength and banking, the House
received "Mr. Macon's Bill No. 2," written by Taylor of South Carolina
and disowned by the committee chairman whose name it bore. With the
Non-Intercourse Act about to expire, this bill left trade entirely free except for a provision that if either Great Britain or France should revoke
its edicts or modify them to exempt American commerce, that fact should
be proclaimed by the President, and if the other belligerent failed to do
likewise within three months, the Non-Intercourse Act should be revived
against it. Take this, Taylor warned, or there would be "not a feather of
opposition" to the detestable oppression of France and England.

Madison viewed the bill with disgust. American goods, he predicted to Jefferson, were certain to glut the English market. British blockades of the coast and France's depredations would complete the disillusionment of American merchants. The bill passed on the day Congress adjourned, thus giving Madison Taylor's "feather." Still, the feather was attached to a quill pen for which either France or England could furnish the ink.

Adjournment left Madison with prestige high from the Jackson affair and in contrast with legislative failures. Considering all the difficulties, wrote a contributor to the *Virginia Argus,* "the President's conduct has been really admirable. . . . Weak members of Congress . . . have cried out, *why does not the President recommend?* Well, sir, he did recommend; but no sooner had he done this, than another would exclaim, why does the President wish to dictate?"

Quite different was the appraisal of Anglophile Senator Timothy Pickering. Having seen Mr. Madison "going hand in hand with Mr. Jefferson, in his crooked paths of cunning, duplicity and deception," he felt it a patriotic duty to unveil his past, beginning with a sell-out to France in the peace treaty of 1783. New England Federalists campaigned on the question: "Did Napoleon Bonaparte say to a foreign minister abroad 'that Mr. Madison was his Vice-Roy . . . ?'" The answer: Every New England state except Connecticut went Republican, and Massachusetts retired Pickering.

With Congress out of the way Madison assessed international affairs. He had little and lessening hope that Wellesley's oral repudiation of Minister Jackson would be translated into action. Even if the marquis had that desire, it would be difficult "to drag his anti-American colleagues into a change of policy; supported as they will be by the speeches and proceedings of Congress." From such conduct they would infer that one party preferred submission to British trade regulation; the other party "confesses the impossibility of resisting it." This was verified by Wellesley's recall of Jackson with modest praise, and a statement that the legation in Washington would be turned over to "a person properly qualified" to carry on ordinary business. Pinkney demonstrated also the existence of his disputed letter: "The account of that interview, as given in my private letter to Mr. Smith of the 4th of January, is so far from exaggerating Lord Wellesley's reception of what I said to him, that it is much below it."

England's failure to send a minister, Madison remarked to Pinkney, was due either to pride or a desire to please pro-British Americans. "On either supposition it is necessary to counteract the ignoble purpose."

Should Pinkney find that Britain intended to degrade diplomatic intercourse, he should pick some American for legation secretary and come home, unless engaged in treaty negotiation. However feeble the Macon Act might be, the President said, it might possibly produce more effect than previous overtures. National pride stood less in the way, since either power could construe the act "not as a coercion or threat to itself, but a promise of attack on the other." He suspected, however, that both belligerents would become more obstinate, thus at least teaching a lesson to the congressmen who abandoned embargo and nonintercourse in favor of "a submission to the predatory systems in force." That might produce a turn from passivity "to the opposite point; more especially as the tone of the nation has never been as low as that of its representatives."

Madison expected the hostile British spirit to continue, and he was "equally distrustful" of France. To stir either nation to a repeal of illegal edicts, the national spirit must be stimulated in the American people and transmitted to Congress.

Madison moved at once to reach that goal. The anger-stirring dispatches from Pinkney were published in a special edition of the *National Intelligencer* two days after their receipt. The same was done immediately afterward with newly arrived dispatches from Armstrong. Sending the newspapers to Jefferson, the President remarked: "The late confiscations by Bonaparte comprise robbery, theft, and breach of trust, and exceed in turpitude any of his enormities not wasting human blood."

These dispatches, he said, were breaking the charm of what was foolishly or wickedly called free trade (unarmed ships running the gauntlet of guns). The next set of dispatches from London and Paris doubled the outcries. At first, Madison commented, Armstrong's picture of the French robbery caused England's attitude to be overlooked. By late June, however, the public was beginning to perceive "that the original sin against neutrals lies with Great Britain."

On the day he wrote this, the *Intelligencer* ("Madison's *Moniteur*,") analyzed the correspondence to show that Champagny conditioned repeal of the Berlin Decree only on repeal of British paper blockades *of prior date*, of which but two were still in force. This hint that France might implement the Macon Act produced a terrific outburst of Federalist hostility. Was America to surrender to the universal tyrant? French policy gave this some weight, for while the ministry was moving toward conciliation, Bonaparte's course continued to be that of a perverse and irrational dictator. Adhering to his naval depredations, he grudgingly approved a modifying decree and at the same time ordered that a new minister be sent to America. "Having little confidence in Turreau," he wanted him replaced by a man "who knows my intentions and who will be adroit enough" to give effect to them. (Quite different from the Federalist picture of Turreau as a ferocious ogre who kept Madison in a closet preparatory to devouring him.)

Revising Champagny's conciliatory decree, Napoleon buried the concessions under a mountain of rhetoric, justifying French depredations and exhorting the United States to save itself from the leaden yoke of England. Published in the *Moniteur*, the translation in London newspapers was thought by some Madisonians to have "gone through the British factory" of forgery.

Armstrong spent weeks with friendly Jean-Baptiste Petry, former legation secretary in Washington, drawing up a treaty that embodied the views of Champagny (lately made Duc de Cadore). Madison, receiving the draft, rejected a clause allowing confiscation of sequestered ships on proof that they had visited England. Napoleon rejected the same clause because such proof could not be obtained. The emperor cancelled the dispatch of a new minister. He stepped up the burning, seizure, confiscation, and sale of American ships as a reply to the American Non-Intercourse Act.

Armstrong's excoriating response to this development was published on receipt, and he was assured that "a high indignation is felt by the President, as well as by the public." Madison had some hope, however, that repeal of nonintercourse might improve the prospects in Paris. On July 5, he instructed Armstrong that if Pinkney failed to secure revocation of the Orders in Council and the earlier blockade of May 1806, Armstrong should communicate that fact to the French government and notify it that the President was ready to exercise the power vested in him. If France would make good the promise of the Duke of Cadore to treat American ships with justice, provided the United States refused to submit to British edicts, the President would prove its refusal "by renewing the nonintercourse against Great Britain."

This prospect was dashed within a week by receipt in mid-July of the March 23 Decree of Rambouillet. After having ignored the Non-Intercourse Act for almost a year, Napoleon made it the excuse for ordering the seizure and sale of all American vessels sequestered in French-held ports after May 20, 1809. The emperor's war chest was almost empty. Confiscation of these ships and cargoes would pour millions into the French Treasury.

Deprived by the French crisis of his usual spring visit, Madison left for home a month earlier than usual in the summer. Before departing, he attended a July 4 Baptist meeting and at noon (said the *National Intelligencer*) opened his house "to a large and brilliant assemblage of both sexes." Dinner with politicos followed, with a toasted pledge to the President of "the confidence of his *real* constituents," and a farewell salute to "the embargo law—proposed by patriots—subverted by traitors."

Reaching Montpelier on July 11, Madison spent the next week in bed with a fever, "owing I conjecture to bile contracted at Washington" or too much sunshine on the journey. Cannon shots followed him. Two were fired by the British sloop-of-war *Moselle* against the smaller brig *Vixen*. There was one casualty—Attorney-General Rodney's son got a splinter of wood in the mouth. Madison approved the judicious conduct of Lieutenant Trippe, who cleared for action but, instead of firing, demanded and received an apology. Trippe's only flaw, the President commented, was in calling George III "His Majesty" instead of "His Britannic Majesty," as a nonsubject should do.

The other cannonading had Gallatin as target. This actually began its crescendo in the spring, with Robert Smith joining his brother Samuel and Senators Leib and Giles, in the political machinations and anonymous attacks that supplemented the open assaults of Duane in the *Aurora*. Rumors of a Gallatin resignation spread over the country, but Speaker Varnum discounted them. "The President and the country are on his side and his enemies are losing popularity every day."

A week after Madison left Washington, London newspapers brought the text of Erskine's dispatches. One recounted a conversation in which Gallatin appeared to say that even though Jefferson might have been partial to France, Madison had no such bias. The *Intelligencer* published this along with Gallatin's reply that instead of calling Jefferson a partisan of France, he had denied the validity of such a surmise.

Tumult resounded. For twelve successive issues, Duane's *Aurora* devoted its editorial page to the "horrible picture of duplicity and cunning" presented by the Secretary of the Treasury. The Baltimore *Whig*, organ of the Smiths, cried out that "the arch apostate Gallatin" should not be kept in office another week. The purpose, commented Congressman Macon, was to hit Madison through Gallatin.

Months earlier Macon had marveled that Madison did not fire Smith. Indeed why not, especially after he found that the Secretary was incompetent to write his own dispatches? Conjecturally, because he did not wish to drive the Smith-Leib-Giles triumvirate into total opposition. More certainly because he was not yet in a position to nominate the desired successor. Madison already had made one effort to restore good relations with Monroe, wrecked by the latter's "third party" candidacy for President in 1808. Late in 1809 he was assured that Monroe had "left no doubt" that he would accept the governorship of Upper Louisiana Territory. Saying that he believed the conclusion to be "totally erroneous," Madison asked Jefferson to probe Monroe's inclination to federal office "without indicating any particular object."

Only three weeks earlier, John Taylor had written to Monroe that "our bureau of state has been accustomed to contain the presidential ermine." If Mr. Madison should sacrifice his private griefs and invite Monroe to become Secretary of State, "I think your sacrifice ought to meet his at the same altar." So, when Jefferson broached the subject of taking office, Monroe had visions of an open road to the Presidency; but Jefferson failed to heed Madison's admonition to say nothing about "any particular object." At the words "Upper Louisiana" Monroe's dream turned into a nightmare.

Jefferson partially repaired the damage by saying that the Louisiana office was his own idea, but the channel of communication between Madison and Jefferson was choked by a new log. John Graham cleared it away in May 1810. Talking with Monroe in Washington, he said that he himself channeled the report, from a Kentucky friend, about Monroe's desire to become territorial governor. The President, Graham said, doubted it, "thinking that the offer of the appointment [to him] would be an insult." The interview led to a meeting with Madison. "The President [Monroe reported to John Taylor] received me with great kindness, as did the heads of departments. Indeed, I had proofs of kindness from every one, many of whom I did not expect it. It shows that they think I have been pushed too hard, for any errors imputed to me."

In September, a visit by the Madisons to Jefferson's home put the President almost next door to Monroe's farm residence. The day after their arrival word was sent to Monroe that the party would dine with him next day. John Randolph was supposed to be there at that time, but (wrote John) he luckily postponed his visit a week, by which time "the royal birds had just taken their flight." Randolph found Monroe in very bad spirits. He protested that all reports of his taking office were groundless, but Randolph had "disquieting reflections" from what he saw. Old Republicans, he advised Taylor, should be alerted to the danger of a reunion with Madison. Taylor agreed—not revealing his latest advice to

Monroe that by stepping into the State Department "you would advance towards the presidency."

Rumors of rapprochement already were rife. In September, the London *Times* reprinted an averment of the Winchester, Virginia, *Gazette*, that Isaac Coles was showing a letter from his brother, Madison's private secretary, saying that Secretary Smith was to be superseded by Monroe. The Alexandria *Gazette* predicted that a place would be made for Monroe by shifting Smith to the Supreme Court.

That hit bottom in probability, but Justice Cushing was dead and Chase dying, so Madison had one vacancy to fill and the certainty of another. Former Attorney-General Levi Lincoln, he found, was going blind with cataracts. Postmaster General Gideon Granger raked up "unsolicited" endorsements of himself from everybody he could coerce. To Jefferson, Granger sent a notice that if he did not get the place, he would give his "vindication to the world . . . by publicity." A resurrection, that meant, of his malaprop attempt in 1804, to defend the chastity of Dolley Madison and Anna Cutts—thus spreading anew the baseless slanders. Also, he would vindicate his "correct and honorable conduct in 1808." That was his aid in quashing a Connecticut indictment for criminal libel, whose trial would have dragged Jefferson's youthful adultery with Mrs. Walker before the public. Jefferson endorsed Granger to Madison: "His abilities are great. I have entire confidence in his integrity." Granger's legal talents, Madison replied, had been publicly displayed only in "his Yazooism."

When Congress convened Madison nominated port collector Alexander Wolcott of Connecticut for the Court. He was strongly supported by Levi Lincoln, who had "met with few men of stronger mind, of greater perceptive and discriminating powers," or steadier adherence to sound principles of government. Wolcott had been heard to say that merchants opposing his strict enforcement of the Non-Intercourse Act "might all go to hell in their own way." The Senate rejected him, twenty-four to nine.

Madison next nominated John Quincy Adams. He was unanimously confirmed but refused the place. By this time the death of Justice Chase made two posts vacant. Rumors of the possible appointment of Ezekiel Bacon or Joseph Story brought a protest from Jefferson. These two, he wrote to Madison, "are exactly the men who deserted us" on the embargo. Story was "unquestionably a tory, and both are too young." Bacon endorsed Story.

Madison nominated 31-year-old Story and Gabriel Duvall, the President's close personal and political friend, at that time Comptroller of the Treasury. Duvall's career on the Court was undistinguished; Story ranked next to Marshall during the next quarter century and remains today the youngest appointee in the Court's history. The record hardly supports the common conjecture that Story was appointed because *Jefferson (the man behind the throne)* overrated his fidelity to Republican principles.

45 / ACTION WITHOUT BENEFIT OF CONGRESS

Foreign policy on all fronts rose to a simultaneous climax in the fall of 1810. Concern over Florida quickened when France and England came to an armed clash on the soil of Spain, with rival kings and juntas as their puppets. Spanish impotence and the threat of French or British occupation roused the spirit of revolt in West Florida. From Mexico to Argentina the Latin American world was full of sparks, where not aflame. An economy move by Gallatin in consular expenses brought the admonition from Madison: "Everything relating to Spanish America is too important to be subjected to a minute economy."

From former Senator Adair, Madison received a report that five-sixths of the wealth of West Florida was located west of the Pearl River and nine-tenths of the inhabitants were Americans (the remainder mostly French). "The people are as ripe fruit; waiting the hand that dares to pluck them; and with them all Florida." Three or four hundred soldiers at Pensacola, half-naked and half-starved, formed the whole armed force of Spain. British agents were at work, promising people a market for cotton from which the states were shut out by trade restrictions.

A Tennessee congressman, urging the President to negotiate for a trade route down the Mobile, received the answer that as long as the Spaniards held the mouth of the river, they would be able "at pleasure to obstruct our passage to the ocean." Since Madison believed that the entire Mobile region was rightfully included in the Louisiana Purchase, the remark clearly pointed to the thought of taking it by force. On June 14, Governor Claiborne of New Orleans dated a letter "From the house of the President." It informed Parish Judge William Wykoff Jr., living opposite Baton Rouge, that by the last accounts from Spain, all hopes of successful resistance to Bonaparte were at an end. "You know," he continued, "that under the Louisiana Convention, we claim as far eastwardly as the Perdido." That claim would never be abandoned: "But under present circumstances, it would be more pleasing that the taking possession of the country be preceded by a request from the inhabitants. Can no means be devised *to obtain such request?* . . . Nature has decreed the union of Florida with the United States, and the welfare of the inhabitants imperiously demands it."

Wykoff was requested to talk to influential Americans on the Spanish side of the Mississippi. The inhabitants could best determine how to express their wishes, but were it done through "a convention of delegates, named by the people, it would be more satisfactory."

A week later Secretary Smith authorized Wykoff to proceed at government expense into both the Floridas, to spread word "that in the event of a political separation from the parent country, their incorporation into our Union would coincide with the sentiments and policy of the United States." At the same time Senator Crawford of Georgia was empowered to send "a gentleman of honor and discretion" into the Floridas for a similar promotion of "the policy of the President in relation to the Floridas."

From Montpelier Madison directed that Governor Holmes of Mississippi Territory be informed of the Wykoff mission and be told to put his militia in shape to deal with either foreign interference or internal convulsions. The intention was "to take care of the rights and interests of the United States by every measure within the limits of the Executive authority." Smith sent Holmes a copy of Wykoff's letter, saying it was "written under a sanction from the President."

Wykoff reported before he received his instructions that the revolt was under way. A convention was set for July 25, with a contest impending between advocates of American union and a composite of oldtime American Tories, army deserters, and other fugitives who were hiding British proclivities under pretended zeal for Ferdinand VII. Receiving this word, the President asked the heads of War and Treasury what measures were within his power concerning the customhouse, in case the people of West Florida offered to place the territory under the authority of the United States. He had no doubt of his authority to take possession.

All territory the United States might claim and possess in West Florida, Gallatin replied, was included in customs districts under the Mobile Act of 1804. Acceptance of a West Florida offer, wrote Eustis, would imply protection and immediate use of force if necessary. Madison's policy was stiffened by a report from Chargé Erving that England was laying plans to govern all Spanish colonies through a nominal regency set up in the name of Ferdinand VII. He ordered the southwestern militia to repel any Spanish armed advance in West Florida.

The West Florida "convention army," mostly American, late in September stormed the Spanish fort at Baton Rouge. The convention thereupon declared "this territory of West Florida to be a *free and independent state.*" The declaration was sent to the President along with a resolution asking the United States "to take the present Government and people of this State under their immediate and special protection, as an integral and inalienable portion of the United States." This was not what Madison expected. With West Florida declared free and independent, accession to the United States was to be negotiated by treaty. Madison recognized the purpose—to validate enormous land grants made by Spanish Intendant Morales to the revolutionaries. However, the immediate question was: should the President act at once or wait until Congress convened in December?

Madison summoned the Cabinet and put the situation before it. Delay would fortify West Florida's sovereignty and strengthen the speculators. A British landing at Pensacola had been reported. Outlaws and army deserters hazarded public order. Two days after the declaration reached him, Madison signed a proclamation directing territorial officials to take possession of the country between the Mississippi and Perdido Rivers.

To combat the land grants, no mention was made of the convention's actions. The President claimed the country as a part of Louisiana conveyed by the treaty of 1803. A crisis subverting Spanish authority made the action necessary. Authority for it was found in acts of Congress framed to cover ultimate American possession.

Neither this proclamation nor a word concerning it was made public in Washington or even hinted at to members of Congress. Numerous copies of it, however, were rushed to Baton Rouge and New Orleans. Secretary Smith informed Turreau that such action *was likely to be taken,* and declared, with his usual truthfulness, "*I swear, General, on my honor* . . . that not only are we strangers to all that passes there," but that reputed agents of the revolutionaries "are the enemies of the Executive."

Not until December 3 did Congress and the public learn about the proclamation of October 27. The delay had two valuable results. It presented Europe with a *fait accompli.* It gave Federalist editors five joyous weeks in which to belabor Madison for not having nerve enough to occupy the province against the will of France. When they learned what he had done they denounced him with equal violence for having taken the territory at Napoleon's demand.

The annexation of West Florida was not the most important Executive action in the fall of 1810. A week before the President returned to Washington in October, the *Intelligencer* printed a letter from the Duke of Cadore to Armstrong, picked up from the official *Moniteur*. Dated August 5, it took note of the repeal of the Non-Intercourse Act, coupled with the authority given the President under the Macon Act to renew it against one belligerent if the other revoked its edicts against American commerce. This new law terminated the authority of the United States to confiscate French ships (none had been confiscated), and thus enabled France to end reprisals. "In this new state of things," wrote the Duke to Armstrong:

> I am authorized to declare to you, sir, that the decrees of Berlin and Milan are revoked, and that after the first of November they will cease to have effect; it being understood that, in consequence of this declaration, the English shall revoke their orders in council, and renounce the new principles of blockade, which they have undertaken to establish; or that the United States, conformably to the act you have just communicated, shall cause their rights to be respected by the English.

From Pinkney in London came cheering promises by Wellesley followed by an unexplained desertion of them. Instead of paper blockades being dropped, a new one was proclaimed covering the Strait of Corfu. This news made Madison ready for action. He sent a directive to Pinkney. Provided the official proceedings of the French government corresponded with the published version: "You will let the British Government understand that on the first day of November the President will issue his proclamation, comfortably to the act of Congress, and that the nonintercourse law will consequently be revived against Great Britain."

The Macon Act gave Great Britain three months after this to escape the ban on trade; but, said Madison, owing to the early notice the British government received of the French action, Congress might not wait that long. Finally, if the British really wanted a good understanding, they would see the need of stopping the insufferable vexation of American seamen by impressment. Pinkney could handle that matter separately, after the *Chesapeake* outrage was atoned for. And if the naming of a minister was still being delayed, Pinkney should return to the United States unless he saw a highly favorable turn in British policies. The congressional elections were nearly over and should carry a warning to London against reliance on the strength of a British party: "And I do not believe that Congress will be disposed, or permitted by the nation, to a tame submission; the less so as it would be not only perfidious to the other belligerent, but irreconcilable with an honorable neutrality."

On the day this was written (Friday, October 19) fresh dispatches arrived from London and were published on Monday. Pinkney had informed Wellesley of "written and official notice" from Armstrong that France had revoked the decrees of Berlin and Milan. He expected that revocation of the British orders of January and November 1807 and April 1809, and all other analogous orders, "will follow of course." Wellesley replied that whenever "repeal of the French decrees shall have actually taken effect," and neutral commerce restored to its condition prior to those decrees, Great Britain would relinquish her retaliatory system.

French repeal unquestionably would end the fictional blockade of the British Isles, but would it *restore prior conditions?* Madison was skeptical. Wellesley's letter, he observed to Pinkney, was "a promise only and that in a very questionable shape." The Orders in Council did not retaliate against the French decrees, but were avowedly founded "on the *unprecedented mode* of warfare against her," evidently meaning the exclusion of British trade from the continent: "These considerations, with the obnoxious exercise of her sham-blockades in the moment of our call for their repeal, backed by the example of France, discourage the hope that she contemplates a reconciliation with us."

Madison laid the situation before his Cabinet. If he waited to find out what Cadore meant by "it being understood" that the United States should cause its rights to be respected, and what Wellesley meant by restoration of trade to its prior condition, the opportunity presented by France would evaporate in French suspicions. The decision was made to issue a proclamation on November 2, using Armstrong's letter to Pinkney as official notice of France's repeal.

Secretary Smith gave notice of the impending action to John Philip Morier, the new British chargé d'affaires, warning that Congress would follow with collision measures. Morier's report to Wellesley was a relay from Federalist dinner tables. Cabinet predictions of congressional actions meant nothing, because "that assembly, instead of receiving, gives the impulse on those questions to the Executive." Madison probably both feared France and was courting her in hope of a return of plundered ships, "Mr. Jefferson and Mr. Barlow being the secret advisers of the President."

The United States, Morier assured Wellesley, could not support a war. Great Britain had an opportunity of "bringing these people to a just sense of the station they hold in relation to her," by simply allowing the Non-Intercourse Act to take effect and by a firm assertion of British rights "tempered with as much justice as was safe."

Morier failed to grasp the fact that nonintercourse was an improvised substitute for a war that would surely come if the substitute failed. His cliches about Madison and Jefferson came from the same sources that caused American historians to keep repeating them for more than a hundred years. The belief that President Madison did not initiate policies was a byproduct of his quiet manner and unimpressive physique.

The "mentor theory" received a great impulse in 1810, when the Federalist postoffice-watcher in Charlottesville spread word that the President wrote to Jefferson twelve times from April through July. What could account for that, except a master and pupil relationship? The correspondence, from beginning to end, concerned the disposition of a lamb born at Alexandria, during the shipment of two pairs of Merino sheep from Portugal as a joint gift to Madison and Jefferson. The two Presidents had to repel the rival claim of the ship captain and then decide which of them owned the lamb. They settled by agreeing to an equal division of the offspring of both ewes, with which they hoped to raise the standard of wool-growing throughout Virginia by giving a ram to each county.

First word to Jefferson of the two great decisions of 1810—the taking of Florida and nonintercourse with England—came to him in the newspapers. However, the general belief that Madison was governed "by the long arm of Monticello" produced an overestimate of his desire for peace and an underrating of his readiness to run the risk of war.

The British government, Madison wrote privately to Pinkney on October 30, should not judge the future of the Non-Intercourse Act by the past. The revived law would permit exports to England, but only in American ships. Effectively carried out, the new policy would reverse the effects of the British navigation laws. From all these hurts she could escape by making her trade restrictions conform to the law of nations.

On October 31, General Turreau was told about the coming proclamation. On November 1, long-expected dispatches arrived from Minister Armstrong. They contained virtually nothing except Cadore's August 5 letter and a private one to the President in which Armstrong said he had scared Napoleon into repeal of the decrees by transmitting a London report *of July 27* that Congress had been called in special session to declare war on France. (The Cadore letter was *drafted on July 25*.) His dispatches did nothing to dispel uncertainties, but Madison held to his determination to act.

On November 2, the President proclaimed that France had met the requirements of the Macon Act. Three months thereafter, unless England similarly revoked her edicts, the Non-Intercourse Act of 1809 would be revived against her. On that same November 2, Turreau was told that a ship was being held for his dispatches. He was to send this message from President Madison: "The Executive thinks that the measures he will take in case England continues to interfere with our communications with Europe *will necessarily lead to war*."

Turreau, whose opinion of Madison had vastly changed during six years, advised his government not to underestimate the threat of war implicit in the proclamation: "It is difficult to believe that England will suffer this new act of emancipation on the part of the Americans, but I will add that I have still more hope for a decided rupture between the two powers from the very firm determination of the Executive to escape from the habitual yoke of Great Britain."

After writing this much Turreau encountered the Secretary of the Treasury. "Mr. Gallatin," he resumed, "told me that he expected war." The minister capped his report with his appraisal: "Such in the last analysis is the disposition of the Executive today that I can no longer reasonably doubt that the Americans will resist England and that these two powers are coming to a rupture."

Madison on the same day directed Armstrong to let France know the grounds on which he acted: (1) That France was extinguishing all decrees actually violating American commerce. (2) That the expression "it being understood" ("*bien entendu*") in Cadore's August 5 letter did not impose *conditions precedent*, affecting the operation of French repeal. (3) That the United States was not pledged against British blockades of later date than the decrees of Berlin and Milan. Moreover, it was "presumed" that France had satisfied the requirement (made on July 5) that American property be restored.

These explanations took account of Federalist outcries over "*bien entendu*." As that party interpreted Cadore's letter, he was saying on August 5 that the French decrees "will be revoked" on November 1, provided the United States *before that time* resisted or got rid of British orders and blockades. This ignored Cadore's statement that the effectiveness of French repeal depended on American resistance to the orders *conformably to the Macon Act*, which gave England three months, after the proclamation of nonintercourse, for her to reshape her policies.

Madison was on weaker ground, and knew it, in his presumption that France had met his July 5 requirement of a pledge to return confiscated property. Armstrong, he discovered, did not receive this instruction until August 7, two days after Cadore delivered his letter. Delay to ascertain facts would wreck the whole arrangement. So Madison merely said that restoration of ships would be a mark of good faith.

Within a week, dispatches from Armstrong shockingly reversed his prediction of the restoration of ships and cargoes. The Decree of Rambouillet was revoked, but would continue to operate as a reprisal against the (never-used) provision in the expired Non-Intercourse Act permitting confiscation of French vessels. In other words, the emperor would continue to fill his war chest by selling American property. Madison flared up at still another restriction. American ships trading to French-controlled ports must obtain licenses from French consuls in the United States. "The government of France," Madison replied, "should not for a moment be misled by the belief that any description of commercial agents whatever will be permitted to exercise" such a nonreciprocal and unlawful power in the ports of the United States.

These developments did not impair the *legality* of Madison's November 2 proclamation; but the political basis of it was shattered. Trade with France in any case would be a trickle, and future confiscations of past-seized ships would infuriate the public. Nevertheless, coupling the possibility of a moderating French attitude with the overriding necessity of putting pressure on England, the President decided to stand by his proclamation.

Eleven years later, as minister to France, Albert Gallatin discovered a still-secret Decree of Trianon, dated August 5, 1810, ordering the confiscation of sequestered American ships and cargoes. Bearing the same date as the announced repeal of the Berlin and Milan decrees, this appeared to convict Cadore of an astounding act of perfidy; but the correspondence of Cadore and Napoleon makes it clear that this Trianon decree was written about September 12, and was predated to furnish a legal basis for actions ordered by Napoleon after August 5.

In his second annual message (December 5, 1810) Madison dealt matter-of-factly with the proclamation against England and revealed the seizure and annexation of West Florida to an astonished Congress and nation. Carefully separating the legally required repeal of the Berlin and Milan decrees from the unjust seizure of property under a "misapplication of the principle of reprisal," he said that the expectation of its restoration by France had not been fulfilled. Notice had been given to England that the blockade of May 1806 was within the purview of the Macon Act and must be revoked to escape re-imposition of the Non-Intercourse Act.

Owing to the state of the Spanish monarchy, the President stated, Spanish authority had been subverted "in that portion of West Florida which, though of right appertaining to the United States, had remained in the possession of Spain" during negotiations for delivery of it. This exposed the province to such hazards that immediate interposition was necessary. He did not doubt that Congress would supply whatever provisions were essential to protect the rights and interests of the people "thus brought into the bosom of the American family."

Domestically, the President suggested further protection of America's expanding manufactures, a navigation act to foster the merchant marine, and establishment of a national university under the congressional power over the District of Columbia. "Such an institution, though local in its legal character, would be universal in its beneficial effects," strengthening the foundations "of our free and happy system of government."

Turning toward an unfree and unhappy aspect of society, Madison asked Congress for further legislation to suppress "a traffic in enslaved Africans," carried on "equally in violation of the laws of humanity" and of the country. His feelings were further indicated in a dispatch to Pinkney approving Britain's condemnation of an American slave ship. He rejected the owners' contention that the Negroes were slaves under American law. They appeared to him to be "prisoners of war liberated by their entrance within a neutral jurisdiction . . . or . . . passengers held in false imprisonment."

Sent to Congress were the year's Anglo-American diplomatic dispatches, revealing unremitting efforts to reach an understanding with England and that country's unyielding adherence to paper blockades. Lazy Armstrong's scanty dispatches were made thinner still by withholding his strictures on Napoleon's stepped-up confiscations. Suppression would ease negotiation and deprive Federalist critics of ammunition. They needed none. For a month they had been assailing the November proclamation—the foolish act, said the New York *Evening Post*, of a man "too weak to be wicked." And in the same paper: "His words are smoother than oil, yet a drawn sword is in his hand." Rather perplexing —a man too weak to be wicked, pointing a drawn sword at the world's most formidable nation.

No milder were Federalist comments about West Florida. Boston's *Columbian Centinel* challenged "the right and authority of Mr. Madison, in face of the Constitution, without any provision to that effect by Law, to order a forcible seizure of a part of *the territory of a friendly State*." Republican editors rose to panegyric over that same action. Declaimed the Richmond *Enquirer:* "We are proud to see such a man as Madison at the head of the nation, so clear in his views, so cool in his decisions, so firm and unshrinking in his purposes. Where is the being who will now complain of Madison's want of nerve?"

That "being" was right at hand. Before the message was delivered, the Baltimore *Federal Republican,* edited by the Federalist chief clerk whom Madison kept in office, had been calling the President "feeble, timid, prevaricating." Wagner greeted the West Florida annexation with the charge that Madison was "arrogating to himself the power of commencing war, without the authority of Congress;" but this "executive usurpation" was the product of weakness, not of strength. It was a just speculation that West Florida had been seized at the special instance of France, probably "to be held in *secret trust* for Napoleon."

Spanish protest reached Madison through the Chevalier de Onís, who for a year had been vainly seeking recognition of himself as minister of the British-controlled junta supporting King Ferdinand. There had been informal contacts. At the Georgetown races in the fall of 1809, the President rode up on horseback to Copenhagen Jackson's awe-inspiring "Landau barouche and four" and found Onís in the carriage. They were introduced. Mrs. Madison invited the Spaniard to her next "Wednesday afternoon." For all of this, Jackson commented to his government, Onís "might as well have stayed at Seville" unless Great Britain wanted to make the refusal to recognize him a cause of war.

Working through Spanish Consul Bernabeu, Onís expressed surprise and concern that the President's message "authorizes an act of hostility and violence against the territory of the king my master." This "Machiavellian policy" contradicted the firm assurances of Secretary Smith that the President would reprobate and punish any American invasion of West Florida. British Chargé Morier, properly shocked by the take over, asked whether it would not "have been worthy of the generosity of a free nation like this" to come to the aid of the gallant Spanish people in their noble struggle for liberty. He did not mention his advice to his own government, less than two weeks earlier, to obtain a cession of Pensacola in the event of war. Pensacola was in East Florida, and that province was in Madison's mind when he asked Senator Crawford to send an agent into the territory. The senator chose General George Mathews, seventy-two-year-old former governor of Georgia. Mathews visited Spanish governor Vizente Folch at Mobile and laid before him Madison's proposition, which foreshadowed the Monroe Doctrine: "That it was the joint interest of the United States and the Spanish provinces to prevent any European nation from obtaining a footing in the new world."

This treated "the Spanish provinces," in effect, as freed from Spanish authority by the subjection of Spain to England and France. Folch, Mathews reported, was solicitous of American aid but seemed unwilling to lose independence "by becoming a component part of the nation." Folch then wrote to Governor Holmes of Mississippi. He had asked Captain General Someruelos of Cuba to negotiate a delivery of the Floridas to the United States, to be held in trust until "an equivalent to Spain should be determined and agreed upon."

Folch wanted firm assurance that the United States would repress an army of adventurers, led by Reuben Kemper and Joseph P. Kennedy, who were threatening to seize Mobile. The President ordered Holmes to capture and prosecute "every person concerned in the unauthorized undertaking." Judge Toulmin reported to Madison that nobody could be found to serve a warrant on the chief conspirators, who were said to have entered into a solemn obligation to murder any public officer who should institute a prosecution.

On December 2, 1810, Governor Folch sent a messenger to Washington with "more positive terms" for delivery of West Florida. Being incomprehensibly abandoned by the vice-regal authorities, he would save the province from rebels and marauders by delivering it to the United States "under an equitable capitulation, provided I do not receive succor from the Havana or Vera Cruz during the present month."

These "more positive terms" were actually less positive. "An equitable capitulation" could mean temporary policing, and the need for this would evaporate if Kemper and Kennedy were restrained. President Madison had his hands full when he came to recommend public measures in the session of Congress that opened in December 1810.

With Folch's remarkable overtures in his hands, the President, on January 3, 1811, sent a secret message to Congress. With it went the letters of the Spanish governor and Morier's protest against the occupation of West Florida—a paper that would stir fear of British military intervention. Madison asked for a declaration (again foreshadowing the Monroe Doctrine) "that the United States could not foresee without serious inquietude any part of a neighboring territory . . . pass from the hands of Spain into those of any other foreign power."

Already empowered to take permanent possession of the country west of the Perdido, he asked now for authority to take temporary possession of any or all parts of Florida east of that river and to govern it during such occupation. Also, Congress should determine what was to be done in the event of a subversion of Spanish authority in East Florida. To stimulate quick action, the President sent in confidence an intercepted letter of Onís saying that Spain and England together could split the United States into two or three republics and make it a perfect nullity.

Within two weeks the President signed a bill and a resolution, passed in secrecy, enacting both of his requests into law. He was authorized to take temporary possession of Florida from the Perdido River to the Atlantic Ocean, by arrangement with the local authority or in the event of attempted foreign occupation. The territory was to "remain subject to a future negotiation."

The United States aimed at permanent acquisition of all the Floridas— a fact made clear in identical instructions to Pinkney in London and Chargé Jonathan Russell in Paris (Armstrong had come home of his own volition). The action of Congress, Madison declared, was "justified by national interest and national policy; an interest founded upon a recognized though unliquidated claim on Spain for indemnities; and a policy imperatively prescribed by a legitimate principle of self preservation."

Events since the acquisition of Louisiana had "increased the solicitude of the United States for the sovereignty of a tract of country whose contiguity renders it vitally important in a military, naval and commercial point of view." Should a foreign power possess itself of the Floridas, the danger to the Union would be too imminent for them "to hesitate a moment as to the conduct which they would be inevitably compelled to pursue." These observations were to be presented in substance with a warning to England patterned on the following to France: "This explicit declaration uttered with sincerity and friendliness, ought to admonish the French government (should it unhappily yield itself up to such improper desires) to check all inclination of gaining a foothold in the Floridas." The assurance should be added concerning East Florida that the United States intend nothing more than preservation of peace and quiet, prevention of anarchy, and exclusion of all external interference, pending amicable adjustment of all matters in dispute.

The President commissioned General Mathews and Colonel John Mc-Kee to receive East Florida and to engage for future "redelivery to the lawful sovereign" if that should be insisted on. Should no agreement be made and foreign occupation be imminent, they must pre-occupy the territory at once.

In Congress, Madison's secret message on East Florida interrupted a fierce partisan debate over his West Florida proclamation. Republicans, supporting a Giles bill to incorporate the occupied country in Orleans Territory, swiftly crossed the Rubicon of forcible expansion. Federalists reined in at the bank and burned their bridges before them. "Sir," asked Senator Outerbridge Horsey of Delaware, "what is the nature and import of this proclamation? In my humble conception—both legislation and war." War—because it directs the occupation of the territory by military force. Legislation—because it annexes the territory to Orleans; "it creates a governor; it enacts laws, and appropriates money."

Everything provided for in the Giles bill, Horsey declared, already had been done by the President. Since that is the case, observed Senator Henry Clay, what reason is there to pass the bill? It was sent back to committee. In the House, a bill implying the right to admit West Florida as a state inspired Josiah Quincy to the most memorable utterance of his career: "If this bill passes, it is my deliberate opinion that it is virtually a dissolution of this Union; that it will free the States from their moral obligation, and, as it will be the right of all, so it will be the duty of some, definitely to prepare for a separation, amicably if they can, violently if they must."

Admission of a state located beyond the 1783 boundaries of the United States, Quincy averred, was unconstitutional. The limits of the power conferred by the Constitution of 1787 were impliedly fixed by Madison's 1780 resolution calling for creation of new states in the American West. "You have no authority," he shouted, "to throw the rights and liberties, and property of this people, into a 'hotch-pot' with the wild men on the Missouri" or the Anglo-Hispano-Gallo Americans who bask on the sands of the Mississippi. Madison had welcomed these same people into "the bosom of the American family."

Criticism touched Madison at another level in the Tory pen of Washington Irving. Taken to a White House levee to see "the sublime Porte," he found Mrs. Madison to be "a fine portly, buxom dame, who has a smile and a pleasant word for everybody . . . but as to Jemmy Madison— ah! poor Jemmy!—he is but a withered little apple-John."

Sixty years, plus the cares of state and Irving's politics, accounted for the description. When the young Baron de Montlezun visited Montpelier a few years later he found Madison immersed in the duties of office; but whenever the President could disengage himself from that "painful honor . . . the wrinkles smooth out of his face, his countenance lights up; it shines then with all the fire of the spirit and with a gentle gayety; and one is surprised to find in the conversation of the great statesman, of the wise administrator, as much of sprightliness as of strength."

Relations with Great Britain were taken up the instant the House ended its last secret session (January 14, 1811) on the East Florida bill. An administration bill provided that the Non-Intercourse Act of 1809, after coming into force against Great Britain on February 2, was to remain in effect until the President proclaimed a revocation of British decrees. To forestall court attack by Federalist judges, the bill provided that the President's November 2 proclamation, and nothing else, was to be admitted in prosecutions as evidence of the revocation or modification of foreign decrees.

Congress was in a belligerent mood, thanks to the national spirit stirred by the diplomatic correspondence published during the recess. (Elected but not yet in session was a new and far more militant House.) Randolphite Richard Stanford wrote the day after Madison sent his secret East Florida message: "The rage for war exceeds any time since the memorable year of 98-9." But the news reaching Madison from France was bad and getting worse. Cadore, capitulating to the emperor, pronounced in the *Moniteur* that "as long as England shall persist in her orders in council, your Majesty will persist in your decrees."

The *Intelligencer* expressed hope that this referred only to decrees operating on the continent; but Madison received word on the same day that the American brig *New-Orleans Packet* had been sequestered under the Berlin and Milan decrees, supposedly revoked. Wild joy seized the Federalists when the President transmitted to Congress Russell's vigorous protest against the seizure. "O Madison! what hast thou not to answer for?" exclaimed lame-duck Senator Pickering. Again the *Intelligencer* expressed palliating doubts. The brig had been at Gibraltar and carried goods of British origin and might have been seized on that account. (That proved true.) Chairman Eppes, however, who did what the President wanted, moved to send his nonintercourse enforcement bill back to committee "until the doubts hanging over our foreign relations were dissipated."

John Randolph (arriving late) moved outright repeal of the Macon Act, calling Madison's proclamation "a bargain which credulity and imbecility enters into with cunning and power." His motion was defeated, 45 to 67, and the Eppes bill was sent back to committee. "We are sold to the French," lamented the Virginia Quid.

Eppes offered a new bill to protect American shipping that left British ports before nonintercourse was reimposed. Debate on it was suspended with an arrival at Norfolk of a new French minister. Ahead of him, came official French announcement in the *Moniteur* that the Berlin and Milan decrees no longer applied to American ships. All captures made under those decrees were to become null and void on February 2, the day nonintercourse was to be restored against Great Britain. Restoration of ships and cargoes would follow. To the Federalist press, however, February 2 was the date on which American ships were to be confiscated unless the United States yielded to the insolence of Napoleon and quarreled with England. The new French minister was coming to impose the will of the perfidious tyrant on a weak and credulous President.

Bachelor Louis Sérurier looked younger than his thirty-five years—a thin, swarthy man with a dark melancholy countenance. Known in France as a diplomat who drew Holland into the Napoleonic fold, he had been advised by Russell not to deal with Americans as he did with brokenhearted Dutchmen. "He would find in the United States a people who feared no one but God."

The President gave Sérurier a cool greeting, confining himself (the minister reported) to laconic expressions of his desire to see a smoothing out of misunderstandings. In his first discussion with Secretary Smith, Sérurier was asked what was meant in Cadore's August 5 letter by "making our rights respected." Was not re-establishment of nonintercourse enough? "Nonintercourse above all," replied the minister, but it seemed natural to include orders to protect coasts and navigation by armaments. What would ensue, Sérurier asked Smith next day, if Great Britain persisted in her Orders in Council and illegal blockades? "War, he replied with decided frankness." The new envoy discussed affairs with his predecessor and sent the result to Paris: "The opinion of General Turreau, still my only guide, is that the government wishes to continue in its system, but that it is hurt, disheartened by the recent sequestrations; that these events make its system unpopular and give arms to the English party, who in their newspapers never fail to class Mr. Madison as the vassal of his Imperial Majesty."

On this day the President placed a 4,000-word letter from Pinkney before his Cabinet. Wellesley was contending that France had merely promised to repeal her decrees on November 1 provided conditions precedent were fulfilled by that time. This view was supported, Pinkney wrote privately, by admiralty judge Sir William Scott and "all that antineutral class to which Stephen and Maryatt belong." Nothing could do more to stiffen Madison's attitude toward England at a time when French perversity might have softened it.

The effect was evident that afternoon, when Smith took Sérurier aside at Mrs. Madison's levee and said he was authorized to give assurance that, in case England adhered to her orders, the government would reinforce nonintercourse, and "give to this measure all the consequences it ought to have." That could only mean war.

The decision freed Eppes to go ahead with his bill to make the President's proclamation binding on the courts. The *Federal Republican*, which had been calling Madison feeble, timid, sullen, wavering, repulsive, and querulous, now saw in him the ruthless dictator, acting "as if invested with kingly prerogatives." To overcome a filibuster, the House was kept in session day and night (twice for eighteen hours running) and the bill was passed at five o'clock in the morning (as Federalists reported it to Chargé Morier) "amidst the drunken shouts of the majority." It whipped through the Senate in two days. Dolley Madison wound up the fight by persuading Eppes and Randolph to shake hands instead of fighting a duel which neither wanted.

Friends of France, Sérurier reported, regarded the new law "as a success in the present temper of things." Let news be received of the absolute abolition of the decrees, they told him, let France display a friendlier disposition, and "the government will easily be induced to take up a stronger and more decided system." Thus, the man who was sent to alter American policies fell at once into the system that caused Turreau's recall: sustaining French conduct in his Washington talk and pleading with his government to alter it.

As Congress approached *sine die* adjournment early in 1811, new attacks burst on Gallatin. The Bank of the United States had three months to live when he renewed the attempt to extend its charter. His arguments for it were sound, and the President was in accord with them. In the Senate, however, Smith, Leib, and Giles cast "the most invidious aspersions" (Crawford's term) on the Treasury head. Vice President Clinton killed the renewal by breaking a tie. Clinton gave a reason drawn from Madison's 1791 speech against the bank: the power to create corporations was "a high attribute of sovereignty," not to be planted in the Constitution by implication. Gallatin translated this into political English: Clinton hoped that a smashing defeat of Gallatin would react against Madison and open the 1812 presidential race to himself or DeWitt Clinton. Samuel and Robert Smith had similar objectives.

In January the Virginia legislature elected James Monroe governor, after he gave a pledge to co-operate with the national administration. John Randolph wrote "Judas" in his diary, but wrote to James M. Garnett that he pitied Monroe. He was "habitually and incurably ambitious . . . he cannot live without office." The terms on which Monroe obtained the governorship spread new reports that he was to succeed Robert Smith and the assaults on Gallatin were seen as a counterpoise. "Gallatin and Smith are at swords points," wrote a New York editor, "whatever outside complaisance they may show to each other."

Smith's political methods were illuminated by his comment to Jefferson (after slurring him to Turreau) that he was endeavoring to uphold "your well digested system," adopted by "our inestimable friend, your worthy successor." Directed by Madison to inform Morier of American acceptance of the repeal of the Berlin and Milan decrees, this was the way he fulfilled the trust: "Mr. Smith declared to me confidentially his opinion that those decrees were not repealed, and that before the rising of the present Congress the whole of their restrictive commercial system should be entirely done away."

Unluckily, Morier referred in a formal note to Smith's admission that Great Britain "had a right to complain." Smith, Madison recorded, reluctantly disavowed the statement, but instead of making a written disavowal, as he was asked to do, he persuaded Morier to withdraw the letter. Members of Congress told the President that Smith was saying the whole policy toward England was contrary to his advice.

On February 20 Smith came to the White House with the draft of a letter to Sérurier, asking categorically whether the Berlin and Milan decrees were revoked on November 1 or at any posterior time. Similar questions followed as to other issues. Barring sabotage, only monumental stupidity could explain the writing of such a letter. The formal sending of it, necessarily followed by disclosure to Congress, would have knocked the bottom out of Madison's foreign policy. Coupled with his intrigues and oral indiscretions, this settled Smith's future.

With the nonintercourse support bill still in the Senate and Congress due to adjourn in eleven days, the President decided against an immediate demand for Smith's resignation. The desire for his ouster, though, was piling up among administration supporters. Judge Nicholson urged Macon to inform Madison that the Smiths were organizing against his program. Macon, after consulting Gallatin, replied that the President was "better acquainted with the intrigue than either you or myself." Randolph, friendly to Gallatin, advised him to go immediately to the President and "demand either the dismissal of Mr. ——— or his own." There was statesmanship in his ensuing remark: "If the cabal succeed in their present projects, and I see nothing but promptitude and decision that can prevent it, the nation is undone."

The President further antagonized the Smiths, at this moment, by nominating Joel Barlow as minister to France. Senator Samuel Smith, who desired that post himself, "raved like a madman about it," (so said George W. Erving), but the Senate, to its own and the country's astonishment, confirmed the nomination twenty-one to eleven. Even Pickering voted for him.

Events moved rapidly after Congress adjourned on March 3. Gallatin submitted his resignation. Personal factions, he wrote, were defeating measures of vital importance. Public confidence in the Executive was being impaired, and he clearly perceived that his continuation in office only "invigorates the opposition against yourself."

Madison instantly rejected the resignation and asked Senator Brent of Virginia to find out whether Monroe would come in as Secretary of State. On its face, this sequence suggests that Madison was unready to fire Smith until Gallatin pressed him to it; but Gallatin knew of Smith's coming ouster before he submitted his resignation. That is evident in a notation he made about a statement by Duane that three intimate congressional friends of Gallatin knew all about the decision before Congress adjourned. Gallatin felt sure *he did not mention it*. If he did not *know about it*, the only rebuttal he needed was to say so. The resignation clearly was a pre-arranged device to ease the firing of Smith.

Senator Brent, in his letter to Monroe, said he was "not expressly authorized to say that this appointment will be offered to you," but he had no doubt it would follow an expression of willingness to take it. Monroe's reply was long delayed by his absence from home.

Hearing nothing from him, Madison on March 19 or 20 asked Robert Smith for his resignation. To avoid an open rupture he was offered the post of minister to Russia. Smith agreed, with retirement fixed for April 1. Given permission to disclose the new appointment, Smith sent his clerk John B. Colvin to the *National Intelligencer* with an announcement that made all eyes bulge: "We understand that the embassy to the Court of St. Petersburg has been offered to the Honorable Robert Smith Esq. Secretary of State."

On the day before this was published Madison directly offered Monroe the State Department post. The letter crossed Monroe's reply to Brent, forwarded to the President—a pro-and-con discussion accompanied by a private note to the senator pointing toward acceptance. In reply to the direct invitation Monroe said he had "every disposition to accept," but candor required him to weigh his belief that the United States ought "to make an accommodation with England, the great maritime power, even on moderate terms, rather than hazard war." He could not accept a station and "act a part in it, which my judgement and conscience did not approve."

Madison saw no obstacle in that reservation. An accommodation with England had been his own desire ever since he entered the Executive councils. Differences of opinion "lie fairly within the compass of free consultation and mutual concession, as subordinate to the necessary unity belonging to the Executive department." He could see nothing in the abortive 1806 adjustment (the rejected Monroe-Pinkney treaty) that would embarrass renewed deliberation. The current questions affecting harmony between the two powers were either of subsequent date or were left in 1806 without any positive decision.

In effect, Madison was saying that an immediate diplomatic settlement with England need not cover impressment or colonial trade—the issues that disrupted the 1806 treaty; but the "necessary unity" of the Executive department would require Monroe to accept presidential decisions on the more recent issues that would determine war or peace.

Had Monroe not been ready to take the post on almost any terms, he would have rejected these. One month earlier he had written that no change from the country's dangerous foreign policy was to be expected "while the present men remain in power." Now John Taylor told him to accept at a flooding tide or float out with it while someone else gained the place "to your irretrievable injury" (in the 1816 election).

Monroe accepted. "The just principles on which you have invited me into the Department of State" he wrote to Madison, "have removed every difficulty which had occurred to me to the measure." Having bound himself to administration measures on all matters in active dispute, he wrote to John Taylor after assuming office on April 6: "I am perfectly at liberty to pursue in all things the counsel which my judgment dictates, as being most likely to promote the public welfare. You will be sensible that I would not have come here on any other principle."

President Madison thus got rid of an incompetent Secretary of State and intriguing enemy and obtained a loyal Secretary who could write his own dispatches and deal competently with foreign diplomats. He had still to reckon with the Smiths and their allies. Robert wrote to Samuel that he availed himself of the Russian offer "without looking at the motives, which conjecture may say produced it." Family protest and inside anger speedily altered Robert's stance. He declined a dinner "made for us at the White House." (Actually for a newly arrived Russian diplomatic staff.) He would "treat with silent contempt" the offer of minister to Russia. "But of this say nothing," he advised Samuel. He was going to make no compromise with Madison. "His overthrow is my object and most assuredly will I effect it." How? By writing a book.

Senator Sam sent his brother a quick warning. If Madison's handling of France and England should pay off, "his conduct and wisdom will be immortalized." In the opposite event the Republican party must rally to him in its own defense. "You will be attacked by a thousand able pens." In any case, "your removal will not be resented out of Maryland."

Duane's *Aurora* was silent until the publisher renewed his bank loans; then he opened up on Gallatin as the man who drove out Smith and was running the government. Duane followed this by reprinting a scurrilous two-column letter from New York assailing Gallatin and Madison as would-be destroyers of "our venerable patriot, Clinton" for his vote against the bank charter. A. J. Dallas named Senator Leib as the transmitter of the New York letter.

Federalists heralded the *Aurora's* continuing assaults as a breakup of the Republican party. The Richmond *Enquirer* called them an attempt to annihilate Madison by sinking him into a mouth-piece of Gallatin. New Yorkers began to talk of DeWitt or George Clinton for President. Garnett, long a Randolphian critic of Madison, denounced "that unprin-

cipled scoundrel Duane." Madison commented about the publisher: "I
have always regarded Duane, and still regard him, as a sincere friend of
liberty, and as ready to make every sacrifice to its cause, but that of his
passions. Of these he appears to be completely a slave."

On April 5 the *Aurora* published a thoroughly misleading account of
the President's rupture with Smith. Recognizing from details that this
could have come from nobody except Smith himself, Madison wrote and
placed in his papers a lengthy memorandum to record the circumstances
whilst "fresh in remembrance." A casual remark by Smith about the dismissal of Secretary Pickering enabled him to speak candidly on a delicate and disagreeable topic. Cabinet consultations, he said, had always
been harmonious. Outside, Smith had counteracted what he himself approved in Cabinet and made representations about the President calculated to diminish public confidence.

The list involved was long: the first and second Macon bills; the
nonintercourse act; disclosures to Federalists of confidential communications from Europe known only to the President and Secretary; disap-
proval to Morier of American policy; the necessity forced on the
President of doing the Secretary's work. To the denial of this, Madison
replied that Smith's letters were "almost always so crude and inadequate
that I was in the more important cases generally obliged to write them
anew myself, under the disadvantage sometimes of retaining, through
delicacy, some mixture of his draft." He must remember that in the cases
of Erskine and Jackson "the correspondence on his part had in a manner fallen entirely on my hands."

Offered the diplomatic post in Russia, Smith asked for London. Madison said he had other plans for that place, and it required talents. Smith
then applied for an appointment to the Supreme Court. When it was refused, he asked if he could say that the Russian appointment was offered.
"I have no objection," the President replied.

Smith's "book," a forty-page pamphlet, came off the press in June
and was copied into newspapers of every political hue. Confidential diplomatic matters were misrepresented at great length. Passages written
by Madison were presented as Smith's language against which the President protested. The *Intelligencer* described Smith's method as "an underhand insidious recurrence to circumstances in which he cannot be chastised by contradiction, the facts being known only to the party attacked,
whose official station forbids a reply even for the refutation of calumny."
Smith, according to his own story, was not fired. The offer of the Russian mission, he wrote, was made with such embarrassment and awk-

wardness that it excited a doubt as to the *real* object, so: "Under the influence of this suspicion, rising from my seat, I, with a decorum due to a President of the United States, distinctly informed him that owing to our different views of many subjects, I had some time since formed a determination to withdraw from his administration."

A few days later, said Smith, he learned with inexpressible astonishment that members of Congress had been told during the last session that the Russian offer would be made "with a view of putting Mr. Monroe in the Department of State." He thereupon went to the President, declined the appointment, and said he would not "allow myself under such circumstances to retain my commission of Secretary of State."

In the country at large there was only one reaction to the pamphlet: "Robert Smith has destroyed himself." William Plumer found in it "such a breach of trust and so much malignancy against Mr. Madison as impeaches his honor and integrity." Samuel Smith quoted in sorrow, and Attorney-General Rodney in jubilation, the same exclamation of Job: "Oh that mine enemy would write a book!"

47 / *GUNFIRE IN THE NIGHT*

Louis Sérurier drew his first impressions of American policy and of Madison from polite, plausible Robert Smith, who was almost as pro-French in talking with him as he was pro-British with Morier. He learned that the "mild, prudent and perhaps too timid" administrations of Jefferson and Madison had depressed the national spirit, which would have carried the nation into war with England "under the administration, for example, of the Vice President General Clinton or any other statesman of that character."

The ouster of Smith filled Sérurier with dismay. "I regard as an evil," he wrote, the removal of a man of such noble views and resolute character. The loss was heightened "by the way in which his place is filled." He was told that Smith, convinced that Madison's weakness would ruin the country, tried to bring either Clinton or himself to the Presidency. This being discovered by Gallatin, "a man much more subtle and cunning than himself," the President was given a warning and sacrificed Smith, to his own security.

Nothing said by Madison offset this Smith-told tale. By design, Sérurier thought, the President turned their frequent conversations onto French literature "which he is fond of and knows well." Probably Madison was awaiting the long-delayed arrival of the frigate *Essex* with dispatches.

That was true, but he also was awaiting the return of Minister Pinkney and the coming of Augustus Foster, whose appointment as British minister had been announced. Foster had advanced markedly in rank and social standing since his service as legation secretary. His mother was now the wife, instead of mistress, of the Duke of Devonshire.

Believing Monroe committed to England, Sérurier, at their first meeting, thought the new Secretary "deliberately exaggerated the disquiet" he felt over a feeble new nonintercourse act. An unnamed friend of Madison undertook to set him right on that point. The administration

459

desired a stronger law, but the seizure of the *New-Orleans Packet* created such a furore that the government's whole system would crumble if it had proposed the bill it wanted. Let France mend her ways, and the administration would stiffen its attitude toward England.

At a White House reception, the President told Sérurier that negotiations in London were definitely broken off. What he wanted was better reports from France. This opened the French minister's eyes. The weakness of American policy, he reported, lay not in the personality of the President but in the constant need of the government to consult public opinion. Otherwise it was "thwarted by the eternal censure of newspapers and the clamor of parties."

Thus reappraised, he found the Madison administration "tardy and without boldness, but honorable and reliable." If France would return the vessels sequestered since the previous November, and open French markets to American trade, "I will venture almost to guarantee that far more energetic measures will be adopted by the Executive against England." In taking this stand Sérurier squarely reversed the position he was directed to take. Sent to draw the United States into the Continental System, he was pleading with his own government to modify that system and make its advantages real. Turreau had made the same shift after six years of ineffectual blustering, and had been recalled because of it.

Sérurier himself felt the sting of the press. He ignored the name "Sérurier-Act" applied to the new nonintercourse law, but it was too much when the *Federal Republican* dubbed him "Minister of Rapine and murder." To his demand for punishment of the editor, Monroe lamented the indignity but remarked that the same paper "daily called Mr. Madison a traitor." If the minister insisted on it, the Attorney-General would prosecute the newspaper for criminal libel, but that would stir the country from the St. Lawrence to the Mississippi. Federalists would cry with fury that the minister was seeking abolition of "freedom of the press so dear to all citizens." Sérurier dropped his request.

The French minister still retained one belief implanted by Robert Smith—that President Madison was ruled by his Cabinet, wherefore he must be on guard against the pro-British leanings of Monroe and Gallatin. That impression was swept away on May 13. "I learn this instant," wrote Sérurier, "that . . . the fine American frigate, the *President* [has been sent to sea] with orders to require the English frigate [*Guerriere*] to depart immediately, and, in case of refusal, to engage in combat with it." This was no decision of a Cabinet reputedly leaning toward England. A new verdict went to Paris: "Mr. Madison governs by himself." The President, Sérurier went on, had "more intelligence and knowledge of affairs than his secretaries, except perhaps that of the Treasury, for whom indeed he has deference without unlimited confidence." With these attributes Madison combined "proper and positive ideas of government," and he proved in this case that he was "not without some toughness of character when he thinks the national honor is involved."

The *Guerriere* had boarded a coastwide brig off New York and impressed a native of Massachusetts. Federalist editors poohpoohed reports that Commodore John Rodgers had orders to capture the *Guerriere.* There had not been time, the *Federal Republican* said, for Madison to receive orders from Monticello, besides which, "we cannot believe [Jefferson] would compel his Vice Roy to be guilty of issuing such orders."

Rodgers' orders repeated those issued in 1810. Remembering the attack on the *Chesapeake,* he must "be prepared and determined at every hazard to vindicate the injured honor of our navy, and revive the drooping spirits of the nation." Observing strict neutrality, he was to maintain the dignity of the flag at every risk, and, "offering yourself no unjust aggression, you are to submit to none, not even a menace or threat from a force not materially your superior."

Barely had the *President* disappeared outside the Virginia capes than nighttime cannonading was reported. A day of suspense followed. Then came a schooner with a report that two large ships of war were seen standing on the same tack at nightfall. Watchers counted 200 flashes and felt the shock of the ten-mile-distant guns. Republicans cheered. Federalists denounced or scoffed. *The Federal Republican* could not believe "that a man of Mr. Madison's character for indecision and pusillanimity would authorize an act so pregnant with mischief, and fearful in its immediate consequences." Yet, "of what rashness and violence will he not be guilty, what unjustifiable and desperate act will he not commit, to retrieve his character with the French party?" But there would be no war with England; that would end him politically.

The mystery ended when Rodgers reached Sandy Hook and reported, with grief, that he had severely damaged the weaker British corvette *Little Belt.* Mistaking her at twilight for a frigate, because of a stern view of her high poop, he had pursued, overhauled, and twice hailed the dimly visible vessel. The response was a heavy shot in the mainmast. An answering shot brought a broadside, and the *President* let loose all her fire power. In ten minutes the enemy guns were silenced. Rodgers then learned the weakness of the opposing ship. His offer of help was politely refused. The death or injury of twenty or thirty men would cause him acute pain for the rest of his life, were it not that the alternative was to remain a passive spectator of insult to his country's flag.

Madison permitted the *National Intelligencer* to say that he approved Rodgers' conduct "in repelling and chastising" the causeless and rash attack. The commodore's "known candor and honor" made his requested investigation unnecessary. British Captain Bingham told a far different story at Halifax. He hove to at 6:30 in daylight, he said, hoisted colors, waited two hours for the *President* to come up and "asked what ship it was." Each captain repeated the question and Rodgers fired a broadside, which I instantly returned." The *President*'s second in command, Captain Ludlow, told the press that "every officer of the ship is ready to pledge his honor that the report of the *President* having fired the first gun is false." Madison ordered a naval board of inquiry.

The same day that Bingham's report was published in Washington— June 29—Minister Augustus Foster stepped off a British frigate at Annapolis. To the same port, on the same day, the *Essex* brought Minister Pinkney home from London; also long-waited Paris dispatches. Questioned again and again by Chargé Russell about the Berlin and Milan decrees, Cadore said after receipt of the November 2 proclamation that they were repealed. The emperor was pleased with what the United States had done, but "could not *throw himself into their arms* until they had accomplished their undertaking." In regard to Florida, however, the United States could proceed as they thought fit.

Sérurier called on Monroe next day and "found him icy." The Secretary "returned for the tenth time" to the universal cry of the people about the condition of commerce. Sérurier observed a change in his own status. People once eager to talk with him now employed a thousand pretexts to avoid him.

The President received Foster on July 2 and interpreted his credentials as "a testimony of amity." Instructed to make an immediate offer of *Chesapeake* reparations, Foster told Monroe that he must wait until the "wanton slaughter" of Britons on the *Little Belt* had been cleared up. The British minister stayed away from the big Fourth of July dinner under tents beside the Potomac, at which General John Mason offered toast No. 18 to Commodore Rodgers: "*Suavitur in modo, fortitur in re*." Translate it, shouted four-fifths of the two hundred guests. It means, said Mason, "Speak when you are spoken to or God damn you I'll sink you." The celebration, Sérurier reported, opened with a White House "at home" attended by all classes of citizens. It ended with a fireworks spectacle to which "I accompanied the President and his family."

Two days later Foster took Mrs. Madison in to dinner. During social contacts Madison urged the impolicy of Britain's conduct, which was turning the United States into a manufacturing rival. Foster pointed to the vast wealth of his own country and the great naval force it could concentrate against France (i.e. against American vessels).

> The arrival of Mr. Foster [Madison wrote to General Dearborn] has yielded nothing that promises an amendment of things with Great Britain. . . . It is required as a condition of the repeal of the orders in council that the French decrees shall be repealed not only as they relate to the United States but as they relate to Great Britain, not only that we may trade with Great Britain, but the ports of her enemy shall be opened to her trade and the idea is held out of retaliating on our non-importation act if it be not forthwith rescinded.

The President reacted to Foster's disclosures by summoning Congress a month early. Relations were not improved by Foster's protest against American occupation of West Florida as "contrary to every principle of public justice, faith and national honor." Monroe retorted that other nations were not so scrupulous. "The President would have incurred the censure of the nation if he had suffered that province to be wrested from the United States [by England or France] under a pretext of wresting it from Spain." A reference by Monroe to undisturbed Spanish troops reflected the failure of the Mathews-McKee mission in East Florida. Angered by discovery that the President had encouraged the Baton Rouge uprising, Folch withdrew his offer to surrender Mobile and Pensacola. Madison rejected the urgings of Claiborne to oust the Spanish garrisons: he would merely hold what had been gained without bloodshed.

American relations with France, Foster reported on July 12, were extremely bad. Monroe in effect said the same to Sérurier when asked once more what was delaying the departure of Minister Barlow for Paris. The lack of good news by the *Essex*, he was told, raised such discontent that Barlow's departure would raise the cry of treason. "You know, sir, that this government is based on public opinion." Sérurier notified his government that to produce war between the United States and England it was imperative to open French markets to American commerce. As matters stood, the affairs of France were "on the verge of perishing in my hands."

In spite of the delicate situation Sérurier no longer postponed one imperative order—to induce the President to address Napoleon as "Sire" instead of "Great and Good Friend." Approaching through Barlow, whose house, "Kalorama," he had just rented, he received Madison's response that if he made this change the political opposition would "cry vassalage and . . . publish a hundred extravagances." Fortunately, Sérurier could answer "yes" to one question asked by Napoleon. Madison used the same familiar language to the King of England and the Emperor of Russia.

News came in mid-July that all American vessels sequestered in France since November 2 had been released. Cadore had resigned, succeeded by Maret, Duke of Bassano, who confirmed the release. Barlow was ordered to sail at once on the frigate *Constitution*. Public opinion, Sérurier reported, was swinging back to the administration. "More than any one else, Mr. Madison seems delighted to see himself confirmed in a system which is wholly his own," but which seemed impossible to maintain: "I have never seen him more triumphant. The Secretaries of State, of the Treasury, and of War are undecided, perhaps, and act more according to events; but happily the President, superior to them in enlightenment as in position, governs entirely by himself, and there is no reason to fear that he will be crossed by them."

It was true that Madison completely dominated the Cabinet. Gone was Monroe's hope of altering policies. Gallatin and Eustis stood by the President in spite of a mild leaning toward Great Britain. Secretary Hamilton (slipping into inebriety) displayed a personal loyalty that glossed his frailty. Attorney-General Rodney, reputedly antiwar, rejoiced at "how rapidly we are progressing as a nation."

Sérurier soon discovered that Madison was not so jubilant as he thought. Paying a farewell visit to the President before his departure for Montpelier, the minister was surprised to find that he was aware of some factors that Sérurier had been directed to conceal. The freeing of sequestered ships and cargoes was welcome, Madison said, but he was profoundly pained to discover, by a careful reading of texts, that vessels *captured at sea* after November 2 were not to be released. This failure to execute the chief engagement "destroyed the good effect of all the rest." Also, selective trade restrictions imposed by France would drain the United States of specie.

Sérurier recognized the President's pen in a *National Intelligencer* article on Foster's position, including a paragraph of "unexpected coldness" about France. This could only be explained by "the stubborness of the President as to the revocation of the decrees, and by the bad reports from the mission at Paris." The dissatisfaction was carried into Barlow's instructions. Revocation of the French decrees had been followed by other oppressive restraints. Ships sailing directly from the United States were charged with criminality or exposed to expensive delays and exorbitant duties. These, if adhered to, would produce countervailing restrictions, leaving no motive to sacrifice British trade for that of France. It was indispensable that France abandon her system of licenses; otherwise the President probably would send French consuls home. Heavy demands were to be made on France for damages inflicted under the decrees of Bayonne and Rambouillet and for the burning of American ships at sea.

The charges against France did not include lack of candor regarding the Berlin and Milan decrees. Doubt about them would have undermined the legal basis of the President's action against England. The instructions made it clear that Madison was not deceived by Napoleon; but French misconduct stemmed from the emperor's military strategy and personal shortcomings. The misconduct of England—conflicting with her military interest—seemed to deny American independence and to be aimed against the country's commercial growth. That, in Madison's mind, outweighed the infuriating outrages of Napoleon and made England's attitude the determining factor in the American choice of war or peace.

Foster was cheered by Cabinet civilities although, unfortunately, "Mr. Madison still shows asperity." He hoped, nevertheless, for a good understanding by the end of the year, provided England persisted in the threat of retaliation against the Non-Importation Act. He had urged a change of American policy by every argument he could think of but it was clear the President would "take no step upon himself." So, counting upon Madison's "known character for indecision" (known to every Federalist), he decided to ask in writing for suspension of the Non-Importation Act. "Mr. Madison," he believed, "would scarcely hazard a refusal to a demand formally made," and thus decline amity with England when the renewed aggressions of France opened the road to an understanding. The indecisive Mr. Madison sent word that even if the Non-Importation Act were extended to France, it was not his intention to remove it as to Britain unless the Orders in Council were revoked. Foster doubted that Congress would support the President in so stern a policy.

This was followed by a formal reply from Monroe which, Foster understood, "was drawn up principally by Mr. Madison himself," for effect on the public. He assailed Foster's extravagant pretension that England could continue to trade with France while excluding the United States from such trade except through England. The penalties of the Macon Act concerned only such violations of neutral commerce "as were committed on the high seas." France had fulfilled this condition; England had not. France, it was true, was interfering with American trade in the continental ports she controlled. That concerned the United States alone. It did not violate the revocation of the French decrees and did not impair the obligation of Great Britain to revoke hers.

The President left for his July-to-October sojourn at Montpelier, after summoning Congress to meet in November. He was followed by the *Federal Republican's* prediction of impeachment for high crimes and misdemeanors, to be revealed by Robert Smith, "throwing far into the shade the crimes of Charles II of England."

At Montpelier Mr. and Mrs. Madison had their first sight of the new one-story wings, under construction for months, that gave the front a 150-foot spread. Public business intruded little on the President for a month. Monroe brought papers late in August, and Jefferson came for a visit from September 2 to 5. Monroe advised the President not to return Jefferson's call, lest hostile newspapers describe it as a policymaking trip. Preferring to be governed by "personal esteem and friendship; and abide whatever may ensue," Madison drove to Monticello and witnessed on September 17 an annular eclipse of the sun.

By this time dispatches were piling up. England demanded a disavowal and reparation in the case of the *Little Belt*. Monroe was directed to repeat the denial that Rodgers had hostile orders, and to say that the United States would take no other notice of the case—"a violent aggression by a British on an American ship"—until there was a settlement of the *Chesapeake* controversy, then in its fifth year. Madison's general attitude was not softened by word that the Orders in Council were being defended as useful "in keeping down the commercial prosperity of the United States."

The *Little Belt* affair took final form late in September with the verdict of an American court of inquiry whose publication coincided with the arrival of a British verdict. The complete proceedings in London consisted of secret written statements by five minor officers who were not put on oath or asked any questions. All said that Bingham hailed twice and Rodgers started the gunfire. In the American inquiry, held in public, fifty commissioned and warrant officers testified under oath that the first shot came from the *Little Belt*. Lord Wellesley, after reading the American testimony, rebuked Foster for letting the affair delay settlement of the *Chesapeake* controversy.

Thanks to slow sailing ships and prevailing uncertainties, the President found this period the most restful of his Presidency. "We passed two months on our mountain in health and peace," wrote Dolley Madison to the Barlows, "returning the first of October to a sick and afflicted city." The unfinished Tyber Creek Canal was blamed for a fatal epidemic of bilious fever. Happily all fear ended with cold weather.

The President was in his carriage, en route to Washington, when his semiofficial mouthpiece declared (October 1, 1811) that further forbearance toward England could "scarcely fail exposing us to the imputation of pusillanimity." The remark reverberated through the country. "Every eye," commented the New York *Evening Post*, "is directed to the *National Intelligencer*, to discover some ray of light there."

Two days after Madison's arrival, the *Intelligencer* toned down its remarks concerning England. The solemn truth is, it said, that our government "will have no feelings but those of amity to her whenever she shall learn to respect our rights, and treat us as she requires all other nations to treat her." Nature had made the two nations friends and "they will again be friends, whenever the British government shall reciprocate to us our treatment of her." The thought exactly duplicated what Madison had just written to Benjamin Rush.

Madison's message to Congress blended force and conciliation. Doubting that British policies would be altered, he said that proofs of change should be met with cordiality, but immediate policies ought to be based on a contrary expectation. France, too, was pursuing a policy that might require retaliation. Under these ominous indications, the Executive had pushed harbor fortifications and recommissioned gunboats and ships of war; but "*the period is arrived*" for the legislative guardians of national rights to provide an ampler system for maintaining them. In spite of multiplied efforts to re-establish friendship the British Cabinet was enforcing measures which had the character and effect of war on our lawful commerce: "With this evidence of hostile inflexibility in trampling on rights which no independent nation can relinquish, Congress will feel the duty of putting the United States into an armor and an attitude demanded by the crisis, and corresponding with the national spirit and expectations."

Recommendations followed: to fill up the existing army, raise an auxiliary force, accept volunteers, summon part of the militia and prepare the rest, develop the military academies, enlarge military supplies, stockpile naval materials, and consider such provisions for the naval force "as may be required." Congress also should protect shipping against foreign discrimination, thereby providing "a growing body of mariners trained by their occupations for the service of their country in times of danger."

The conditional language concerning the Navy has sometimes been construed as evidence of disinterest. It was in fact phrased to avoid stirring the long-existing prejudice against high naval power. On the subject of the navy, Sérurier wrote in September, "the opinion of the Executive Power is not in doubt. It wants a Navy, but wants it on a larger scale than it is today." To promote that objective, the government was stimulating nationwide debate "by way of its newspaper," on the question: "Does it suit the Republic to have a navy" and if so should it not be "such as can make the American flag respected?" This "questioning and deferential form" was chosen, Sérurier said, so as not to excite the jealousy of the states over federal power. The *Intelligencer* was still publishing responses, all but one affirmative, when Congress reassembled.

Press reaction to the message placed only the toughest Federalists in opposition. The President had firmly and coolly done his duty, said the Richmond *Enquirer;* it was for Congress to do theirs. The Baltimore *Federal Republican* accused him of overcoloring British misconduct and ignoring the most obvious injuries received from France. "Forlorn and gloomy is our prospect."

Major General Andrew Jackson rejoiced to his Tennessee militiamen that the President had taken a "firm and manly stand" to preserve national honor and independence. William Plumer, who once thought Madison fearful and timid, cast off that idea with his abandoned Federalism. In this document, he wrote, the federal camp "must see a refutation of their groundless charge so often reiterated against the President, that he is nerve-less and his measures pusillanimous. His message does him and the nation honor." John Adams, now a man of no party, saw "great honor to the President, to his minister and ambassadors" in the message and accompanying documents.

Sérurier weighed the popular response and reported a unanimous verdict: "The message is considered . . . as equivalent to a declaration of war on Great Britain." A few days later he reported the impression on Congress. All parties except the English "say that never has the government assumed a language and an attitude more worthy. They talk boldly of war, if the dispatches from Mr. Barlow are satisfactory."

The message as originally written was still more militant toward Great Britain. Gallatin, to whom the draft was submitted, preferred continuation of nonintercourse. He argued that "the measures necessary to carry on the war must be unpopular and by producing a change of men [Madison's defeat in 1812] may lead to a disgraceful peace" and absolute subservience to Great Britain. Also, he doubted whether the Constitution authorized the President to adopt a tone on war that might influence Congress, in whom the power of declaring it was vested. Comparison of the first and final drafts reveals that the President dropped a request for authority to make reprisals and softened "direct and undisguised hostility" to "hostile inflexibility." The fundamental alternatives stayed in it: cessation of attacks on commerce, or war.

British Minister Foster regretted that the President said nothing about his new offer of *Chesapeake* reparations. The settlement, accepted on November 12 and announced to Congress next day, was a virtual duplicate of the one repudiated by the British Cabinet.

Madison had little confidence that Congress would respond to his call for military preparations. Measures of resistance, he predicted to John Quincy Adams, would be put off until the close of the session, except for a license to merchantmen to arm in self-defense. Arming them "can scarcely fail to bring on war in its full extent unless such an evidence of the disposition of the United States to prefer war to submission should arrest the cause of it."

Monroe told both the British and French ministers that the President's disposition was unyielding. The government had lost every illusion as to repeal of the Orders in Council, and it would not retreat. Now that the French decrees were repealed, the coming military measures could strike only at England. Monroe declared (Sérurier reported) that the administration in taking this resolution had seen perfectly where it would lead—"he regarded war as well nigh decided."

President Madison, talking with Foster, remarked that anything was better than remaining in the present state of things. Could they not hope, Foster asked, for a solution without a sacrifice of principle? The President avowed "his sincere desire that so salutary an object could be brought about." There would be no sacrifice of principle in the "indispensable preliminary." The Orders in Council must first be withdrawn, because "he must consider the French decrees as revoked as far as Great Britain had a right to expect America should require their revocation." Napoleon's Continental System, which excluded British goods from the countries he controlled, was not a measure that America was bound to resist.

After this talk the President directed Monroe to make a clarifying restatement, even though he was told to say "governments on the eve of being at variance did not usually disclose their intentions." The United States government "could not recede from the ground they had taken, neither was it probable they would remain as they were, war now existing in fact on the one side since the revocation of the French decrees, and not on the other." Foster committed their lengthy talk to writing and submitted it to Monroe to be sure of accuracy. The Secretary asked that several expressions be altered to remove "the idea of menaces to either France or England," or of such strong complaints about France.

Since this appeared to modify what the President himself had said, Foster made another ostensibly social visit to the White House. Madison, he reported, "said explicitly that America would never acquiesce in the Orders in Council," and declared that Great Britain would be the loser even if she gained every point—an English market glutted with American goods would not provide the means for American purchase of British goods. He "darkly hinted" at British motives (trade monopoly) but would not discuss them out of respect to the British government. Foster asked Madison what he had done about the abominable treatment received from France. "He again assured me . . . that America would certainly ask what she had a right to claim of France, but he said if the ruler of France was to burn and destroy every American ship and article in the European ports, this would not be a reason for the interference of England."

America by herself, Madison asserted, would obtain justice from France and would not blend it with what she had a right to claim of England. Foster asked about the arming of merchantmen—an uncontrollable hazard to peace. In ordinary times, the President replied, "nothing was to be more deprecated," but the times were extraordinary. However, the President led Foster to suppose "that nothing would arise to make a serious change in our relations before the return of the *Hornet*."

This was a crucial talk. The distinction Madison drew between measures against England and France was legal, not political. The President had just written privately to Barlow that proceedings against England would be greatly influenced by the French choice between "crafty contrivance and insatiate cupidity," and "open, manly and upright dealing with a nation whose example demands it." The licentiousness of French privateers in the Baltic was kindling a fresh flame, and were it not for the risk of a clash with the British Navy, he would not scruple to send some frigates to the Baltic to suppress French and Danish depredations.

Madison's remark about awaiting the return of the *Hornet* was equivalent to saying, in November 1811, that there would be no decision for war or peace before April or May 1812. Aside from the President and Secretary of State, Foster drew his American impressions almost entirely from Federalist congressmen. In December he sent a forecast which, if acted on by London, would make war inevitable:

> It is the opinion of most of the sensible men here that this government will not be pushed into a war with us, but that their object is to secure the support of their party at the next election of a President by obtaining the credit of having forced us to a change of system by the line of conduct they have adopted. . . . To judge from present indications there never was a more favorable moment for Great Britain to impose almost what terms she pleases upon the United States, provided an appearance of conciliation be exhibited.

Foster sent that report to London just after clearsighted Sérurier wrote to Bassano: "Only the recall of the Orders in Council can now prevent war. I do not doubt that Mr. Foster has advised his government of this." He wrote it just after Dolley Madison wrote to her sister: "I believe there will be war. Mr. Madison sees no end to the perplexities without it."

Had the President known of Foster's dispatches, it might have altered a decision that magnified the effect of the British minister's incompetence. Although England had restored her representation to the ministerial level, Madison decided not to send an American minister to London (Foster was told) as long as Britain was warring on American commerce. That was a bold pressure move, but results depended on the accuracy of Foster's reports. In actual effect, it deprived the President of the only means—presence of a topnotch diplomat in London—by which governmental contacts might have led to peace-preserving negotiations.

Dolley Madison's statement that the President expected war ended with the prediction that Congress "will sit until June." Combined with Madison's intention to wait for the *Hornet*'s return in April or May, and the need to bring the merchant fleet into port, that virtually marked June as the time for a beginning of hostilities. At the time this was written (December 20, 1811) there had been no conspicuous effect from a huge change in the personnel of Congress. The Senate was much the same, but feeling against submissiveness to foreign powers sent sixty-three new members to a House that totaled 140. They swelled mightily the element known as War Hawks, who elected as speaker Henry Clay of Kentucky, now in the House after one year in the Senate.

Men of all parties were inflamed against France, but the Republicans lacked the partiality for England that turned the Federalists into anti-Gallic fanatics. Economic interest heightened the division. New England shipowners were growing rich carrying flour to the British armies in Portugal or trading from England to French-controlled ports under British license.

Madison's political party shared his feeling that Britain's war on trade menaced the development of the United States. Ancient antagonisms made every seizure of American seamen a personal and national degradation. The spirit of territorial imperialism, which threatened New England's political and economic power, ran high in the West and South. It was primary as to Florida, secondary as to Canada, which was looked upon as a source of arms and incitement to northwestern Indian tribes.

The House divided Madison's message into nine parts and referred them to seven select and two standing committees. This enabled Speaker Clay to ignore seniority and put foreign relations, military, and naval affairs into militant hands. In the Senate the Giles-Leib-Smith cabal linked up with the Federalists and Vice President Clinton and delivered those three subjects to a single anti-Madison committee headed by Giles.

Madison and Clay held almost identical views regarding foreign policy. In August 1811, Clay had written to Attorney-General Rodney that if Britain persisted in her Orders in Council "and France is honest and sincere in her recent measures, I look upon war with Great Britain [as] inevitable." Madison more than once said the same but with less regard to French policy. Rodney resigned late in the year—unwilling to move to Washington and give up his Wilmington law practice. Appointment of William Pinkney to succeed him gave the President a firm defender of his policies and staunch political backer without the necessity of moving from nearby Baltimore.

Just as this change took place news came that General William Henry Harrison, sent to protect western settlers from the Shawnee "Prophet," had been treacherously attacked before dawn in front of the Prophet's Town, losing 20 per cent of his thousand men. At dawn the troops charged through and burned the town. This was the famous battle whose chanted fame put "Tippecanoe and Tyler too" successively in the White House. More slowly came the true story: that Harrison advanced fifty miles into Indian territory which Madison forbade him to enter; camped in a menacing posture without taking adequate precautions; had his troops cut to pieces, and then burned the Indian village after it had been evacuated. These trivialities were not known when the President praised "the dauntless spirit and fortitude" of the troops and "the collected firmness which distinguished their commander."

On November 29 Chairman Peter B. Porter presented a report on foreign relations that was completed after three conferences with Secretary Monroe. It added "the unhappy case of our impressed seamen" to the causes of war given in the President's message and advised six military measures already called for by him. Principally, the army should be brought up to its authorized level of ten thousand, an equal number of additional regulars enlisted and fifty thousand volunteers accepted. Congressman John Harper, one of New Hampshire's five new Hawks, told what went on in committee: "The *motives*, the *views* and the *wishes* of the Executive were made known to us through an *official* organ . . . I feel no hesitation in saying that the present session will not be closed, without an *arrangement*, or an actual *war* with Great Britain."

Richard M. Johnson of Kentucky, Madison's closest friend on the committee, reported the Executive "pledged for war if Great Britain should not recede." Felix Grundy of Tennessee wrote to Andrew Jackson that the committee was unwilling to act until assured of presidential approval, and William Lowndes of South Carolina spelled that out: "Mr. Monroe has given the strongest assurances that the President will co-operate zealously with Congress in declaring war, if our complaints are not redressed by May next."

The record as revealed in the British, French, and American archives, the papers of Madison, and the words of militant members of Congress, totally refutes the historical picture of the President as a passive observer or helpless opponent of congressional policies. The May date specified by Monroe gives the key to Madison's thought. Desiring peace but believing war to be inevitable, he guided Congress toward that event and stimulated preparation for it, while restraining a declaration in hope that the *Hornet* would bring final means of a peaceable accommodation.

Chairman Porter, opening debate on the committee report, presented the same policy in a far different tone. England's "miserable shifts and evasions" were such that the committee would ultimately recommend war unless England repealed her Orders in Council and did something satisfactory about impressment. Porter trusted that "the howlings of newspapers" would not push Congress into hostilities before the nation was ready.

Randolph leaped to his feet with an attack on the army as ten thousand vagabonds, pickpockets, and mercenaries picked up from brothels. Were Republicans to become instruments of Bonaparte, "who had effaced the title of Attila to the 'Scourge of God' "? Richard Johnson asked the House to look at Madison's message: "I feel rejoiced that the hour of resistance is at hand, and that the President, in whom the people have so much confidence, has warned us of the perils that await them, and has exhorted us to put on the armor of defense, to gird on the sword, and assume the manly and bold attitude of war."

John C. Calhoun spoke in similar vein: American rights were attacked, and war was the only means of redress. Middle-ground Republicans supported the military measures while rejecting the seeming inference of Calhoun and Porter that the report committed the nation to war. All proposals were approved by heavy majorities.

In the Senate Chairman Giles let six weeks go by without action, then assailed the President's proposals as far too weak. He wished to protect Mr. Madison (he said amidst Federalist laughter) against the aspersions of a Quebec writer of newspaper doggerel. He then read the whole "poem," pitting the President's "syllogisms" and "abstract rights" against the "three-deckers" of the British Navy. To protect New Orleans against a surrender by the President, Giles declared with mock alarm, Canada must be invaded at once. Giles and Smith helped the antiwar Federalists and confused Republicans carry a motion to enlarge the army to 35,000 men.

Senate and House fought for a month before adopting the Giles program on January 11. The President, Sérurier reported, now had authority to raise 35,000 men with no funds to enlist, arm, or clothe them. Federalists voted for the program in hope that the resulting taxes would lead to Madison's downfall. Nevertheless, said the minister, "Everything moves toward war with greater rapidity than was to be expected from this government." Congress was supporting the Executive, and "public opinion blazes out everywhere in favor of his system."

Taking up the bill for 50,000 volunteers, the House wrangled for weeks over the constitutional power of the President to order such troops onto foreign soil. Madison prodded the lawmakers with late correspondence with Foster and a one-sentence covering message: The continued "hostile policy of the British government against our national rights, strengthens the . . . [need] of adequate means for maintaining them." Separately, the President reported that 6,200 impressed American seamen were held by force in the British Navy. The bill for 50,000 volunteers passed, weakened by terms implying that they were militiamen, hence ineligible to foreign service. The House's supporting appropriation of $3 million was cut to one-third of that in the Senate. Madison described the general conduct of Congress: "With a view to enable the Executive to step at once into Canada they have provided, after two months delay, for a regular force requiring twelve [months] to raise it, and after three months for a volunteer force, on terms not likely to raise it at all for that object."

Madison's comment disclosed the intended war strategy. He wanted a small army, speedily raised, to make an immediate occupation of Halifax and Quebec, before the tiny British garrisons in Canada could be reinforced. Canada would then be held hostage for a speedy and satisfactory peace.

Having met its military responsibility in this fashion Congress turned to the Naval Establishment, for which Secretary Hamilton had submitted the administration's program on December 3. Hamilton asked for the construction of twelve 74-gun ships of the line and ten frigates in addition to the ten already in being, five of which should be reconditioned.

The committee on Naval Affairs, headed by Langdon Cheves of South Carolina, recommended ten frigates but submitted the ship-of-the-line request without opinion, accompanied by Hamilton's letter. When the report was taken up late in January, War Hawk Republicans split down the middle. Land-militants from the West joined traditional anti-navalists and eastern economizers. At this point Secretary Gallatin submitted a report on war costs that threw Congress into a panic. Estimating total cost at $50 million, he advised raising $3 million in direct taxes and $2 million in additional excises, the remainder to be borrowed at the rate of $10 million a year.

The tumult grew louder with Gallatin's revelation that in the first year of restored trade, exports to Great Britain and her satellite-allies, Spain and Portugal, totaled $38.5 million; those to France and vassal Italy only $1,194,000. The House voted down every proposed number of new frigates—ten, six, five, four, three—and then struck out the whole authorization, 62 to 59, overriding Federalists and seaboard war men.

That left the Navy with five frigates in commission, five awaiting heavy repairs. The Senate cut out two-thirds of the repair appropriation and limited the work to the *Chesapeake*, the *Constellation* and the *Adams*. The House then defeated a bill to arm and classify the militia.

From the President's language and that held in Congress, Foster advised London, "it would almost appear that hostilities actually existed between America and England." That, however, did not mean anything. Madison was merely adapting his tone to that of the War Hawks (so said the *Federal Republican*), and Federalist leaders assured Foster that they would do no more pushing for war. (That is, they felt that they had hooked Madison on war costs.) Ship insurance had not risen— a fact "of itself sufficient to show how little in earnest the government are supposed to be." Had Foster been gifted with the slightest acumen, he would have seen that Congress was going pell mell in two directions—toward a declaration of war and away from the responsibility of waging it—a combination that made nothing certain except war itself.

Madison's eyes were on Westminster as well as the Capitol. The Prince of Wales, reputedly friendly to America, was now Regent. His first action—a noncommittal reply to an appeal for American trade— was construed by Madison to indicate adherence to the Orders in Council. A talk with the President on that subject persuaded Federalist Senator Bayard of Delaware "that we shall have the war, not instantly but before the year goes round." Within a fortnight the Prince Regent's address to Parliament confirmed the President's appraisal. Conciliation must be consistent "with the due maintenance of the maritime and commercial rights and interests of the British Empire."

From Barlow came mildly optimistic reports concerning a new commercial treaty, which he was discussing with Jean-Baptiste Petry. Federalists who decried the Connecticut poet as an impractical visionary and worshiper of France would not have recognized Petry's account of him. "My first talks with Mr. Barlow yielded me nothing," he wrote to Bassano. "I thought that with a man so cold, who seemed to me to wish to know the ground on which he stood, I should place long intervals between my visits, in order to show him that, like him . . . I was not governed by desire and curiosity to learn his secrets."

Madison told Barlow to work for a reduction of French tariffs. Also, the system of licenses must be abolished. The present footing of commerce was intolerable. Trade "will be prohibited, if no essential change takes place."

Monroe pointed out to Sérurier the thirteen-to-one discrepancy in trade with England and France. To renounce so great a market, and induce a peaceful trading people to pay war taxes, it was necessary to present them with very real advantages. Instead, France was still holding American ships and capturing more. The French minister, in reply, complained of the cold, laconic article in the *National Intelligencer* announcing the arrival of the *Constitution* with dispatches. It would have been imprudent, Monroe answered, to announce anything without certainty. Sérurier explained to his government the status of this Madisonian organ: "The *National Intelligencer* is the official newspaper. It is not avowed as such by the government, but it has all the characteristics of it and is so used. It is edited by a man wholly in the hands of the President, and the greater part of its articles on political relations and other great subjects come to it from the Department of State, or have been examined there."

Late in February Foster panicked and wrote to Wellesley that if Britain made no concession "war may ensue in the course of a fortnight." A week later he sent directions in quintuplicate to disregard the warning. He had learned (from Federalists) that the administration was trying to induce England to strike the first blow and thereby "enable this government to raise an army." On that same day (March 6), the President wrote to Jefferson that the House of Representatives had swallowed "the dose of taxes—strong proof that they do not mean to flinch from the contest to which the mad conduct of Great Britain drives them."

The rumor of "war in a fortnight" was connected, undoubtedly, with spreading reports about the Count de Crillon, "son of the celebrated Count de Crillon," who arrived with a letter to Madison from Governor Gerry of Massachusetts. The count, described as "a thick-set man, monstrous thick legs," almost bald and heavily bearded, dined at the White House on January 30. He went to see Sérurier, presenting a letter from the Duke of Istria, hero of Austerlitz. He showed copies of letters held by British Captain John Henry who, he said, was hiding in Washington. Henry would deliver them to the government for "certain pecuniary advantages." Sérurier sent the count to Monroe. Report seeped through the city that Madison was to send a special message on the subject. He did so on March 9.

The impact of the message can be gauged by an incident recorded by Sérurier. Presidential Secretary Edward Coles, leaving the Capitol, ran across A. St. John Baker, British Secretary of Legation, who asked him what the message was about. "Nothing," answered Coles, "just the communication of the correspondence of a man named Henry." "With whom," gasped the horrified Baker, "with Sir James Craig?" "There you are," responded Coles with a profound bow.

Madison's brief message set forth that while the United States was peaceably negotiating with Erskine in 1809, the British government employed a secret agent to foment disaffection in Massachusetts and other states, with the aim, eventually, of destroying the Union and connecting the Eastern states with Great Britain. The documents included the "most secret" instructions of Governor Craig of Canada, numerous reports by Henry of his 1809 subversive activities, and a batch of 1811 letters covering his futile efforts to collect the promised reward.

Federalists had been calling Crillon an impostor—which he was, and a clever one, his aim being to swindle Henry. His letter from the Duke of Istria was forged, but Captain Henry's documents were not open to question. To obtain them the State Department paid $50,000. "Crillon," who was actually a gambler named Soubiron, got nearly all of the money from Henry by selling him an imaginary French estate. The two men left the country on different ships, Henry sailing toward disillusionment, Soubiron to a French dungeon.

The fantastic facts about "Crillon" developed too slowly to diminish the sensation of the "Henry letters." As they were read in Congress, Federalists squirmed in agony, but they had one consolation. The letters, replete with proof of disaffection, did not name a single American. By the President's order, *all names were erased.* Sérurier explained the suppression: The administration "sees only the crime of the foreigner." If any citizens are guilty, "it hopes this warning will suffice for them," and that all Americans will "see in this fortunate discovery only reasons for coming together and reuniting against the common enemy."

After their initial dismay the Federalists were infuriated. All but one of them boycotted the next White House levee, but that produced such an outpouring of Republicans on the following Wednesday that (wrote Dolley) the Federalists were "alarmed into a return." Nothing in the entire session, reported Congressman Harper, had mortified the

Federalists more than "finding that the Republicans, in consequence of their conduct, paid their respects to Mr. Madison almost to a man." The Henry letters, in spite of the "Crillon" fiasco, gave deliberately planned impetus to the many forces that were bringing the country to the brink of war.

On Sunday morning, March 15, 1812, one week after Madison submitted the Henry papers, Secretary Monroe and Speaker Clay met for a strategy decision. Later in the day Clay put two propositions on paper: "That the President recommend an embargo to last say 30 days, by a confidential message. That a termination of the embargo be followed by war."

The ultimate decision, wrote the Speaker in his covering letter, need not be absolute. "By the expiration of the embargo," needed to bring American property under shelter, "the *Hornet* will have returned with good or bad news and of course the question of war may then be fairly decided." He then dealt with Madison's feeling that constitutional principles did not permit him to press for a declaration of war: "Although the power of declaring war belongs to Congress I do not see that it falls less within the scope of the President's constitutional duty to recommend such measures as he shall judge necessary and expedient, than any other which being suggested by him they alone can adopt."

The correspondence does not indicate whether the move for a prewar embargo originated with Clay or the President. It does establish that Monroe knew Madison's attitude. Without consultation, he was able to lay down Madison's condition as to the *Hornet* and present the point of constitutional authority.

Within a week London and Paris furnished dark news. England, Foster stated, intended to keep on searching American ships at sea. Arming them would be likely "to produce the calamity of war." Asked to put that statement in writing, Foster refused. The effect was visible in Sérurier's dispatch next day. All available troops were being sent to the Canadian frontier, artillery assembled for the defense of New York, and they were talking "of an embargo which will be ordered in a week . . . as the indispensable preliminary to the declaration of war" that depended on the return of the *Hornet*.

The next day (March 23) produced the deposition of a ship captain who brought home the crews of two American ships burned at sea. The French commander told the captain that he had orders to destroy all vessels bound to or from Lisbon. Sérurier quoted Monroe: "Well sir, it is then decided that we are to receive nothing but outrages from France!" The administration, he said, used Henry's documents to arouse the nation and Congress. "Within a week we were going to propose the embargo . . . to carry the declaration of war, and it would have passed almost unanimously."

It was at such a moment, said the "agitated and discomposed" Secretary, "that your frigates have just burned our ships, destroyed all our work, and put the administration in the most false and terrible position in which a government can find itself placed." Monroe, Sérurier commented, often exaggerated his griefs, and he doubted whether the President would draw back from the course in which he was so deeply engaged. That was a correct forecast. In an editorial described by Foster as a substitute for a presidential message, the *National Intelligencer* said there was no hope of expecting Britain to respect American rights "except at the cannon's mouth": "Let us then no longer deceive ourselves; the period is arrived when the rights and honor of our country must be asserted by an appeal to arms, or ignominiously surrendered to the dictation of a foreign power."

"The period is arrived" was from the President's annual message. Madison's intention to press for the embargo was evidenced in Dolley's March 27 note to Anna Cutts in Maine: "Where are your husband's vessels? And why does he not get them in?" On the thirty-first Monroe appeared before the House Committee on Foreign Affairs. John Randolph recorded his words: "the President thought we ought to declare war before we adjourn, unless Great Britain recedes, of which there was no prospect." Would he recommend that by message? "He would, if he could be assured it would be acceptable to the House. . . . the unprepared state of the country was the only reason why ultimate measures should be deferred."

On April 1, President Madison asked for immediate passage of a general embargo law, to be laid for sixty days "on all vessels now in port, or hereafter arriving." Barely taking time to leave the chamber, the House Committee on Foreign Affairs presented a bill that emanated, it said, from the Secretary of the Treasury.

Questioned about the purpose, Speaker Clay and Felix Grundy both called it a measure meant to lead directly to war. Clay "felt a pride that the Executive had recommended this measure." Randolph promptly denied that the embargo was a measure of the Executive. It had been engendered on him "by an extensive excitement." It was a retreat from the battle. There would be no war because "the Executive dare not plunge the nation into a war in our unprepared state." He would not "be guilty of such gross and unparalleled treason."

This assault was answered by John Smilie of Pennsylvania, described by Foster as the member "most in the confidence of the President." He had heard "but one sentiment from the President, which is *that we must make war* unless Great Britain relents. The President had always supposed that the embargo must precede war. . . . the embargo is intended as a war measure." Madison said the same to Jefferson two days later.

The House passed the bill on the day it received Madison's message. The Senate lengthened the embargo to ninety days, and Madison signed the bill into law three days after he asked for it. The lengthening, he said, proceeded from those who wished to make it a negotiating measure, those who wished to put off war as long as possible, and a few who hoped for a declaration of war by surprise before the embargo expired.

In the bitterness of defeat, Randolph threw the full blame onto the President he had pretended to regard as a victim of War Hawk coercion. It had been demonstrated once more that the Executive could "indisputably carry his measures in Congress . . . The President of the United States for fourteen years has been omnipotent."

Monroe, queried by Foster, deprecated the embargo "being considered as a war measure." Foster went to see Madison and expressed pleasure at Monroe's comment. He answered, "Oh no, Embargo is not war," but the United States would be amply justified in going to war because "Great Britain was actually waging war upon them." He then offered England one more way out. If Foster's government would stop defending the Orders in Council as measures of retaliation, and turn to *a complete blockade* of the enemy's dominions as a measure of self-preservation, an effective appeal might be made to American public opinion.

Foster failed to realize that "Embargo is not war" was a correction of Monroe's use of the term, not an agreement with it. Nor did he grasp the fact that by a *complete blockade* Madison meant a *completely effective* blockade, not a paper one. In consequence, he advised London that the embargo was a presidential measure of which the nation would soon weary, and all that the President wanted from England was a mere change in the name of the Orders in Council. The whole thing was presidential politics. Whatever would secure the re-election of Mr. Madison, from war to reconciliation, "will be recommended by the government," and the session of Congress would probably wind up with repeal of the Non-Intercourse Act. If Foster wanted to make war absolutely inevitable, that dispatch echoing Federalist chatter ought to perform the trick.

The impulse toward war was checked momentarily by a report published in London that France was forcibly detaining the *Hornet*. That being disproved by a Barlow dispatch, the *National Intelligencer* carried a clarion call for "open and manly war." The wrongs of the nation were great; its cause was just; France could be dealt with later: "Let war therefore be forthwith proclaimed against England. With her there can be no motive for delay. Any further discussion, any new attempt at negotiation, would be as fruitless as it would be dishonorable."

Those words produced a national sensation. The New York *Evening Post* gave "Mr. Speaker" the credit of authorship. "Depend on it, it is *not* the language of the cabinet." Foster, also ascribing it to Clay, wrote that "it was supposed that the government by no means approved of the language of excitement that had been used."

These reports planted a belief, widely accepted by historians, that Clay seized national leadership from Madison and dragooned the President into acceptance of war as the price of renomination. The editorial actually was written by Secretary of State Monroe. The working draft of it lies in his papers, heavily interlined with changes that brought it to its published wording.

The exhortation that war be "forthwith proclaimed against England" was designed to halt a move to repeal nonimportation and check the talk of "two wars or none," occasioned by the conduct of France. Madison followed it with a request that Congress provide the War Department with two assistant secretaries. Its total personnel consisted of the Secretary and six clerks, all overloaded with work. Federalists assailed Eustis as incompetent; War Hawk Republicans praised his "zeal, ability and industry," asking where was the individual who could carry such a load. The bill passed both houses, but Senator Leib killed it by securing postponement of a House amendment.

The President and Secretary Eustis, by this time, had chosen high army officers. In doing so they faced a dilemma. Twenty years of virtual disarmament forced them to select either Revolutionary veterans of low rank or young officers of similar rank and no battle experience. They chose age and prestige, partly to help recruiting. Major Generals Dearborn and Thomas Pinckney were placed above Brigadier Generals Wilkinson, Wade Hampton, and Peter Gansevoort.

New brigadiers were former Governor Joseph Bloomfield of New Jersey, Governor William Hull of Michigan Territory, and Tennessee Indian-fighter James Winchester. These eight generals ranged in age from fifty-eight to sixty-two. They ranged in *wartime* rank from captain to lieutenant colonel. Former Governor Morgan Lewis of New York was picked for quartermaster general. For adjutant general Madison wanted General William North, trained under Baron Steuben, but Federalists persuaded him to reject the offer.

The President had other troubles. General Mathews in his East Florida mission was "playing a strange comedy, in the face of common sense, as well as of his instructions. His extravagances place us in the most distressing dilemma." (This to Jefferson.) Mathews had been instructed that if he discovered a disposition in Governor Folch or the existing local authority "amicably to surrender that province into the possession of the United States," he was to accept it on terms prescribed. In case of an attempt by foreign forces to take possession, he was to pre-occupy the territory and exclude the invaders. Mathews mistook palmetto fronds for the local authority, and proceeded to sweep the province with two hundred American adventurers. A Georgia expatriate, J. H. McIntosh, who had eight followers, issued a declaration of independence. Commodore Campbell, commanding gunboats in the boundary river, misconstrued the instructions to Mathews and gave him backing. The Spanish commander surrendered the province as far south as the St. John's River, and McIntosh's revolutionary government ceded that area to the United States.

Madison discharged Mathews and turned his powers and duties over to Governor D. B. Mitchell of Georgia, with instructions to restore the occupied territory to Spain, subject to assurances of no reprisals against Florida inhabitants. But as war with England drew nearer and the danger of British invasion of Florida heightened, Madison ordered Mitchell to remain unless he could withdraw with safety to the inhabitants. This was a virtual directive to hold the occupied territory.

More disturbing to the President was Jefferson's report that the embargo had caught Virginia (also Pennsylvania) farmers with much of their wheat, flour, and tobacco unmarketed. A clamor for peace would result if war came without a foreign market for farm produce. Madison replied that "in a state of war, the Spanish and Portuguese flags and papers, real or counterfeit, will afford a neutral cover to our produce," as far as needed. In other words, farmers would be held in line by supplying Wellington's armies.

Madison probably was not so explicit when the French minister described American ships burned at sea as "floating warehouses of the English army." Unfortunately, he wrote, "the President and his cabinet refused to see all this as I did." Another angle was presented in Massachusetts, where Federalists were sweeping the spring elections on a charge that the embargo was not a war measure but a ruinous instrument of economic coercion. The *Intelligencer* took up both subjects in a string of editorials concerning which Minister Foster wrote: "Bayard told me that he knew it for a fact positive that the President (Madison) furnished the articles."

No doubt Madison outlined them, but the language is identifiable as Monroe's. They stamped it as "undoubted truth, that the Embargo is meant to be the precursor of war," and war would ensue as soon as physical resources permitted unless the British government evinced a very different temper. Again through Monroe and the *Intelligencer*, the President gave notice that it would be futile to attempt to intimidate the government by reprisals in the coming presidential campaign: "What has the Presidential Election to do with avenging our wrongs? If they call for energetic measures, and if energetic measures require united councils, let us without dissension take the attitude the times demand, and settle afterwards, as we please, who shall be our next President. But let us, in the meantime, distrust the man who blends these topics."

This article, published May 5, took account of a rumor that President Madison had attempted to send Senator Bayard to London as a peace emissary but was thwarted by Clay and other War Hawks, who called on the President and forced him to agree to a declaration of war as a condition to renomination. The story was rendered absurd by Bayard's reaction to the May 5 article. "When the President has made the war," he commented bitterly next day, "I presume Congress will not be too modest to declare it."

The story was tied to the unusually late date of the congressional caucus for nomination of candidates. That delay, however, was caused by uncertainty concerning the two Clintons. Would ailing George Clinton seek another term as Vice President? If not, would DeWitt Clinton accept that nomination or seek the Presidency? George Clinton settled it for himself by dying on April 21. His nephew kept silent while henchmen boomed him for President.

The selection of a candidate actually did not depend on the congressional caucus. DeWitt Clinton had no chance unless Pennsylvania supported him. Madison's nomination was made certain on March 7, when the Republicans of the Pennsylvania legislature, following the February example of Virginia, selected a solid slate of Madisonian electors. Governor Snyder (whom Madison coerced into obeying a Supreme Court edict) led the way with a toast at the pre-caucus dinner: "The present will be the next President of the United States." The Philadelphia *Democratic Press* saw nothing reluctant about Madison's adherence to a militant policy: "We venture to say that there is not an individual in the United States more disgusted with our wrongs, or more resolved to avenge and terminate them by war, than the distinguished person at the head of the government . . . The mild Mr. Madison is as determined and straight-forward a statesman as any country can boast."

Republican members of Congress caucused on May 18. The result: "For James Madison, 82, no other person being voted for." Most New Yorkers stayed away. Ten other absentees put themselves on record for Madison. Elbridge Gerry of Massachusetts was put up for Vice President after John Langdon declined because of age. On May 29 New York Republican legislators, at a meeting of which only supporters of DeWitt Clinton were notified, presented him as the state's choice for President. The Federalists had still to decide whether to support Clinton or put forward a ticket of their own. The only certainty, they assured Minister Foster, was the defeat of the President. Those out of power could "hold out what prospects they please of relief to the people," while Madison must either lose the North by going to war or lose the South by failing to do so.

Part VI

Citing the distress of farmers and millers, opponents of the embargo launched a repeal campaign midway of its sixty-day life. An Albany petition signed by 800 citizens touched off the debate on May 6. How could the embargo be the precursor of war? asked Federalist Hermanus Bleecker of New York. "Where are your armies? your navy? Have you money?" To John Randolph the talk of war was a pretense for restoring Jefferson's celebrated embargo—"pork still, without even changing the sauce." What! Go to war when Congress had not courage to lay taxes? "The people will not believe it." Calhoun denounced Randolph's insinuation that the embargo was "*engendered* from a fortuitous concourse" between the Executive and the Committee of Foreign Relations. "No, sir, it was not engendered, but adopted by both the Executive and committee, from its manifest propriety as a prelude to war."

Madison, according to Augustus Foster, took this occasion to spread reports "that neutral flags will be allowed to come to trade in the American ports, and the surplus produce of the country be thus enabled to find a vent whatever course affairs may take." This meant, wrote Foster, that American ships would be allowed to trade in wartime under the flag of Portugal. Thus, at a time when mythologians pictured Madison as resisting War Hawk pressure, he was actually making it easier for hardpressed Middlestate congressmen to vote for war.

What the President wanted was a firm assurance that if he asked for a declaration of war, Congress would declare it. That assurance he obtained, apparently on May 13, on which day the House passed a resolution calling upon all absent members to return "forthwith." On that evening Harper of New Hampshire sent a detailed forecast of future events to William Plumer: "The great question will undoubtedly be taken early in June. The President probably will send an important and very argumentative message to Congress. A manifesto will be brought forward by the Committee of Foreign Relations and a declaration that 'war exists' between the United States and the crown of Great Britain and its dependencies."

That forecast was correct in every detail. The preliminaries to it were described forty years later by Editor Joseph Gales of the *Intelligencer*. The President, Gales wrote, hesitated to ask for a declaration of war "not from any backwardness on his part . . . but deterred by a remaining doubt in his mind as to the House sustaining the Executive." After a private conference "a deputation of members of Congress, with Mr. Clay at their head, waited upon the President, and . . . [assured him] of the readiness of a majority of Congress to vote the war if recommended."

Foster inferentially confirmed this on May 15. The government was diligently spreading intimations of having reached "a final decision to declare war against England if the majority will support them." Sérurier wrote one day earlier that the Executive and Foreign Relations Committee "profess loudly in concert" that they only awaited the *Hornet*'s arrival to propose a declaration of war. In the meantime the opposing party in Congress "grows daily more insolent and more numerous and the cries of commerce more resounding."

The long-awaited *Hornet* glided into New York harbor on May 19 and brought—nothing. Barlow, after holding the vessel four months, merely sent her home when the *Wasp* reached France. The vessel did indeed bring indecisive dispatches which, the President observed to Jefferson, rebutted the allegation that the French decrees were not revoked; but in other respects French conduct "betrays the design of leaving Great Britain a pretext for enforcing her Orders in Council." This made the business truly puzzling: "To go to war with England and not with France arms the Federalists with new matter, and divides the Republicans . . . To go to war against both presents a thousand difficulties, above all, that of shutting off the ports of Europe against our cruisers [privateers] who can do little without the use of them."

Moreover, the President added, a "triangular war as it is called" was unlikely to bring over the Federalists, who would turn all these difficulties against the administration. The faint hope of peace flickered a little when Foster on May 27 asked for an appointment with Monroe to convey exceedingly important information. It turned out to be a dispatch from Foreign Secretary Castlereagh which (to block "trick, falsehood and artifice") Foster allowed Monroe to show to the President but not to copy. With it was a report by Bassano to Napoleon pointing to the exemption of the United States from the decrees of

Berlin and Milan; but even if the exemption was genuine, Castlereagh continued, the United States had "not a pretense" for demanding repeal of the Orders in Council. England never had offered to repeal her orders as applied to the United States even though France did so: "What Great Britain always avowed was, her readiness to rescind her orders, so soon as France rescinded absolutely and unconditionally her decrees. *She never engaged to repeal those orders, as affecting America alone, leaving them in force against other states, upon condition that France would except singly and specially America from the operation of her decrees.*"

Foster allowed time for Madison to read the dispatch and then visited him and Monroe. Bassano's outrageous pretensions, Foster reported, "scarcely drew from them a single remark." To Foster's assertion that Bassano's report did not exempt the United States by name, Madison replied "that it was useless to discuss the matter further"— not a single American ship had been captured under the French decrees since November 1810, and Barlow's treaty project plainly proved their· repeal as to the United States. The President regarded Castlereagh's refusal as an actual extension of British demands, and he would so inform Congress.

Foster refused again to allow the dispatch to be copied but promised to embody its substance in a note of his own. In doing so, he informed Castlereagh, he blocked the intended use of it by omitting the crucial sentence (italicized above) which revealed the British position. For maximum effect in upsetting policy, he was holding this note back until the morning of June 1, the day he understood to be set for the war message. (This by the man who accused Madison of "trick, falsehood and artifice.")

In the meantime Foster made a final offer, sanctioned by Castlereagh. If the United States would resume commercial relations with England, Americans would be admitted to an equal share of the licensed trade Britain carried on with her enemies. The offer was spurned. Foster then threw down his last card. If the United States would trade with England and accept the blockades, England would turn over to the United States her entire lucrative trade with the enemy—"a sacrifice of profit made for the sole purpose of conciliating the United States." The proposal, Foster reported, "met with even a worse fate than the former one." Monroe and Madison both replied that the United States would never bargain away its rights, and the President said it "as if he had been prepared for the proposal."

On June 1 Madison's war message was read in Congress behind closed doors. Listing British actions hostile to the United States as an independent and neutral nation, the President opened with the violation of the American flag on the great highway of nations. On the pretext of a search for British subjects thousands of American citizens were torn from their country, forced to risk their lives in the battles of their oppressors. British cruisers had "engaged in the most lawless proceedings in our very harbors" and wantonly spilt American blood within the territorial sanctuary.

Under pretended blockades, "our commerce has been plundered in every sea." The blockades were at length sweepingly embodied in the Orders in Council—orders defended as retaliation against a blockade of the British Isles by a French naval force that dared not issue from its own ports. "When deprived of this flimsy veil" by France's repeal of her prohibition of Anglo-American trade, Great Britain formally avowed that she would enforce her orders against the United States "until the markets of her enemy should be laid open to British products." She was now demanding that French repeal as to the United States should be extended to all other neutral nations.

It had become evident, said the President, that Great Britain was intent on sacrificing American commerce, "not as supplying the wants of her enemies, which she herself supplies; but as interfering with the monopoly which she covets for her own commerce and navigation. She carries on a war against the lawful commerce of a friend that she may the better carry on a commerce with an enemy"—a commerce polluted by forgeries and perjuries.

The President revealed (for the first time) that he had gone as far as he constitutionally could to lead England to expect that repeal of her edicts "would be followed by a war between the United States and France, unless the French edicts should also be repealed." Even this did not reduce Britain's hostile attitude, revealed also in the repudiation of the Erskine agreement and the Henry mission. He added a suggestion (not a charge) of British responsibility for renewed Indian warfare. To sum up: "Such is the spectacle of injuries and indignities which have been heaped on our country, and such the crisis which its unexampled forbearance and conciliatory efforts have not been able to avert. . . . We behold, in fine, on the side of Great Britain a state of war against the United States, and on the side of the United States a state of peace toward Great Britain."

Whether the country should continue to be passive under these accumulating wrongs or oppose force to force, avoiding entanglements with other powers, was "a solemn question which the Constitution wisely confides to the legislative department of the government." In recommending it to their early deliberations he was "happy in the assurance that the decision will be worthy the enlightened and patriotic councils of a virtuous, a free, and a powerful nation." A final paragraph condemned the conduct of France but postponed definitive measures until current discussions should enable Congress to decide "on the course due to the rights, the interests, and the honor of our country."

As had been pre-arranged in mid-May, Acting Chairman Calhoun on June 3 presented a spirited war manifesto drafted by Secretary of State Monroe. (Joseph Gales of the *Intelligencer* stated "positively" that Monroe wrote it, and numerous passages duplicate his exact language elsewhere.) After a lengthy historical review, the manifesto appealed to "the free-born sons of America" to resist multiplied wrongs that turned the contest into one for national sovereignty and independence: "Relying on the patriotism of the nation, and confidently trusting that the Lord of Hosts will go on with us to battle in a righteous cause, and crown our efforts with success, your committee recommend an immediate appeal to arms."

Debate on the message and manifesto was secret, but John Randolph in effect opened the doors before either document was presented. For hours, on May 29, before crowded galleries, he defended the British blockades and pilloried the Madison administration as basely subservient to France.

Foster carried out his plan of doctoring Castlereagh's dispatch. First word of results came from a pro-British congressman who wrote that after the reading of the President's message "Calhoun got a letter from Monroe which he gave to Grundy who looked grave." The next day, Foster recorded, Monroe asked him to alter his letter to make it agree with what the President had said about the sentence that Foster deleted. "I declined." Would he answer a written request for an explanation? He would. Monroe quoted the sentence in asking for the explanation. Foster's reply was a polite refusal to discuss it. Madison sent the full correspondence to Congress, frustrating the planned assault.

On June 4 the House secretly voted for war, 79 to 49. Opposed were the Federalists and fifteen Republicans, including the Quids and some Clintonians. Foster had not a hint of it when he wrote in his diary on the seventh: "Met Mr. Madison, coming from church in a coach and four, being but the second time he has been out these seven months. He now went to show he is not afraid." Mrs. Madison wrote to Sister Anna: "My dear husband is overpowered with business, but is in good health."

When people began asking Foster if his horses were for sale, he countered by remarking that he had just bought an icehouse for the winter. He was disturbed, however, when Secretary Eustis tried to buy his marquee. Still, he jotted in his diary, he was told that not four senators north of the Potomac would vote for war. The House, he understood, had passed a shuffling sort of a bill on letters of marque— a device to postpone the crisis until after the election.

The truth came through on June 9, when Foster learned that the House-passed bill was "an absolute declaration of war." Still, he was assured, the Senate had an indicated majority of two against the bill, and Madison probably counted on its defeat in that chamber. A few days later that belief faded: "Nine tenths of the people will not yet believe it possible that Mr. Madison will go to war, but it is too apparent that he is now obstinately bent on it as a solution of his difficulties."

Foster did not dream that the President's greatest difficulty was the minister's own unintentional misleading of his government under the spell of Federalist delusions and misrepresentations. The people knew nothing of what was going on in Congress. The *Intelligencer* adjured them on June 13 to disbelieve a thousand rumors. Congress was certain to adopt some measure "having the effect and character of war." That reflected the tie vote by which, on the previous day, the Senate refused to limit the war to naval reprisals and privateering. On this crucial test, Smith of Maryland and Giles upset forecasts by joining the administration forces led by Crawford. Six Republicans, including all Pennsylvanians and New Yorkers, voted with the Federalists. On June 17 the Senate beat down, 18 to 14, an attempt by Giles to make war at sea against both England and France. Foster sent his military aide to make Senator Brent of Virginia drunk, "an easy matter," but Lieutenant More came back drunk himself.

On that same day, June 17, the Senate voted 19 to 13 for immediate and unrestricted war. German of Pennsylvania, Gilman of New Hampshire, and Worthington of Ohio cast the only Republican votes in opposition. That evening Foster went to Mrs. Madison's drawing room. The President "made me three bows—he was remarkably civil," talked of Russia and British successes in Spain; but he "looked ghastly pale . . . very naturally felt all the responsibility he would incur."

The House on June 18 accepted minor Senate amendments, and President Madison immediately signed the declaration of war. He followed it with a proclamation exhorting "all the good people of the United States, as they love their country, as they value the precious heritage derived from the virtue and valor of their fathers," to exert themselves in preserving order, promoting concord, and supporting all measures "for obtaining a speedy, a just and an honorable peace."

Madison's attitude toward the War of 1812 was then and long remained a matter of dispute. Federalists, for partisan reasons, promptly labeled it "Mr. Madison's War," but the belief became fixed that he was forced into it by popular and congressional pressure. His wartime secretary, Edward Coles, denied this in 1856, when biographer William C. Rives put the question to him.

"It was congenial alike to the life and character of Mr. Madison," wrote Coles, "that he should be reluctant to go to war." He did not "entirely despair of preserving peace" until the British government "contended that France must not only repeal her decrees against us, but against all the world," before England would repeal or modify her orders. This "closed the door to peace in Mr. Madison's opinion," and from that time his mind was "irrevocably fixed on war as the only course left us" by Britain's conduct.

That makes the date of decision July 23, 1811, when Madison first rejected Foster's condition of universal repeal of the French decrees. With a war policy decided upon, Coles continued, Madison announced it to Congress in his November message. From November until June he stood between "the hotspurs of the day," who demanded an immediate declaration without preparations for defense, and the "sound, prudent and patriotic men" who wanted one more diplomatic effort for peace while the nation prepared for hostilities. The war, Madison believed, "should be declared by a large and influential majority." To that end: "He endeavored to moderate the zeal and impatience of the ultra belligerent men, and to stimulate the more moderate and forbearing. To check those who were anxious to rush on hastily to extreme measures without due preparation and to urge those who lagged too far behind."

By this course, Coles asserted, Madison increased the vote for war in both houses and added to its popularity, but at the same time "brought into question the ardor and sincerity of his own conduct." The

Coles appraisal is completely supported by the diplomatic and legislative record. At no time until the final vote, however, was the course so completely settled that news of an altered attitude by England would not have averted bloodshed.

In that respect, unknown in America, dramatic events were taking place in Europe. On April 30, responding to Barlow's almost peremptory demand that repeal of the French decrees be officially proclaimed, Napoleon published a repeal decree dated April 11, 1811. The date was manifestly fictitious, but the document was legally valid and satified the announced requirement of the British Prince Regent. On May 11 Prime Minister Perceval, the unyielding supporter of the Orders in Council, was shot to death by a maniac.

The Cabinet, pounded with repeal demands by British manufacturers and committees of Parliament, resigned on May 22. George Joy, Madison's confidant, convinced Lord Sidmouth that the President's position varied widely from Napoleon's. The American embargo alerted the headless Cabinet to the imminence of war. On June 16 it was announced in Parliament that the Orders in Council would be suspended. They were revoked next day—the very day on which the United States Senate joined in the decision for war.

In 1830 Madison told Jared Sparks that Castlereagh's final letter, submitted to him five days before he sent his war message to Congress, "shut out all prospects of conciliation." Had it "been of a different tone war would not have been at that time declared, nor is it probable that it would have followed, because there was every prospect that the affair of impressment and other grievances might have been reconciled after the repeal of the obnoxious Orders in Council."

This was not to be, and the War of 1812 began one day after the principal cause of it disappeared.

For all the responsibilties he bore in public life up to June 18, 1812, James Madison was admirably fitted by his native qualities and experience. He carried the world's history in his mind and knew the springs of human conduct. He was quick in thought, cautious in conduct, always looking to the consequences of action before acting, but firm and tenacious when the course was set.

Madison's one besetting fault was lack of ruthlessness toward subordinates. If a head of department faltered he would take on additional duties rather than force a resignation. As Secretary of State he had been an assistant President. As President he was his own Secretary of State. Now, a commander-in-chief untrained in the arts of war had to lead a nation totally unprepared to fight and sharply divided in its loyalties.

From the day he entered the White House, in 1809, President Madison had employed the secret threat of war to support diplomatic pressures inappropriate to a government of divided powers ruling a divided people. Worse than disunity was the universal repugnance to taxation. For three years, all administration defense programs had been ignored, whittled down or given only paper substance. When on March 31, 1812, he declared his readiness to ask for war, the President told congressional leaders that he would not assume "the responsibility of declaring that we are prepared for war."

Had the United States been wholly the master of its course, this anomaly could have been avoided; but the European conflict subjected the country to unbearable humiliation. American seamen were impressed onto British warships which aggressively patrolled the American coast. England and France alike seized and confiscated American ships and cargoes. Aggravating Britain's conduct were commercial restrictions designed to reduce the United States to semicolonial status. Magnifying the effect was the spread of an expanding population over an almost empty continent. All factors combined to produce a compound of overconfidence, national ambition, commercial aggressiveness, and sensitivity to foreign insults—without a corresponding spirit of sacrifice.

In Madison himself, Revolutionary patriotism heightened his reaction against British navigation laws that destroyed American trade with the West Indies and held down the development of a merchant marine. Napoleon's "crafty contrivance and insatiate cupidity" stirred his anger, but these excesses were seen as the temporary product of European strife. England's "monopoly and piracy," in contrast, marked a systematic assault on American sovereignty, evidenced both in governmental actions and in the *Delenda est Carthago* campaign of the ministerial pamphleteer James Stephen.

Totally absent from Madison's thinking, and nonexistent as a factor leading to war, was the motive of annexing Canada, charged by Federalists. The thought of a future union was omnipresent. "When the pear is ripe," said Madison to Turreau, "it will fall of itself." Kentuckians looked upon Canada as a stimulator of Indian warfare and hailed the thought of conquest on that account. Congressman John Harper of New Hampshire was an open advocate of annexation. But commercial New England, a beneficiary from that course, opposed the war. The South, which wanted no addition of Northern territories, was clamorous for hostilities. The conjecture has been made that Senator Crawford of Georgia and Congressman Harper teamed up, Crawford agreeing to the conquest of Canada in order to gain northern support for the taking of Florida. There is no evidence of that, and it is refuted by logic. Florida, already occupied by an American force, could have been taken more easily without an Anglo-American war than by means of it.

Canada's true relationship to the war was spelled out by Monroe a few days before war was declared. That country was to be invaded "not as an object of the war but as a means of bringing it to a satisfactory conclusion." That was clarified in the first message Madison sent to London after the declaration. If England wanted a satisfactory peace she should take quick steps to reach an armistice. Otherwise a successful invasion, by its effect on the public mind, might make it "difficult to relinquish territory which had been conquered." The war quickly produced that spirit, although that spirit would not have produced war.

On the afternoon of June 18 Congress lifted its June 1 injunction of secrecy and (in the words of the *Intelligencer*) stamped "reality on what was before mere inference and conjecture." Expresses raced north, south, and west. In Richmond, wrote William Pope, consternation reigned among Tories; friends of their country exulted and many gave Madison all the credit: "You have politically regenerated the nation and washed out the stain in their national character, inflicted on it by England." Kentucky Congressmen Clay and Johnson, riding westward, found Pennsylvania and Ohio strong for the war and their own state so ardent that it was almost alarming.

The flour millers of Pennsylvania's Lehigh Valley, suppliers of the British army, were "thunderstruck at the news." The Boston *Repertory* asked whether the people of Massachusetts would submit to be slaves of the slaves of Napoleon. "You must bow to the yoke, or break it to pieces." All through New England, pulpits shook with outcries against the war.

Justice Story, at his home in Salem, witnessed the tumult and suggested that Congress repress it by giving the federal courts a common-law jurisdiction to punish any act injurious to the United States. Madison, who had written that such a power would open "the hideous volumes of penal law," ignored the proposal. Jefferson, witnessing the Tory reaction, thought that "a barrel of tar to each state south of the Potomac" would keep all in order, but in the North they might need "hemp and confiscation."

In Baltimore the *Federal Republican* reiterated its chronic charge that Madison was obeying the orders of Napoleon. Enraged citizens smashed press and types and tore down the plant. In Congress, both parties recognized that nobody wanted to pay for the war. Federalists, looking toward the fall elections, challenged the Republicans to be prompt and fearless in laying internal taxes. The Republicans, seeking to fill the Treasury without emptying their seats, voted to borrow $5 million.

With invasion of Canada lying ahead, Congress heeded the President's request for authority to appoint commissioned officers of the Volunteer Corps. That converted the corps from militiamen into regulars, thus removing the bar to service on foreign soil. Privateering was authorized and trade with the enemy forbidden.

Dissident Republican senators, Representative Jonathan Roberts of Pennsylvania commented, voted for these measures only after they had vented their feelings "against anything Madison might be for." The President, he added, "preserves his cheerfulness wonderfully," although "the factious temper of the Senate is enough to cast a gloom over a mind of more than common strength." Mrs. Madison was singularly discreet. "By her deportment in her own house you cannot discover who is her husband's friends or foes." Roberts himself, he disclosed to his brother, had been criticized in Congress for sharing Mrs. Madison's box at an overcrowded theater: "The world are pleased to suppose I am on good terms at the White House, which by the way is no advantage for the cry of mad dog is not more fatal to its victim than the cry of executive connection here."

Madison drew increasing criticism in Congress and from the public for failing to proclaim a day of public humiliation and prayer. On June 30 Congress requested him to do so, first amending the resolution to insert "dependence on Almighty God" in place of "a just confidence [of the people] in the vigor of their own arm." On July 9, three days after the session ended, Madison issued a carefully worded proclamation. *In response to a request of Congress*, he invited religious "societies *so disposed*, to offer, at one and the same time, their common vows and adorations to Almighty God, on the solemn occasion produced by the war, in which he has been pleased to permit the injustice of a foreign Power to involve these United States."

This was recognized instantly as a satirical response to Governor Strong of Massachusetts, who called for prayers *against the war*, which the Almightly had permitted "us to be engaged in . . . against the nation from which we are descended and which for many generations has been the bulwark of the Religion we profess." Madison himself said he worded the proclamation to avoid a call on the people to pray, which he regarded as an encroachment on freedom of religion. New Hampshire Federalists, observed Congressman Harper, were not blind to the nature of the proclamation, but "none, in my presence, had the presumption to attack it."

Federalist opposition to the war took an upward turn with the publication, upon adjournment of Congress, of a minority address by thirty-four Federalists and Quids. It upheld Britain's orders in council and described Madison's position on impressment as "a standing invitation to the subjects of a foreign power to become deserters and traitors." John Randolph gloated over Madison's reputed reaction to it: " 'Tis said our sovereign lord the P[resident] is exceeding wroth at the address of certain heretics to their constituents; that he has pronounced that (except the overt act) it is treason." And so it was, measured by the effect in England.

The administration devoted three issues of the *National Intelligencer* to rebuttal of the address, using documents sent to Congress. They showed that under the paper blockades, Great Britain had been waging war on American commerce for three years before France issued the decrees against which the Orders in Council were said to be retaliation. Coupled with this, the President sent statistics on impressment which, he said, would have been far more voluminous if there had been time to prepare them. This strategy enabled him, by a cut-off date, to present figures showing huge impressments during the Washington and Adams administration, with their protests against them. The record showed that Timothy Pickering, the most vociferous assailant of Madison's contention that the American flag protected *all* seamen sailing under it, had himself formulated that doctrine as Secretary of State. The revelation did not deter Pickering from writing, in July 1812, that French money produced the declaration of war.

The black passions of the war of words took on a crimson hue at the end of July. Alexander Contee Hanson, youthful publisher of the Baltimore *Federal Republican*, shifted it to Georgetown after his office was destroyed but carried the printed papers to his Baltimore home for distribution. Fifty armed defenders, headed by General Henry Lee, occupied the house. Boys threw stones at it. Shots were fired from the house to disperse them. A mob assembled and attacked with rocks and rams. A volley from inside the house killed a bystander and wounded several, one fatally. The militia placed the defenders in jail for safe-keeping. The mob reassembled, stormed the jail, killed General Lingan, and trampled Lee almost to death.

Correspondence revealed later that the "defenders" plotted in advance to provoke an attack, but the immediate reaction was one of national horror. The Federalist press promptly accused President Madison of having inspired the onslaught. The affair came before him officially because the jail was in the same building as the post office. Writing after an investigating committee made its report, he said he never considered an assault probable nor had he doubted the ability and willingness of the local authorities to cope with one if made. The investigation furnished "a seasonable antidote" to the misrepresentations of factionists who were seeking to blame the atrocity of the mob "on the friends of true liberty." County mass meetings defended Madison against "the slanderous insinuations" leveled at him in the affair.

By this time Federalist newspapers were printing a nine-part serial, "Mr. Madison's War: A Dispassionate Inquiry," written "By a New England Farmer." In it Boston lawyer John Lowell passionately recounted Madison's complete vassalage to France, which began in the Revolution and culminated in this war "undertaken for *French* interests, and in conformity with repeated *French* orders." Each American citizen, he declared, had a constitutional right to refuse military service. Collectively, the people should go into the presidential campaign determined to "displace the *man who alone is responsible for this war—* I mean Mr. Madison."

Matthew Carey, the spirited Philadelphia publicist, appealed to Madison to help organize nationwide committees to counter the "gross and abominable lies" of shameless printers. Madison replied that except in extreme cases he would prefer local efforts without government sponsorship. "But I cannot suppress my hope that the wicked project of destroying the Union of the states is defeating itself." The great body of New England people had too palpable a stake in national prosperity to be seduced into a foreign connection. That thought, applying the principles of the Tenth Federalist, reinforced his determination to maintain complete civil liberty in a passion-torn country rife with disloyalty. He held to that course throughout the war, in spite of slanders directed against himself unparalleled in American history.

In the war the first moves were toward peace. The day after it was declared, British Minister Foster proposed that hostilities be suspended until he could carry news of the declaration to London. The President declined the offer but arranged for contacts through Chargé Russell and Legation Secretary Baker as nondiplomatic agents.

On June 22, press reports from London indicated that the Orders in Council were nearing revocation. Madison sent word to Foster that he "would not be displeased" by a farewell visit. They met, and Madison expressed his wish to see the causes of the war removed. Foster asked whether repeal of the orders would be sufficient to restore peace. It would, Madison replied, if coupled with a promise of negotiation on the question of impressment.

Foster wanted to know whether this would produce an immediate armistice. That would depend on Congress, Madison told him. Foster said he would guarantee the proclamation of an armistice by Admiral Sawyer if the President would take similar action. That was impossible, Madison replied. He had a mandate to carry on the war and could not modify it. The President entrusted Foster with armistice terms Chargé Russell was to present, stiffer on impressment than their talk had indicated: "If the Orders in Council are repealed, and no illegal blockades are substituted for them, and orders are given to discontinue the impressment of seamen from our vessels, and to restore those already impressed, there is no reason why hostilities should not immediately cease."

Russell was to inform England that the United States was under no engagement of any kind to the French government, and nothing except a calamitous prosecution of the war by England could produce one. That disclaimer reflected growing anger against France over the burning of American ships. From the President down to the most obscure members of Congress, wrote Sérurier, after his great July 3 dinner was boycotted, "everybody thinks himself obliged to avoid me." Madison undoubtedly wrote the toast at next day's banquet managed by presidential Secretary Coles: "The war—we have selected an adversary without electing an ally . . ."

The navy was toasted: "An infant Hercules, destined, by the presage of early prowess, to extirpate the race of pirates and freebooters." That reflected the firing of the first shots of the war. Two days after its declaration Commodores Rodgers and Decatur were ordered to sea from New York and Hampton Roads, their squadrons to cruise south from Sandy Hook and north from the Virginia capes. They were to unite if necessary with Rodgers in command, protect commerce and, if possible, destroy the powerful British warships *Belvidera* and *Tartarus*.

These orders and the resulting action totally disprove a remarkable story forgetfully recounted in 1845 by Captain Charles Stewart, that when he went to Washington on June 21 to ask for an active assignment he was told by Secretary Hamilton that the Navy was to be kept safe in port for harbor protection.

According to Stewart's recollection, he and Captain Bainbridge protested to President Madison, who overruled the Secretary and said to the two officers: "It is victories we want; if you give us them and lose your ships afterwards, they can be replaced by others." Navy records show that Bainbridge was in Charlestown, Massachusetts, on June 21. Stewart was in Washington, and on that day was ordered to sea in command of the brig *Argus*, but was left shipless because the *Argus* already had sailed in Rodgers' squadron.

Both Stewart and Bainbridge, however, were in Washington at the end of February 1812. Hamilton at that time spoke of holding the vessels in port; the officers protested. Hamilton delivered their letter to Madison, who called the trio before him, listened to their arguments, and said the Navy should go to sea. His remark about victories bringing replacements suited the day: the House had just defeated the administration bill to construct ten additional frigates.

A month of silence settled down after Rodgers put to sea. His immediate object, he sent word, was pursuit of a large West India convoy reported to be headed for England along the edge of the Gulf Stream. It was mid-July before news reached Washington that the American squadron encountered the *Belvidera* and pursued her toward Halifax. Rodgers' flagship, the *President*, far outdistanced the other vessels and finally overtook the British frigate which escaped (said the reports from Halifax) because the *President* mysteriously yawed each time she came up in the stern chase.

The British flight from a vessel of equal force set crowds to cheering, but months passed before the yawing was explained. The explosion of one bow gun silenced the other (also killing or wounding sixteen sailors and breaking Rodgers' leg). Forced to yaw in order to bring her broadsides to bear, the *President* dropped out of range every time she fired, and Rodgers finally gave up the chase. Before he came into port his reassembled squadron neared the coast of England.

Taken as a whole, the naval confrontation in the war of 1812 was Leviathan against a dingey. The ready-for-action United States Navy consisted of five frigates, one 20-gun ship, and eight small swift sloops and brigs. Great Britain in June 1812 had nearly 700 warships actually at sea, including about 260 ships of the line (three-deckers) and frigates. Great Britain had three *warships* for every American *gun*. The American officers were trained in Mediterranean service and had one great superiority in tactics. *They aimed at the waterline*, puncturing hulls. Shots that fell short ricocheted onto deck or into the rigging. British gunners aimed at masts and spars. The difference was destined to determine the outcome of almost every ship-to-ship encounter, but the overall odds were insuperable in favor of the "mistress of the seas."

In land warfare, the only American advantages lay in spread of territory and distance from Europe. The forces in being consisted almost literally of eight aging and inexperienced general officers without an army. On June 18 the enlisted personnel numbered 6,744 in old regiments, with 5,000 recruits in training, plus some thousands of volunteers in Kentucky and Tennessee and a sprinkling in the East. New York alone had militia ready for Canadian frontier duty. New England refused to fight.

In Canada, 2,257 British regulars were strung out from Montreal to Detroit—745 in Montreal, about as many at Kingston, 400 along the Niagara River, and 280 at Fort Malden below Detroit. In Lower Canada (Quebec) British troops numbered 4,744, whose availability for service in Upper Canada depended on New England's attitude. Captain General Sir George Prevost considered the Canadian militia disloyal, but he had an ardent Indian ally in Tecumseh, in whose breast the embers of Tippecanoe still burned.

The American military forces had no supreme field commander. A report spread, after the war, that Madison wished to appoint inexperienced Henry Clay to this post but was dissuaded by members of Congress who said Clay could not be spared from that body. Edward Coles traced the story to General John T. Mason, who gave it a very different twist: Congressional friends of Clay urged his appointment on the President, who assented to his fitness "but said he could not be spared out of Congress."

Major General Dearborn, assigned to the northeastern command, recommended a main advance on Montreal by way of Lake Champlain, while three corps were to enter Canada from Detroit, Niagara, and Sackett's Harbor. Capture of Montreal would cut off the entire Canadian West from supplies and reinforcements. Unanswered: what would the enemy be doing during the required year of preparation?

Brigadier General Hull, governor of Michigan Territory and a former Massachusetts Federalist, was hailed by that party as the only competent man appointed to command. He had an excellent Revolutionary record at regimental level. Hull in an April conference with Madison urged immediate dispatch of troops to Detroit. A fleet, he said, ought to be built on Lake Erie (controlled by British warships), but the same results could be achieved by driving eastward from Detroit. Hull was directed to gather troops and "repair with as little delay as possible to Detroit."

Desiring to build a fleet on Lake Erie, the President offered command there to Captain Stewart, but congressional anti-navalism and Stewart's rejection of the post ended that project. Hull's plan was accepted in full, with no thought of the gigantic mobile advantage the British would have through control of the lake.

Starting north from near Dayton, Ohio, on June 1, Hull's 1,200-man army grew to more than 2,000 by the time he approached Lake Erie. A dispatch from Secretary Eustis, dated June 18, urged haste, but neglected to mention the declaration of war. The British were better posted. On that same June 18, John Jacob Astor innocently sent an express to Canada to notify his partners in the fur trade. A swift boat carried the tidings to Fort Malden, and Hull's hospital ship, carrying all of the army papers, was captured as it sailed past the British fort.

Hull occupied Fort Detroit on July 5 and there received orders from Eustis to "take possession of Malden and extend your conquests as circumstances may justify." General Dearborn at the same time was directed to prepare for an advance on Niagara, Kingston, and Montreal. "You will take your own time," wrote the Secretary, as it was "altogether uncertain at what time General Hull may deem it expedient to commence offensive operations."

Fort Malden was a scrawny fortification of earthworks and wooden palings, dominated by surrounding hills. On the day Hull reached Detroit, the fort was defended by 280 British regulars, 600 Canadian militiamen, and about the same number of Indians. Two days later 460 of the militiamen and all but 240 of the Indians had fled, and fifty of the regulars were chasing the militia.

Glowing reports reached President Madison from Hull. The general crossed the Detroit River on July 12 without opposition and was about to march on Malden. British General Brock, stationed opposite Niagara but commanding the entire West, wrote despairingly to Prevost: "The enemy was not likely to delay attacking a force that had allowed him to cross the river in open day without firing a shot."

The President was well satisfied with the western position. Fifteen hundred more troops, he wrote to General Dearborn, were on their way to Detroit. With these, Hull would be able to descend toward Niagara. Slow enlistments had destroyed the possibility of a simultaneous advance on Montreal, but operations against Kingston should be pushed. Its occupation would place in American hands "not only all the most valuable parts of the upper province, but the important command of the lakes."

Madison was disturbed when Hull reported that the British had captured the 63-man garrison at Michilimachinac, fronting the country of the Sioux and other tribes. Hull's situation, the President commented, would be very ineligible if his reinforcements did not enable him to take Malden and "awe the savages emboldened by the British success" at Michilimachinac. Having mortars and cannon, Hull should be able to reduce or invest the fort and still press on to hem Brock's troops between himself and Dearborn. Brock had the same thought. "My situation," he wrote to Prevost, "is gettting each day more critical." With fifty regulars and 250 militiamen he sailed on August 8 for Amherstburg, to take command at Fort Malden.

During the summer of 1812 relations with France grew steadily worse, while evidence piled up that the British Orders in Council were being repealed. That was still uncertain on July 16, when Monroe furnished an editorial to the *National Intelligencer* (the draft is in his papers) defending the authenticity of Napoleon's predated repeal decree of April 28, 1811. Whether written then or later, Napoleon's signature made it the kind of document England was asking for, thus ending all pretext for continuing the Orders in Council.

Madison, writing privately to Barlow, said that the conduct of the French government would be an everlasting reproach to it. Its predated decree was the more shameful because, departing from the 1810 declaration of Cadore, it made the revocation of the Berlin and Milan decrees the *effect*, when in fact it was the *cause*, of the break-off of trade with England.

That feature was instantly seized on by Robert Smith, deposed head of the State Department. Filling several columns as "A Spectator" in the Baltimore *Federal Gazette*, he treated the 1811 date as genuine and cried out in pretended indignation: "In the name of common decency, wherefore has this document been so long withheld from the government of the United States?" It typified "all the wily arts" by which the deceived and humiliated Madison, whom the writer deeply pitied, had been seduced into the Continental System.

Boston's *Columbian Centinal* achieved an equal pitch of condemnation by recognizing the falseness of Napoleon's dating: "If it should be proven that Mr. Madison was privy to the scandalous *juggling*, . . . he is lost forever. . . . the public will be much surprised if some one does not blab the secret." In the official realm, Monroe informed Barlow of the President's "great surprise and concern" that France clung to her system of licenses and, instead of making indemnities, was perpetrating outrageous new wrongs in the burning of American ships.

The next packet to England broadened Russell's authority to conclude an armistice. All that was needed, preliminary to it, was revocation of the Orders in Council and an informal understanding on blockades and impressments—the terms Madison first stated orally to Foster.
Monroe then left for his Virginia farm and Madison took over the
task of stating national policy in the *Intelligencer*.

On August 4, the semiofficial organ published an editorial that
startled the nation, as well as Paris and London. George Joy, reading
it in the London *Star*, at once told Lord Sidmouth that "the style and
composition of the President" marked it as "the immediate product of
his own pen." Petry, in Paris, did not need to rely on style. Madison,
he wrote to Bassano, had avowed his authorship in a private letter to
Barlow.

"We have seen with regret and surprise," the President's editorial
began, "the many misrepresentations of the views of the government
which are daily published in the federal prints." To end them "so far
as is in our power, we will remark, that altho' the government are
making the most vigorous efforts to prosecute the war against England
with effect, they are disposed to accommodate all differences on the
most reasonable conditions." An offer already had been made to exclude British seamen from American vessels if Great Britain would
stop making impressments from them. As for the other European
belligerent:

> We state with pleasure another fact which we believe to
> be equally true—that our government will not under any
> circumstances that may occur, form a political connection
> with France. . . . It is not desirable to enter the lists with
> the two great belligerents at once; but if England acts with
> wisdom, and France perseveres in her career of injustice and
> folly . . . from that moment we have no doubt that the
> United States will assume a correspondent relation with
> both.

Here was an indirect but recognizable presidential statement of
readiness to change sides in the European war, made before it was
positively known that England had repealed her Orders in Council.
That information swiftly followed. On August 5, young George Barclay, son of the British consul general at New York, arrived from Halifax with dispatches from Foster to Baker covering a message from
Castlereagh.

The British government accepted Napoleon's predated decree as an official repeal of the Berlin and Milan decrees as far as they related to America. Baker was authorized to say that the Orders in Council, in relation to the United States, "would be repealed on the first of August, to be revived on the first May, 1813," unless French conduct and the result of Franco-American communications rendered their revival unnecessary. Baker also delivered a message from Foster, containing an almost solid assurance that British authorities in Canada would agree to a suspension of hostilities.

The President authorized Chief Clerk Graham to reply that the communication was received with sincere satisfaction, as opening the way to peace and solid friendship. The particular armistice proposal seemed to be beyond the President's authority, but the pacific advance being made through Chargé Russell would, if favorably received, become operative as soon as any other arrangement that could now be made.

Madison actually had doubts about authority at Halifax to agree to an armistice. Nothing disclosed from British sources, he wrote to General Dearborn, "ought in the slightest degree to slacken our military exertions." In spite of these reservations the President was moved to intensify his warnings to France. On August 11, he wrote privately to Barlow, but with instructions to use the letter:

> In the event of a pacification with Great Britain the full tide of indignation with which the public mind here is boiling will be directed against France, if not obviated by a due reparation of her wrongs. War will be called for by the nation almost una voce. Even without a peace with England, the further refusal and prevarications of France on the subject of redress may be expected to produce measures of hostility at the ensuing session of Congress. This result is the more probable, as the general exasperation will coincide with the calculation of not a few, that a double war is the shortest road to peace.

This letter, fortified by the avowal of Madison's authorship of the *Intelligencer*'s threat of war, created a swift aboutface in France. Napoleon was with his army in Moscow, and Bassano was at winter headquarters at Vilna. In thirty-eight days, Petry wrote to Bassano, Congress would reconvene. France had that many days to forestall war: "Thus the question now is, *do we desire a rupture with the United States, or do we desire it not?* If we desire it, our views will easily be fulfilled—

let things be. If we do not desire it, there is no time to lose to prevent it."

The Americans, Petry said, were slow in their resolutions, but once these were taken they would not renounce them "without having obtained satisfaction for all the grievances they claim to have against us." French alarm was increased by the interception and decoding of Barlow's reply to Madison. He argued so vigorously against a double war as to leave no doubt that he took Madison's threat seriously. Bassano asked Barlow to come to Vilna to complete a treaty. The American minister set out in October, followed by Petry.

At home, meanwhile, General Dearborn agreed to a proposal by Captain General Prevost that hostilities cease until the President's decision on Foster's armistice proposal should reach both sides. Madison overruled Dearborn's action. Considering the need of a diversion to aid General Hull, wrote Eustis, "the President thinks it proper that not a moment should be lost in gaining possession of the British posts at Niagara and Kingston, or at least the former." Dearborn should give Prevost notice and "proceed with the utmost vigor in your operations."

Dearborn replied that as it was too late for him to take effective command at Niagara, he would go ahead with his original plan to push toward Montreal while the force in western New York struck at Niagara. Prevost found Dearborn's unauthorized armistice helpful. It so uplifted Canadian morale that he no longer feared internal tumult. Colonel Baynes, who carried the truce offer, brought back word that General Dearborn, although strong and healthy at sixty (one), did not appear to possess the strength of mind called for by his assignment. Neither Eustis nor Madison had discovered that exceedingly relevant fact.

Madison fared better with peace efforts on another front. Early in August two dozen Indian chiefs from Missouri Territory were brought in by General William Clark (of Lewis and Clark) to visit the President. Although some were at war with others, they all shook hands amicably with the President and went to the theater. The Madisons entertained twenty-nine of them at dinner, plus five interpreters, and the whole Cabinet, with the band playing. On August 15 the Sioux arrived, and these "terrific kings and princes" likewise had a White House dinner.

Madison had a double peace task, to end intertribal wars west of the Mississippi, and dissuade the Sioux and Sacs from their half-formed connection with the British Army. Forty warriors reciprocated the

White House dinners with "an Indian feast, war dance and war whoop" on Greenleaf's Point. They represented "the most magnificent, imposing, native human pageantry" Richard Rush ever saw. Madison's salutation probably was furnished by General Clark: "My Red Children: . . . I love to shake hands with hearts in them."

The President desired that the bloody tomahawk be buried among the Osages, Cherokees, and Choctaws: the Shawnees and Osages; the Sacs and Foxes, and the Osages; the Osages and Ioways. "They must put under my feet their evil intentions against one another." He warned that "the people composing the 18 fires" covered the land as the stars fill the sky. One little fire—Canada—was trying to decoy the red people into war on the British side. "I warn all the red people to avoid the ruin this must bring upon them."

Madison spoke of the factories that had been established for Indian trade. He advised the red men to breed cattle and sheep, plow the earth, spin and weave, that they might have good houses and more than enough to eat. Above all, they should be at peace with one another. Indian chiefs responded approvingly, but each wanted a factory in his own village, to avoid being killed on the way to trade. "All is pleasing to us," said Big Soldier of the Little Osages, "but being killed." A Sac leader approved of peace, but said he could not control his young men. One of them, Quash-quam-ma, proved it by saying to the President: "You have war. It is very well—defend yourselves. We will do the same with our neighbors. . . . I wish to see you and enquire . . . whether it was by your directions that [your] people settled on [our lands]."

Madison must have been doubly pleased with the words of The Buffalo that Walks, chief of the Sioux: "My great father. I am a small man, but I am regarded as a man." He gave a pledge of peace. Big Thunder delivered the valedictory address: "I am tired of rolling about on the floor and wish to return home."

On August 12, the text of Britain's repeal of the Orders in Council reached Washington—outright repeal as to the United States, to be void unless the law barring trade with England was repealed "as soon as may be" after formal notice of the British action was received. Pressed by Baker for a suspension of hostilities, Madison said he must first learn what effect the declaration of war would have on British policy. Russell was notified that if the new spirit of conciliation was extended to impressment a durable and happy peace could not fail to result. There need be no precise pledge on that point: evidence of

514	The Fourth President: James Madison

a sincere disposition to settle that difference by treaty would be enough. Another problem remained: to receive or confiscate the enormous shipments of British goods sent out on repeal of the Orders in Council, with no knowledge that war had been declared. Baker was told that if Congress denied relief, arrangements would be made to protect the British owners by treaty.

Canadian newspapers told of a sharp repulse of the Americans near Fort Malden, just when, on August 28, Monroe's return from his farm enabled the President to leave Washington. In eight months he had been out of the presidential square only twice—to church on June 7 and to the July 4 oratory in the Capitol. "I find myself much worn down," he had written, "and in need of an antidote to the accumulating bile . . . which I have never escaped in August on tide water."

Heading for Montpelier via Fredericksburg, the President and Mrs. Madison reached Dumfries on the first evening. From Washington came a galloping horseman with a message from Secretary Eustis. General Hull had surrendered his entire army of 2,500 men without firing a shot. The President headed back to the White House.

Virtually all that was known when he reached Washington was that Hull abruptly ordered his army back to Detroit and sent out several hundred regulars to clear a cut supply line (which they did). The President's reaction was implicit in what Dolley wrote: "Do you not tremble with resentment at this treacherous act? Yet we must not judge the man until we are in possession of his reasons." The worst of the expedition's failure, commented the President to John Nicholas, "was, that we were misled by a reliance, authorized by himself, on its securing to us the command of the lakes."

Summoning his Cabinet, Madison placed two questions before its members: whether to build at once a naval force on the Great Lakes, and whether to attempt an immediate recovery of Detroit. All approved both. Brigadier General Winchester, whose 2,000 men were slated to reinforce Hull, was given the recovery assignment, to be joined by Brigadier General William Henry Harrison, lately commissioned. Orders were issued to replace artillery and call up 3,000 Virginia and Pennsylvania militia and more Westerners. Naval command on Lakes Erie and Ontario was given to Commodore Isaac Chauncey; and on Lake Champlain, to Lieutenant Thomas Macdonough. British warships controlled all three lakes.

These steps taken, the President on September 1 left once more for Montpelier, where details of the Detroit debacle kept coming in a steady stream. First reports disclosed a total loss of confidence in Hull among his officers. His civilian soldiers, released in Ohio on parole, filled the countryside with their denunciations of him as a traitor and a coward.

The amazing story piled up—the unexplained and needless retreat to Detroit—Hull's statement to Colonel Brush of the Michigan militia that a capitulation might be necessary—an agreement by five colonels that they would divest him of command if he attempted to surrender. (Colonel Cass, paroled, brought the account to Washington.) Then, on August 15, came a written demand by General Brock for surrender of the fort to avoid extermination by his uncontrollable Indians. Hull sent back a refusal. Next morning 700 British troops crossed the river below Detroit, together with 600 Indians who disappeared in the forest.

At Fort Detroit, soldiers watched the British, two-thirds militia, march in close platoons up the road, straight toward 24-pounders loaded with grapeshot that could enfilade the whole column. Hull sat on an old tent, tobacco juice drooling down his beard and vest. In a tremulous voice he forbade the firing of a shot. Then, without consulting a single officer, without their knowledge, he ordered a white flag hoisted. The absence of Colonels Cass and McArthur, who with 350 men had been sent to escort a supply train, upset the plan to depose the general. Had a firing been heard, wrote Cass, the advancing column, only three miles away, would have attacked the British in the rear and "very few would have escaped."

The British account, more than corroborative, was not yet known. "When I detail my good fortune," wrote Brock to Prevost, "Your Excellency will be astonished." Reaching Fort Malden three days earlier, Brock was shown an intercepted letter from Hull to Eustis showing the American commander to be in a state of total panic over the Indians he expected to swoop down from Michilimachinac. Soldiers' letters revealed that confidence in the general was gone. Brock undertook to force Hull's army into the open by carrying two cannon across the river and opening a cross fire from there and the east shore. Once on the road, he found that he was caught between the fort and the returning column under Cass and McArthur.

As the only chance to escape annihilation Brock ordered his little band—330 regulars, 360 militia—to march on the fort. As they did so, a white flag fluttered above the wall. Unable to believe his eyes, Brock halted and sent an officer ahead to ask what it meant—capitulation.

Lieutenant Richardson, Canadian historian of the campaign, described their advance into the cannons' mouth. They were on a narrow road between rowhouses and a picket fence. (Behind it, farther ahead, Ohio and Michigan troops lay in ambush.) "We distinctly saw . . . the gunners with their fuses burning." Had they fired, "fearful . . . must have been the havoc, for there was not the slightest possibility of deploying."

Hull's defense, accepted by many historians, was that he had less than a day's supply of powder and that he could not subject Detroit civilians to massacre by Indians who, loosed from their northern hive by surrender of Michilimachinac, were "swarming down in every direction." When Hull gave his powder excuse to Prevost, the British commander handed him "the return of the large supply found in the fort; it did not create a blush."

As for the Indians, not one had come down from the "northern hive." On the very day of Hull's surrender, British Captain Charles Roberts wrote from Michilimachinac that when the Indians heard that the American army had entered Canada, all but thirty of the Sioux left for home and, the Ottawas determined "to go down to Detroit and implore forgiveness on their knees from the Americans for what they had done and to demand of me the restoration of this fort to that government."

Among supporters of the war, news of Hull's surrender produced calls for the resignation of Secretary Eustis. Federalist editors accepted Hull's account as if it were Holy Writ. Infamous attacks were being made on him, said the *Columbian Centinel*, "in order that an imbecile and improvident Administration may escape the execration of the People."

Emotions were at their peak when news arrived that the frigate *Constitution* under Captain Isaac Hull (the general's nephew) had captured and destroyed the British frigate *Guerriere* between Halifax and Bermuda. Close action lasted less than half an hour, but the *Guerriere*'s hull was so shattered that she had to be burned and sunk. Better marksmanship and superior tactics decided the conflict between two evenly matched vessels—the American with thirty per cent heavier guns, the British with fifty per cent faster firepower.

Following the *Constitution* into port came Commodore Rodgers' squadron after a seventy-day sweep almost to England and to the Azores. He had sighted not a single enemy warship, after the *Belvidera*, and took only seven prizes. Yet the mere fact that so powerful a group of American warships was at sea forced the British to concentrate their own naval force, and thus gave American merchantmen an open road to safety. Together the two exploits invigorated the whole war effort and emphasized the need to uplift land operations.

Monroe, a colonel in the Revolution, knew the best man to command both in East and West—himself. He first was denied a temporary appointment over Dearborn, then volunteered to accept the personal danger and political hazards of an attempt to retake Detroit. By pre-arrangement, recommendations for that task came to the President from Richard Rush, General John Mason, and Justice Duvall. Rush, sending Monroe the draft of his letter, said he had not expressed himself "as if possessed of your determinations." Madison told Monroe he would willingly consent to any arrangements Eustis might make with him, but he was inclined to think that the best antidote to Hull's surrender would be found in successful operations under Dearborn.

That hope was dashed by a confidential note from Quartermaster General Morgan Lewis saying that Dearborn's army was "but the shadow of a regular force," inadequately staffed and ill supplied. Dearborn's own letters left his objective in doubt—whether Montreal or Niagara—but it was clear that he did not have troops enough for either. "I am thus led," wrote Madison to Monroe, "to the idea which I find by letters from Rush, Mason, etc., occurs to the best judges among our best friends, of availing the crisis if possible of your services."

Monroe wrote joyously to Rush that he was to set out in a few days to manage the western troops. This set the stage for the real purpose of Rush, Mason, and Duvall—to create a vacancy in the State Department and induce the President to give the place to Thomas Jefferson. Nobody but Jefferson, Rush wrote to the President, could fill the chasm vacated by Monroe's departure. "May not his venerable and almost canonized form be seen to step forth . . . at such a time, at such a call?"

Madison dismissed the Jefferson suggestion without even mentioning it to Monroe. He knew what the Federalists would say—that Madison had abdicated the Presidency to the man who cut down the Army and froze naval development by shifting from frigates to worthless gunboats. The President ended the Monroe assignment by shifting Winchester's command to the Kentuckians' idol, William Henry Harrison, United States brigadier and major general of Kentucky militia.

Monroe told Henry Clay how it all happened. The President originally made a "sudden and unexpected" proposal that Monroe take command in the West, but on mature reflection concluded that he could not be spared from his present post. "I had no opinion on the subject, but was prepared to act." Monroe's fidelity to truth had remarkable elasticity.

Dearborn displayed resentment when he learned that his command included the Niagara operations. He transferred a large part of his regulars from "what I considered my immediate command Lower Canada," and now was unable to move against Montreal. The disaster at Detroit, he said, enabled Brock to concentrate enough troops at Niagara to drive out General Van Rensselaer before reinforcements could reach him. Brock actually ordered his Detroit forces to invest Fort Wayne and came back alone. "I expect an attack almost immediately," he wrote to Prevost. The Americans could easily turn his left flank at Fort George, using boats on Lake Ontario at the mouth of the Niagara.

Dearborn, postponing his Montreal campaign until 1813, told the President that for it the Army needed five new major generals, four brigadiers and 50,000 regulars. He hoped that his command would be cut down to exclude distant points (meaning nearby Niagara). Madison replied that the mutual relations between the objectives required a common command. He agreed that the lateness of the season made an immediate advance into Lower Canada impracticable, but they should keep in mind that Quebec was the *nerve center* of British North America.

The President almost regretted that the disaster at Detroit did not come earlier, thus speeding up the building of ships to gain control of the lakes. That method, he observed to Dearborn, would have been adopted at the outset if Hull had not promised an easy conquest of them by land. Naval command of those waters "ought to have been a fundamental point in the national policy from the moment the peace" of 1783 took place, thus making Canada "a hostage for peace and justice." Richard Rush told John Adams of a remark the President made at this time: "If the British built thirty frigates upon [the lakes] we ought to build forty." Replied Adams: "No President of the United States ever said a wiser thing."

Major General Stephen Van Rensselaer of the New York militia saw his force on the Niagara front double in a fortnight, rising from 2,600 to 5,170. Inspector General Alexander Smyth, transferred to field duty, brought 1,650 regulars and straightway claimed supreme command. A brigadier general in the regular army, he asserted, outranked a major general of militia. Dearborn quashed that unwarranted idea, whereupon Smyth halted his troops at Buffalo, saying that he disapproved of a decision to cross the Niagara below the Falls. He disregarded a summons to attend a conference at Lewiston.

Second in command under Van Rensselaer was his cousin and chief strategist, Colonel Solomon Van Rensselaer. *Smyth would outrank him in the field.* Apparently to avoid that, the two Van Rensselaers abandoned a well-conceived plan to outflank Fort George while storming across the river at Lewiston, and chose only the latter move. Smyth was ordered to bring his brigade to Lewiston, but the order was so timed as to permit his arrival only for mopping up after Solomon carried the Queenstown Heights.

The Van Rensselaers took 1,000 men across the Niagara when 5,000 were available. They used only thirteen boats, although eighty were at hand. Their slow movement allowed General Brock to ride from Fort George to direct the battle. (He came alone, supposing it was a feint to cover an easier attack on Fort George.) Colonel Van Rensselaer and his men courageously charged up the Queenstown Heights. The militiamen on the American side refused to cross the river to support him. The invading force was overwhelmed, 60 killed, 170 wounded, 764 surrendered. In one sense it was an important American victory that stirred no thrill of pride. General Brock was killed.

General Van Rensselaer made his report and resigned, the command passing to Smyth. That valiant officer, bypassing Dearborn, wrote to Eustis: "Give me here *a clear stage*, men, and *money*, and I will retrieve your affairs or perish." Eustis chillingly ordered him to direct all communications to his superior officer. Smyth replaced the decamped militia in a month, then issued a public manifesto, denouncing the Van Rensselaers and announcing that in a few days his troops would "plant the American standard in Canada." Madison, reading it, sent a command that if Smyth received such an order from Dearborn he should obey it; otherwise he should take the opinion of his general and field officers on the expediency of the measure.

Before that message arrived Smyth outdid himself. In a new proclamation he announced to his own and the British Army that "the time is at hand" to conquer "a country that is to be one of the United States." Rewards and honors for the brave, infamy and contempt for cowards! "Come on my heroes!"

There was no time for the President to deal with this before news of Smyth's "invasion" arrived. He spent half a day putting his army in boats. When all was ready, he sent a "flag" across the river with a demand for the surrender of Fort Erie. Receiving a refusal, he unloaded his boats.

Fearful of being shot by his own men, Smyth fled from his command and asked leave to retire from it. He received the reply: "The President desires that you may do so." From the pen of Colonel Isaac Coles, Dolley Madison's cousin and commander of a regiment under Smyth, the President received (via Jefferson) a twenty-eight-page description of the general's conduct. It could have been boiled down to four words: martinet, ignoramus, fool, trickster. Congress eliminated him from the Army by merging his permanent post of inspector general with that of adjutant general.

These incredible performances on land, displaying the incompetence of general after general, all took place in the final months of the 1812 presidential campaign in which James Madison was a candidate for re-election. As handicaps, that piled several Ossas on Pelion.

53 / RE-ELECTION

Few were surprised when DeWitt Clinton, boss of New York State, continued to seek the Presidency after the Republican (Democratic) congressional caucus, 82 to 0, presented James Madison for a second term. Federalist leaders held off until they should discover whether the combined *anti*-feelings of the day—against war, taxes, France, and trade restriction—would warrant the presentation of a ticket of their own.

The Clintonian press charged Madison with incompetent management of the war. The outcry in New England was against him as maker of the war and agent of Napoleon. In Massachusetts, wrote William Plumer, "sedition and a spirit approaching to revolution and treason displays itself in the face of day." The object of all this Federalist bluster, commented patriotic John Adams, was to get Madison out. But who was to get in? Jay? Clinton? Pinckney? "I own I prefer Madison to all three, at the present moment." None of them, however, could "essentially or materially depart from Madison's present system."

Ben Stoddert, former Secretary of War, astutely told other Federalist leaders that support of a second-string Democrat was the prelude to defeat. In politics as on the stage, it took a hero to defeat a villain. His hero was Chief Justice John Marshall, the only person who might defeat Madison in his own state. Should Virginia persist in fastening "the obnoxious and fatal administration of Mr. Madison" upon the country, he wrote anonymously in the Alexandria *Gazette*, "we may bid adieu to the Union, and prepare for the horrors of intestine commotion, civil war, and all the calamities that have desolated the old world."

Marshall, sounded out by various Federalists, showed relish for the overtures without indicating acquiescence. Opposed to the war, he gave advice to Robert Smith: "The lines of subdivision between parties, if not absolutely effaced, should at least be convened for a time; and the great division between the friends of peace and the advocates of war ought alone to remain." The Clintonians dismissed Marshall. Madison could not be beaten if he carried New York, and who but Clinton could defeat him there?

On August 15 the Federalists convened an Assembly of Notables (so dubbed by Madisonians) in New York City. Deep secrecy surrounded the three-day meeting, until the *National Intelligencer* published so accurate an account of it that Clinton's principal organ labeled it a complete FALSEHOOD in capital letters. The convention was told that at a meeting with Gouverneur Morris and others (Jay and King), Clinton declared that "all political connections between himself and the Democratic party in the United States had ceased and would not again be renewed." The conclave on hearing this adopted resolutions, using no names, but pledging to support the candidate who would best promote Federalist objects.

Morris (after writing to Clinton that he was disgusted at the weakness of the resolutions) denied publicly that any had been adopted or that he had seen Clinton during the period involved. (The secret meeting was held in advance, on August 5.) Robert Goodloe Harper wrote to Colonel Lynn of Maryland describing the assurances received from Clinton and the resulting plan "to let the Clintonian Democrats take the lead . . . and to support them silently with our votes." Keep this strictly secret, he adjured. After the storm broke he used two columns in the *Federal Republican* to pronounce it "utterly untrue" that any person or persons at the meeting communicated with Clinton or that any representation of his political sentiments was made to that body. Of course, he said, the convention gave thought to the fact that Clinton's election would prevent Madison from hiring 20,000 to 30,000 French troops and would avert a dissolution of the Union.

Although Rufus King attended the secret meeting with Clinton, he opposed the alliance with him. A memorandum in his papers coincides with the *Intelligencer*'s account of the conference. He wrote to his Republican half-brother, Major General William King of the Massachusetts militia: "It is well known that I do not approve of Mr. Madison's administration—but between him and Mr. Clinton for reasons which in my judgment deeply concern the public liberties, I prefer the election of Mr. Madison."

The President was in a perilous situation. His only opponent was a leading member of his own party, who had the solid support of the Federalists. Democrats (as rank-and-file Republicans were now almost universally calling themselves) could vote for Clinton because of opposition to the war or dissatisfaction with its conduct, without abandoning their own party.

Clinton and his diverse supporters adjusted themselves to that situation. Throughout New England they offered the alternatives, "Madison and War! or Clinton and Peace." In militant Pennsylvania, wrote Samuel Carswell to Madison, Clinton's commissioners pledged that the war "shall be prosecuted till every object shall be attained for which we fight." Sérurier described Clinton as the thunderbolt of war and angel of peace. His emissaries were proclaiming in the South and West that three months after his election "the colors of the Republic would float over Quebec." In New York and Massachusetts he gave assurances "that he would hasten to finish so disastrous a war."

Except for "one poor rickety print" in New York City (so wrote Maturin Livingston), Clinton controlled the entire press of the state through distribution of public printing. Its powerful metropolitan publications were able to "poison the public mind in the remotest parts of the state." Eustis formed an easy target, but Gallatin was a bigger one. Only a change of Presidents could rid the government of that French monster of chicanery.

The catastrophe at Detroit at first drew Clintonian suspicions that Madison had appointed "the imbecile and inefficient Hull" from inherent sympathy of character; but on reading Hull's defense the same New York *Columbian* had naught but praise for his soldierly report, "simple, frank and manly." A capable general had been done in by Executive incompetence.

Clintonian agents were soon swarming through the Pennsylvania mountains, laden with pamphlets blaming the administration for the loss of Hull's army and general lack of energy. A fiery ex-chaplain of the Continental Army, 76-year-old David Jones, relayed the latter charge to the President with the comment: "I am sorry that for months past, you have given them so much room for their assertion. . . . My dear sir, if you must die politically, die gloriously." Madison instantly re-appointed him chaplain, to put spirit if not saintliness into the armed forces.

Needing a vice-presidential candidate, the Clinton managers were reluctant to name a Federalist. They already had that party's votes and putting a member of it on their ticket would drive away Republican votes. Three North Carolinians rejected offers of the nomination in exchange for their state's electors, who were to be chosen by the legislature. Clinton finally settled on Jared Ingersoll, a prominent Pennsylvania Federalist. His pulling power matched that of Madison's partner Elbridge Gerry—both zero.

Hull's defeat produced a drive among Madison's supporters to push Eustis and Hamilton (the latter far gone in alcoholism) out of office.

Retain them, declared Senator Crawford, and the President "must be content with defeat and disgrace in all his efforts during the war." Congressman Adam Seybert of Pennsylvania warned that the rising critical torrent against these men endangered Madison's re-election.

Richard Rush drew Jared Ingersoll's rebellious son Charles (Republican candidate for Congress) into the anti-Eustis campaign. Write a letter to be shown to the President, he requested, but not in Ingersoll's usual vocabulary. Avoid the terms "damnation, infernal, scabby, rotten and such like." Ingersoll complied. With all this before him, Madison suggested to Gallatin a shift of places within the Cabinet (presumably sending Monroe to the War Department, Gallatin to State). It would be politically disastrous, Gallatin replied. Madison decided to ride out the storm.

Through the pen of Thomas Addis Emmet, Irish refugee and state attorney-general, the New York Clintonian committee put out a manifesto assailing Madison's nomination by a congressional caucus and attacking him as a Virginian. The Pennsylvania Democratic committee replied with a broadside decrying the attempt to sow jealousy among the states. It pointed out that eight Republican legislatures had endorsed Madison, against New York's solitary approval of Clinton, then launched into a eulogy of the candidate. Madison's writings as Secretary of State "were among the ablest state papers, and the best defense of neutral rights, which modern times have produced." The firm, impartial course of his administration commanded respect and admiration. His messages as President proved him to be a profound public jurist, "intimately acquainted with the rights and wrongs of his country, able to defend the one and avenge the other."

A month later the Pennsylvania committee took up the charge of misconducting the war. Congress alone could provide the means of defense, while "to impute to Mr. Madison the failure of every military expedition, or the defection of every military chief," was to place his reputation on a foundation that could not have supported a *Washington*.

One Clintonian charge was true: Madison tolerated wartime trade that supported British arms in Portugal and Spain. The Pennsylvanians turned this into a political asset. "Never did the abundant harvests of Pennsylvania find a quicker or a better market." And were American manufacturers complaining? "Why, the war is the main spring of the hopes of every manufacturer and mechanic for property and wealth." Exclude British competition, and the *second American war* would serve to perpetuate "that independence which the first war so gloriously achieved." High farm prices and a huge market may have won more votes for Madison than all the utterances of supporting editors and politicians.

Personally the President was a bystander in the contest. Charles Ingersoll recorded "on high authority, that while a candidate for the presidency, no one, however intimate, ever heard him open his lips or say one word on the subject." He did comment on the *experimentum crucis* in mid-October, as successive state and federal polls were held. Maryland, New Jersey, New Hampshire, and North Carolina were doubtful, he reported to Jefferson; Pennsylvania shaken but reputedly safe; the other states "pretty decided on one hand or the other."

Presidential electors were to be chosen at various times by statewide voting in New Hampshire, Rhode Island, Pennsylvania, Virginia, and Ohio. The decision would be by electoral districts in Massachusetts, Maryland, Tennessee, and Kentucky. In the nine other states, the legislatures would choose the electors. New Jersey's Federalist legislature switched to that system at the last moment, after the October state election clearly forecast a Madison victory.

Madison was conceded Virginia, South Carolina, Georgia, Kentucky, Tennessee, and Louisiana. Clinton was sure of New York, New Jersey, Connecticut, and Rhode Island. Vermont and New Hampshire, voting early, divided, Madison carrying the former. On October 30 and November 2, Pennsylvania and Virginia went overwhelmingly for Madison. Maryland split its vote, Madison carrying six districts, Clinton five.

That left the decision to North Carolina and Ohio, and Clinton needed both to win. A rumor swept Washington and was forwarded by North Carolina congressmen, that a New Yorker with a bag of money had taken the stage to Raleigh. Back from Raleigh came word that two suspicious-looking men got off the stage, took one look and decamped. Twenty Federalists thereupon joined the Republicans in piling up a 130-to-60 majority for Madison. They did so, lamented one of the faithful sixty, on the argument "that as agents were at hand to buy their voices, they must, to prove their incorruptibility, vote for Madison." The year ended before Ohio's belated returns completed the final tally—Madison 128; Clinton 89.

Sérurier made a shrewd appraisal of the contest. Clinton's fatal weakness was his obligation to the Federalists, which required him, if he won, to reverse the whole system of the administration. This conviction alienated nearly all Republicans "while the honorable and lofty conduct of Mr. Madison rallied to him the minds which his first military reverses had swept away." His friends were united in saying that he forbade intrigue, declaring that he committed himself to the judgment of the Republic: "If it continued him in the direction of affairs, he would acquit himself with all the zeal possible, and in case it retired him, he would be satisfied with having been four years honored with its confidence, and with having done, for its dignity and dearest interests, all that the times permitted to him."

Madison's margin of victory was narrow indeed, but the marvel was that he won at all. The outcome was a testimonial both to the personal confidence felt in him during military misfortunes and to the enduring loyalty of Republican voters to their party.

The election was still uncertain when Madison addressed Congress on November 4. It was consoling that the misfortunte at Detroit had roused new ardor and determination among the people. The expectation of gaining control of the lakes by invasion of Canada had been disappointed, but "measures were instantly taken to provide on them a naval force superior to that of the enemy."

The President denounced the refusal of Massachusetts and Connecticut governors to furnish militia for coast defense. They were construing the Constitution as if the United States were "not one nation for the purpose most of all requiring it." He gave Commodore Rodgers credit for the safe return of American merchant vessels. Captain Hull and all on board the *Constitution* were applauded for the "commanding talents" and courage that brought them victory at sea.

Madison reviewed the steps he had taken toward a pacification with England, but said that the British attitude toward impressment made it "unwise to relax our measures in any respect." Affairs with France were at a standstill.

The President called for vigorous measures to fill up the army and enlarge the navy. Enlisted men must be paid higher wages to match the general rise. More high officers were needed; the staff establishment required reorganization; militia laws should be revised.

In conclusion Madison affirmed that the spirit and strength of the nation were equal to the support of all its rights. Americans knew that the war in which they were engaged "is a war neither of ambition nor of vainglory." It was being waged for the maintenance of our own commercial rights and maritime independence. "To have shrunk under such circumstances from manly resistance would have been a degradation blasting our best and proudest hopes." It would have acknowledged that on the sea, equally open to all independent nations, the American people were vassals. Entangled in no connection with other powers, ever ready to accept peace with justice, "we prosecute the war with united counsels and with the ample faculties of the nation," until, under divine blessing, peace be speedily obtained.

Federalist Congressman Taggart pronounced the message to be "smooth, jesuitical, abounding with erroneous statements and false coloring." Sérurier noted the skill with which Madison fulfilled the need in a republic of offering something to everybody. The East, disliking the war but wanting a larger Navy, was to get it. The call for military vigor pleased the warlike faction. The conspicuous silence as to flour exports mollified commercial interests. The minister performed his duty by protesting the unfriendly attitude toward France. He would discover, Monroe retorted, "that the President had feebly expressed the discontent of the nation." That prediction, Sérurier observed to Bassano, was fulfilled when the House of Representatives overwhelmingly defeated a bill to stop the exportation of grain and flour to British armies in Spain.

British Admiral Warren (Sawyer's successor) concentrated on Madison's intention to gain naval superiority on the Great Lakes. If that comes about, he warned his government, "all the Indian force will be destroyed" and defenses weakened against the "efforts of Madison to wrest the Canadas from the British Empire." Build more ships of thirty-two and twenty guns, he advised.

From Chargé Russell, arriving home, the President received confirmation of Castlereagh's intransigent position on impressment. It included evidence, contrary to American belief, that there never had been any thought of yielding on that point in the past. Minister King in 1803 and his successors had mistaken British cordiality for tentative acceptance of their proposals. Castlereagh's adament position upset Madison's belief that once the Orders in Council were out of the way, impressment would be easy to dispose of. That left no acceptable way out of the impasse except by gaining the national objectives in war.

On December 3—the same day the Electoral College cast its ballots for President—William Eustis resigned as Secretary of War. Madison, concurring, praised his zeal and constancy "under difficulties peculiarly arduous and trying." The President would have kept him in office, Congressman Harper believed, but yielded to congressional criticism of him for want of energy.

Actually, Eustis had extraordinary energy which he exhausted on the detailed work of his understaffed department. What he lacked was a full grasp of military strategy and the ability to appraise the capabilities of army commanders. Madison, as yet, had acquired no competence in those fields, nor did he realize the deficiencies of the Secretary.

When Nancy Spear, javelin-tongued relative of the Baltimore Smiths, heard that Eustis was out she exclaimed: "Lord, how it will startle poor Mr. Hamilton; it seems so like saying 'be ye also ready.' " Hamilton, to offset his compulsive tippling, was fortified by the continuing naval spectaculars. Following the return of Rodgers and Decatur, he approved Rodgers' suggestion that the ships go out in squadrons, thus compelling the enemy to concentrate and reducing his ability to attack merchantmen. Once at sea, they would separate for raiding purposes. In September Rodgers, Decatur and Bainbridge were ordered to sea with the frigates the *President*, the *United States*, and the *Constitution* as their respective flagships. Their successful departure brought a wail from the British Admiralty to Admiral Warren. With 97 ships of war under his command he had allowed these American squadrons to go to sea and thus forced the British Navy to employ heavy convoys and set up four strong patrolling squadrons to cover the Atlantic as far south as St. Helena.

Out of the Atlantic, in November, came word that the 18-gun *Wasp* boarded and captured the 22-gun British brig *Frolic*. With neither ship able to sail, both were captured by the 74-gun *Poictiers*. The glory won by the smaller vessel gave an opening for Madison's naval program. Hamilton urged the building of 74-gun ships of the line. The House committee agreed but needed help to overcome an alliance of antinaval members and opponents of big ships. Under the management of presidential secretary Coles, a grand entertainment for members of Congress was given by Captain Stewart on board the almost-rebuilt *Constellation*. President Madison broke custom and attended.

The festivities put the House in a proper mood, but conversion of the Senate required a second celebration. Madison did not attend. Dolley and her house guests, Maria Mayo and Eliza Coles, drove past wildly cheering crowds. For word had come that the frigate *United States*, under Decatur, had captured the British frigate *Macedonian* west of the Canary Islands and brought her to Rhode Island. During the evening, Decatur's dispatches were brought to the White House; the *Macedonian*'s flag was paraded at the naval party.

When the news reached London the Admiralty could not believe it. The newest, largest frigate in the British navy, timbered with oak against weaker American fir, had been reduced (in Captain Carden's words) to "a perfect wreck and unmanageable log." "In the name of God," cried the *Times*, what was being done with a naval strength between Halifax and the West Indies seven times as great as the entire United States Navy? Congress voted to build four ships of the line and six 44-gun frigates.

There was one notable casualty, not of the naval battles but of the celebrations. Navy Secretary Hamilton became publicly intoxicated at both parties. On December 30 Hamilton authorized the *Intelligencer* to announce his resignation. Until that time, wrote Congressman Harper, it would have been treason to speak aloud what everybody knew. On the 29th, the President summoned Hamilton to the White House. The Secretary went with his commission in his pocket. In the United States, Madison observed to him, an officer could not be useful when public opinion was sufficiently set against him. Hamilton replied that the only glory the country had won came from his department. The navy, Madison responded, could not operate without appropriations. "Sir, I understand your meaning," replied the Secretary, "and here is my commission." In formally accepting his resignation, the President testified (with good reason) to the faithful zeal and unimpeachable integrity with which Hamilton had discharged his trust.

The War Department was not attractive to men with political ambition. Monroe, taking the assignment temporarily, refused a permanent appointment after consulting Crawford about presidential prospects in 1816. General Dearborn refused it. So did Crawford. That virtually reduced the field to John Armstrong, whose appointment was pressed by Gallatin.

Madison cited his own and Monroe's objections to him: he was reputed to be indolent and bad-tempered, and he had many enemies. The public, Gallatin argued, had a confidence in Armstrong that would shield the administration from attacks. Indolence would be overcome by a sense of duty and fear of disgrace. Richard Rush and Thomas Leiper of Philadelphia joined the chorus of praise for Armstrong. Madison reluctantly sent Armstrong's name to the Senate, in the hope (he wrote afterwards) that his "objectionable peculiarities" could be diminished by conciliating confidence and presidential control.

For the naval post, Madison chose William Jones of Philadelphia, sea-captain, merchant, and ex-congressman, who had refused the same post in the Jefferson Cabinet. Congressman Roberts of Pennsylvania described the general reaction to the two appointments: "The public voice says these two men in qualification are the fittest in the nation. . . . Madison has now formed a cabinet that will conduct us to peace if any human means can do it."

Madison's attempt to lift Army pay from five to eight dollars a month raised congressional cries of extravagance, but the House Military Committee reported it "in compliance with the urgent wishes of the cabinet." Exemption of soldiers from arrest for debt was denounced by Federalists as an unconstitutional invasion of sacred property rights. Lowering the enlistment age to eighteen robbed parents of their control of children. The government, intoned Josiah Quincy, was welcome to recruit from jails and brothels. "But here stop . . . have compassion for the tears of parents." He knew it was useless to speak, since "the will of the Cabinet is the law of the land." But there was a way to deal with recruiting officers: New England should invoke the old laws against kidnaping.

Ezekiel Bacon of Massachusetts explained the need for exemption from arrest for debt. It was to stop the scandalous collusion in his own state by which pretended patriots enlisted, collected the federal bounty, then were arrested for fictitious debt and released on bail. Collusive judges postponed their trials indefinitely.

A weepy Senate kept the enlistment age at twenty-one but stuck to the exemption from arrest: the scandal in Massachusetts could not be overlooked. The bill passed, but the partisan pattern deepened when the administration asked for enlargement of the army and reorganization of its staff departments. The attempt to raise 35,000 regulars had failed because of the five-year enlistment forced on the President by Congress. Congress was asked to authorize twenty new regiments of twelve-months men, the President to appoint all officers under the rank of colonel without senatorial confirmation. This meant, in practical effect, that colonels instead of congressmen would select the junior officers.

Congress clung to part of its patronage by limiting unconfirmed appointments to periods when the Senate was not in session. Federalists hardly debated the bill at all but took this opportunity, as Harper expressed it, "to deliver themselves of their war speeches with which they were pregnant last session." Quincy took the lead, denouncing Cabinet government by three Virginians and a foreigner—Jefferson (the invisible master), Madison, Monroe, and Gallatin. Daily and nightly these men stirred antipathy to England and cringed before Bonaparte. To say such things, Quincy knew, would loose a thousand tongues with cries of "traitor" and "British gold," but he did not heed the yelpings, the howlings, and snarlings of the native curs and imported hounds and spaniels whom corrupt men kept in pay. Eastern Democrats (but this was expunged from the published record), were "reptiles which spread their slime in the drawing room;" administration supporters haunted the Executive "like toads, that live on the spittle of the palace and [Dolley's] levee." Worse vulgarities about the Madisons went wholly unrecorded.

For these "foul and undeserved aspersions," Rhea of Tennessee had "one only answer—'*Let him who is filthy be filthy still.*'" Speaker Clay spoke for two days rebutting Quincy, emphasizing Castlereagh's rejection of Madison's peace terms, ridiculing the idea of Virginian presidential plots. If, as Quincy charged, Madison was designated for the Presidency before his predecessor retired, he was so designated by "public sentiment which grew out of his known virtues, his illustrious services, and his distinguished abilities."

Harper described the impact of Clay's reply to Quincy: "Never was man more severely castigated or one who more richly deserved it." Editors Hanson and Wagner transferred the whispering campaign against Dolley Madison to their own columns in a pretended review of a nonexistent book containing a chapter entitled "*L'Amour et al fumée ne peuvent se cacher,*" dealing with sexual infidelity in the wife of an allegedly impotent husband. "The attack on Mrs. Madison," wrote Federalist Charles Carroll, "is very reprehensible and the calumny unfounded."

The House approved Madison's request for six additional major generals and six brigadiers after Chairman Williams denied that it was part of a scheme to make Monroe a lieutenant general. Eustis, the chairman said, had favored creation of the higher post, but "the people in the white house" turned it down. Gallatin redrafted Acting Secretary Monroe's bill revamping the general staff and reorganizing the supply system. Three offices were consolidated under a Superintendent General of Military Supplies—total budget, $10,000. On the administration's repellent request that $5.5 million be raised by taxation, Congress did nothing until it was too late. So the President called a special session for May. To close the yawning financial gap, the Treasury was authorized to borrow $21 million.

To ease the way to peace, Madison asked Congress to confront England with an actual law, instead of a presidential promise, excluding British seamen from American vessels after the close of the war. Federalists inconsistently called it a *temporary* scheme to obtain peace by subterfuge, a crippling *permanent* blow to the American merchant marine. Advocates replied that it would either bring the war to a satisfactory end or have no effect whatever. It became law.

Far stronger resistance met the President's request for authority to occupy East Florida, immediately to thwart a British occupation, but with the thought of securing the province as reparation for commercial spoliation. The United States already held Amelia Island and other coastal territory. Spanish agent Onís announced in September that he had power from the (British-controlled) Ferdinand junta to cede the territory. An interview verified Monroe's belief and Madison's certainty that he was lying (seeking to delay an American occupation). Seminole, Creek, and Choctaw Indians began using both the Floridas as bases for border raids. Intercepted letters showed Spanish stimulus.

Madison called on the governor of Tennessee for 1,500 militiamen, to be marched to New Orleans, and directed Major General Pinckney to assemble forces on the East Florida frontier. He then drafted a message asking for invasion powers to cope with savages incited by Spanish officials "to a merciless war against the United States." He would occupy the territory, not as an act of hostility "but subject to future amicable negotiations for adjusting all differences between Spain and the United States." (In that settlement, of course, East Florida was to be acquired in payment of spoliation claims.)

The message never was delivered. Senator Anderson of Tennessee jumped the gun with a bill to grant this authority, and the Senate cut it to a power, already exercised, to take Mobile. By this strategy, wrote Senator Gilman, "an effectual and humiliating check was given" to the unwarrantable proceedings of the Executive. The decisive votes came from factional Republicans.

General Armstrong took over the War Department on February 5 and gave an immediate demonstration of his "objectionable peculiarities." Forced, through the Senate's action, to recall the Tennessee militia expedition, he sent a cold, curt note to high-spirited General Andrew Jackson. The causes of taking the corps to New Orleans having ceased to exist, "you will on receipt of this letter, consider it as dismissed from public service." He was to deliver all public property to General Wilkinson and accept the thanks of the President.

Jackson forwarded the "astonishing order" to Madison, disbelieving that he could be responsible for dismissing 2,000 men 800 miles from home, without money or supplies, disarmed in a savage wilderness. Armstrong made amends with high praise and a direction to retain arms.

The advent of two secretaries did not change the pattern of events. General Winchester, reaching the Raisin River with 750 men, disbelieved his own scouts and allowed himself to be surprised at dawn by British and Indians. He surrendered his entire force. The shock of the news deepened to rage when paroled prisoners told what followed—indiscriminate massacre of the wounded, with many burned alive by the Indians. Congress authorized the President to retaliate.

The Navy, as usual, dissipated the gloom. The President, on Washington's Birthday, sent Congress a special message telling of the capture and destruction of the 49-gun frigate *Java* by Captain Bainbridge in the *Constitution*—"another example of the professional skill and heroic spirit which prevail in our naval service." The *Java*, being beyond salvage, was burned.

Another message followed, citing a British order licensing importations to the West Indies from "ports of the Eastern States exclusively." This "insulting attempt on the virtue, the patriotism, and the fidelity of our brethren of the Eastern States," he was certain, would attach them more closely to the Union; but he wished Congress to prohibit any trade whatever under special licenses, or any exportations in foreign bottoms, mostly counterfeit. John Randolph assailed the President's "angry, undignified, yea scurrilous message." Sectionalism took over. Middle-state war supporters hated to give up the lucrative trade to Portugal. Calhoun offered amendments stopping only Northern produce. Quincy came back with others hitting the South. Administration forces accepted both restrictions and passed the bill, but the Senate killed it.

Sérurier got into the picture when the mulatto chief, Pétion, sent a ship to the United States flying the unrecognized flag of Haiti. Madison refused to order the ship away and thereby aid British efforts to stir a slave revolt in the United States. The President, Sérurier remarked, was displaying "a great deal of ill humor against our government" but this would vanish whenever good news came from Minister Barlow.

Not a word had been heard from Barlow since January, when he wrote of his reluctant departure for Vilna. Federalists called him a chambermaid carried around by the emperor to humiliate the United States. Then came report after report of French disasters in Russia. These were offset, on February 17, by (misinterpreted) news of Napoleon's safe return to

Paris. Sérurier, at Mrs. Madison's party, was deluged with congratulations, but not from Madison, who could think of nothing but Barlow's "painful journey of 1,200 leagues to accomplish nothing."

News about Barlow arrived next day. He was dead in Poland. His own letters and those of his companion Petry reveal the story. He joined Bassano at Vilna just as Napoleon wrote that his shattered, starved, and frozen army would soon be streaming into that city. "Food! Food! Food!" exclaimed the emperor. "Without it there is no horror to which this undisciplined mass will not resort." He would meet Bassano and the foreign envoys in Warsaw. Barlow and Petry set out, Barlow taking with him his last poem, "Advice to a Raven in Russia," asking: "Black fool, why winter here?" Was it from fear that milder climes no longer furnished

> Your human carnage, that delicious fare
> That lured you hither, following still your friend
> The great Napoleon to the world's bleak end. . . .
> Fear not, my screamer, call your greedy train,
> Sweep over Europe, hurry back to Spain.
> You'll find his legions there; the valiant crew
> Please best their master when they toil for you.

That from the man pictured by Federalists as the devotee and tool of Bonaparte! Stricken with pneumonia, Barlow died on December 26 in the little village of Zarnowiec, north of Krakow. "We paid the last respects to him today," wrote Petry on the 27th. His death, chortled the Alexandria *Gazette*, was a divine interposition frustrating a *formal* alliance with the French despot.

In spite of Federalist resistance and Republican factionalism, Congress when it adjourned on March 3 had given the Executive nearly everything he asked for to carry on the war. His second term began the next day.

Cavalry, marines, and artillery units escorted President Madison to the Capitol on March 3, 1813. He was profoundly moved, he told the large audience, at this evidence that faithful endeavors to discharge arduous duties had been favorably estimated. An enlightened people shared his conviction that the war was "stamped with that justice which invites the smiles of Heaven on the means of conducting it to a successful conclusion." On the issue of it were staked American sovereignty on the high seas and the security of a cruelly suffering class of citizens. (Impressed seamen.)

The justice of the war, he said, was made more conspicuous by the disposition of the United States to arrest its progress. "The sword was scarcely out of the scabbard, before the enemy was apprized of the reasonable terms on which it would be resheathed." The forbidding reception left no reliance except on military resources. These, fortunately, were ample, and systematic exertions alone were needed to render the war short and its success sure: "Already have the gallant exploits of our naval heroes proved to the world our inherent capacity to maintain our rights on one element. If the reputation of our arms has been thrown under clouds on the other, presaging flashes of heroic enterprise assure us that nothing is wanting to correspondent triumphs there also, but the discipline and habits which are in daily progress."

The "presaging flashes," presumably, were the dash of Colonel Zebulon Pike to the Canadian boundary, which his men refused to cross; and the thrilling conduct of Lieutenant Colonels Winfield Scott and John Christie, who waived rank and fought bravely as volunteers in the Battle of Queenstown Heights. Had Pike or Scott commanded at Detroit, the war would have been of a different complexion.

The inaugural address drew the usual Republican praise and Federalist castigation. Opposition newspapers spread the "despicable falsehood" (as the *Intelligencer* called it) that Chief Justice Marshall totally unnerved the President by a fixed and scornful gaze. A Philadelphia newspaper located the stare during the outdoor delivery of the inaugural address; Jacob Wagner (*in absentia*) saw the "guilty effusion spread" over Madison's face in the Senate chamber as the oath was being administered.

From this theme the Federalist press turned to hearty endorsement of a six-column declaration by the British Prince Regent on the causes of the war. He proceeded from two false assumptions—that Napoleon's antedated decree of April 11 correctly portrayed American policy and that Madison accepted Napoleon's contention that a legal blockade required investment of a port *by land* as well as by sea. The "real origin" of the war lay in America's long-continued policy of "assisting the aggressive tyranny of France." Every descriptive phrase echoed the Essex Junto.

Within a week the *Intelligencer* startled the country by saying: "It is understood that the Emperor of Russia has offered to the U. States and Great Britain, his mediation, with a view to promote peace between them, and that a communication to this effect has just been made to our government by Mr. Daschkoff." The semiofficial organ presumed that the government would "not hesitate to accede to a measure, which, having peace solely and simply for its object, may be beneficial, and cannot be injurious, to the U. States."

Timed like a postscript to Madison's warlike inaugural, the pacific tone of this announcement convinced Federalists that it was political chicanery. Its true meaning, declared the *Federal Republican*, was to be found in "Mr. Madison's character for cunning and his habitual deceit and hypocrisy." The Russian offer, the newspaper charged, had been made *and rejected* more than a month before. In evidence, the *Federal Republican* reprinted an item from its own issue of February 1: "It is said that the Russian Minister lately offered his mediation for the restoration of peace between the United States and Great Britain, but it was declined by Mr. Madison."

That statement, the paper now said, could not have resulted from divination. It did indeed seem to impair the President's credibility, but it was a careful perversion of what editor Wagner heard from Danish Minister Soderstrom about an unauthorized Daschkoff overture. Soderstrom repeated the story to Senator Pickering. The following is from Pickering's memorandum:

On January 30, Daschkoff told Soderstrom that two days earlier he remained at Madison's dinner table after other guests withdrew. He told the President that, in the light of what was happening to the French in Russia, he thought it was time for the United States to make peace with Great Britain. "Although he had no instructions from his court yet he would on his own risk offer the Emperor's interference as a mediator." The President said the offer was very liberal and the moment favorable, "but will you or can you guarantee to us all the rights we claim?" That, said Daschkoff, "is out of my power. Mr. D. and the President then went into another room and joined the company."

On February 24, dispatches arrived for Daschkoff and from American Minister John Quincy Adams. Those from Adams pointed toward mediation but made it plain that Daschkoff then had no powers. Madison wanted no peace publicity before his war bills were passed, nor until, by his firm inaugural address, he could convince Great Britain that acceptance of mediation was not based on weakness. He therefore stalled Daschkoff's urgent request for an interview with Monroe until after March 4. The emperor's "humane and enlightened" offer was accepted by the President as soon as his minister presented it.

Madison hoped to gain something, he wrote privately, from the affinity between the Baltic and American ideas of maritime law. Also, Russia was "the only power in Europe which can command respect from both France and England," and Russian prestige was at its zenith. To gain advantage from this the President decided to create a three-man commission, headed by Adams, without waiting for England's response to the Russian offer.

Peace prospects gave a greatly needed stimulus to the $16 million war loan, one-third raised. Anybody who subscribed to it, said the New York *Evening Post*, would "be buying powder and ball to blow his own brains out." Gallatin lifted the interest rate to 7.5 per cent. Combining that with patriotism, David Parish, Stephen Girard, and John Jacob Astor took the entire unsubscribed $11 million. Other bankers rushed in to oversubscribe the loan. Gallatin accepted a place on the mediation commission, taking a leave of absence from the Treasury.

The *Evening Post* continued its patriotic course by republishing, from the Montreal *Herald,* a string of letters from Barlow to Madison, said to have been taken from a Barlow servant on the trip to Poland. The *National Intelligencer* was astonished that the factious American press dared to print such absurd and monstrous forgeries, embodying a supposed offer by Napoleon to make Madison President for life and pay him half a million francs annually in exchange for a declaration of war on England. The concoction was not too monstrous for the *Federal Republican.* "TREMBLE THOU WRETCH," it cried. The American people had "been betrayed, basely betrayed into the hands of France." Forgery was impossible because the fourth letter, dated December 26, 1811, forecast an event totally unknown and unexpected at the time of the 1813 publication in Montreal.

Quite puzzling, until one consults the files of the Montreal *Herald* and discovers that there was no fourth letter. It was written in the office of the New York *Evening Post,* as were, probably, the three others, sent to Montreal for publication. Domestic political references were much too intricate for a Canadian origin.

For third place on the peace commission the President selected Senator James A. Bayard, a Federalist who voted against war but said afterward in debate that there was cause enough to declare it. Instructions to Adams, Gallatin, and Bayard laid heavy stress on impressment, the only important grievance that remained unmitigated. British seamen, it was proposed, should be excluded from the American service, naturalization of seamen be mutually prohibited, deserters surrendered. In return the President expected a clear and definite provision against impressment and no concession of the right to search American vessels for British seamen.

Gallatin and Bayard sailed for Russia on May 9, taking with them two secretaries, George M. Dallas, twenty-year-old son of the noted Philadelphia lawyer, and John Payne Todd, Mrs. Madison's twenty-one-year-old son. The latter was to top off his education with a sight of the old world, financed by his paternal inheritance.

When William Jones took over the Navy Department, four frigates lately at sea were being repaired. Also, the captured *Macedonian* was getting new masts at New York; the rebuilt *Constellation* was bottled up at Norfolk. The *Chesapeake* and *Essex* were at sea. As British concentrations made squadron cruising hazardous, Jones approved the requests of Decatur and Captain Jacob Jones (late of the *Wasp*), to cruise separately with the *United States* and *Macedonian* and perhaps draw off blockading forces. High naval morale went higher yet when Captain James Lawrence brought in the little sloop *Hornet* with survivors of the much heavier brig-of-war *Peacock*, which had been sent to the bottom in fifteen minutes.

In a more vital area, Jones revealed presidential policy by telling Commodore Chauncey that success on land "will depend absolutely upon our superiority on all the lakes." The President's "solicitude on this important subject is only equalled by his . . . confidence in . . . your skill and valor." On Ontario, Chauncey was to build a new corvette to supplement the brig *Oneida* and nine small purchased schooners. On Erie he was to build a second brig. One had been captured from the British in a daring raid by Navy Lieutenant James D. Elliott and Artillery Captain Nathan Towson with two boatloads of volunteers.

Land strategy was taken up at the first Cabinet meeting attended by Secretary Armstrong. The enemy, he reported, had ten or twelve thousand effectives on the Montreal front. They could not be attacked before the mid-May breakup of ice in the St. Lawrence River. To fill the hiatus, he suggested American capture of Prescott, Kingston, York (Toronto), and Forts George and Erie on the Niagara. Warships iced in at Kingston and frigates building at York could be destroyed. Madison approved the plan. Dearborn was ordered to assemble 4,000 men at Sackett's Harbor to attack Kingston by boat and then move against York, capital of Upper Canada.

Next came the appointment of new generals authorized by Congress. Four brigadiers were promoted to major general: James Wilkinson (reputed to be Armstrong's political ally), William Henry Harrison, Wade Hampton, and Morgan Lewis (then quartermaster general). Two Federalists were offered commissions but refused. For greater freedom in naming seven brigadier generals, the President gave recess appointments after Congress adjourned. Here at last the accent was on youth and demonstrated ability. Promoted were Colonels Pike, George Izard (trained in foreign military schools), McArthur and Cass of the Detroit expedition (released by exchange), William Winder (brother of Maryland's Federalist governor), and Thomas Parker. Monroe recommended Winder, Parker, and the seventh appointee, Ben Howard, governor of (Upper) Louisiana Territory. Excepting Howard and Revolutionary veteran Parker, the average age of the brigadiers was thirty-three. Of the new major generals, Harrison was forty, the others in their middle fifties.

In Armstrong's assignment of commanders to nine military districts, Dearborn and Harrison retained command in the North and Northwest. A surprise came in the transfer of Major General Wilkinson from New Orleans to Sackett's Harbor. Armstrong had his own reasons for this assignment which also satisfied the demand of Louisiana senators that this "abandoned and profligate man" be removed from New Orleans.

The national capital was verbally menaced in the spring of 1813 by loud threats from Admiral Cockburn, uttered after he destroyed Havre de Grace and other towns above Annapolis. (His name rhymes with "go burn.") He intended to "make his bow" at Dolley Madison's drawing room before burning the White House and government offices. "I do not tremble at this," wrote Dolley, "but feel affronted that the Admiral (of Havre de Grace memory) should send me notice" of his intention. Secretary Armstrong thought the city safe because the British had no land troops or artillery. The President sent two regiments of regulars to Norfolk and asked Governor Winder to strengthen Fort McHenry, at Baltimore, with fifteen hundred militia.

A presidential order cutting off unopened mail between American citizens and British cartel vessels brought a scream from the Georgetown *Federal Republican* that "James Madison, after the manner of his master, Napoleon of France," had committed "a most profligate and daring act of usurpation and tyranny." Madison went back to *The Federalist* in justifying his order. The President, wrote Armstrong, holds that although his order was based on no specific law, "if the duty of defending the United States be imposed by the Constitution upon the executive authority of the Union, the powers incident to the discharge of that duty must necessarily go with it."

Owing to erroneous reports of heavy British concentrations at Prescott, Armstrong shifted the initial attack to York. Early in May the newspapers disclosed that General Pike and his brigade had sailed for York in Admiral Chauncey's squadron. Dearborn was in supreme command to avoid an army-navy clash of authority based on rank.

Twelve days of silence, and news came that York was captured, 700 prisoners taken. General Sheaffe and 200 regulars escaped to Kingston after burning a nearly completed 30-gun frigate. The 16-gun *Duke of*

Gloucester was captured. There was one tragic American loss. General Pike, whose skill and drive brought victory, was killed, along with thirty-eight other Americans, by an explosion of the powder magazine. The fuse was too short, lamented a British officer, "or the whole column would have been in the air."

Other incidents followed and developed into a long-lasting mythology. It became a pseudo-fact of history that American sailors ransacked the House of Parliament, discovered a scalp in it, and set fire to the building, carrying away the scalp, the mace, a British royal ensign, and destroying the library except for the books they stole.

The truth can be found in official records *of that time*, both Canadian and American. The city was captured on April 27 and capitulated on the 28th. *The Parliament House burned on April 30.* On April 27, a party of sailors looted the public library located in the Elmsley House. There is no doubt about the date. The Reverend John Strachan of York wrote that Commodore Chauncey had gathered up and promised to return the books carried away "*on the 27 April.*" On that same day a detachment of sailors *entered* Parliament House. Commodore Chauncey sent to Secretary Jones "the British standard taken at York *on the 27th of April* last, accompanied by the mace over which hung a human scalp." These articles, said Chauncey, "were taken from the Parliament House *by one of my officers* and presented to me."

All this was three days before the Parliament House burned. When that fire broke out, Major Grafton, commander of the American detachment *guarding York*, was on horseback less than 300 yards away. He rode over to the burning building, about which a crowd was standing, and asked how the fire started. Nobody knew. "At this time there was not in sight an American soldier."

General Dearborn inferred from the reports to him that the building —two connected wooden 24x40 foot halls—was burned by "some exasperated subjects of Canada." Of these there were plenty. The general's proclamation against disorder, wrote a York magistrate, "produced a good effect on the turbulent minds of some wretches of our own population, whose thirst for plunder was more alarming to the inhabitants than the presence of the enemy."

Citing the fire, the magistrates unitedly requested General Dearborn to restore their civil functions—a move (as they described the situation to General Sheaffe) to deal with "a great number of traitorous people [who] had come from the country." At the end of the occupation the magistrates sent a message to Dearborn gratefully acknowledging "a line of conduct so conducive to the protection of a number of individuals, and so honorable to himself."

More than a year later, after Admiral Cockburn carried out his threat to burn Washington, Chancellor Vansittart declared in Parliament that at York the Americans destroyed not only the public buildings but "every house belonging to the meanest individual." Six months after that alleged conflagration, Lieutenant Peter Pelham was captured in battle. When British officers learned that he had been adjutant of the guard during the occupation of York, they appealed to Captain General Prevost to set him free. He was given a special parole on the stated ground that he had been on duty with the regiment that protected the property of the inhabitants of York.

Instead of searching for the truth that was available in the public archives, numerous masochistic American writers have built up a myth that had its origin in the deliberate invention of British and Federalist politicians and editors—not, be it noted, in the contemporaneous utterances of the Canadians most affected.

55 / GREAT LAKES VICTORY; MONTREAL FIASCO

Spring elections in 1813 appeared to reverse the autumnal Federalist trend. The movement toward a Northern confederacy was dashed by the re-election of New York's Governor Daniel D. Tompkins over a Federalist-Clintonian coalition. Governor Plumer almost pulled through in New Hampshire. In Massachusetts, Madison reported to him, loyal citizens had strength enough to curb the dissident majority if not to control policies. Congressman Roberts of Pennsylvania, returning for the special session in May, reported that "the President looks better than I have ever seen him and seems cheerful and affable."

Part of this cheerfulness, probably, was due to the defeat of John Randolph by John W. Eppes—a gain for comfort too great to be offset by the election to the House of Alexander C. Hanson, mendacious publisher of the Georgetown *Federal Republican*. Speaker Clay's 89-to-54 re-election spelled solid Democratic control of the House. The party's nominal two-vote margin in the Senate was negated by the anti-Madison, anti-Gallatin alliance of Republicans Smith, Giles, Leib, German, and Gilman.

Addressing Congress, the President told of the appointment of peace commissioners and his proposal that the United States and England each exclude from its vessels the nationals of the other. Unfortunately, the fairness of this policy did not ensure acceptance. The true assurance of peace lay in vigorous prosecution of the war—a conclusion emphasized by the Raisin River Massacre of prisoners and the naval plunder and conflagration along the Atlantic Coast.

The Treasury, Madison reported, held $1,857,000 on April 1, with about $20 million in loans and $9.3 million in revenue to be received in the coming nine months. Debt payments and war and civil expenses would almost exactly match this. The heavy dependence on loans pointed to the need of additional taxes.

542

This request cued the Federalist response. "The Treasury Bankrupt" was the heading in Hanson's newspaper. To the New York *Evening Post* the call for taxes was a bloody dagger held before the nation's face. If there must be taxes, where was the Secretary of the Treasury who was to define the taxable objects? "Fled from his station, like a coward, as he is, fled to hide himself from the evil in a distant land." That was no sudden thought: the canard already had been spread throughout the country.

With confirmation of the peace commissioners before the Senate, the bipartisan coalition struck by asking whether Gallatin retained the office of Secretary of the Treasury, and if so, who was performing its duties. Madison reported that they were being handled by Secretary Jones under the authority of a 1792 statute. Senator King replied that this law was meant to cover unavoidable absences, not one created by the President himself in defiance of the Constitution and laws.

Gallatin's nomination was referred to a special committee "to inquire and report" upon it. Chairman Anderson called on the President, who said that "inquire and report" did not authorize an official visit of the committee. He would receive a committee instructed to see him.

Besides rewording the Gallatin resolution, the coalition secured the appointment of another committee authorized "respectfully to confer" with the President about his nomination of Jonathan Russell to be minister to Sweden—against which senators were protesting as a needless expense. The Russell committee—a hostile one—reported two postponements of a conference, followed by a June 16 note regretting that the President's continuing indisposition "will not permit him to see the committee of the Senate today, nor can he at present fix a day when it will be in his power."

Word spread quickly that Madison was critically ill of bilious fever. "The thought of his possible death," wrote Sérurier, "strikes everybody with consternation. It . . . would be a veritable national calamity." Vice President Gerry was "a respectable old man, but weak and worn out. All good Americans pray for the recovery of Mr. Madison."

No such concern was visible among House Federalists, led by a bull-necked, bullheaded newcomer named Daniel Webster. He offered five resolutions, embodying the Senate objections to Gallatin's appointment and demanding also to know "when, by whom, and in what manner" the first word of Napoleon's (predated) repeal decree was brought before the President. The motion was full of insinuations that Madison had brought on the war by concealing the decree. It could not be voted down without creating the appearance of presidential guilt. Calhoun's attempt to remove the innuendoes by amendment loosed the vituperative tongues of the Federalists at a moment when Madison was thought to be dying. The President, said Grosvenor of New York, "must soon appear at the bar of Immortal Justice." How would his soul recoil if he must do so bearing the guilt of this bloody crime! Grosvenor did not believe him capable of a crime "combining all the blackest attributes of official turpitude, murder, and treason." Yet if the House failed to investigate his conduct, "Guilty, guilty, guilty, will be the universal verdict."

Congressman Lovett thought that Grosvenor overdid things a trifle. Better tactics were those of fellow New Yorker Oakley, who assailed the President in the most shrewd and cunning manner, "yet in such cautious phraseology, that no old foxes can check him." Grundy of Tennessee sarcastically complimented "these new guardians of the Executive honor," and then spoke "the language of truth" about them. They were systematically at work to destroy national credit, damp the ardor of citizens, paralyze the national energies, "and multiply chances of getting new men into power."

The Webster resolutions were adopted unchanged on June 21, and their author went with Rhea of Tennessee to deliver them to the President. "I found him in his bed, sick of a fever," wrote Webster. "I gave them to him, and he merely answered that they would be attended to." Hanson's newspaper, anticipating Madison's death, employed Shakespearean allusions to cloak a prediction that (there being then no president pro tempore of the Senate) Speaker Clay would seize the Presidency by murdering Vice President Gerry. There was an actual move, Monroe reported, to put Giles in the line of succession by giving him the "pro tem" post as soon as Gerry should succeed Madison.

The hopers and schemers underrated Madison's recuperative powers. On July 2 Dolley wrote that quinine was producing a good effect. "It has been three weeks since I have nursed him night and day. Sometimes I despair! but now that I see he will get well, I feel as if I should die myself from fatigue." On July 7 the *Intelligencer* announced that the President had resumed the most urgent public business.

The resumption consisted of his dictation, in bed, of a defiant refusal to meet with the special Senate committee on the subject of a minister to Sweden. On such a subject, he said, the Executive and Senate were independent and co-ordinate. If the Senate wished information, the Executive would furnish it, or the committee could communicate with the head of the proper department. He was willing to *receive* the committee, but only to explain why he declined to *confer* with it officially.

On hearing this, the Senate swelled up in all its majesty. This body, said Senator King, was "the greatest power in the Constitution, created . . . to impart wisdom, stability and safety to the laws." To pass on a nomination, it needed the same information that caused the President to make it, and he was "bound to impart such information to the Senate when requested." The suggestion that the Senate confer with a mere head of department "tends to degrade the Senate."

Madison had the last word on procedure, but the Senate's word was final on appointments. It resolved, on economy grounds, that it was inexpedient to send a minister to Sweden. The anti-Gallatin committee was then received by the President. It handed him a Senate resolution calling Gallatin's diplomatic appointment incompatible with his Treasury position. Madison regretted that the Senate's action deprived him of its "aid or advice." He said no more. The committee said no more, except, after a minute of silence, goodby. The Senate confirmed Adams and Bayard and rejected the Gallatin nomination, 17 to 18.

Word went to A. J. Dallas that if Madison had declared the Treasury office vacant the Senate would have confirmed Gallatin, but, wrote Dallas, "he firmly refused to do so." Worse than the Federalists was the "malcontent junto of self-called republicans," and Secretary Armstrong "was the devil from the beginning." Dallas doubted that Gallatin would remain in the Cabinet when he learned that the Secretary of War had solicited votes against his confirmation to the Russian mission.

During these developments news reached Washington that France and Russia had signed an armistice. This convinced Madison that England would reject Russian mediation. Such a result, Jones reported to Dallas, would allow Gallatin to determine his own future. It strengthened the President's determination not to weaken the executive power by yielding to the Senate's demand for Gallatin's retirement as a precondition to temporary diplomatic service.

Writing to Gallatin on August 2 (by which time Madison was again riding in public) he said that friendly senators had overstated the support the nomination would receive. Had he made a bargain, founded on a vacancy in the Treasury, he doubted whether it would have succeeded, but even if it were otherwise, he could not accept such a "degradation of the Executive." The whole proceeding, "according to every friendly opinion, will have the effect of giving you a stronger hold on the confidence and support of the nation."

Actually, the President's defeat was caused by the transfer to Paris of his most powerful supporter, Senator Crawford, and by his own illness and the consequent shutting down of the influential White House levees. This reduced Madison's position to a cold, curt assertion of Executive prerogative that struck chillingly upon senatorial self-esteem. Yet from his sickbed he halted the most ambitious attempt yet made to subordinate the President to the Senate in their co-ordinate activities.

Madison's first task upon recovery was to answer Webster's Resolutions. It was easy enough to prove what everybody knew, that he had no knowledge, in 1811, of a predated decree written in 1812. Webster's intended "bitter pill" was his inquiry whether the President had ever remonstrated to France about the decree. Without revealing his personal excoriation of that document to Barlow, the President disclosed his protest, through Monroe, against the "outrageous character" of the French action. Using the Webster Resolutions as a handle, the President furnished a 6,000-word description, by Monroe, of the whole course of diplomatic events, culminating in England's acceptance of the predated decree as a legal basis for repeal of the Orders in Council. Webster was knocked flat by the recoil of his own weapon.

In spite of Federalist obstruction, the special session produced thirty-eight laws, embracing all except a minor one of Gallatin's twelve revenue measures. They included a direct tax of $3 million and authority to borrow $7.5 million. Late in the session the President enlarged his request for a ban on trading with the enemy. The House, in two days, put through a total embargo. "So servile are the majority," wrote John Lovett, "that the little booby at the palace is as much a despot as the Dey of Algiers." The Senate's bipartisan alliance reduced the measure to a penalty on American users of British licenses, thus, said Lovett, ending "Executive Omnipotence."

Madison countered with an order to the navy to halt "the palpable and criminal intercourse" with the enemy, carried on by foreigners under the specious guise of friendly flags. It reached the same end as the defeated embargo and, commented Secretary Jones, was perfectly within the military powers of the President. That same trade had helped re-elect him.

Once more, responding to a congressional resolution for a day of prayer, Madison invited those "piously disposed" to give thanks and offer supplications to the Great Parent and Sovereign of the Universe. He stirred up partisan and religious critics by saying that to be worthy of reception by the Omniscient Being, public homage must come from those who "are guided only by their free choice, by the impulse of their hearts and the dictates of their consciences." A newspaper contributer signing himself "Bible Christian" was unable to find one word in the proclamation "which could be offensive to the ear of a pagan, an infidel, a deist, and scarcely to that of an atheist." The Baltimore *Patriot* praised its spirit of elevated piety and patriotism.

New England's continuing sedition led Justice Story to propose amendments to the "grossly and barbarously defective" criminal statutes. The President ignored the advice and gave similar treatment to Mathew Carey's appeal for action to suppress the "daring, powerful, unprincipled and formidable conspiracy" in Massachusetts. Suppression of free speech, in Madison's opinion, was more damaging than the license it engendered.

The succession of naval victories was interrupted when Captain Lawrence, hero of the *Hornet*, took the frigate *Chesapeake* to sea with an untrained crew and encountered the British frigate *Shannon*. His dying cry, "Don't give up the ship," echoed long after the *Chesapeake*'s surrender. The offsetting victory of the American brig *Enterprise* over the evenly matched *Boxer* gave the President "a just cause of congratulations." Plans for ocean raiding, however, received a blow when Decatur's three ships were intercepted in Long Island Sound by two British squadrons and forced to take refuge in the Thames River. This at least gave Madison the unexpected pleasure of thanking Governor John Cotton Smith for bringing the Connecticut militia vigorously into the national defense.

The tying up of Atlantic frigates released seamen for service on the Great Lakes, where a shipbuilding race was going on. Commodore Chauncey, Secretary Jones reported to the President in June, was following "the course which you were so solicitous he should have done"— make no attack on Admiral Yeo before completion of the *General Pike* assured control of Lake Ontario. Commandant Perry, on Lake Erie, asked for and received permission to take the offensive as soon as his crews were built up.

By this time Dearborn's unfitness for command was becoming too apparent to be ignored, and a temporary illness eased the way to his removal. Armstrong's callous one-sentence letter of dismissal was forwarded by Dearborn to the President, who replied that his esteem had undergone no change, but retirement "was pressed by your best personal friends."

Armstrong had plans which he did not reveal to the President. The day after Dearborn was dismissed he planted a letter from "An Army Officer" in the *Intelligencer*, saying, concerning the Northern command: "I languish for the sight of a man who, understanding his business, will do justice to the army and the country. Under such a man there is both

honor and renown—under any other, confusion, disaster and disgrace."
On the same day he wrote to Major General Lewis: "I shall set out for
the frontier of the North in a few days."

Several months earlier Armstrong had told Gallatin that he wanted to
"make an excursion" towards the Northern front. Although Gallatin had
no wish to see Armstrong "unite the character of general to that of secretary" (so he wrote to Madison) his strategic ideas seemed sounder than
Dearborn's and a visit of a few days might be useful. The Secretary's
departure was delayed for several weeks by the slow progress of General
Wilkinson, from one banquet table to the next, en route from New
Orleans to Washington and his Niagara post. Armstrong's yearning for
command did not inspire his naval colleague with confidence. "Many
begin to believe," wrote Jones, "that the 'Old Soldier' is not a legitimate
son of Mars."

Late in July, Secretary Armstrong outlined Northern campaign plans
to the President. He asked for a concentration of troops at Sackett's
Harbor, on Lake Ontario, with the commending general there to choose
between an attack on Kingston or a movement down the St. Lawrence to
capture Montreal. The plan, approved, was put in the hands of General
Wilkinson when he passed through Washington. That military genius replied that if land and naval forces were strong enough he would make
"a bold feint" against Montreal (how much boldness is required for a
feint?), clear the Niagara Peninsula and send a detachment to Detroit
(thus moving away from both objectives), and then attack either Kingston
or Montreal if the season was not too far advanced. The most useful
action at that moment would have been to deliver General Wilkinson to
the British.

Armstrong overruled the Niagara operation but left the choice between
Kingston and Montreal to Wilkinson, thus giving himself an alibi if things
went wrong. The Secretary and the general left for the North and Madison, recovering from a post-bilious bout with influenza, set out for Montpelier, a journey "prescribed by my physicians as indispensable." Surmis-
ing his departure (unannounced for security reasons), Congressman
Roberts commented: "Poor gentleman, his health needed it. I never saw
a man I commiserated more, not because I think him unequal to his station, but because it is a spectacle of no common interest to see 'a good
man struggling in the storms of fate.' Though he be brave and virtuous
he is put to trial. My best wishes are for his triumph."

The President reported that the four-day journey gave him strength, but his enemies were gleefully pessimistic. His recent illness, the *Federal Republican* asserted, "has made havoc of his constitution, and left him, it is confidently believed, but a few months, perhaps a few days to live." Visitors, moreover, "have left his chamber under a full conviction of the derangement of his mind." John Adams rejoiced when he learned the falsity of a report that Madison "lives by laudanum and could not hold out four months." Within a few weeks the President was riding "a gay saddle horse" to view his plantation, and Dolley was barely able to write letters because of the ever-changing "crowd of company."

The President eagerly awaited news from the lakes. From Ontario it was not good. Pursuing Yeo, Chauncey had lost two schooners in a midnight storm and two more through over-eager attack by their commanders. The situation on Lake Erie caused optimism and concern. Commandant Perry used pumped-out pontoons to lift two brigs over the Presqu' Isle bar and had eight warships ready for action. (British Captain Barclay helped by lifting the blockade while he visited the widow of an army officer.) However, Barclay's new *Detroit*, largest ship of war on the lake, was receiving long-range land guns that would tilt the weight of metal in Britain's favor. Then, on September 23, a speeding express brought Madison this brief dispatch from Perry: "It has pleased the Almighty to give to the arms of the United States a signal victory over their enemies on this lake. The British squadron, consisting of two ships, two brigs, one schooner and one sloop have this moment surrendered to the force under my command, after a sharp conflict."

The messenger carried back Madison's order promoting Perry from master commandant to captain. As a squadron commander, that made him commodore. Dispatches followed with the story of the battle. Outranged by the heavier guns of the *Detroit*, the *Queen Charlotte* and the *Lady Prevost*, Perry's *Lawrence* and *Niagara* and two-gun schooners had greater fire power at close range. He drove at the enemy until the *Lawrence* was disabled, then shifted by boat to the *Niagara* and cut through the middle of the British squadron, raking five British warships with both broadsides. He said not a word about the conduct of the *Niagara*'s jealous commander, who backed his main topsail and delayed by two hours his ship's entry into the battle.

"Perry's triumph," commented John Adams, "is enough to revive Mr. Madison, if he was in the last stage of a consumption." To Congressman-Publisher Hanson the world turned black. "The vanity of a people cannot bear these brilliant naval victories," he lamented, ". . . unless we shortly meet with some reverses, administration will find more friends than enemies in this state by a great deal." The feared result—election of a Republican Maryland legislature which would choose a pro-war governor —was happily averted when the Alleghany County Court stole the county election and reversed the statewide majority.

The war, like politics, was becoming more savage. Twenty-three naturalized Americans were sent to England to be tried as traitors. Madison retaliated by placing forty-six British officers in close confinement, with a notification to Prevost that executions would follow if any of the Americans were put to death. Also, retaliation would follow if Prevost carried out his public threat to destroy American cities, towns and villages. Tempers were not improved when capture of Admiral Warren's tender, the *High Flier*, turned up its journal with entries chronicling the destruction of Frenchtown, Havre de Grace, Frederick and Georgetown —all coastal villages and towns.

From Armstrong in October came reports of near readiness to move down the St. Lawrence against Montreal. Owing to Wilkinson's illness the Secretary was going to accompany the army. He had previously said he would do so because there was bad blood between Wilkinson and General Hampton, who was to attack Montreal from Lake Champlain. Acting thus, Armstrong could claim credit for a victory.

Good news came from Detroit. Harrison's army had occupied Fort Malden and won a decisive victory over the British and Indians on the River Thames, in Canada. (It was not yet known that the great Tecumseh was slain.) The impression made on the Indians, Madison commented, would have a far-reaching effect—even, probably, upon the Southern Creeks, who had slaughtered a hundred men, women and children at Fort Mims and were due for a chastising by General Andrew Jackson and his Tennessee militia.

The President returned to Washington on October 24 and threw Federalist editors into deep depression by attending the Georgetown races. Wrote Richard Rush: "The little President is back, and as game as ever. He mounted his horse on Tuesday and attended by Mr. Monroe and General Mason spurred off to the course Virginia-like—where too he saw a Virginia horse carry the day."

The gaiety was increased by word that General Harrison's threatened eastword movement had caused the British to evacuate the entire Niagara Peninsula. Colonel Winfield Scott, lately exchanged, hastened their retreat by brilliant capture of Fort George. Further cheering news came from Sackett's Harbor, where a British landing party of about a thousand men was driven off by the tactical skill of Brigadier General Jacob Brown of the New York militia. The President promptly gave Brown the same rank in the regular army.

Michigan Territory, reclaimed from British rule and Indian terror, was put under the governorship of Brigadier General Cass. Feed the Indians, Madison directed, and do not let them plunder the whites. The latter too must receive food supplies "imperiously required by humanity," even though such an application of money was "not contemplated by the law."

When Russia entered a new coalition against France, Madison was not impressed by Sérurier's cheerful remark that the coalition had ten heads and France only one. The minister recorded: " 'And what a puissant head!' the President instantly replied, with *even less* grace than conviction in his entire deportment."* Sérurier assured Bassano that the President really felt grieved by French misfortunes (as no doubt he did in relation to American military fortunes); but Rush wrote that every high official from Madison down regarded Napoleon as "personally and peculiarly a deadly enemy to us," the greatest stumbling block to America's commercial objectives in the war.

Late October dispatches from Armstrong suggested indecision and apprehension of failure. He lamented the slow gathering of Wilkinson's forces while the British at Kingston doubled theirs. "With nine days' start of the enemy what might not have been done? At Kingston we shall no longer find him naked and napping"; but, "as the General is now compos, I shall forbear my visit to Canada until a future day." Armstrong did not reveal that on that very day he overruled Wilkinson and ordered a descent on Montreal. Nor could he reveal that instead of Kingston being reinforced, all except two battalions of regulars had been shifted to Montreal. Finally, Wilkinson did not know that he had recovered his health. Armstrong, smelling discomfiture, was leaving the field just when he was most needed to cope with Wilkinson's disability and his feud with Hampton. Madison's reply to Armstrong carried a distant optimism: "In the worst event, I hope an immediate establishment between Kingston and Montreal can be secured, which adding to the advantages already gained in the present campaign, one having so favorable a bearing on the next, will preserve the tone of the nation, and inculcate on the enemy a disposition to peace."

---

*Innocently for once, Historian Henry Adams converted this sarcasm into adulation because his copyist left out the word "*encore*" in "*avec moins de grace encore de la conviction.*"

Reports of the campaign reached the President from various sources. A Canadian newspaper carried Adjutant General Baynes' report that General Hampton's 4,000 men were turned back at the frontier by 460 French-Canadian militiamen. Hampton said he retreated because he received no word of an American army coming down the St. Lawrence.

A single sentence from Armstrong told the Montreal story: "You will find in the enclosed letters [exchanged between Wilkinson and Hampton] the probable termination of the campaign on the St. Lawrence." The correspondence consisted of mutual recriminations followed by decisions of both commanders to go into winter quarters. Armstrong enclosed the Albany *Argus*, for which he had written a carefully inaccurate account of the American descent of the St. Lawrence, presenting the Battle of Chrysler's Farm as an American victory. Unmentioned was the fact that Wilkinson left his rear uncovered against pursuing boats. Armstrong mentioned "three charges of the bayonet," omitting that all were repulsed because Brigadier General Boyd, with 1,800 men against 860, divided his force into three detachments, making each one inferior in successive charges.

For shrewd personal reasons, Armstrong printed the accusatory letters of Wilkinson and Hampton in the *Argus*. To the extent that the two incompetents killed each other off, they absolved the Secretary. He had knowingly assigned the joint operation to two personal enemies, failed to supervise them, assumed direction of operations for his own aggrandizement, and ran for cover when he saw how it was going to end. Madison was not free of blame: Wilkinson's unsavory reputation should have been sufficient warning against approval of the Northern command.

For both President and public, the Montreal failure was tempered by a smashing victory of militia Major General Andrew Jackson over the Creek Indians—a victory that made Jackson the man of the hour in the Southwest. New talent was appearing near the top—Brown and Jackson; Colonel Scott; Colonel Edmund P. Gaines, who handled his regiment so well under Boyd that the British commander sent a flag of truce to ask for postwar friendship; General Izard, who steadied the Champlain army when Hampton fizzled. The war was generating the means of its own prosecution.

On that subject, Secretary Armstrong had his own ideas. He had set the stage for victory; incompetent generals had flubbed it. There was no need for him to put his name to the letter, signed "An Officer of the Army," that appeared in the Albany *Argus* just as he left that city for Washington. Urgently advocating the appointment of a *lieutenant general* to command all the Northern armies, the "Officer" continued: "On whom this important trust should be conferred, will rest with the wisdom of government. I can only add, that if the genius which marked the outlines of this campaign, had shown in its execution, it might have pointed to the individual who is worthy to rule the destinies of the American army."

Addressing Congress on December 7, 1813, President Madison reported that Great Britain, perhaps "mistaking our desire for peace for a
dread of British power," had declined Russian mediation. "Under such
circumstances a nation proud of its rights and conscious of its strength
has no choice but an exertion of the one in support of the other."

The President surveyed the war scene. Captain Perry's adroit and daring conduct had furnished a victory on Lake Erie never surpassed in
luster. In Lake Ontario the enemy avoided decisive conflict. American
naval superiority there permitted offensive operations on the St. Lawrence, but "circumstances attending the final movements of the army"
nullified the efforts. Against this failure he was able to list ten successes
on land, including recovery of Detroit, reduction of York, and occupation of Forts Erie and George on the Niagara River.

Chastened by home-state sentiment, Senate and House took only
eight days to pass an embargo act asked for by Madison to cut off supplies to the enemy. Congressman Hanson's newspaper, no longer jeering
at "poor Madison," so weak and timid, cried out that the President's
whipping-in system had produced "a dictatorship, little, if any, less stern
and griping than the iron despotism of France." John Randolph, decapi-
tated politically, did not expect to survive "the first year of Mr. Madison's
dictationship." The country had been made "one vast prison-house" by
"our merciless and remorseless tyrants."

Sérurier reported things differently. People agreed "that nothing more
energetic and more warlike" than the President's message had ever come
from the Cabinet. In the speedy enactment of the embargo "one sees a
new proof of the stubbornness of Mr. Madison." In Connecticut, the
President was told, the embargo was received with astonishing approval,
as it lowered prices for consumers; but Boston merchants were jubilant
because it would render the government unpopular.

Congressman Hanson regained form. His newspaper published an
English translation, abstracted from the State Department by Robert

Smith, of Turreau's 1809 letter assailing former President Jefferson. Intimating treason in concealment, Hanson moved that the House ask for all correspondence on it. He then withdrew his motion. Administration forces re-introduced and passed it. The House received from Chief Clerk Graham (the translator) an assurance that Turreau withdrew the letter to escape a demand for recall.

Secretary Armstrong returned to Washington on Christmas morning and troubles began at once. An alarmed senator found him lobbying (without authorization) for conscription. General Hampton, en route to a well-earned retirement, informed Madison of Armstrong's promotion system: promising young officers higher rank "without your knowledge . . . and exciting their resentment against you if it did not take effect."

Armstrong's continuance in office, wrote Monroe, "will ruin not you and the administration only, but the whole republican party and cause." He saw additional reason for it in Armstrong's failure to place troops at Fort George (which the British re-occupied) and the burning of nearby Newark "if done by his order." Armstrong denied that he ordered General McClure to burn the town. He authorized it "only in case it should be necessary to the *defence* of Fort George." Madison directed the Secretary to send a frank statement to Prevost "that the burning of Newark was the effect of a misapprehension of the officer," and was being disavowed.

This impelled Armstrong to disclose an order he had just sent to General Harrison, to convert the British settlements on the Thames "into a desert," then conciliate the Indians and turn them loose upon the British inhabitants. Madison ordered a quick reversal of the savage directive. Complying, Armstrong wrote that *the President, on reflection*, thought the measure too severe.

The Secretary sent Prevost a copy of his order giving McClure discretion to burn Newark, then placed a garbled account of it in the *Intelligencer* (signed, as usual, "An Officer of the Army"), absolving himself and convicting McClure of outright disobedience. Prevost responded by proclaiming it his "imperious duty to retaliate on America the miseries" inflicted on Newark. British soldiers and Indians overran the almost undefended Peninsula, burning Buffalo, Lewiston, and Manchester, killing and scalping inhabitants. The Fort Niagara garrison surrendered, and all but three of the 150 soldiers were slaughtered by the Indians.

Navy Secretary Jones, overworked as acting Secretary of the Treasury, begged for relief. Hold on a little longer, the President urged: Gallatin would soon be back from Russia. Jones reported that military expenses for 1814 were anticipated at $24,550,000; naval, $6,900,000. Unless taxes were raised, $29,350,000 would have to be borrowed.

The House sustained Madison's proposal to stimulate recruiting by a financial incentive: bounties were lifted from $16 to $124—a scheme, Webster charged, to raise a mercenary army to conquer Canada. In the Senate, Chairman Campbell presented alternative plans from Armstrong —larger bounties for regulars or a conscripted militia. This, said the Secretary, represented the sentiments of the President. That could be doubted, but not by the Federalists, who cried out that Madison, "the father and patron of this war," was secretly supporting "the hideous system of conscription."

To support his request for total exclusion of imported articles of British origin, the President submitted a book-length report by Tench Coxe on the remarkable spread of manufacturing, especially textiles, leather, iron goods, pottery, shipbuilding. Senator Gore, Massachusetts Federalist, protested against this attempt to "prematurely seduce the capitalists of the country into new and untried employments." In textiles, an idiot could operate a machine as skillfully as a mechanic. Unfeeling war-supporting senators voted to force the textile industry onto New England, but Calhoun, to protect Southern exports of cotton, pigeonholed the bill in the House.

Peace rumors spread through Washington on the last day of 1813. Castlereagh, though rejecting mediation, had been in touch with the American envoys. On January 6 the President notified Congress that he had accepted an offer of direct negotiations. Peace talks, he said, would not be impeded by vigorous war measures.

In the exchange of formal notes, Castlereagh reserved "the maritime rights of the British empire"; Madison stood for "the rights of both parties as sovereign and independent nations." In other words, there was no meeting of minds on impressment of seamen. Former Speaker Macon pointed out some American disadvantages at the conference table. Recruiting was at a standstill. Conscription was political suicide. New England was unwilling to let militia go into Canada. Federalists were at work to deprive the government of men and money.

The President now had to reappoint the peace commission. Secretary Gallatin, whose absence was limited by law to six months, could not be renominated without declaring his Cabinet post vacant. Without him, there might be a deadlock between Adams and Bayard over impressment. Madison decided to add Henry Clay and Jonathan Russell to the commission. The four were confirmed.

Federalists and even some Republicans were appalled at the choice of Clay. Western voracity for Indian lands, held in check by British influence, might cause him to insist on the cession of Canada, even though the effort would desolate the entire Atlantic seaboard. So said one Virginian. To Sérurier, however, Madison's appointment of Clay was a guarantee "to the nation of his inflexible resolution to maintain its rights and honor up to the last extremity."

The peace, Sérurier told his government, would ratify war results already achieved and unchangeable. He saw a symbol of the American future in the adulation of Commodore Perry. Daily testimony confirmed his opinion that "this people was irresistibly called to a great naval destiny." England was imprudently building up a rival maritime and manufacturing power. "I repeat, the greatest object of the war is accomplished, and the peace can but perpetuate it."

At this point Mrs. Gallatin learned that her husband expected to spend the winter in Europe. Attorney-General Pinkney resigned because of a pending bill requiring that officer to live in Washington. Madison nominated Gallatin to the peace commission and offered Alexander J. Dallas his choice of the two vacant positions. He declined both—the Treasury (he intimated) because he could not stand it to be associated with Armstrong, the other post because he could not afford to leave his Philadelphia law practice. For Attorney-General the President chose brilliant young Richard Rush and nominated Senator George W. Campbell of Tennessee for Secretary of the Treasury. Both were quickly approved by the Senate, as was Gallatin.

Madison faced a personal problem in Postmaster General Gideon Granger who, by law, had power to appoint postmasters without the approval of the President. For twelve years Granger had been building a personal machine powerful in Congress and for seven years hostile to the administration. Now he intended to make Senator Leib, who faced defeat, postmaster at Philadelphia. A score of Pennsylvania congressmen told Granger that if he appointed Leib he would be dismissed next day. He announced the appointment and was summoned instantly to the White House.

Told that he was to be dismissed, Granger declared that he would ask Jefferson's aid in a public vindication. He wrote to Jefferson, saying that a letter silencing the calumnies against him would make it unnecessary to revive "that unhappy affair of Hunt" or to explain the circumstances under which he suppressed certain common-law sedition indictments in Connecticut. In other words, if dismissed from office he would revive the

1804 unchastity slanders against Dolley Madison and parade the Jefferson-Mrs. Walker liaison. Jefferson replied that if he did so, he would be overwhelmed by the public reaction. Madison dismissed him, and Granger kept silent. Leib resigned from the Senate and Jonathan Roberts, ardently pro-Madison, succeeded him. The Federalist press called it all a Madisonian plot to get rid of Leib.

On the peace front, Gallatin was the natural leader of a strong five-man team. The President gave them trading material (to secure peace on the Indian frontier) by authorizing them to seek Canadian annexation. He offered also to pledge the return of British seamen deserting in American ports. England's peace move discomfited the Federalists. Their political hopes, which had rested on American military misfortunes, now depended on misfortune at the peace table. Their only recourse, wrote Pickering, was "to discourage and prevent loans, by rendering the lenders infamous in the eyes of the people." With the bill for a $25 million loan before them, the minority denounced conquest of Canada and charged the President with deliberately fomenting war.

The new Speaker, Cheves of South Carolina, led the defense, emphasizing that the peace ultimatum was confined to mercantile protection and reasonable security against impressment. The desire of the British to retain Canada was a strong inducement to an honorable peace. The loan went through, 97 to 55.

At this time—February 1814—every ship from Europe chronicled French collapse. Peace proposals by the continental powers were in the emperor's hands. Wellington's veterans were being released for American service. With the Orders in Council already revoked and the reason for impressment disappearing, the United States had nothing to gain or lose in the war except prestige. England had no reason to continue it except for mercantile domination and revenge at sea. New England's support of British intransigence would further idle that region's ships and keep Gloucester fishermen off the Banks of Newfoundland.

To aid the Treasury, the administration revived the attempt to re-establish a national bank. Jefferson's son-in-law Eppes adhered rigidly to the 1791 Madison-Jefferson denial of constitutionality. Madison kept silent but allowed the *National Intelligencer* to give unofficial assurance, "from conviction, not from knowledge," that the administration wanted it. Federalist support was needed but could not be obtained for a bank that would help the Treasury. The bill died.

On March 30 the President startled Congress with a request that the embargo and nonimportation laws be immediately repealed. Instead, he wanted a tonnage tax on foreign vessels. Calhoun presented the administration's reasoning. Denmark, Germany, Holland, and Italy were being opened to commerce; trade with Spain and Portugal no longer aided the enemy. Sérurier reported additional reasons. England, the President believed, probably had signed peace already (she did so four days earlier), leaving the United States alone at war with her. Repeal of nonimportation would swing the manufacturing cities of England to the American side, while double duties would enable American manufacturers to hold their own. And, with defense needs immense and the loan unfilled, American merchants were crying: "Give us freedom and we will give you money." Federalists chuckled as the Republicans abruptly reversed themselves and obeyed a bidding for which (said Sérurier) the President had not "in the least prepared their minds."

The huge bounties began to fill the army, for which new generals had been appointed. Among the regulars who had failed, Hull was sentenced to death but spared, Smyth was squeezed out, Dearborn was sidetracked, Winchester was a prisoner, Hampton resigned, Wilkinson was awaiting court-martial.

On January 21, the President nominated Brigadier Generals Izard and Brown to be major generals. The selection of Brown has been glowingly cited as evidence that Secretary Armstrong, by himself, regenerated the army. But Armstrong did not recommend Brown. In December, writing to the President from his home in Red Hook, New York, he spoke well of Izard and then said: "There are now two vacant major generals' places. Flournoy and he ought immediately to be nominated to these."

Why Flournoy, an obscure brigadier serving under militia Major General Andrew Jackson at New Orleans? The cue can be found in Monroe's report to Madison, a few weeks later, that Armstrong was urging congressmen to create the post of lieutenant general for himself. The logical choices for that rank were Brown and Jackson. By elevating Flournoy, Armstrong at one stroke would block the promotion of Brown and drive the fiery Jackson out of the army by lifting his subordinate above him. Madison foiled that game and thus fortified the army.

Where self-interest did not enter, Armstrong did indeed vastly strengthen the army. His slate of brigadiers included Colonels Winfield Scott, captor of Fort George; Edward P. Gaines (recommended by Brown); and Alexander Macomb, who handled his regiment skillfully on Hampton's abortive march.

General Brown transferred his 2,000 men from Lake Champlain to Sackett's Harbor, where he received from Armstrong the "command of the President" that he recapture Fort Niagara. A more detailed order would follow. It did, directing him to cross the ice and attack Kingston if Commodore Chauncey approved, using the first order as a mask. Brown, Gaines, and Chauncey puzzled over the two orders and sent word to Armstrong that the army was setting out for Fort Niagara. A message from the Secretary caught up with them. "You have mistaken my meaning." An attack on Fort Niagara was not intended; but "go on and prosper. Good consequences are sometimes the result of mistakes."

The blunder was Armstrong's ambiguity; but to avoid confessing this to the President, he diverted the main attacking force to an objective that would fall automatically if Kingston fell. The potential results of the year's campaign were correspondingly minimized.

Madison left for Montpelier at the end of April, where he received Armstrong's later proposals for Brown's operations. Ferried across Lake Erie, 8,000 troops assembled in five weeks could move against Burlington Bay and encircle Lake Ontario, capturing York. This would force evacuation of the entire Niagara Peninsula.

The President expressed surprise that so many troops could be brought together so soon. (Fewer were assembled in a longer time.) He doubted whether control of Lake Erie would make it possible to encircle Lake Ontario. After all, offensive operations there "must have some dependence on the naval command." With that in British hands, "sudden concentrations at any point chosen may thwart measures otherwise the best planned." (Madison's remarks anticipated those of Admiral Mahan a century later.) Two new ships of sixty and forty-four guns actually gave control to Admiral Yeo at this moment.

Armstrong's field orders consisted of a copy of his (unapproved) letter to Madison, thus showing that he was running things. Breaching military rules, he addressed the directive to Brigadier General Scott, who deduced from it that he was on his own. Brown, thus bypassed, wrote to Armstrong: "I cannot suppose that you would have said a word to weaken my hands or diminish my authority with any part of the forces that you placed at my command." The Secretary, indeed, had no such intention. He was merely playing the generalissimo.

The President knew nothing of this, but he did discover, via the *National Intelligencer*, that the Secretary had usurped presidential authority by deciding what officers should be retained or dismissed in the consolidation of regiments. The President's responsibility, Madison sharply informed him, could not be satisfied without "weighing well the whole proceeding."

At Montpelier Madison read a proclamation posted on the Georgia-Florida frontier by Admiral Cochrane, new British naval commander.

The admiral invited Southern slaves to join the British land or naval forces or be "sent as FREE settlers" into British dominions. Coupled with the release of Britain's continental forces for invasion, this proclamation convinced Madison that a new level of ruthlessness was in prospect. It would culminate, he concluded, in a devastating attack on the City of Washington.

The enemy's inveterate spirit against the South, the President wrote to Armstrong, could be expected "to show itself against every object within the reach of vindictive enterprise. Among these the seat of government cannot fail to be a favorite one." The news from Europe and Cochrane's proclamation, he told Monroe, "warn us to be prepared for the worst measures of the enemy and in their worst forms."

General Jackson's total defeat of the Creeks brought up the question of his promotion. Madison approved a suggestion by Armstrong that he be made a brigadier in the general army and be breveted major general. The Secretary forwarded the brevet for signature without the brigadier's commission. This would make the regular army connection temporary. He also disclosed the resignation of Major General Harrison but gave no reason for it. The Harrison vacancy, the President replied, could be filled directly by the appointment of Jackson, without a brevet. "I suspend a final decision, however, till I see you, which will be in two or three days after the arrival of this."

Reaching Washington, Madison found a letter *to himself*, from Harrison, which Armstrong had not forwarded. It revealed that Harrison needed only a friendly word from the President to induce him to withdraw his resignation. Already, Madison discovered, Armstrong had written to Harrison that the President had accepted his resignation, and he had just sent notice to Jackson that he was to succeed Harrison. It was fairly obvious that, disliking both officers, he had made sure of eliminating one and getting credit for the other's promotion after failing to block or limit it.

However, the regeneration of army command was complete. Youth, skill, and valor succeeded age and incompetence. Izard, the senior general officer, was thirty-nine; Brown, thirty-seven; Jackson, forty-seven. Scott was twenty-eight and six brigadiers averaged thirty-three. At the lower level, credit was due to Armstrong. At the highest, it belonged to Madison by protecting merit from intrigue.

The new leadership, though misdirected in strategy, showed quick results in the field. Early in July General Brown's army crossed the Niagara Strait and captured Fort Erie and its garrison. A few days later he smashed the whole British peninsular force on Chippewa Creek. Brown heaped praise on Scott: "To him more than to any other man am I indebted for the victory."

It was time now for co-operation between Brown and Commodore Chauncey to clean up Fort George. The days stretched out with no word from either and with reports of British troops in transit from Europe to Quebec. In this critical situation, wrote Sérurier on July 20, "the Executive shows himself calm to maintain confidence, and up to now he has succeeded." Urged to summon Congress to vote more arms, Madison refused to spread alarm "by thus sounding the tocsin."

Word came at last that Brown, hearing nothing from Chauncey, had lifted the siege of Fort George and dropped back to his old position at Chippewa Creek. At sundown of the day Brown wrote, the bloodiest land battle of the war erupted at Lundy's Lane. From conflicting reports, both sides were victorious, both sides defeated. Brown and Scott were wounded and out of action. British General Riall and two hundred men were captured.

Official reports made the situation sound much better. Lieutenant General Drummond's larger army "was completely defeated and our troops remained on the battle ground." But at midnight, with Brown and Scott disabled, Brigadier General Ripley returned the exhausted army to camp for rest. Next morning the British re-occupied the battlefield and claimed victory. The battle, Sérurier reported to Paris, doubled the American Army by giving it confidence in its generals and itself.

Without help from Chauncey an American advance would be futile. General Gaines, placed in command during the convalescence of the two major generals (Scott was promoted) drew back to Fort Erie, where he smashingly defeated an attempted surprise attack by Drummond.

On the day he returned from Montpelier (June 3) the President requested "a consultation with the Heads of Departments" on Tuesday, the seventh. "The object is to decide on the plan of campaign which our means naval and military render most eligible." Armstrong and Jones were directed to report on the number and distribution of American and British military and naval forces.

The wording of Madison's note was significant. The term "heads of departments," Attorney-General Rush discovered, was invariably used to indicate that the United States had no "Cabinet government" of the British majority-rule type (tacitly followed by Presidents Washington and Jefferson). The object specified, "to decide on a plan of campaign," rebuked Armstrong for having ordered operations without the President's approval. Finally, Madison was deviating from the rule he had followed in the war (according to Gallatin) of consulting only the department head directly involved.

Armstrong reported 20,000 men ready for action, with 7,000 recruits about ready to report and other thousands of men going home. Nearly half of the army was in coastal districts; 2,121 on the Detroit front; 5,000 on Lake Champlain; 3,000 under Brown in the Niagara sector. These meager numbers ruled out a drive on Montreal. On Lake Ontario, to offset Britain's *Prince Regent*, the 44-gun *Superior* was being boosted to fifty-eight, and ten extra cannon were being placed on the 32-gun *Mohawk*. On all-important Lake Champlain, completion of the 26-gun *Saratoga* gave Commodore Macdonough freedom to cruise and transport troops.

The President laid Armstrong's plan of encircling Lake Ontario before the Cabinet, stipulating, however, that the expedition was "to depend on Commodore Chauncey's gaining the command of the lake." Armstrong joined in the vote by which the President's disregarded advice was converted into a mandate.

The happy situation on Lake Champlain did not last. Commodore Macdonough reported that a British warship far surpassing the *Saratoga* was nearing completion. Only the quick building of a 20-gun brig could prevent loss of control and the descent of Wellington's assembled veterans on New York State. Navy Secretary Jones threw up his hands. The brig could not be built. There was no time, no money. It *must* be built, Madison told him. Jones sent ship carpenters from New York City. The brig was launched three and one-half weeks after its timbers were growing in the forest.

Following the July 1 Cabinet meeting, the President directed Armstrong to send him all correspondence of recent months with Generals Harrison, Jackson, Izard, Brown, and Gaines. From this he learned how Harrison was finessed out of the army and how, after trying to block Jackson's promotion, Armstrong took credit for it. Major General Harrison's resignation, the Secretary had written after receiving the President's near-decision, had "created a vacancy of that grade, which I hasten to fill with your name." Jackson, penetrating the maneuver, accepted the appointment "made by the President."

For more than a month Madison studied Armstrong's orders, overruling several as he went along. On August 13 he confronted the Secretary of War with his findings: (1) Armstrong had consolidated regiments without presidential sanction. (2) He had issued hospital and medical rules in violation of law. (3) He had decreed dismissal for duels and challenges without the trial prescribed by law. (4) He had issued important instructions regarding plans and operations, without previous or even subsequent communication with the President. (5) Letters expressly intended for the President had been acted on without being previously communicated.

This supplemented an interim accusation (which led Armstrong to change the dates of letters) that the Secretary had utterly failed to maintain communication and co-ordination between the armies of Generals Izard and Brown.

A sensitive Secretary of War would have resigned on receipt of this rebuke. A President possessing the ruthlessness required in wartime would have fired him on the spot. Neither did either.

On May 24, at Montpelier, President Madison had predicted a British attempt to devastate Washington. Later developments in Europe were ominous. Napoleon was a prisoner on the Island of Elba. There was talk in London of excluding Americans from the Newfoundland fisheries and of returning Louisiana to Spain. The Madison Cabinet on June 23 and 24 approved the rejection of such terms, but it unanimously backed an instruction that various issues be deferred because "the essential causes of the war . . . and particularly the practice of impressment, have ceased."

There followed a spate of stories from London calling for "punishment of America." *Cobbett's Weekly Register*, anti-government, denounced "such monsters" as the *Times* of London, who "revel at the idea of *burning* the cities and towns, the mills and manufactories" of America. The least of their talk was "of forcing Mr. Madison from his seat, and new-modelling the government." Gallatin and Bayard reported 15,000 veterans about to sail from Bordeaux to Quebec. In Salem, Massachusetts, July 4 banqueters toasted Wellington and the prospect that President Madison would "be *Elb*-owed out of office."

From Bermuda, via Portsmouth, New Hampshire, came the report of an American sea captain that an expedition was on its way to attack Washington and "devastate and attack everything valuable" in the South. Admiral Cockburn already was doing that along Chesapeake Bay, as well as recruiting slaves for the British Navy and their wives for the officers. Sending one "very fair" in color to the warship *Jaseur*, the admiral remarked that she "will make a valuable addition to Mr. Fenwick's coterie."

Again and again after his return from Virginia (so wrote Attorney-General Rush) the President "dwelt upon the probability of an attack upon Washington." Nobody agreed with him. Navy Secretary Jones considered other points "more inviting to the enemy." Monroe thought

(June 25) the unsettled condition of Europe made a British expedition hazardous, especially one "affording so little prospect of success." The Secretary of the Treasury was no less skeptical and Armstrong scoffingly so.

With his apprehension heightened by the Gallatin-Bayard report, the President created Military District No. 10, embracing Maryland, the District of Columbia, and Virginia's northern neck. Brigadier General Winder was given command. On July 1, summoning the Cabinet once more, the President pointed to "the fierce aspect which British military power now had." It was his unequivocal belief (Rush recorded) that "the capital would be marked as the most inviting object of a speedy attack." He proposed that a force of 10,000 men, including a thousand or more regulars, be got in readiness and that depots of arms and equipment be established.

Years later Madison's close friend George Tucker wrote that the President repeatedly suggested the likelihood of a British attack on Washington, but "his cabinet did not concur with him . . . and especially General Armstrong." Secretary Jones told Congress that he "accorded in the expediency of the preparations" but was "not equally impressed" with the danger. "In this sentiment I was not alone."

Among the papers of James Monroe is the draft of a letter to Madison, dated July 3, 1814, excitedly warning him of imminent danger to the capital city and charging fellow Cabinet members with blindness to the crisis. Unfortunately for himself, Monroe inserted conclusive evidence that this "letter" (not found in Madison's papers) was drafted after memory grew faulty. It contains the advice that the President call Congress in special session for the purpose of "establishing a national bank." Such a bank was proposed in the fall of 1814, but Monroe wrote letter after letter opposing it. On May 4, *1815*, he wrote to the President suggesting a special session for its establishment.*

The seven weeks following the July 1 preparedness meeting produced a sort of competition between Secretary Armstrong and General Winder —the former to see how little could be done to get ready to meet an attack on Washington, the latter to see how vigorously he could waste his efforts. The President authorized the calling of 6,000 Maryland mili-

---

*The device thus employed was not new to Monroe. Lying in Madison's papers is a two-sentence note from Monroe, dated February 25, 1813, concerning a military appointment for himself. Among *Monroe's papers* is the draft of a letter of that date opening with the same two sentences and proceeding with 1,800 words of complaint about plans and actions of Armstrong, relating to the Northern front, including events that developed from April through July of that year 1813.

tia. Winder soundly proposed that they be embodied at once for training. Armstrong refused; militia could best be used "upon the spur of the occasion." It would be impossible, Winder replied, to collect a force quickly enough after the enemy arrived.

True, but Armstrong did not expect an enemy. Notified by the commander at Norfolk that a new British squadron had entered Chesapeake Bay and that 12,000 troops were reported to be following, the Secretary of War doubted the naval part and dismissed the invasion story as "palpably a fable." On that day Admiral Cochrane absorbed Admiral Cockburn's squadron and asked him where he should land the invasion forces. Replied Cockburn: "I consider the town of Benedict in the Patuxent to offer us advantages for this purpose beyond any other spot in the United States. . . . Within 48 hours after the arrival in the Patuxent of such a force as you expect, the city of Washington might be possessed without difficulty or opposition of any kind."

The day after Armstrong scoffed at the invasion report he cut down the militia authorization by including Baltimore's 2,000 as part of the Maryland total. The President stepped in by authorizing calls for 2,000 Virginia militia and 5,000 from Pennsylvania, directing also that two or three thousand Marylanders be stationed between Washington and Baltimore. Armstrong sent his own cutdown order *by an express*, the President's buildup directive (on the same day) *by ordinary mail*. Winder received it twenty-two days later, after meetings with Armstrong in which the Secretary did not mention the subject.

During the interval Maryland's militia General Philip Stuart wrote personally to the President, begging for heavy weapons with which to cope with Cockburn's raiding parties and adding privately: "To the Secretary of War I shall make no further communications." Madison sent a terse order to Armstrong: "The Secretary of War will cause the supply of ammunition requested to be furnished," and the cannon if available.

Through John Graham, the President suggested to Winder that he exercise his existing authority to summon 2,000 Virginia volunteers who had courageously halted Cockburn raids. Winder's prompt order, sent to Armstrong, reached the President for signature three weeks later. Winder meanwhile was running himself ragged, riding all over the Patuxent-Potomac peninsula instead of organizing an army and planning a campaign. He had no staff until, after five weeks of dinning at Armstrong, he was given one adjutant.

The President, in successive orders, had authorized the calling of 15,000 militia from Maryland, Virginia, and Pennsylvania. Winder's order summoning 3,000 from western Maryland produced 300. There were 3,000 militia in Baltimore, 2,000 in the District of Columbia, all subject to Winder's call but none embodied for action. Major General John P. Van Ness, commanding two District brigades, sought to have his men encamped. Armstrong's reply, Van Ness recorded, fitted his habit of "treating with indifference, at least, if not with levity, the idea of an attack by the enemy."

Such was the situation when, on August 18, news reached Washington that fifty-one British warships and military transports had dropped anchor at the mouth of the Patuxent River. Excitement seized everybody except Armstrong. Monroe went with dragoons to scout the Patuxent. Winder ordered mass assembly of the Columbian, Baltimore, and nearby Maryland militia. Emergency requisitions were dispatched to the Pennsylvania and Maryland governors. Naval commanders were ordered to bring seamen and marines from Philadelphia and New York. Armstrong saw no need to worry. Urged by Van Ness to speed things up he replied: "Oh yes, by God they . . . [mean] to strike somewhere, but they certainly will not come here; what the devil will they do here . . . Baltimore is the place, sir; that is of so much more importance."

Claiming that a major general of militia outranked a brigadier of the regular army, Van Ness sought overall command. The President supported Armstrong's rejoinder that the general's rank did not count because the two Columbian brigades had been summoned separately. However, Madison asked that Van Ness be given a separate station. Instead, Armstrong told the general he was not in service at all. Van Ness resigned and organized a civilian corps to construct defenses at Bladensburg.

Ordering three Baltimore regiments to Washington, Winder sent cavalry down the roads to Benedict with orders to block them with trees. They did not do so. Hearing that night from Monroe of the enemy's landing at Benedict, the President personally sent orders to throw in "all sorts of obstructions in the routes." None were thrown in. Monroe's message next morning reported the enemy to number about 5,000. With so small a force and no cavalry, Madison replied, "it seems extraordinary that he should venture on an enterprise to this distance from his shipping. He may however count on the effect of boldness and celerity in his side, and the want of precaution in ours." True indeed!

Government papers of all sorts, the President told Monroe, were being moved to safety. All arriving troops would be hastened forward, but few could be expected before the crisis was over. Under a direct prod from the President, Secretary Armstrong ordered a scattered brigade of

Virginia troops to come to Washington. Madison sent John Graham to call Colonel George Minor and his Fairfax regiment from Falls Church.

Armstrong was still skeptical. Observing Clerk Stephen Pleasonton packing the Declaration of Independence and other State Department documents, he observed "that he did not think the British were serious in their intentions of coming to Washington." That was on August 22, at which time, wrote the French minister, the roads were covered with inhabitants "fleeing in wild disorder."

"The President [Sérurier continued] has just gone to the camp to encourage, by his presence, the army to defend the capital. It appears that the idea of fighting the English in the field has been rightfully abandoned, in view of the poor quality of the troops, and that they will limit themselves to disputing the crossing of the Eastern Branch at Bladensburg, six miles from the capital."

Madison left, wrote Dolley, after inquiring "anxiously whether I had courage, or firmness, to remain in the President's house until his return on the morrow, or succeeding day; and . . . beseeching me to take care of myself, and of the cabinet papers, public and private." Accompanied by Secretary Jones, General Mason, and Attorney-General Rush, and two aides, the President rode to the army camp at Long Old Fields, nine miles east of Washington. Secretary Armstrong followed them.

At camp they found Commodore Joshua Barney and 500 seamen who had marched overland after scuttling their fourteen boats on the Patuxent. Next morning the President reviewed the troops who (he wrote to Dolley) "are in high spirits and make a good appearance." The enemy, as reported by Winder, were not in a condition to strike at Washington, but they might have a greater force than was represented or "their temerity may be greater than their strength."

Madison's concern deepened after he interrogated two British deserters brought in by Major Thomas L. McKenney. Their reports of an advancing army reinforced McKenney's prediction of an immediate assault on Washington. Armstrong still scoffed: "They can have no such intention. They are foraging, I suppose, and if an attack is meditated by them, upon any place, it is Annapolis."

Madison disagreed. His second note to his wife is known only from hers to her sister Lucy: "The last is alarming, because he desires I should be ready at a moment's warning to enter my carriage, and leave the city; that the enemy seemed stronger than had been reported, and that it might happen that they would reach the city with intention to destroy it." She had filled a carriage with state papers, but she would not leave "until I see Mr. Madison safe, and he can accompany me,—as I hear of much hostility towards him."

Late that afternoon a letter reached camp from John Graham saying that Colonel Minor needed an order from General Winder (who was scouting) to change the destination of his regiment from Alexandria to Washington. Militia General Smith submitted the letter to Armstrong with this result: "He treated the matter with great indifference, and . . . declined to give any order. I then carried the note to Mr. Madison, also in camp, who entertained a different view; and on being told of Gen. Armstrong's course, gave the order direct to Col. Minor to move on to Washington so as to unite with us."

Madison, Jones, and Armstrong left for Washington at two o'clock, not knowing that the army of British General Ross was only three miles behind them. "At candlelight" the President found Colonel Minor at the door and sent him to Armstrong for arms and ammunition. Armstrong told him it was too late: he should see Colonel Carberry at the Armory in the morning. After Minor left, Armstrong ordered his aid, Lieutenant Colonel John Tayloe, to go *to Virginia* with the following order:

"Lieutenant Colonel Minor will repair to Washington, with the regiment under his command, with the utmost dispatch. He will report on his arrival to Colonel Carberry of the 36th regiment of United States' infantry, and make a requisition for arms and ammunition."

Knowing that Minor was in Washington, Tayloe delivered the order to him at the home of Dr. Ewell. Armstrong submitted this fictional paper to a congressional investigating committee, and it has been quoted by historians as evidence of the speed and zeal with which Armstrong rose to the defense of Washington in the face of presidential inaction.

Madison had another visitor that night. At nine o'clock General Winder came to the White House. Fearing a night attack in which he could not use artillery, he had brought his inferior army on the run to Washington and camped near the Navy Yard. His Baltimore brigade, after an all-day advance from Bladensburg, had been sent back to that location. Thus, Winder had two armies of 2,500 men each, five miles apart and worn out by futile marching, and he had wasted 500 men by leaving them to guard Fort Washington, a dozen miles down the Potomac. At midnight the President was wakened by a courier from Monroe with the word: "The enemy are in full march for Washington." It was the last night the Madisons ever spent in the White House.

Early in the morning, responding to Winder's request for speedy counsel, the President rode to the Navy Yard, where he found Secretary Jones with the army commander. Monroe and Rush soon joined them. A vidette brought word that the British were moving toward Bladensburg, so Winder ordered his men to make the five-mile march. An hour or so later (Madison recorded) Armstrong showed up ("impatiently expected, and surprise at his delay manifested"). He was asked whether he had any advice to offer in the emergency. "He said he had not; adding that as the battle would be between militia and regular troops, the former would be beaten."

Commodore Barney joined the President's party. General Winder, he said, had ordered him to remain with his seamen at the Navy Yard to blow up the bridge if necessary. The commodore remarked that 500 very efficient men were being left to do a job that could be done by half a dozen. Madison ordered him to march his men immediately to Bladensburg. As the presidential party mounted horses, Treasury Secretary Campbell told the President that Armstrong had said he would voice no opinions unless the President invited him to do so. Madison directed the Secretary of War to hasten ahead and give Winder all the aid in his power. If a dispute over authority arose, the President would be at hand to settle it.

After a brief stop at the Marine Barracks, Madison's horse went lame and he borrowed the mount of his aide, Charles Carroll. Galloping past Barney's men, they came upon 2,000 militiamen a mile or more from Bladensburg. At length they rode down the long slope to the Eastern Branch of the Anacostia River, passing Baltimore militia, riflemen, and artillery. Winder, they thought, must be in Bladensburg.

As Madison and Rush started to cross the bridge they were met by William Simmons, a discharged War Department accountant, who told them they were within gunshot of a British advance party not in uniform. They went up the hill considerably faster than they had gone down. At the summit, where he found Winder, Armstrong, and Monroe, the President asked Armstrong if he had spoken with Winder about the military arrangements. "He said he had not." Told to do so, he rode over to the general. The unruliness of Madison's borrowed horse kept him out of hearing, but in response to a question Armstrong said the arrangements "appeared to be as good as circumstances admitted."

He should have said "as bad." General Stansbury of the Baltimore militia had abandoned Bladensburg, whose brick houses and the Van Ness fortifications provided a strong defense. He gave them a good cover in a hillside orchard. Monroe, the would-be lieutenant general, ordered them back onto the open hillside, not only exposing them to attack but depriving the advanced artillery of support. The main line of defense was more than a mile to the rear. The result was that a British Army, superior in discipline but badly outnumbered, was given a decisive advantage in *available numbers* at every stage of the conflict.

At the outset, the Baltimore artillery almost wiped out a British company on the bridge. The enemy then began firing Congreve rockets—a weapon of terror against raw troops. Some rockets, Monroe and Rush reported, fell near the President and others went over his head. Madison's narrative said nothing of this but recorded that "when the battle had decidedly commenced, I observed to the Secretary of War and Secretary of State that it would be proper to withdraw to a position in the rear . . . leaving military movements to the military functionaries who were responsible for them."

The trio retired to the main line of defense, Rush joining them. There Madison received a message from Winder that his forces had been driven back, but he hoped to make a stand somewhere short of the Capitol. He was abandoning the main position without a fight. At that, wrote Madison, "Mr. Rush accompanying me, I fell down into the road leading to the city and returned to it." The President did not witness the flight of the first line under rocket fire and a hail of lead from the enemy-occupied orchard. Nor did he view the one redeeming feature of the battle—the valiant resistance of Barney's seamen and marines after the second line of 2,000 men (pursuant to Winder's order) melted away without firing musket or cannon.

The President reached the White House shortly after four o'clock and found it empty. At three, Dolley had written to sister Lucy: "I am still here within sound of the cannon! Mr. Madison comes not; may God protect him. Two messengers covered with dust come to bid me fly; but I wait for him." She had filled a wagon with plate and other valuables, and Charles Carroll had come to hasten her departure, "in a very bad humor" with her because she stopped to have the large picture of General Washington unscrewed from the wall. The frame was then broken for speed "and the precious portrait placed in the hands of [Jacob Barker and Robert de Peyster] for safekeeping."

The French minister, watching from the nearby Octagon House, witnessed the militia streaming past "in the greatest confusion" after Madison's return. Writing to Talleyrand, he told of the Executive's departure: "It was then, my lord, that the President, who, in the midst of all this disorder, had displayed, to stop it, a firmness and constancy worthy of better success, but powerless in regard to militia . . . coolly mounted his horse, accompanied by some friends, and slowly gained the bridge that separates Washington from Virginia."

Madison, Mason, and Rush crossed the Potomac, not on the Long Bridge (which had been blown up) but on Mason's Ferry. This followed a double change of plan. The first arrangement was for the Madisons, Secretary Jones and family, and Charles Carroll to gather at Bellevue, the Carroll home in Georgetown, and go from there to Virginia by way of the Little Falls Bridge, five miles upstream. Carroll escorted Mrs. Madison to Bellevue, where they were joined by the Joneses and Navy Clerk Edward Duvall.

Owing to the turmoil in the streets, Madison sent a message that he would join them at Foxall's cannon foundry near the river. The crush of fleeing humanity made that unfeasible, so he sent Monroe's aide Tench Ringgold to Foxall's with a notice that he would cross on the ferry and join them in Virginia.

The separate travels of President and Mrs. Madison became a modern odyssey of changeable mythology. Dolley was said to have slept in an army encampment and then to have crossed into Virginia, where she was chased out of a house at night by an irate landlady and went on to a tavern. The President was portrayed (in scurrilous verse which he quoted in laughter) as bobbing on horseback from Bladensburg to Frederick. By an alternative tale, he joined Dolley at the Virginia tavern but fled from it at midnight, fearing capture, and spent the rest of the night in a miserable hovel in the woods. Three Virginia houses, Rokeby, Salona, and the home of Mrs. Minor, competed for the honor of having sheltered the President's wife.

Shreds of some of these stories are visible in the true account, found in the papers of Secretary Jones and Richard Rush, the memoirs of Matilda Love Lee, and the narrative of Mordecai Booth, a naval clerk who hunted for Madison through half the night and next day, seeking an order for the disposition of naval gunpowder carried to Falls Church.

The scheduled stopping place was Salona, the home of the Reverend John Maffitt, three miles above the Little Falls bridge. Night coming on, Dolley and her party stopped one mile short of it, at Rokeby, the home of Richard Hendry Love and his young wife, who had been house guests at the White House. Wrote Mrs. Love in her memoirs: "Mrs. Madison and a number of city people took refuge at my house the night the British took Washington." They arrived, she recorded, shortly after Monroe (and Ringgold) finished supper and left. "Oh, it was a trying time, for Mr. Love's company . . . was called out, and I was in a peck of trouble." (She was the "irate landlady" of erroneous tradition.) Mrs. Madison, the Joneses, the Carrolls, and Duvall, went on next day to the ultimate stopping place, Wiley's Tavern on Difficult Run near Great Falls.

Richard Rush forgot after forty years that the presidential party crossed on Mason's Ferry instead of at Little Falls, but he had in indelible memory of the "columns of flame and smoke ascending throughout the night" as they rode into the hills away from the burning White House and Capitol. "If at intervals the dismal sight was lost to our view, we got it again from some hill-top or eminence where we paused to look at it."

Madison, Mason, and Rush at a late hour reached Wren's Tavern at Falls Church. They went from there to the home of Mrs. Minor and on to Salona, where they spent the night. Next morning Madison rode back to Wren's Tavern, where he was given a guard of two Virginia dragoons. Returning to Salona, he learned that Mrs. Madison and party had gone by, en route to Wiley's Tavern. He and Rush hastened after them (Mason being detained for a time), but they were forced to sit out a terrific hurricane at "the Crossroads" two miles down the Old Dominion Road. Resuming their journey, they were overtaken by Mordecai Booth, who accompanied them to Wiley's Tavern.

At midnight, Booth recorded, the President set out with Jones, Rush, Mason, John Graham, and the dragoons for Conn's Ferry above Great Falls. Conn refused to make the dangerous, rocky crossing at night. Jones returned to the tavern; the others stayed at Conn's farmhouse (the "midnight hovel" of the myth). All next day they traveled, seeking to rejoin the army, which they followed from Montgomery Courthouse (Rockville) toward Baltimore. The next night was spent at Brookeville in the home of Caleb and Henrietta Bentley. Getting word in the morning that the British were returning to their ships, Madison headed for the national capital, followed by the troops.

For more than four days the 64-year-old President had spent up to twenty hours a day in the saddle. Accused of fleeing to safety, he had been with the army at its farthest point of advance, followed it to battle, was under fire, and came back to Washington ahead of the army after the debacle. He found the White House, the Capitol, and all public buildings, except the Patent Office, a mass of gaunt and blackened ruins.

Responsibility for the capture of Washington was easier to fix than to explain. The immediate blame lay overwhelmingly on Armstrong, whose obstinate refusal to initiate or carry out defensive measures produced the same effect as deliberate sabotage. Completing the failure was the too-late-discovered incompetence of General Winder. Though energetic and courageous, he allowed the British to advance for four days without throwing a single obstruction in their way. The British chronicler of the expedition, Lieutenant George R. Gleig, wrote that if the Americans had "permitted us to advance as far as Nottingham, then broken up the roads and covered them with trees, it would have been impossible for us to go a step beyond." With similar tactics in the rear "we would have been . . . obliged, in all probability, to surrender."

Winder's incompetence produced amazing casualty figures. Gleig put the total British losses at 500 killed or wounded. (Civilians buried 200 enemy dead.) American casualties totaled thirty or forty dead and fifty or sixty wounded, nearly all in Barney's naval force. (Barney himself, near bleeding to death, was paroled in the field by General Ross.) The main American Army never heard a bullet zing.

President Madison bore a responsibility for the debacle that was increased, not lessened, by his unshared expectation of the attack. Had he booted Armstrong out of office on July 1, when the Secretary began his course of stubborn resistance, the defenses the President ordered would have been built. Had he done so on August 13—the day he catalogued the Secretary's misfeasances—the regulars and Virginia militia he called for could have been brought in. The inadequacy of Winder was not so easy to spot. His first test as a tactician was the one in which he failed.

From Brookeville, the President had sent notes to Mrs. Madison and Secretary Jones advising their immediate return to Washington. He was just setting out with Monroe and Rush to inspect the devastated capital when Jones rode up, alone. He had crossed on Conn's ferry with his family, headed for Baltimore, leaving Duvall and a dragoon to look after Dolley, and learned of the British withdrawal en route.

During the night a thunderous cannonade announced the fall of Fort Washington, blown up by its inept commander. There was no surprise when a British squadron came in sight below Alexandria. Riding from Greenleaf's Point toward Georgetown, with Monroe choosing artillery positions, the President was informed by Dr. William Thornton that the citizens of Washington were preparing to send a deputation to the British commander for the purpose of capitulating. Monroe wrote in his diary: "The President forbade the measure."

A pleasant sight greeted Madison when he returned to the house of sister-in-law Cutts. His wife was there, escorted to Washington by Duvall. The Cutts house became presidential headquarters, with eleven dragoons sleeping outside at night—lying down "like dogs upon straw," said the *Federal Republican*, to protect "Little Jemmy, or poor Madison." A paradox followed. Four citizens, including the publisher of that scurrilous newspaper, came to the President with "a confidential caution against designs said to be in agitation against his person." They evidently shared the feeling that caused Monroe to write: "I am satisfied that if by any casualty the President's return had been delayed 24 hours, that a degree of degradation would have been exhibited here and elsewhere . . . of the most disastrous character."

Banker John Barnes put the testimony in positive form: "Our good President is out animating and encouraging the troops and citizens not to despair."

Alexandria saved itself from the torch by pledging delivery of all naval and ordnance stores, shipping and private merchandise. The loot filled seventy-one seized vessels, with which the enemy retreated as shoreside batteries were being emplaced downstream.

Now Secretary Armstrong came back from Frederick. He visited a militia camp on Windmill Point just after Madison left it, with results that were quickly reported to the President. The soldiers throwing up fortifications all laid down their shovels. Their commander, Brigadier General Smith, sent word to Madison "that every officer would tear off his epaulets if General Armstrong was to have anything to do with them." Major McKenney recorded the President's answer: "Say to General Smith *the contingency* (namely, that of any future orders being given by General Armstrong) *shall not happen*."

On that same evening (a memorandum by Madison reads), "being on horseback I stopped at General Armstrong's lodgings" and told him of the message from General Smith and the threats of personal violence "thrown out against us both, but more especially against him." The Secretary replied that the excitement against him was inspired by intrigue and founded on falsehood. He was ready to resign, or "with my permission, retire from the scene, by setting out immediately on a visit to his family in the state of New York." The latter course, Madison told him, would avoid the existing embarrassment and leave the future open.

Armstrong insisted that he had omitted no defensive step "which had been enjoined on him." The President replied that it was the Secretary's duty not only to execute plans but to devise them. In dealing with the danger to the capital Armstrong "had never himself proposed or suggested a single precaution or arrangement for its safety, everything done on that subject having been brought forward by myself." The President's own suggestions had been held to a minimum "to obtrude the less on a reluctant execution."

Madison remarked that he had appointed Armstrong out of respect for his talents and had treated him with friendliness and confidence. Wishing to close his own public career in harmony, he had "acquiesced in many things, to which no other consideration would have reconciled me." The meeting closed with renewed permission for Armstrong to visit his family.

Instead of going to Red Hook, Armstrong spent the next few days in Baltimore, then resigned his office and published a long explanation in the Baltimore *Patriot*. The President, he averred, told him of the message from the militia officers and suggested a temporary departure. He replied (he said) that it was not for him to say why the President was yielding "to an impulse so vile and profligate." He himself would never bow to the humors of a village mob and if the President intended to do so he should "accept my resignation." This Madison declined to do, citing the Secretary's "general zeal, diligence and talent."

Since coming to Baltimore, Armstrong went on, he had been told as a fact that *prior to his return to Washington*, a deputation including Alexander C. Hanson of the *Federal Republican* obtained a promise from the President "that I should no longer direct the military defences of the District. On this fact all commentary is unnecessary." Hanson, whose visit was to warn Madison of a plot against him, killed this distortion by inserting the word "FALSE" in the narrative. It was denied also by Major John S. Williams, brigade inspector. Navy Secretary Jones bade Armstrong a glad farewell: "With much cunning, an insufferable degree of vanity, a caustic pithy pen, and the affectation of military science, has this man imposed himself upon society without one useful and valuable quality either social, civil or military. He is gone and has told his story, which is as destitute of candor as of truth."

Unanswered when the enemy left Washington was the question why nonmilitary buildings had been systematically destroyed. Admiral Cockburn was an eager arsonist, but he took part as a mere volunteer under General Ross, who was subordinate to Admiral Cochrane. Six days after the holocaust, Secretary of State Monroe received a letter from Cochrane, dated August 18 (six days before the torch was set). He stated that in retaliation for American outrages in Upper Canada, it had become his duty "to destroy and lay waste such towns and districts upon the coast as may be found available." He would stay his hand if the Executive would make reparations to the Canadians.

This was predated afterthought harking back to prior policy. Cochrane had used precisely the same words in his Bermuda proclamation months before. The Canadian incident now referred to was the unauthorized burning of the village of Dover on Lake Erie by Colonel Campbell, for which Prevost had asked retaliation. Cochrane knew on August 18 that Campbell had been courtmartialed and condemned for his action. That excuse was so flimsy that the British government disregarded it and proceeded to convert the occupation of York, and the burning by unknown persons of the small wooden Parliament House, into an American-set holocaust that justified destruction of the American capital.

Only the guiltiest of consciences could produce such a defense. Perhaps the British Admiralty was acting on Canning's 1813 observation that a vigorous system of coastwise destruction would have prevented Madison's re-election. Gleig, future chaplain-general, had similar Christian thoughts about the way to make war on nations governed by popular assemblies. Lamenting the failure to destroy Baltimore he wrote: "Burn their houses, plunder their property, block up their harbors, and destroy their shipping in a few places; and before you have time to proceed to the rest, you will be stopped by entreaties for peace."

The failure to ravage Baltimore was not due to tenderheartedness. With that city facing attack, the President added naval personnel and army regulars to the Baltimore militia, commanded by militia Major General (Senator) Samuel Smith. The highways of Pennsylvania, Virginia, and Maryland were thronged with citizen soldiers headed for Baltimore and Washington. Smith had 15,588 men under his command when Cochrane's near-fifty vessels anchored on September 11, fourteen miles below Baltimore.

Three days later, hour by hour through day and night, battle news came to the President. The British had landed and were repulsed, with General Ross fatally wounded. The militia were forced back but retired fighting. Fort McHenry ("We'll take it in two hours," boasted Cockburn) withstood a twenty-five-hour bombardment. ("*O! say can you see by the dawn's early light*," wrote a young emissary from the President, held on shipboard while seeking the release of a civilian physician.) And then! the enemy was retiring in great confusion, pursued by the same militia that had fled at Bladensburg. They were re-embarking; the fleet was leaving.

Jubilation rose higher with publication of a dispatch from Commodore Macdonough: "The Almighty has been pleased to grant us a signal victory on Lake Champlain, in the capture of one frigate, one brig, and two sloops of war of the enemy." General Macomb was pursuing Prevost's 14,000 men in precipitate retreat into Canada. There would be no invasion of New York, designed to split the Union.

Admiral Mahan wrote that the battle of Lake Champlain, "more than any other incident of the War of 1812, merits the epithet 'decisive.'" Among the millions of rejoicing Americans, scarce half a dozen knew that President Madison, by personal intervention, furnished the twenty guns of the brig *Eagle* that enabled Macdonough, by superior position and marksmanship, to snatch victory from a more powerful enemy.

Congress convened in special session on the day this heartening news was published. Expectations of peace, Madison said in his message, were created by the pacification of Europe, which withdrew the occasion for impressment of seamen; but the enemy's conduct implied a spirit of hostility more violent than ever—based, he thought, on overbearing naval power and possession of disposable armaments. Whatever inspired these violent passions, the need was to provide means of defeating them.

The current campaign, said the President, gave the enemy little to exult over unless he found it in his wanton expeditions against Washington and Alexandria. The splendid victories of Generals Brown, Scott, and Gaines had triumphantly tested the discipline of American soldiery. At Baltimore and Plattsburg, enemy attacks were turned into hasty retreat. Macdonough's triumph on Champlain matched that of Perry on Erie. The recent loss of Captain Porter's *Essex* (dismasted by high wind and lawlessly attacked in a Chilean port) was "hidden in the blaze of heroism with which she was defended."

To meet the enemy's extended warfare, Madison asked for measures to fill the regular army, classify the militia (i.e. turn portions into regulars by lengthening service) and enlarge the provision for special corps. The American people would "cheerfully and proudly bear every burden of every kind which the safety and honor of the nation demand." Congress did not seem to think so. They "have met in a bad temper," commented Secretary Jones, "grumbling at everything," refusing to provide revenue measures, yet they "expect the war to be carried on with energy." One can only imagine what their temper would have been without the Niagara, Baltimore, and Champlain victories, to which General Brown now added another that sent Drummond reeling back to Chippewa Creek.

The House of Representatives investigated the capture of Washington, the testimony consisting importantly of the lies of Armstrong and the refutation of them by Monroe, Jones, Rush, Campbell, Commodore Barney, and Generals Winder, Smith, Van Ness, and other officers. The President, Armstrong declared, first gave him full direction of the battle of Bladensburg, then interposed and prevented it. All of this was drawn from Madison's direction to Armstrong to give Winder all the aid in his power (which he did not do) and the President's remark in the course of the battle that it was time for civilians to withdraw. The committee submitted the evidence without opinion.

With Armstrong out, Campbell in miserable health, and Jones desperately oppressed by old commercial debts, Madison faced a major Cabinet reorganization. The difficulties were happily surmounted. Jones was relieved of the Treasury and persuaded to hang onto the Navy for a time. Dallas changed his mind about the Treasury, persuaded by Jones's plea that he was needed: "The President is virtuous, able and patriotic, but finance is out of his walk." Monroe proved willing to shift the word "Acting" from one department to another. From Secretary of State and Acting Secretary of War he became Secretary of War and Acting Secretary of State.

The alteration produced a Federalist outcry that Monroe had ousted Armstrong to gain the Presidency. Monroe met this by his usual proceeding. He placed a letter-draft to Madison in his papers, *asking* for a *permanent* appointment in order to avert the suspicion that he obtained the *temporary* one by intrigue. This fantastic illogic bore the very date on which Secretary Jones casually wrote that Monroe was to be Secretary of War—the day before his name was sent to the Senate.

With news from the peace envoys four months in arrears and all of it gloomy, Madison and his advisers reached a crucial decision in October. The commissioners were authorized "to agree to the *status quo ante bellum* as the basis of negotiation." They were forbidden to relinquish the fisheries or territorial or trade rights, and must not sanction impressment or paper blockades. Thus, all objectives for which the United States went to war were given up; but all had been obtained, in substance, by repeal of the Orders in Council and the automatic ending of impressment by peace in Europe. Peace now depended on the balance between England's desire to punish America and, on the other hand, British longing for trade and the new cast given to the conflict by the striking American military victories on the Northern frontier.

Excitement was followed by depression at the Octagon House (which Sérurier had given up to the President) when George Dallas came in from Ghent with dispatches up to August 20. London was making demands as if upon a defeated nation—everything north of the Ohio to be "Indian dominions," the Great Lakes to be wholly incorporated in Canada, part of Maine to be ceded. The American answer, the envoys said, would be a unanimous rejection, probably bringing the negotiation to an end. Gallatin wrote privately that Britain's main objective was to make New Orleans a sugar colony and through it dominate the West. For that purpose a large expedition was to sail in September. Madison's reaction, expressed at a dinner party, was recorded by a newly arrived French legation secretary, Roth: "If the English force us to continue the war, they will make us do in ten years what we perhaps would not do in half a century."

Madison at once made these dispatches public, along with the June instructions abandoning original demands. Republication of them in London, contrasting British intransigence with American moderation, induced 60,000 textile manufacturers and workers to petition for peace and trade.

To meet the threat to New Orleans, the President made requisitions on Kentucky, Tennessee, and Georgia that would raise General Jackson's force to 15,000 militia plus 2,300 re-classified as two-year regulars. With 200 British troops at Pensacola, the spirited Jackson notified the Spanish governor that future diplomatic efforts to eliminate them would be "by the mouths of my cannon." Monroe (October 21) conveyed the President's approval of the Tennessean's manly tone and his caution to "take no measures which would involve this government in a contest with Spain." Before the letter reached him Jackson drove the British out to sea and returned to New Orleans.

With the President's approval, Monroe asked Congress to conscript as well as re-classify the militia on a two-year basis. (Bladensburg had taught its lesson.) Madison's argument supporting its constitutionality, "An unqualified grant of power gives the means necessary to carry it into effect," paraphrased his forty-fourth *Federalist*. If that is true, cried the *Connecticut Mirror*, "we are a nation of abject slaves—slaves to tyrants, which we voluntarily create once in four years." The supporting bill for 80,000 such troops lay fallow.

In the House, Chairman Eppes presented a Ways and Means report asking for a fifty per cent increase in the direct tax on land and numerous additional duties and excises. With the Treasury full, its small notes could supply the country with currency. The alternative to these notes was a national bank. Dallas had been two days in Washington when he asked Congress to set up a bank, forty per cent of its $50 million stock to be furnished by the United States. Monroe worked vigorously to persuade Dallas to drop the bank and rely on Treasury notes but, wrote Monroe to Jefferson, Dallas "adhered to his own plan."

By late fall of 1814, New England's ruling faction was deep in illicit trade across the Canadian border, resisting war loans and defying presidential requisitions of militia. Underneath, however, there was a groundswell of patriotic response to American military victories. A Bostonian writing to British Undersecretary Hamilton lamented that these events, "so contrary to all our expectations, created such a military spirit here, and so tarnished the glory of the British arms." John Low moved in the Massachusetts legislature that an interstate delegation be sent to inform Madison "that he must either resign his office as President" or remove those ministers "who have, by their nefarious plans, ruined the nation."

The design took shape in a committee report calling for a conference with nearby states aimed at a refusal to pay federal taxes and a convention of all the states to amend the Constitution by other than the ordinary method. The legislature appointed twelve delegates to attend a meeting set for December at Hartford. William Wirt described the impact of this on Madison: "[John] Page and I called on the President. He looks miserably shattered and woe-begone. In short, he looked heartbroken. His mind is full of the New England sedition."

Madison had no fear that Massachusetts would dissolve the Union or lead to defeat, but her conduct darkened the prospect of a just and early peace at the moment that good and bad events alike should have led to national unity. Sérurier gave the President chief credit for the nation's ability to keep on fighting. He could only marvel "that a government so badly armed should be able to fight alone, and with success," against powerful England, "with so active a hostile faction at the heart of the nation. This proves beyond reply the great firmness of the President and the wisdom of the counsel he is given." Madison agreed with Wilson Cary Nicholas that the conduct of the Eastern states presented the greatest difficulty in carrying on the war, adding that it was the greatest if not the sole inducement of the enemy to persevere in it:

> The greater part of the people in that quarter have been brought by their leaders, aided by their priests, under a delusion scarcely exceeded by that recorded in the period of witchcraft; and the leaders themselves are becoming daily more desperate in the use they make of it. Their object is power. If they could obtain it by menaces their efforts would stop there. These failing, they are ready to go every length for which they can train their followers.

Gallatin wrote of the effect this had in England. But for "the New England traitors," a good treaty could have been obtained by midsummer. Madison's refusal to employ force or vigilante methods against New England brought cries of despair from Mathew Carey. For years he had begged, prayed, and implored for action but "you remained inflexible. As well might I have attempted to arrest the torrents of the Niagara as to prevail upon you. . . . The die is now cast. The Union will not last a year."

The President's policy looked better when New Hampshire and Vermont spurned the Hartford invitation, but army bills and financial relief lagged in Congress. American seamen were unpaid, and the navy had "not a dollar" to move them in case of crisis. Yeo's 105-gun flagship would control Lake Ontario when the ice melted in May. The President directed Secretary Jones, without waiting for congressional action, to shift an oceanic fund and build three ships of the line on Ontario, to be completed by May 15. Jones protested. There was no money. It would strip the seagoing fleet of personnel. Could Chauncey build them in time? Find out, Madison directed, but send the necessary naval guns (284 of them) up the Hudson before the ice shuts in. Chauncey began work on two 94s and a 44-gun frigate.

In Congress, Federalists decided to assent to taxes (since the war made them inescapable) and raise such a storm against Madison that both he and Gerry would resign. Rufus King would then be made President pro tempore of the Senate and by law would become President of the United States. Their speeches, charging Madison with incompetence either to run the war or make the peace, blazed on the pages of London newspapers.

Taxes were voted, but Calhoun wrecked the bank bill by stripping it of all provisions that aided the Treasury. It passed and the President vetoed it not as unconstitutional but *because it lacked the features that he had called unconstitutional in 1791.*

During the congressional turmoil Vice President Gerry died. This forced the election of a senatorial president pro tempore who would be next in line for the national presidency. To Congressman Hanson's *Federal Republican,* Gerry's death was a divine intervention to give Madison, by resigning, the opportunity to "prevent a great and rising empire from being deluged with blood" in civil commotion. The Senate elected Gaillard of South Carolina over King. When, moaned Hanson's organ, "did distress ever oblige a Prince to abdicate his authority?"

The *Times* of London thought in similar personal terms. Stung anew by the repulse at Fort Erie, it cried out: "Something must be done to strike terror into the blind faction that has hitherto supported Madison. So long as a man like him is kept in power,—a man who sticks at no fraud, no baseness, no falsehood to gratify his unnatural and deadly malice against England,—so long peace cannot exist between the two countries." Thrilled from type to press, the *Times* announced next day that "Washington—the proud seat of that nest of traitors"—Washington was captured, "and all its public buildings destroyed."

The cry of barbarism rolled over the continent, to which the *Times* replied that England was fighting, and fighting honorably, to save Europe from "the infant marine of America" which had rapidly become "so formidable an engine of hostility." The paper warned the people of England against a spreading belief that the burning of Washington would cause the Americans to yield at Ghent and hide their disgrace in the revival of commerce: "This is to understand but ill the mulish obstinacy of Mr. Madison's mind. Not an iota will he ever concede, but to downright force."

The British disasters on Lake Champlain and at Baltimore turned the Thunderer's anger against its own government. No choice was left except to win by main force or retire from the contest "with our flag disgraced on the ocean and on the lakes." England must go on, forced to do so by the changing attitude of the European powers:

"Already do they begin to relax in their deep and merited contempt of the servile hypocrite Madison. Already do they turn a compassionating look on the smoking rafters of the would-be Capitol. . . . Therefore . . . let not another autumnal sun go down in disgrace to the British arms."

With the negotiations at Ghent apparently ruptured, "the servile hypocrite Madison" thought this a proper time to publish "an explanation to the impartial world of the causes and character of the war." It was being continued by England, he said in a lengthy booklet outlined by him and enlarged by Dallas, in "the hopes of strangling the maritime power of the United States in its cradle and cutting off their commerce with other nations having an interest in it."

Such was the state of things as an event neared that loomed large in the President's thoughts—the Hartford Convention. Early in its development Colonel Jesup of the regular army, assigned to recruit a regiment in Connecticut, was instructed to watch the convention leaders closely, to determine whether there was any connection between them and the British naval command in Long Island Sound. Governor Tompkins of New York was asked to have troops ready in the event of a New England uprising.

Closely related to this was the refusal of Governor Strong of Massachusetts to obey Madison's call for militia to repel an invasion of Maine (a part of Massachusetts) by seaborne British troops. The President, relying on a bill that had passed only the Senate, gave patriotic militia Major General William King direct authority to call the state troops into active federal service. Federalists shouted dictator.

The Hartford project, lighted with a gigantic torch, sputtered along its fuse and finally exploded with the deafening fizz of a wet firecracker. Madison's military measures, their report to the New England governors declared, cloaked a military despotism. It should be countered by constitutional amendments. If the Union must be dissolved, "it should, if possible, be the work of peaceable times, and deliberate consent."

Convention Secretary Theodore Dwight "heard it said that Mr. Madison laughed when he saw the Report of the Convention . . . If, however, this New England caucus should . . . GIVE THE COUNTRY A *Chief Magistrate*, Mr. Madison will probably terminate his laughing fit in a groan." The thought was that with New Orleans about to fall to the British, only New England could save the country from being overrun, and Madison would have to buy its support by resigning.

At ten o'clock Sunday night, January 8, 1815, word came from New Orleans that sixty British warships were sailing across Lake Pontchartrain with the invading army.

59 / PEACE AND JUBILATION

A January flood of the Tennessee River produced a two-week gap in the New Orleans mail, while tension mounted. "The suspicion gains ground," said the *Federal Republican*, "that the government is in possession of the official account of the capture of this important city." On January 20 a courier struggled through with news of indecisive fighting, Jackson retiring to a stronger position.

The next evening, twenty-three-year-old George Ticknor of the Harvard faculty was one of the President's twenty guests. Before dinner a servant called Madison out: the New Orleans mail had arrived. Madison, wrote Ticknor, "returned with added gravity and said that there was no news! Silence ensued." Nobody knew what to say "and said nothing at all."

At dinner, the modest Ticknor took a chair at the foot of the table, whereupon the President came around and "fairly seated me between himself and Mrs. Madison." To his surprise, Ticknor found Madison "free and open" in conversation, "making remarks that sometimes savored of humor and levity . . . but his face was always grave." Madison was "curious to know how the cause of liberal Christianity stood with us. . . . He pretty distinctly intimated to me his own regard for the Unitarian doctrines."

At the end of January, Jackson reported another indecisive battle in which his 5,500 men, fortified behind a dry canal, connecting a cypress swamp with the Mississippi, repulsed 8,000 British troops commanded by Wellington's brother-in-law, Major General Sir Edward Pakenham. The report did not inspire confidence in all. "Turn your eyes to New Orleans!" exclaimed Congressman Hanson's newspaper. The only measure likely to produce lasting beneficial results "would be the impeachment and punishment of James Madison. While this man, if he deserves the name, is at the head of affairs . . . there can be nothing but dishonor, disappointment and disaster."

Disaster speedily followed, but not as foretold: Pakenham's army was utterly cut to pieces between river and swamp, 2,600 killed, wounded, or captured, with Pakenham among the dead. American losses: seven killed, six wounded. It was truly impossible, but impossibly true. Jackson had withheld his fire, as the serried thousands advanced with scaling ladders, then mowed them down as they kept on coming and coming but unable to deploy.

The terrain did not permit pursuit without reversing the odds, so for ten days the two armies remained within cannonshot. Then the British spiked their guns and sailed out to sea. The President on February 13 reduced his call for western militia in the expectation that offensive operations would soon bring the war to a close.

Twenty-four hours later the treaty of peace was in Madison's hands. The swing from diplomatic stalemate to settlement was almost as startling as the battle of New Orleans. Hostilities were to end upon the exchange of ratifications *in Washington*. The Prince Regent already had ratified and the Senate did so, unanimously, in twenty-four hours. On February 17, 1815, the President proclaimed the conflict ended—two years and eight months after it began.

The treaty followed the formula laid down by President Madison on June 4: a return to the *status quo ante bellum:* no gains and no concessions by either side. Disputed boundaries were to be settled by joint commissions. The conditions asked for and abandoned by the United States were those which *had come into effect, de facto*, just before the start and during the course of the conflict. The Orders in Council had been revoked: impressment was at an end.

In giving up its demands, the United States relinquished the assurance that the practices would not be resumed; but why did the British government suddenly abandon its punitive counterclaims, so vigorously put forward after the American demands were dropped? The documents accompanying the treaty threw no light on this, but time revealed three reasons:

> (1) The mounting cry of British manufacturers, mechanics, and merchants for trade in place of a war of vengeance.
> (2) The Duke of Wellington's reply to Lord Liverpool, when asked to direct the 1815 campaign, that he would do so if the war should continue, but (in Liverpool's paraphrase) "there was no vulnerable point of importance belonging to

the United States which we could hope to take and hold except New Orleans, and this settlement is one of the most unhealthy in any part of America."

(3) The report of Major General Sir Phineas Riall and Major Sir John Moryllion Wilson, wounded and captured at Lundy's Lane and sent to London on parole, that the American Army had undergone a complete metamorphosis in regulars, volunteers, and militia. That wrote off British victory.

The President displayed quiet satisfaction when he submitted the treaty to the Senate. It terminated "with peculiar felicity a campaign signalized by the most brilliant successes." The war, reluctantly declared but necessary to assert national rights, had been waged with a success which was the natural result of legislative wisdom, the patriotism of the people and the valor of the military and naval forces: "Peace, at all times a blessing, is peculiarly welcome, therefore, at a period when the causes of the war have ceased to operate, when the Government has demonstrated the efficiency of its powers of defense, and when the nation can review its conduct without regret and without reproach."

Federalist editors called the treaty an ignoble defeat, but the people reacted with wild rejoicing that matched British and Canadian gloom. "It is inconceivable," commented the Montreal *Herald*, "to see to what a pitch illuminations and rejoicings are carried throughout the United States. . . . What a contrast is exhibited in this country! You scarcely meet a cheerful countenance from one end of the province to the other when you speak of the peace."

The *Times* of London had hailed Federalist bombast over the Hartford resolutions as proof that the "assassin" Madison was "beaten down on his knees" by the New England states. "With them let us treat, and not with the traitor Madison." A week later the *Times* presented the "fatal intelligence" that the treaty was signed and outlined "the terms of the deadly instrument" which had ended the war "without wiping off our naval and military disgraces." Summing up: "Our complaint is that with the bravest seamen, and the most powerful navy in the world, we retire from the contest when the balance of defeat is so heavily against us." The *Morning Chronicle* welcomed peace but damned the statesmen who had subjected their country to humiliation: "Great Britain *was* the first naval power in the world. Woe to those who have put to stake her maritime pre-eminence. . . . It must, indeed, be encouraging to Mr. Madison to read the logs of his cruisers. If they fight, they are sure to conquer; if they fly, they are certain to escape."

The diplomatic exchanges, made public by the President, produced a wave of accusation in Parliament. As Earl Gray saw it, England had "rejected moderate overtures in the hour of elation and success, to which we had afterwards acceded when the time came of reverse and defeat." The Marquis Wellesley (Wellington's brother) declared that the British Cabinet, *in forma pauperis*, "laid the British crown at the foot of the American President." In his opinion "the American commissioners had shown the most astonishing superiority over the British, during the whole of the correspondence."

They, in fact, had driven both the British commissioners and Cabinet from one untenable position after another. John Quincy Adams wrote to his father that Gallatin "contributed the largest and most important share to the conclusion of the peace," but all five had displayed a basic harmony that made minor disagreements harmless. Madison informed the Senate confidentially of the crucial decision. The American envoys offered a choice: confirm American fishing rights off Newfoundland and British rights (recognized in 1783) to navigate the Mississippi, or omit both. The Cabinet proposed confirmation of both rights plus a boundary concession. The Americans rejected that, but offered to omit all three subjects. To their happy surprise, the Cabinet agreed.

The joyous American reaction took account of the new national standing that Sérurier had recognized at the time of Perry's victory. The treaty, he now wrote, restored prewar rights and possessions, but "in all other regards, all is loss for England; all is gain for the United States." American naval victories were "a prelude to the lofty destiny to which they are called on that element." On land "three great attacks saw Wellington's best corps flee before their militia." The war had produced an expansion of manufactures that could not have been achieved in twenty years of peace. It had proved the Union to be indissoluble.

With this, said the French diplomat, had come a revolution in political thinking. Three years of trial had proved the capacity of republican institutions to sustain a state of war. It had destroyed the illusions, the prejudices and the mental habits of too prolonged peace and reconciled the people to the idea of taxes and sacrifice: "Finally the war has given the Americans what they so essentially lacked, a national character founded on a glory common to all. . . . The United States . . . are at this moment, in my eyes, a naval power. . . . Within ten years they will be masters in their waters and upon their coasts."

Kindred thoughts were in the mind of Justice Joseph Story: "Peace has come in a most welcome time to delight and astonish us. Never did a country occupy more lofty ground; we have stood the contest, single-handed, against the conqueror of Europe; and we are at peace, with all our blushing victories crowding on us."

Story prayed to God that the golden moment would not be thrown away: "Let us extend the national authority over the whole extent of power given by the Constitution. Let us have great military and naval schools; an adequate regular army; the broad foundations laid of a permanent navy. . . . Let us prevent the possibility of a division by creating great national interests which shall bind us in an indissoluble chain."

The war intensified the trend toward federal power in an expanding nation. Carried far enough, these developments would violate Madison's concept of a federal republic; but his contribution to them was not open to question. In the Continental Congress, the Virginia legislature, and the Federal convention of 1787, he had worked to build a strong federal government. In the Congress of the United States, as Secretary of State and as President, he was unremitting in stirring national resistance to maritime aggressions, with a resort to arms rising higher and higher in the calculations.

As President in the War of 1812, Madison foresaw and strove to overcome weaknesses which Congress refused to remedy. He held the nation to its course with unfaltering determination in the face of military adversities and New England sedition. His refusal to abridge freedom of speech and press saved the country from civil war.

As Commander-in-Chief Madison's deep and serious flaw was reluctance to cut off the heads of incompetent department chiefs and generals. He entered the conflict, as did the military branch itself, with little knowledge of strategy, tactics, or the essentials of command. His growth in that respect matched that of the army itself. To this he notably contributed by foiling the machinations of Armstrong against Generals Brown and Jackson, architects of the principal victories. At the outset, Madison contributed to military discomfiture by accepting General Hull's inept plan for gaining control of the Great Lakes. At the last stage of the war he determined its outcome by building the means of victory on Lake Champlain. The words of Richard Rush expressed the sentiment of the American people when he wrote to the President: "Your anxious moments sir will now be fewer; your labors abridged; your friends more than ever gratified; an unmanly opposition more than ever confounded; the nation in your day advanced anew in prosperity and glory."

Madison's own appraisal of the war was made with modesty, insight, and paramount regard for peace: "Whatever be the light in which any individual actor on the public theater may appear, the contest exhibited in its true features can not fail to do honor to our country. . . . If our first struggle was a war of our infancy, this last was that of our youth; and the issue of both, wisely improved, may long postpone if not forever prevent a necessity for exerting the strength of our manhood."

In a special message of February 18, 1815, the President warned against a sudden and general revocation of war measures. A disposition toward peace could not exempt a nation from the menace of strife. He asked Congress to provide for an adequate regular army, gradually build up the navy, and take other defensive measures. Legislation was needed to foster navigation and promote manufactures.

A week later Madison asked for and obtained a declaration of war against the Dey of Algiers, who for three years had been engaged in "open and direct warfare" against the United States. Commodore Decatur was dispatched with a strong squadron following the return of one commanded by Bainbridge. Work was halted on the almost completed Lake Ontario warships but deep-sea construction went ahead. Asked by the President to keep 20,000 troops under arms, the House cut the figure to 5,000. The Senate got 10,000 in conference.

With *sine die* adjournment approaching, Madison again made Monroe Secretary of State and nominated Crawford for Secretary of War. Gallatin was appointed minister to France, Adams to Great Britain, Bayard to Russia. (He died on reaching home.) The Madison-Dallas *exposé* of the causes and conduct of the war, having expository value, was "leaked" by Rush to Ingersoll and published in the Philadelphia *Aurora* without (in Madison's words) "any indelicate participation" by the government. Republished in London as Madison's work, it led the *Times* to call him a scoundrel who ought to be hanged.

Through Dallas, the President mildly chastised General Jackson for continuing martial law after news of peace arrived, thereby interfering with freedom of the press and resisting the courts. Martial law, the President commented to Dallas, "results from a given military situation," not from the discretion of military authority. However, Jackson's conduct should be judged "with a liberality proportioned to the greatness of his services, the purity of his intentions, and the peculiarity of the circumstances." The reprimand informed the general that his action might be justified by the law of necessity, but he could not resort for vindication to the established law of the land.

The President by this time was at Montpelier, briefly recovering in the mountain air from long-sustained fatigue. There, however, he plunged into a new crisis. Napoleon had returned from Elba, the French Army had rallied to his support. If England and France renewed their struggle, Madison wrote to Monroe, "our great objects will be to save our peace and our rights from the effect of it; and whether war ensue or not, to take advantage of the crisis to adjust our interests with both."

The President analyzed future prospects. Revival of the European coalition, with civil war in France, would lead to Napoleon's speedy overthrow. Given united French support and allied disunity, the Emperor would quickly triumph. On other suppositions the issue would be doubtful. Unless Napoleon profited from experience, he would either invite American commerce in order to snare England into attacking it, or resume his own attacks. England had commercial and military reasons for respecting the United States but might be influenced by a spirit of revenge or a wish to retard American maritime growth. In spite of these hazards, Madison decided that the reduction of the army should continue, and the Mediterranean fleet should sail to protect American commerce in the corsair-infected seas. "Peace without tribute" was the instruction to Decatur.

On July 4 Monroe toasted "American Neutrality . . . founded in justice, and maintained with firmness." That toast, Sérurier reported, foreshadowed a renewal of the war if England resumed her blockades and France favored American commerce. The French minister, as instructed, gave assurance that the emperor placed the greatest value on the President's friendliness, but Madison told Dallas that he "had no intention to acknowledge the government of Napoleon during the uncertainty of the issue of the contest."

That question never had to be faced. The Madisons were in Virginia for their summer-long stay, the Cabinet had scattered, when Napoleon's revival shrank into "The Hundred Days." In a three-day battle near Waterloo, Belgium, his armies were totally defeated with a loss of 50,000 to 60,000 men, and their leader abdicated. "The same comments probably occur to all of us," Madison wrote to Rush at the seat of government.

The world was spared a new era of bloodletting, the United States escaped the hazards of a commercial or a shooting war; but the new order of things ran deeper. United States Consul Maury reported that instead of searching American ships in port for British seamen (a right recognized by the United States) the Liverpool authorities had used the utmost courtesy towards the crews of our ships. From Holland came more striking testimony. American minister Eustis received complaint of an impressment in a Dutch harbor. Regarding the complainant as a great villain and no American, Eustis protested only the *act* of impressment. The British minister ordered the seaman released and sent the captain of the warship home "to account for his conduct." The Treaty of Ghent was silent, but the major objective of the War of 1812 had been achieved.

More good news came from London in September 1815. Clay and Gallatin had negotiated a treaty of commerce, equalizing navigation laws almost in the words of a draft by Madison. Trade with British India was opened but not with the rest of the colonial empire. "Good as far as it goes," was the President's comment. Other international issues rose and vanished. Commodore Decatur captured a 46-gun Algerine frigate and obtained a peace "dictated at the mouth of the cannon." The President thwarted a filibustering force about to sail from New Orleans to liberate Texas. Deeply as he sympathized with Spanish colonials seeking liberty, the President observed to Rush, "a respect for authority of the laws alone obliges the Executive to prevent these enterprises in violation of them."

There was real alarm, however, when a French Army of invasion landed at New York, recruited a supporting force from the United States Navy and marched on Montpelier. It consisted of ex-King Joseph Bonaparte and Commodore Jacob Lewis. Under orders from the President, Attorney-General Rush called out the Horse Marines (Navy Clerk Duvall) who, splashing through torrential rains, brought the expedition to a halt near Baltimore. Joseph's quest for a personal presidential grant of sanctuary might have menaced relations with England.

Then home came a welcome European traveler, Dolley Madison's beloved son John Payne Todd, now a cultured young gentleman. He had enjoyed quasi-royal status in St. Petersburg ballrooms, lost at cards to Clay what he won from Russell, and deserted his secretarial duties for a several months' fling in Paris. There, combining dissipation with discriminating purchase of art objects, he exhausted the patrimony that financed his trip and finally forced Gallatin to sanction a $6,500 draft on Madison, sold to Baring Brothers to cover Payne's debts. With his mother begging him to hurry home, he missed the sailings of two ships, one of which carried his baggage. Much was told, months after his return, by a peace commission secretary whom Payne was to meet at the Georgetown races. "Our friend Todd was semper Todd," wrote Christopher Hughes, "and came to the race after it was over." Payne was well-set for his mission in life.

On October 12 the President was once more in Washington, moving from the too-damp Octagon House to the Seven Buildings on Pennsylvania Avenue. Foreign diplomats, who moved to Philadelphia after the fire, came streaming back, but not the Russians. Consul General Kosloff raped a twelve-year-old servant girl and spent eighteen hours in jail before bail and diplomatic immunity came to his rescue. Minister Daschkoff (whose own conduct, Rush thought, "made him wonderfully kind towards the failings of Mr. Kosloff"), raised such a ruckus in Philadelphia and St. Petersburg that President Madison sent private Secretary Edward Coles to Russia in the sloop of war *Prometheus*. He bore corrective documents which, the President believed, would turn imperial resentment against Daschkoff.

The dispute ran on for a year, in the course of which Madison issued a mandamus requiring foreign diplomats to live in Washington. ("The Republic does not stoop," remarked Rush.) Daschkoff proclaimed that diplomatic relations were severed between Russia and the United States. Then, partially recovering his sanity, he told his government that the State Department broke them. Daschkoff and Kosloff were recalled.

The fall elections of 1815 produced Republican gains in Federalist strongholds, foreshadowing presidential results. Two questions were being asked: Would Madison seek a third term? Would the Virginia dynasty be continued in Monroe? From London, via George Joy, Madison received John Quincy Adams' assurance "that if you consent to remain you shall have his support." Both questions were answered when the *National Intelligencer* republished a Worcester, Massachusetts, editorial opening with the statement: "It is well understood that President Madison will retire from office at the expiration of the present term." The editorial cracked sectional hostility to a Virginia succession, and republication in Madison's organ cleared the way for Monroe.

From Adams came a newspaper report that Great Britain intended to build up its armaments on the Great Lakes. Madison made a double decision. He asked Congress for funds to complete the three big warships on Ontario and instructed Adams to propose mutual reduction of armaments on the lakes. The farther England would go, the more it would conform to the President's preference.

Madison's 1815 annual message was the first in which he was able to give primary attention to domestic affairs. He dealt briefly with military matters: peace forced on Algiers and negotiated with the Indians, the army reduced and pensions needed. The militia should be classified, the navy and coast defenses strengthened, military academies enlarged. A "corps of invalids" might be organized to help support the aged and disabled through useful stationary services.

Madison pointed with satisfaction to the revival of public credit, the great increase in revenues, but said that the absence of a uniform national currency suggested the probable need of a national bank. (Coming from him, this was equal to an ardent exhortation.) In adjusting import duties, he advised, part of the purpose should be the introduction and maturing of manufacturing establishments.

The country, he said, greatly needed "roads and canals which can best be executed under the national authority." No objects within the circle of political economy would "so richly repay the expense bestowed on them," nor contribute so greatly to binding the extended country together. Any defect of constitutional authority could be supplied by amendment. Once more he called for establishment of a national seminary of learning within the District of Columbia.

In closing he felicitated Congress and the country on the "tranquil enjoyment of prosperous and honorable peace." The fruits of the trials of war and the reputation gained by arms were growing respect abroad and a just confidence of the nation in itself. It remained for the guardians of the public welfare to persevere in justice and good will toward other nations, to cherish civil and religious liberties, and to combine a liberal system of foreign commerce with the "protection and extension of the independent resources of our highly favored and happy country."

Unrest among friendly Southern Indians was allayed when Madison sent soldiers to drive white intruders off their lands. A similar order to United States marshals, regarding squatters on public lands in Mississippi Territory, went unenforced after "James Maderson" heard from Clabon Harris that there had Been Some Rong Misrepresentations about his and 500 other families who had been encouraged by genneral Jackson to Settle on the allebarmer, and how to get back to North and South Carolina and georgia god only knows.

Reacting to a deputation of Cherokees who called to protest boundary demands on them and the Creeks, Madison obtained their promise to let a military road to New Orleans cross their domain and sent this direction to Commissioner Andrew Jackson: "The President is determined to obtain no lands from either of those nations, upon principles inconsistent with their ideas of justice and right."

After the commercial treaty with England was ratified, House and Senate squabbled for two months over the scope and nature of legislation needed to bring its provisions into effect. The House contended that every clause had to be implemented by a law. The Senate sought to preserve its treaty power intact by a simple bill declaring any act conflicting with the treaty to be null and void. The Senate won from the House but lost to the President. At the midway point of the fight, telling congressional committees of his intention, Madison brought the treaty into full effect by exercising the discretionary power it gave him to reduce import duties.

Madison's plea for a national university produced a favorable committee report but, lamented the *Intelligencer*, it "fell still-born" into the House. Not so his proposal of roads and canals. Disregarding his doubt about constitutionality, Congress took preliminary steps for a Delaware-Chesapeake canal, a road from Ohio to Louisiana, and a broad general program. President Madison, it was noted, had continued to sign appropriation bills for Jefferson's interstate Cumberland Road. On April 10, 1816, Madison signed a bill creating the second Bank of the United States, asked for by him twenty-four years after he denied the power of Congress to create it. Unwilling to admit error, he later called it expedient and "almost necessary," rendered constitutional (that is, "necessary and proper") by the unchallenged operation of the First Bank.

Congress passed a steady stream of presidential measures. Manufactures were protected and revenue stabilized by a new tariff. Internal taxes were continued, the land tax cut in two. Veterans' pensions were voted. An Army General Staff was created, fortifications extended, the militia improved, money voted for nine ships of the line and twelve frigates. The administration, wrote John Randolph, "out-Hamiltons Alexander Hamilton."

On March 16, 1816, James Monroe won the Republican congressional nomination for President, 65 to 54, over George Washington Crawford of Georgia. The contest, limited to two adherents of the Madison administration, furnished convincing proof of the President's popularity and public satisfaction with the outcome of the war. These factors, combined with Monroe's connection with the fortunate final phases of the conflict, overcame the cry against "the Virginia Dynasty." The Federalists, sinking in the bog of their own sedition, despairingly put up Rufus King.

French Chargé Roth, Sérurier's successor, sensed a profound alteration in American society and politics. A new manufacturing class was growing up in the interior states, fostered by the Madison administration in order to break the country's dependence on English goods and to build a counterweight to the British-oriented Northeast. Federalists complained that the administration, to preserve its own popularity and power, was borrowing Federalist policies. Republicans, in turn, chided their opponents for opposing those policies with arguments which they had called false and vulgar when directed against themselves.

The truth, thought Roth, lay deeper. "The government of this country, Federalist or Republican, moves with giant strides toward an extension of strength and power which insensibly changes its nature." The free and rude habits of an earlier age of society were giving way to the advance of civilization and the development of wealth and industry. The new order would rule.

This estimate, which Roth drew from leaders of both parties, took no account of the roll of population into the western wilderness and the future brief supremacy of a still ruder democracy. It amounted to a consensus of opinion that the Madison administration had set the country on the road to internal development, national strength, and economic independence, without weakening the fabric of self-government. That was the legacy of the War of 1812.

The final year of Madison's Presidency was one of unaccustomed ease and tranquillity. After the adjournment of Congress in April 1816 he pressed for the goal of disarmament on the Great Lakes. A favorable reaction by Castlereagh led to a presidential directive to Minister Adams. Unlike impressment and blockades, lake disarmament involved not public law but prudence and reciprocity. Congress had declined to complete the lake warships (out of penury, not policy), but British construction there would incite the Indians and bring an opposite decision. Speedy arrangements were necessary to forestall this.

Late in May the President and Mrs. Madison went to Annapolis in a navy barge to inspect the 74-gun *Washington.* As the trip was unofficial he insisted on paying the $25 cost for boatmen. On June 5 the family left for Montpelier where the President hoped to spend the whole summer. He stayed until October—the longest absence of a President from the capital in American history.

July 4 saw ninety guests at one long dinner table on the Montpelier lawn, all men except the President's mother, wife, a sister, and a niece. On that same day, the annual Independence Day dinner in Washington was one long panegyric of the President. He was toasted as "a ruler more respected for his merit, than his power, and greater in the simple dignity of his virtues than the proudest monarch on his throne." The orator of the day, Benjamin Lear, son of Tobias, traced the Second War of Independence to the peace by which "our Republic has taken her stand among the nations. Her character established—her power respected, and her institutions revered." The most powerful enemy and the most inveterate opposition at home had both been withstood without one trial for treason or even for libel. Of President Madison Lear said: "His name will descend to posterity with that of our illustrious Washington. One achieved our independence, and the other sustained it.—What proud and happy feelings will he carry with him to that retirement to which he will also carry the acclamations and the prayers of a grateful nation."

To escape hearing anti-French toasts at that banquet, the new French minister Jean Guillaume Hyde de Neuville had been cajoled by Monroe into a trip to Montpelier. There Madison entertained him and three of his staff, putting him entirely at his ease, Hyde de Neuville reported, by talking as if "Louis XVIII had just succeeded Louis XVI." (Napoleon never existed.) However, the minister was smitten with fury when he returned to Washington and learned that the Baltimore postmaster in a toast had referred to Louis XVIII as "an imbecile tyrant."

With Secretary Monroe supposed to be at Montpelier, the French minister sent his private secretary there with a demand for the postmaster's immediate dismissal. The tone of the note was so arrogant, Madison wrote to Monroe, as to forfeit all respect. It would seem as if he "hoped to hide the degradation of the Bourbons under a blustering deportment in a distant country." The reply should be conciliatory but couched in terms to arouse the monarch to his minister's indecorum. Hyde de Neuville gnawed his fingers until Madison returned to Washington and entertained him at dinner. To his boundless joy he found himself sitting beneath the side-by-side portraits of Louis XVIII and George Washington.

The President's long stay at Montpelier encompassed one of the coldest and driest harvest seasons within memory. Attorney-General Rush visited him late in September. Never, he wrote after his return, had be "seen Mr. Madison so well fixed anywhere . . . not even before he was burnt out here." He was reputed to be an excellent farm manager, was a model of kindness to his slaves, lived with a profuse hospitality, and "was never developed to me under so many interesting lights" as during that week.

Hardly had Rush departed when the young Baron de Montlezun arrived, bearing a letter from Lafayette. Invited to remain a week, he kept discovering "new lights and very extensive learning" in his host.

"With a great deal of modesty, Mr. Madison has a precise and quick mind, infinite wisdom, an excellent tone in conversation, never dogmatic." He showed high regard to a stream of visitors, with the very rare art of leaving to them the comfort and freedom they enjoy in their own homes. This helped him also to attend to public duties: "Work is easy for him; he reads and writes almost all day, and often part of the night. . . . Madame his wife is sweetness, honesty and goodness itself."

Congress convened on December 2 with presidential election returns pouring in. It was a sweep for Monroe, King carrying only Massachusetts, Connecticut, and Delaware. Had Madison been the candidate, John Adams believed, he would have won all New England.

Madison's final message to Congress was on the face of it an impossible list of requests. In reality it was a blueprint for the American future. He asked for a decimal system of weights and measures—not yet achieved; a revision of the criminal code (accomplished in 1825); a Department of the Interior (created in 1849); federal aid to education (begun in 1862); a system of appellate circuit courts (established in 1911).

Madison reviewed public affairs and gave high praise to Secretary Dallas for the improved condition of the Treasury. Exclaimed Dallas to Rush: "To be praised by such a man! upon such an occasion! I am content."

In a closing valedictory the President beheld his country blessed with tranquillity and prosperity at home, peace and respect abroad. The American people lived under a Constitution that reconciled public strength with individual liberty. In the devotion of the American people to true liberty and the Constitution, Madison could read sure presages of the country's destined career. It would exhibit a government watching over the purity of elections, the freedom of speech and of the press, trial by jury, separation of religion and the state. It would be a government that made persons and property secure; that promoted the general diffusion of knowledge on which public liberty depended; a government whose conduct bespoke "the most noble of all ambitions—that of promoting peace on earth and good will to men."

Richard Rush called the message "the last act of one of the purest and wisest of statesmen; a statesman out of the career of whose genius and virtues some future American Plutarch will make up some of his brightest pages." During Madison's final months in office no man in Congress spoke a sharp word against him. Even John Randolph tempered his ancient animosities. On one occasion, when Randolph seemed to be depriving Madison of credit for an action of the Virginia legislature, Congressman James Pleasants chidingly remarked that the united force of all its advocates would not have carried it "but for the weight of character of James Madison." Randolph agreed, adding that as he had not been bred to worship the rising sun, he would not be deterred from saying, now that Madison's orb was temperately setting, "that he was a great man . . . and he sincerely wished him all happiness in his retirement."

Madison's last official act was to veto a bill whose purposes he thoroughly endorsed. Congress seized on his renewed request for federal roads and canals but gave no heed to the suggested necessity of a constitutional amendment. Under Calhoun's mentorship, the $1.5 million bonus paid by the National Bank for its charter was appropriated to internal improvements in order to promote interstate commerce and national defense. The power proposed to be exercised, Madison declared in his veto message, was not enumerated in the Constitution. To base it on a power to spend for the common defense and general welfare would give Congress a sweeping power of legislation on all subjects, money being the ordinary means of executing all important measures.

Federal development of roads and waterways, Madison agreed, would greatly promote the nation's prosperity; but believing that this power could not be deduced without inadmissible construction "and a reliance on insufficient precedents," believing also that the success of the Constitution depended on a definite partition of state and federal powers, he must withhold his signature. Congress promptly repassed the bill over his veto.

The word "insufficient" meant that Madison did not regard half a dozen appropriations for the Cumberland Road, signed by himself and Jefferson, as adequate precedents. Yet a single antecedent action made him accept the bank bill. He now ignored the convincing argument of Representative (ex-Senator) Pickering that if Congress could improve coastal navigation for the benefit of foreign and coastal commerce it must have a corresponding power to aid interstate commerce.

There were other precedents. In 1813 Madison unhesitatingly signed a bill establishing a salaried United States Agent of Vaccination. When Congress abolished the office in 1816, the President gave a naval surgeon's commission to a private physician, with instructions, "predicated upon the general principles of humanity," to vaccinate men in service and "such others of the class of seamen as may apply." Had there

been as much immediate need for roads as for the bank, or the conquest of smallpox, he might have found the precedent to be not only
sufficient but sound.

Madison's note of retrenchment of power was sounded out of concern for the nation's future. It did not, however, alter the basic fact
that in thirty-five years of federal service, then coming to a close, he
had been the most effective of all Americans in advocating and obtaining
national powers equal to national responsibilities.

Two days after he stepped out of office Madison was presented by
Mayor James H. Blake with the resolutions of a Washington mass
meeting. "We come, sir," they read, to mingle congratulations and
regret—congratulations as Americans participating "in the untarnished
glory that accompanies you;" regret at the personal loss about to be
experienced. "We shall never forget that when our city felt the tempest
of war, it was your wisdom and firmness that repaired the breach." The
world was in chaos when Madison entered the Presidency. Violence
and injustice forced a resort to arms.

> Its fruits are a solid peace, a name among the nations of
> the earth, a self respect founded upon justice and common
> strength. . . . Power and national glory, sir, have often before
> been acquired by the sword; but rarely without the sacrifice of
> civil or political liberty. . . . When we reflect that this sword
> was drawn under your guidance we cannot resist offering
> your our own as well as a nation's thanks for the vigilance
> with which you have restrained it within its proper limits,
> the energy with which you have directed it to its proper objects
> and the safety with which you have wielded an armed force
> of fifty thousand men . . . without infringing a political, civil
> or religious right.

The legislature of Virginia adopted resolutions of like tenor, conveyed by Governor Preston with his own satisfaction that Madison
"presided over the Union during this wonderful march of national
prosperity and glory." Albert Gallatin wrote from Paris: "Few indeed
have the good fortune, after such career as yours, to carry in their
retirement the entire approbation of their fellow citizens with that of
their own conscience. Never was a country left in a more flourishing
situation than the United States at the end of your administration; and
they are more united at home and respected abroad than at any period
since the war of the independence."

The eight years of James Monroe's Presidency became known as "The Era of Good Feeling." The spontaneous tributes poured upon Madison, at the close of his presidency, highlight a little observed fact. The "era of good feeling" was a donation to Monroe by his predecessor.

As President, Madison upheld executive prerogatives when threatened by Congress but ruled his own course strictly by his concept of the Constitution. Desiring peace but not shrinking from war, he stood up to the battling Titans of the Old World, first in diplomacy and ultimately by challenging the mightiest of naval powers. His steadfast courage carried the country through the trials of a war rendered divisive by politics and greed. His unyielding maintenance of the right of dissent prevented sedition from swelling into civil strife. Notwithstanding a thousand faults and blunders, wrote former President John Adams to his successor, Madison's administration "has acquired more glory, and established more Union, than all three predecessors, Washington, Adams and Jefferson, put together." If James Madison was not a great President, greatness has no meaning.

Part VII

Part III

61 / AT MONTPELIER

For a month the Madisons attended farewell balls and dinners, and packed personal belongings for a train of wagons brought from home. Informed of the overseer's safe return "with the plunder," they left Washington on April 6. Madison never went back, nor did Dolley during her husband's lifetime. Their mode of travel bespoke the industrial revolution—by steamboat from Washington to Aquia Creek, where their carriage awaited them.

James K. Paulding, secretary of the Navy Board, went with them on the boat and, he wrote, "if ever man sincerely rejoiced in being freed from the cares of public life," it was Madison. "During the voyage he was as playful as a child; talked and joked with everybody on board, and reminded me of a schoolboy on a long vacation."

Paulding was one of the earliest invited guests that summer. Madison's 5,000 acres, he noted, stretched from the Rapidan River eastward to the summit of the Southwest Mountains. The ground rose abruptly behind the house, while in front lay a broad field nearly a mile in length, leading the eyes to the sweep of the distant Blue Ridge. The center section of the large brick house, with its fine Doric portico, was flanked by two lately built wings, one of them used exclusively by Madison's 85-year-old mother.

Each morning, after breakfast, Madison would join his guest on the portico and open a conversation about political, literary, or philosophical subjects, speaking without reserve about his own public life. "He was a man of wit, relished wit in others and his small bright blue eyes would twinkle most wickedly when lighted up by some whimsical conception or association." After a time they would set out on horseback to watch farming operations. Using a crooked stick, Madison would open the gates without dismounting—a trick in which Paulding could not arrive at his host's "matchless dexterity." One day an old slave accompanied them as they inspected a once-fine riverside meadow on which a flash flood had deposited several inches of gravel. Paulding recorded the conversation.

> " 'Why, this is bad business, Tony,' said Mr. Madison.
> " 'Yes masser ver bad—ver bad indeed,' answered Tony. Then scratching his gray head he added with perfect simplicity, 'I tell you what, masser—I think Gor Amighty by and large, he do most as much harm as good.' "

On the portico a telescope brought the mountains and distant neighbors close. Mary Cutts, Dolley's niece, recorded that the nearly impassable roads did not keep the Madisons at home: "With their coach and four, skillful driver and outriders" to prevent an overturn, they would journey five to thirty miles to dinner. The longest drive, made often, was to Jefferson's home near Charlottesville.

Madison declined an appointment to the Virginia Board of Public Works but accepted one to the Board of Visitors of Central College— the prenatal name of Jefferson's University of Virginia. He replied to Jeremy Bentham's five-year-old offer to draw up a complete body of law, converting the English common law into statutes for the American states. It was doubtful, he said, that even Bentham, with his penetrating and accurate judgment, could completely codify unwritten laws that had been constantly altered by varying statutes in all the states. Admiral Sir Isaac Coffin received from Madison a gift of wild turkeys. Great horned owls disposed of the pheasants Sir Isaac sent in return.

Richard Rush, temporarily handling diplomatic affairs, sought Madison's advice on a breach of etiquette by Correa de Serra, minister from Portugal. Reproved for publishing notice of the blockade of rebel-held Brazilian ports, he had said his purpose was to protect the standing of the United States in Europe. "A silly reason from a wise man," replied Madison, "is never the true one." The blockade was illegal because unenforceable. Congressman Rhea of Tennessee thanked Madison for the advice that enabled him to make a political comeback: "Put your enemies in the wrong."

Madison was pleased with the selection of John Quincy Adams for Secretary of State. His competence did not prevent Monroe from submitting diplomatic questions to Madison. What signified Russia's rejection of a British proposal of joint mediation between Spain and Buenos Aires? It accounted, Madison replied, for Spain's stiff attitude toward the United States concerning Florida, and for England's reluctance to adopt a definite policy toward Spanish America. The Russian Emperor's ambition to conserve peace (through the Holy Alliance), he observed, seemed to be spiced with fanaticism. This might either end in hypocrisy or grow into stronger delusions of supernatural guidance and "transform the Saint into the Despot. Already he talks of *coercion*, though he disclaims the sword."

Madison advised full recognition of Argentine independence, even though England held back and all Europe would resent it. The sense of the nation toward the South American struggle could not be mistaken. "Good wishes for its success, and every lawful manifestation of them, will be approved by all, whatever may be the consequences." Unknown to Monroe and Madison, Spain about that time gave up hope of European aid and ceded Florida to the United States. Sixteen years of effort by Madison reached a consummation under Monroe.

Accepting Madison's position on roads and canals, Monroe in his first annual message denied the power of Congress to build them. The House, in reply, cited Madison's signing of Cumberland Road appropriations. Monroe vetoed the next Cumberland bill, accompanying his message with a 25,000-word elaboration of Madison's argument against its constitutionality. Reading this treatise, Madison discovered that Monroe had demolished his position by conceding that Congress had power to build roads with the consent of the states. If such a substantive power existed, Madison wrote to him, "it would seem like the others to be entitled to all laws necessary and proper to carry it into effect."

In 1803 Madison had been elected first president of the American Board of Agriculture. He was a natural choice, therefore, to head the five-county Agricultural Society of Albermarle, organized in 1818. In his presidential address, published throughout America and in Europe, he advocated contour plowing and horizontal planting of slopes, greater use of manures and composts, rotation of crops, noncultivation of inferior land, improved breeding of livestock, avoidance of grass and forest fires, reduction of timber cutting, reforestation. In short, he advocated and practiced the methods of farming taken up as new and revolutionary by government agencies more than a century later.

More fundamentally still, the address could have been entitled: "Will the human race destroy the earth it lives on?" The ultimate question was whether all the productive powers of the surface of the earth could be devoted to the use of man. Such a course, he said, would destroy the symmetry of nature. Plants, birds, quadrupeds, fishes, reptiles, insects ran to uncountable numbers. Added to these were invisible forms of life whose existence was probably connected with the larger forms. Disaster would ensue if the profusion and multiplicity of beings were destroyed in order to multiply the few best fitted for human use. So vast a transformation might so alter the vital air that it no longer would support the life and health of organized beings. He pointed to the relationship between animal and vegetable life—plants restoring the chemicals removed by animals. Could either live without the other? If not, a vast change in the *proportions* of the two classes might not be compatible with the continued existence and health of the remaining species.

More than half of the twentieth century went by before alarmed scientists developed these unheeded truths into a portent of calamity. In correspondence resulting from this address, Madison skirted the theory of evolution. "The tendency of the earth to vary its spontaneous productions," he observed to Judge Peters of Philadelphia, more likely resulted from "equivocal generation" than from long-dormant seed. That implied "no more than that Omnipotence has bestowed on nature greater capacities than is generally supposed."

In 1819, to combat slurs in British journals, Robert Walsh asked Madison to describe the state of slavery, morals, religion, and education in Virginia. Of education, he could only say that the intelligence of the masses had risen greatly since the colonial period. With respect to morals, the pictures drawn of Virginia were outrageous caricatures: separation of church and state had reformed the clergy.

The condition of slaves, Madison said, was incomparably better than before the Revolution. They were better fed, better clad, better lodged, and better treated. This was due to the sensibility to human suffering growing out of the Revolution and to the decreasing proportion of slaves to the owners of them—a reduction resulting from the breaking up of estates by abolition of entails and the right of primogeniture.

With the country lashed by the rising dispute over slavery in the coming state of Missouri, Madison outlined his views on emancipation to a Philadelphia abolitionist, Robert J. Evans. The freeing of slaves ought to be gradual, equitable to those concerned, and "consistent with the existing and durable prejudices of the nation." Owing to those prejudices, the freed blacks ought to be permanently removed beyond the regions of white occupation. If the two races remained together in freedom, most of the whites would have insuperable objections to a thorough incorporation. The blacks, suffering "under the degrading privation of rights political and social," would regard their condition "as a change only from one to another species of oppression." With them set apart by physical differences, having vindictive recollections, held to a lower level in society by a people holding them in contempt, collisions would result for which it would be unfair to put the blame "wholly on the side of the Blacks." Reciprocal antipathies would double the danger.

Madison had a plan for financing universal manumission. Six hundred million dollars would free the million and a half slaves then in the country. The whole sum could be raised by selling 300 million acres—a third part of the disposable public land—at two dollars per acre. The place for resettlement, he believed, was Africa, and it might be begun by making the existing American Colonization Society (organized in 1816 with Madison as a life member) a government corporation superintended by the National Executive.

That project died at conception, but Madison's portrait of free blacks in a hostile white society might have been put on paper 150 years later. It did not represent his own attitude toward them, or his concept of Negro capabilities. Witness the management of a Madison farm by the slave Sawney.

Walsh presented another angle of the slavery issue to Madison during the debate over the Missouri Compromise. Did the words "migration or importation" in the Constitution's clause on the slave trade apply only to slaves brought in from abroad, or did they authorize Congress to forbid interstate movements? Not a man in the Federal Convention or the ratifying bodies, Madison answered, ever thought of the latter construction. It would have been fatal to ratification. The word "migration" was used to strengthen the concept of slaves as persons rather than property.

Madison approved the effort to settle the Missouri dispute by conciliation but doubted the power of Congress to exclude slavery from any state after it was admitted to the Union. He was filled with anxiety at the tendency to divide the country into slave and free areas with a corresponding political cleavage. Uncontrolled dispersal of existing slaves combined with the ban on importation, he believed, would promote universal emancipation by reducing the ratio of slaves to freemen, thus encouraging voluntary manumission and prohibition by state action. The other course opened a dreadful prospect: "Should a state of parties arise, founded on geographical boundaries and other physical and permanent distinctions which happen to coincide with them, what is to control those great repulsive masses from awful shocks against each other?"

The answer was given forty-one years later at Fort Sumter, in cataclysmic tones. Madison's concern over broadening concepts of federal power increased as Marshall's Supreme Court handed down its nationalistic decisions, but he did not share the alarm of the Virginia State Rights zealots. When Judge Spencer Roane sent him his "Hampden" articles attacking *McCulloch* v. *Maryland*, Madison offered no criticism of the decision denying the state's power to tax the national bank. He protested the dangerous latitude taken by the Court in defining the power to pass "necessary and proper" laws. His reference was to Marshall's famous utterance, "Let the end be legitimate, let it be within the scope of the Constitution, and all means which are appropriate . . . plainly adapted to that end . . . not prohibited . . . are constitutional." Yet this was hardly more than a paraphrase of Madison's assertion in *The Federalist* that "wherever the end is required, the means are authorized; wherever a general power to do a thing is given, every particular power necessary for doing it is included." Madison's main objection seemed to be that Marshall was employing their common thought as a legal maxim by which to determine specific powers, instead of (as Madison put it) letting the meaning of the Constitution result from a series of decisions in particular cases.

Virginia's revolt against the Court reached a climax in John Taylor's book, *Construction Construed*, and Roane's vitriolic "Algernon Sidney" articles of 1821, both of them denying that the Supreme Court had constitutional power to override state court decisions. Roane appealed to Jefferson and Madison to help him slay the dragon. Jefferson complied with a warm endorsement of Taylor's book and his own opinion that state and federal governments were co-ordinate, "each equally supreme" as to its delegated powers, and neither one authorized to decide on the division of power between them.

Roane's strongest appeal was to Madison. All in Richmond who cherished the Constitution, he wrote, "see in your pen . . . the only certain antidote to the ingenious and fatal sophistries of Marshall. Other and inferior pens may no doubt take up the subject; but to yours an universal homage would be paid." In Madison's view, the sophistries of Marshall were trivial compared with those of Taylor and Roane. If the states individually were given power to settle federal-state disagreements, he replied, the national Constitution would soon have a different meaning in different states. The vital principle of equality that cemented the Union would be destroyed. Knowing how sensitive Jefferson was to criticism, Madison waited two years before writing to him that "I have never yielded my original opinion indicated in the 'Federalist' No. 39 to the ingenious reasonings of Colonel Taylor against this construction of the Constitution." He combated the Taylor-Roane thesis for the rest of his life, but he dared not give a handle to the State Righters by admitting the extent of his 1787 nationalism, as revealed in the published convention notes of Judge Yates. (*Cf* Chapter 18 *ante*.)

Latin-American affairs continued to be placed before the former President. In 1822 he gave strong approval to Monroe's recognition of all revolted Spanish colonies from Mexico to Argentina. On July 22, 1823, Madison wrote to Richard Rush, American minister in London, that England was failing to grasp a great opportunity to retrieve her reputation. She had broken with the Holy Alliance—the emperors of Russia, Prussia, and Austria—over their support of tyranny in Spain and Naples, but England's concern was for endangered royal families, not for oppressed peoples. Bourbon France was resurrecting "the obsolete and impious doctrine of the divine right of kings" and claiming the right to overthrow neighboring governments bent on reform. Were such principles sustained by powers to match, the government of the United States would face "a crusade as bigoted and bloody as the original one against the Saracens."

This letter was on its way when Rush expressed his hope to Foreign Minister Canning that England would not permit France to seize Spanish-American territory. Canning instantly asked whether the United States would go hand in hand with England on that subject. The conversation led to two notes from Canning on which, in October, President Monroe asked the advice of Jefferson and Madison. (Secretary of State Adams was in Massachusetts.)

Recovery of the colonies by Spain, wrote Canning, was hopeless. England did not aim at possession and "could not see any portion of them transferred to any other power with indifference." If the United States had the same opinions, "why should we hestitate . . . to declare them in the face of the world?"

Monroe submitted the question: should the United States risk entanglement in European politics and wars by joining England in this move? His own impression was "that we ought to meet the proposal" and make it known that any interference with or attack on the colonies would be regarded "as an attack on ourselves."

The answers of Madison and Jefferson could not be in doubt. Madison, as Secretary of State, had declared to Chargé Pichon, for Napoleon's ear, that the United States "held the balance in the new world," desired it to remain unravaged by the wars of Europe, and "it would depend in great part on them, one day, to guarantee it this tranquillity." As President, in 1810, he declared it to be "the joint interest of the United States and the Spanish provinces to prevent any European nation from obtaining a footing in the new world." Jefferson in 1808 expressed a desire "to exclude all European influence from this hemisphere." He now saw an opportunity to bring England's "mighty weight into the scale of free government."

Madison gave England no such moral credit. He interpreted Canning's course as a cool and calculated move to extend British commerce to the former Spanish colonies. England would make that move regardless of what the United States might do, but if she acted alone, and war resulted, the United States would gain the South American trade. However, doubt about England's motive ought not to divert our country from what was just and proper in itself. All considerations, Madison wrote, "unite in calling for our efforts to defeat the meditated crusade. . . . Our co-operation is due to ourselves and to the world."

Jefferson returned an emphatic "No" to the question whether the United States ought to risk entanglement in European politics. Madison, in contrast, was ready to join England in condemning French aggression against Spain, and in some "declaratory act in favor of the Greeks," unsuccessfully revolting against Turkish despotism.

At this juncture Secretary Adams returned to the capital. His diary records agreement with Madison that England was impelled "more by her interest than by a principle of genuine liberty." Monroe at this moment, said Adams, was thrown into a panic by the surrender of Cadiz to the French. "He will recover from this in a few days; but I never saw more indecision in him." Adams and Monroe both wished to ask Madison to go to London but dropped the idea as impractical. Then, hearing from Rush that Canning had gone silent on South America, they decided on unilateral American action.

From this came the "Monroe Doctrine," expressed in the President's annual message. The first draft in substance recognized Greek independence (based on Madison's suggestion), but Adams pointed out that unilateral recognition would constitute a summons to arms against all Europe. It was cut down to mere sympathy. The final declaration resembled an earlier warning to Russia by Adams against attempts at colonization in California.

Basing his stand on "the rights and interests of the United States," Monroe declared "that the American continents, by the free and independent condition which they have assumed and maintain, are henceforth not to be considered as subjects for future colonization by any European powers." The United States could not behold with indifference any attempt of the allied powers to extend their political system to any portion of either continent. Madison gave this his hearty approval.

Canning's mysterious silence, it developed, covered an effort to induce France to disavow any South American adventures. The foreign minister suggested American participation in a European conference on the subject. Asked by Monroe for his opinion, Madison said that taking part under the wing of England would reduce American prestige and lead the country "into a wilderness of politics and a den of conspirators." The conference was not held. Monroe's message, Canning commented, gave it the *coup de grace*.

European diplomats and editors raged at the arrogance of the Monroe Doctrine. This caused no surprise to Madison. "I never had a doubt," he wrote to Monroe in 1824, "that your message, proclaiming the just and loftly sentiments of ten millions, soon to become twenty, enjoying in tranquil freedom the rich fruits of successful revolution, would be received in the present crisis of Europe with exulting sympathies by all such men as Lafayette, and with envenomed alarm by the partisans of despotism."

Visited later that year by Daniel Webster and Mr. and Mrs. George Ticknor, Madison declined to take a side in the presidential rivalry of his four friends, Adams, Clay, Crawford, and Jackson. His guests agreed that they had never passed time more pleasantly than in the division of it between Madison and Jefferson. Madison, nearing 74, wrote Ticknor, is "certainly the gayest person of that age I ever saw." His conversation, much of it humorous historical anecdote, "was marked with such a richness, variety and felicity of expression" as his guest had seldom heard. Jefferson was a frank and easy conversationalist but, excepting for strong opposition to Jackson, he was "singularly ignorant and insensible on the subjects of passing politics." In this he differed signally from Madison, who received multitudes of newspapers and eagerly awaited the arrival of the post.

A few weeks later the Marquis de Lafayette made a triumphal journey across Virginia. Madison met him at Jefferson's home on November 4. "My old friend," Madison wrote to his wife, "embraced me with great warmth." The three were central figures among 400 dinner guests at the University Rotunda, provoking, wrote Lafayette's secretary Levasseur, enlivening sallies of wit and humor. "Mr. Madison . . . stood out among all of them for the originality of his mind and the delicacy of his allusions." Madison offered a toast: "Happy the people who have virtue for their guest and gratitude for their feast."

Lafayette and party spent four days at the Madison home. Work and reflection, Levasseur noted, had given Madison's countenance a severe aspect, but his well-preserved frame contained a still-youthful soul full of gentle sensibility and gaiety. Among neighboring farmers Lafayette raised the question of slavery and was delighted to find confirmation of "the noble sentiments of the majority of Virginians upon this deplorable subject." Lafayette (Mary Cutts recalled) was fascinated with the log cabin of "Granny Milly," aged 104, who presided over daughters and granddaughters, the youngest nearly seventy, all permanently retired from their labors. "Old Sawney," now ninety, had given up farm management and sold chickens and eggs to "Miss Dolley." His sole duty was to hand a daily glass of water to still-older "Mother Madison."

At a courthouse dinner for Lafayette, Madison wrote nine of the thirteen formal toasts and was himself toasted as "pure in private as illustrious in public life, we love the man and venerate the statesman." As Lafayette and his military escort departed for Fredericksburg, Madison (Levasseur recorded) "nimbly mounted his horse and returned alone through the woods to his peaceful dwelling."

The Wright sisters, Lafayette's unofficially adopted daughters, paid a delayed visit to Montpelier in February 1825, and Madison's views on slavery were plainly visible in Fanny's emancipation plan published that summer. He endorsed her subsequent purchase of Tennessee land to colonize manumitted slaves but was differently impressed when she added free love and racial amalgamation to her ideas. "With her rare talents and still rarer disinterestedness," he wrote to Lafayette, "she has I fear created insuperable obstacles" to good results by her defiance of "established opinion and vivid feelings."

Robert Dale Owen's New Harmony colony in Indiana came to Madison's attention when Owen called on him in 1825. A Socialist enclave, Madison predicted, would share the economic ills of the larger communities. Owen replied that labor would be relished without the ordinary impulses to it. Madison retained his skepticism. "Custom," he commented, "is properly called a second nature. Mr. Owen makes it nature herself." Still, it would be interesting to see how far he could carry the combined force of education and habit, in order to prove the perfect natural equality of men.

The economic ills of society were then pressing heavily on Madison. The years had brought a succession of hot rainless summers broken by crop-destroying downpours; years of recurring insect pests. Two typhoid epidemics struck his family, "and among the black members of it not a little mortality." The Swift Run Turnpike company became insolvent, forcing seven neighbors, including Madison, to divide its $12,000 bank debt. With more than a hundred persons to support, he turned part of his laboring force to household manufactures, chiefly woolens from his Merinos and flax.

Farm losses could have been absorbed easily except for personal complications. Dolley's brother-in-law Richard Cutts, entrusted with $12,000 by Madison, used it to make quick profits in Washington real estate, and lost his property on Lafayette Square through foreclosure. Other creditors threw him into debtors' prison, from which he escaped by a declaration of insolvency. The bank then sold the house and lots to Madison at an appraised price (between $5,000 and $6,000), and Cutts undertook to buy it back by installment payments. Continued occupancy by Cutts led to a rumor that it was a collusive sale to protect him from creditors. Madison assured inquirers that he was the bona fide and absolute owner. He was not only that, but the principal sufferer.

As a token of things to come, a Baltimore storekeeper sent Madison a large unpaid bill that Payne Todd had run up as a schoolboy. Payne, now in his thirties, was roaming the East and pursuing his course as a compulsive gambler, receiving letter after letter from his mother and squandering the money sent to pay his stagefare home. Madison paid $500 to a Washington lottery house but was unable to take care of a Philadelphia board bill at once and pleaded with the landlord to let Payne return instead of imprisoning him. The Philadelphia postmaster saved him from prison by taking up his worthless draft for $300, whereupon Payne went to New York and tapped John Jacob Astor for $700. Other obligations piled up, $600 more in Philadelphia, $2,700 in Georgetown. Madison guaranteed payment of $3,600 of these debts and begged Edward Coles in Philadelphia to use all efforts to send Payne home:

His career must soon be fatal to everything dear to him in life; and you will know how to press on him the misery he is inflicting on his parents. With all the concealments and alleviations I have been able to effect, his mother has known enough to make her wretched the whole time of his strange absence and mysterious silence; and it is no longer possible to keep from her the results now threatened.

A few days later Madison had calamitous confirmation of his fear that a promissory note for $1,300, sent to Payne to cover a Georgetown debt, had been discounted and cashed by him. Tobacco sales and bank loans enabled Madison to clear away $3,000 of Payne's debts, and a $2,000 loan from Coles helped him to handle the bank indebtedness when it became due.

For the next three years Payne Todd was in and out of debtors' prison, Madison paying for his release each time. A sealed record of payments, *about which Dolley knew nothing*, was placed in the hands of her brother John C. Payne to be given to Dolley after Madison's death. They totaled $20,000 and amounted, Madison stated, to about half of the total cost of his stepson's misbehavior.

Madison's public activities after retirement had a tranquil opening. On February 26, 1819, struggling through heavy snow, Thomas Jefferson and General John H. Cocke joined him at Montpelier for the first meeting of the five-man Board of Visitors of yet unopened Central College. On that day they converted it into the University of Virginia and assigned a division of work in its creation. Jefferson was made Rector (President), Joseph C. Cabell was to seek appropriations, Jefferson and Cocke took charge of construction, and Jefferson and Madison began the search for a faculty.

The preliminaries covered six years, during which Madison devoted time and thought to what was essentially Jefferson's project. He agreed that they should seek professors in Europe but induced Jefferson to delete that purpose from his report to the antiforeign legislature. A majority in that body revolted against the selection of Dr. Thomas Cooper of Philadelphia, scientist, lawyer, and prominent Unitarian, for the chairs of law and chemistry. "His religious views are damnable," exclaimed Joseph Cabell's influential brother. The choice was postponed and finally dropped.

The penurious legislature deceived itself into a belief that a tiny annuity granted to the university would pay off huge loans for construction. By the time they discovered the truth the buildings were ready for use. Madison scorned the popular objection that attention to architecture added to the expense. He defended the exclusion of chairs of theology. Setting them up would produce either a sectarian monopoly or a battle of theological gladiators.

Young Francis Gilmer, sent to Europe as a scout, brought back four Englishmen and a German, all younger or barely older than himself. Their youth pleased Madison: "They will be the less inflexible in their habits, the more improvable in their qualifications and will last the longer." The addition of an Irish-American and a native of Bermuda left John Tayloe Lomax, professor of law, the only native American on the faculty. The Bermudan, George Tucker, was praised by Madison for the acuteness and elegance of his philosophical writings, which offset his fear that Tucker might be intent on the production of fashionable novels, with which emulators of Walter Scott were satiating the public.

Prior to the choice of Lomax, Madison suggested Henry St. George Tucker for the law seat, in spite of the fact that as a member of Congress he had upheld its power to cut canals. The will of the nation, Madison said, was omnipotent for wrong as well as for right, and the building of roads and canals had been "sanctioned by the nation under the permanent influence of benefit to the major part of it." Jefferson suggested that to diminish the influence of "Richmond lawyers" (i.e., Chief Justice Marshall) the law course be based on the Declaration of Independence, the *Federalist Papers*, and Madison's 1800 *Report* on the Alien and Sedition Acts. With his usual delicate handling of Jefferson's undigested ideas, Madison praised the suggestion but asked whether use of the *Report*, which referred to a political partisanship not yet extinct, might not stir up prejudices against the entire university.

In 1825 the University of Virginia opened its doors under the European "academical village" system of independent professorships, completely elective studies and self-discipline through a student board. This, Jefferson predicted, would bring only earnest and intelligent young men, stirred by pride and ambition. Instead the campus was overrun by a rabble from wealthy families, who stormed out of classes, assaulted professors, got drunk in taverns, and turned dormitories into gambling houses. In September 1825 the crisis came when a stink bomb was thrown into the house of the talented professor of English, Long. A masked mob surged through the campus shouting "Down with the European professors," and assaulted Bermudan Tucker and Irishman Emmet.

Madison was at Monticello on the night of the riot, preliminary to a meeting of the Board of Visitors, which now included three ex-Presidents of the United States. Next day, faced with two resignations and the threat of the entire faculty to resign, the Board met with the students at the University Rotunda. Student Henry Tutwiler, afterwards a professor, described the session: "Jefferson arose to address the students. He began by declaring that it was one of the most painful events of his life, but he had not gone far before his feelings overcame him, and he sat down, saying that he would leave to abler hands the task of saying what he wished to say."

The scene was so affecting that when Chapman Johnson asked the rioters to come forward and give in their names, nearly all did so. The Board then established a disciplinary system and the two professors withdrew their resignations.

Within a few months Jefferson was deep in financial trouble and broken in health. Expecting death, he was comforted to know that the university would be left in Madison's care. Hearing, erroneously, that Madison was writing a history, the sinking statesman wrote: "To myself you have been a pillar of support through life. Take care of me when dead, and be assured that I shall leave with you my last affections."

If our long period of friendship and harmony "are a source of pleasure to you," Madison replied, "what ought they not be to me?" To both of them, he believed, another generation would ensure "after we are gone, whatever of justice may be withheld whilst we are here. The political horizon is already yielding in your case at least, the surest auguries of it."

Jefferson died on July 4, 1826, leaving to Madison "my gold-mounted walking staff of animal horn" as a token of their cordial and affectionate friendship. Madison received the peculiarly personal gift "with all the feelings due to such a token of the place I held in the friendship of one whom I so much revered and loved when living, and whose memory can never cease to be dear to me."

Jefferson, creator of the university, lived less than a year after it opened its doors. Madison succeeded him as Rector and member of the Executive Committee. Thereafter, wrote one professor, he never missed a board meeting except when sick. He upheld the European professorships in spite of complaints, but joined in letting the German professor go after he cowhided his wife in public. With student disorders persisting in spite of severe rules, Madison sided with the boys on their chief complaint, the compulsory wearing of expensive uniforms. "I retain the opinion," he wrote to Cabell after four years of agitation, "that a cheap black gown, such as is used in other institutions, would answer all purposes better." The board was stubborn, and the Rector kept silent when students blamed him for perpetuating the hated garb. On a major matter, Madison triumphed. He held the board steadily to the exclusion of sectarianism in the faculty or on the campus, even though this gave a handle to the charge of irreligion spread by rival colleges. His hope, he wrote to Chapman Johnson, was that students or their parents would arrange for clergymen to hold services in the college building set aside for nonsectarian use. Being voluntary and unofficial, this would interfere neither with "the consecrated principle of the law nor the spirit of the country."

Appointment of University Secretary Nicholas P. Trist (grandson of Eliza Trist and grandson-in-law of Jefferson) greatly lightened Madison's routine chores as Rector. When Trist resigned to enter the State Department, the talented young lawyer John A. G. Davis took his place, and Jefferson's grandson Thomas J. Randolph was appointed to the Board of Visitors. His selection, Davis wrote to Trist, foiled great efforts "by the religious people to gain ascendancy in the Board." Davis, shifted to law after Lomax resigned, faced defeat for a permanent appointment: he was a political radical and a Unitarian. Unable to attend the crucial meeting because of illness, Madison carried the day for him by the force of his written appeal.

No helping secretarial hand aided Madison in his major public activity, forced on him by South Carolina's revolt against the constitutional power of Congress to enact protective tariffs. This denial came first in Virginia resolutions by William B. Giles, adopted in 1826 and 1827, illogically based on Madison's Resolutions of 1798 and *Report* of 1800.

Appealed to by Cabell, Madison stated for private use the position he had always taken, that the power to regulate commerce included the power to protect manufactures. His letter checked the nullification spirit of the legislature until Giles posthumously published an 1825 letter from Jefferson declaring that Congress, under the pretense of regulating commerce, had assumed indefinite power to transfer earnings from agriculture to manufactures.

Multiple falsehoods in newspapers forced Madison to deny, in the Lynchburg *Virginian*, that he had ever called Giles a "dog in the manger" or that he (Madison) was the author of published letters assailing Andrew Jackson's fitness to be President. This gave him a natural opening to state his constitutional views on the tariff. His letter, widely republished, led Charles J. Ingersoll, on October 26, 1827, to deliver a toast at a dinner of Pennsylvania manufacturers: "I offer for your acceptance, gentlemen, as a sentiment becoming this meeting, 'The health and happiness of James Madison, the father and guardian of the Constitution.'"

This was the first time the precise words "father of the Constitution" had been applied to him. His paternity was not acknowledged in South Carolina, where the Giles resolutions and Jefferson's 1825 letter produced a surge of resistance to the 1828 "tariff of abominations."

At Virginia's anti-Jackson convention in January 1828, Madison was placed on the Adams electoral slate in the face of Cabell's assurance that he would not accept. Cabell himself then begged Madison to abandon his neutrality. "The opinion is general that your decision on this call will essentially determine the presidential contest." Acceptance would "be the rallying point of the good and the wise throughout the republic." Madison held to his refusal, as did Monroe.

Cabell begged Madison for more material on the tariff. From South Carolina came word that secession as well as nullification was in the air. Responding to Cabell's request, Madison aimed his letter at the Carolinians. "You must consent to its publication," wrote Cabell. It "is the property of the nation and calculated to do infinite good to our distracted country." Madison consented but advised that for fuller effect it should be withheld until after the presidential election. He employed the interval in drafting a second letter on the legitimate uses of the protective tariff.

The *National Intelligencer* prefaced the letters with a eulogy of Madison: "His is the wisdom of age—the fruit of experience, plucked from the tree of knowledge." Starting with the premise of worldwide use of taxation to regulate trade, he combined precedent and policy in upholding the constitutional power to levy protective duties. A month after publication, Attorney-General Wirt and editor Gales reported to Cabell that nothing could exceed the influence of these letters at the seat of government and in the nation. The *constitutional croakers* were as "frogs frozen up in a pond." However, the Richmond *Enquirer* belabored Madison for two months in anonymous articles, nine of them by Governor Giles. They shed tears that so virtuous a man had so debased his great talents. Despicable rigamarole, Trist called the outburst.

Madison's letters counteracted, in Virginia, the effect of Calhoun's South Carolina "Exposition" of December 1828. Among other misrepresentations of Madison's position, Calhoun credited his 1800 *Report* with denying the power of the Supreme Court to overset state laws. Madison warned Cabell against replying to the misstatement. Many Virginians were anti-Court but pro-tariff. Let the tariff fever spend itself, then "take up both the judicial and the anti-Union heresies." Outlining his argument for possible future use, Madison contended that controversies over the boundaries of state and federal power were to be settled by the Supreme Court. There were constitutional remedies for usurpations: remonstrances and instructions; recurring elections and impeachments; amendment of the Constitution. Finally, should conditions be absolutely intolerable, the yoke could be thrown off by force, but such a prospect must be shuddered at by every friend of his country: "The happy Union of these states is a wonder; their Constitution is a miracle; their example the hope of Liberty throughout the world. Woe to the ambition that would meditate the destruction of either!"

Madison's determination to keep put of political life was broken in the fall of 1829 when he—the only surviving delegate to the Federal Convention of 1787—was prevailed upon to help draft a new constitution for Virginia. At the opening session of the state convention, October 5, 1829, he escaped the presidency of it by nominating James Monroe, whose impaired health later forced him to resign.

A year earlier, Madison and Monroe had taken part in a state-wide meeting on internal improvements, whose session in Charlottesville coincided with a meeting of the university Visitors. A newspaper correspondent wrote: "Mr. Madison, I think, looks very well—Mr. Monroe is the most perfect figure of woe I ever beheld—exceedingly wasted away, and manifesting in his countenance the deepest and most fixed melancholy." Madison was pressed into the chairmanship by Chief Justice Marshall, but the united efforts of himself, Marshall, and Monroe failed to sanction a purchase by Virginia of stock in Maryland's Chesapeake & Ohio Canal. The argument: the canal was receiving federal support, and a Virginia contribution would surrender the sacred principle (enunciated by Madison!) that the federal government had no power in that field. The true reason: unwillingness to spend Virginia's tax money in Maryland for the benefit of Virginians living on the south bank of the Potomac.

Jealousy on a vastly greater scale, between tidewater Virginians and western mountaineers, between slaveowners and other freemen, ruled the constitutional convention of 1829-30. East of the Blue Ridge the population was more than fifty per cent black; west of the Alleghanies, ten per cent. Slaves could not vote but were counted in apportionment of the legislature. The West demanded a "white basis" of representation. The East fought to continue its "rotten borough" system.

This trip to Richmond marked the first departure of James and Dolley Madison from their neighborhood in twelve years. Stormy days in convention were followed by gay and friendly evening parties. Dolley was in her element, and Madison (George Tucker recorded) seldom missed a party. "He seemed to be rejuvenated, and his cheerfulness and amenity and abundant stock of racy ancedotes were the delight of every social board."

Made chairman of the committee on representation and suffrage, Madison led in securing committee approval of the "white basis" in the House and rejection of it in the Senate. A memorandum circulated by him, on increase of population and the danger of basing government on a landowning minority sustained by military force, led to an extension of the ballot to all householders and heads of families who paid taxes.

The East-West committee compromise on representation, designed to bring peace, created fury. The East spurned it, even though it would have produced an 89-to-27 House majority east of the Alleghanies. Only simpletons and natural idiots, roared Benjamin W. Leigh (future United States senator), would give up the present system. The convention rocked with laughter (Hugh B. Grigsby reported) while "Mr. Madison elongated his upper lip, and assumed a serious air that was irresistibly comic."

Madison proposed a new compromise—counting three-fifths of the slaves. Members from all parts of the hall (chronicled the Richmond *Enquirer*) crowded around him when he took the floor on December 2. Justice, truth, and humanity, he argued, required that slaves be considered, as much as possible, as human beings and not as mere property. Under the system now proposed, one House would be disposed to protect the slaves as persons, the other to protect them as property.

Such a ratio had been accepted nationally as a solution of competing property rights, when Madison proposed it in 1787. Now he was addressing a majority that could not care less about the protection of slaves as persons, and his words went forth to a likeminded electorate. A dozen horsemen (J.A.G. Davis told Trist) rode through Orange County telling the ignorant that under the "white basis" eastern Virginia would be taxed to level the western mountains. Hundreds were signing petitions against it. Within the convention, shaken moderates joined the East, which demanded and secured a constitution giving perpetual control of both houses to the counties east of the Blue Ridge.

Madison's principles were just, his proposals were sound, but put forward in an open slavery-controlled convention they were like a stick thrown into the side wall of a tornado. In his optimistic memorandum on suffrage, Madison had predicted that a properly amended state constitution might well last more than a hundred years. Virginia itself, as an undivided state, survived the adoption of this constitution only thirty-one years.

At adjournment in January all of the delegates shook hands with Madison, who was so visibly affected that (said Grigsby) "I could scarce refrain from shedding tears." Madison wrote to Monroe: "We reached home the fifth day after leaving Richmond, much fatigued, and with horses almost broken down by the almost impassable state of the roads."

Early in 1830 came the great debate between Senators Daniel Webster and Robert Y. Hayne. The Carolinian thrust at New England's defection during the War of 1812, when " 'the island of Elba! or a halter!' were the alternatives they presented to the excellent and venerable James Madison." Hayne taunted his opponent with having contended, years before, that protective duties were unconstitutional. Unwilling to admit that New England's manufacturing expansion had changed his mind, Webster credited his reversal to Madison's recent letters. "He has placed [the power], I must acknowledge, upon grounds of construction and argument which seem impregnable."

Hayne went to the same source for contrary evidence. The South Carolina doctrine of interposition, he asserted, is the doctrine of "that celebrated report which is familiarly known as 'Madison's Report,' and which deserves to last as long as the Constitution itself." Hayne quoted extensively from the *Report,* omitting the clarification—which completely refuted his interpretation—that interpositions by a state "are expressions of opinion," having no judicial force. Webster pointed to the absurd contradiction in the nullifiers' position: "Mr. Madison himself deems this same tariff law quite constitutional. Instead of a clear and palpable violation, it is, in his judgment, no violation at all. So that, while they use his authority for a hypothetical case, they reject it in the very case before them."

The two continued to fight over Madison's views. Hayne quoted his statement that the Constitution is "a compact to which the States are parties," with powers divided between states and nation. This, he said, made the Constitution a compact between federal and state sovereigns. "All sovereigns are of necessity equal," wherefore, in disputes between them, the states and federal government must be their own judges. Webster's devastating reply on that point was in harmony with Madison's concept of a *sovereign people* who divided their sovereignty between state and federal governments and placed a superior power of decision in the federal branch.

In his encounter with Hayne, wrote Trist to Madison, Webster was "the mammoth deliberately treading the canebrake," crushing all obstacles. There was, however, a dangerous difference between Webster's and Madison's identification of "We the people" who established the Constitution. To Webster, these were the American people in the aggregate. To Madison, they were the American people organized in states. Webster's view, not essential to his general position, produced the cry that the federal government was swallowing up the states. Senator Rowan of Kentucky led off on that, and Madison drafted a refutation averring that the people of the states, *in whom all sovereignty resided*, had divided it and declared a federal supremacy in exposition, as well as execution of the instrument.

Before this could be used, both Hayne and Webster sent their speeches to Madison. Replying, Madison congratulated Webster on the overwhelming effect of his speeches, then set forth his view of "We the people." Webster silently dropped his interpretation of the phrase.

For Hayne, following praise of his "ability and eloquence," Madison wrote a 4,000-word rebuttal of doctrines "from which I am constrained to dissent." An unidentified copy of this letter, for private use, was sent to Edward Everett, member of the House and editor of the *North American Review*. From all sides now, requests poured in on Madison to make a public correction of Hayne's misstatements of his position on nullification. South Carolina newspapers were citing him to justify forcible resistance to the collection of duties. The Richmond *Whig* reprinted one such article that it might move Madison "to vindicate himself, and arrest the deadly poison circulated under the authority of his name." Wrote Cabell: "The most alarming doctrines are abroad. The adverse party are using your name to prepare the people of the South for the worst, the most horrible measures. We know your real opinions to be the reverse, and think they may again save our country from the most dire calamities."

Responding to the request of a South Carolina Unionist, Madison sent him a rebuttal of Hayne's concept of state sovereignty. Published in Charleston under the heading, "Mr. Madison and the Nullifiers," it was reprinted in the Richmond *Enquirer*, followed by a shift in editor Ritchie's position. He still contended that the Resolutions of 1798 justified nullification, but "this inestimable Union" must not be destroyed for the sake of the tariff! Madison's position, rejecting the extremes of both Webster and Hayne, united Virginia nationalists and State Righters who placed the Union above the tariff issue. "Nullification is dead in this state," wrote Cabell late in 1830.

It was lusty enough elsewhere. Responding to repeated requests of Edward Everett, Madison recast his letter to Hayne into an article published in the *North American Review* of October 1830. In it he assailed the efforts of the nullifiers to ground their doctrines on the 1798-1800 proceedings of Virginia. A long analysis of state and federal sovereignty, under the Constitution, brought him to two fundamental conclusions:

(1) The Constitution, being a compact among the people of *all* the states, could not be altered or annulled by the states individually.

(2) The Constitution, laws and treaties of the United States were expressly declared to be the supreme law of the land, binding on the states and enforceable by the federal judiciary.

Without this supremacy, the diversity of state court decisions, breakdown of federal laws, and revival of interstate conflicts would speedily put an end to the Union itself.

The effect of the *Review* article was enormously increased by the prior reliance on Madison's authority by Hayne, Rowan, and others. Chief Justice Marshall exclaimed, "Madison . . . is himself again." Cabell said it would have "an effect as great as ever was produced by any document in any age or country." South Carolina Unionists chortled over the lightning switch of the nullifiers, the most lavish praisers of Madison turning into "his most embittered revilers and denouncers."

Where did President Jackson stand? At a Washington dinner dominated by State Righters he gave the toast, "The Federal Union—it must be preserved." The dismayed "Nullies" told each other that he meant preserved from consolidated federal power. Madison and Jackson were on cordial terms. Though opposed to the spoils system, Madison was not shocked by it. When Mrs. William C. Rives remarked that a lot of office-seekers were going to be disappointed, Madison "suspected there were 'more pigs than teats' and that there could not fail to be some squealing." In 1830 Secretary of State Van Buren asked Madison to answer a set of questions on roads and canals, based on the assumption that President Jackson regarded the power of Congress to be settled (as did Madison himself). He answered all queries and gave the general advice that local and national projects be strictly separated and costs be split between state and nation when the benefits were divided. The vast modern system of federal aid to states was thus foreshadowed.

As a side-effect of the great Cabinet shake-up over Peggy Eaton, *declassée* wife of the Secretary of War, Nicholas Trist became private secretary to the President. Some months later Edward Livingston succeeded Van Buren as Secretary of State. Livingston credited Madison with shaping his views on nullification, and Trist was virtually Madison's agent in dissemination of material on that subject. Jackson made his position clear on July 4, 1831, when Charleston, South Carolina Unionists publicly read his pledge to perform "at all hazards" his high and sacred duty to resist any disorganizing plan.

On that same day the governor of South Carolina assured a different set of banqueters that "a distinguished politician" of Virginia unequivocally assured him that South Carolina was placing a true construction on Madison's papers of 1798 and 1800. Commented Cabell to Madison: "I always did believe Mr. Giles to be at the bottom of all the mischief in the state of South Carolina."

With the reputed assurance overset by Madison himself, the nullifiers fastened on Jefferson, pointing out that in 1799 a supplementary set of Kentucky Resolutions used the actual word "nullification." Madison wrote to Trist and Everett that Jefferson had nothing to do with the 1799 proceedings. Then he found, in his own papers, a draft of Jefferson's 1798 resolutions with the 1799 sentence in it. Kentuckians had struck it out but used it a year later. Sending corrections, too late for Everett but in time for Trist, he expressed his belief that Jefferson thought of nullification only as a natural or revolutionary right, not as a constitutional one. To one disturbed inquirer he answered, correctly but uncandidly, that Jefferson did not write the Kentucky Resolutions of 1799, and what he *might* have thought about the meaning of nullification was to be gathered from his language elsewhere. On that point, citing Jefferson's approval of federal coercion of delinquent states, Madison wrote to Trist: "It is remarkable how closely the nullifiers, who make the name of Mr. Jefferson the pedestal for their colossal heresy, shut their eyes and lips whenever his authority is ever so clearly and emphatically against them."

By this time, in 1831, Madison was bedridden with severe and lasting general rheumatism which especially crippled his arms and legs. Undiminished were his cheerfulness and his determination to keep on fighting nullification. Unable to move his wrists in writing, he could only twitch the finger tips that held a fine quill. "In explanation of my microscopic writing," he observed to Monroe, "I must remark that the older I grow the more my stiffening fingers make smaller letters, as my feet take shorter steps." Thanking Dr. Carr of the university medical school, who sent him a remedy, he said that with *faith*, he *hoped* in the effect of the *charity*. If the medicine achieved anything, he wrote after a month's trial, it merely slackened the rate at which the complaint was spreading, and he must rely on the healing powers of nature. But his fingers were as busy as ever.

Hayne clung to his contention that Madison's Resolutions of 1798 sustained South Carolina's revised doctrine, which asserted the right of a single state to stop the execution of a law until it should be upheld by three-fourths of the states in convention. "For this preposterous and anarchic pretension," wrote Madison to Trist, "there is not a shadow of countenance in the Constitution; and well that there is not, for it is certain that, with such a deadly poison in it, no constitution could be sure of lasting a year." Equally invalid was South Carolina's denial of the supremacy of the federal judiciary in determining state and federal jurisdiction: "A supremacy in the Constitution and laws of the Union, without a supremacy in the exposition and execution of them, would be as much a mockery as a scabbard put into the hands of a soldier without a sword in it."

This material, Trist was told, was not sent for immediate publication, but "that a discreet and friendly hand should possess and preserve an antidote to misstatements." In other words, it was to be shown at his discretion to President Jackson, Livingston, and other key figures in the controversy.

At this time (September 1831) Madison's illness was complicated with a bilious fever which, wrote Dolley, "has reduced him so much he can hardly walk from one bed to another." Physicians advised a stay at Warm Springs, but he could not travel unless in his bed and "we dare not think of it at present." In December his swollen legs were wrapped in oiled silk bandages which did no good.

Briefly, in March 1832, Madison regained almost full health. At this juncture the Richmond *Enquirer* published the original draft of Jefferson's Kentucky Resolutions with the fatal word "nullification" in it. South Carolina flamed anew, and sparks showered over the whole South. Madison appealed to Henry Clay for tariff reductions great enough to detach moderates from extremists and thwart the project of a disunionizing Southern convention. A note from Trist sustained his alarm: "Things are in a dreadful state here. The Union in imminent peril. The very devil in the heart of John C. Calhoun." Unable to hold a pen, Madison dictated a reply designed to remove the nullification tag from Jefferson, for whom, he added, allowance ought to be made for a habit, "as in others of great genius, of expressing in strong and round terms impressions of the moment." (An appraisal of him too seldom made.) A tariff compromise, Madison thought, might "arrest the headlong course in South Carolina" toward the appalling alternative: "The idea that a Constitution which has been so fruitful of blessings, and a Union admitted to be the only guardian of the peace, liberty and happiness of the people of the states comprising it, should be broken up and scattered to the winds, without greater than any existing causes, is more painful than words can express."

In the House former President John Quincy Adams was a leading defender of the tariff power and the Union. To combat his "latitudinarian" construction of that power, Speaker Andrew Stevenson dug out a letter Madison had written to him two years earlier on the history and meaning of the General Welfare Clause. (See page 189 *ante*.) This he published in the *Intelligencer*, saying it proved the protective tariff to be unconstitutional. Adams replied in the same newspaper: "If there be one living man to whom this country is indebted for greater and more eminent services than to any other, it is James Madison." Adams felt a similar personal debt. "It is impossible for me to hear his name mentioned but with sentiments of reverence and affection." Both he and Madison, however, affirmed the legality of the protective tariff. Surely all members of the House must have read Madison's letters to Cabell, which left not a scintilla of doubt as to the lawfulness of the protective system:

"If you appeal to Mr. Madison as authority, you must submit to his authority. . . . The *authority* of Mr. Madison upon this question is against you; clearly and unequivocally against you."

In May 1832, Madison was hit again by bilious fever and wrote as he recuperated: "I am still confined to my bed, with my malady, my debility, and my age, in triple alliance against me." President Jackson paid a call at the end of July, and Henry Clay, his rival in that year's election, escaped a confrontation by riding on down the road, returning after Jackson left. In November, thanking Speaker Stevenson and his wife ("Cousin Sally") for a warm cap and gloves, he wrote that Mrs. Madison had provided equally well for his feet:

> I am thus equipped cap-a-pie, for the campaign against Boreas, and his allies the frosts and snows. But there is another article of covering, which I need most of all and which my best friends cannot supply. My bones have lost a sad portion of the flesh which clothed and protected them, and the digestive and nutritive organs which alone can replace it, are too slothful in their functions.

A few days later Madison received South Carolina's nullifying ordinance, adopted November 24, 1832, forbidding federal officers to collect duties within the state and decreeing that any forcible attempt to execute the tariff laws would sever South Carolina's connection with the Union. Following this was an address to the people, basing nullification on Madison's 1798-1800 writings but savagely attacking him for the 1787 hostility to state sovereignty revealed in the constitutional convention notes of Judge Yates. The pertinacity with which Madison urged that Congress be given power to veto state laws, the address contended, proved that no such power was given to the Supreme Court. (Madison's actual contention was that judicial action was not speedy enough.) The address then accused Madison of giving a current interpretation of the 1798 resolutions "contrary to the most obvious import of the terms." To support this by quotation, Madison's phrase "the states . . . have the right" was changed to "the state . . . has."

Reading this perversion of his text and views apparently improved Madison's health. Using his rheumatic fingers, he wrote to Trist and Cabell that in the 1798 resolutions he used the *plural* number, *states*, in *every* instance where paramount rights were concerned. In a solitary reference to the "respective" states, the meaning was that all states having the same rights, they could jointly endeavor to secure them to each. Had abuse of the expression been foreseen, it would have been varied.

The attack on Madison had more behind it than angry reprisal. South Carolina could get nowhere without Virginia's support, and to obtain that Madison's influence had to be destroyed. The situation was brought to a crisis by President Jackson's December 10 proclamation against nullification, written by Secretary Livingston. Besides warning that national laws would be upheld, Jackson vigorously challenged the right of a state to secede from the Union. Trist informed Madison that he pleaded in vain with Livingston to base that denial on Madison's contention that in a government founded on compact, one party had no greater power to break off the bargain than the others had to compel its observance. Instead, Livingston caused Jackson to declare that the Constitution transferred both sovereignty and citizenship from the states to the nation.

In Richmond, Madison replied on December 23, these passages "created an alarm against the danger of consolidation, matching that of disunion." Three days before he wrote those words the Virginia legislature took up the subject, with Madison's name swirling in the vortex of the storm.

Virginia's leading secessionist, Thomas W. Gilmer of Charlottesville, moved in the House of Delegates on December 20, 1832, to print 500 copies of Madison's 1800 *Report*. Campbell of Brooke County attempted to include Madison's letter in the *North American Review*. "It was useless," replied Gilmer, "to lumber the journal with such trash."

"Trash!" exclaimed Campbell. Surely Madison was the best judge of his own writings. "We do not believe," replied Carter of Prince William, "that the fabric raised by a youthful Hercules can be thrown down by him in the weakness and decrepitude of old age." Was the *mere name* of Madison to rule the legislature? asked Goode of Mecklenburg. Before they got through, the 1800 *Report* was Holy Writ, and the Almighty, said Gregory of Williamsburg, had never been called on to explain the meaning of his own words.

Cabell assured Madison that his personal friends in the House "do not think *you* are the sufferer from such a scene." The most damaging charge was that Madison had reversed himself in affirming federal judicial supremacy. Cabell wanted to disprove this by a legislative reading of Madison's 1821 letter to Judge Roane, but Madison dissuaded him. Better not revive bitter issues when the same thing could be proved from *The Federalist*.

The Virginia debate drew national attention. "All eyes are at this moment turned to the Old Dominion," said the *Age* of Augusta, Maine. ". . . Should she adopt South Carolina principles in practice, disunion would seem inevitable." Campbell's motion to include Madison's letter was rejected, 65 to 45, but the leaven of it remained at work. Secession was stricken out of the resolutions supporting South Carolina, sent to the State Senate. Even so, Madison believed, that doctrine still retained "more adherents than its twin heresy nullification, though it ought to be buried in the same grave with it."

In the Senate, Madison was told, secession support shrank from two-thirds to a minority. The final resolves entreated South Carolina to rescind or suspend its nullification ordinance and earnestly requested Congress to lower the tariff. The reshaped appeal could as well have been written by Madison himself. Virginia was salvaged, but elsewhere the "consolidation" aspect of Jackson's proclamation wrought havoc.

Calhoun, who resigned as Vice President to enter the Senate, offered resolutions denying that the people of the United States formed one nation. Under slightly veiled language it affirmed that each state could nullify federal laws and secede at will from the Union. Senator John Tyler of Virginia, in an exchange with Holmes of Maine, dragged Madison into the debate. He recalled a previous remark on the floor that there once existed a firm under the style of "James Madison, Felix Grundy, John Holmes and . . . the Devil." Holmes, interrupting, said if Tyler wanted to know how the firm stood at present, he "would inform him that his Satanic Majesty had gone over to the nullifiers, and much about the same time with the Senator from Virginia."

A warning from Trist about the revival of Calhounism reached Madison at a time when William C. Rives, minister to France, was returning to enter the Senate. Madison had just written a treatise on nullification and secession for the use of the senator's brother Alexander, a pamphleteer. This he greatly expanded and sent to Speaker Stevenson to be given to Senator Rives. A week after he stepped off the boat from France, Rives astonished the Senate with a discourse that produced this comment in the Philadelphia *Pennsylvanian:* "Mr. Rives . . . has met Mr. Calhoun on his own ground, and by one of the ablest speeches delivered this session, has demolished the doctrine of nullification, root and branch. . . . You have no idea how Mr. Rives's facts and arguments made Mr. Calhoun wince in his seat."

Rives cited Madison's public papers and Jefferson's correspondence as the chief sources of his argument, affirming federal supremacy in a system of divided sovereignty. Calhoun, replying next day, could do nothing but charge Rives with "explaining away" the true meaning of the Resolutions of 1798, and reiterate his own misinterpretation of them. Calhoun was so excited and infuriated, the Richmond *Enquirer* heard, that his speech was a total failure. He was followed by Webster, who likened Calhoun's position to "a man struggling in a morass; every effort to extricate himself only sinks him deeper and deeper."

Webster sent his speech to Madison, who said it crushed nullification "and must hasten the abandonment of 'secession.' " By placing all secession in a single category, however, his argument allowed the secessionists to dodge the blow. The claim of a *free right* of secession answered itself, "being a violation, without cause, of a faith solemnly pledged." Secession justified by intolerable oppression was "another name only for revolution, about which there is no theoretic controversy." As long as the constitutional compact remained undissolved, it must be executed according to its terms.

Clay lightened the tension with a bill for gradual reduction of the tariff. Its passage, Madison wrote to him, "had the effect of an anodyne on the feverish excitement" of the public mind in Virginia. An accompanying "force bill" for the collection of duties brought Clay into a clash with Calhoun. The Kentuckian agreed with Calhoun that the Constitution was a compact, but that created no right to nullify the laws of the United States. On that point Clay "adhered to the doctrines of that ablest, wisest and purest of American statesmen, James Madison," whose writings put an end to the Alien and Sedition Laws.

The South Carolina convention re-assembled, repealed the antitariff ordinance and adopted a new one nullifying the "force bill." The legislature failed to implement this, and nullification was reduced to Southern politics and emotions. This did not allay Madison's fears for the future. South Carolina, he wrote to Clay, had bequeathed "the torch of discord" to the country. By insidiously suggesting a permanent hostility of interests between North and South, "by contagious zeal in vindicating and varnishing the doctrines of nullification and secession," South Carolina's course had a tendency to create disgust with the Union and then to open the way out of it. The hope must be "that as the gulf is approached the deluded will recoil from its horrors, and that the deluders, if not themselves sufficiently startled, will be abandoned and overwhelmed by their followers." At the time he wrote, secession and civil war lay twenty-eight years ahead.

As an octogenarian, intermittently bedridden with rheumatism, Madison bore up under work and responsibilities that would have taxed a healthy man in the prime of life. His mother had died in 1829 at the age of ninety-seven. In 1831 Payne Todd gave up jails and travel (except for the ensuing summer in Washington) and took up the inexpensive study of geology. Dolley's brother John C. Payne was living at Montpelier and serving usefully as amanuensis. Wading through lawsuits against collusive Kentucky defrauders, Madison managed to collect a final $2,500 from the purchasers of his Panther Creek lands.

The money helped Madison make his 1832 annual purchase of 10,000 pounds of pork from neighbor David Weaver, from whom he could "git" more if this "ante as meney as you want." William Patterson of

Baltimore made Mrs. Madison a gift of four North Devon calves descended from the stock of "Mr. Coke, M. P.," the "celebrated agriculturalist" to whom Sir Isaac Coffin had given some of Madison's wild turkeys. Madison named the breed "Coke Devon."

Visitors continued to overrun Montpelier; some invited, others, he said, who fell like public finance into two catagories, "some were taxes and others bounties." One of the invited guests was historian Jared Sparks, who made a five-day record of "topics and anecdotes" in 1830. John Jay, Madison told him, "had two strong traits of character, suspicion and religious bigotry." Washington was taciturn in general society, talkative and even eloquent when with intimate friends.

"The intellect and memory of Mr. Madison," Sparks recorded, "appear to retain all their pristine vigor." He was gay, full of anecdote, "sprightly, varied, fertile in his topics and felicitous in his descriptions and illustrations." Add the accomplishments of Mrs. Madison and rarely would one encounter "so many of the essential means of social happiness as at Montpelier."

In 1833 Madison's improved health permitted three-mile horseback rides. In that year came three portrait artists, Longacre, Chapman, and Durand. A French visitor paid for board and lodging with a poetic tribute: "Madison! *a ce nom l'Amerique s'eveille/L'Anglais tremble.*" Princess Victoria of England sought Madison's autograph for her collection. Acknowledging the resulting note, her social chargé d'affaires wrote that when Victoria read the touching and flattering reference to her endowments and virtues, "the blush which crimsoned her cheek . . . exhibited a modest innocence" hardly to be looked for in one born to a throne. The Victorian age was rising from the cradle.

In that same year Madison succeeded John Marshall as president of the American Colonization Society, then resettling freed slaves in Liberia. His first act was to write to Professor Thomas R. Dew of William and Mary College who, echoing Senator Hayne, had charged in a pamphlet that the secret objective of the society was to extinguish the divinely sanctioned institution of slavery. That, said Madison, was indeed its purpose. It was a slow and difficult process, but was it not "preferable to a torpid acquiescence in a perpetuation of slavery, or an extinguishment of it by convulsions more disastrous in their character and consequences than slavery itself?"

To Edward Coles, who had freed his own slaves and begged Madison to do the same, he replied that there would be an emancipation provision in his will. Meanwhile they were a burden on himself. The Virginia depression (combined with Payne Todd's $40,000 expense account) had forced him to sell three farms, but he refused to part with the slaves who worked them. These he brought to Montpelier, adding to an over-population that was exhausting the land and impoverishing himself. In 1834, under still heavier pressure, he sold sixteen ablebodied slaves, with their consent, to a kinsman for $6,000. This fell several thousand short of clearing his debts and increased the proportion of those too old or too young to work.

England's Harriet Martineau, a visitor in 1834, devoted a full chapter to the Madisons in her *Retrospect of Western Travel*. Though confined to one room from nine in the morning until ten at night, Madison was "a wonderful man of eighty-three. . . . His voice was clear and strong, and his manner of speaking particularly lively, often playful." Madison had inexhaustible faith in an American commonwealth made immortal by the spirit of justice, Miss Martineau recorded—except on the one topic on which he talked the most: "With regard to slavery he owned himself almost to be in despair . . . acknowledging . . . all the evils with which it has ever been charged."

Conditions in Virginia, Madison said, were growing swiftly worse because of the disproportionate increase of the black population under licentious conditions. Every slave girl was "expected to be a mother by the time she is fifteen." One-third of his own slaves were less than five years old. The only hope he saw was in the African Colonization movement, but that, he admitted, amounted only to a lessening of despair. The "glad consent" of his own slaves to a sale to his cousin was due to "their horror of going to Liberia." That statement, Miss Martineau wrote, increased her mystification that "such a mind as his" should put any reliance on colonization. It must be the result of "his overflowing faith."

Madison told his English visitor of the astonishment of some strangers from afar when they saw his slaves trooping off to church, gaily dressed and raising umbrellas against a sudden shower. How happy they were! No, Madison told his visitor, they were not happy. The institution of slavery degraded their minds, ruined family relationships and instilled a spirit of cruelty to animals.

The saddest slavery of all, he remarked to Miss Martineau, was that of conscientious Southern white women who could not trust their slaves and were kept in a state of perpetual fear and anger by misconduct inspired by free blacks. He spoke strongly "of the helplessness of all countries cursed with a servile population in a conflict with a people wholly free." He ridiculed "the idea of the Southern States being able to maintain a rising against the North." Finally, "He believed that Congress has power to prohibit the internal slave-trade."

Here is a clear indication that although Madison saw no such power in the constitutional clause on the "importation or migration" of slaves, he believed it to exist under John Marshall's broad interpretation of the Commerce Clause.

Madison's opinion on public questions was constantly sought. Edward Coles asked him to rebut the claim that new states were entitled to the public lands within their boundaries. He had always viewed such a claim, he replied, "as so unfair and unjust; so contrary to the certain and notorious intentions of the parties to the case and so directly in the teeth of the conditions on which the lands were ceded to the Union, that if a technical title could be made out by the claimants it ought in conscience and honor to be waived."

Late in 1834 the New York State Temperance Society proposed that the three living Presidents—Madison, Adams, and Jackson—jointly advise American citizens to disuse ardent spirits. They did so, and Dolley won the Society a $1,000 contribution from John Jacob Astor. Madison carried a stock of wines in one of his portico pillars and was renowned at parties for his ability to identify name and year of vintage. Dolley recorded that he "was ever temperate, but reasonably fond of generous diet and good wines, tea and coffee." His valet Paul Jennings wrote that he took one glass of wine at dinner, but none at all for the last fifteen years of his life.* Though a raiser of tobacco, he was not a smoker, but placed Dolley "among the amateurs of the snuff box."

Inability to make trips to Charlottesville led Madison to resign in 1834 as Visitor and Rector of the University of Virginia—a position that he held, after it opened its doors, eight times as long as Jefferson, the real founder of the institution. At this point Thomas Gilmer (who had called his writings "trash") invited him as "the patriarch of another age" to attend a July 4 dinner of citizens "opposed to Executive usurpation and misrule." Recognizing this as a secessionist attempt to drag in opponents of President Jackson's bank policies, Madison declined, deftly turning Gilmer's words into an attempt to go back to the imbecility of the Confederation. Exclaimed the *Enquirer:* "With what dignity does the old Patriarch parry this insidious appeal!" The Columbia

---

*Paul Jennings, *A Colored Man's Reminiscences of James Madison* (1865). A letter in Jenning's hand marks him as a well-educated man. Upon Madison's death he was purchased, set free, and employed by Daniel Webster.

(South Carolina) *Times* lamented: "The poor old Patriot is controlled by the influence of Jackson partisans," prostrating in his last days "that very liberty for which the toils of his youth and manhood were expended."

Madison sensed ominous trends in Southern opinion. Urged by Coles to take a stand against Jackson's removal of government deposits from the national bank, he said this was at worst only an abuse of power which was rapidly reducing the President's popularity. On the other hand what was more dangerous than nullification, both in its original shape and its disguises?

> Nullification has the effect of putting powder under the Constitution and Union, and a match in the hand of every party to blow them up at pleasure: And for its progress, hearken to the tone in which it is now preached; cast your eye on the increasing minorities in most of the Southern States without a decrease in any one of them. Look at Virginia herself and read in the gazettes and in the proceedings of popular meetings, the figure which the anarchical principle now makes, in contrast with the scouting reception given to it but a short time ago.

The danger, he went on, might be increased by restless political aspirants or diminished by closer interstate commercial ties or foreign danger; but in the meantime, local prejudices and ambitious leaders might be too successful, through the nullifying experiment of disunion, in breaking the empire "into parts which a miracle only could reunite." To Coles' rejoinder that executive misrule was turning the country's attention away from nullification, Madison replied that this was part of the danger. Nullification was "propagating itself under the name of State Rights," and presenting itself as their only defender. The old North-South tariff cleavage, he pointed out to another correspondent, had been replaced by the threat of disunion and border wars "engendered by animosities between the slaveholding and other states."

These letters to Coles, in the fall of 1834, were written by Madison in the normal clear penmanship of the 1820's. Free of rheumatism, he had regained strength. This enabled him to make a great expansion of the notes on nullification on which Rives had based his Senate speech of February 14, 1833. By the end of March 1835 renewed illness left him "very feeble and indisposed." On April 17 he drew up his will.

All real estate was left to his wife, except 240 acres to John C. Payne for his devoted labors, subject to bequests totalling $9,000 to numerous nephews and nieces. Other bequests were conditioned on publication of his *Debates in the Federal Convention*. His library was bequeathed to the University of Virginia. The slaves were not set free. The consequence of manumission was one he could not accept: to leave his wife in poverty.

On July 6, 1835, Chief Justice Marshall died, leaving Madison as the only surviving national figure of the Revolution. The differences between them had never been personal. Justice Story, speaking at a Massachusetts memorial for Marshall, told his auditors that Marshall's "bold and steady support" of Madison in the Virginia Convention of 1788 preserved their friendship when other measures widely separated them: "Nothing, indeed, could be more touching to an ingenuous mind than to hear from their lips, in their later years, expressions of mutual respect and confidence; or to witness their earnest testimony to the talents, the virtues, and the services of each other."

That link heightened Madison's pleasure when he was elected to succeed Marshall as president of the Washington National Monument Association. Time passed for him, in 1835, with octogenarian speed and invalid slowness. In September three hours of dictation to Dolley were followed by feverish sleep. By November, debility and rheumatism scarcely permitted him to walk across the room, but even then (wrote George Tucker) nothing in the newspapers worth noting escaped his observation. In the spring of 1836, an attack on Senator Leigh for disobeying state instructions produced a lengthy letter approving his conduct. Sending in place of it a shorter note, he converted the original into a memorandum. In this he placed his expression of confidence that the great American experiment in free government would survive as "the hope of the world."

Charles J. Ingersoll arrived for a visit on May 2, and to him Madison revealed his fear of the results of abolition societies springing up in the North and pro-slavery sentiment hardening in the South. Ingersoll, in Congress and in the Washington *Globe*, told of the days he spent with Madison: "Infirm as his body is, his understanding is as bright as ever; his intelligence, recollections, discrimination and philosophy, all delightfully instructive." Madison "spoke often and anxiously of slave property as the worst possible for profit, unless employed in manufactures." He did not doubt that Richard Rush's ten-acre farm near Philadelphia was more profitable than his 2,000-acre one. On abolition:

"He was extremely feeble, unable to sit up. But he raised his almost exanimate body from the couch, when speaking to me of modern abolition; he said that, to it alone we owe not only the lamentable arrest of onward emancipation; but till it obtruded, no governor in Carolina extolled slavery as a happy balance of her government, no Virginia professor vindicated its moral advantages."

All that was true, but Madison had hit a deeper truth when he told Professor Dew that the economic ills of the South resulted from slavery itself. Unable to realize this, the South clung desperately to its own destroyer.

At their parting, Ingersoll expressed hope that Madison's health was improving. He replied "with perfect composure and resignation, that he believed he had a proper sense of his situation; that he felt he was on the descending, not the ascending line." The excitement of these stimulating talks produced a quick reaction. On May 8 Madison was "unable to write, or even to exert his thoughts without oppressive fatigue." Yet within a week he was predicting to Ingersoll that with the American Navy soon to equal England's, "she can no longer hope to continue mistress of the seas. The trident, if there be one, must soon pass to this hemisphere." In this last recorded writing on public policy, Madison spanned the years since 1789, when he asked Congress "to form a school for seamen, to lay the foundation of a navy."

As he grew weaker, in June, Dolley was unable to conceal her dejection, while "Uncle Madison" (wrote Anna Payne) begged and entreated her "to be composed if not cheerful." He had to be carried on a couch between bedroom and sitting room, but, wrote John C. Payne on the twentieth, there was no impairment of intellect: "In his views on important subjects, the same soundness, clearness, vigor and felicity of expression now prevail that have ever distinguished his compositions; and the same richness and playfulness of imagination, the same draughts from the stores of memory."

On June 26 Madison insisted that he must acknowledge George Tucker's dedication to him of his biography of Thomas Jefferson. Hours were spent dictating a short letter with a closing reference to "the permanent liberty and happiness of the United States." The trembling signature "James Madison" was barely legible. Paul Jennings, Madison's valet, who as a boy of fifteen rode on the ferry with him at the burning of Washington, described in his book of recollections this final crossing of another ferry. At breakfast on the morning of the twenty-seventh Madison could not swallow:

"His niece, Mrs. Willis, said, 'What is the matter, Uncle James?'

" 'Nothing more than a change of *mind*, my dear.' His head instantly dropped, and he ceased breathing as quietly as the snuff of a candle goes out."

Except for the keen anguish of it, the cry of John C. Payne to Edward Coles expressed the feeling of the nation: "Oh, MY FRIEND, where shall we find his parallel in life or in Death!" The last great light of the Revolution, said the *National Intelligencer*, "has at last sunk below the horizon. It has left a radiance in the firmament." Supporting President Jackson's invitation to Congress to pass measures of respect, John Quincy Adams asked what he could say about Madison that was not already impressed upon the hearts of everyone: "Is it not in a pre-eminent degree by emanations from his mind, that we are assembled here as the representatives of the people and the states of the Union? Is it not transcendantly by his exertions that we address each other here by the endearing appellations of Countrymen and fellow-citizens?"

Henry Clay wrote to the widow: "And yet why should we be grieved? Mr. Madison . . . after having rendered more important services to his country than any other man, Washington alone excepted, has sunk down into the grave as tranquilly as he lived. . . . His was not a case of death but of transition."

Madison was buried in the family cemetery half a mile south of his house, followed in August by a county memorial at which James Barbour was the speaker. "Many of you were at his funeral," he said. "You must have seen his slaves decently attired in attendance, and their orderly deportment; the profound silence was now and then broken by their sobs." None could forget "how it pierced our souls" when the body of "our Madison" was lowered into the grave. It was not only the personal servant (Paul Jennings) who wept, "standing directly by me . . . but the hundred slaves gave vent to their lamentations in one violent burst that rent the air." Like Clay and Adams, Barbour gave credit to Madison "more than to any other mortal, unless Washington be an exception," for the existence of the Union. There were so many memorial services throughout the country that Barbour summed them up as "a national funeral."

John Quincy Adams, at the Boston memorial, made Madison's 1783 "Address to the States" the beginning of a transition from feudal baronies to the components of a nation. As Secretary of State, said Adams, his analyses of the law of nations were not inferior to the works of any writer since Grotius. He carried the nation through the ordeal of war and into a period of prosperity for which "a tribute of gratitude and applause" was due him, and his conciliatory policy healed the internal wounds. It was the duty of later generations to cherish and improve their inheritance, not in the earthquake of revolution or the fire of civil dissension, but seeking guidance "in the still small voice that succeeds the whirlwind, the earthquake and the fire." For that voice, "may you and your children's children 'to the last syllable of recorded time,' fix your eyes upon the memory, and listen with your ears to the life of James Madison."

Congress purchased the *Notes of Debates* for $30,000, and Dolley had $9,000 left after all bequests were paid. In 1837 she returned to Washington, welcomed by an unforgetful public, and established herself in the house taken over from Richard Cutts. Payne Todd remained at Montpelier to mismanage the estate and make his mother penniless. Congress rescued her once more by purchasing Madison's correspondence.* She still was forced to sell Montpelier at a price made low by the requirement that slave families be kept together and the aged ones supported. "Oh, for my counselor!" she often was heard to say. On July 12, 1849, she died at the age of eighty-one.

Inevitably, the close association between Madison and Jefferson led to animated comparisons of their standing as statesmen. Margaret Bayard Smith chronicled a conversation on that subject between Henry Clay and her husband, the first editor of the *National Intelligencer*. "Mr. Clay preferred Madison, and pronounced him after Washington our greatest statesman, and first political writer." Clay thought Jefferson had the most genius, Madison excelled in judgment and common sense— Jefferson a rash and imprudent visionary and theorist. Samuel Harrison Smith contended that Jefferson's greater power and energy carried the country through dangers Madison could not have dealt with. "Prudence and caution," Clay insisted, "would have produced the same results."

---

*Payne Todd abstracted a considerable portion of these papers before delivery to Congress and sold them to James C. McGuire, whose heirs sold them to Marshall Field for the Chicago Historical Society in 1892. They were restored to the government in 1910 for Field's purchase price. Todd similarly disposed of the books bequeathed to the University of Virginia. A larger portion of the Madison Papers, loaned to Senator William C. Rives for the writing of his unfinished biography of Madison, was inadvertently retained in the Rives family papers until that collection was purchased by the Library of Congress in 1940.

Clay did not know to what an extent those traits in Madison, plus quiet power and energy, helped carry the country through the dangers faced in the Jefferson administrations. The then-hidden records of diplomacy reveal instance after instance in which Madison was the first to take a position common to both, or in which Jefferson, as President, swung over to the stand of his Secretary of State. And Madison, as President, carried the country through far greater dangers without once seeking or following advice from his predecessor. Caution, commonly mistaken for indecision, was for him the timing instrument of boldness.

Gallatin called Madison "the ablest man that ever sat in the American Congress." Ingersoll approved the saying as "perfect truth, that give Mr. Madison the right side of a good cause, and no man could equal him in its vindication." John Marshall said that if eloquence included the art of "persuasion by convincing, Mr. Madison was the most eloquent man I ever heard." Justice Story concurred with Ezekiel Bacon in his "estimate of Mr. Madison—his private virtues, his extraordinary talents, his comprehensive and statesmanlike views . . . in wisdom I have long been accustomed to place him before Jefferson." Story added: "I wish some one who was perfectly fitted for the task would write a full and accurate biography of Madison. I fear that it can hardly be done now; for the men who best appreciated his excellences have already all passed away. What shadows we are!"

Belief that Madison was a mere political lieutenant of Thomas Jefferson and derived his ideas from that source was widely prevalent during their lifetime, due, undoubtedly, to Jefferson's immensely greater power to stimulate a political following and to his gift of expression. Madison paid no heed to this disparagement, but it rankled with Dolley. She left a memorandum remarking that Jefferson, who was in Paris when the Constitution was being framed, "is looked up to by many as its father and almost unanimously as its only true expositor." Yet all of Jefferson's information about the motives and intents of the framers "was derived from Mr. Madison whose opinions guided him in the construction of that instrument."

No doubt that was true as to information, but Madison's best efforts could not prevent Jefferson from indulging in dangerous constitutional aberrations. Jefferson was sounder than Madison as to the basic need of a Bill of Rights; Madison was infinitely superior to Jefferson in the application of those guarantees to specific circumstances.

Both during Madison's life and thereafter, the deepest underrating of his work has been as President and wartime Commander-in-Chief.

His talents were not military, but he kept a firm hand on the helm during a contest that rent the American people asunder. Most of all, the underrating resulted from the quiet methods of President Madison and from historians' disregard of the titanic difficulties heaped on him by the refusal of New England to take part in the war. By his unflinching stand for freedom of speech and press he prevented sedition from flaring into civil war. Ingersoll recorded the extent of the temptation he resisted: "I have heard Governor Coles say, who was his Secretary, when he was every day called tyrant, murderer, despot, etc., that he was never known to speak harshly of those who vilified him. His patience and forbearance were inexhaustible."

Primarily Madison was a molder of national government and national directions. That was his role in the Continental Congress and the Congress of the United States; as Secretary of State and as President. In the convention that framed the Constitution he had to convince conservative property holders that by federal organization of republican government, with powers divided and balanced, with class action impeded by sectional diversity of economic interests, a continental area could safely be entrusted to government by the great body of the people.

To that belief he held throughout his life, enlarging on it, indeed, as he saw how the system worked under strain. The federal principle, he wrote not long before his death, could be modified to indefinite extents of space, expanding or contracting its attributes "by a pyramid of federal systems." Under such a plan "nothing but time and space could control the practical expansion over the globe." If, in his lifetime, there were physical obstacles to worldwide extension "how much are they reduced by mechanical improvements, *made and to be made.*"

While thus looking forward to world federation, Madison was beset with anxiety for the fate of the American republic, faced with a rising threat of dissolution under the strains of the slavery issue. There is nothing in American history comparable to his battle in old age to protect the Union he so dearly loved. Thoughts he put on paper in October 1834, during the brief return of his handwriting to nonrheumatic firmness, were left by him for publication after his death:

ADVICE TO MY COUNTRY

As this advice, if it ever see the light will not do it till I am no more it may be considered as issuing from the tomb, where truth alone can be respected, and the happiness of man alone consulted. It will be entitled therefore to whatever weight can be derived from good intentions, and from the experience of one who has served his country in various stations through a period of forty years, who espoused in his youth and adhered through his life to the cause of its liberty, and who has borne a part in most of the great transactions which will constitute epochs of its destiny.

The advice nearest to my heart and deepest in my convictions is that the Union of the States be cherished and perpetuated. Let the open enemy to it be regarded as a Pandora with her box opened; and the disguised one, as the Serpent creeping with his deadly wiles into Paradise.

Madison had been fourteen years in his grave, and the country was in pro- and antislavery turmoil over the Wilmot Proviso and California's admission into the Union, when Richard Rush produced this paper, described by the *National Intelligencer* as "The Dying Injunction of Mr. Madison." Shocked secessionists cried forgery. Why had it not been published before? They were silenced by Edward Coles' production of a copy in the handwriting of deceased Mrs. Madison. Unknown for another hundred years was the fact that the original lay in Madison's papers, written, it appeared, with the very pen to which he shifted while warning Coles that nullification, disguised as State Rights, was furnishing powder and matches with which to blow up the Union.

Three things Madison held to throughout his life with undeviating fidelity and zeal: Complete freedom of conscience and other personal rights and liberties; firm adherence to the republican form of government, broadly based on the will of the people; passionate devotion to the American Union as the bulwark of security and justice.

' Had none of the Presidents of the United States held that position, only three of them—Washington, Jefferson, and Madison—could conceivably be given first rank among American statesmen: Washington, for holding the country together during the Revolution; Jefferson, as author of the Declaration of Independence; Madison, as political philosopher and principal framer of the Constitution. When Madison's standing as a President is brought up to the level of greatness compelled by the historical record, he is still set apart from all great Presidents except Washington and Jefferson. Others—Jackson, Lincoln, Wilson, the Roosevelts—rose in the Presidency to a pinnacle of greatness; the earlier trio lived on a mountain-high plateau.

To know what ultimate position James Madison will hold in his country's history one must know what the country's future will be. If the American people abandon the rights and liberties he worked so hard to establish, he will be forgotten along with them. If those rights and liberties are cherished and maintained, the memory of James Madison will be as enduring as the mountains at which he looked so often across field and forest from his Virginia home.

NOTES

Complete annotation of this book would force the division of it into two volumes. Nearly all factual material contained in it, and quotations in particular, are to be found in my six-volume biography of James Madison, with full citation of sources. For those who wish to determine the sources or expand the references, the following notes give the volumes and chapters of the six-volume work covered by each chapter of the present book.

PART I

Chapter 1. Irving Brant, *James Madison: The Virginia Revolutionist* (1941), hereinafter called *Madison* I, chapters 1, 2, 3, 4.
Chapter 2. *Madison* I, chapters 4, 5, 6.
Chapter 3. *Madison* I, chapters 7, 8, 9.
Chapter 4. *Madison* I, chapters 9, 10, 11, 12.
Chapter 5. *Madison* I, chapters 10, 13, 14, 15, 16, 18.

PART II

Chapter 6. Irving Brant, *James Madison: The Nationalist* (1948), hereinafter called *Madison* II, chapters 1, 2, 3, 4.
Chapter 7. *Madison* II, chapters 4 (page 48), 7, 8.
Chapter 8. *Madison* II, chapters 5, 6, 13.
Chapter 9. *Madison* II, chapters 9, 10, 11, 12.
Chapter 10. *Madison* II, chapters 13, 14, 17.
Chapter 11. *Madison* II, chapters 15, 16.
Chapter 12. *Madison* II, chapters 17, 18, 19.
Chapter 13. *Madison* II, chapters 20, 21.
Chapter 14. *Madison* II, chapters 22, 23.
Chapter 15. *Madison* II, chapters 24, 25.

PART III

Chapter 16. *Madison* II, chapter 26. Irving Brant, *James Madison: Father of the Constitution* (1950), hereinafter called *Madison* III, chapter 1.
Chapter 17. *Madison* III, chapters 1, 2, 3, 4.
Chapter 18. *Madison* III, chapters 6, 7, 8.
Chapter 19. *Madison* III, chapters 8, 9.
Chapter 20. *Madison* III, chapters 9, 10.
Chapter 21. *Madison* III, chapter 11.
Chapter 22. *Madison* III, chapters 12, 13, 14.

Chapter 23. *Madison* III, chapters 15, 16, 17.
Chapter 24. *Madison* III, chapters 18, 19, 20.
Chapter 25. *Madison* III, chapters 21, 22.
Chapter 26. *Madison* III, chapters 22, 23, 24, 28.
Chapter 27. *Madison* III, chapters 25, 26, 27, 28.
Chapter 28. *Madison* III, chapters 28, 29, 30.
Chapter 29. *Madison* III, chapters 31, 32.
Chapter 30. *Madison* III, chapters 32, 33, 34.
Chapter 31. *Madison* III, chapter 34. Irving Brant, *James Madison: Secretary of State* (1953), hereinafter called *Madison* IV, chapters 1, 2.

PART IV

Chapter 32. *Madison* IV, chapters 1, 2, 3, 4, 5, 6, 7.
Chapter 33. *Madison* IV, chapters 7, 8, 9, 10, 16.
Chapter 34. *Madison* IV, chapters 11, 14, 15, 16.
Chapter 35. *Madison* IV, chapters 12, 13, 15.
Chapter 36. *Madison* IV, chapters 16, 17, 18, 19, 20.
Chapter 37. *Madison* IV, chapters 21, 22, 23.
Chapter 38. *Madison* IV, chapters 23, 24, 25.
Chapter 39. *Madison* IV, chapters 26, 27, 28, 29.
Chapter 40. *Madison* IV, chapters 30, 31, 32, 33.

PART V

Chapter 41. Irving Brant, *James Madison: The President* (1956), hereinafter called *Madison* V, chapters 1, 2.
Chapter 42. *Madison* V, chapters 3, 4, 5, 6.
Chapter 43. *Madison* V, chapters 6, 7, 8.
Chapter 44. *Madison* V, chapters 9, 10, 11.
Chapter 45. *Madison* V, chapters 12, 13, 14, 15.
Chapter 46. *Madison* V, chapters 16, 17, 18, 19.
Chapter 47. *Madison* V, chapters 20, 21, 22.
Chapter 48. *Madison* V, chapters 23, 24, 25, 26.
Chapter 49. *Madison* V, chapters 27, 28, 29.

PART VI

Chapter 50. *Madison* V, chapter 30. Irving Brant, *James Madison: Commander in Chief* (1961), hereinafter called *Madison* VI, chapter 1.
Chapter 51. *Madison* VI, chapters 1, 2, 3, 4.
Chapter 52. *Madison* VI, chapters 5, 6, 7.
Chapter 53. *Madison* VI, chapters 8, 9.
Chapter 54. *Madison* VI, chapters 10, 11, 12, 24.
Chapter 55. *Madison* VI, chapters 13, 14, 15.
Chapter 56. *Madison* VI, chapters 16, 17, 18, 19, 20.

PART VII

INDEX OF NAMES

INDEX OF SUBJECTS

INDEX TO THE WAR OF 1812

A distinguished historian and journalist, deeply involved in public affairs, Irving Brant is the celebrated author of *Dollars and Sense* (1934), *Storm Over The Constitution* (1936), *The Bill of Rights* (1965), and the widely acclaimed definitive six-volume biography of James Madison, published from 1941 to 1961.